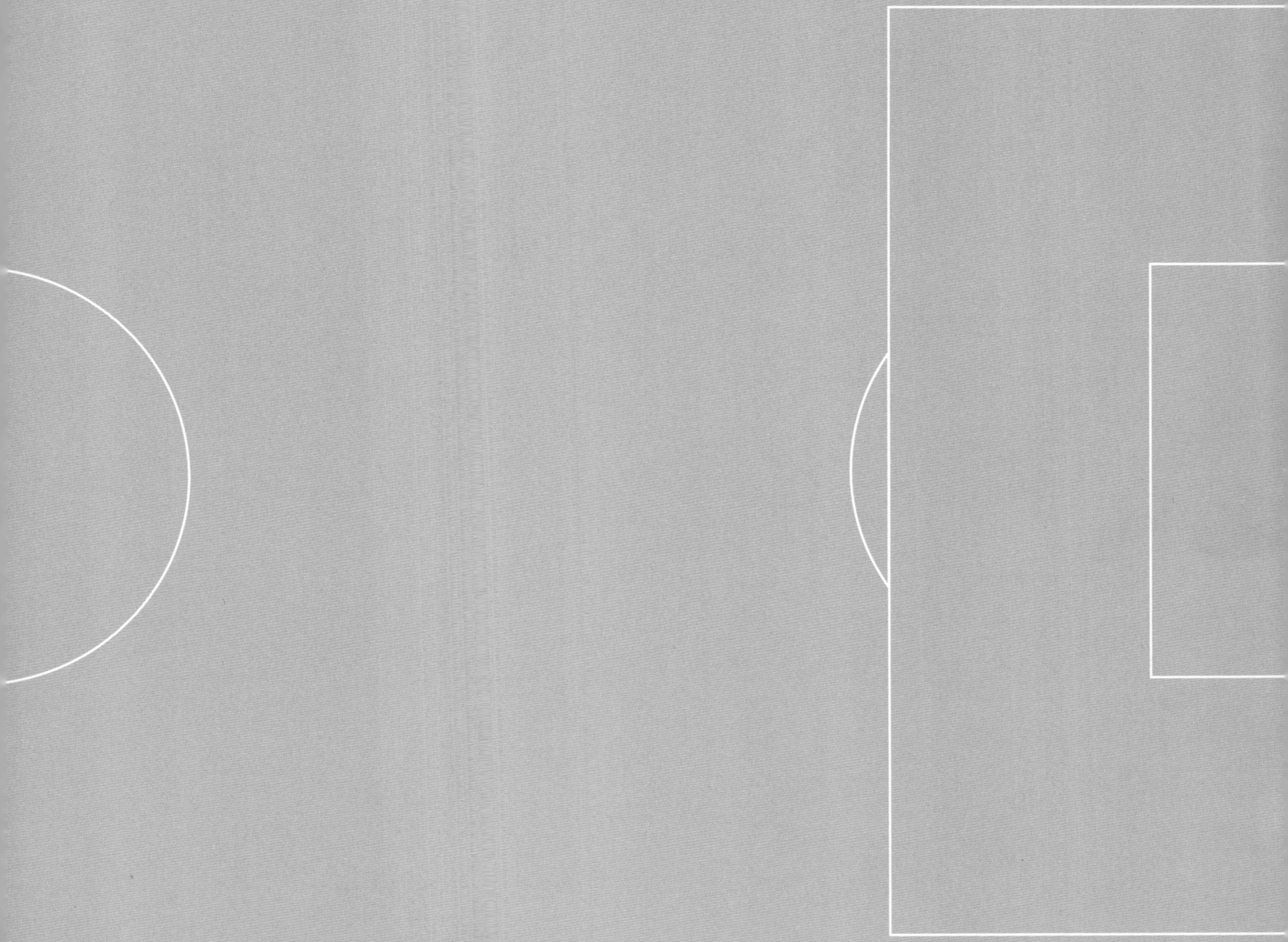

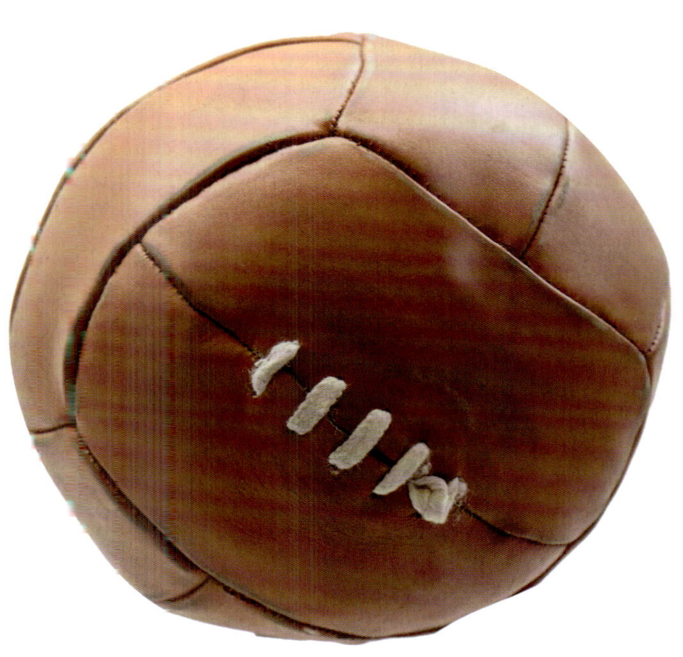

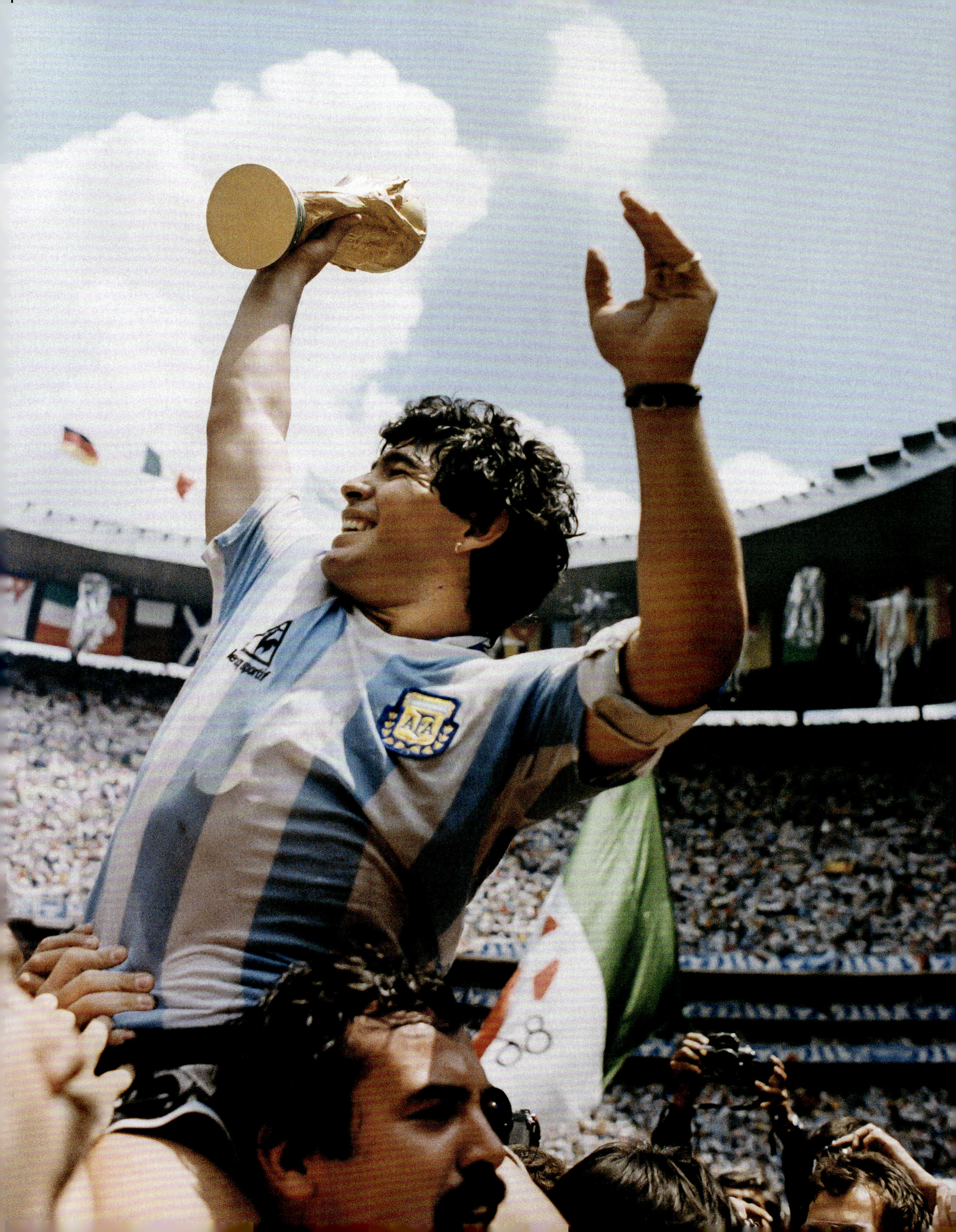

# IMMORTAL MOMENTS
# THE WORLD CUP

## BY RICK BARBA

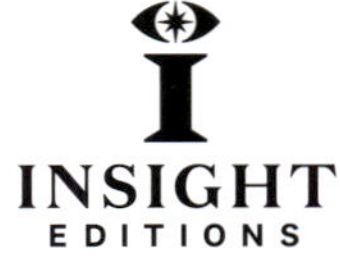

INSIGHT
EDITIONS

SAN RAFAEL · LOS ANGELES · LONDON

## EVERY FOUR YEARS, THE WORLD STOPS FOR FOOTBALL

**For the skeptics, a statistic:** The 2022 FIFA World Cup tournament in Qatar drew in an estimated TV viewership of 3.57 billion and engaged another 1.8 billion across digital and streaming platforms. The most watched and celebrated happening on the planet with no true equal, not even the Summer Olympic Games, World Cup football is not just a sporting event — it's a global cultural phenomenon.

Held quadrennially since 1930 (minus a decade interrupted by the Second World War), the Cup brings together nations from all continents, ignites passions and hopes across borders and languages, and binds cultures together through a shared love of what the legendary Pelé crowned 'the Beautiful Game.'

Association football — more commonly known as just 'football' or, in a handful of countries, 'soccer' — has been played in its current form for more than 150 years. With an estimated 240 million registered participants worldwide, it is easily the world's most popular sport. The Fédération Internationale de Football Association (FIFA), the international governing body for football, oversees member associations in 211 countries and territories. Within those nations, over 300,000 football clubs. And, of course, billions of avid fans globally.

The origin of the FIFA World Cup dates to the early twentieth century, during a period when football was growing rapidly in popularity around the world. Europe and South America saw the most widespread interest, but confederations grew in other regions, too. The creation of the World Cup was a response to rapid globalisation and the surging demand for an organised international competition to showcase the sport.

After staging three successful tournaments in the 1930s, the 1940s saw FIFA join the rest of the world in pausing international activity during the terrible conflagration and aftermath of the Second World War. With such a long break kneecapping the tournament just as it was getting off the ground, many predicted its ultimate demise. But football was not to be stopped, and the World Cup returned full force in 1950, with ever-bigger tournaments being staged every four years.

In the 1960s and 1970s, advances in TV-broadcast technology began to bring Cup action to millions, and eventually billions, of viewers. In 2022, the live broadcast of a single match, the World Cup Final between Argentina and France, drew a live TV audience of 1.5 billion people. It was the seventh-most-watched single event in television history. The number of qualifying nations also increased steadily over the years. The first tournament in 1930 had thirteen teams participate, then increased to sixteen in 1934, twenty-four in 1982, and thirty-two in 1998. The upcoming 2026 tournament will feature a staggering forty-eight teams, representing more nations around the globe than ever before.

Like all sports, football is about competition, rivalries, winning, and losing. In many nations, the sport is deeply interwoven into the fabric of society, and success on the world stage is a source of immense national pride — a pride on full display as fans don national team jerseys, wave banners, bang drums, blow vuvuzelas, and sing anthems like 'Cielito Lindo' ('Beautiful Heaven') in Mexico, 'Que bonito é' ('How beautiful it is') in Brazil, 'Muchachos' in Argentina, 'Sweet Caroline' in England, and the universal and ubiquitous football chant Olé, Olé, Olé, Olé! Host countries invest billions in sports infrastructure in preparation for the Cup and go to great lengths to showcase their cultural heritage, history, and identity in massive opening ceremonies.

Whereas national pride certainly unites folks *within* countries, every World Cup turns the host nation into an amazing cultural melting pot, bringing dozens of nationalities together in a spirit of celebration. Since 1930, the Cup has been hosted by twenty-four different countries, each one drawing millions of fans from every corner of the globe into a monthlong intercultural exchange, sharing music, food, languages, and traditions on the streets and stadiums of the host's venue cities.

In this way, the World Cup has been a vanguard against the divisive strains of nationalism that have historically bred xenophobia and bigotry. World Cup football revels in the common human experiences that bring diverse peoples together: moments of joy, despair, hope, and passion. Despite the Cup's complex and deeply interwoven relationship with turbulent global events, it has consistently managed to inspire the world as a beacon of hope and healing. Songs like Ricky Martin's 'La Copa de la Vida' ('The Cup of Life') in 1998 or Shakira's 'Waka Waka' in 2010, composed specifically for those years' respective tournaments, became global hits that celebrated and spread the Cup's unifying spirit.

Few events have the power to make people across all twenty-four global time zones stop what they're doing and gather in homes, pubs, stadiums, and public squares to collectively awe at raw moments of unfiltered drama and glory. A stoppage-time winner, a penalty shootout, a scandal, an underdog taking a heavyweight to the wire. On the international stage, only football can deliver.

It seems that most everybody is connected in 'the beautiful game', which on the pitch transpires something deeply human. It certainly has something to do with the raw physics of football, its dynamic and unregimented flow across ninety minutes, but it goes beyond. The interplay between individual brilliance and collective effort reveals a fundamental emotion.

There can be no greater expression of this essence than when donning the national team shirt, the whole world watching, cheering . . .

*Olé, Olé, Olé, Olé!*

# THE 1930s

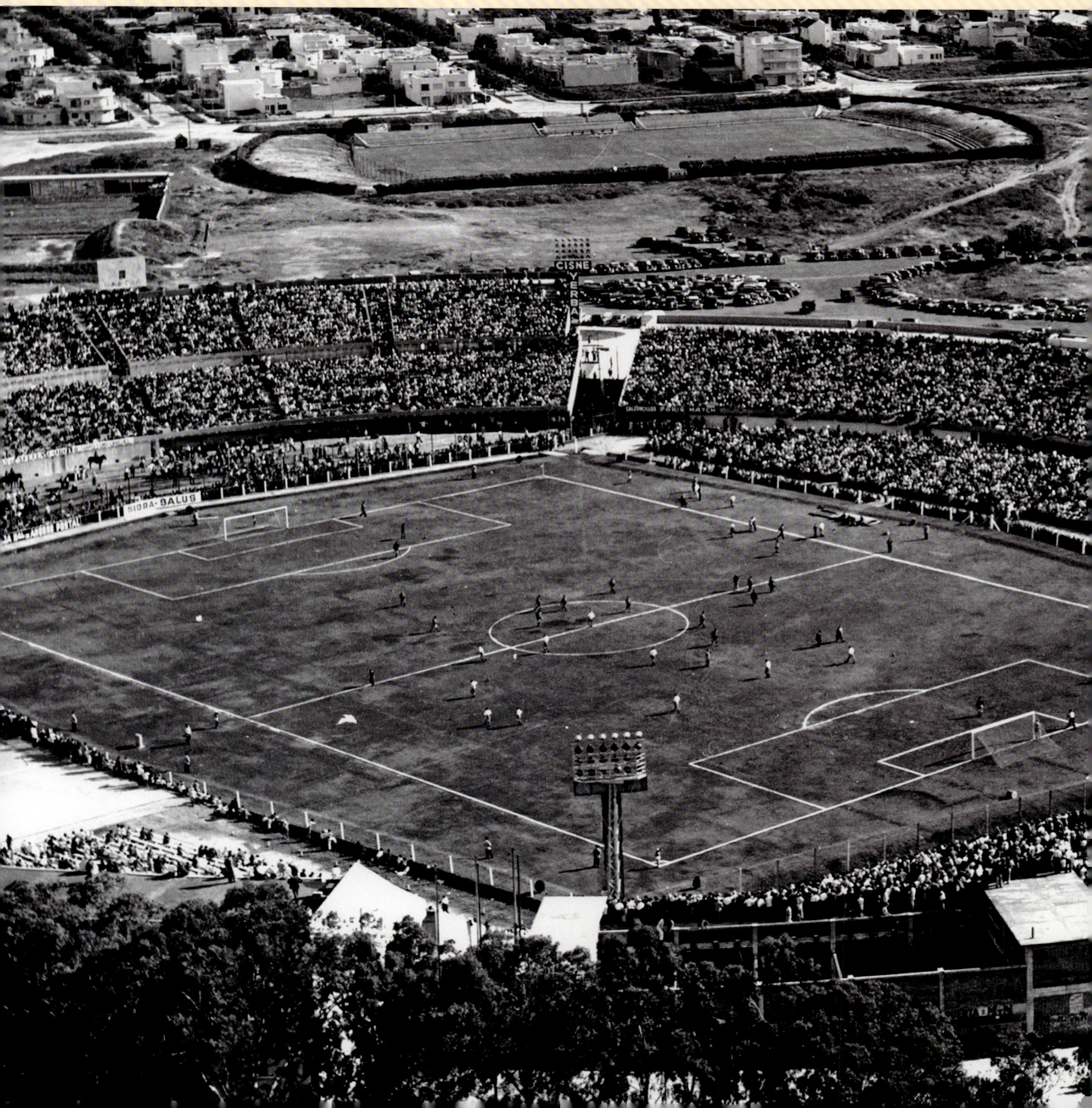

# CHAPTER 1

# Origins & Early Days

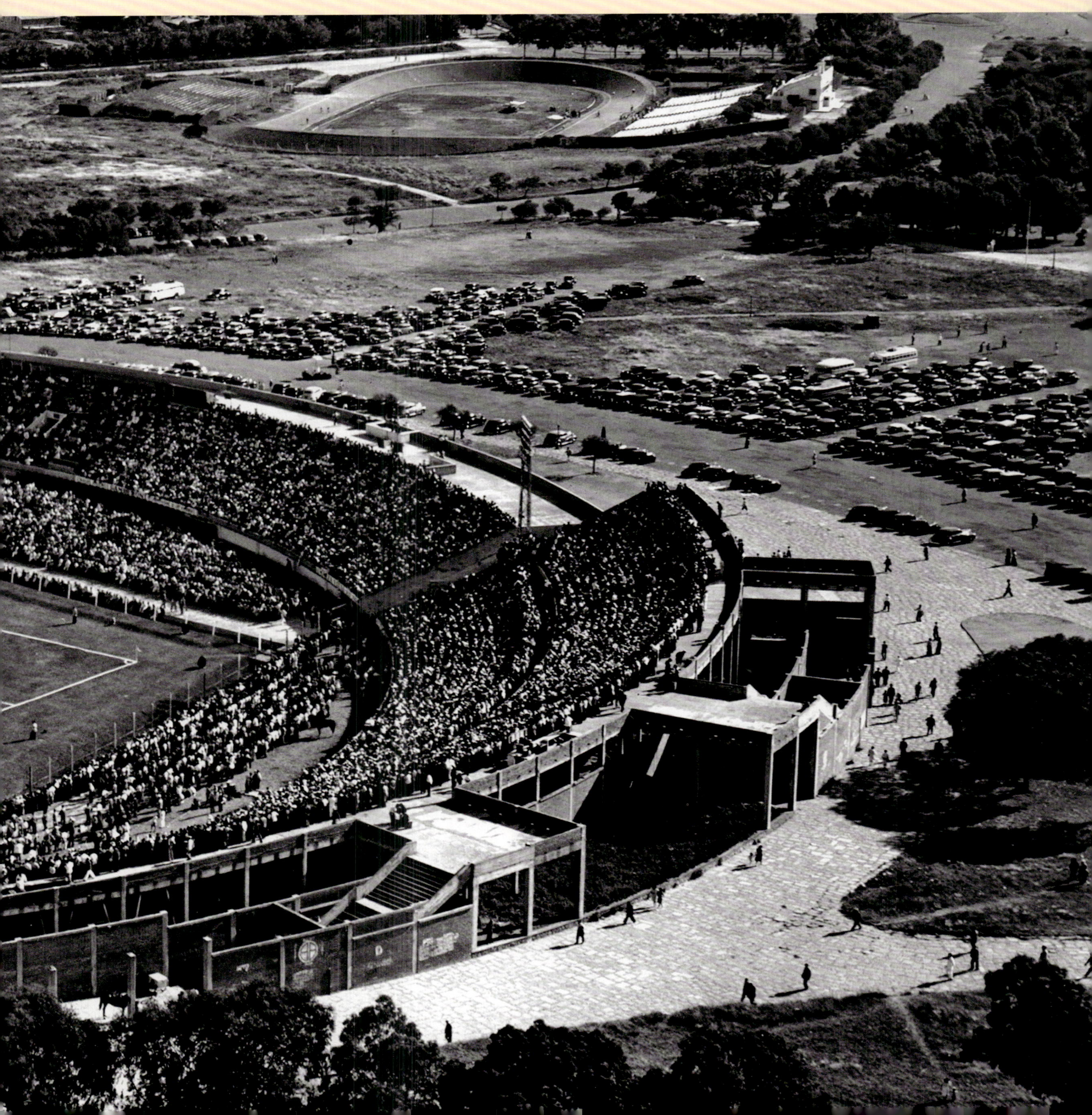

# THE CUP IS BORN

**On 30 November of 1872,** when England battled its neighbour Scotland to a scrappy 0–0 draw at Glasgow's Hamilton Crescent, 4,000 eager spectators saw just a spirited 'local scrum.' Today, however, that hallowed meeting is officially recognised as the first international football match. And it took off.

In response to the remarkable growth, an organisation called FIFA (Fédération Internationale de Football Association) was founded in Paris in 1904. Created to standardise the rules of the game and facilitate international competitions, FIFA focused mainly on Europe in those early years. But football was to be a global phenomenon, and it steadily spread from Europe to the Americas and Asia in the early twentieth century. The sport that Pelé would one day dub 'the beautiful game' had begun to dig its claws into impassioned fan bases worldwide, and so the yearning grew for an international tournament that featured competing nations from every continent, not just club sides.

To help satisfy the demand for premier international competition, football officially debuted as an Olympic sport at the 1908 Summer Olympics in London. For the next two decades, the gold medal–winning country would be considered the world champion of football until the next Games. The Olympics, of course, adhered to a strict code of amateurism for all athletes. For years, many footballers maintained their Olympic amateur status by subterfuge, earning generous wages while 'employed' in fictitious positions at football-loving businesses. English pro clubs like Blackburn Rovers and Darwen often signed 'amateurs' in this manner. As a result, those years are often referred to as the 'Shamateur Era.'

**But by the 1920s, football** had transitioned to a much more open professionalism, with most national teams filling their squads with pro players. As a result, many countries stopped sending squads to the Olympics altogether. In response to this troubling trend that threatened to undermine global football competition, FIFA president Jules Rimet and French Football Association secretary Henri Delaunay began to organise an international football championship that would be open to all players, regardless of status. On 26 May, 1928, the FIFA Congress in Amsterdam officially founded a World Cup tournament to be played in 1930 and every four years thereafter — designed to take place halfway between editions of the Summer Olympics.

After much negotiation, Uruguay was selected as the inaugural host nation. It was a sensible choice for several reasons. First, Uruguay was considered the best national team in the world, having won Olympic gold in both 1924 and 1928, and in dominant fashion. Second, FIFA wanted football to shed its Eurocentric image, and Rimet believed a South American site would add a more global sheen to the Cup. Finally, 1930 would also see Uruguay commemorating its centenary as an independent nation, and such a celebration would certainly supercharge the festive aura of the Cup proceedings.

Unfortunately, several European teams dropped out of this first tournament to protest the decision, including England, Austria, Italy, Sweden, Hungary, and Spain. But viewed through a wider scope, selecting Uruguay as the first World Cup host was clearly a wise and prescient choice. Football fever spread with astonishing speed across South America, a joyous continental contagion that eventually produced some of the most thrilling teams and players in the history of the game. Rimet's bold inaugural choice helped pave the path to a future that would bring us the magnificent likes of Pelé, Maradona, Ronaldo, and Messi.

**PREVIOUS SPREAD** *The Estadio Centenario in Montevideo, Uruguay, dubbed a 'temple of football' by Jules Rimet. It was built to host the inaugural World Cup and was later named by FIFA as the first Historical Monument of World Football in 1983.*

**BELOW** *Jules Rimet, then-president of the Fédération Internationale de Football Association (FIFA) and the driving force behind the creation of the World Cup, opens the 1931 FIFA Congress in Berlin. It was the first session held after the success of the 1930 inaugural tournament.*

**OPPOSITE** *Scottish artist W. Ralston's illustrated rendition of the first-ever international football match, originally published in The Graphic. Held on 30 November, 1872, the match saw England and Scotland battle to a 0–0 draw at Hamilton Crescent in Glasgow.*

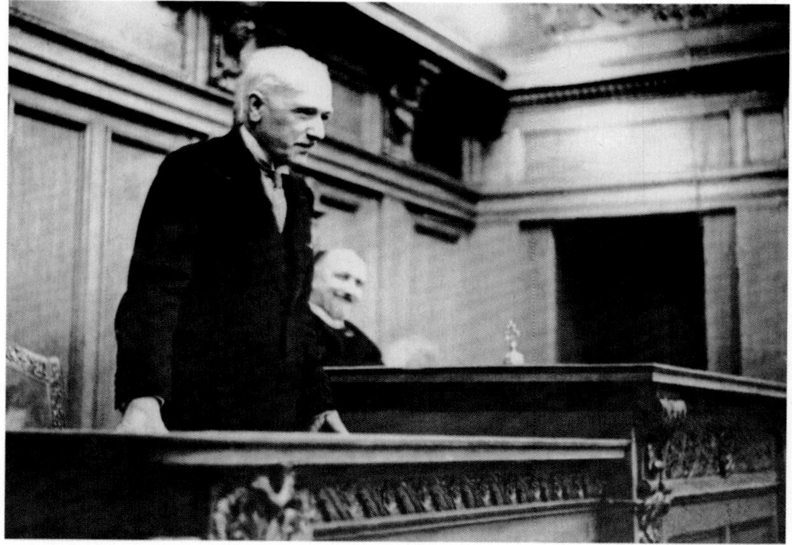

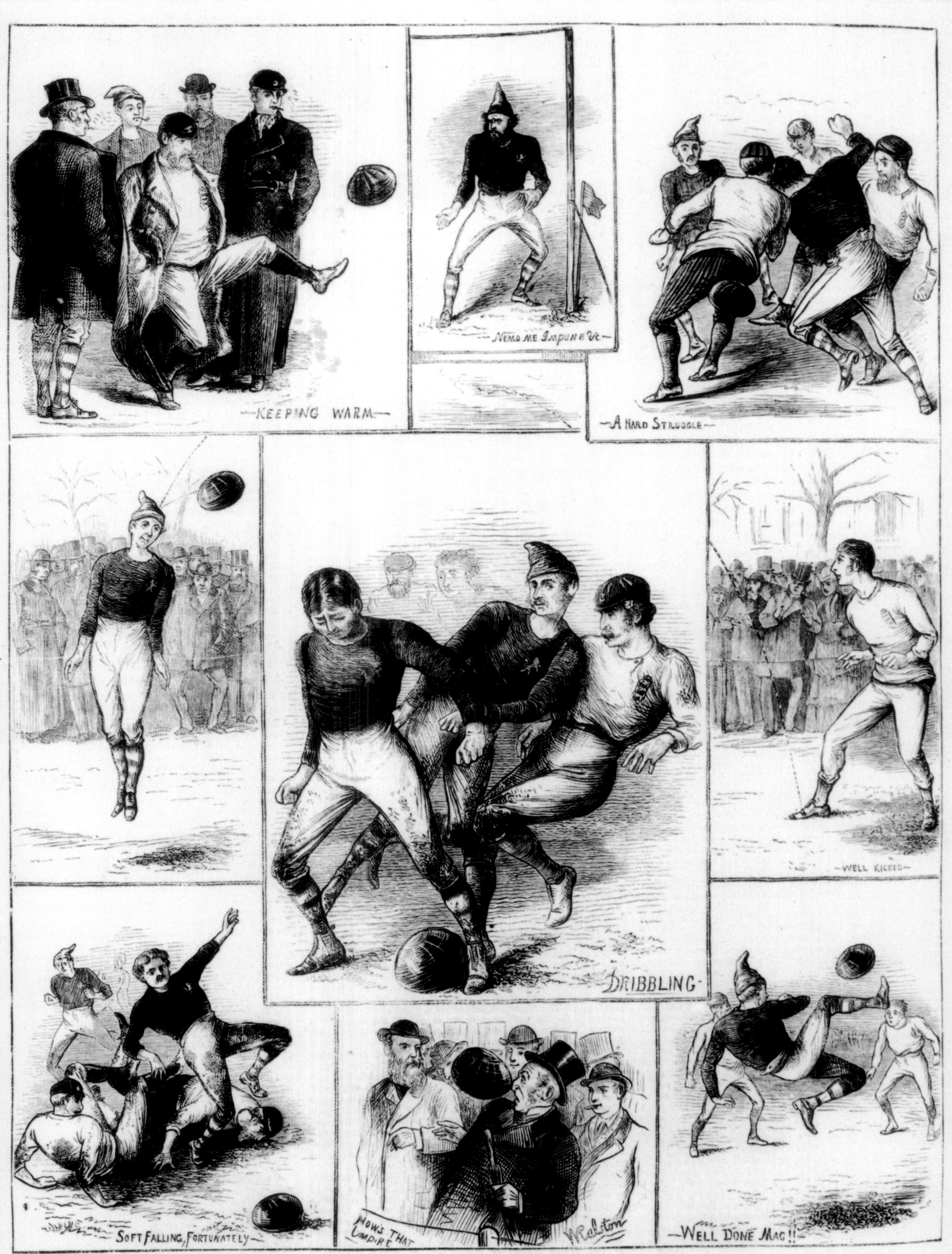


SKETCHES AT THE INTERNATIONAL FOOTBALL MATCH, GLASGOW

# 1930



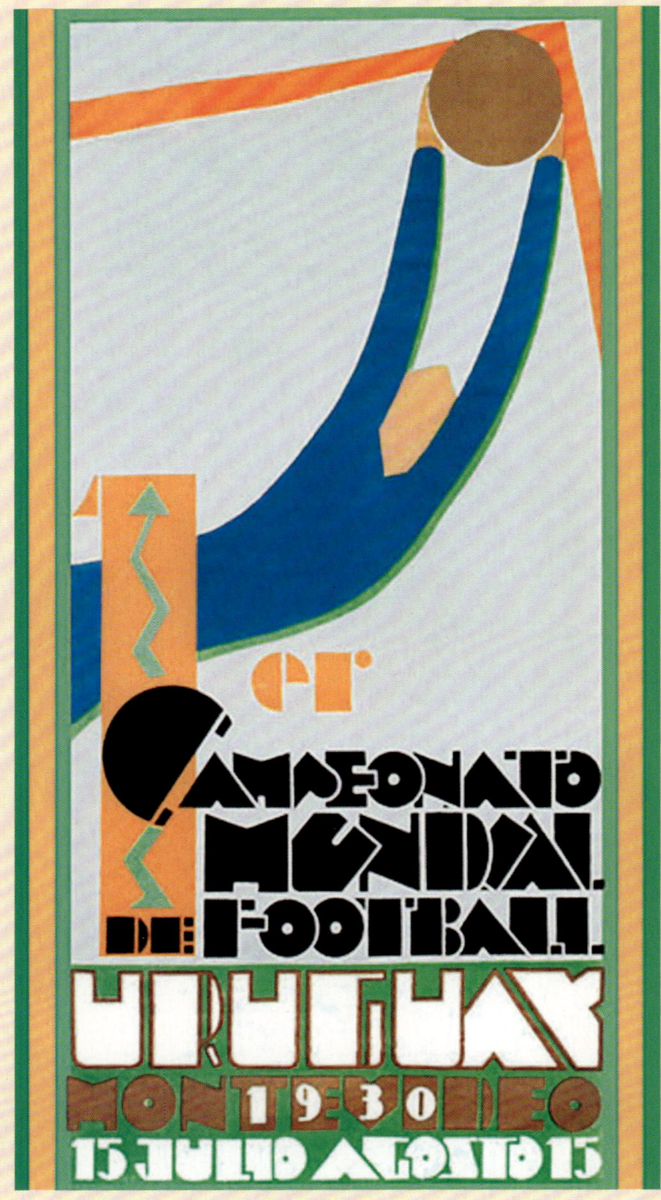



**FIFA's first World Cup competition** took place in the summer of 1930, 3 July to 30 July, in the Uruguayan capital of Montevideo. This would be the only World Cup with no qualifying tournaments to narrow the field, as FIFA invited all forty-one member nations. At first, only ten countries agreed to send a team, a truly lacklustre response, partly due to the boycott by European nations protesting the site selection. Initially, nobody in Europe would commit; FIFA President Jules Rimet, a Frenchman, had to badger his own home team to participate, as did FIFA's Belgian vice president, Rodolphe Seeldrayers. Eventually, France, Belgium, Romania, and Yugoslavia agreed to go. But the significant cost and logistical challenges of a long voyage to South America was a tough roadblock for FIFA to get past.

The rest of the line-up included seven South American sides (host nation Uruguay, as well as Argentina, Bolivia, Brazil, Chile, Paraguay, and Peru), two from North America (Mexico and the USA), and just one team from outside Europe and the Americas: Egypt.

**LEFT** *The official poster of the 1930 World Cup. Designed by Uruguayan artist Guillermo Laborde, it incorporated elements of Planismo, a prominent art style in 1920s Uruguay characterised by flat geometric shapes and bright colours.*

## THE KING'S SIDE

**In Romania, a new monarch,** Carol II, took the throne just a month before the start of the World Cup. The king was a rabid football fan and, despite the boycott sentiment rippling across the rest of Europe, he unequivocally demanded that his country send a team to Uruguay.

To facilitate this, Carol II granted amnesty to any Romanian suspended from football for any reason (including, unsurprisingly, some *very* good players), decreed that businesses that employed national team players must offer them the three months of paid leave necessary to play in the Cup or else be shut down, and hand-picked the Romanian squad himself. 'By force of the king's will', reported *The New York Times*, 'a mostly urban team was plucked from the industrial centres of Bucharest and Timișoara and bundled off to Genoa, Italy, where they boarded an ocean liner and sailed three weeks across the Atlantic to compete in Montevideo'.

On top of all that, King Carol spent a significant amount of political capital to convince neighbouring Yugoslavia to send a team of their own. As a result of his insistent lobbying, Carol II was personally responsible for deploying half of the European sides that participated in the inaugural World Cup!

As the *New York Times* summed up so eloquently: 'Though much enlarged, the World Cup is still at its core what it was in King Carol's day: a pageant of nation-states . . . Along with a flag and an anthem, a soccer team gave a country a tangible form, tracing the contours of a people in the collective striving on the field. The memorable stories of each World Cup are often ones of national apotheosis and national calamity'.

## THE GREAT VOYAGE

**A huge barrier to Cup participation** in 1930 was the logistical difficulty and cost of commercial travel, especially during the fraught early days of the Great Depression. Team travel from Europe to South America required a three-week sea voyage, costing not just money but also the loss of critical pretournament training sessions. After finalizing their participation plans, the Romanian, French, and Belgian teams boarded the giant transatlantic ocean liner *SS Conte Verde* for the long haul. The ship also picked up the Brazilian team in Rio de Janeiro en route to the Uruguayan coastal city of Montevideo, the site of the tournament.

Meanwhile, Yugoslavia and Egypt were booked for travel aboard a pleasure cruiser, the *Florida*, bound for Uruguay from Marseilles. Unfortunately, a heavy storm in

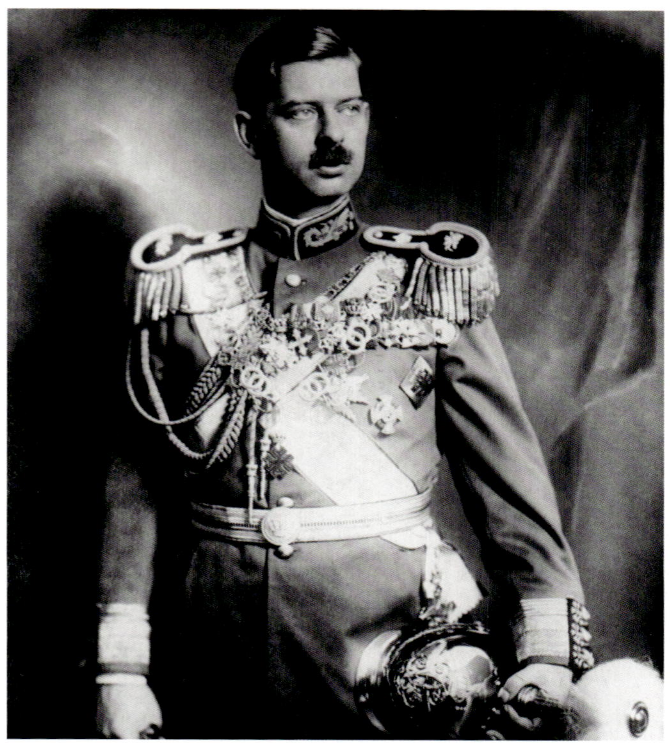

ABOVE *Carol II, King of Romania from 1930 to 1940. An unlikely protagonist of the World Cup's early history.*

BELOW *An illustration of the SS Conte Verde.*

BOTTOM *Members of the French squad aboard the Conte Verde.*

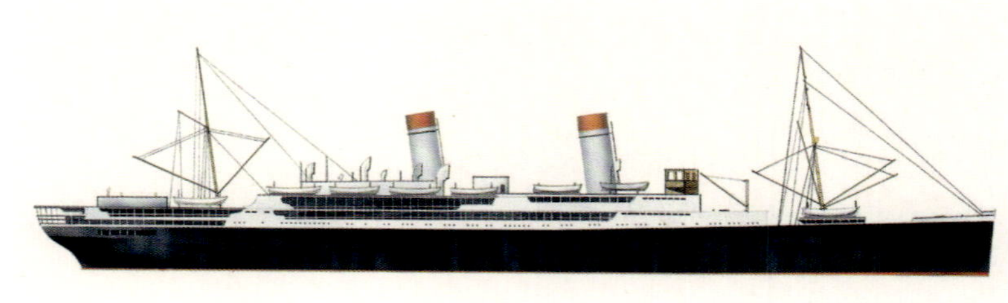

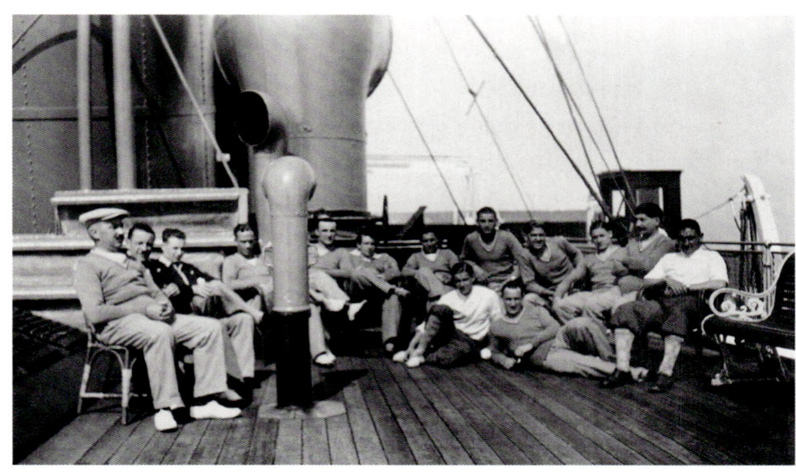

the Mediterranean forced the Egyptian team to miss the connection, and the whole tournament, as a result. The first World Cup was down to just thirteen nations.

# Tournament: GROUP STAGE

**Once all the pretournament drama** was surmounted, the tourney itself proved a great showcase for the sport. Teams were organised into four groups for round-robin play, with the four group winners moving on to the tournament semi-finals. Again, Uruguay's centenary celebration sparked a festive atmosphere as the group-stage matches unfolded in Montevideo's three stadiums, including the brand-new Estadio Centenario ('Centenary Stadium').

## WORLD CUP FIRSTS

### FIRST-EVER WORLD CUP MATCHES

The first pair of Cup matches kicked off simultaneously at two separate stadiums: France vs Mexico and USA vs Belgium.

### FIRST-EVER WORLD CUP GOAL

Lucien Laurent of France scored the tournament's first goal in the nineteenth minute against Mexico. France went on to win the match 4–1.

### FIRST-EVER WORLD CUP SHUTOUT

In the other match, the United States beat Belgium 3–0. Thus, USA goalkeeper Jimmy Douglas posted the first-ever World Cup 'clean sheet'.

### FIRST SENDOFF

In Romania's 3–1 victory over Peru, the referee expelled Peruvian midfielder Plácido Reynaldo Galindo in the seventieth minute for rough play.

### FIRST-EVER HAT-TRICK

This one took seventy-six years to officially settle. On 19 July, Argentine forward Guillermo Stábile scored three goals in a 6–3 thrashing of Mexico. However, two days earlier, USA forward Bert Patenaude scored two goals against Paraguay, with a third goal initially marked as a poke-in by a teammate. For decades, Stábile's feat was listed as the first hat-trick in World Cup play. But after a careful review in 2006, FIFA confirmed that it was, in fact, Patenaude who had scored the Americans' third goal . . . and officially declared his hat-trick as the first in World Cup history.

OPPOSITE *USA's Bert Patenaude beats the Belgian keeper and is challenged by defender Nicolas Hoydonckx. At the fiftieth minute, Patenaude notched the first hat-trick in tournament history.*

### GROUP 1: ARGENTINA, CHILE, FRANCE, MEXICO

| | | |
|---|---|---|
| France 4 | 1 | Mexico |
| Argentina 1 | 0 | France |
| Chile 3 | 0 | Mexico |
| Chile 1 | 0 | France |
| Argentina 6 | 3 | Mexico |
| Argentina 3 | 1 | Chile |

**Group Winner: Argentina**

The Argentina–Chile match was marred by a series of brawls so unruly that police had to restore order at half-time. Against Mexico, Argentine forward Guillermo Stábile scored yet another hat-trick.

### GROUP 2: BOLIVIA, BRAZIL, YUGOSLAVIA

| | | |
|---|---|---|
| Yugoslavia 2 | 1 | Brazil |
| Yugoslavia 4 | 0 | Bolivia |
| Brazil 4 | 0 | Bolivia |

**Group Winner: Yugoslavia**

Like Romania, a latecomer to the tournament roster, Yugoslavia showed great grit in dispatching the two South American sides. Its win over group favourite Brazil was decisive, with the Yugoslavs leading 2–0 after just thirty minutes. Afterward the Brazilians claimed they were unaccustomed to the unexpectedly cold temperatures in Montevideo.

### GROUP 3: PERU, ROMANIA, URUGUAY

| | | |
|---|---|---|
| Romania 3 | 1 | Peru |
| Uruguay 1 | 0 | Peru |
| Uruguay 4 | 0 | Romania |

**Group Winner: Uruguay**

Romania versus Peru was played before a crowd of just 300 people, the smallest in World Cup history…a record unlikely to be 'surpassed' in the future.

### GROUP 4: BELGIUM, PARAGUAY, USA

| | | |
|---|---|---|
| USA 3 | 0 | Belgium |
| USA 3 | 0 | Paraguay |
| Paraguay 1 | 0 | Belgium |

**Group Winner: USA**

The USA was surprisingly dominant in Group 4 play, with striker Bert Patenaude knocking in a goal against Belgium and three more against Paraguay. The USA–Belgium match drew an unexpectedly large crowd of nearly 20,000 spectators, mostly Uruguayan—an early sign that football fans were fascinated by international matchups, no matter who or where they were played.

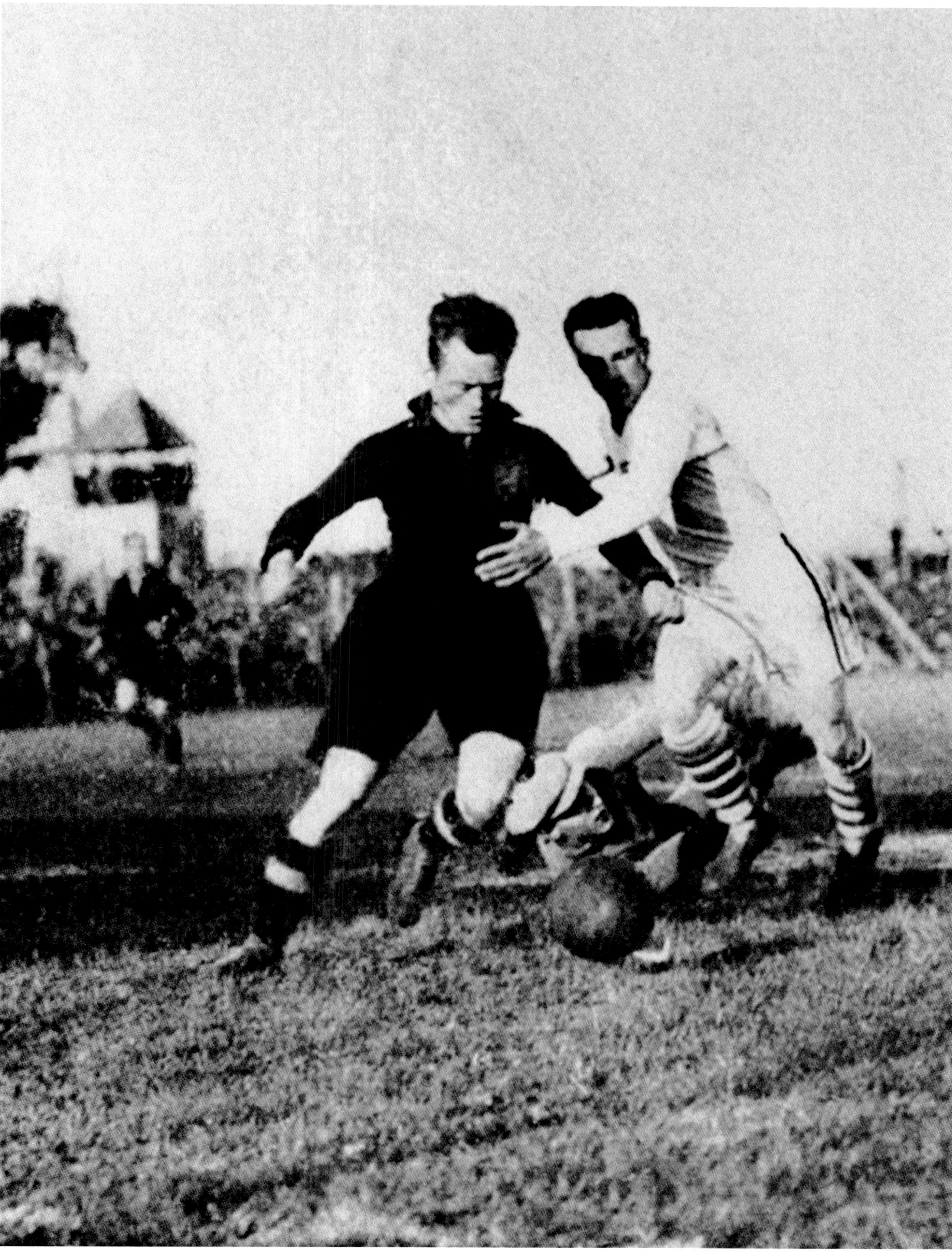

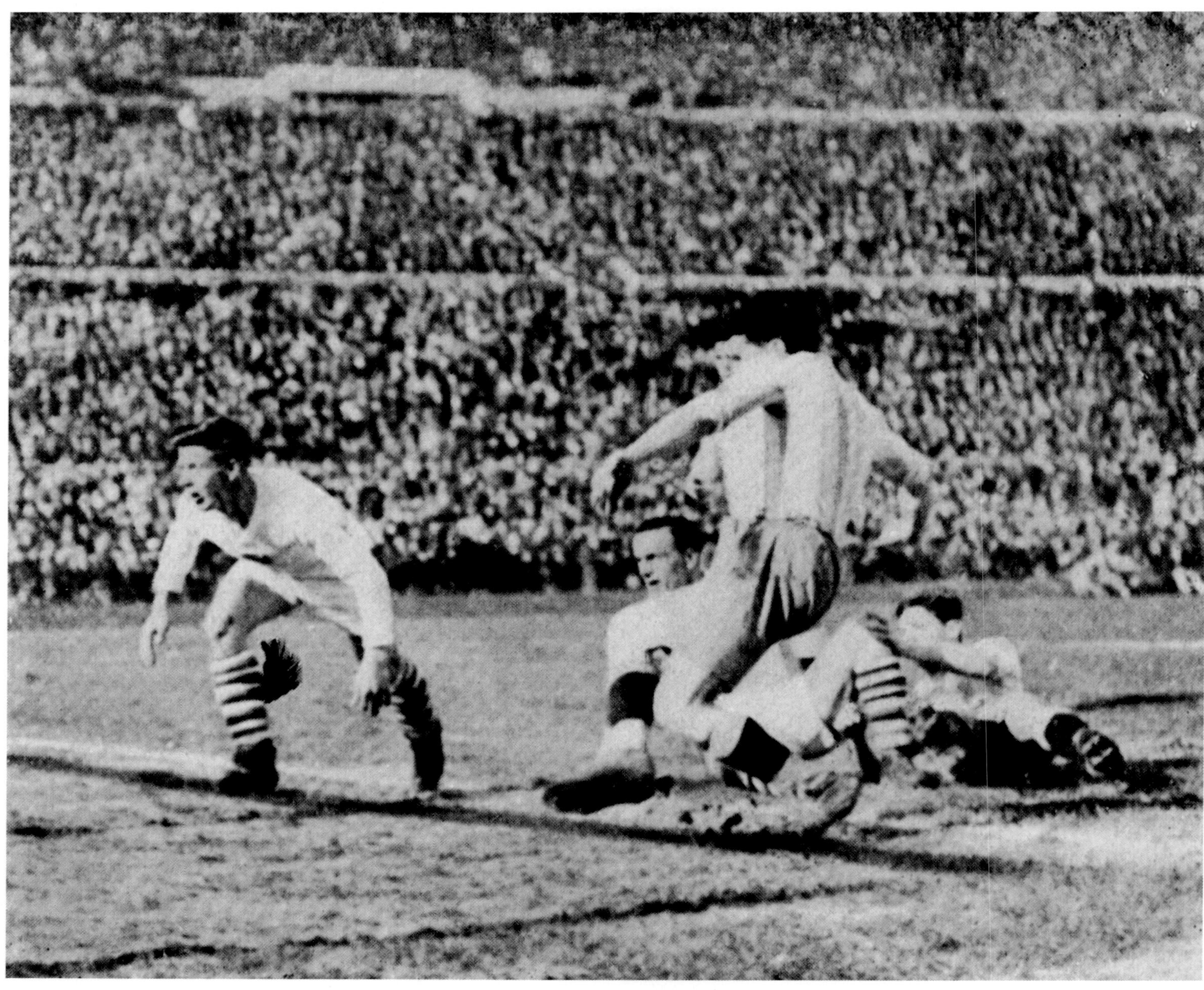

## SEMI-FINALS

Argentina 6 | 1 USA
Uruguay 6 | 1 Yugoslavia

In the first semi-final, Argentina punished the USA, to the tune of a 6–1 scoreline, in a brutal match marked by extremely physical play and multiple injuries. FIFA policy at the time included the odd rule that no substitutions were allowed for any reason, not even an injured player. So, when USA centre-half Raphael Tracey suffered a leg injury in the nineteenth minute, he struggled to stay on but, ultimately, had to exit the match for good at halftime with his team trailing only 1–0. Facing a side of only ten in the second half, the skilful Argentines broke down the bigger but slower Americans (nicknamed 'the shot-putters' by the French) and ended up netting a barrage of three goals in just seven minutes late in the match.

The second semi-final pitted the tourney host against the tournament's Cinderella team. The upstart squad from Yugoslavia had won Group 2 with a shocking 2–1 victory over group favourite Brazil. The valiant *Plavi* (The Blues) scored like a bolt of lightning in the fourth minute, but after that, they were no match for the reigning Olympic champion. It was 3–1 Uruguay by half, with the final tally reaching 6–1, capped off by a hat-trick from the prodigious forward Pedro Cea.

# THE FIRST WORLD CUP FINAL

Uruguay 4 | 2 Argentina

With as many as 100,000 fans packed into the gleaming Estadio Centenario, the 30 July final featured the resumption of a red-hot rivalry that raged both on the field and in the stands. 'The Battle of Archenemies' was a rematch of the fevered 1928 Olympic gold-medal final that saw Uruguay win 2–1 in a full replay after the first game had ended in a 1–1 tie. (In that era, knockout games that ended in a tie had to be replayed in their entirety. Penalty-kick shoot-outs were not used to settle World Cup knockout games until 1982.)

A pregame controversy over which side's ball to use started things off poorly, but FIFA worked out a compromise with a team ball swap at halftime. Many of the Argentine players, including their star Luis Monti, felt threatened by hostile fans of the host team. Monti had even decided to opt out at first but changed his mind at game time. Meanwhile, the Belgian centre referee, John Langenus, demanded a guarantee of safe postgame passage back to the ship.

Buoyed by an adoring crowd on its home soil, Uruguay controlled the pace early and took a 1–0 lead in the twelfth minute. But Argentina regrouped to score twice before half-time and went in with a 2–1 lead. Pedro Cea tied the match early in the second half, and Uruguayan winger Santos Iriarte knocked in a shot for the lead at the 68' mark. The action grew unbearably tense over the final twenty minutes as Argentina made a series of dangerous runs in pursuit of an equaliser. But Uruguay's goal in the final minute put the match away and the hosts emerged with a hard-fought victory.

In Uruguay, 31 July was declared a national holiday. In Argentina, a furious mob threw stones at the Uruguayan embassy in Buenos Aires.

And thus, World Cup passion was born.

**OPPOSITE** *Argentina's Guillermo Stábile scores one of his two goals in the 6–1 rout of USA.*

**BELOW** *A close view of the Estadio Centenario's pitch before the 1930 World Cup Final between Uruguay and Argentina.*

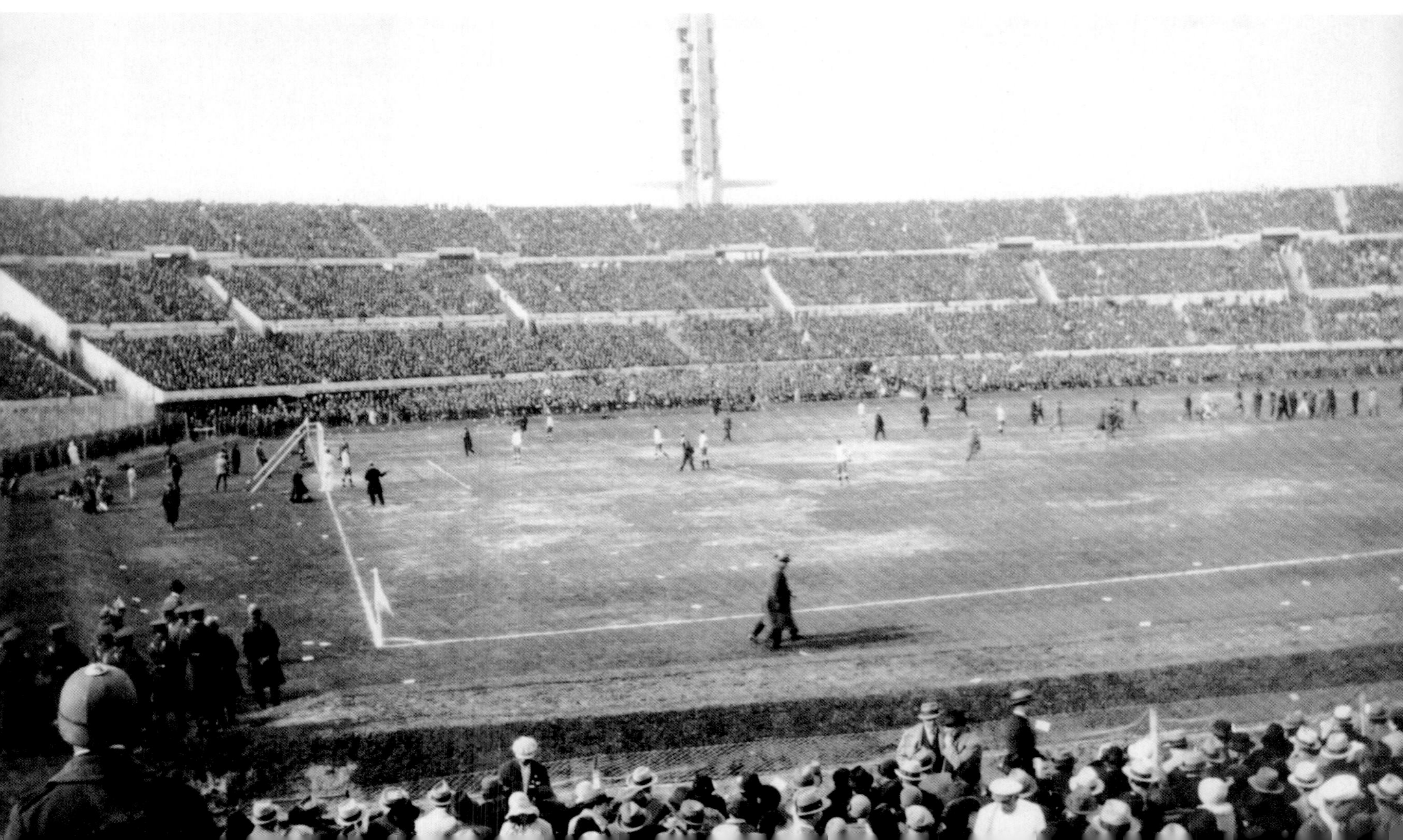

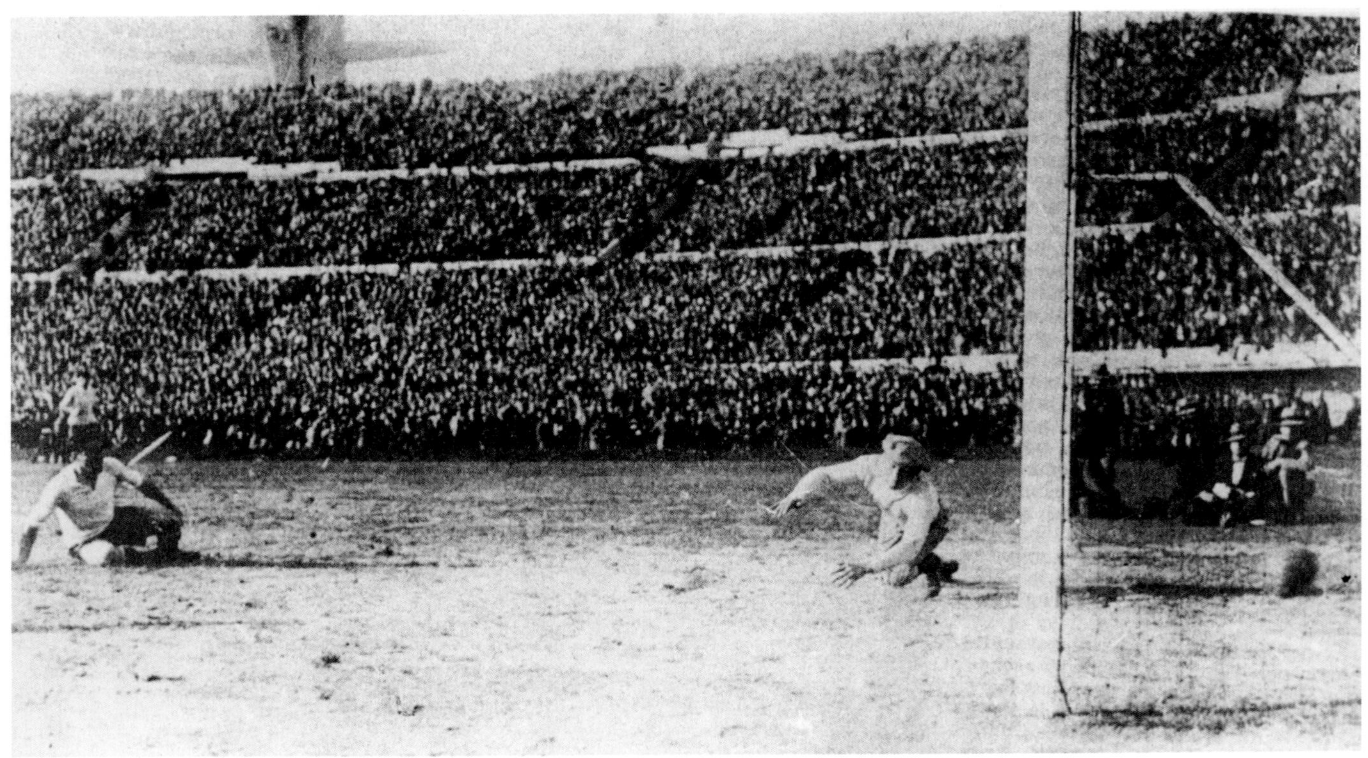

**TOP** *The ball hits the back of Argentina's net for one of Uruguay's four goals.*

**BOTTOM** *Uruguay captain José Nasazzi and Argentina captain Manuel 'Nolo' Ferreira shake hands before the final. Between them John Langenus, the Belgian centre referee.*

**OPPOSITE TOP** *An illustration of Jules Rimet and his eponymous trophy from the 1966 Campionati Mondiali di Calcio ('Football World Cup') series of Liebig trading cards.*

**OPPOSITE BOTTOM** *Jules Rimet hands over the championship trophy to Raúl Jude, president of the Uruguayan Football Association.*

# THE JULES RIMET TROPHY

**Originally named simply 'Victory',** the original World Cup Trophy was re-christened as the Jules Rimet Trophy in 1946 in honour of the World Cup founder and longtime FIFA President (1921–1954). The trophy — a gold-plated sterling-silver cup on a lapis-lazuli base, depicting Nike, the Greek goddess of victory — was passed to each new World Cup winner from 1930 until 1970, when the trophy was permanently awarded to Brazil for its third Cup win. (Jules Rimet himself had stipulated in 1930 that the first three-time World Cup winner would receive the trophy in perpetuity.)

Thus, the 1974 Cup tournament would see the Rimet Trophy replaced by the familiar 18-karat gold FIFA World Cup Trophy still used today. Sadly, in December of 1983, the original Jules Rimet Trophy was stolen from its bullet-proof display case at the headquarters of the Brazilian Football Confederation (CBF) in Rio de Janeiro . . . and was never recovered. But Rimet's vision lives on. As *The Independent* once noted, he believed football could unite nations, a powerful means by which one day 'people could meet in confidence without hatred in their hearts and without an insult on their lips'.

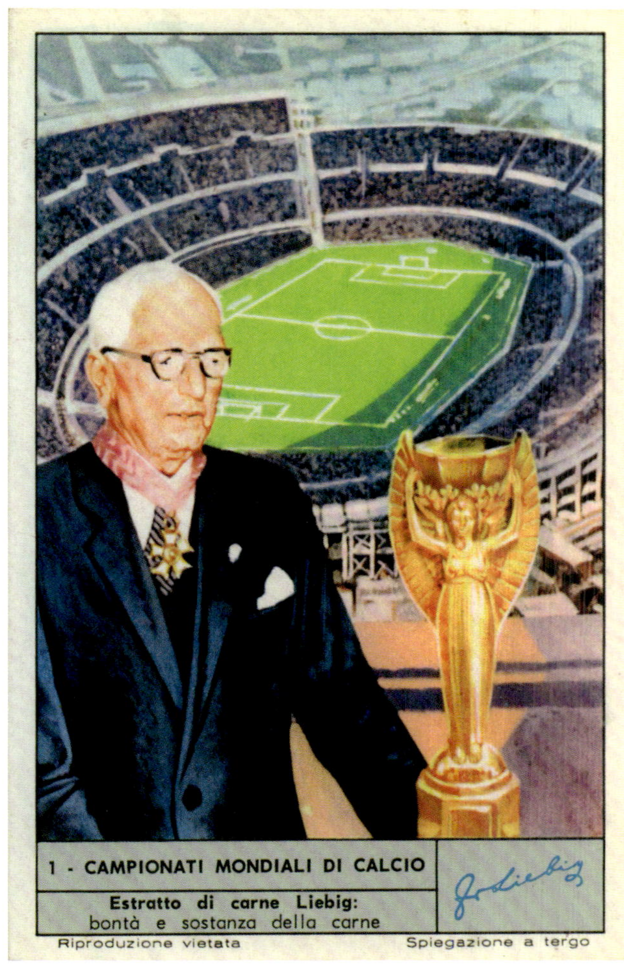



# THE MOST INFAMOUS FOOTBALLER OF 1930

**The celebrated captain** of the 1930 French World Cup squad, Alexandre Villaplane, had also played on France's 1928 Olympic team. But by the mid-1930s, his involvement in the French criminal underworld led to fines for match-fixing scandals and then imprisonment for fixing horse races.

During the Nazi occupation of France, Villaplane descended into racketeering, stolen goods, and the Parisian black market. This led to work with German security services, helping them root out members of the French Resistance. He even held a rank and uniform as a Nazi SS leader in what was considered the 'French Gestapo'. As *The Guardian* reported, Villaplane went from beloved captain of his national team to a brutal SS sublieutenant running the infamous Brigade Nord-Africaine (BNA), a murderous counterinsurgency unit that killed hundreds of Frenchmen.

After D-Day and the liberation of France, Villaplane was convicted of treason. He was executed by a French firing squad on 27 December, 1944.

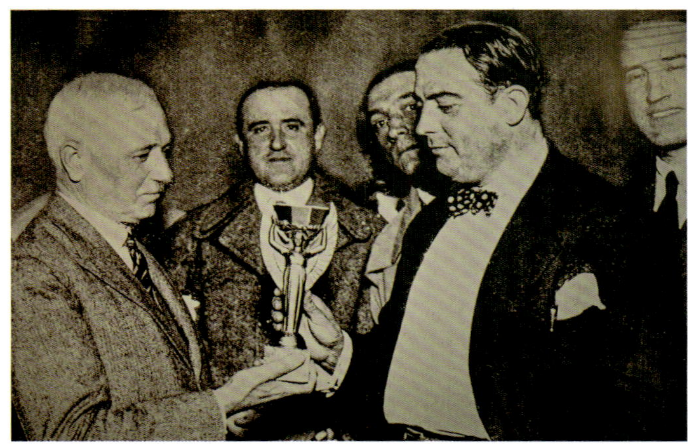

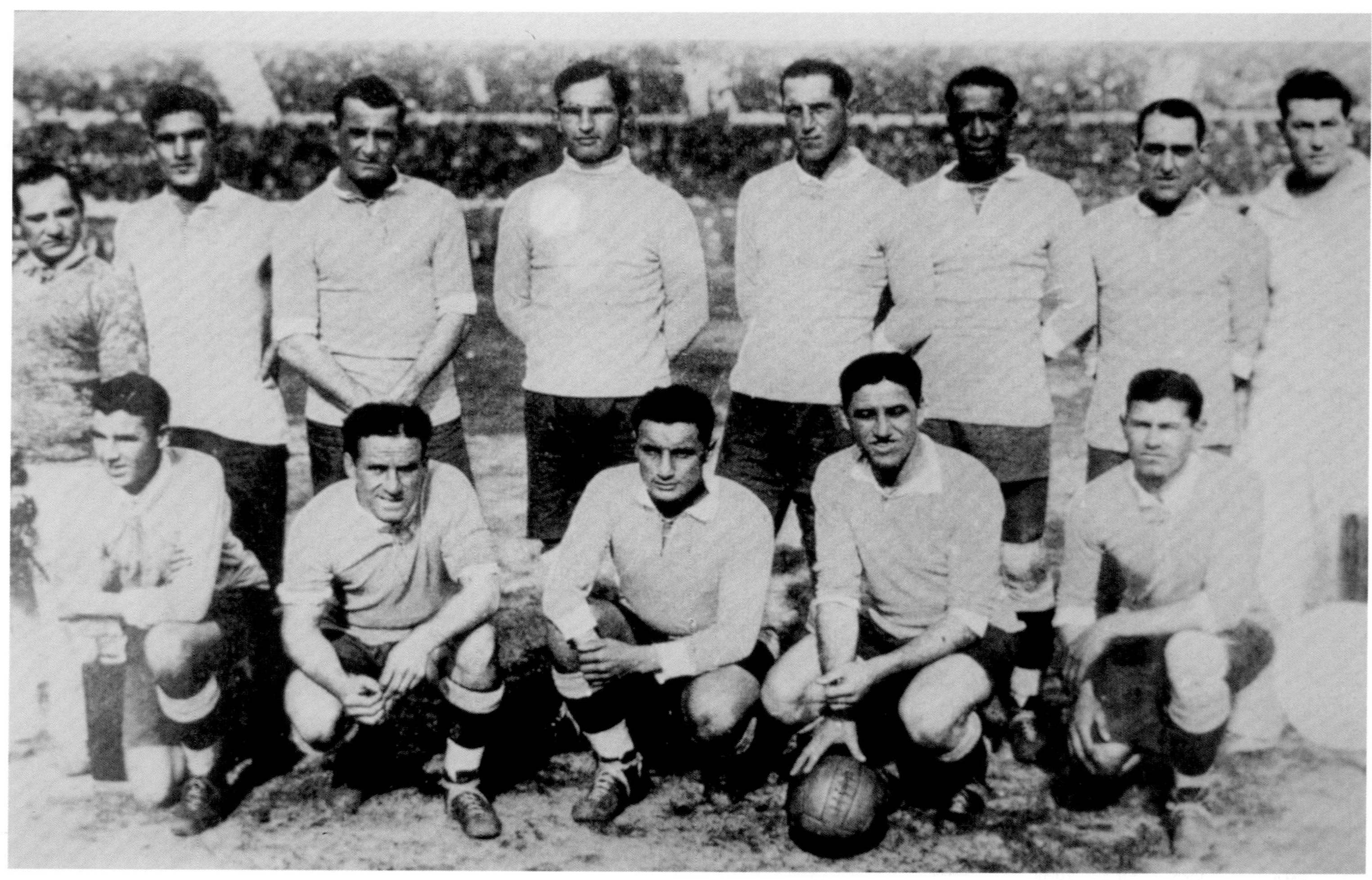

**ABOVE** *Uruguay's starting line-up for the 1930 World Cup—and the first-ever world champions of football.*

**OPPOSITE** *The 1930 World Cup Final as depicted in a stamp issued by the Hungarian Post, part of a series leading up to the 1966 World Cup.*

*'In Uruguay, 31 July was declared a national holiday. In Argentina, a furious mob threw stones at the Uruguayan embassy in Buenos Aires. And thus, World Cup passion was born.'*

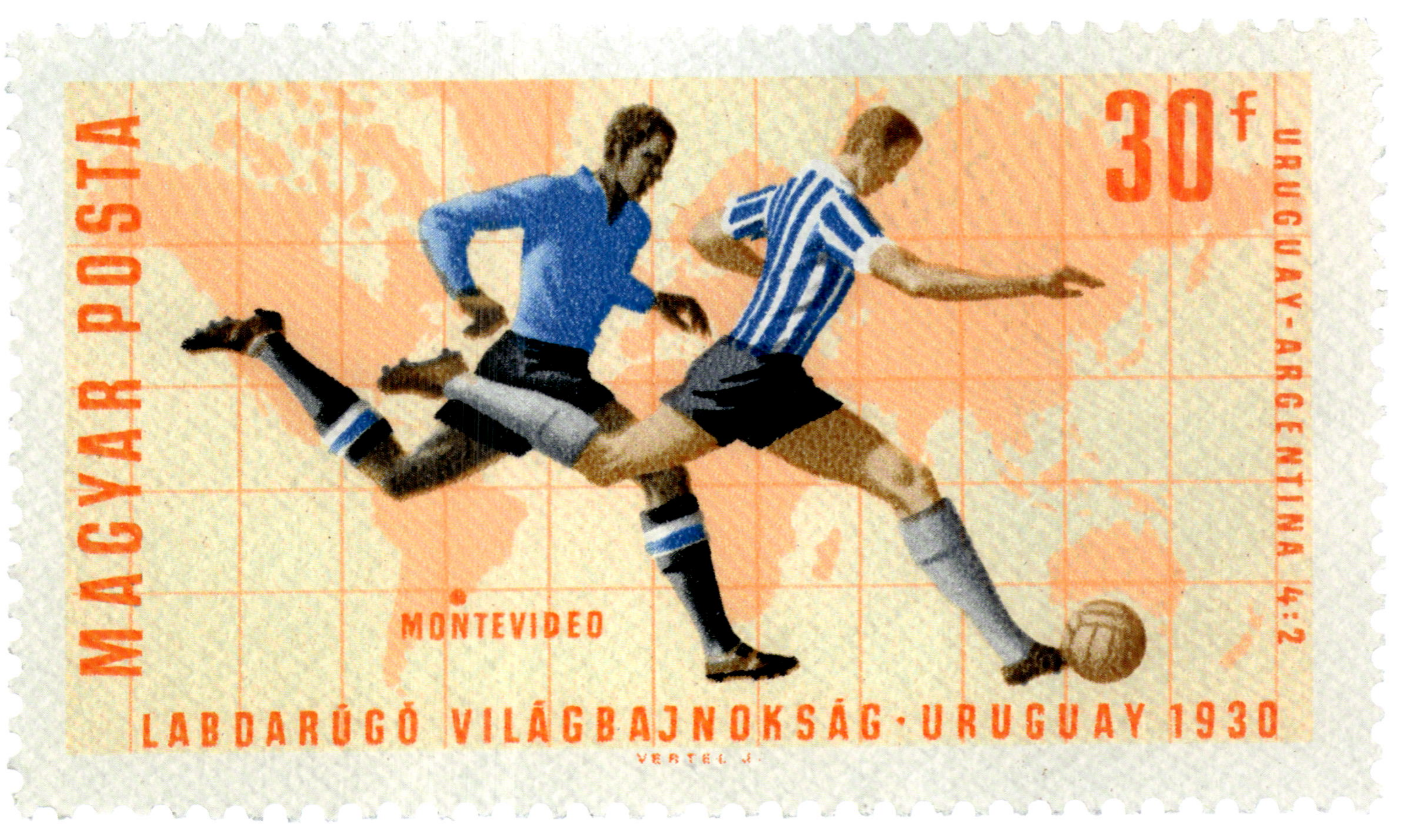

# 1934

HOST COUNTRY: **ITALY**
CHAMPION: **ITALY**
RUNNER-UP: **CZECHOSLOVAKIA**
THIRD PLACE: **GERMANY OVER AUSTRIA**

COPPA DEL MONDO • WORLD'S • COUPE DU MONDE • WELTMEISTERSCHAFT • CUP • COPA DEL MUNDO

ITALIA

A. XII

**CAMPIONATO MONDIALE DI CALCIO**

27 MAGGIO
10 GIUGNO

F.I.F.A.
F.I.G.C.

**In October of 1932,** after eight gruelling FIFA Committee meetings and much controversy, Italy was chosen over Sweden as host of the 1934 World Cup. The bidding process was marred by suspicions of bribery and corruption as Benito Mussolini aggressively sought a propaganda showcase for his Italian Fascist Party. Scheduled for 27 May to 10 June of that year, the second World Cup would feature the first-ever pretournament qualification phase, with thirty-six national teams competing for the fifteen open spots. The host country Italy automatically qualified, a tradition continued in all subsequent Cups.

Sadly, the reigning Cup champion and 1930 host Uruguay declined to participate, boycotting in protest of the top European teams that had refused to travel to South America four years prior. As a result, the 1934 tourney became the only Cup in history where the previous champ did not defend its title. Peru and Chile withdrew as well, in support of Uruguay, and the British Home Nations (England, Scotland, Wales, and Ireland), valuing their independent identity and disputing FIFA's policies about payments to amateur players, refused to join FIFA or play in the Cup tournament—despite FIFA offering England and Scotland direct qualification.

# THE INFLUENCE OF *IL DUCE*

**Benito Mussolini, *Il Duce*** ('The Leader') of the Italian Fascist movement, saw football as a tool for promoting the superiority of his regime. Thus, he pushed hard to host the 1934 World Cup, believing it would shine a favourable international spotlight on Italy's new fascist order — what is now commonly referred to as 'sportswashing'. Some historians suspect Mussolini exerted improper influence on the tournament's outcome as well — he was seen dining with referees and officials before and during the tournament, often prior to Italy's matches.

'The tournament left a bitter taste outside Italy,' wrote Ian Morrison in his history of the World Cup. 'There was little doubt that Italy had won because they were the host nation, and local fanaticism had intimidated referees.'

Even though the tampering rumours were almost certainly true, there is no doubt that Italian football was indeed ascendant in the 1930s: The Italian Serie A was one of the world's most competitive football leagues, Italy's national squad would go on to win the 1936 Olympic gold medal in Germany, and then they repeated as World Cup champs in France 1938. Mussolini likely greased a few official palms, yes, but the fact remains that Italian football didn't need fascist help to become the decade's dominant international side.

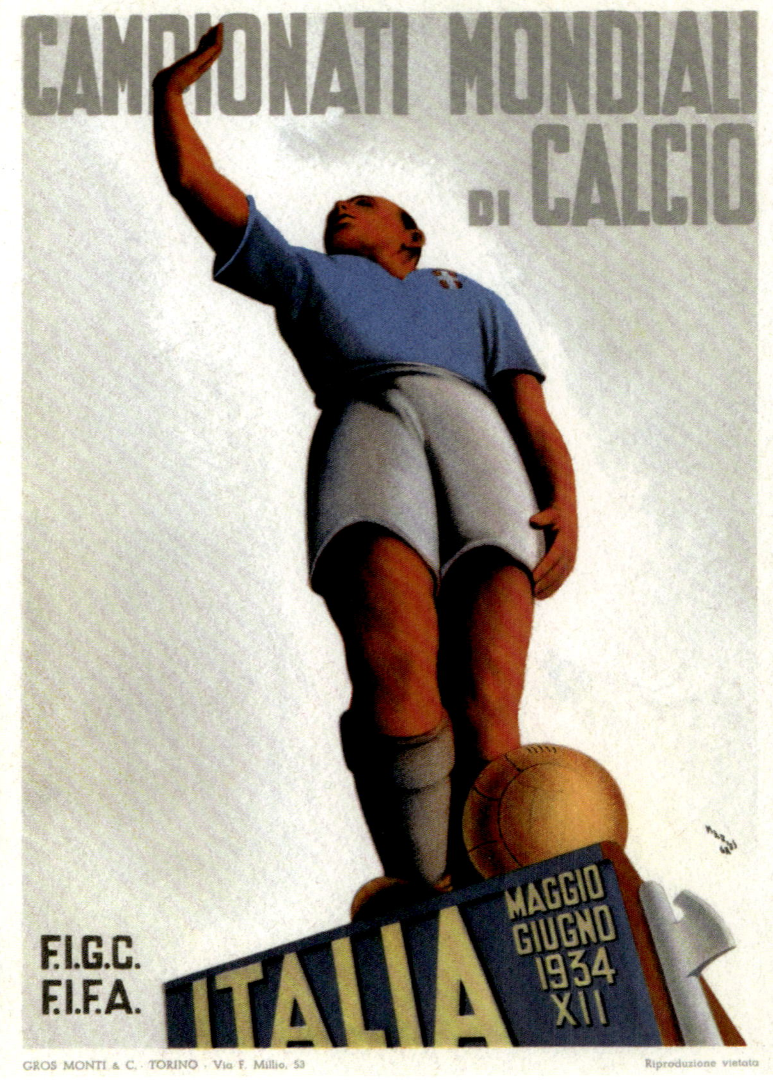


*OPPOSITE The official poster for the 1934 World Cup by Italian artist Gino Boccasile. Boccasile was a well-connected artist and often employed by the National Fascist Party to produce propaganda material for Mussolini and his Italian government.*

*ABOVE An alternative poster design, believed to be the work of Mario Gros, features a prominent display of the fascist salute.*

## THE FORMAT

Matches would be played in eight different stadiums, all in separate Italian cities, with the final played in the Stadio Nazionale PNF (for *Partito Nazionale Fascista*, Mussolini's National Fascist Party) in Rome. The format was a full knockout tournament, pairing off teams in brackets with no group play — one loss sent your team home. Eight top teams — Argentina, Brazil, Germany, Italy, Netherlands, Austria, Czechoslovakia, and Hungary — were seeded so they wouldn't play each other in the first round. Games tied at the end of regulation time would add thirty minutes of extra time. If a match was still tied after that, a full replay would be scheduled the next day.

# Tournament: ROUND OF 16

| | | |
|---:|:---:|:---|
| Italy 7 | | 1 USA |
| Sweden 3 | | 2 Argentina |
| Spain 3 | | 1 Brazil |
| Austria 3 | | 2 France |
| Hungary 4 | | 2 Egypt |
| Czechoslovakia 2 | | 1 Romania |
| Switzerland 3 | | 2 Netherlands |
| Germany 5 | | 2 Belgium |

As a nice touch, all eight first-round matches were timed to kick off at the same moment in their venues at the eight separate cities. Italy's 7–1 thrashing of the USA featured a dazzling hat-trick by Angelo Schiavio. Three seeded favourites —Argentina, Brazil, and Netherlands—were knocked out in the round. Those results, along with Egypt's loss to Hungary and Uruguay's absence, ensured that all eight quarter-finalists would be European teams…a frustrating result given FIFA's desire to give the World Cup a more global character and reach.

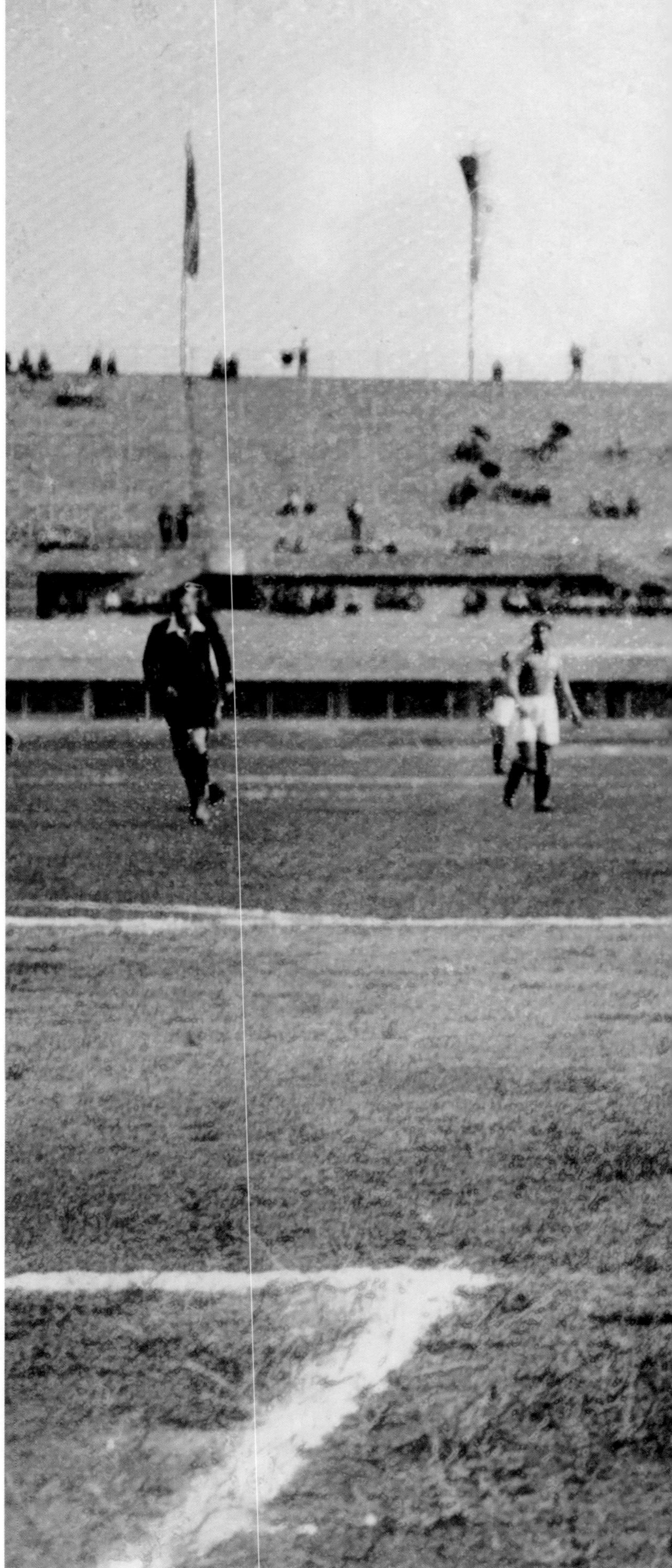

**RIGHT** *Austria's Anton Schall sees his shot blocked by France's Jacques Mairesse in the opening Round of 16.*

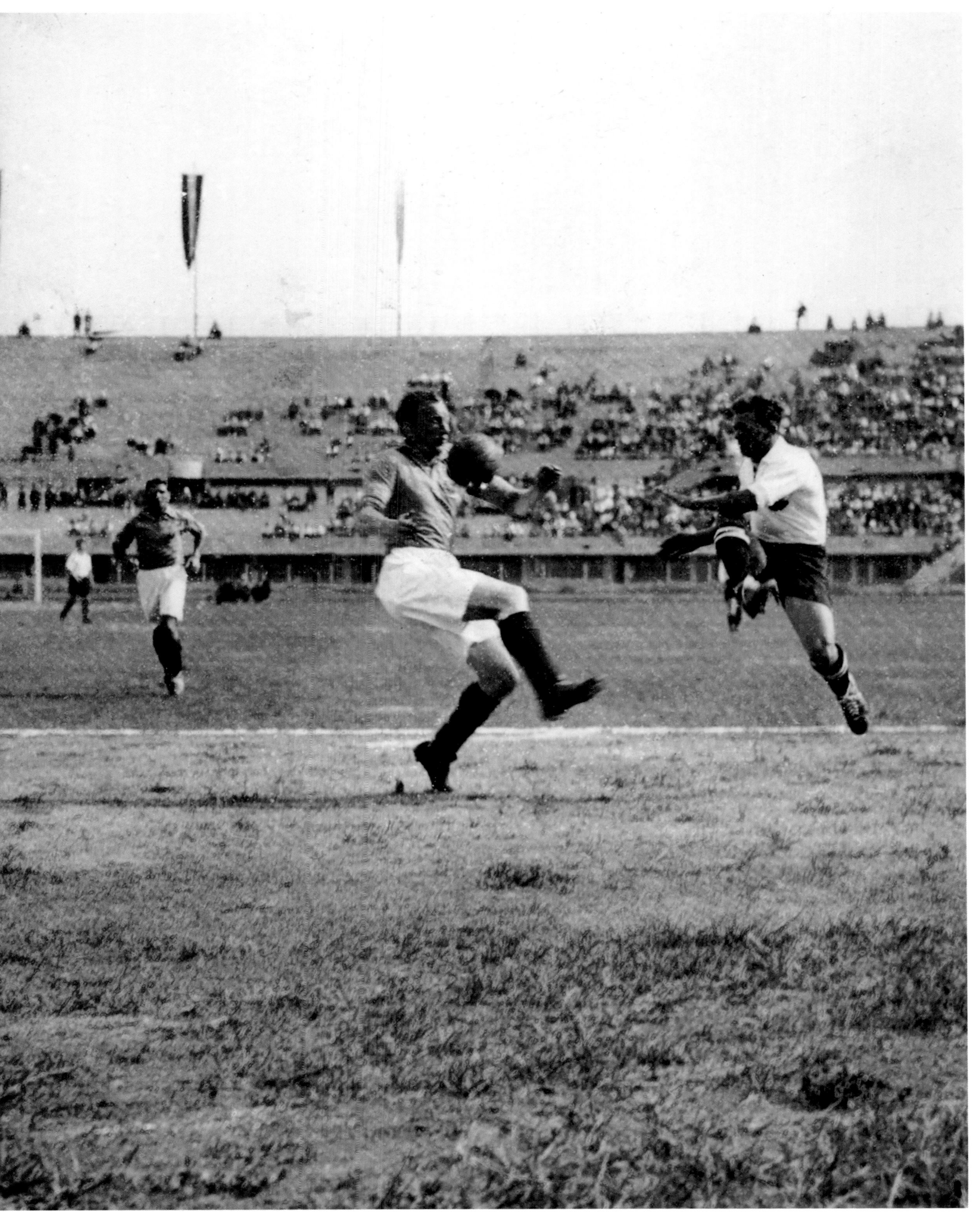

*'The format was a full knockout
tournament, pairing off teams in
brackets with no group play—
one loss sent your team home.'*

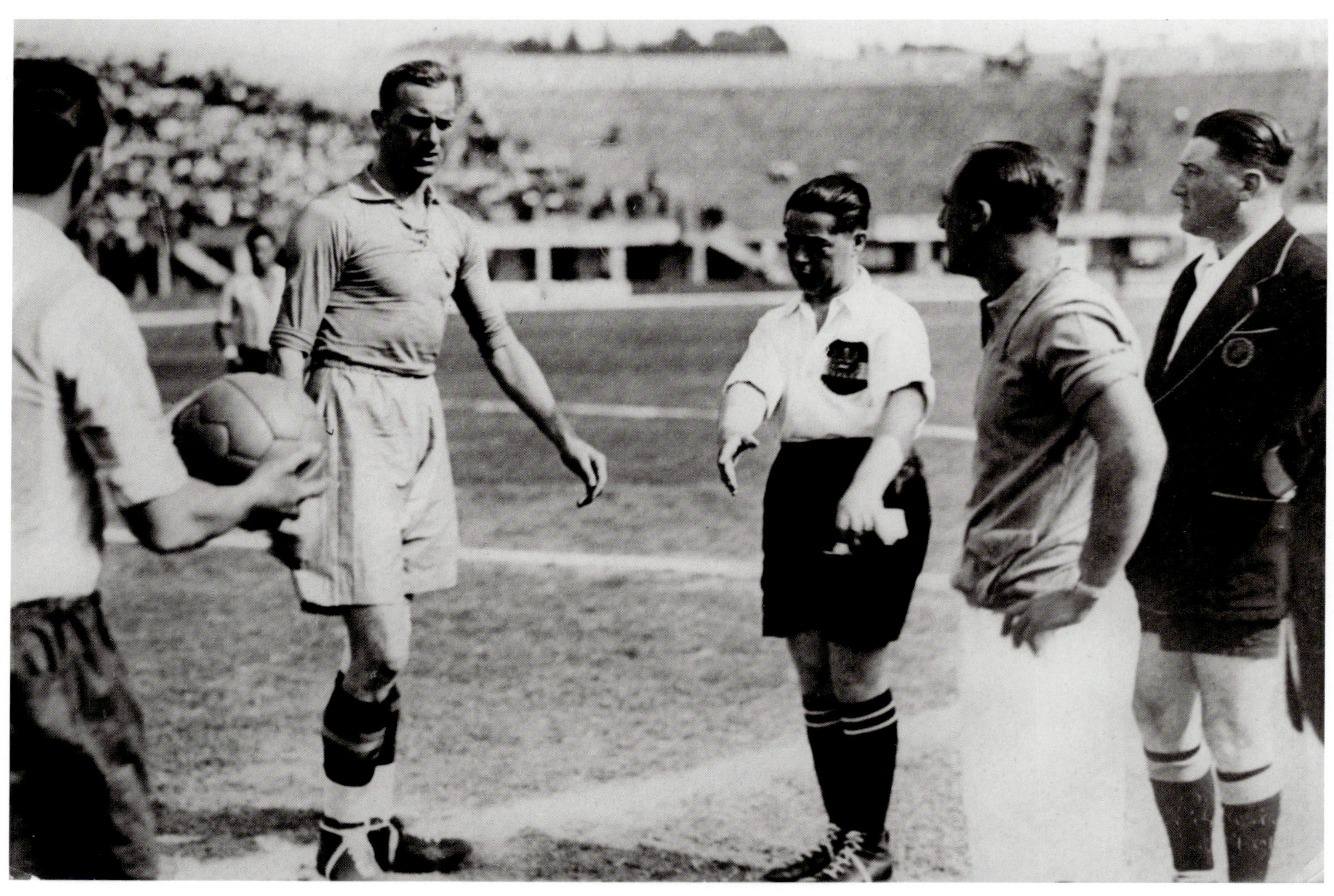

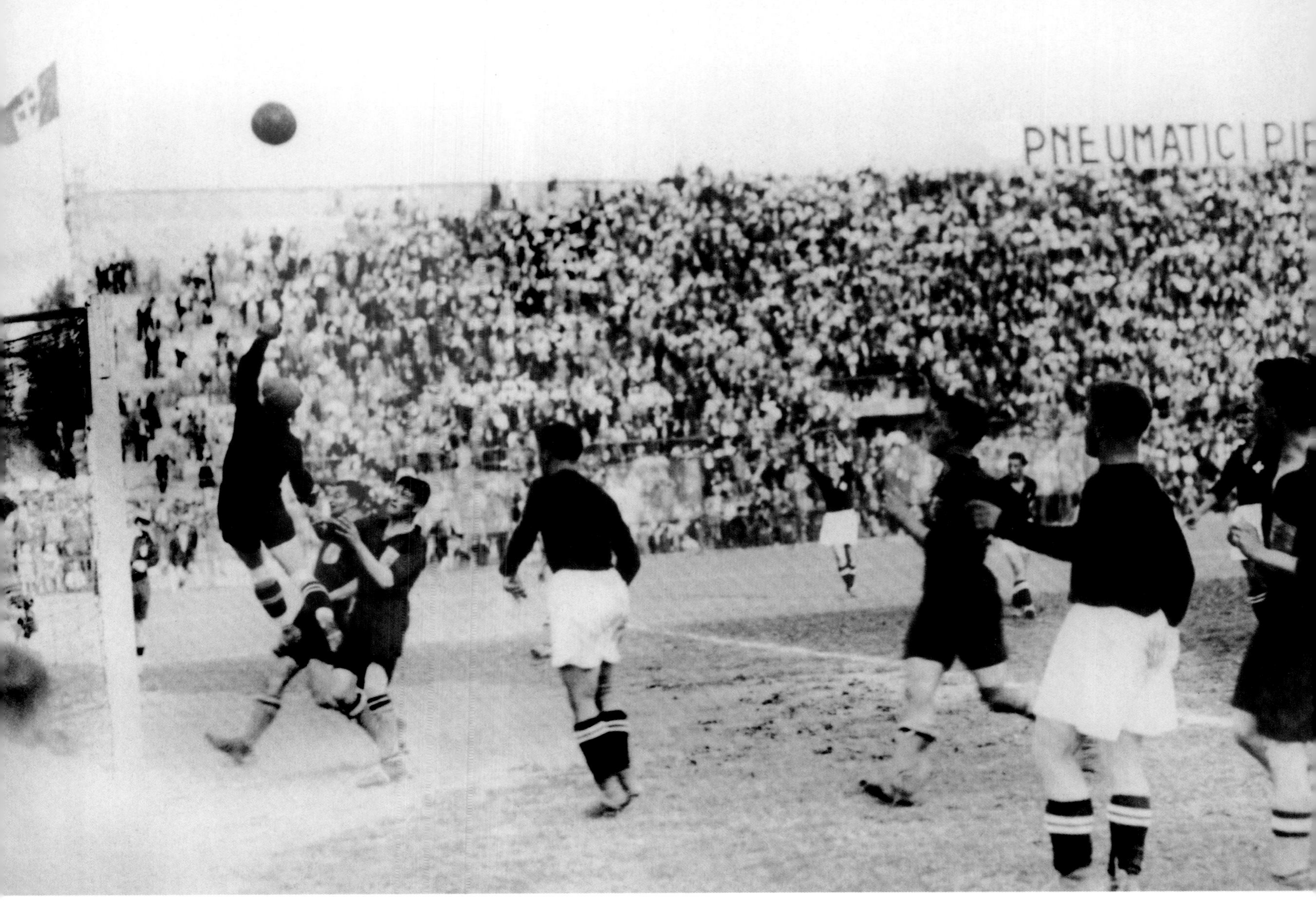



**OPPOSITE** *Argentina and Sweden prepare to face off.*

**ABOVE** *Swiss keeper Frank Séchehaye makes an aerial challenge on the ball against the Netherlands.*

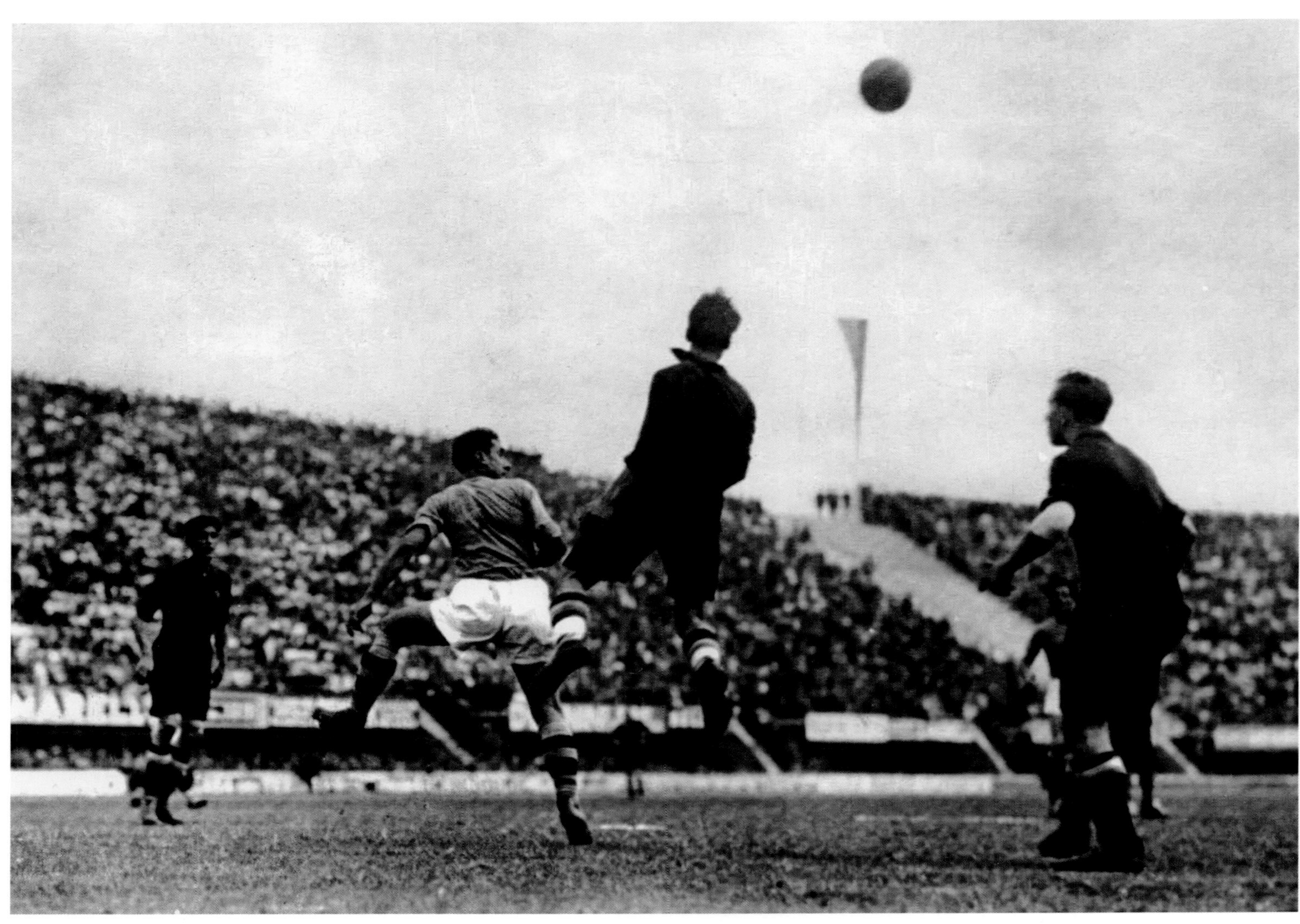

## QUARTER-FINALS

| | |
|---|---|
| Austria 2 | 1 Hungary |
| Czechoslovakia 3 | 2 Switzerland |
| Germany 2 | 1 Sweden |
| Italy 1 | 1 Spain |
| | (Replay: Italy 1 \| Spain 0) |

Again, all four matches were played simultaneously. Austria versus Hungary was rife with fouls and emotions ran high. Hungarian players hounded the referee after the match, blaming him for their defeat. But that game's violence paled in comparison to Italy versus Spain, a contentious slugfest marred by fights, brutal play, and multiple injuries on both sides. At one point, the Italians knocked out the brilliant Spanish keeper and team captain, Ricardo Zamora, while the Spaniards broke the leg of Italian midfielder Mario Pizziolo. The match ended in a 1–1 tie, forcing a replay the next day, where the hostilities fully resumed despite both sides being depleted by injuries and exhaustion. In the end, Italy prevailed 1–0, but many of the Swiss referee's calls were considered so questionable—he disallowed two likely Spanish goals in the second half—that FIFA permanently suspended him after the tournament. And so the dark spectre of *Il Duce*'s tampering hovered over the result.

# SEMI-FINALS

Czechoslovakia 3 | 1 Germany
Italy 1 | 0 Austria

In Rome, Oldřich Nejedlý provided all the Czech scoring with a remarkable hat-trick performance against a very physical Germany. Nejedlý would, in fact, lead the tournament in scoring with five goals. In the other semi-final, played in Milan, a torrential downpour and Italy's stellar defence combined to clamp down Austria's star forward Matthias Sindelar. Italy scored in the nineteenth minute when Enrique Guaita pounced on a ricochet off the post, and the rugged Italian back line repeatedly stymied the Austrian attack to log a shutout victory.

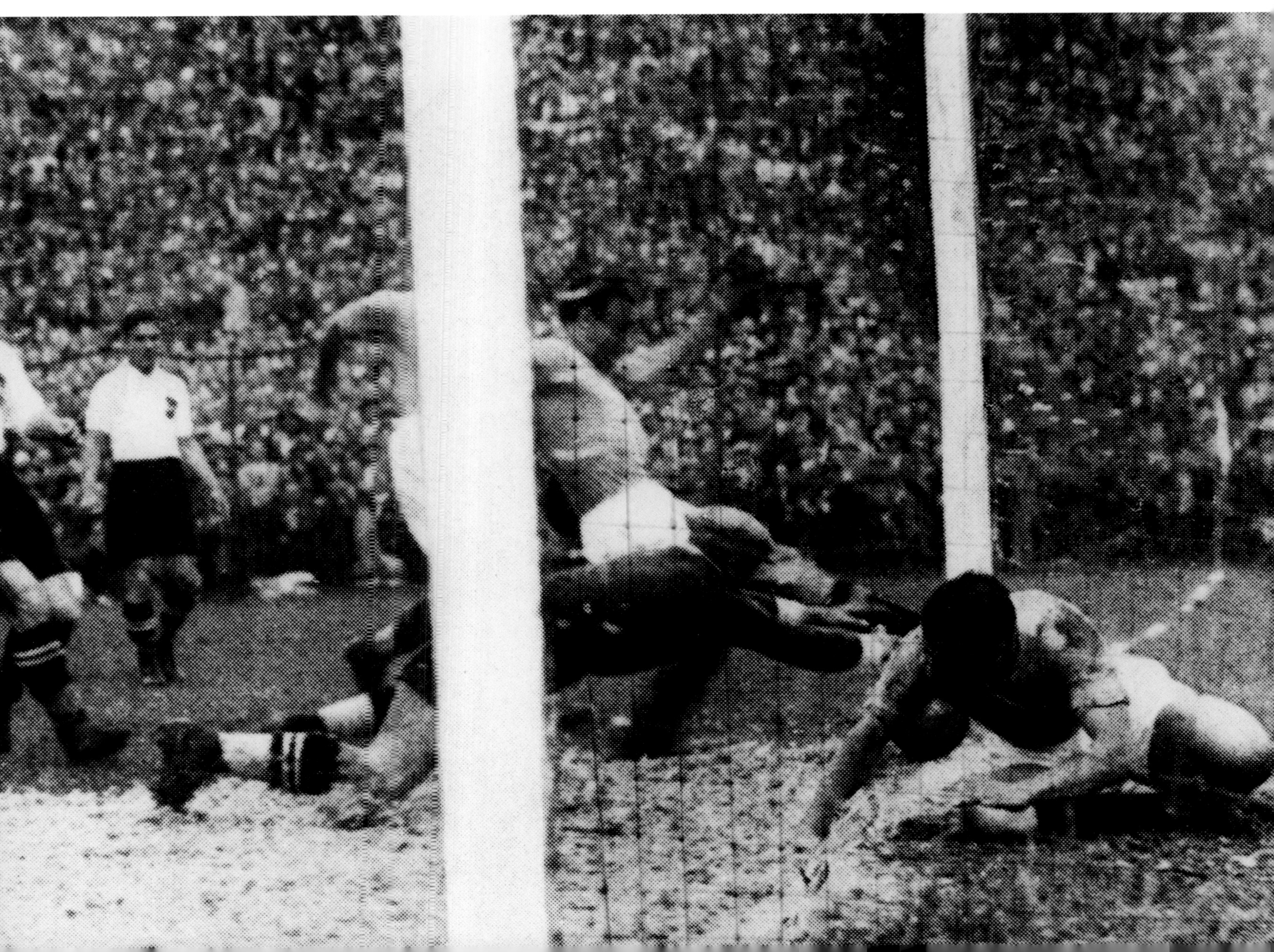

**BELOW** *Enrique Guaita, nick-named Il Corsaro Nero ('The Black Corsair'), scores a scrappy goal to put Italy ahead of Austria. The match was played at the now-historic San Siro in Milan.*

**OPPOSITE** *Italy and Spain in their quarter-final match.*

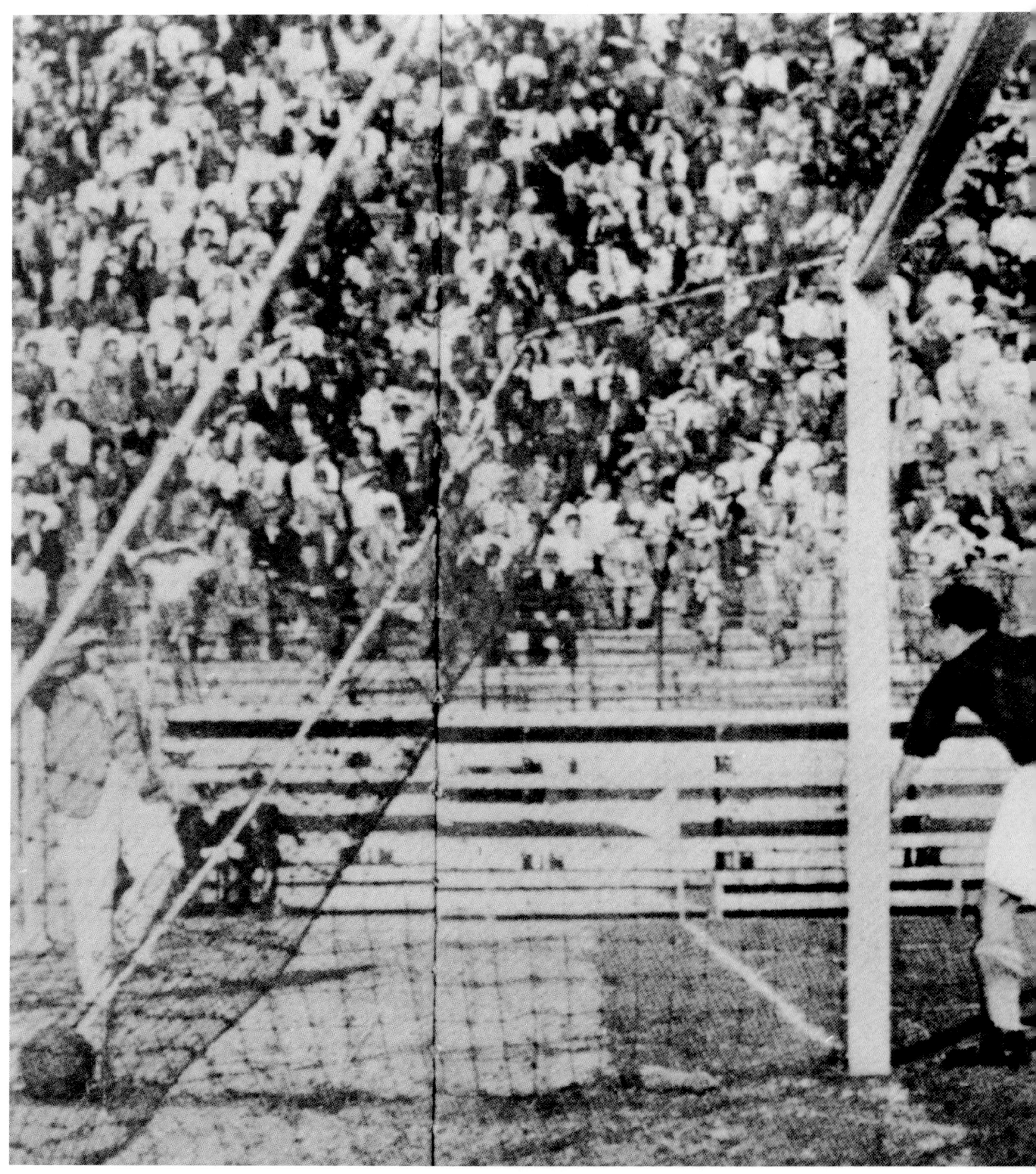

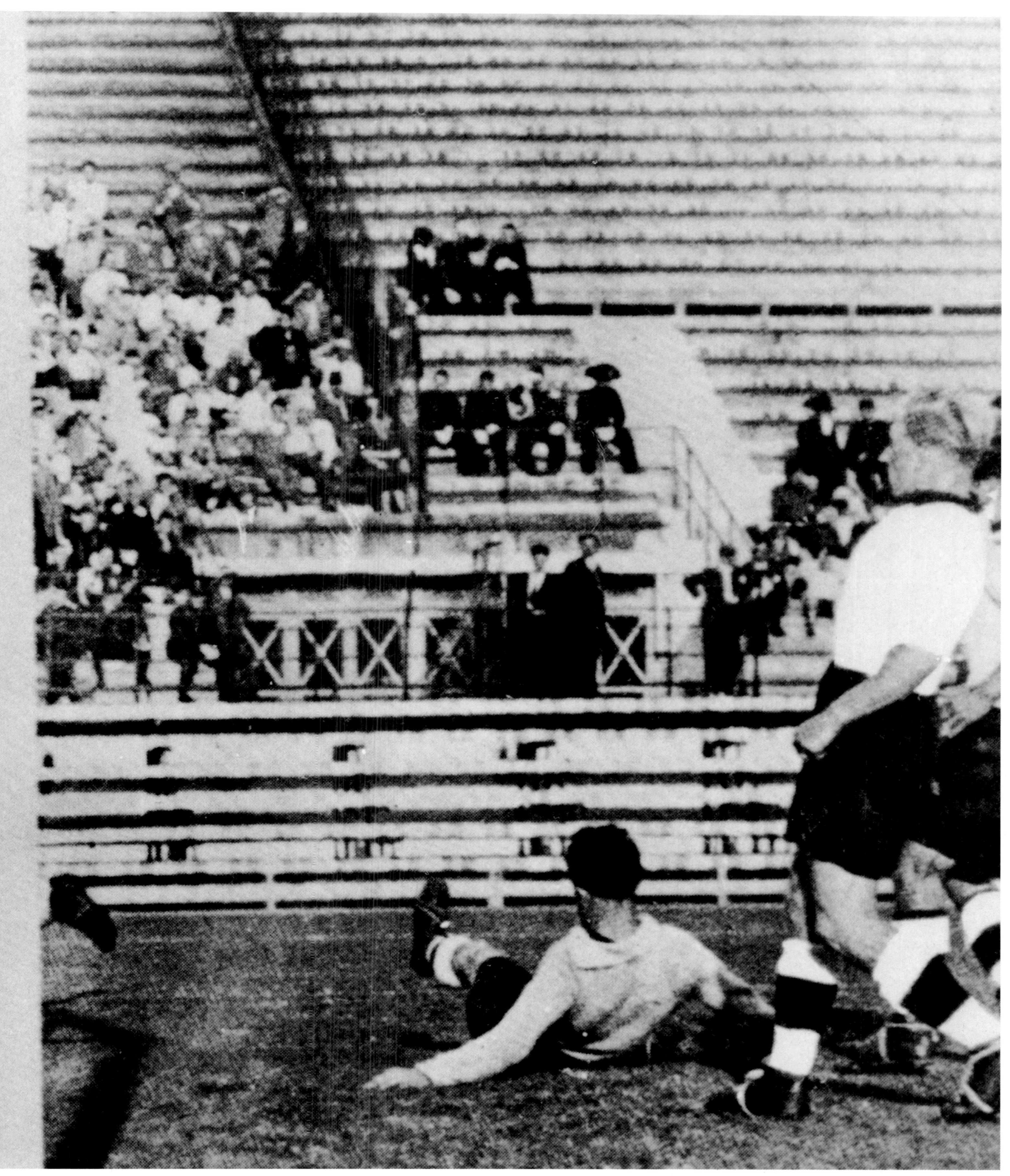

**ABOVE** *Oldřich Nejedlý scores one of his three semi-final goals against Germany.*

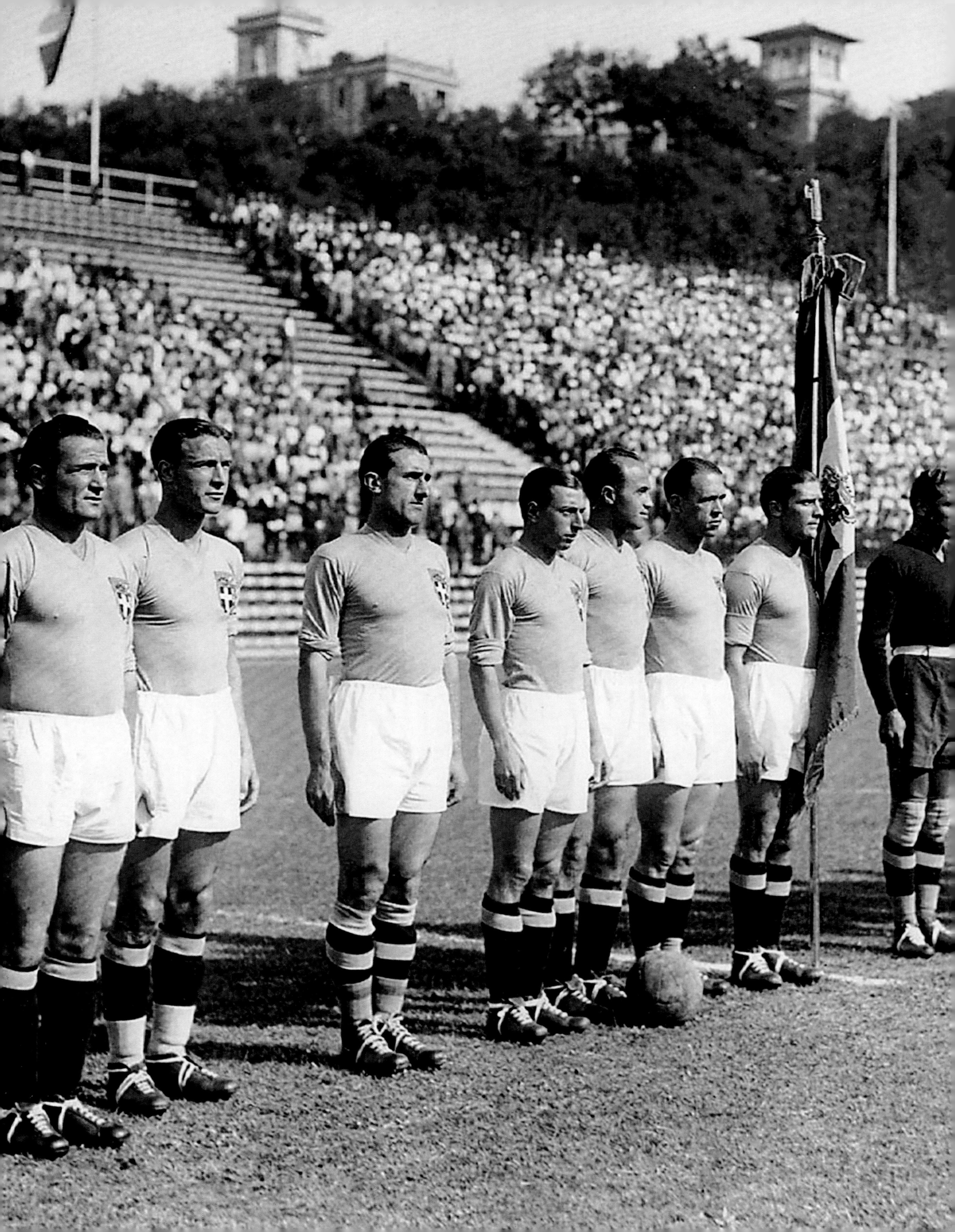

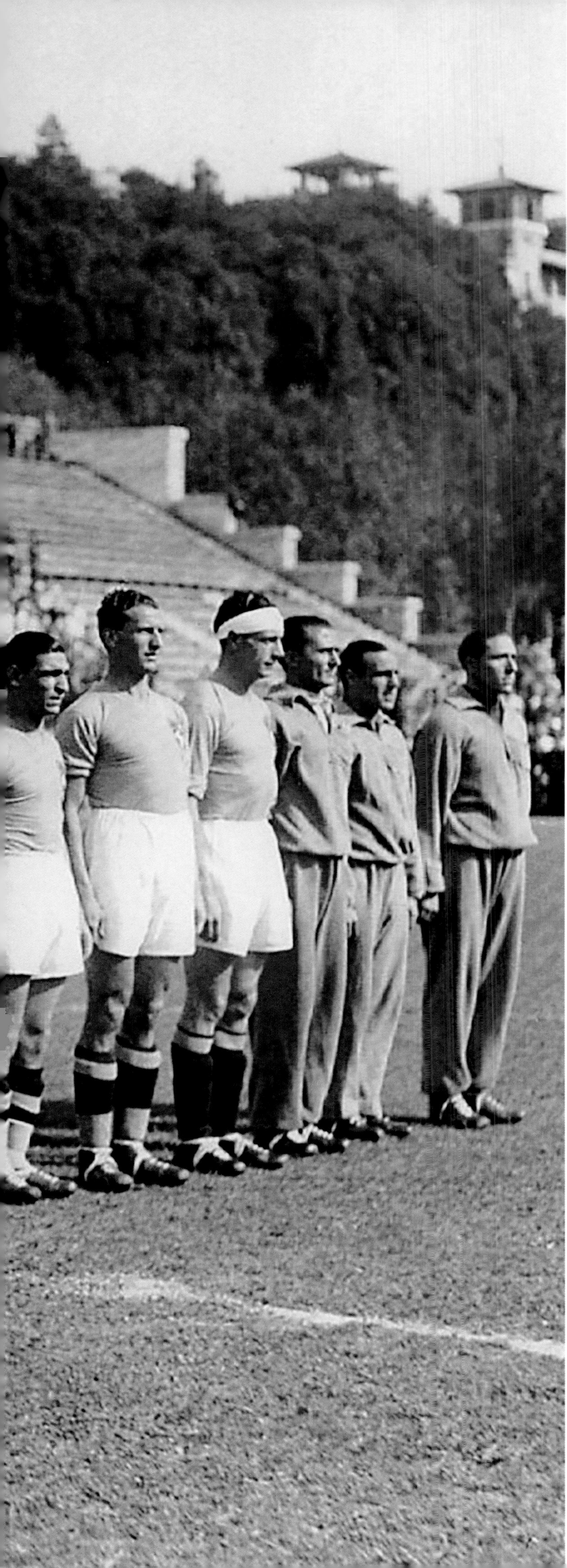



# FINAL

|  |  |
|---|---|
| Italy 2 | 1 Czechoslovakia (First Place) |
| Germany 3 | 2 Austria (Third Place) |

Germany and Austria met on 7 June in Naples for the first-ever consolation game in World Cup history. The match was politically charged, as the Austrian government was resisting unification pressure from the German Nazi regime. German winger Ernst Lehner scored just twenty-five seconds in, which would stand for twenty-eight years as the fastest goal in a World Cup Final. Another Lehner goal before halftime padded the German lead to 3–1, but Austria scored once more in the fifty-fourth minute to make the match's final half hour a fascinating flurry. Despite relentless Austrian pressure for an equaliser, the Germans held on for a 3–2 victory and a third-place finish in the tournament.

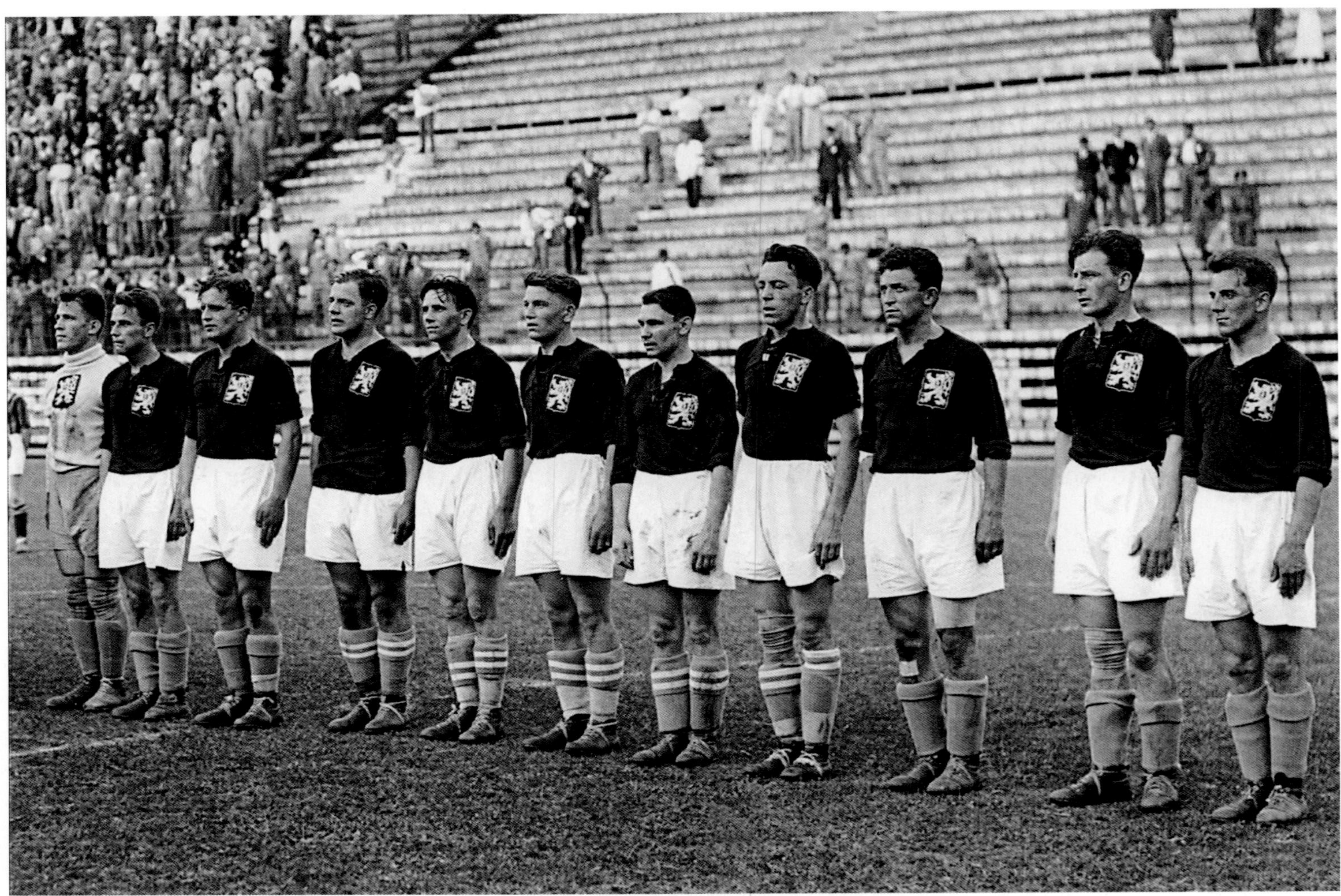

The dramatic Cup Final was played on 10 June in Rome's Stadio Nazionale PNF in front of an overflow crowd of 55,000 largely rooting for the home side. With temperatures climbing over 38°F down on the pitch, the game was a gruelling, scoreless slog for more than seventy minutes. Finally, the Czech side, known for its technical prowess and finesse, broke through with a goal off a corner kick for a 1–0 lead at the seventy-one-minute mark. But the lead wasn't for long, as Italy rallied to level the score just ten minutes later in stunning fashion. FIFA has called Raimundo Orsi's brilliant chip-shot equaliser 'one of the most legendary goals in the history of the World Cup'.

The 1–1 score held to the end of regulation, and so both teams girded for thirty minutes of extra time in the unbearable heat—and, as you may recall, no substitutions were allowed back then! Just five minutes into the overtime, Angelo Schiavio scored to boost Italy into the lead. The Italians desperately clung to this 2–1 advantage as the two haggard squads battled through the final twenty-five minutes. When the final whistle sounded, both teams collapsed in exhaustion as the Stadio stands erupted in jubilation.

'The game was a gruelling, scoreless slog
for more than seventy minutes.'

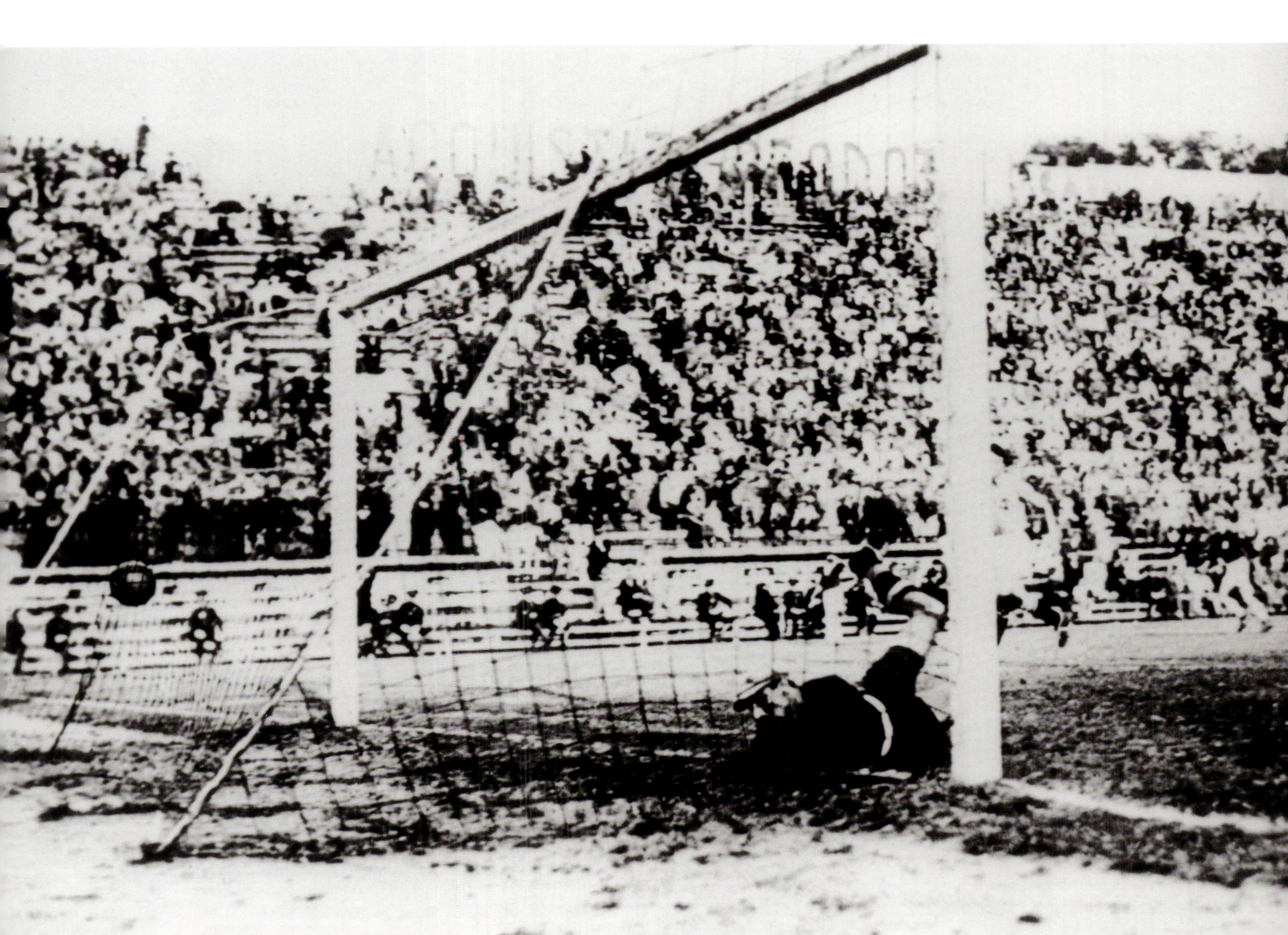

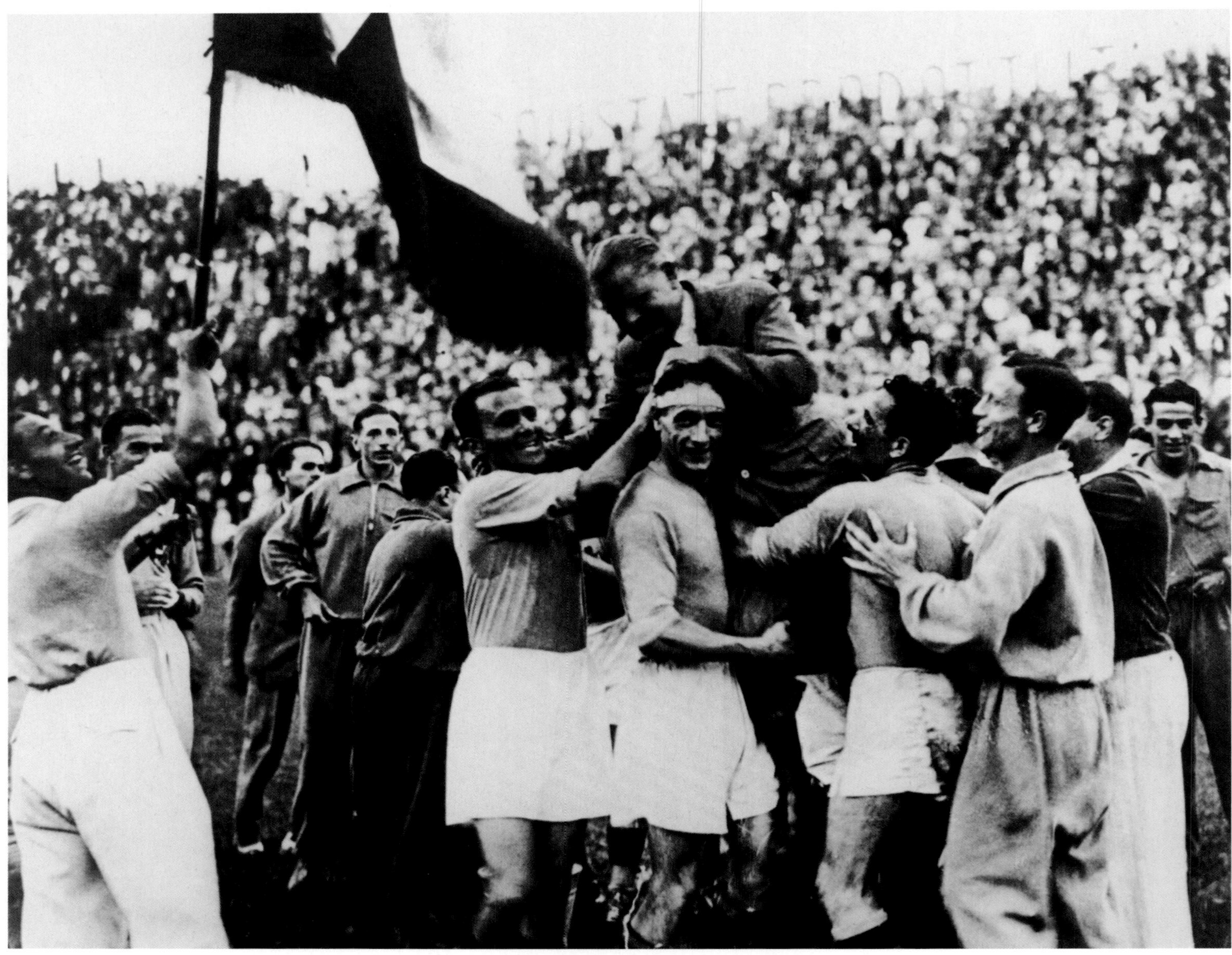

**ABOVE** *Head coach Vittorio Pozzo is lifted by his players after securing a hard-won victory in the final.*

**OPPOSITE TOP** *Italy's commemorative postage stamps for the 1934 World Cup. They were denoted in Italian lira, the host country's official currency from 1861–2002.*

**OPPOSITE** *The Italian team performing the fascist salute before the final. A testament to football's weight on the international stage and a reminder of its often-complicated relationship with global geopolitics.*

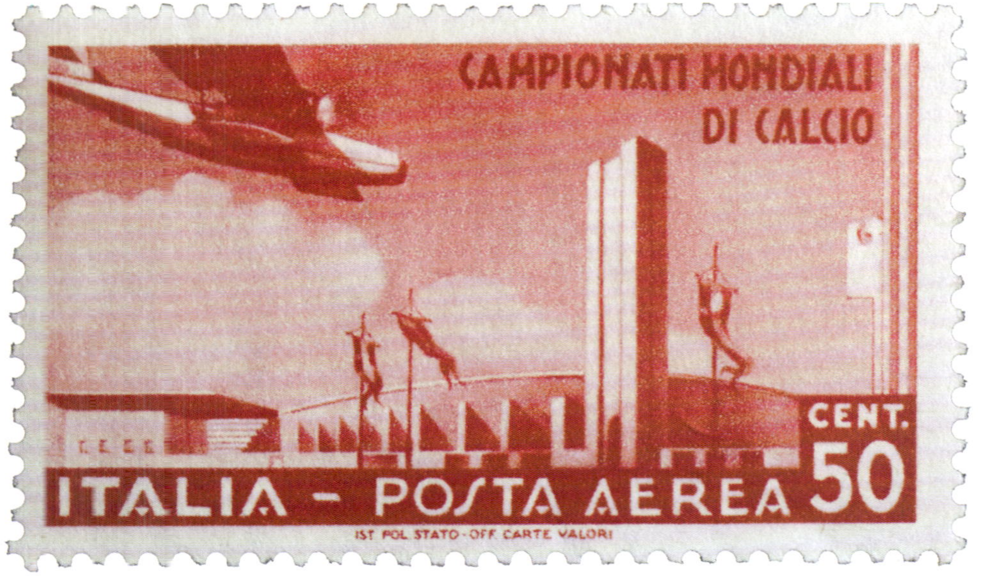
CAMPIONATI MONDIALI
DI CALCIO
ITALIA - POSTA AEREA
CENT.
50
IST. POL. STATO - OFF. CARTE VALORI

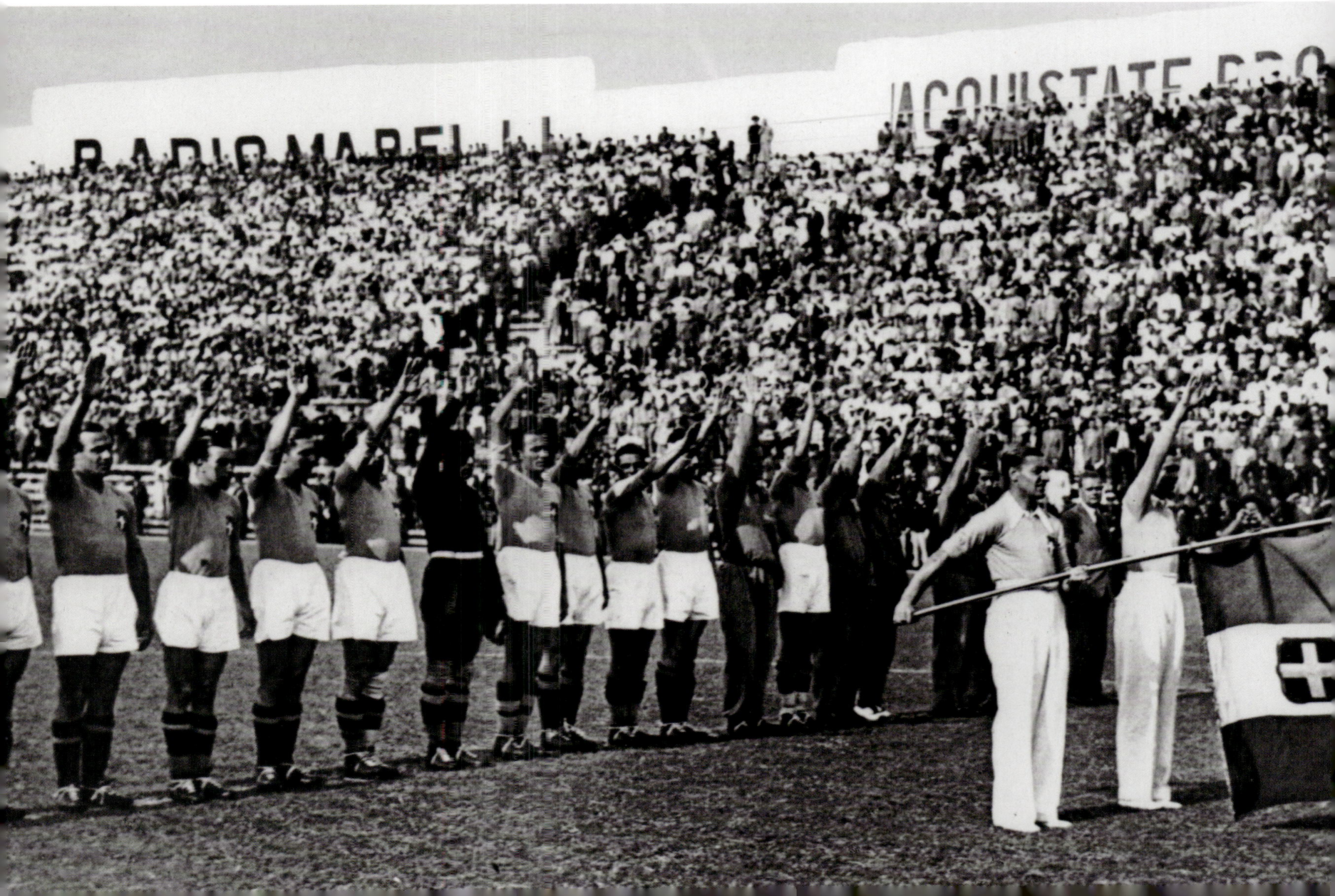

# NEW TACTICS

**The 1934 World Cup tournament** ushered in new trends that allowed better-organised sides to see more success, even when playing against teams with more skilful players. For years, most football clubs played a very loosely organised 2-3-5 system — two defenders, three midfielders, and a forward wall of five attackers, with many long passes sent upfield 'over the top', putting an emphasis on speed and individual play. But in 1934, new tactical subtleties, based on better spacing, shorter passing, and collaborative defending, were introduced that could better neutralise individual talent.

One variation was called the 'W-M' system, named for how the on-field formation reflected the shapes of those two letters when stacked. Another, called the 'Metodo' (Italian for 'method'), was developed by the Italian coach Vittorio Pozzo and contributed much to Italy's ultimate victory in the Cup. That system used a 2-3-2-3 formation, which pulled back the two inside forwards from the front five to create better spacing for passes, more control of the midfield, and more effective counterattacks.

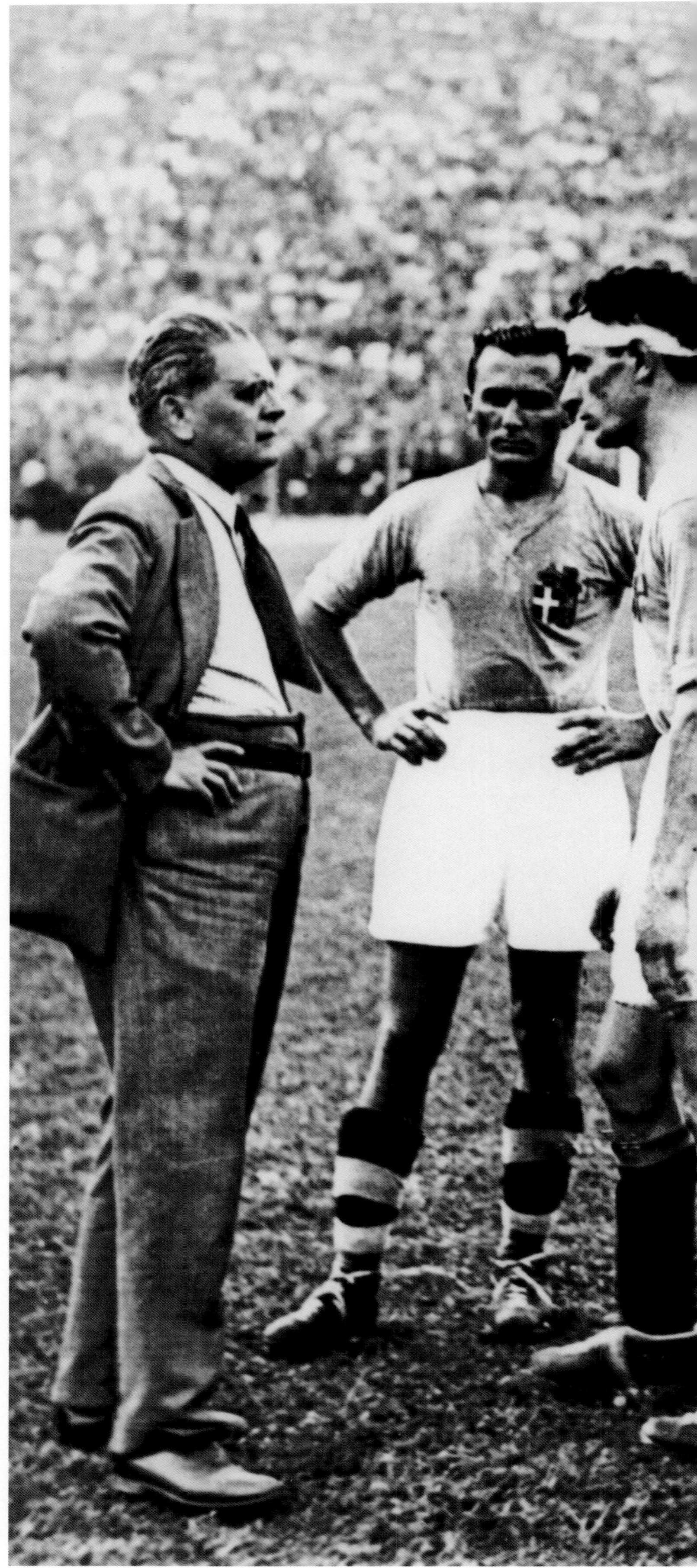

**RIGHT** *Vittorio Pozzo in the final, strategising with his players before extra time.*

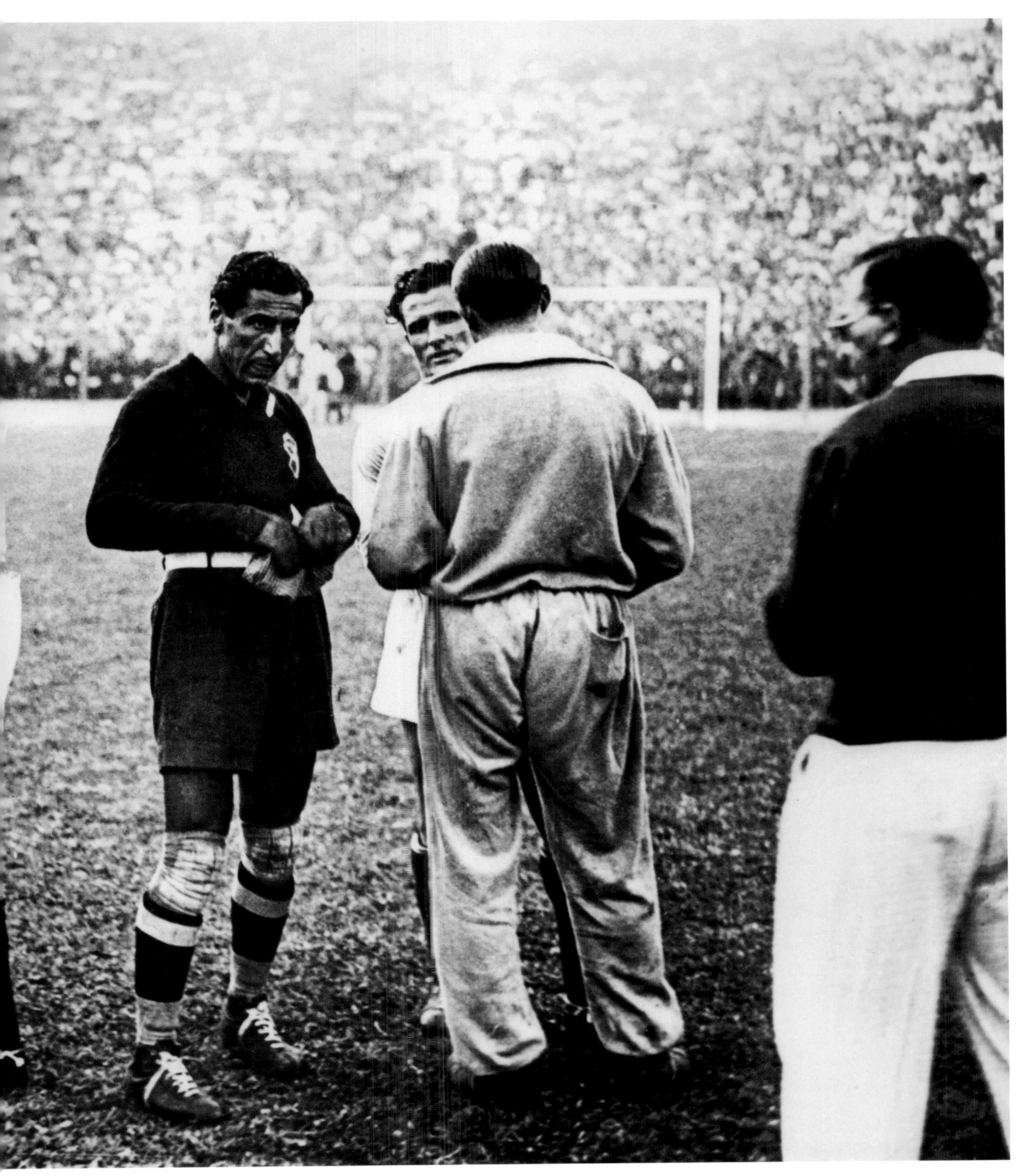

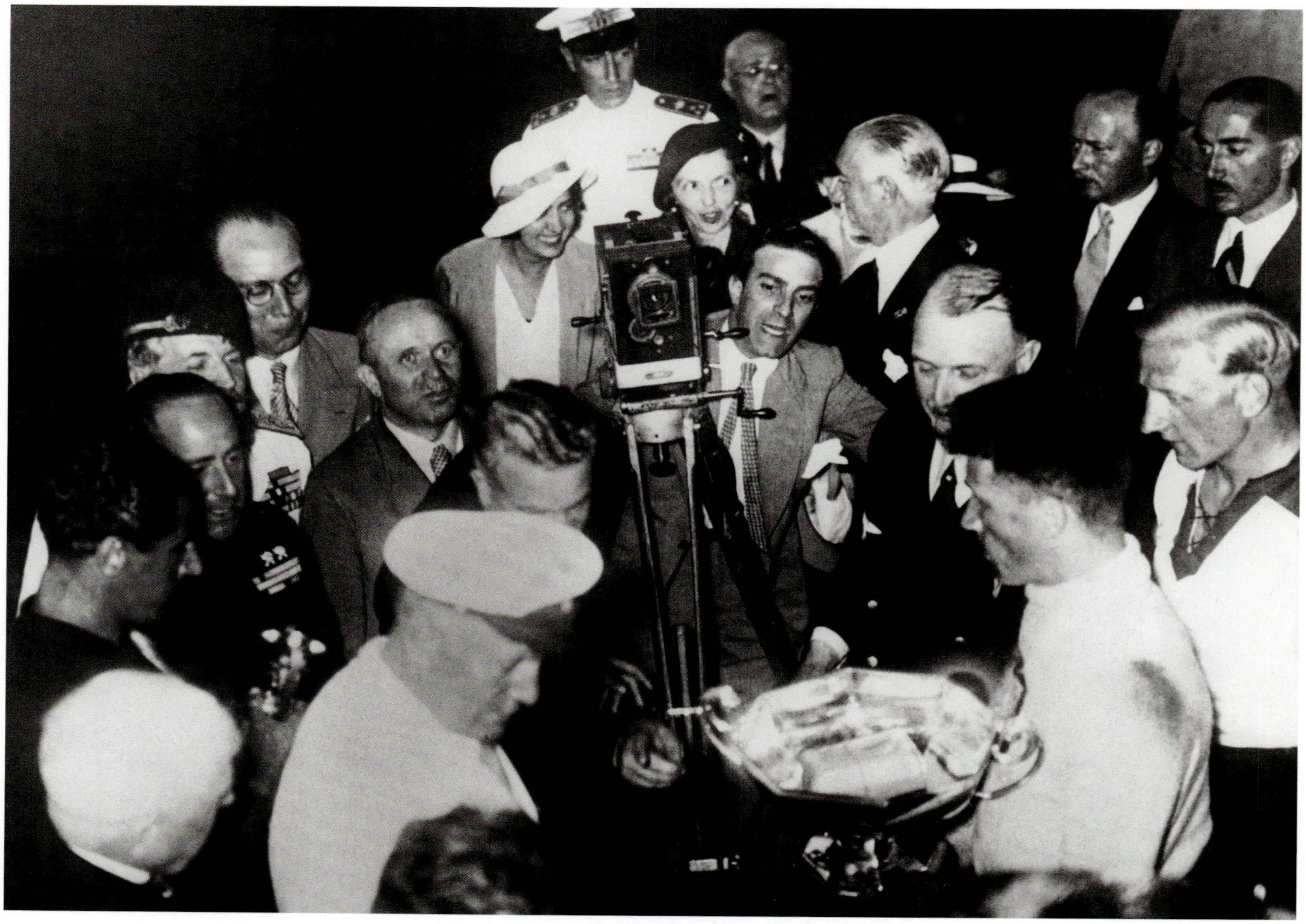

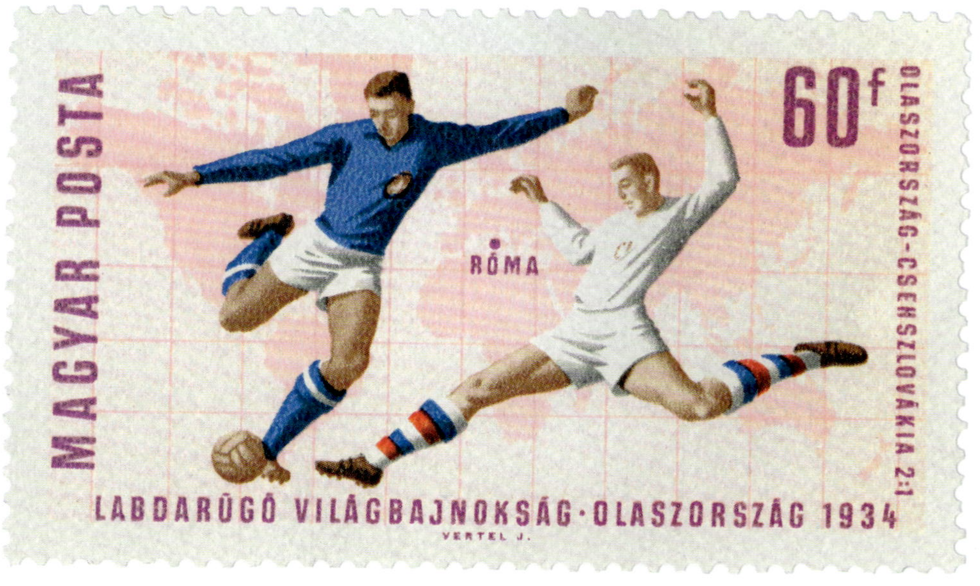


**ABOVE** *Italian dictator Benito Mussolini (front, white cap) after handing the trophy over to the team.*

**LEFT** *The 1934 World Cup Final as depicted in a stamp issued by the Hungarian Post, part of a series leading up to the 1966 World Cup.*

**OPPOSITE** *La Gazzetta dello Sport: [The Blues win the world championship in the presence of Mussolini]*

1934 - Anno XL - N. 139

TARIFFA INSERZIONI

# La Gazzetta dello Sport

LUNEDÌ
11
Giugno
— Anno XII —

EDIZIONE UNICA

Un numero Cent. 20

Esce tutti i giorni esclusa la domenica
Conto corrente con la posta

Direzione — Amministrazione
Milano - Via Galileo Galilei, 5 bis
Pubblicità - Abbonamenti
Piazza Duomo 22 - Telefono 12-785

## LE GRANDI VITTORIE DEGLI ATLETI FASCISTI NEL NOME E PER IL PREMIO DEL DUCE

# Gli azzurri conquistano alla presenza di Mussolini il Campionato del Mondo
# Learco Guerra inscrive il proprio nome sul libro d'oro del Giro d'Italia

## La volontà e il gioco irresistibile dei calciatori italiani

### sono stati i coefficienti decisivi della vittoria azzurra che ha coronato nei due tempi supplementari la partita di tutte le emozioni
### Italia-Cecoslovacchia: 2-1 (0-0, 1-1, 1-0 0-0)

(Puc, Orsi, Schiavio)

### Soldati dello Sport

ROMA, 10 giugno.

Fino a quel momento la partita è di colore grigio. Aspra è la volontà di lottare nel cuore degli atleti, ma le due squadre, a furia di contendersi il terreno palmo a palmo, hanno finito per irrigidirsi in un gioco uniforme, per impaniarsi in una gara tutta nervi e niente fantasia. Fino a quel momento è la partita di chi ha paura di perdere, più che la partita di chi ha la smania di vincere; gli avversari si temono, la tattica è guardinga, i due portieri passano lunghi minuti inoperosamente: potrebbero agganciare un'amaca ai pali delle porte rispettive, e dormirci su.

D'un tratto la comune partita di calcio si trasforma in una tenzone guerriera. Alza verticalmente i suoi toni, scatena nelle squadre scariche elettriche, diffonde nella moltitudine un'ondata di passione. Diventa, per l'incantesimo d'un episodio di gioco, la vera, l'autentica finalissima del campionato del mondo. E' quando Puc, al 25', prima che la gara si concluda, sorprende Combi con un tiro violento ed insidioso e slancia la sua squadra in vantaggio. Mancano venti minuti al fischio dell'epilogo. E' come se una mazzata abbia percosso gli azzurri. Venti minuti, e la squadra boema non si raggomitola in difesa, ma sparpaglia le azioni allo scop...

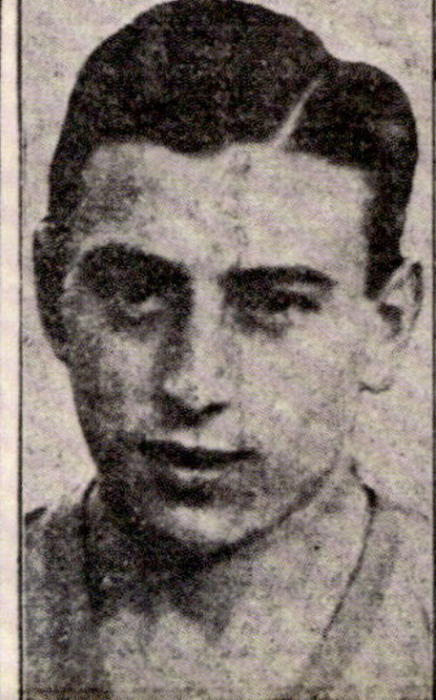

RAIMONDO ORSI

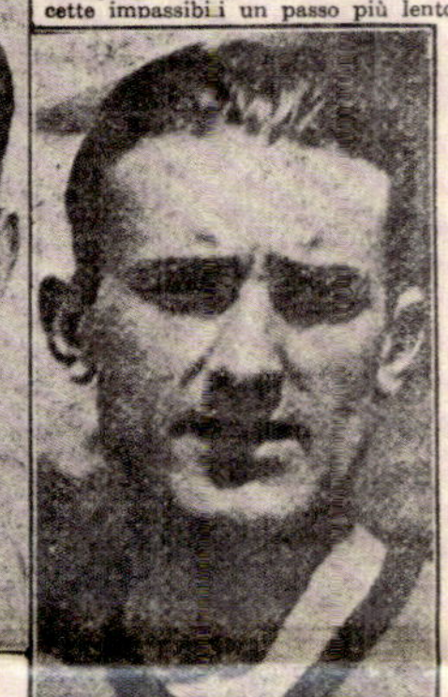

ANGELO SCHIAVIO

# La grande corsa a tappe conclusa all'Arena di Milano

### in uno scenario fantastico di folla ed in una vibrante atmosfera di passione sportiva - Gli altri premi del Capo del Governo, del Partito e del C. O. N. I. a Camusso, secondo a 51" dalla maglia rosa, e ai nuovi campioni Giovanni Cazzulani e Giuseppe Olmo

### Nella luce della realtà

Il XXII Giro d'Italia e il suo meritevole vincitore han voluto che la folla trepidasse sino all'ultimo istante. L'atleta vittorioso e la manifestazione imponente e complessa, vissuta in uno scenario che il nostro cuore non dimenticherà, hanno concluso la loro differente vicenda in modo trionfale. Nemmeno l'ultima tappa è stata un giuoco per fanciulli. Ed anche nell'episodio finale la prova e il campione sono risultati l'uno degno del proprio prestigio e l'altra delle tradizioni che la distinguono.

Learco Guerra ha trionfato. Mancava alla collana dei successi conseguiti dal corridore mantovano la perla più interessante. Due volte secondo nel Giro di Francia, Guerra non aveva ancora vinto il Giro d'Italia. Nè era riuscito a conseguire, nella corsa nazionale a tappe, classifiche così onorevoli come quelle raggiunte al « Tour ».

#### Vincitore e campione

Strano atleta Guerra; strano nella sua stessa espressione di poderosità e nel nervo della sua altissima classe. Forse è nella possanza fisica che distingue il campione d'Italia, la spiegazione di qualche mancanza che farà sorgere a scrivere di Guerra come di un meraviglioso campione del ciclismo mondiale, ma anche come di un concorrente di rango poi temibile in provare in volata, non pare a tappa. Siano nella realtà: che infatti è di quel periodo la maggior massa del tappeto, ma riguardi del vincitore del Giro d'Italia, di una questione sportiva e tecnica di diciassettesimo la F. C. I. chiamata ad occuparsi del desiderio o meno di Guerra di partecipare al Giro di Francia, e preoccupata della scelta degli azzurri che dovranno difendere il buon nome dello sport ciclistico nazionale nel Campionato del Mondo s'è dichiarato assai più fiducioso delle possibilità di Guerra nella disputa del massimo titolo che non in Guerra vincitore nello stesso anno del « Tour » e del « Giro ».

Ad esso lo genio e d'nella collana, e il campione, che si applica, un qualche massaro dell'avvenimento concluso ieri all'Arena, in maglia rosa piuttosto che nella suggestiva vivacità del drappo tricolore, rifulge comunque nel mistero di una perfidoma. A termine di ogni grande manifestazione atletica è buona consuetudine quella di illustrare i protagonisti del...

## La classifica definitiva

1. **GUERRA LEARCO** di Mantova che ha compiuto la complessiva distanza di km. 3706.2 in ore . . . . . . . . . 121.17'17" tempo reale, dedotti i due minuti di abbuono ricevuti per le vittorie di tappa a Teramo e a Firenze, ore 121.15'17"; media generale km. 30,548.

2. CAMUSSO FRANCESCO di Cumiana in ore . . . . . . 121.18'08"
3. *Cazzulani Giovanni* di Lardello Cremonese in ore . . . . 121.22'16"
4. Olmo Giuseppe di Celle Ligure in ore . . . . . . . 121.22'56"
5. Gotti Giovanni di Sedrina in ore . . . . . . . . . 121.25'16"
   Primo degl'isolati
6. Bertoni Remo di Varese in ore . . . . . . . . . . 121.28'10"

|  |  |  |
|---|---|---|
| 7. | Piemontesi Dom., Boca | 121.32'47" |
| 8. | Vignoli Adriano, Sasso — Secondo degl'isolati | 121.42'03" |
| 9. | Giacobbe L., Boscomarengo | 121.43'15" |
| 10. | Barral Luigi, Chargeoir | 121.50'35" |
| 11. | Demuysère Jeff, Verwick — Primo degli stranieri | 121.51'30" |
| 12. | Rogora B., Solbiate Olona | 121.52'28" |
| 13. | Scorticati R., Reggio Em. — Terzo degl'isolati | 121.54'15" |
| 14. | Mealli Adalino, Malva | 121.54'20" |
| 15. | Zanzi Augusto, Varese | 122.00'24" |
| 16. | Como A., Cassano Spin. | 122.05'25" |
| 17. | Teani Orlando, Massa | 122.06'50" |
| 18. | Orecchia M., Testona Tor. | 122.10'18" |
| 19. | Morelli Ambrogio, Nerviano | 122.15'11" |
| 20. | Masarati Attilio, Caorso | 122.25'11" |
| 21. | Piubellini Isidoro, Caccivio | 122.31'52" |
| 22. | Battesini Fabio, Mantova | 122.32'12" |
| 23. | Astrua B., Graglia Biellese | 122.32'25" |
| 24. | Sella N., Caresana Vercell. | 122.42'30" |
| 25. | Oria C., S. Mauro Torinese | 122.45'29" |
| 26. | Grassi Clemente, Corbetta | 122.46'13" |
| 27. | Meini Ettore, Cascina | 122.54'54" |
| 28. | Merlini Ernesto, Rho | 122.58'19" |
| 29. | Baroni Giuseppe, Bareggio | 123.08'33" |
| 30. | Vervaecke Fel., Dadizeele — Secondo degli stranieri | 123.09'01" |
| 31. | Ghesquiere Alfonso, Ypres — Terzo degli stranieri | 123.21'22" |
| 32. | Giuppone Stef. Demonte | 123.26'44" |
| 33. | Scacchetti P., S. Giac. Seg. | 123.37'50" |
| 34. | Carlotti L., S. Bart. Bosco | 123.39'51" |
| 35. | De Paolis G., Palestrina | 123.46'24" |
| 36. | Andretta Antonio, Tombolo | 123.48'18" |
| 37. | Trueba Vic., Torrelavega | 123.59'38" |
| 38. | Zucchini Armando, Albedo | 124.05'15" |
| 39. | Pancera G., Castelnuovo V. | 124.06'26" |
| 40. | Guarducci U., P. V. Ceppi | 124.09'54" |
| 41. | Moretti C., S. Maria Rossa | 124.25'42" |
| 42. | Galateau F., Nantoi-la-Foss | 124.29'25" |
| 43. | Merlino Vincenzo, Tunisi | 124.40'53" |
| 44. | Salazard Vincent, La Celle St. Cl. | 124.54'42" |
| 45. | Sieronski H., Berlino | 125.02'15" |
| 46. | Rinaldi Angelo, Basaluzzo | 125.11'39" |
| 47. | Bulla Max, Vienna | 125.13'52" |
| 48. | Fraccaroli Antonio, Verona | 125.32'52" |
| 49. | Abondio Gius., Mazamet | 125.39'01" |
| 50. | Gulli Francesco, Bertonico | 126.12'05" |
| 51. | Mammina Nicolò, Monreale | 126.19'44" |
| 52. | Pavesi Attilio, Caorso | 128.02'48" |

Emilio Colombo

(Vedere la continuazione in terza pagina)

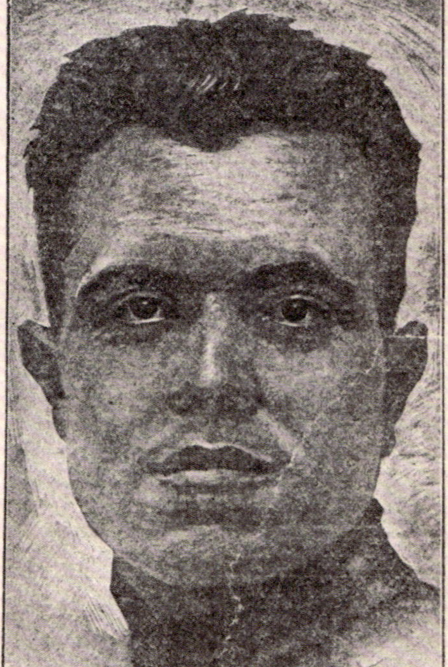

LEARCO GUERRA

(Continua in seconda pagina)

# 1938



**Controversy often accompanies** the quadrennial selection of the World Cup host country — which is understandable, considering hosting a Cup is one of the most prestigious (and lucrative) plums in international sports, rivalled only by hosting a Summer Olympics. In August of 1936, FIFA President Jules Rimet convinced the FIFA Congress to select his home country France as host of the third World Cup, with tournament dates set for 4–19 June of 1938. The choice of a second successive European site infuriated teams from the Americas, who'd been led to believe that World Cup hosting would alternate between Europe and the Americas every four years. The outrage led Uruguay, Argentina, USA, and Mexico to withdraw. And once again — for the third World Cup in a row — the British Home Nations of England, Scotland, Ireland, and Wales refused to participate. Finally, Spain's ongoing civil war forced it to withdraw from consideration as well.

This left thirty-four national teams still eligible to qualify. The tournament field would include just sixteen teams again, so qualification playoffs would be necessary. Host France and defending-champion Italy were slated as automatic qualifiers, reducing the available slots in the tournament bracket to fourteen — eleven allocated to Europe, two to the Americas, and one to Asia. Thus, only three non-European nations played — Brazil, Cuba, and Dutch East Indies (now Indonesia), the first Asian country to participate in a FIFA World Cup.

After qualification playoffs set the tourney field, world politics seeped into the tournament yet again when Austria was infamously 'annexed' (i.e., invaded) in early 1938 by Nazi Germany, forcing its withdrawal from the Cup. Latvia was the runner-up in Austria's qualification group, but FIFA offered the open spot instead to England . . . who still said no. Then, to Latvia's woe, FIFA decided not to replace Austria at all, leaving just fifteen

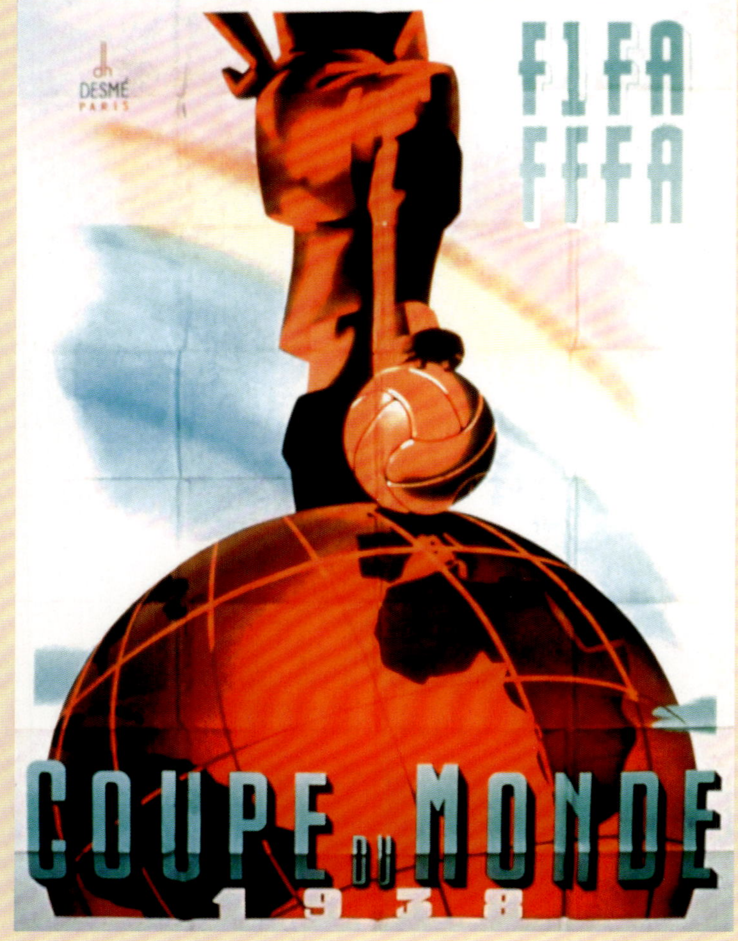


teams in the tournament. In the end, the football squads from both Nazi Germany and Fascist Italy would be pelted with debris by angry French crowds as the world teetered on the brink of a global conflagration.

Sadly, the world's worst fears would ultimately be realised: the 1938 edition would be the last World Cup until 1950, as the Second World War cancelled all international tournament play in the 1940s.

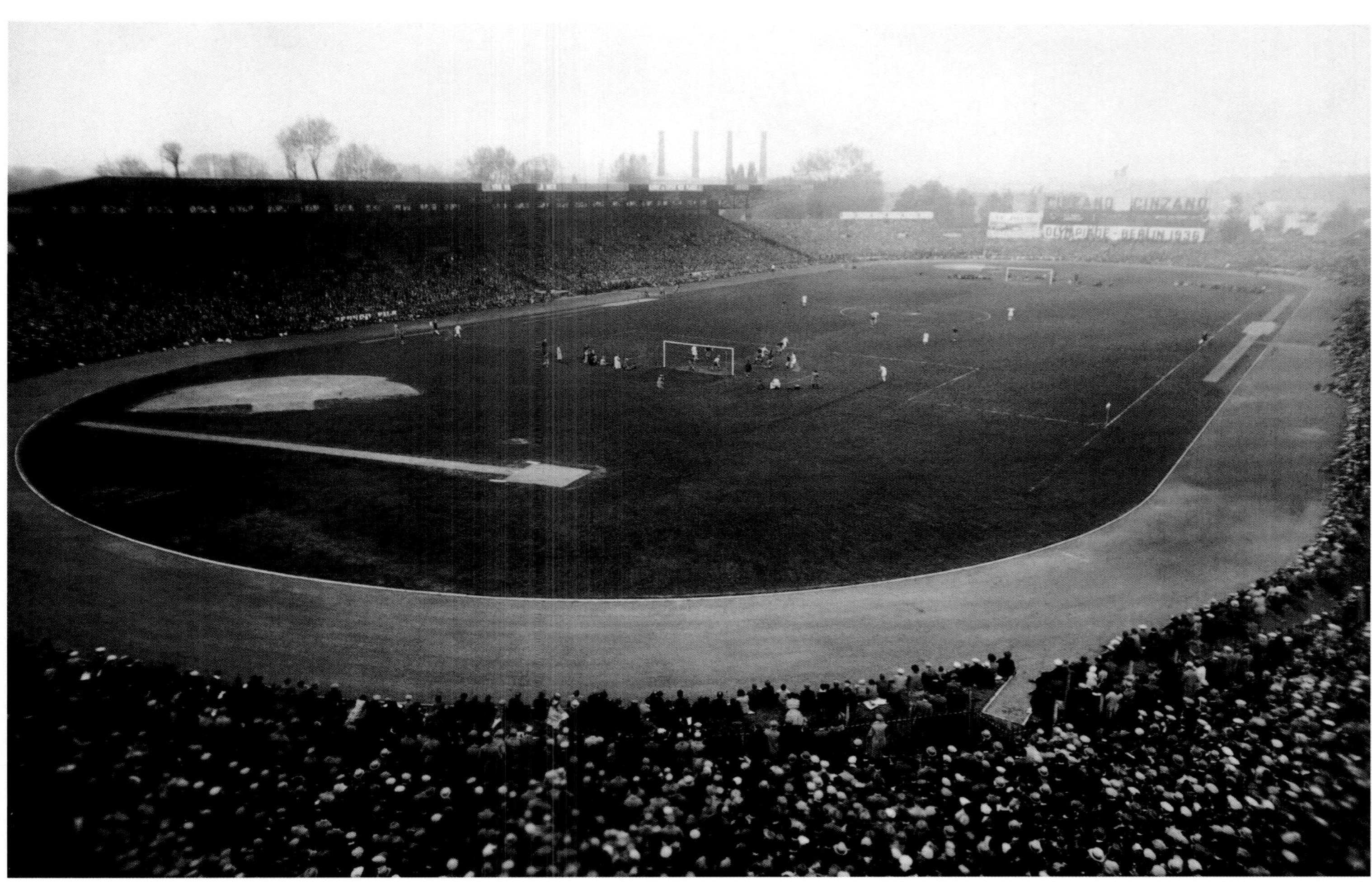

## THE FORMAT

**This World Cup retained** the same basic tournament format as the previous one in 1934: eight seeded teams in a single-elimination bracket, thirty-minute overtimes if tied, with any final ties fully replayed the next day. This was the last time a full knockout, one-loss-and-done format starting with the very first round of play, would be used in a World Cup. Teams would play at ten venues in nine host cities around France, with the final match played in Stade Olympique de Colombes outside Paris.



**OPPOSITE** *Leading up to the 1938 World Cup, FIFA sponsored a design contest for the official tournament poster. The winner was this now-iconic lithograph by French artist Henri Desmé, who employed an Art Deco stencil technique to render his image in the heroic-realist style commonly seen in the political propaganda of the day.*

**ABOVE** *The Stade Yves-du-Manoir in Colombes was renovated in 1938 to increase seating capacity from 45,000 to 60,000.*

# Tournament: FIRST ROUND

| | | |
|---:|:---:|:---|
| Italy 2 | | 1 Norway |
| France 3 | | 1 Belgium |
| Brazil 6 | | 5 Poland |
| Czechoslovakia 3 | | 0 Netherlands |
| Hungary 6 | | 0 Dutch East Indies |
| Switzerland 1 | | 1 Germany |
| (Replay: Switzerland 4 | | 2 Germany |
| Cuba 3 | | 3 Romania |
| (Replay: Cuba 2 | | 1 Romania) |

***Sweden automatically advances to quarter-finals
after Austria withdraws***

In a rematch of the torridly competitive semi-final at the 1936 Olympics, the Italian coach Vittorio Pozzo deployed his *Metodo* system against Norway for better control of the midfield and a lethal counterattack in Italy's 2–1 win. Meanwhile, Brazil and Poland unleashed a scoring explosion featuring two hat-tricks—one by Leônidas of Brazil, and an astounding *four goals* by Ernst Wilimowski for Poland…all four after the fifty-three-minute mark! Football historians and journals like *FourFourTwo* magazine have called it 'the best World Cup match you've never heard of'.

On the other side of the bracket, Cuba's strong play surprised Romania in the 3–3 tie of their first match. But the replay was a shocker, as the Cubans scraped out a 2–1 lead and then relied on the superhuman goalkeeping of Juan Ayra to fend off wave after wave of Romanian attacks to secure the win.

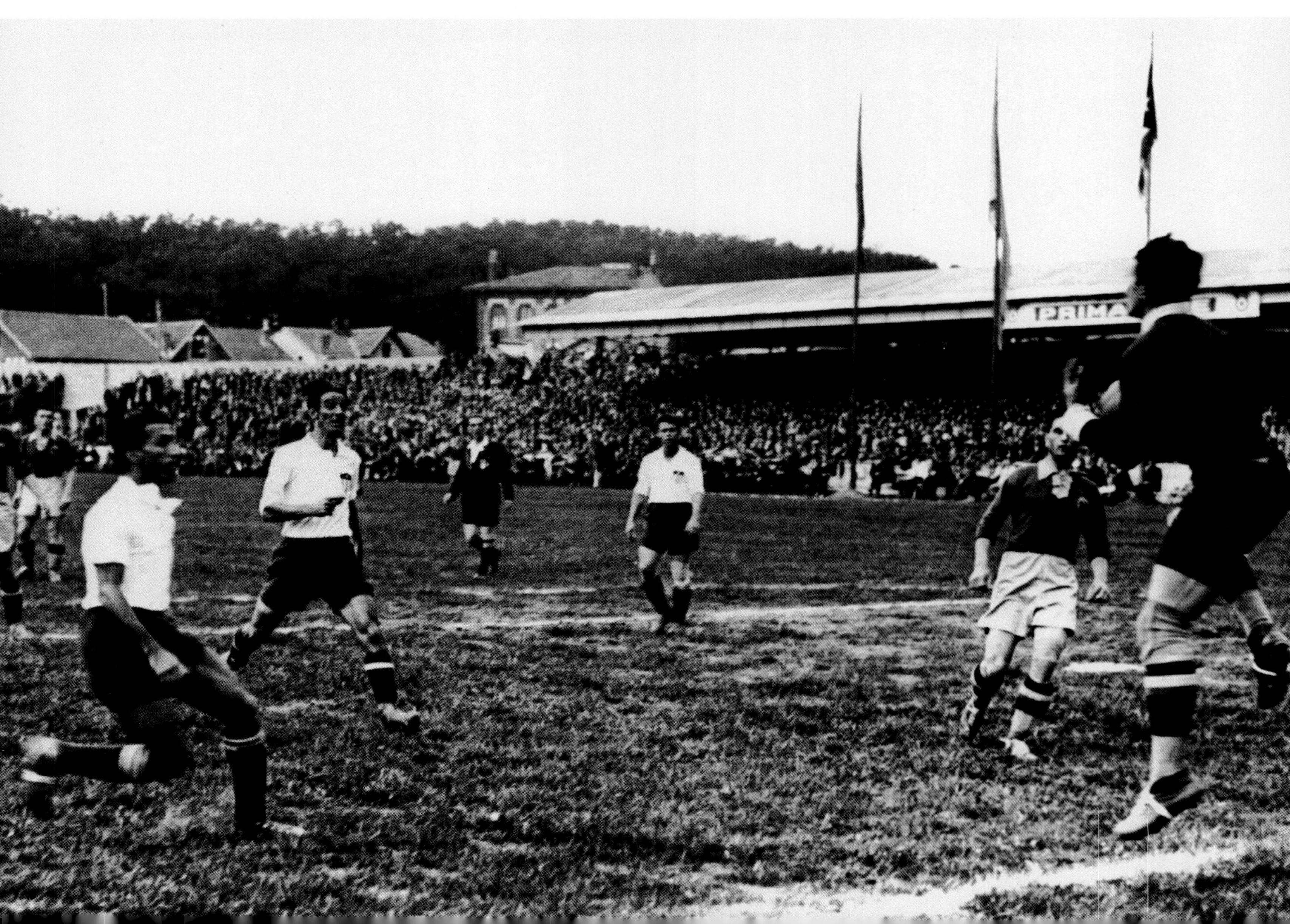

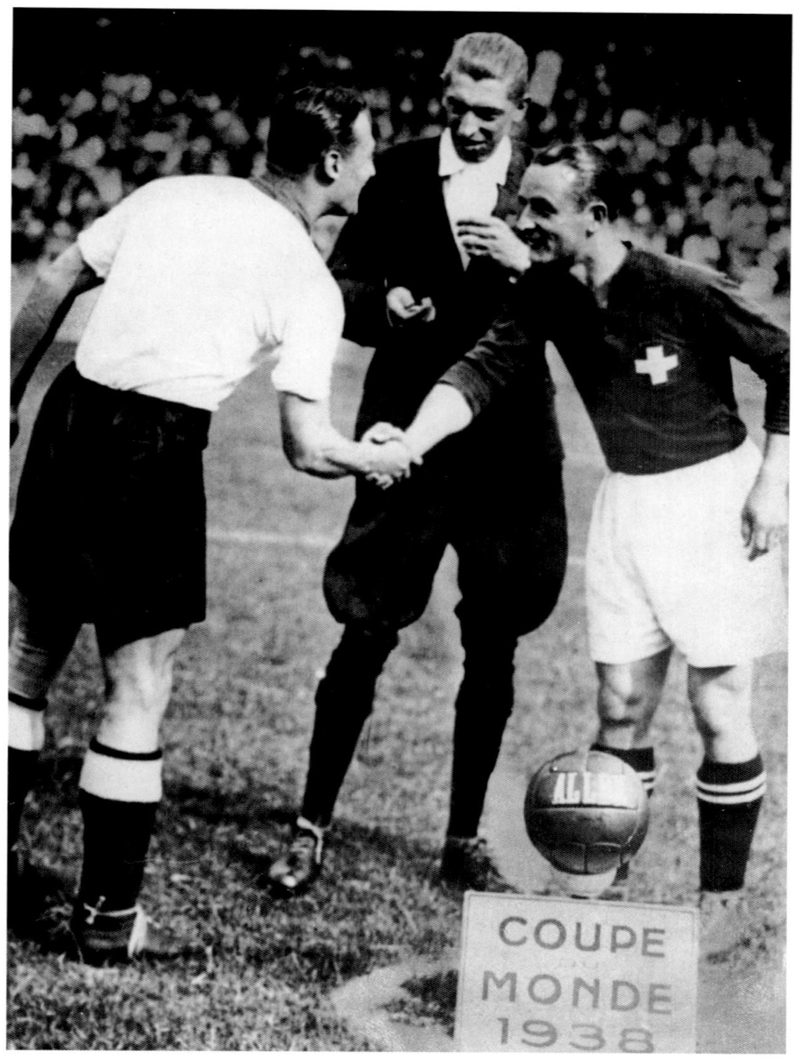


## SWISS PRECISION vs GERMAN BLITZKRIEG

In 1938, Germany's feared forward line featured much individual brilliance. To counter, Swiss coach Karl Rappan — a legendary tactical genius — deployed an innovative four-man defensive structure he called 'the bolt' system. He placed an extra defender — typically referred to later as a sweeper or *libero* — in a support position slightly behind his three-man back line. Unlike the other backs, this 'security bolt' was largely free from individual marking assignments: His job was to cut off passing lanes, provide instant support to the other defenders, and 'sweep up' loose balls coming into the back third.

Rappan's formation conceded some midfield possession in exchange for disciplined, relentless defensive work that frustrated the talented German front runners and generated occasional sudden Swiss counterattacks. This system was a precursor to the famous Italian *Catenaccio* ('door-bolt') system that also featured a defensive focus, with a sturdy, organised back line paired with swift, deadly counterattacking.

In the tournament's first round, Switzerland and Germany ended up playing each other in two full-length matches because the first ended in a 1–1 draw; FIFA's Cup rules then called for a complete replay. When the German team gave its pregame Nazi salute before the first match, a predominantly French crowd responded with a barrage of eggs, tomatoes, and bottles. In the second match, an early injury forced the Swiss to play with just ten men at first, and Germany took a 2–0 lead into halftime. When the injured player finally returned in the second half, the Swiss unleashed a furious fusillade of four goals to stun the Germans, 4–2.

**BELOW** *The German squad performing the Nazi salute ahead of their
match against Switzerland.*

**OPPOSITE TOP** *The German and
Swiss teams take to the field for
their rematch.*

**OPPOSITE BOTTOM** *Lauro 'Lajo'
Amadò of Switzerland twists for an
acrobatic volley and German goalkeeper Rudi Raftl moves to contest.*


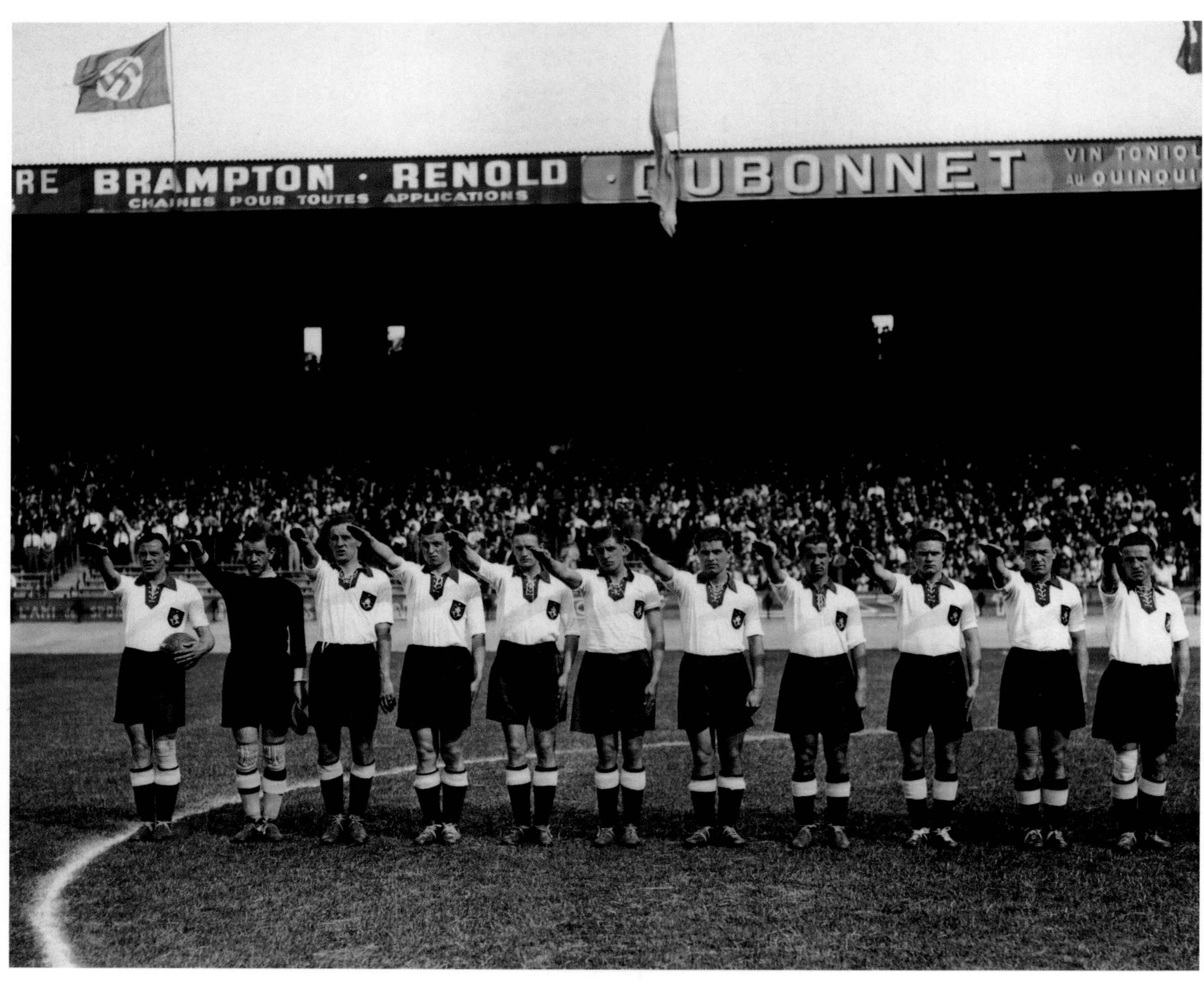

RE BRAMPTON · RENOLD · DUBONNET VIN TONIQU
CHAÎNES POUR TOUTES APPLICATIONS AU QUINQUI

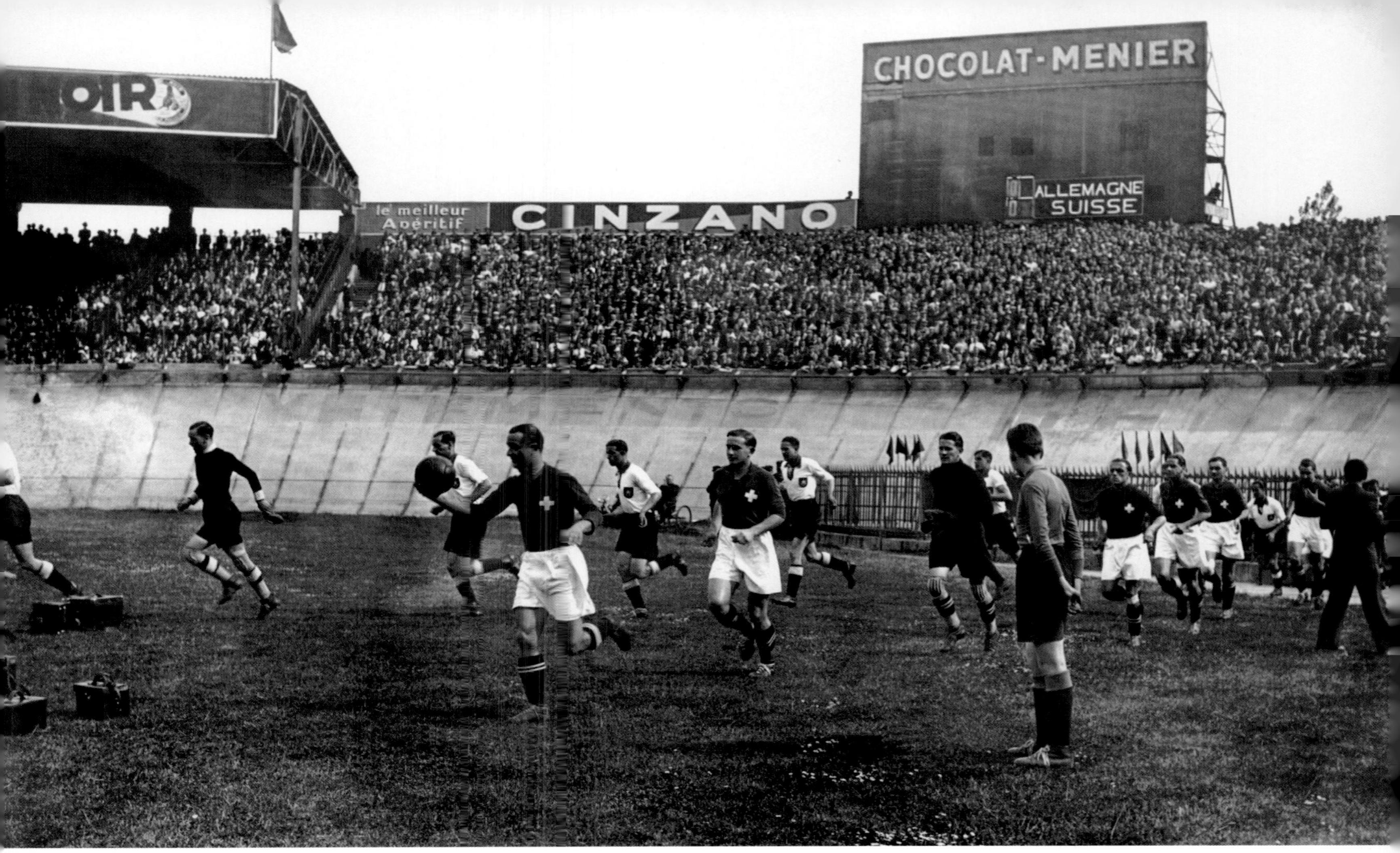

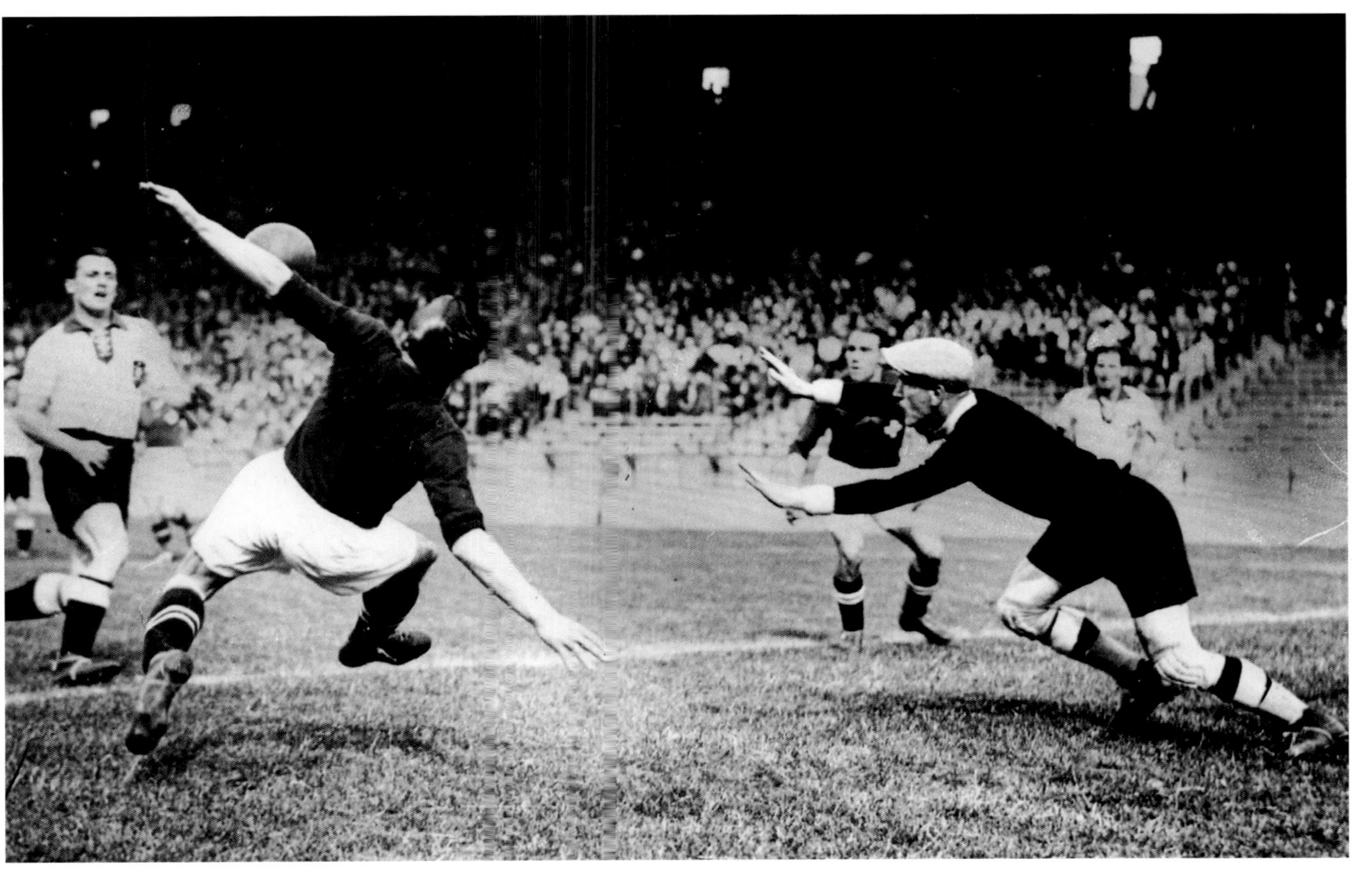

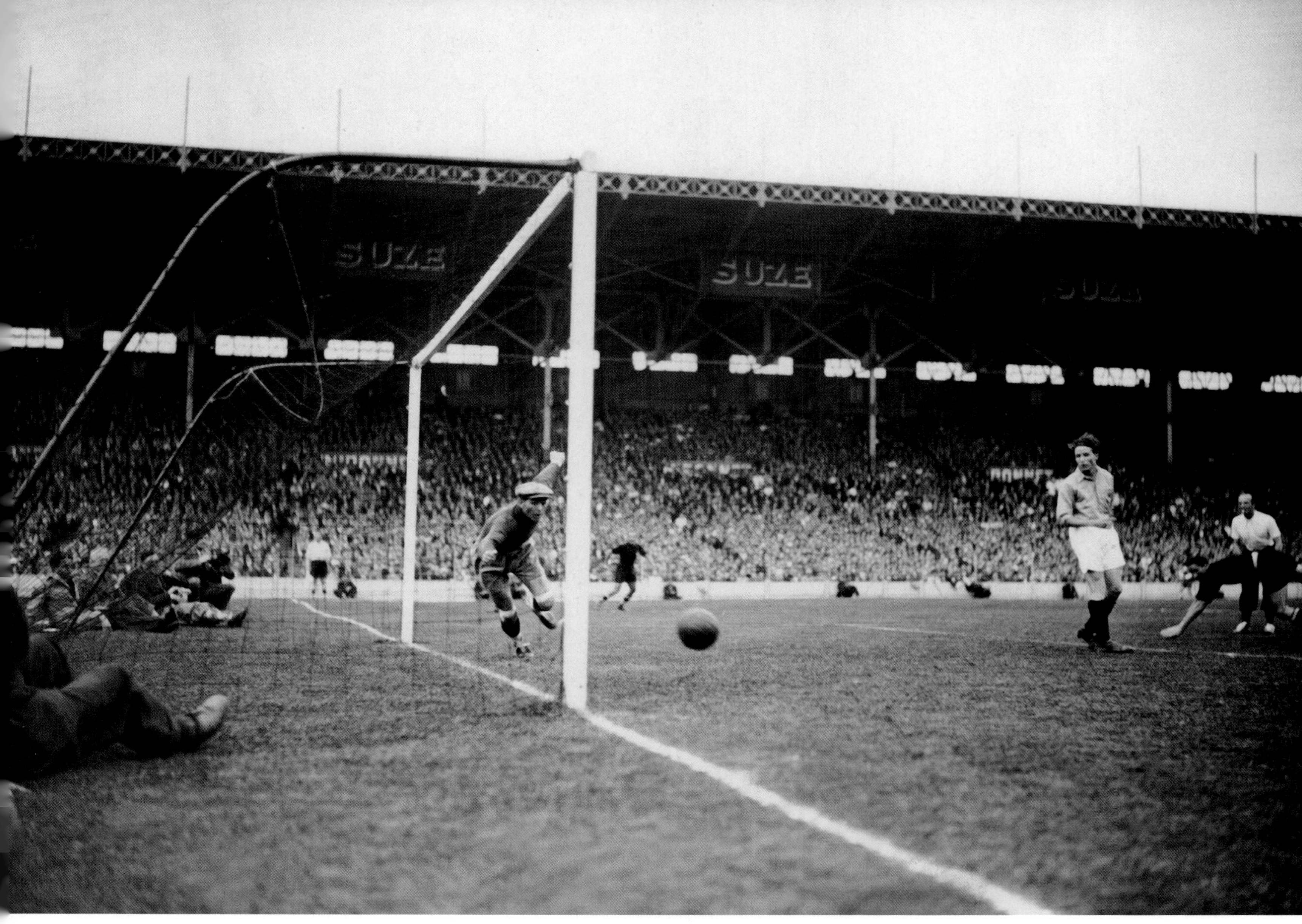

## QUARTER-FINALS

| | | |
|---:|---|---|
| Italy 3 | 1 | France |
| Brazil 1 | 1 | Czechoslovakia |
| (Replay: Brazil 2 | 1 | Czechoslovakia) |
| Hungary 2 | 0 | Switzerland |
| Sweden 8 | 0 | Cuba |

The Swiss lost several of their best players in the gruelling pair of games against Germany and, despite a valiant effort, finally fell to a very strong Hungarian side that ended up in the final. In Sweden's ferocious route of Cuba, the Swedish forward Gustav Wetterström netted a hat-trick before halftime.

Many observers consider Brazil's 1–1 tie with Czechoslovakia one of the most brutal games in Cup history, so violent it was dubbed 'The Battle of Bordeaux'—three ejections and multiple serious injuries, including two broken bones. Brazil's win in the replay marked the last match ever replayed in a World Cup tournament. Both teams were so beat up from the first match that a total of fourteen reserves debuted in the second match.

**ABOVE** *French goalkeeper Laurent Di Lorto caught in poor position for one of Italy's three quarter-final goals.*

**OPPOSITE** *Jan Říha (left) and Romeu Pellicciari (right) of Czechoslovakia and Brazil, respectively, prepare to make a play on the ball.*

'So violent it was dubbed
"The Battle of Bordeaux".'

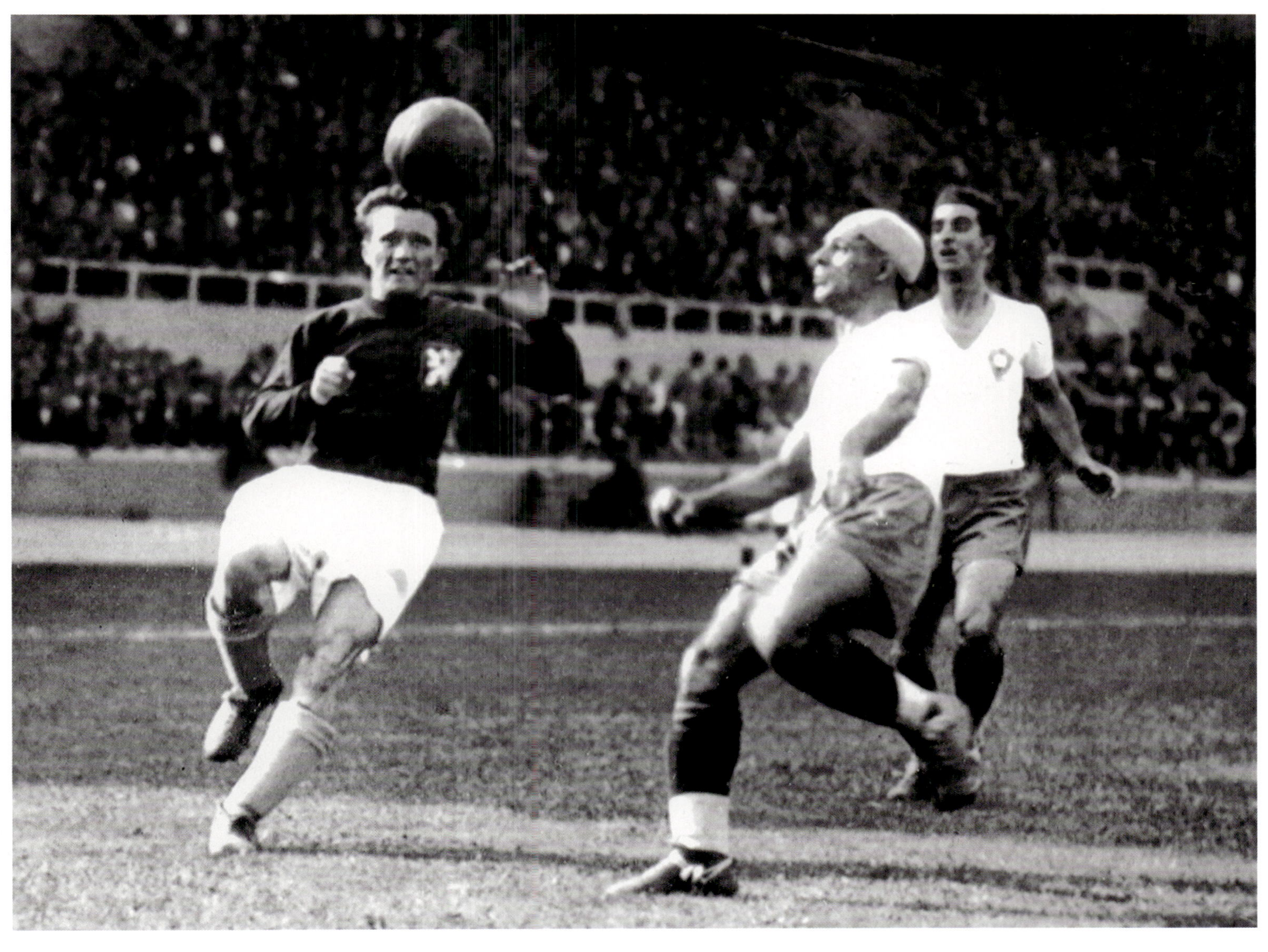

# SEMI-FINALS

Italy 2 | 1 Brazil
Hungary 5 | 1 Sweden

Upstart Sweden stunned the Hungarians with a goal just thirty-five seconds after the opening kickoff, but Hungary took charge from that point on, wearing down the overmatched Swedes with relentless runs and three goals before halftime. Hungarian forward Gyula Zsengellér scored once in each half for a brace.

The other semi-final was a highly anticipated clash between the reigning Italians and the swiftly rising Brazilians. The first half was a seesaw affair, with Brazil's cat-like keeper Walter snuffing out multiple Italian threats. In the second half, Italy scored early and then converted from the penalty spot just nine minutes later for a 2–0 lead. Brazil managed a late goal off a corner kick and pressed hard in the tense final minutes, but the Italians were determined to fend off the several late runs.

**RIGHT** *A Hungarian defender clears the ball in the semi-final against Sweden.*

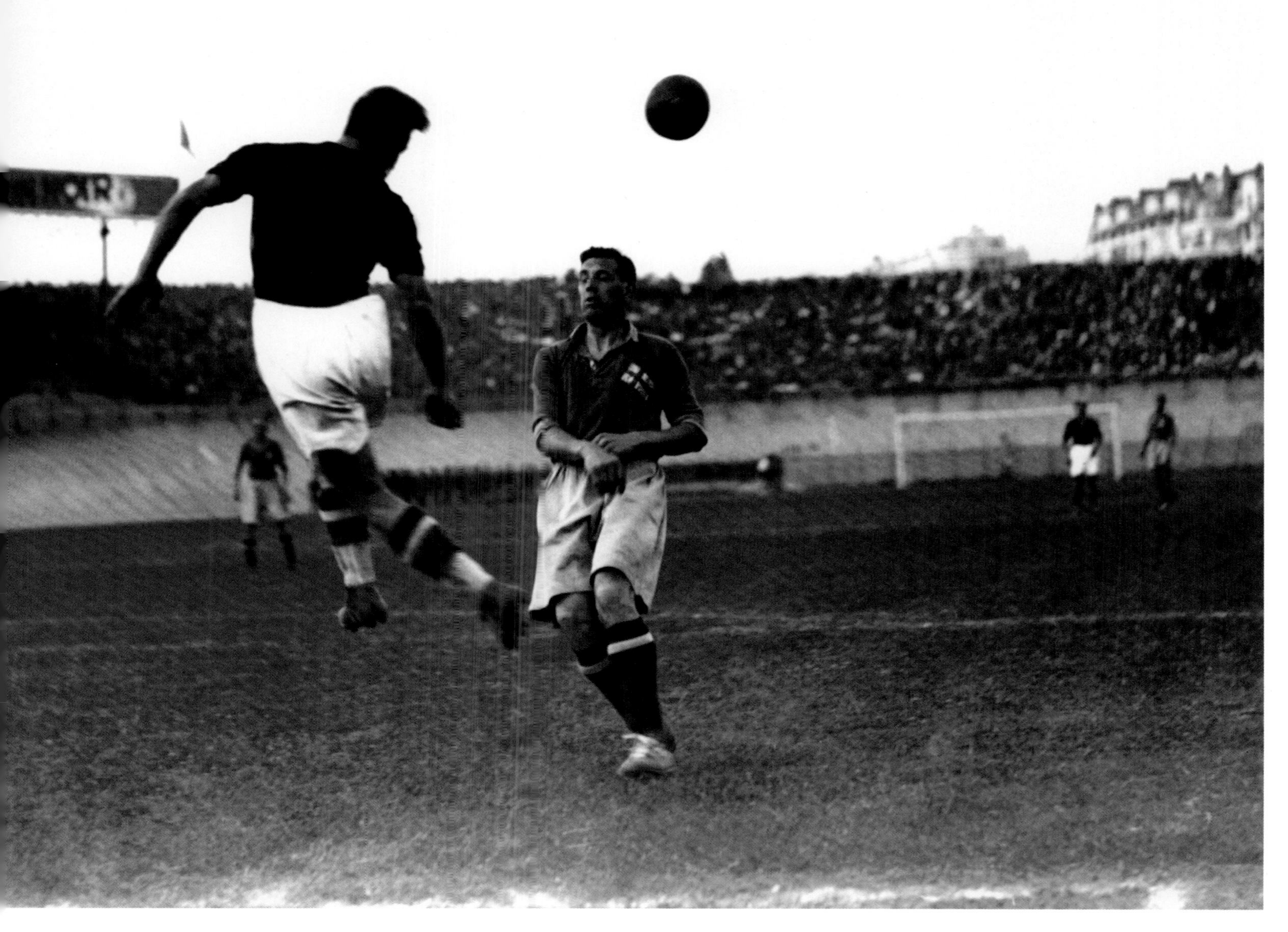

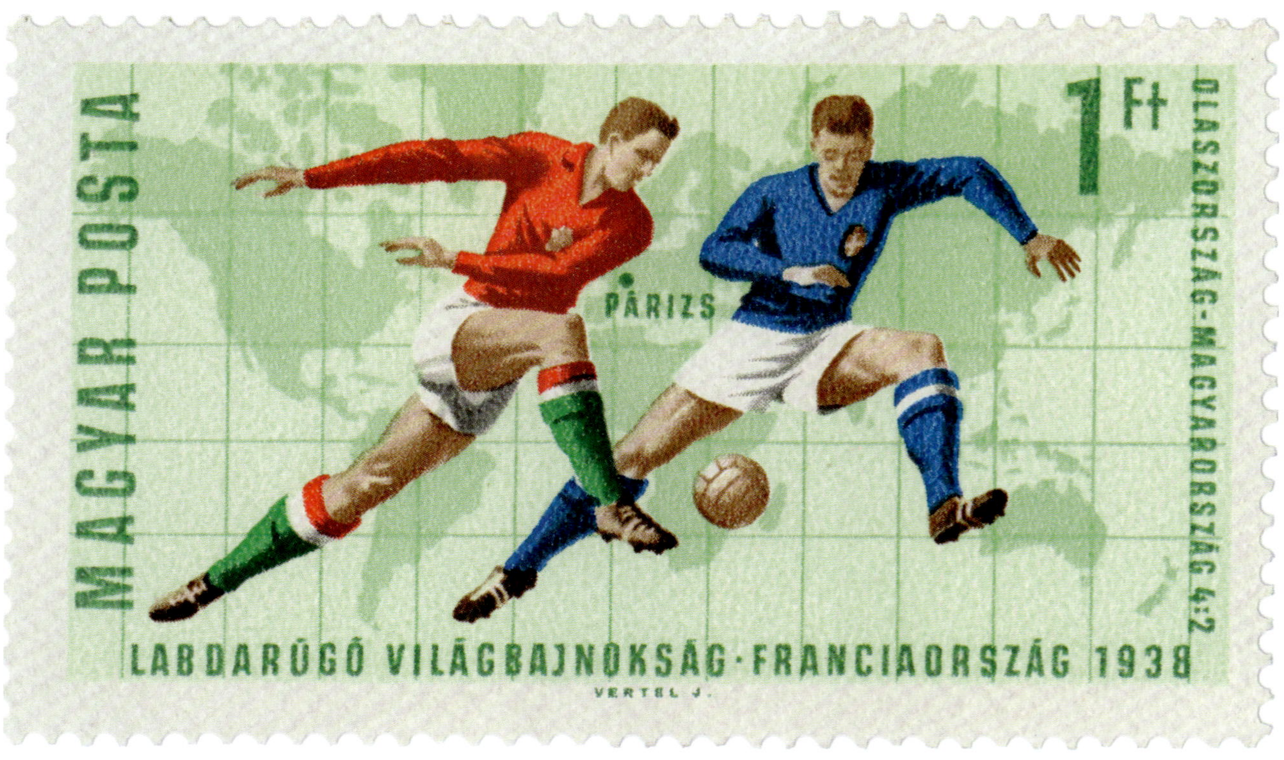


## FINAL

Italy 4 | 2 Hungary
(First Place)

Brazil 4 | 2 Sweden
(Third Place)

Even though it would be twenty years until Brazil won its first World Cup, the 1938 tournament gave the world its first glimpse of an emerging global force in football. After pushing eventual-champion Italy to the brink in its semi-final, Brazil came out uninspired against Sweden in the consolation match at Parc Lescure in Bordeaux, falling behind 2–0 at halftime. But the second half was a Brazilian attacking clinic as star forward Leônidas finished beautiful chances eleven minutes apart to give his *Canarinhos* (Canaries) the lead. A capper by Perácio put the final touch on a four-goal second-half blitz that gave Brazil a 4–2 victory…and gave the sport a preview of the Brazilians' bright future. Leônidas ended up the tournament's top scorer with seven goals.

The first-place final in the majestic Stade Olympique de Colombes, near Paris, matched the defending Cup champion Italy against an intimidating Hungarian side that had stormed through the tournament, overpowering its three opponents by a total of 13–1. Italy jumped out to a quick lead in the sixth minute, but Hungary equalised just two minutes later. Italian star Silvio Piola took the lead back with a rifle shot and then Gino Colaussi scored his second goal of the game to give the Blues a 3–1 lead at halftime. The Hungarian captain György Sárosi scored his fifth goal of the tournament to bring his side within one, but Piola finished his brace at the eighty-two-minute mark to seal a 4–2 victory for the back-to-back World Cup champions.

Thus, Italy proved that its controversial 1934 Cup title was no fluke. And to this day, the immortal Vittorio Pozzo remains the only football manager to steer a national team to two FIFA World Cup titles as a coach.

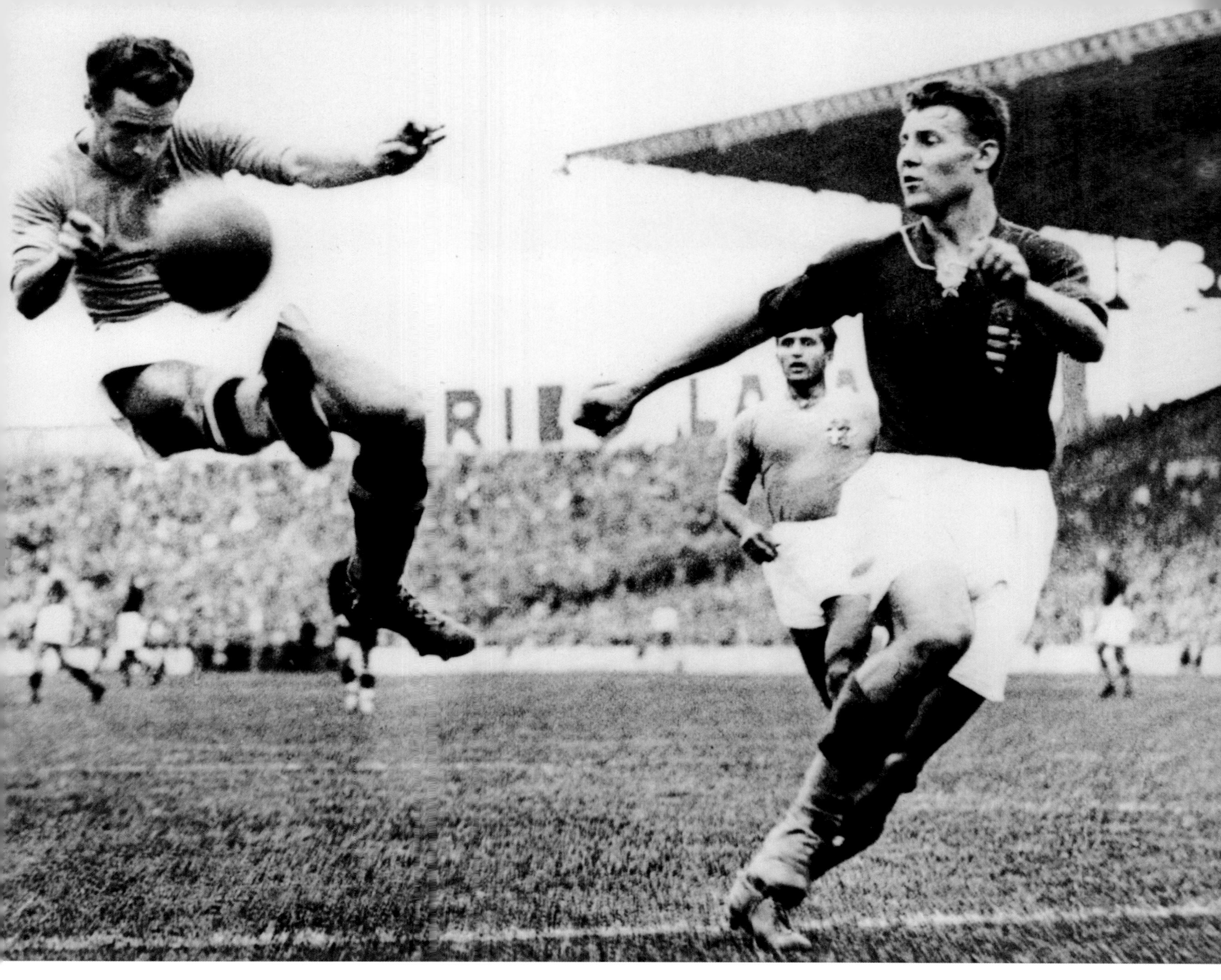



**OPPOSITE** *The 1938 World Cup Final as depicted in a stamp issued by the Hungarian Post, part of a series leading up to the 1966 World Cup.*

**ABOVE** *Facing off against Hungary in the final, Alfredo Foni of Italy attempts to bring down the ball in the opponent's box.*

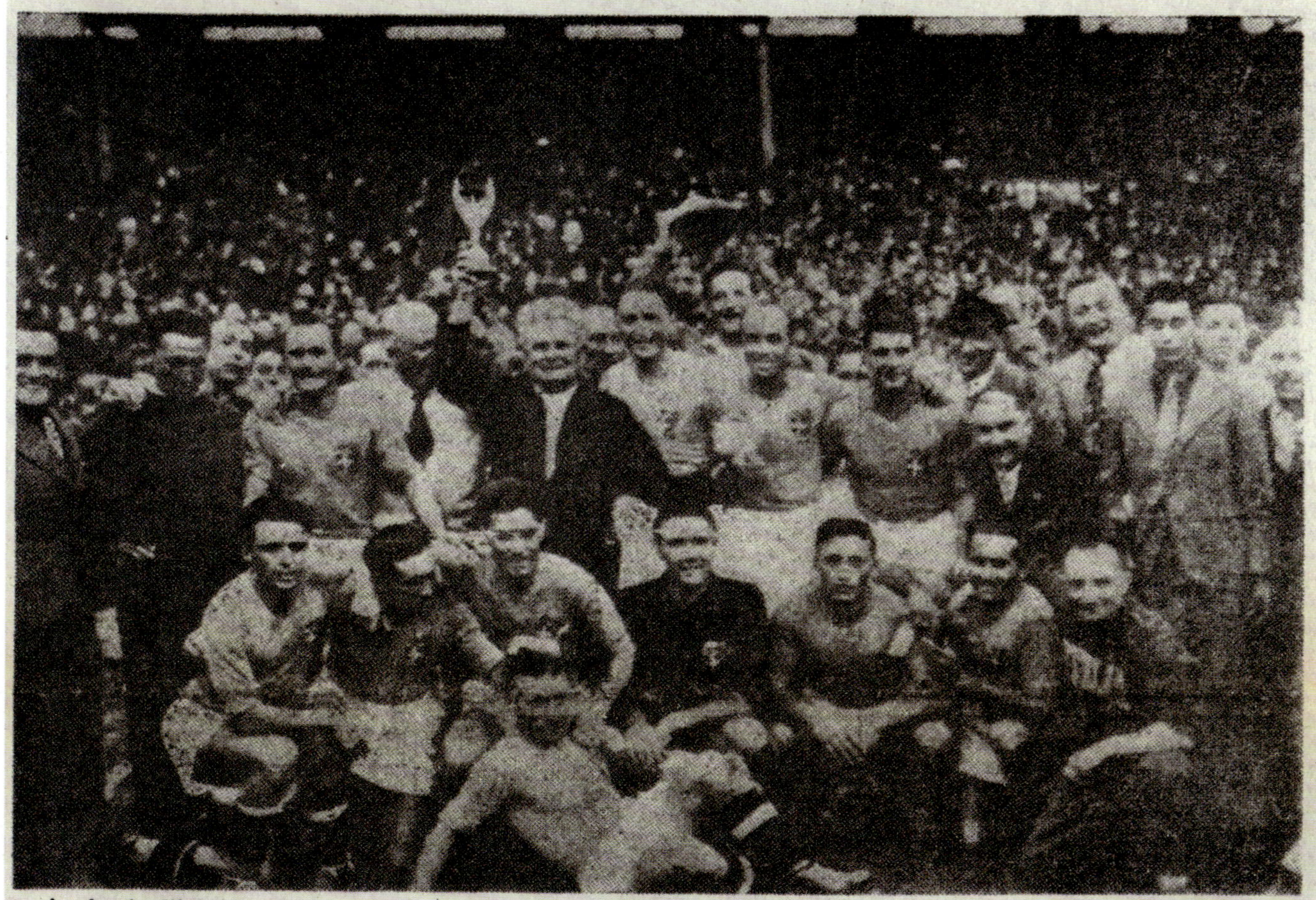



**ABOVE** Il Popolo d'Italia: *[The Italian footballers conquer the third World Cup by clearly defeating the Hungarians: 4–2]*

**OPPOSITE** Il Popolo d'Italia: *[Italy wins their third World Cup, closing the tournament with a masterful match]*

# L'Italia conquista la III Coppa del Mondo

## chiudendo il torneo con una partita magistrale

### (DAL NOSTRO INVIATO SPECIALE)

**Parigi 20 giugno**

La scena finale è quella che tocca da vicino il cuore e lo fa traboccare di entusiasmo e di commozione. E allora — siccome al cuore ci vuole affidare nel descrivere quest'ultima partita del campionato del mondo, assai più che al concetto tecnico e al quadernetto degli appunti — cominciamo dall'epilogo che sportivamente parlando è un'apoteosi di trionfo e di vera gloria.

Siamo allo scoccare del tempo regolamentare. Sulla parete nera che domina lo stadio, in enormi lettere gialle, stanno scritti due nomi e due numeri: Italia 4, Ungheria 2. Su quello non c'è da discutere; di quello non ci si preoccupa. La partita è stata vinta nei primissimi minuti. È stata condotta sempre vittoriosamente, ha avuto momenti di così schiacciante superiorità italiana, di così alta bellezza estetica, da far gridare anche i più calmi e i più riflessivi finchè la voce moriva in gola, troppa povera voce per troppa grande gioia.

### L'arbitro e il pallone

Ecco che la palla passa vicino all'arbitro. Lui fischia, rincorre la palla, corre via portandosela sotto il braccio. Con una mano fa dei grandi gesti per far comprendere a tutti che la lotta è finita, che il titolo di campione del mondo è assegnato.

Dal centro della tribuna opposta a quella in cui noi ci troviamo, una banda militare di 128 elementi — a prego di credere al particolare perchè i suoi componenti sono stati contati uno per uno — muove verso gli azzurri che, dopo di essersi serrati l'uno contro l'altro in un vigoroso e appassionato abbraccio, si irrigidiscono sull'attenti e alzano il braccio nel saluto romano, mentre nell'aria calma della splendente serena mattina si levano cavalcanti, imperiose, gagliarde le note care della « Marcia Reale ». Dalle tribune, dalle gradinate, dalle curve, gruppi di italiani ebbri di frenetica contentezza agitano bandiere tricolori, scandiscono a gran voce il nome fatidico: « Italia! Italia! ».

Ecco che le battute della « Marcia Reale » sono finite e il dignitoso comandante della musica, dopo aver segnato per tre volte il tempo con le mani guantate di bianco, attacca « La Marsigliese ». Come si fa a resistere? Siamo a Parigi, sessantamila persone ci guardano e noi italiani — un manipolo di giocatori in maglia azzurra in gruppo in mezzo al campo, centinaia e centinaia di persone venute con ogni mezzo dalla Patria, migliaia di connazionali che aspettavano questo momento da anni — udiamo suonare da una banda militare francese, l'inno della nostra Patria, il canto della nostra fede, il giuramento della nostra dedizione al Duce. Come si fa a resistere — si diceva — perchè una lagrima non corra giù per la guancia a rigare il viso...

### L'incasso totale: 6.000.000 di franchi

Gli incassi della terza Coppa del Mondo avevano raggiunto, prima delle due partite di finale di ieri, la cifra di 4.900.000 franchi.

La finale di Parigi ha fruttato 820.000 franchi e quella di Bordeaux, fra il Brasile e la Svezia, ha dato un incasso di 220.000 franchi. Pertanto il totale generale raggiunge la rispettabile cifra di 5.940.000 franchi.

...tio, testimone muto di quello che il cuore, di quel grande tumulto che si ha nel sangue e che le parole non sapranno mai rendere?

Poi Meazza si stacca dai compagni, entra nella tribuna d'onore, riceve dalle mani del signor Lebrun, Presidente della Repubblica, la Coppa d'oro che la Francia ha voluto offrire alla Nazione vincitrice e ritorna giù sul prato verde dove con gli altri dieci suoi camerati, ha vinto la battaglia più bella della sua carriera sportiva.

### Canzoni e applausi

Nell'aria volano cento e cento vivi scaraitti in segno di esultanza; scocciano i primi applausi, il trepidano carezzanti di inmalzano gossenti evviva.

La folla parigina non si muove. Ammira in silenzio. E forse si associa a questa nostra vittoria sportiva accomuna questo nostro entusiasmo ad altri affetti che ferono, tanti anni presenti davanti agli occhi, ad altri entusiasmi che un dì non si possono più. Ma è cuore, che trabocca da every tumore e ricordare e sorridere dire come che non può e non sa dire, non deve prendersi la mano non dove non si lontano.

Ritornando alla partita, ripensando al nostro dovere professionale, ci si sente incapaci di far rivivere tutto, si comprende benissimo che il lettore prendendo in mano il giornale non potrà — sarebbe eccessiva modestia — vibrare come noi abbiamo vibrato, esultare come noi abbiamo esultato. Si vorrebbero conoscere parole sonanti come squilli di tromba, fragorose come uno scoppio di castagnole per far rivivere ad un giorno di distanza gli episodi, le vicende, il clima della nostra grande partita.

E questa gara la vogliamo raccontare subito perchè è troppo bella, perchè la squadra si è imposta di colpo con il ritmo serrato di una carica di cavalleria, perchè l'impeto delle nostre offensive ha ragione di ogni barriera, perchè nello stile e nella sicurezza dei giocatori italiani c'è tutta la genialità estrosa della nostra razza latina, c'è tutto il fuoco del nostro temperamento, c'è tutta la volontà che noi italiani sappiamo mettere in ognuna delle nostre imprese.

Il cerimoniale di stretta etichetta si compie a tambur battente. Le due squadre sono affacciate all'imbocco del sottopassaggio, in attesa dell'arrivo del presidente della Repubblica. Quando il signor Lebrun entra nella tribuna, la banda intona la « Marsigliese ».

Gli ungheresi in maglia rossa escono per primi e a passo cadenzato si portano al centro del terreno; gli azzurri irrompono di corsa ed è come una folata di giovinezza che entra impetuosa nello scenario imponente e suggestivo dello Stadio. Lento e solenne l'inno magiaro; vivi, appassionati, vibranti gli inni nostri. Il signor Lebrun scende sul terreno di giuoco, si porta sulla linea dove i 22 uomini sono schierati e, cominciando da Olivieri che è il primo dei nostri, stringe la mano a tutti i giocatori, che il generale Vaccaro gli presenta uno ad uno.

Poi, rapidissimo, il via. È passato appena un minuto e i nostri sono in angolo per un salvataggio di Foni su Titkos sfuggito in velocità a Serantoni. È passato un altro minuto e sono in angolo gli ungheresi per una fuga di Colaussi, imbeccato da Piola, e per un suo tiro violento che costringe Szabo ad una parata audace. La previsione di ieri, che si sarebbe cominciato da parte nostra a tutta andatura, era troppo facile da imbroccare. Difesa, mediana, attacco azzurri si muovono rapidissimi, guizzano via per ogni dove, invano inseguiti dagli avversari, che accusano nettamente il disagio della troppo celere andatura.

### Si pone la prima pietra

Prima fase fondamentale al 5' di giuoco. Una carica di Andreolo è fischiata dall'arbitro e il centro mediano Szucs tira la punizione da una trentina di metri, contro la nostra rete. La palla batte sulla schiena di un azzurro, si alza, va in angolo...

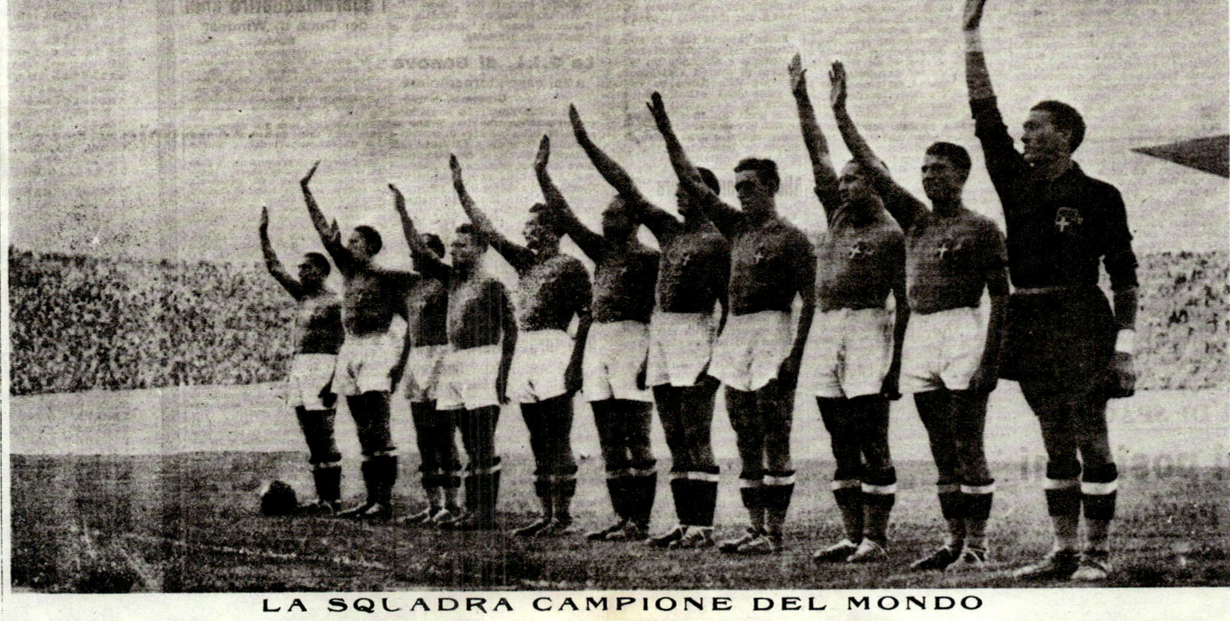

### LA SQUADRA CAMPIONE DEL MONDO

...

Colaussi aspetta che il mediano gli si avvicina in rete. Siamo all'8' di giuoco. Ci sorride la gioia di un bel giuoco. Il primo colpo di testa gli fa passare la palla sfila rapido, poi, entrando con uno scarto a una finta. Ma serra la porta ungherese. Questo spettacoloso giocatore, che è tutto decisione, forza, coraggio, è un centro mediano che fa più suoi tiri nel deciso, più felice nel tiro. È un eroe, Piola...

### Botta e risposta

La ripresa, dal punto di vista della cronaca, è più povera del primo tempo. Si presta a qualche breve digressione tecnica, che sarà fatta a dopo. I primi venti minuti passano senza tiri notevoli, se si eccettua un tiro contro la base del palo, e poco dopo di Biavati, a quello della legge incidente — Piola-Biro, Serantoni-Titkos immediatamente represso dall'arbitro.

I nostri sono lenti, piuttosto apatici. Dopo una lunga incubazione, maturano secondo rete magiara. È Titkos che fugge tutto solo e dal fondo campo tira verso la porta. La palla, piena di effetto, anziché il momentaneo solo, modificarsi fatto a Sarosi, leggermente anticipato il tiro. Non si fa spettatore, e non guarda il tuoi compresi dal distante sono diminuite: una sola delle nostre ne guardo. Il prezioso posizione la rete dà di testa. Quattro a due. Nove minuti di giuoco ancora. Questi nove minuti non mettono da paura alla stessa. Quelli che vengono dopo sono lungamente descritti in principio.

### Tattica di gare

Descritta minutamente nelle sue particolarità — sei reti, tutte notevole, tutte impeccabili, tutto frutto alla bravura di attaccanti, veemente ed errore di difensori — la partita va riepilogata nelle sue fasi, analizzata...

### Tutti bravi

Che dire dei protagonisti? Quelli italiani vanno citati tutti sullo stesso piano. Olivieri è stato pochissimo impegnato. Lo si attendeva alla prova, contro dei cannonieri che ci avevano garantito essere pericolosissimi. Non si sono visti quasi mai. Un solo tiro serio, quello citato di Szengeller, è stato fermato da Olivieri con intuito e scelta di tempo perfetta. La coppia dei terzini non ha sbagliato un rimando. È la nuova grande forza della Nazionale, è un reparto che non ha dubbi, che non ha debolezze, che costituisce garanzia sicura in ogni situazione. Rava, abbandonandosi al suo temperamento, è stato più audace, più impetuoso, più combattivo. Foni è il giocatore dalla tecnica perfetta, che ha il dono grandissimo di fare di ogni pallone un passaggio, che sa sempre dove manderà la palla, che riesce a vedere il compagno in posizione migliore e a servirlo a dovere.

Nella mediana Andreolo ha dominato con quel suo modo di giocare tutto decisione, forza, coraggio, le due ali mediane di copertura che gli danno aiuto una volta portandosi davanti al portiere. Si sa che i tiri di Piola sono fuciliate che non si freno-prodigiosi a caso di necessità, anche indispensabile per la prima linea che serra la figura e ci sorride. Gli attaccanti: il peso grande e giovane cuore grande e generoso, con la prima linea di scorta e sempre bene a posto.

### Ghiaccio sulla testa

Lo stadio di Colombes deve avere una certa ritrosia a lasciare soddisfatti i calciatori italiani dopo il loro successo. Come già contro la Francia, il pareggio dopo la prima nostra rete è stato fulmineo, così anche questa volta gli ungheresi si portarono alla pari. Diceva sulla strada per Vincere e Vincere: Locatelli interçetta, rimpalga troppo corto a Vinçce riprende ancora e l'azione è ripresa. Altra palla porta a giuoco e poi si schiude la tela. Fonte copre la palla di testa, non arriva; irrompe Titkos, debolmente ostacolato da Serantoni e scaraventa in rete. Siamo all'8' di giuoco. Ci sorride la trepidazione al pallido scherzo, sol ritardo con uno scarto e una finta. Ma serra la porta ungherese. Questo spettacoloso giocatore...

...Piola che ha seguito l'azione del compagno spostandosi davanti a lui sulla destra del campo, riceve la palla. L'altro terzino ungherese Polgar, vista la mala parata, gli va incontro e Piola, cogliendo l'attimo di tempo giusto, sposta il giuoco sulla sinistra, dove Colaussi è rimasto completamente solo. Per il triestino, piombare sul pallone, riprendere al volo e saettarlo imparabilmente in un angolo della rete è affare di un centesimo di secondo. Szabo non ha potuto muoversi. La rete italiana è fatta, sulle gradinate qualcuno non ne può già più. Siamo al 6' di fuoco. L'applauso si fa scrosciante quando già i giocatori italiani hanno ripreso le loro posizioni di partenza. La folla, prima di battere le mani, ha dovuto superare 30 secondi di assoluto sbalordimento per la rapidità, la semplicità, la straordinaria percisione della manovra azzurra. Proprio così: Serantoni-Biavati-Piola-Colaussi-rete: tre passaggi, un tiro, un punto.

...ridoi miracolosi, non alzandosi di un palmo da terra, evitando sempre al millimetro gli avversari. È una rete indescrivibile. La più bella rete, su azione manovrata, che si sia vista da un paio d'anni a questa parte.

Voi penserete che, paghi di questa prodezza gli azzurri rallentino l'andatura. Nemmeno per scherzare. Mentre gli ungheresi non sanno a quale santo votarsi per tenere gli azzurri, che sgusciano da ogni parte come anguille imprendibili, i nostri insistono nella loro accademia meravigliosa, che provoca ondate di ammirato entusiasmo. Ecco un tiro di Meazza, proprio sotto la sbarra, che Szabo inchioda con una presa a tenaglia impeccabile; ecco una nuova discesa di Biavati che porta una minaccia seria alla rete ungherese. Un salvataggio di Rava in angolo, su discesa di Titkos, un brutto scarto a Meazza, punito immediatamente dall'arbitro. Qualche minuto di rallentamento verso la mezz'ora e poi al 35' la terza rete italiana.

Nasce da un'azione ungherese. Foni intercetta e rimanda corto, appena fuori della nostra area il...

...quando è giornata di grazia, non conosce cosa impossibili: in grandi di lui, seguiva un terzino resta alla carica dell'altro terzino e in vincola da un paio di metri in un raggio di almeno 20 metri, Szabo e terzino del terzino resta alla riva a barba e capelli. Da altra parte dei punti violentissimi in rete. Szabo meraviglioso, dei difensori ungheresi che rincorrono, dei difensori che si serrano in schiena in angolo, quando già la nostra ala sinistra arriva sparato secco. Dopo salvataggio meraviglioso. Al 45' Gli ungheresi dopo magistralmente l'unica partita delle difese, il primo Piola, Riccardo la palla da Biavati e Piola. Ricdda in rete e difese, la compressione di volere passare a limitista, e invece — buttando tutto sulla destra con una di quelle conversioni fulminee che soltanto gli ungheresi sanno — si trova libero davanti al portiere. Si sa che i tiri del Piola sono fuciliate che non si fermano, e prima di riprendere quando serve. A contatto con gli ungheresi vi sono due nostri...

tra, e invece — buttando tutto sulla destra con una di quelle conversioni fulminee che soltanto gli ungheresi sanno — si trova libero davanti al portiere. Si sa che i tiri del Piola sono fuciliate che non si fermano, e prima di riprendere le posizioni serve con precisione. A 45' gli ungheresi dopo magistralmente l'unica partita delle difese, proprio alla fine...

### Grosso premio ai calciatori italiani

**Parigi 20 giugno**

Ci risulta che, in seguito alla brillante vittoria conseguita dai calciatori italiani nella terza Coppa del Mondo — vittoria che conferma la legittimità del titolo di campioni del mondo conquistato nel 1934 allo stadio del Partito a Roma alla presenza animatrice del Duce — è stato concesso ai nostri atleti un grosso premio. Si tratterebbe di ventimila lire per ciascuno giocatore.

L'Italia calcistica conclude vittoriosamente il suo secondo campionato del mondo. Moltissime vodi straniere avevano espresso dubbi che era stata ottenuta la vittoria netta. Questa volta la critica mondiale deve essere più di una riserva ad ammettere — in terra straniera, con la base sottile ricordo di Marsiglia. Forse qualche volenteroso...

**Nino Nutrizio**

*Italia:* Olivieri — Foni, Rava — Serantoni, Andreolo, Locatelli — Biavati, Meazza, Piola, Ferrari, Colaussi.
*Ungheria:* Szabo — Polgar, Biro — Szalai, Szucs, Lazar — Sas, Vincze, Sarosi, Szengeller, Titkos.
*Arbitro:* Capdeville (Francia).
*Terreno:* partita disputatissima. Spettatori: 55.500. Incasso: 820.600 franchi.

### Piola migliore di Drake

Piola, la meraviglia del calcio italiano, ha disputato ieri una partita sbalorditiva. Dei tecnici inglesi quei tali signori di cui ieri si parlò a proposito del famosissimo Drake, perchè di più veloce, più deciso, più felice nel tiro. È non avendo Piola, che di tutte le difese, ci ha fatto vedere ieri come così capace e quanto possa compiere un solo uomo quando da mezza forza, classe ed audacia, abbiano diretto indissolubile patto di alleanza fra loro.

Colaussi è stato per il migliore uomo che abbia giocato ieri a Colombes. Siccome pochi in ballo i fischietti per il triestino elogio possa bastare. Se Colaussi dovesse giocare sempre come ieri ed essere servito sempre a quel modo dai compagni abili come Piola, Meazza e Ferrari, nessun portiere potrebbe arreschiarsi di mettergli contro per un'ora e mezzo, senza conoscere la violenza e la precisione dei suoi tiri imparabili.

Resta ancora Biavati: quando di bolognese avrà la sicurezza nel tiro, come l'ha Colaussi ogni, sarà più pericoloso alla destra che possa sentare il calcio non solo italiano, ma forse anche europeo. L'ungherese Sas che ci assicuravano essere un asso del ruolo, ha toccato meno bene — la ventesima porte di quello che Biavati è riuscito a combinare nel corso della partita.

Degli ungheresi non parleremo perchè più di tanto non ci intéressano. Essi e i loro sostenitori si saranno convinti che contro l'Italia il migliore è stato Szabo, non fosse altro che per aver parato due tiri sensazionali di Piola.

Il franzese Capdeville ha arbitrato ella di sottile perfezione, lasciando alle valle che è tutto l'azione, intervenendo ove gli strumenti di richiamo e infliggendo i calcio di punizione. Questi interventi sono stati, al massimo, al punto. Tre volte una parola di richiamo severa agli straneri di buona volontà svolge effettivamente arbitrato la partita senza lasciarla svolgere con quella massima libertà d'azione che è tutta l'espressione e il fascino di quel giuoco.

La cronaca della partita ha riportato vinto dalla squadra locale per 3 a 0.

| CAMPIONI MONDIALI 1934 | CAMPIONI OLIMPIONICI 1936 | CAMPIONI MONDIALI 1938 |
|---|---|---|
| Combi | Venturini | Olivieri |
| Monzeglio | Foni | Foni |
| Allemandi | Rava | Rava |
| Ferrarsi IV | Baldo | Serantoni |
| Monti | Piccini | Andreolo |
| Bertolini | Locatelli | Locatelli |
| Guaita | Frossi | Biavati |
| Meazza | Marchini | Meazza |
| Schiavio | Bertoni | Piola |
| Ferrari | Biagi | Ferrari |
| Orsi | Gabriotti | Colaussi |

## Per poco non ci scappava la sorpresa!

## Brasile-Svezia 4-2 (1-2)

**Bordeaux 20 giugno**

(G. B.) — È mancato poco che la partita che ha deciso del terzo posto, non terminasse con un colpo di scena. I brasiliani erano così convinti della facilità del loro compito, che almeno nel primo tempo sono stati traditi dalla loro eccessiva fiducia. Gli svedesi, con il loro giuoco sobrio, basato soprattutto sulle incursioni in profondità, hanno costretto la difesa avversaria ad un duro lavoro. I nordici hanno, anzi imposto una netta prevalenza, prevalenza concretata con il vantaggio di una rete.

Gli svedesi avevano infatti aperto il punteggio per merito del centro avanti Nyberg e collocavano un secondo punto su una veloce discesa di Anderson. I brasiliani avevano invece segnato verso la fine per merito di Peracho. Ma alla ripresa la fisonomia della partita ha cambiato aspetto. I brasiliani hanno cominciato veramente a giuocare e la loro superiorità di classe si è allora manifestata nel modo più evidente. Il quintetto sud-americano, ritrovava la buona equilibrazione e insisteva in una serie di attacchi condotti con tale rapidità da scompaginare la squadra nordica. Gli svedesi erano allora costretti ad asserragliarsi in difesa e le loro fugaci reazioni si infrangevano inesorabilmente sulla salda difesa avversaria. I brasiliani, che all'inizio del secondo tempo non sapevano approfittare di un rigore concesso dall'arbitro per un fallo di un terzino svedese, coglievano il pareggio dopo una ventina di minuti di giuoco e da questo momento la partita si svolgeva su una porta sola.

Leonidas, il famoso centro avanti brasiliano, si prodigava nelle sue puntate velocissime e segnava uno dopo l'altro due bellissimi punti. Infine al 35' Romeo Pellicciari portava a quattro il punteggio per il Brasile.

*Brasile:* Lorenzato - Domingos, Machado - Procopio, Martin Silvera, Alfonso Guimares - Roberto Cunha, Romeo Pellicciari, Leonidas, Peracho, Patesco.
*Svezia:* Abrahamas - Eriksson, Nilson - Almgrem, Linderholm, Swanson - Jonassonn, Personn, Nyberg, H. Andersson, A. Andersson.
*Arbitro:* Langenus.

● **RISULTATI** delle principali partite amichevoli di calcio disputate ieri: a Biella: Juventus-Biellese 5-2; a Padova: Torino-Padova 2-0; a Genova: Genova-Liguria 3-0 (la Coppa del Federale è quindi assegnata al Genova).

● **IL TRADIZIONALE INCONTRO** fra gli avvocati di Milano e di Genova, disputato ieri a Genova è stato vinto dalla squadra locale per 3 a 0.

# THE 1940s

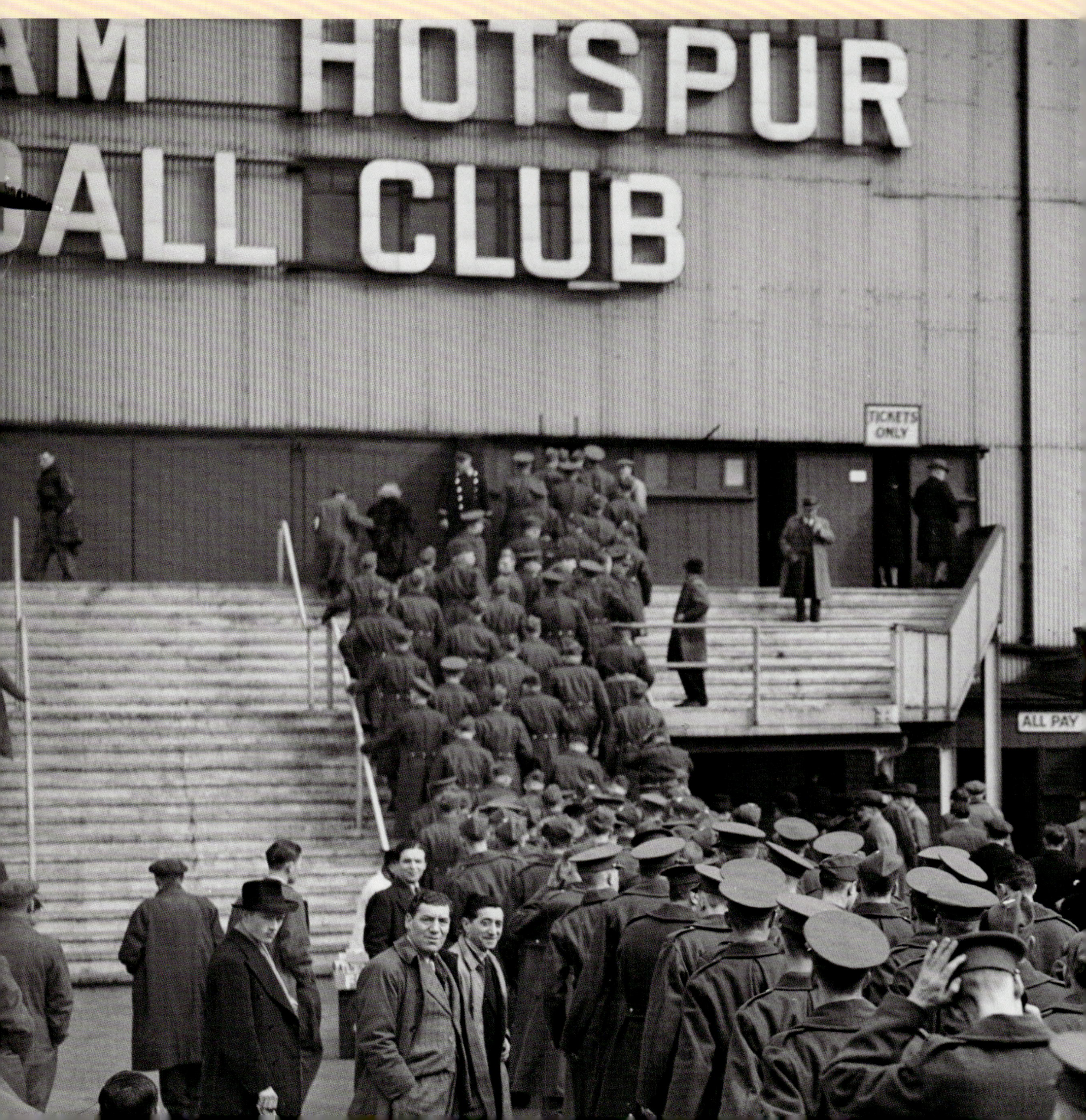

# CHAPTER 2

# The Lost Decade

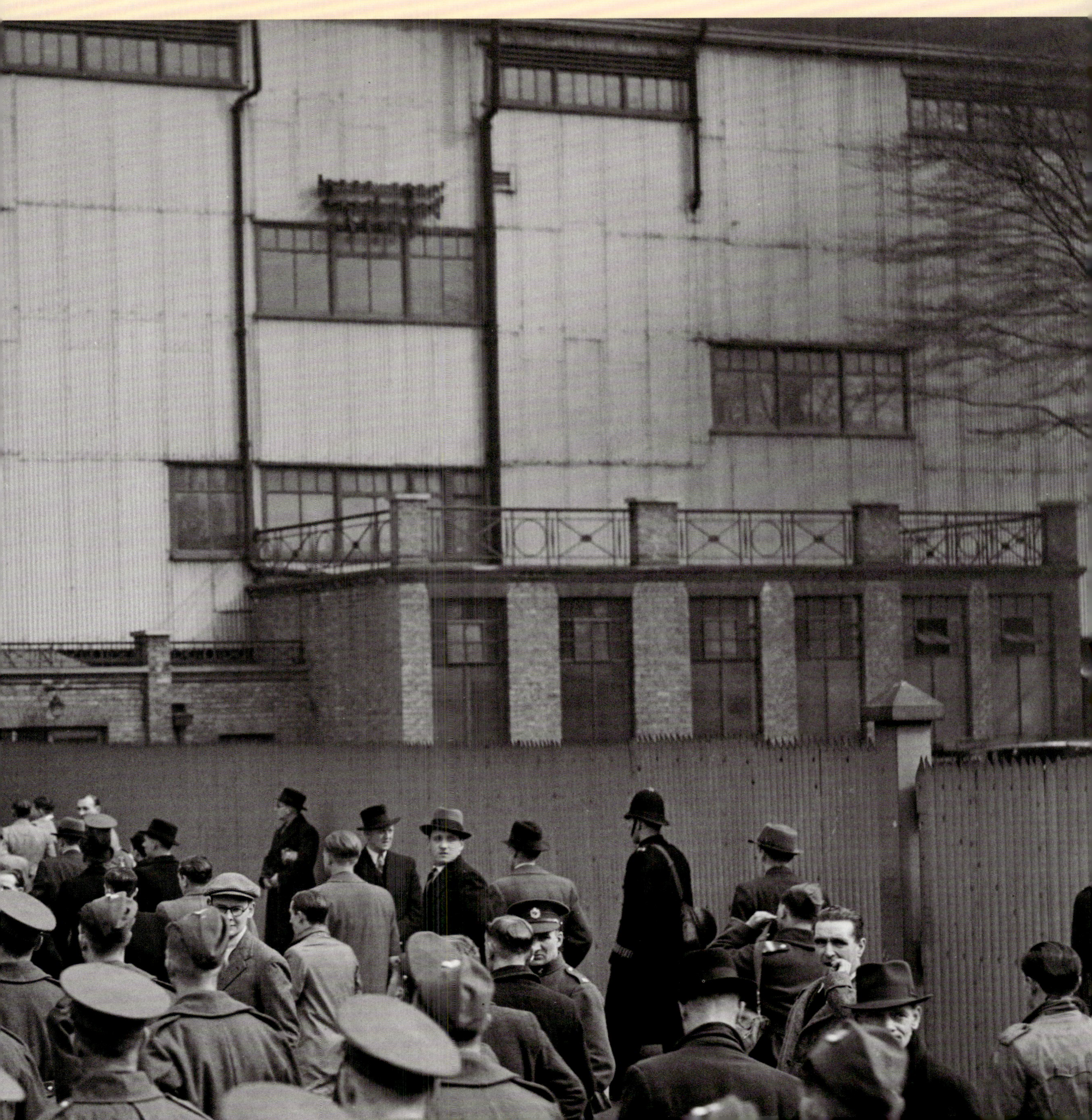

# FOOTBALL DURING WARTIME

When Italy defeated Hungary in the World Cup Final on 19 June, 1938, the European continent had already been steeped in political hostility and growing tensions for years. Then Nazi Germany's invasion of Poland on 1 September, 1939, triggered a series of war declarations that tipped the world over a precipice, plunging it into the most catastrophic conflict in human history: the Second World War. Ironically, Germany had applied to host the next Cup tournament, set for 1942. That pending competition, of course, was cancelled.

Certainly, the continuation of football was the least of concerns as war machines ramped up across Europe. Most professional athletes joined their nation's armed forces or contributed to the war effort in factories or community service. But even though many European pro leagues like the English Football League and Division 1 in France were suspended and player contracts cancelled, Allied military leadership saw football as a great way to keep troops fit, boost morale, and forge tighter bonds within units. Competitive matches between service branches flourished—the British military even organised a Brigade Association Football Cup for teams formed of military units.

Football helped on the home front as well. Local exhibition matches often featured soldiers who'd been famous footballers before the war, and thus excitement ran high and raised civilian spirits. Paid attendance at some of the larger exhibitions also helped raise money for critical wartime services and charities.

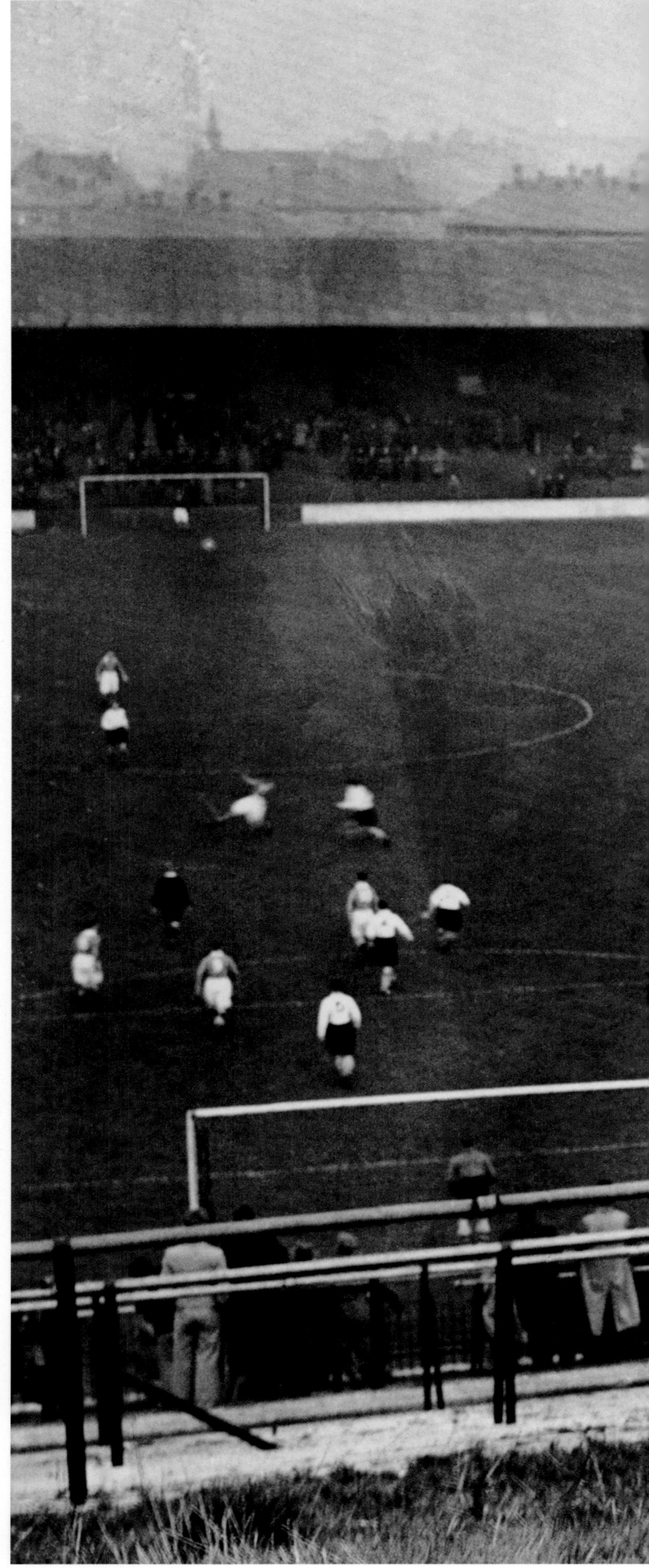

**PREVIOUS SPREAD** *British soldiers on leave attend a match between English clubs Arsenal and Chelsea, the Tottenham Hotspur's White Hart Lane serving as the venue, 1940.*

**RIGHT** *A match between Arsenal and Charlton is surveilled by an air raid warden, 1940.*

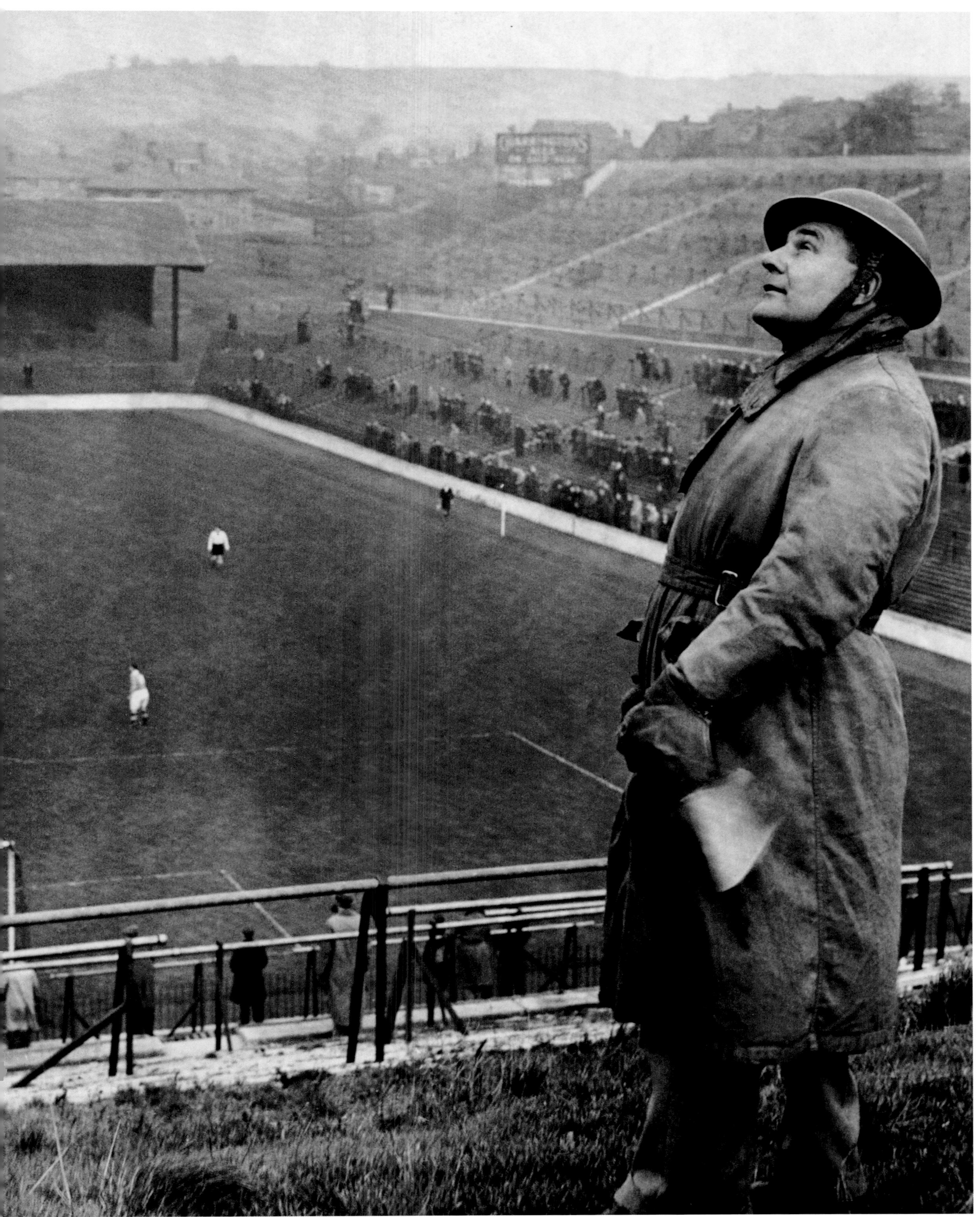

# THE ULTIMATE TEAM PLAYER

**During the Second World War,** the British Home Office saw football as a compelling recruitment tool. For example, the great Harry Goslin, captain and longtime star defender of the Bolton Wanderers, not only volunteered for active service but made an impassioned plea to the Burnden Park crowd before his last game as a civilian in 1939, urging spectators to enlist in the cause, too.

'We are facing a national emergency,' he announced. 'This is something you can't leave to the other fellow. Everybody has a share to do.'

Two days later, Goslin and sixteen of his teammates joined the 53rd Field Regiment, Royal Artillery. By April 1940, according to *Picture Post* magazine, 629 British professional footballers had joined the services — 514 in the Territorial Army, eighty-four in the RAF, and thirty-one in the Royal Navy. Others went into war work. In 1940, one factory in Oldbury employed eighteen West Bromwich Albion players.

The Bolton soldiers would continue to play a handful of matches at small venues across the country — large assemblies were banned, with air raids a constant threat — raising not only local spirits but also wartime charity funds. Goslin himself was selected to play for England in unofficial 'international' matches against Scotland and Wales in 1941. Sadly, after earning an officer's commission and serving with distinction under Field Marshal 'Monty' Montgomery in the North African campaign, Goslin would be killed by a mortar round during the Allied invasion of Italy in December of 1944.

**BELOW** *An unofficial wartime match between England and Wales at Wembley Stadium in London, 1940. Alexander Cambridge, 1ˢᵗ Earl of Athlone, shakes hands with the visiting Welsh players.*

**OPPOSITE** *Harry Goslin, playing for the Bolton Wanderers, before a match against Chelsea at Stamford Bridge, 1939.*

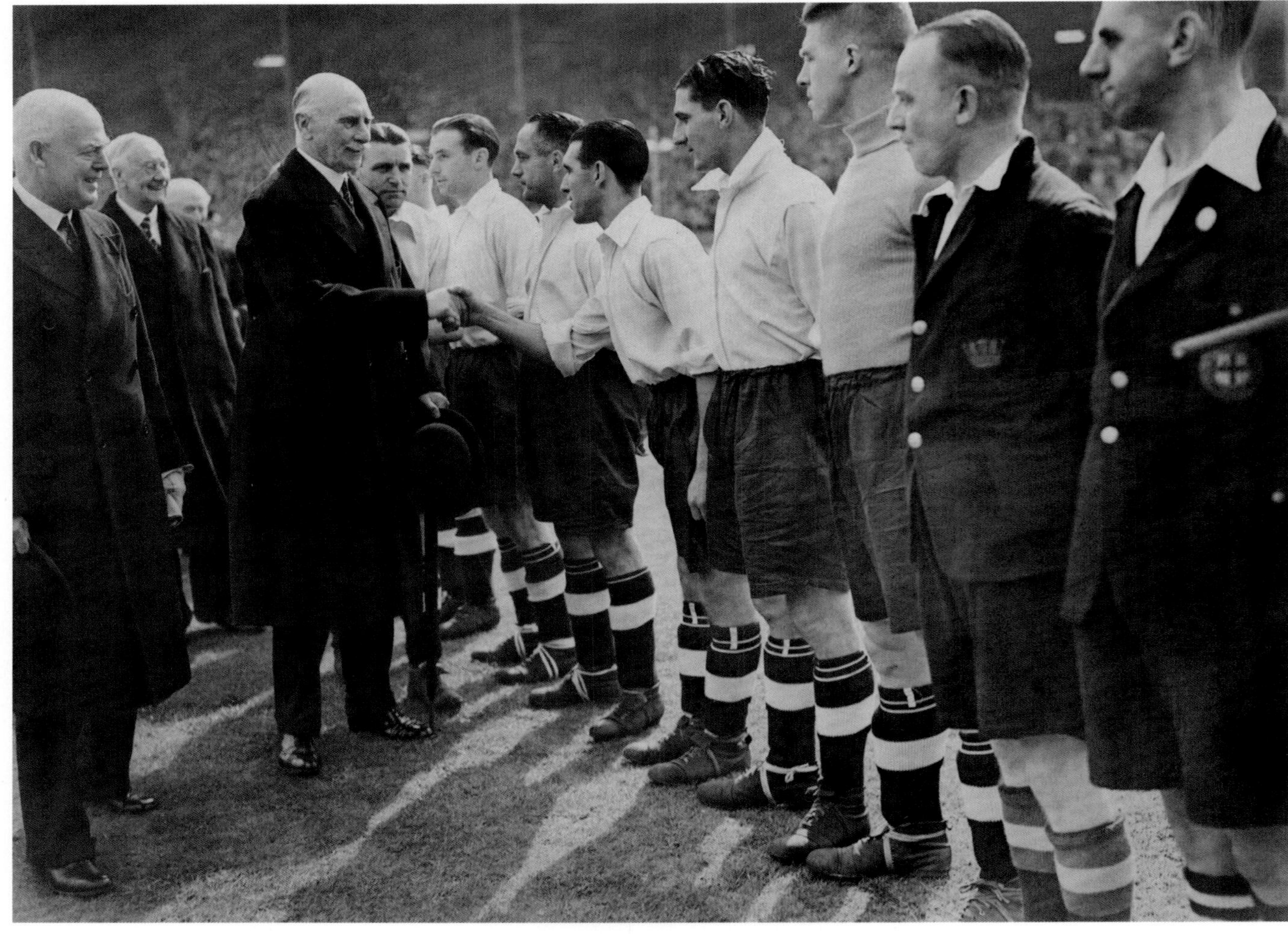

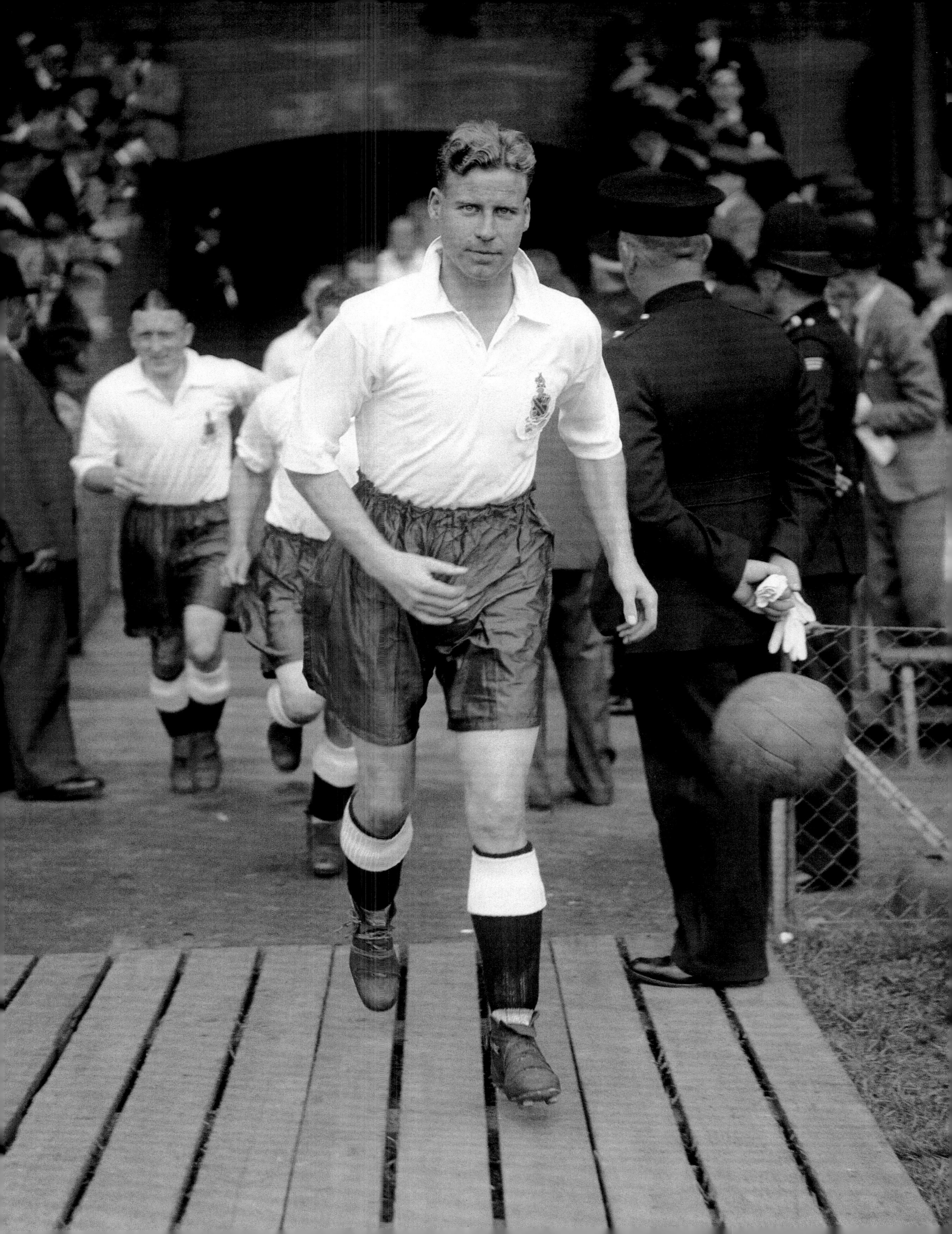

# FOOTBALLERS ON THE FRONT LINES

**Thousands of well-known athletes** served as soldiers, sailors, airmen, or resistance fighters on both sides of the conflict in the Second World War, including celebrated footballers. Many earned honours for bravery and outstanding service: Rangers forward Willie Thornton served in the Scottish Horse regiment and won the Military Medal for 'acts of gallantry under fire' during the Allied invasion of Sicily. The brilliant German goalkeeper Bert Trautmann joined the Nazi's Luftwaffe and earned five medals, including the prestigious Iron Cross — after the war, he put in 508 performances in goal for Manchester City. French winger Rino Della Negra, active in the French Resistance, became a national icon in France and a hero to fans of his club, Red Star Olympique.

And yet, many hundreds more lost their lives in combat. The above-mentioned Della Negra, just twenty years old, was captured and faced a Nazi firing squad in 1944. Nor were footballers insulated from the terror and tragedy of the Holocaust. A significant number of Jewish players and coaches were victims, including former members of the German and Austrian national teams.

Two of football's greatest heroes of the Second World War were Géza Kertész and István Tóth, former teammates on the Hungarian national team. Both coached high-level professional clubs, including Roma, Atalanta, and Inter Milan in the 1930s. But after the war broke out, both were conscripted to serve as officers in Nazi-occupied Hungary. During these commissions, Kertész and Tóth worked together to set up a secret network that rescued hundreds of Jews and members of the Hungarian resistance from deportation to Nazi concentration camps. Betrayed to the Gestapo by an informant, the valiant partners were executed in Budapest in 1945, just days before the city was liberated by Allied forces.

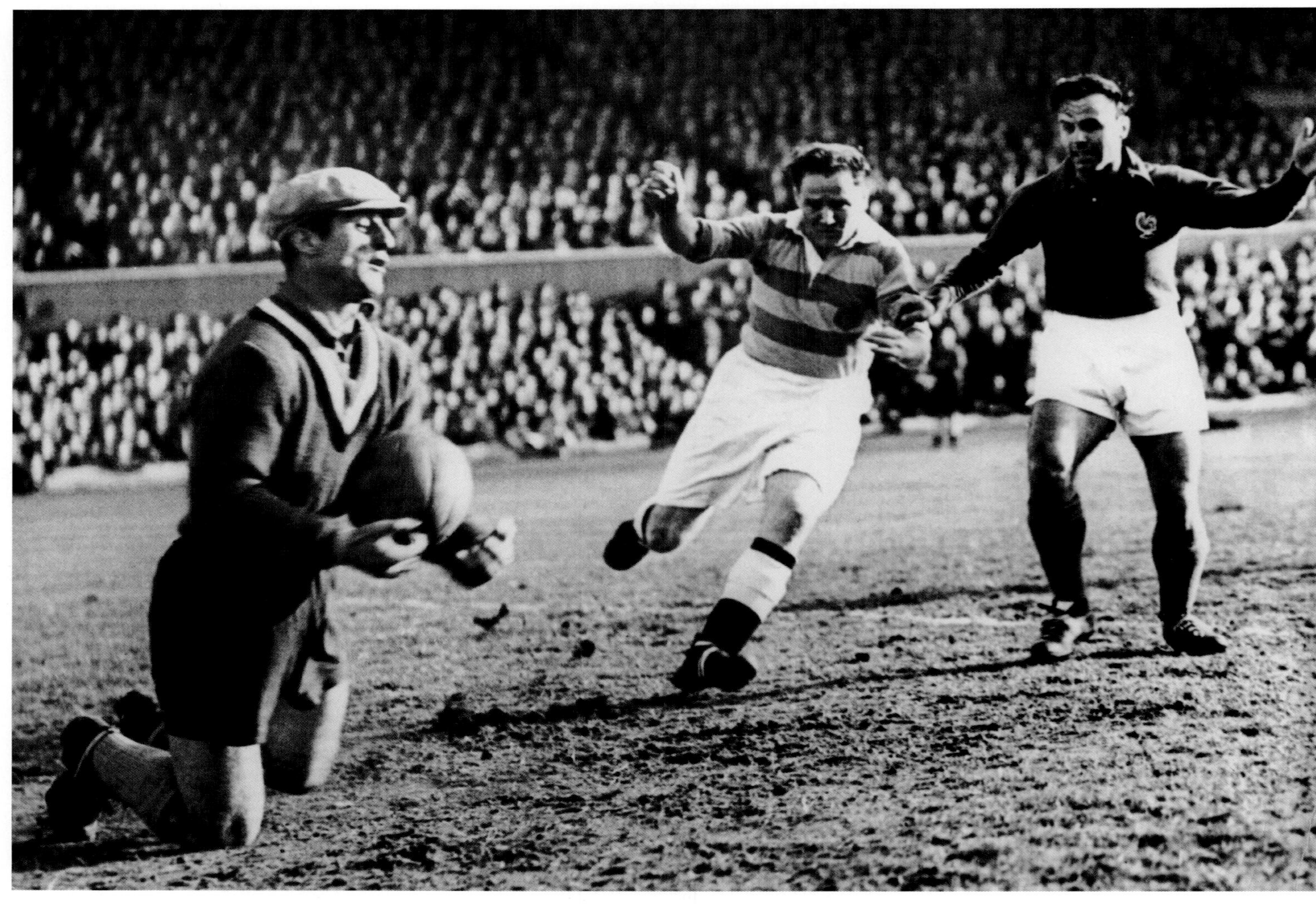

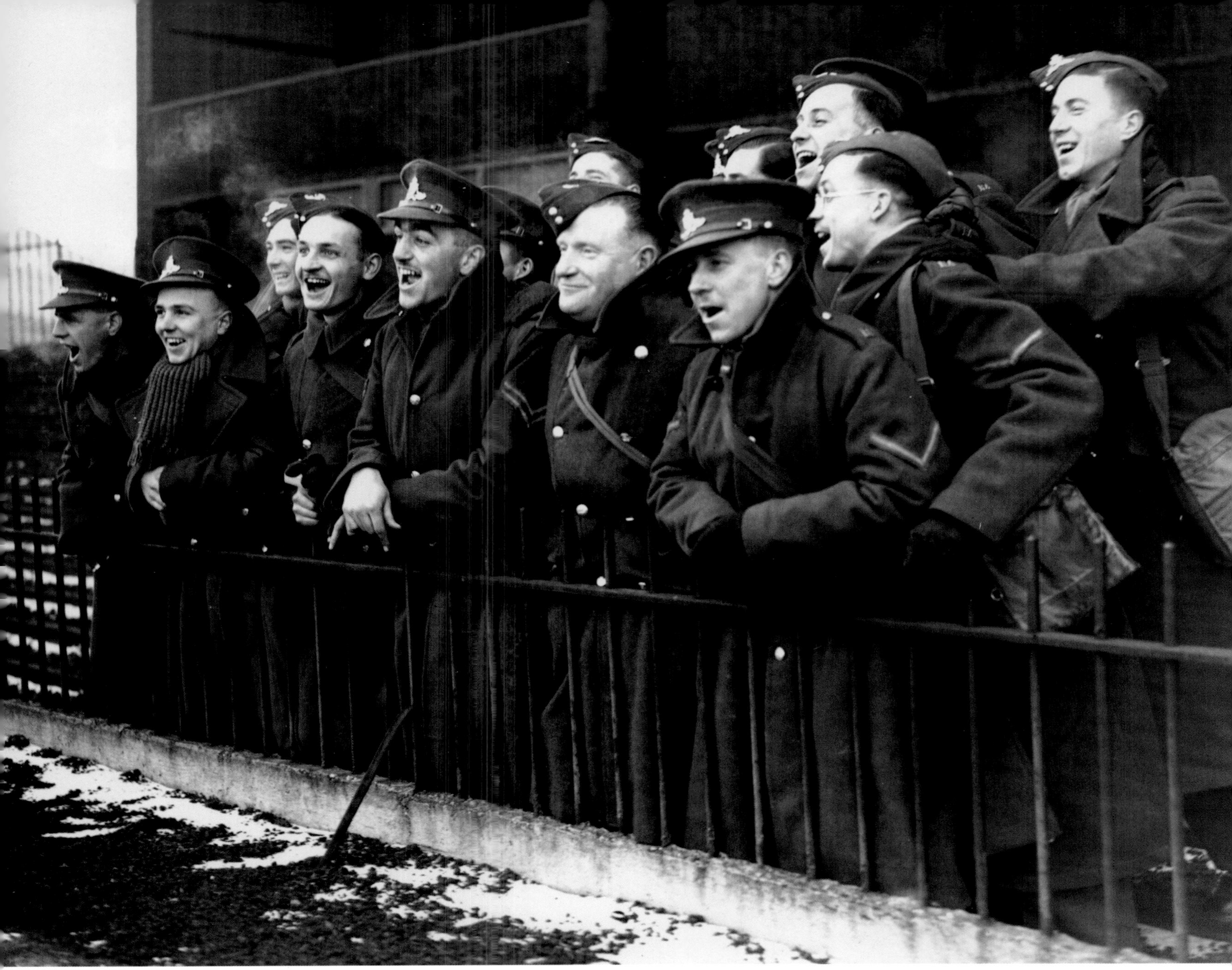



**OPPOSITE** *Scotland's Willie Thornton battling through the physicality of a French defender. The wartime hero was able to resume his professional career after the Second World War. Glasgow, 1949.*

**ABOVE** *English troops supporting the Army football team in a friendly match against the England national team. Played at Selhurst Park in London, the match was a trial for the Army team in preparation for a fixture against France's army squad. 21 January, 1940.*

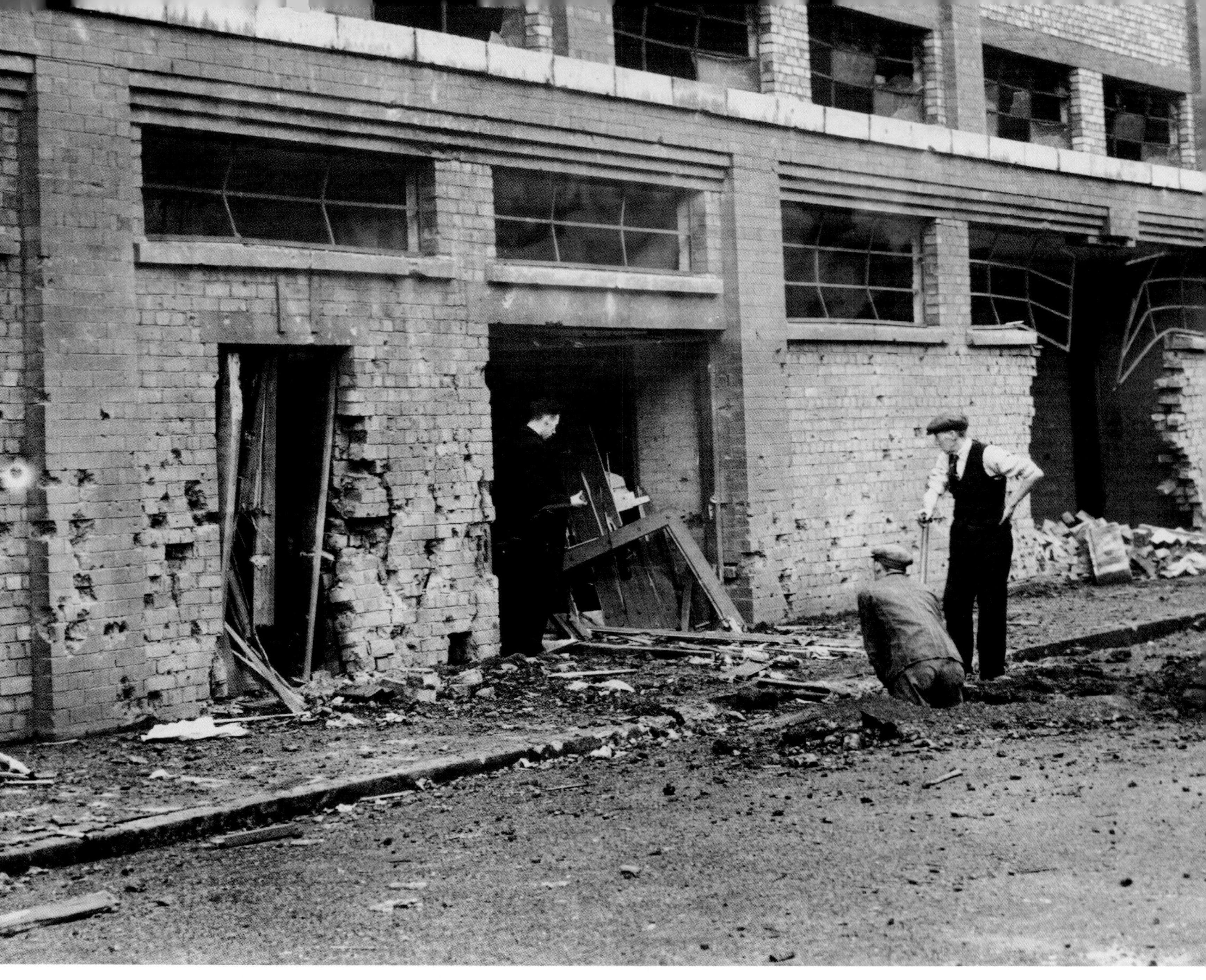

## A NEW DAWN ON THE PITCH

**Even though fighting** finally ended in 1945 — Germany surrendered in May, followed by Japan in August — much of Europe lay in ruins, and FIFA was in no position, financially or otherwise, to plan a World Cup tournament for 1946. At first, the reconstituted FIFA Congress set its sights on 1949 for the next Cup, but Brazil presented an attractive bid to host in 1950 instead. This Brazilian bid was accepted at FIFA's meeting in Luxembourg on 26 July, 1946.

And so, the FIFA nations began to work together again, hoping that a World Cup might help usher in a new spirit of international co-operation . . . and perhaps offer some small measure of healing to a war-torn world.

**ABOVE** *Everton FC's home stadium, Goodison Park, with bomb damage after an air raid, 1940.*

**OPPOSITE** *Footballs from the early '40s.*

*'Hoping that a World Cup might help usher in a new spirit of international co-operation.'*

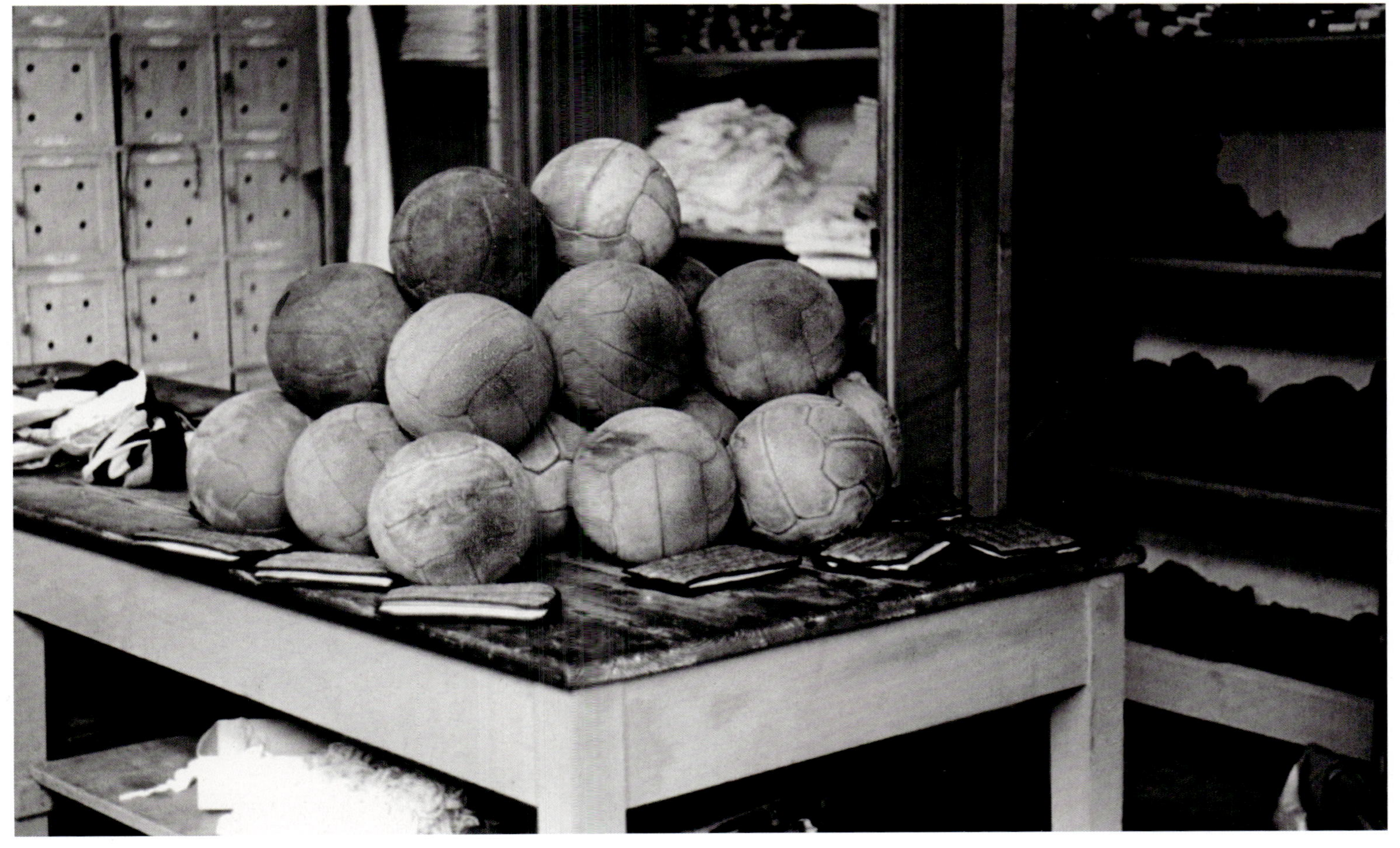

# THE 1950s

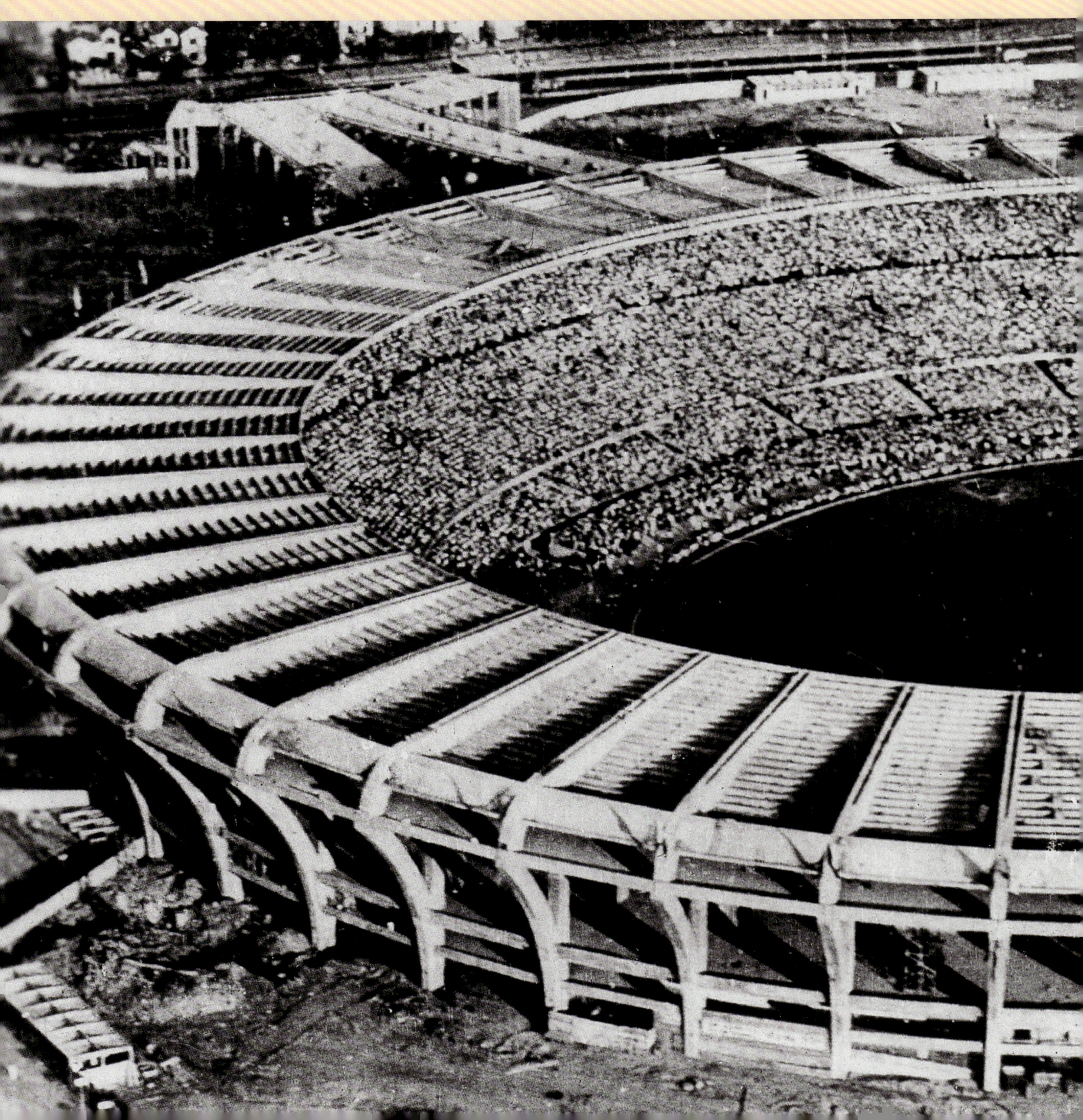

# CHAPTER 3

# The Post-war Boom

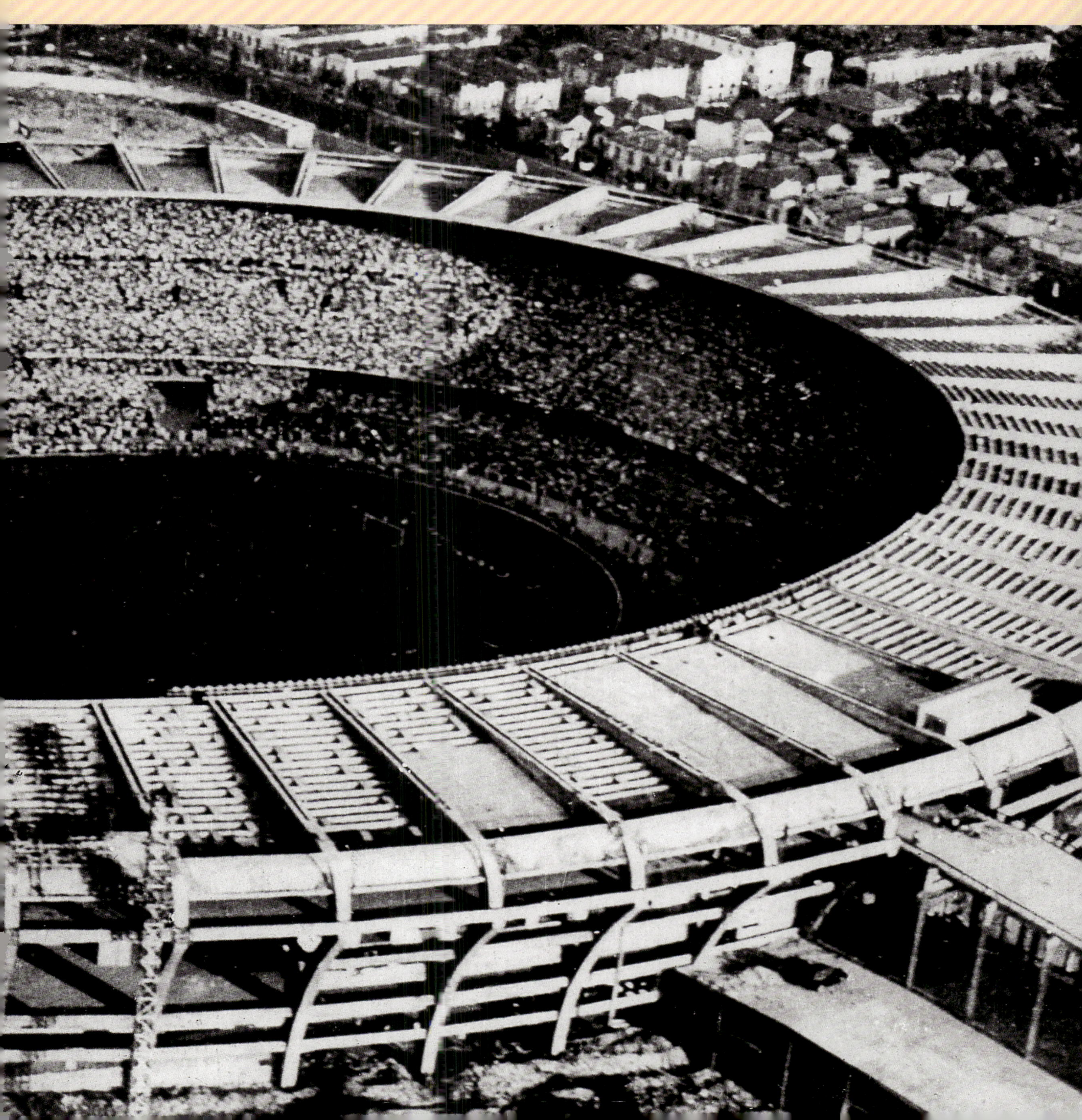

# 1950

HOST COUNTRY: **BRAZIL**
CHAMPION: **URUGUAY**
RUNNER-UP: **BRAZIL**
THIRD PLACE: **SWEDEN OVER SPAIN**

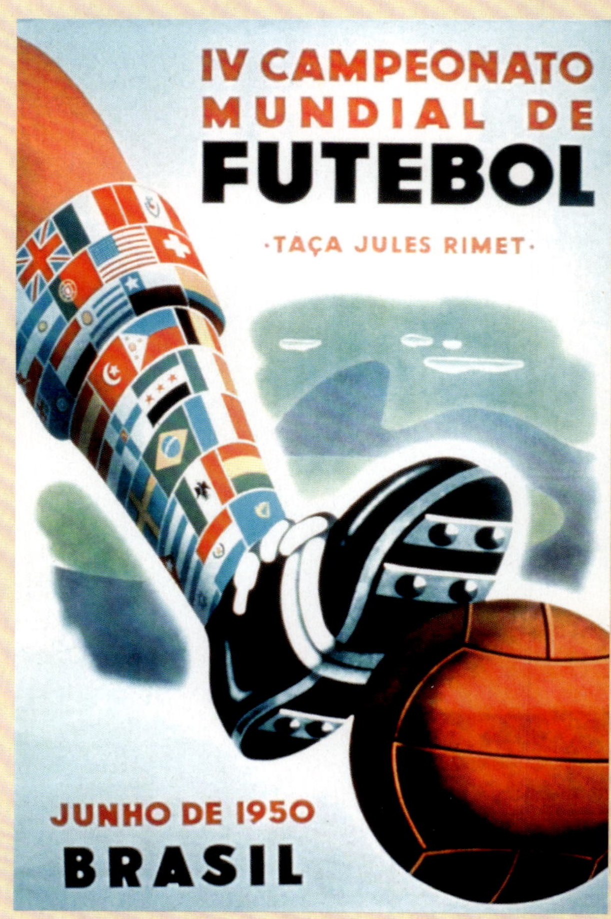


**Although Brazil's bid** for the 1950 tournament reignited global interest in the World Cup, post-war realities limited international participation. On the upside, the mighty England, after finally rejoining FIFA in 1946, made it to a Cup at last. But emergent Cold War friction between the Soviet Union and the West prompted Eastern Bloc countries to opt out, including previous Cup Finalists Czechoslovakia and Hungary. And defeated Axis powers Germany and Japan, still occupied by Allied troops, were denied entry.

Sixteen countries originally qualified for the final tournament, but a string of late withdrawals plagued the process — Scotland and Turkey pulled out just before the group draw, so France was added to bring the total to fifteen. After the draw, however, France decided against going after all. India withdrew soon after. This left just thirteen teams in the tournament, with just three nations in Group 3 and only two in Group 4.

**PREVIOUS SPREAD** *The Estádio do Maracanã in Rio de Janeiro, Brazil, 1950.*

**ABOVE** *The official poster for the 1950 World Cup. The designer is believed to be J. Ney Damasceno, a Rio de Janeiro resident.*

**OPPOSITE TOP** *Inside the Maracanã.*

**OPPOSITE BOTTOM** *Il Grande Torino in Lisbon on 3 May, 1949 — just one day before the tragic 'Superga Air Disaster'. The squad was returning home from a match against Benfica.*

# A NEW FORMAT AND A FLAGSHIP STADIUM

**Scheduled for 24 June to 16 July,** the 1950 World Cup featured several interesting format changes. Brazil wanted to host a bigger, better tournament with more games, more international buzz, and *much* greater attendance figures. To reach these goals, the planning committee staged a first round of four groups (then called 'pools') engaged in round-robin play, with teams earning two points per win and one point per draw. This would guarantee multiple games for every entrant.

Then, instead of playing semi-finals and a final, the four group winners would play *another* round-robin competition, adding six more high-quality games. This format led to a total of twenty-two matches played over the course of the tournament. It would also make this the only Cup in history that wasn't structured to end with a championship match between two finalists.

To further ensure a record-setting attendance, Brazil constructed the massive Maracanã Stadium in Rio de Janeiro.

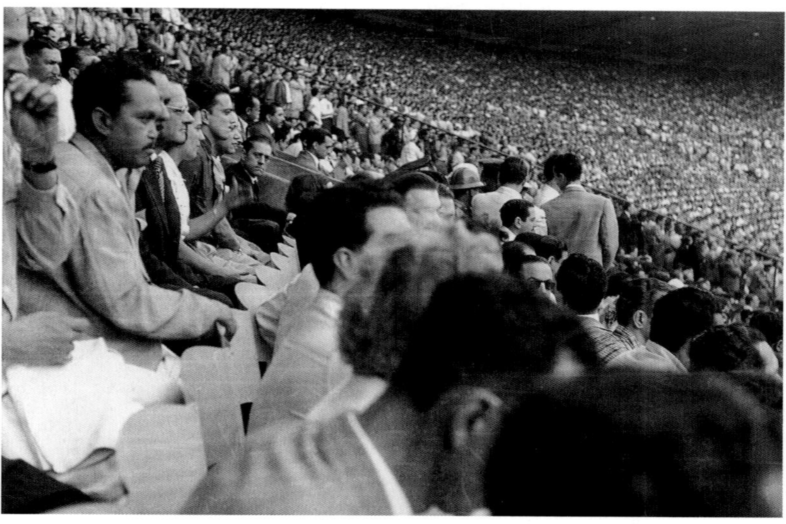

With an astounding capacity of 200,000, the venue drew huge crowds to its eight matches during the tournament, including five of the six played by the Brazilian home team. In the end, the 1950 World Cup tournament boasted a total attendance of 1,045,246, with an incredible average of 47,511 per match.

# ITALY'S SUPERGA AIR DISASTER

One of FIFA's goals in 1950 was to ensure that Italy could participate despite being on the losing side of the Second World War. As the two-time defending champion (1934 and 1938), Italy automatically qualified ... but a shocking tragedy nearly derailed its appearance. On 4 May, 1949,

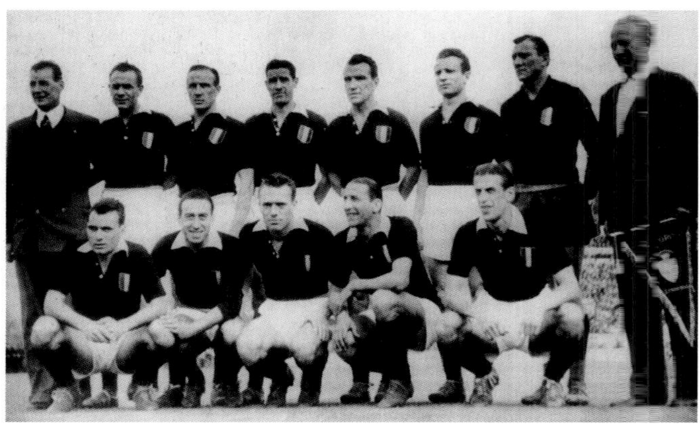

an Italian Airlines flight carrying the entire roster of the Torino Football Club encountered thick fog and crashed into the rock wall of the Basilica of Superga outside Turin. All thirty-one people on board were killed.

Known as *Il Grande Torino* ('The Great Torino'), the historic club had won five consecutive Italian Serie A league championships. Its roster also served as the backbone of the Italian national team—ten of the eleven starters for Italy's international appearances in 1949 were Torino FC players, including the national team captain, Valentino Mazzola. The crash was devastating, not just for Italy but the wider sporting world. On the day of the funerals, the streets of Turin were filled with half a million people paying their respects.

The next year, Italy did manage to send a team to Brazil for the World Cup, travelling by boat instead of air, but they were eliminated in the first round.

# Tournament: GROUP STAGE

### GROUP 1: BRAZIL, YUGOSLAVIA, SWITZERLAND, MEXICO

| | | |
|---|---|---|
| Brazil 4 | 0 | Mexico |
| Yugoslavia 3 | 0 | Switzerland |
| Brazil 2 | 2 | Switzerland |
| Yugoslavia 4 | 1 | Mexico |
| Brazil 2 | 0 | Yugoslavia |
| Switzerland 2 | 1 | Mexico |

**Group Winner: Brazil**

### GROUP 2: SPAIN, ENGLAND, CHILE, USA

| | | |
|---|---|---|
| England 2 | 0 | Chile |
| Spain 3 | 1 | USA |
| Spain 2 | 0 | Chile |
| USA 1 | 0 | England |
| Spain 1 | 0 | England |
| Chile 5 | 2 | USA |

**Group Winner: Spain**

Brazil had two dominating shutout wins en route to the final round but were also surprised by the Swiss, who held them to a 2–2 tie. Both Mexico and Switzerland brought only red kits to the tournament, so before they faced off in Porto Alegre, a coin was tossed. Mexico won the right to play in their own kit—a right they promptly waived in the spirit of sportsmanship. The Mexicans borrowed blue-and-white-striped jerseys from local club Cruzeiro EC.

England went into the tournament as a Cup favourite, so its stunning 1–0 loss to a lowly USA squad absolutely shocked the football world. A subsequent loss to Spain kept the Lions out of the final round and sent the Spanish through.

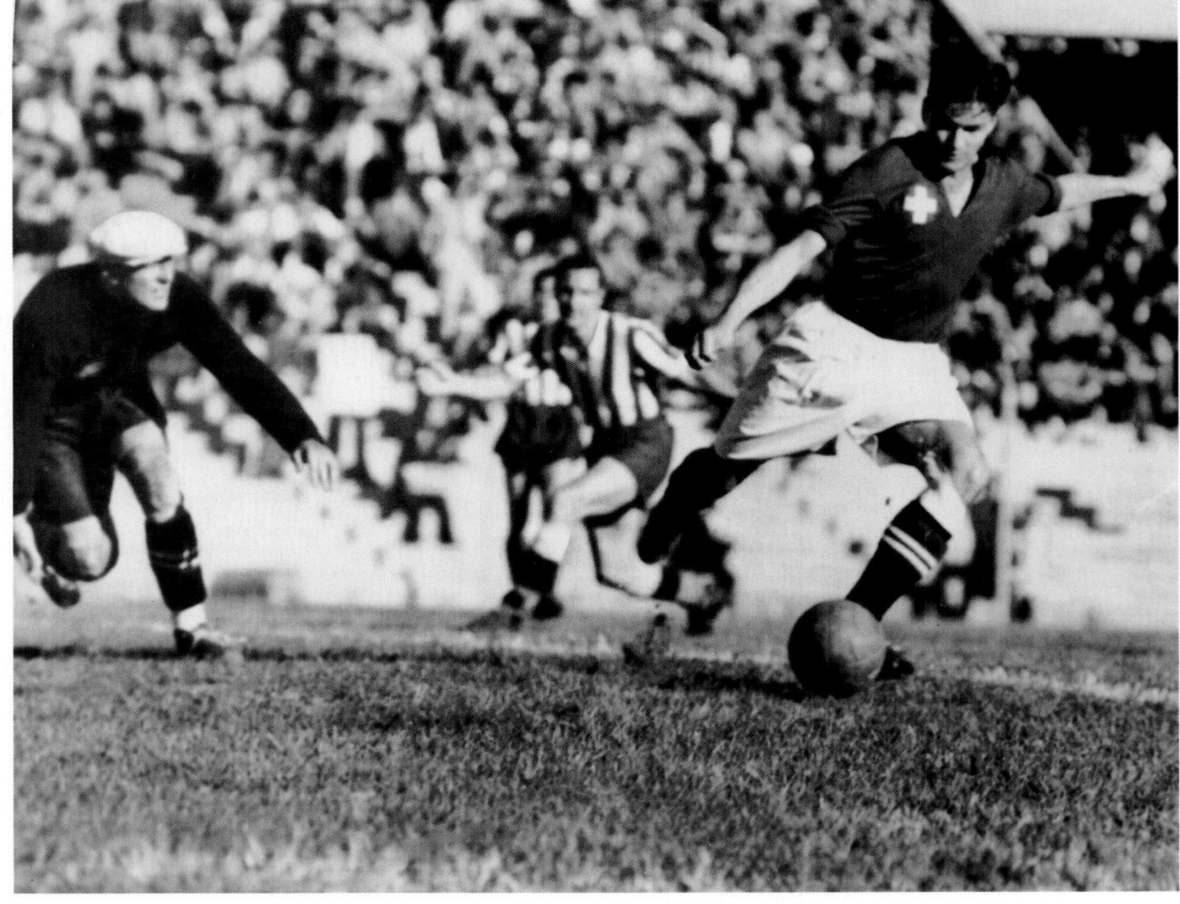

**LEFT** *A Swiss defender clearing the ball from his own penalty area. In the background are two Mexican players wearing the blue-and-white stripes of Cruzeiro EC.*

**OPPOSITE** *England's Thomas Finney (centre) makes an aerial challenge on the ball, contested by USA's Charlie Colombo (left) and Ed McIlvenny. USA's eventual 1–0 victory would go on to be one of the greatest upsets in World Cup history.*

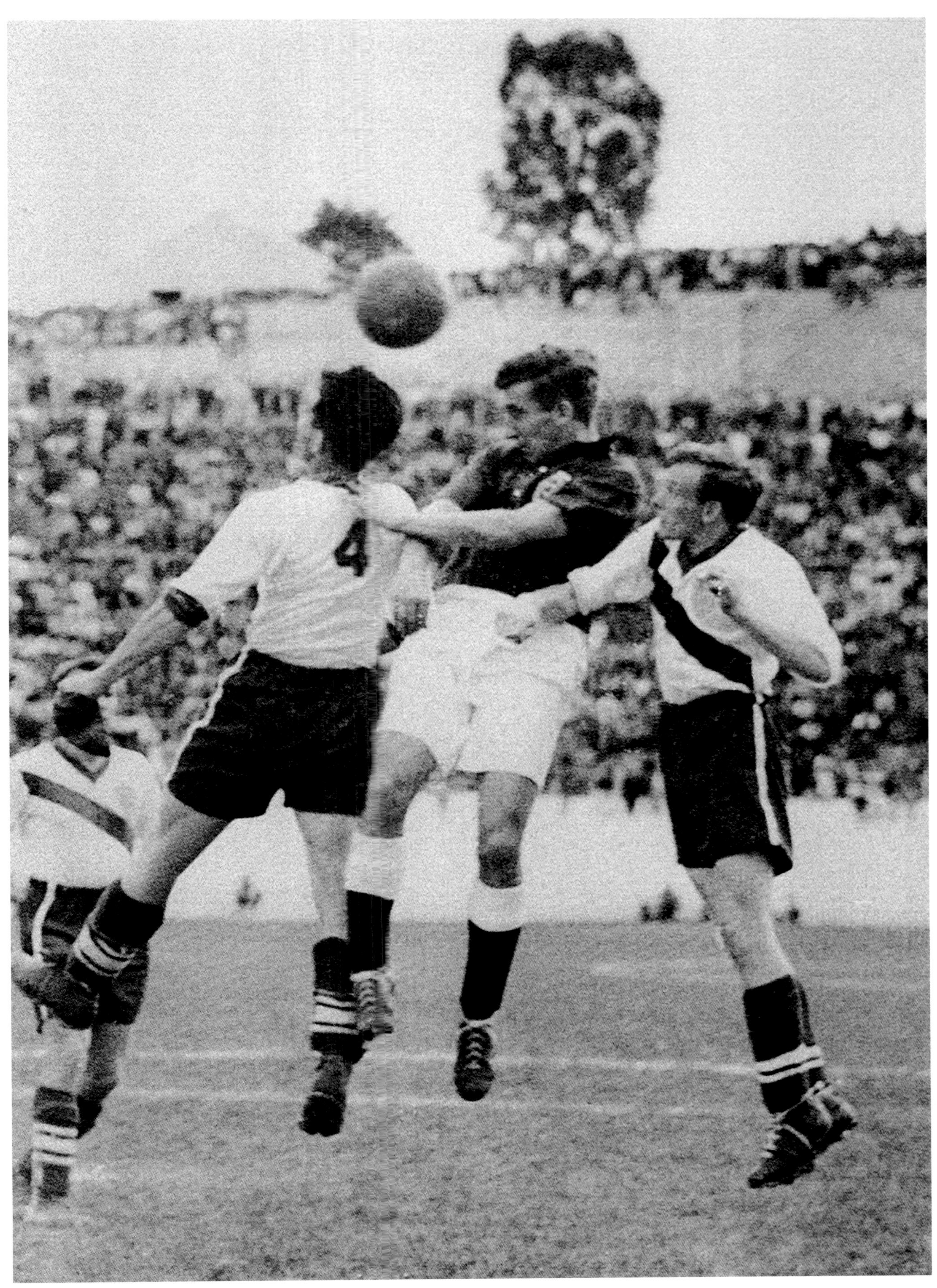

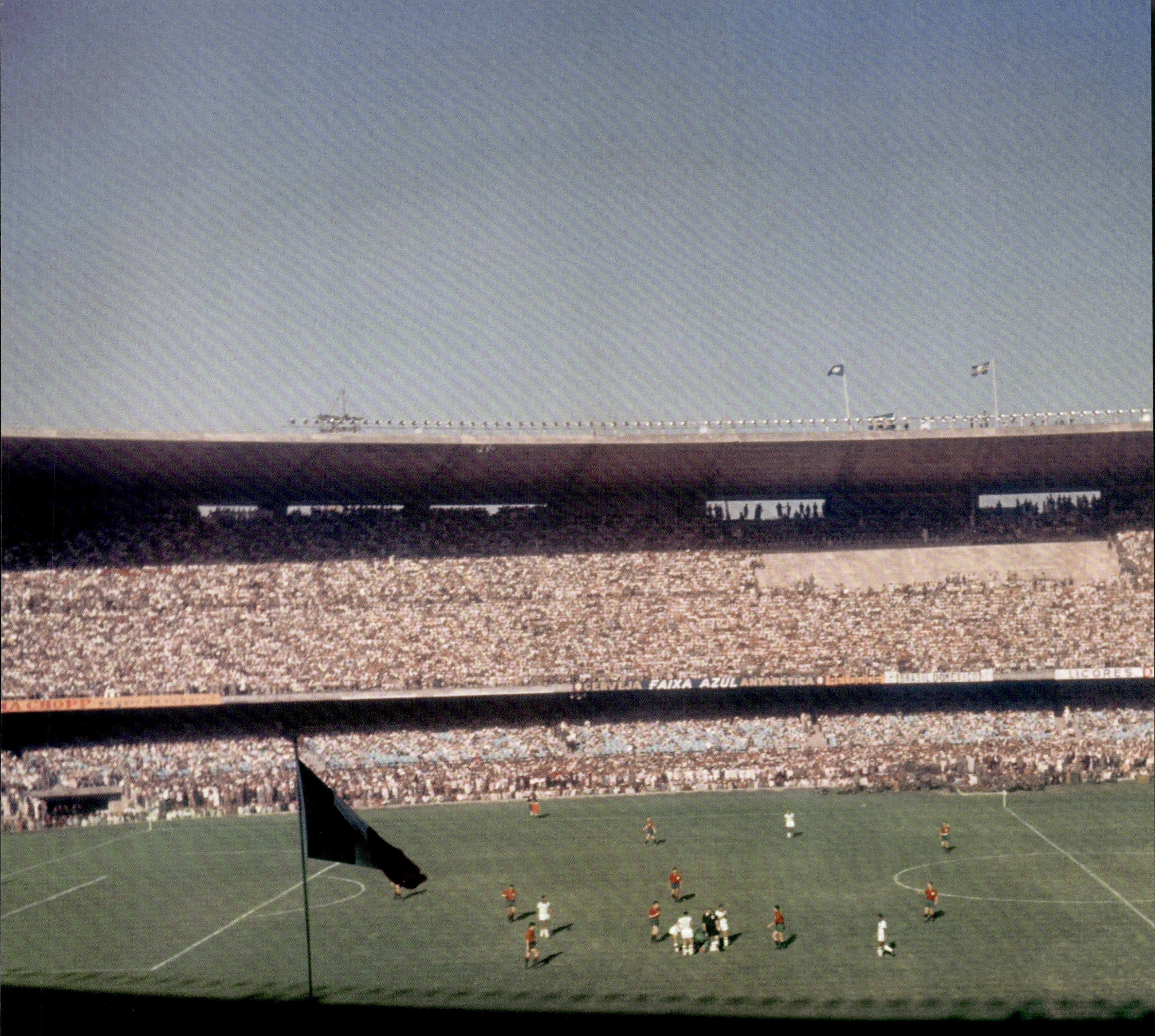
CERVEJA FAIXA AZUL ANTARCTICA
LICORES

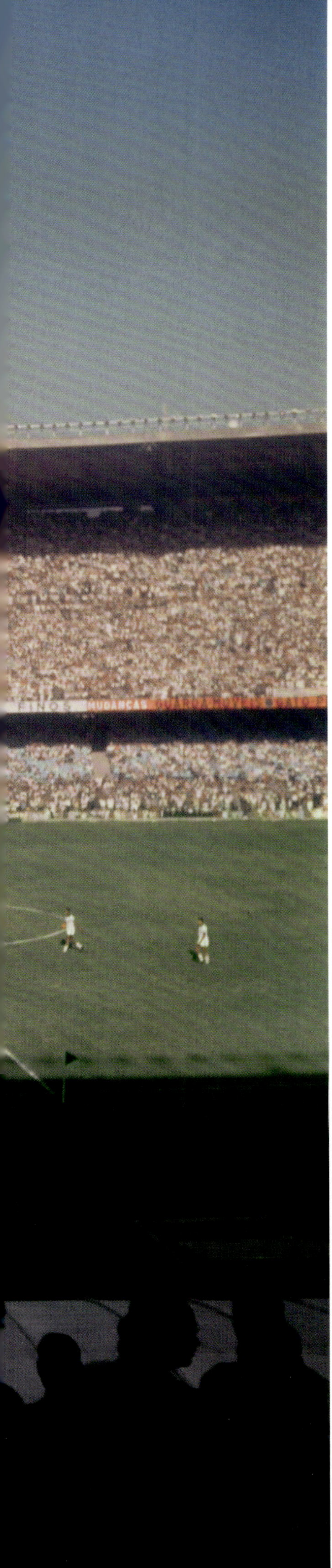



## GROUP 3: SWEDEN, ITALY, PARAGUAY (, INDIA)
### (NOTE: India withdrew before playing)

| Sweden 3 | 2 Italy |
|---|---|
| Sweden 2 | 2 Paraguay |
| Italy 2 | 0 Paraguay |

**Group Winner: Sweden**

Italy's 3–2 loss to Sweden was the nation's first in a World Cup tournament. They would rebound with a win over Paraguay, but the latter's 2–2 tie with Sweden eliminated Italy and sent the Scandinavian side on to the final round.

## GROUP 4: URUGUAY, BOLIVIA

| Uruguay 8 | 0 Bolivia |
|---|---|

**Group Winner: Uruguay**

France's withdrawal left Group 4 with only two teams and just one group match. There is some debate as to whether Uruguay's easy 8–0 romp over Bolivia blessed them with fresh legs for the final round or left them less prepared for more competitive play. Perhaps it was a bit of both… Uruguay struggled to tie its next game against Spain, but the squad certainly had the juice it needed down the closing stretch of the tournament.

**OPPOSITE** *A colour photograph — rare in 1950 — of the tournament's opening match between Brazil and Mexico at the Maracanã Stadium. Brazil won the match 4–0.*

**BELOW** *The Paraguay squad that managed a surprising 2–2 tie with Sweden. The result prevented powerhouse Italy from advancing.*

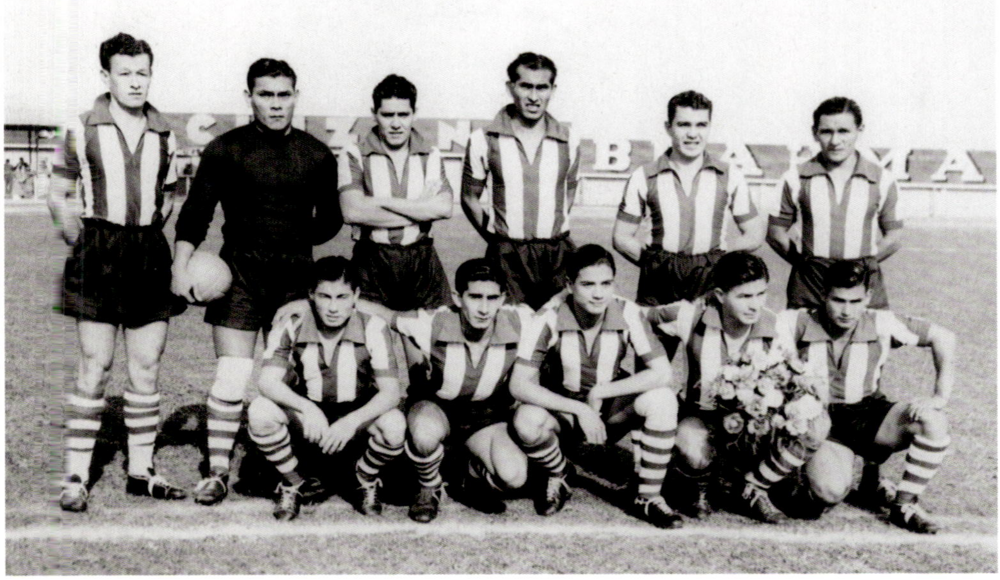

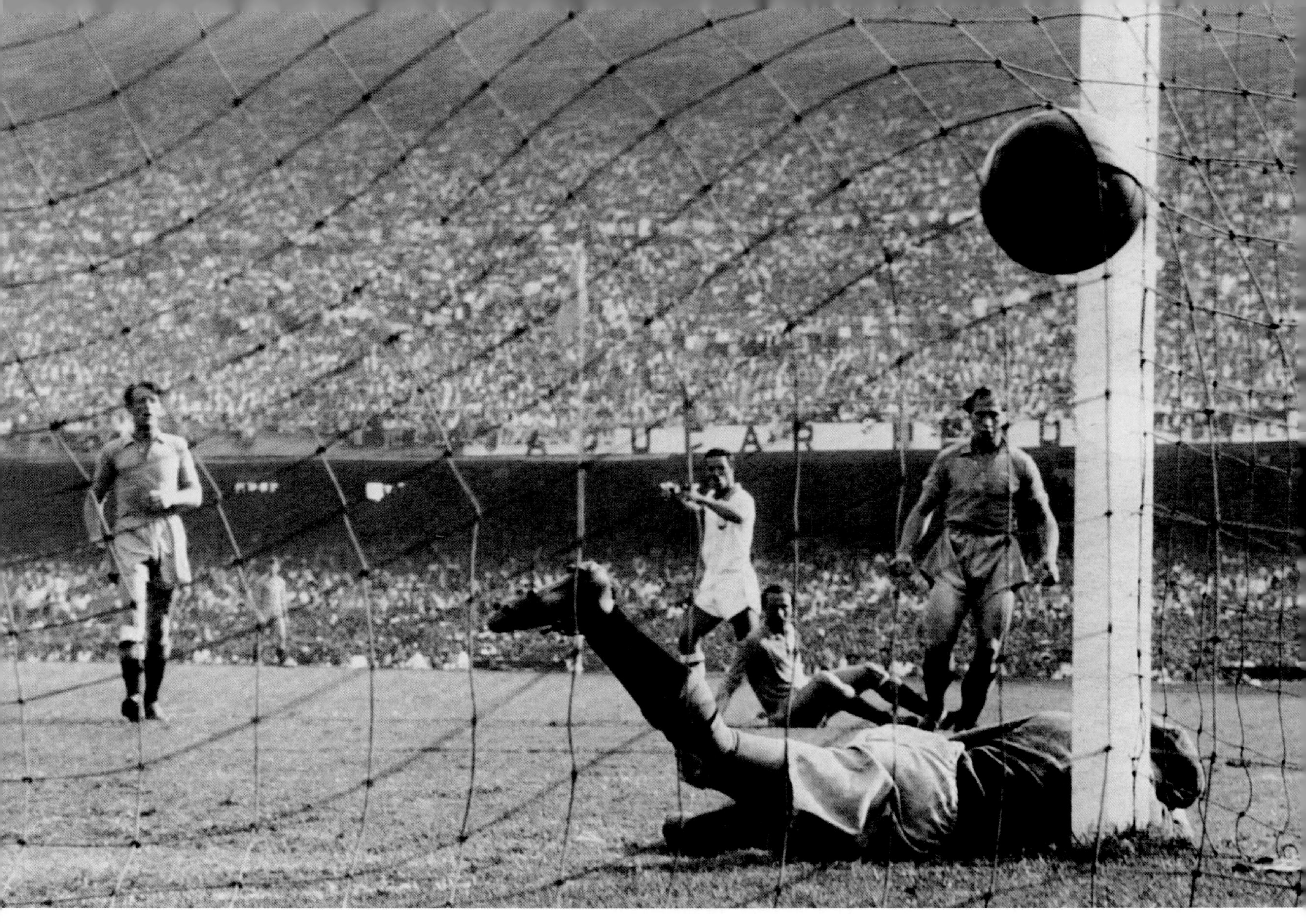

# FINAL ROUND

**FINALIST GROUP: URUGUAY, BRAZIL, SWEDEN, SPAIN**

| | | |
|---:|:---:|:---|
| Uruguay 2 | | 2 Spain |
| Brazil 7 | | 1 Sweden |
| Brazil 6 | | 1 Spain |
| Uruguay 3 | | 2 Sweden |
| Sweden 3 | | 1 Spain |
| Uruguay 2 | | 1 Brazil |

**Group & World Cup Winner: Uruguay**

Brazil played all three of its final round matches in its imposing new Maracanã Stadium in Rio de Janeiro, drawing huge crowds in favour of the host nation. Brazilian forward Ademir was on fire in these finals, scoring four goals against Sweden and two more against Spain, ending up as the tournament's leading scorer with nine goals. Alcides Ghiggia, who tallied Uruguay's winning goal against Brazil, scored in every game his team played.

**ABOVE** *Swedish keeper Karl-Oskar 'Kalle' Svensson is beat by a strike from Brazil's Ademir (white).*

**OPPOSITE** *Brazil's Jair (white) puts one past Spanish goalkeeper Antoni Ramallets.*

'Brazil played all three of its final round matches in its imposing new Maracanã Stadium in Rio de Janeiro.'

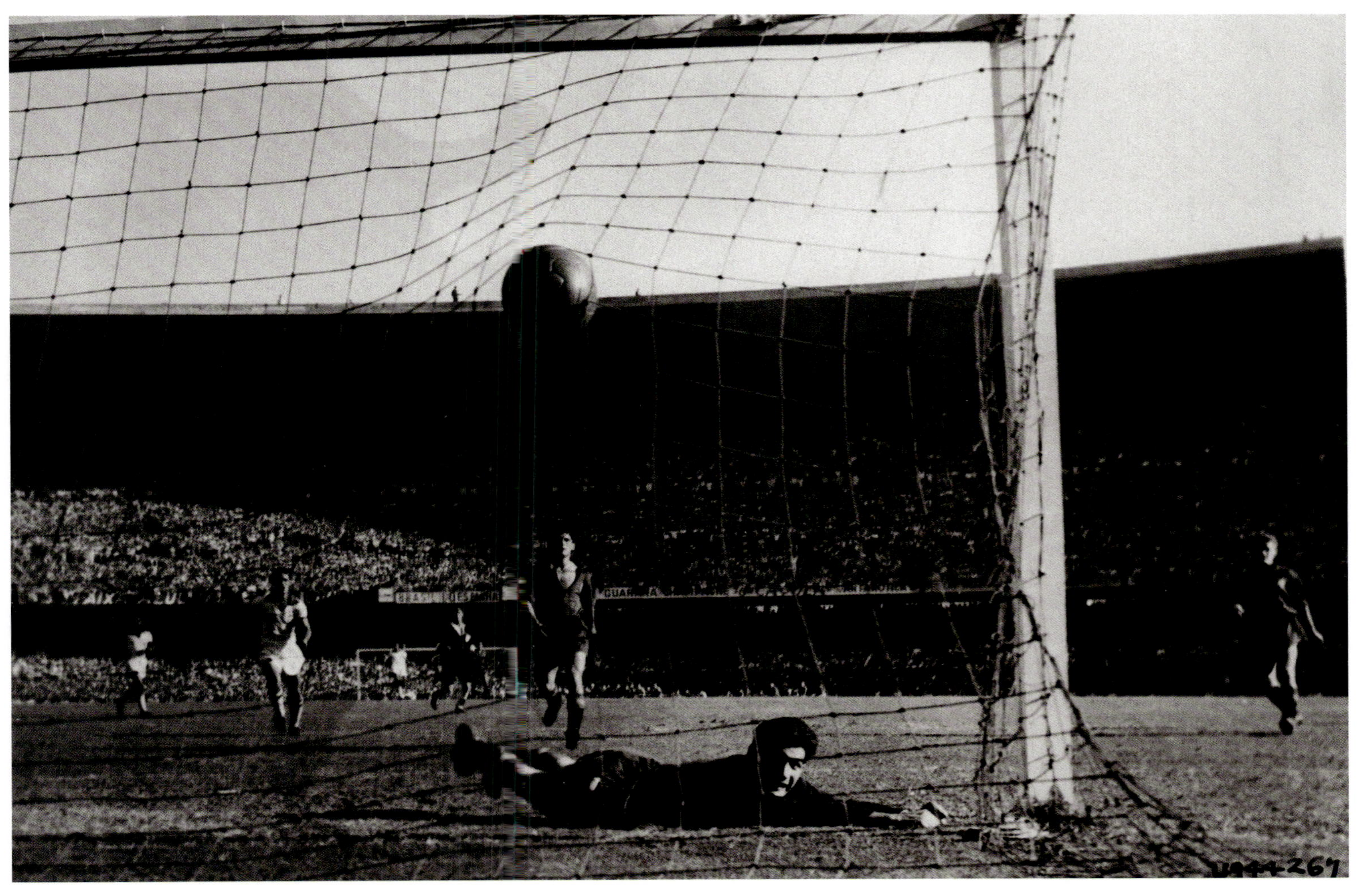

# TWO MIGHTY UPSETS

## *'THE MIRACLE ON GRASS'*

**On 29 June, 1950,** one of the biggest mismatches in twentieth-century sporting history kicked off in the Brazilian mining town of Belo Horizonte. Going into that year's World Cup tournament, England was generally seen as one of sport's pre-eminent powers, often called 'The Kings of Football.' Its post-war international record of twenty-three wins and only four losses was among the best in the world, and its national team was stacked with professional players from clubs of the vaunted Football League of England and Wales.

The USA squad, on the other hand, was a ragtag band of mostly part-time, semipro players that included midfielder Walter Bahr (high-school teacher), forwards Frank Wallace (mailman) and Gino Pariani (dock worker), centre halfback Charles Colombo (meat-packing supervisor), and goalkeeper Frank Borghi, who drove hearses for his uncle's funeral home. The USA national team had lost its last seven international matches by a combined score of 45–2, and 1950's hastily gathered squad had only one practise together — the day before they departed for Brazil.

In London, the *Daily Express* wrote: 'It would be fair to give the US three goals of a start.' Internal sentiment was hardly more optimistic. 'We have no chance', new coach Bill Jeffrey told reporters. Later, he compared his team to sheep ready to be slaughtered.

The first half proceeded as expected, with the English peppering the USA goal with no fewer than six clear scoring chances, hitting the woodwork twice and forcing multiple diving saves. After the game, US goalkeeper Frank Borghi said, 'I was hoping to hold them to only five or six goals.' But at the thirty-eight-minute mark, American Joe Gaetjens — a part-time dishwasher of Haitian descent — connected with a diving header that nudged the ball past England's keeper Bert Williams. Gaetjens landed face down in the grass and never saw the ball go in. Suddenly, impossibly, mighty England trailed the lowly USA 1–0.

The furious second half saw an increasingly desperate English side send wave after wave of attacking runs into the American third. The resilient Americans not only fended off each run, but they also managed to create some dangerous counterattack chances of their own. In the end, the USA held on for the upset win. Players and coaches staggered around the postgame pitch in delirious disbelief. Joyous Brazilian fans in attendance even carried Gaetjens off the pitch. Back home in England, the press coverage was excoriating and brutal.

The blue kit England wore that day was never worn again.

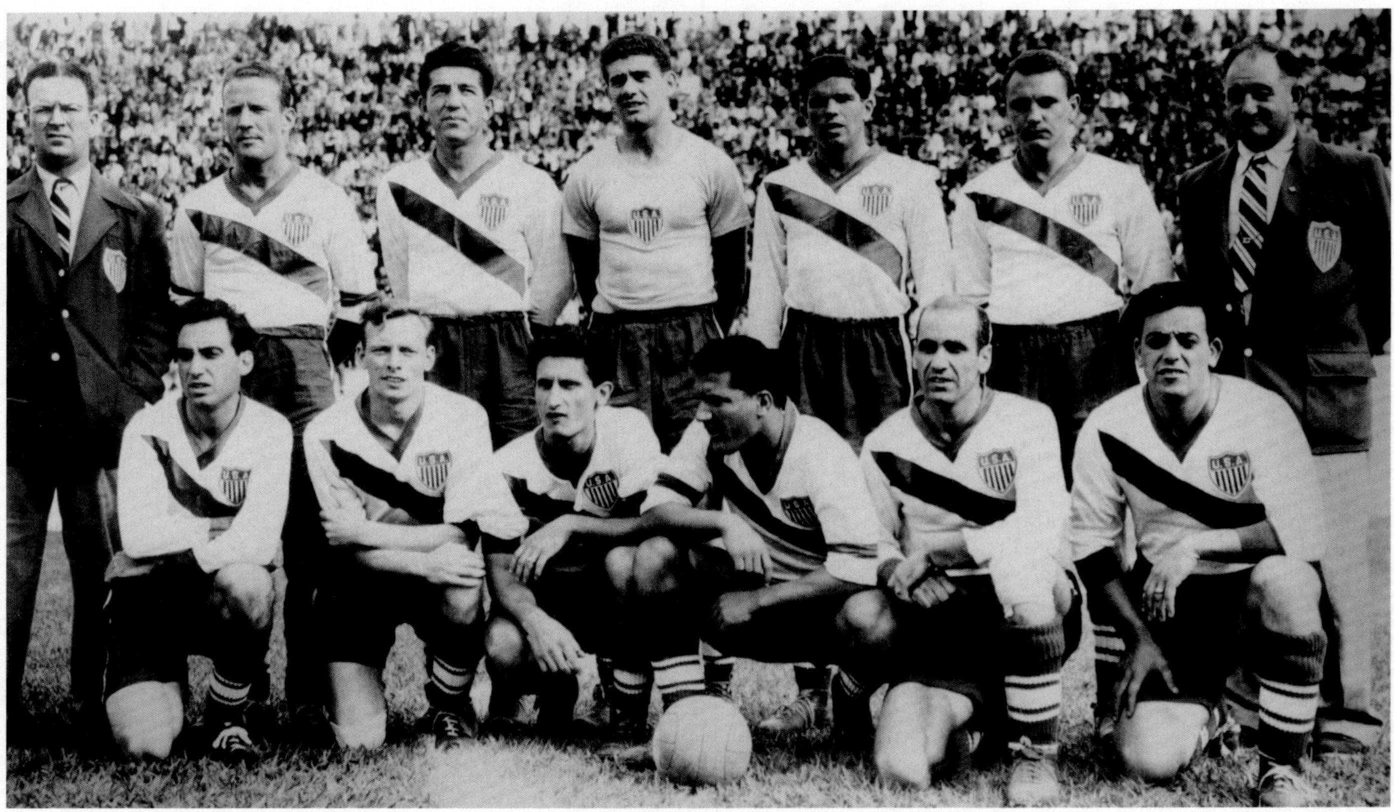

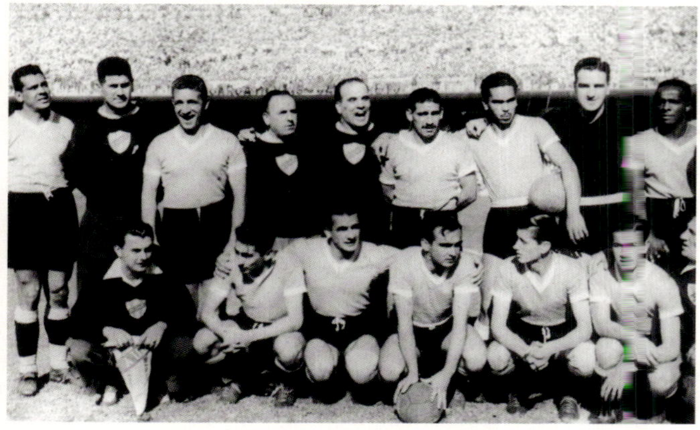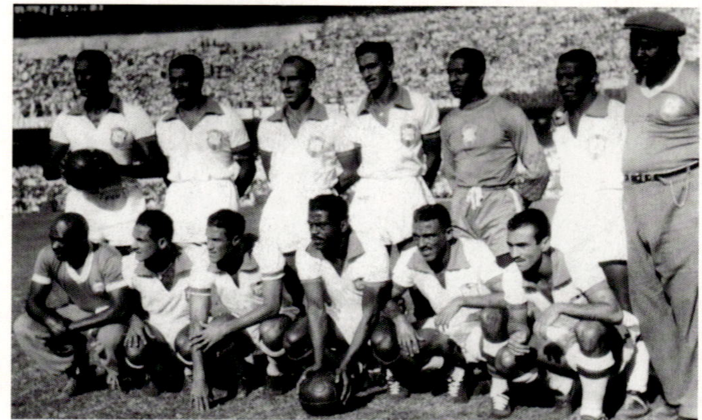

## 'EL MARACANAZO'

**By scheduling luck** (and perhaps a bit of foresight by the schedulers), the last match of the finalist group's round-robin — the last match of the entire tournament, in fact — proved to be the World Cup decider. Historically, Brazil versus Uruguay seemed evenly matched. The two sides had played each other in a trio of very close matches just months prior in the Copa Río Branco. The results were two wins for Brazil, one for Uruguay, and just a one goal difference in each game.

But going into the final, Brazil had outscored its Cup opponents 23–4, demolished its other two finals foes Sweden (7–1) and Spain (6–1), and seemed virtually unstoppable on its home soil. The great English sportswriter Brian Glanville called Brazil's level of play, 'The football of the future'. Meanwhile, Uruguay struggled to a 2–2 tie with Spain and a tight 3–2 victory over Sweden. They were even down 2–1 late into both matches. With a one-point lead in the group standings, Brazil needed just a tie against Uruguay to win the final group and take the Jules Rimet Trophy. Best of all, the game was in the brand-new Maracanã Stadium — where a Brazilian crowd of 200,000 raucous fans arrived fully expecting to crown their local heroes as World Cup

kings. *El Mundo* even printed a photo of the team in its morning edition with the caption: 'Champions of the World.'

'It was a fantastic atmosphere,' said Uruguayan winger Alcides Ghiggia in a 2014 interview with BBC World. 'Their supporters were jumping with joy as if they'd already won the World Cup.'

Football is funny. The best side usually wins, sure, but anything can happen during the ninety minutes of an elimination match. Even the strongest of teams (on paper) can be thrown into a gruelling duel given that a matchup presents a troublesome blend of talent, tactics, and tenacity.

On 16 July, 1950, the Brazilians played a strong first half, keeping Uruguay on the defensive, and then finally broke through early in the second half. A goal by right winger Friaça gave Brazil what appeared to be a comfortable 1–0 cushion, as Brazil only needed a tie.

But Uruguay's Juan Alberto 'Pepe' Schiaffino finished a crossing ball from Ghiggia to equalise in the sixty-sixth minute. Then, late in the game, Ghiggia broke free around the right wing again. The Brazilian goalkeeper Barbosa, expecting another cross, took a half-step out from the near post . . . and so Ghiggia hammered a low, hard shot that nicked the inside of the post and went into the net. The sudden silence in the massive stadium was otherworldly.

'Only three people have silenced the Maracanã,' said Ghiggia. 'The Pope, Frank Sinatra . . . and me.'

The great Pelé, who was ten years old at the time, had said that when the final whistle blew, it was the only time he ever saw his father cry. The game became a national tragedy known as 'El Maracanazo'—and lives in infamy in Brazil to this day.

**OPPOSITE** *The legendary USA team that performed 'The Miracle on Grass' by upsetting massive favourites England.*

**ABOVE** *Uruguay's squad (left) ahead of the final. Brazil's squad (right) would be on the receiving end of an infamous upset known as 'El Maracanazo'.*

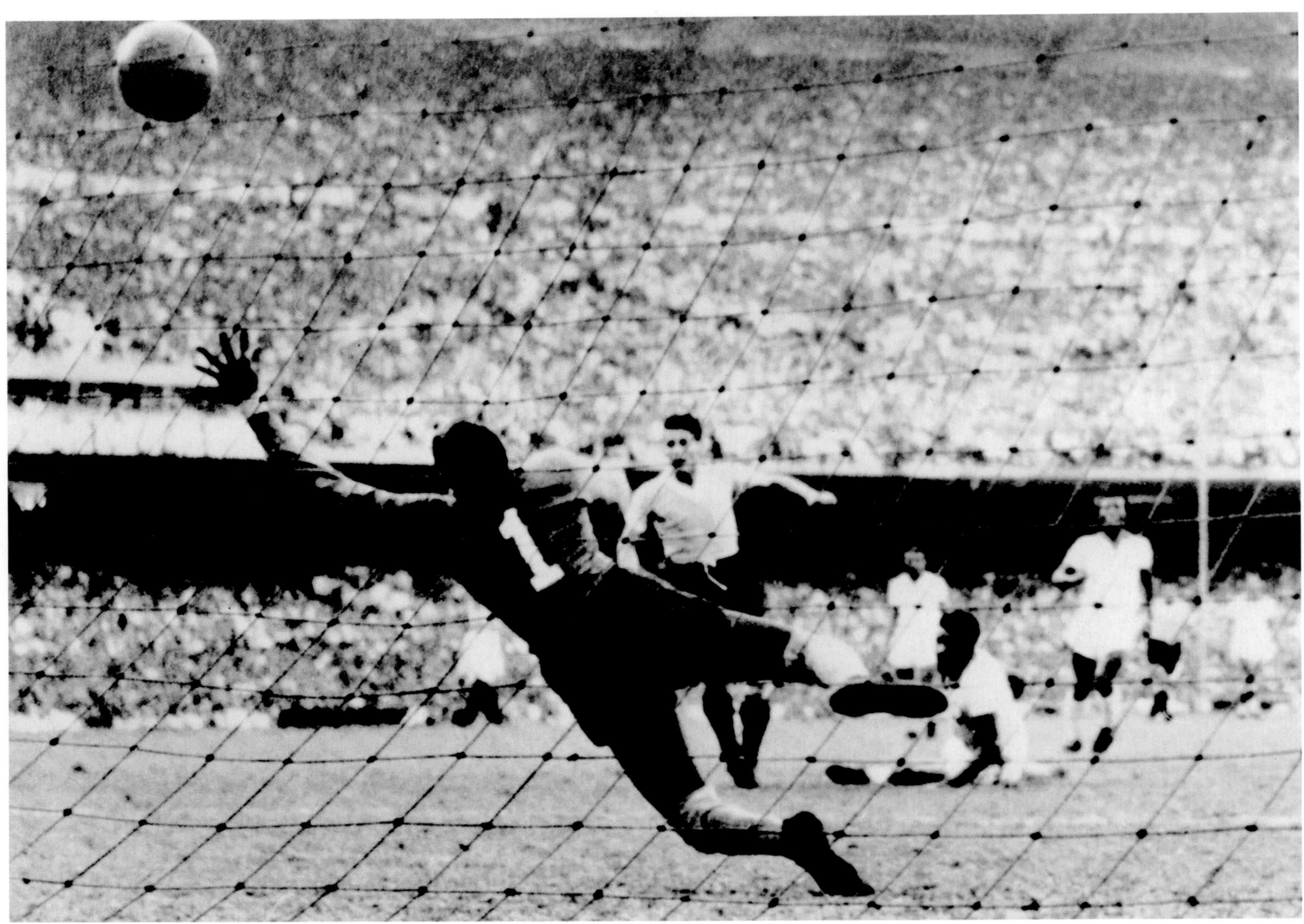



**ABOVE** *Juan Alberto 'Pepe' Schiaffino's one-touch equaliser thunders past Brazil's Moacir Barbosa.*

**OPPOSITE** *An example of the fiercely competitive, physical play that character-ised 'El Maracanazo'.*

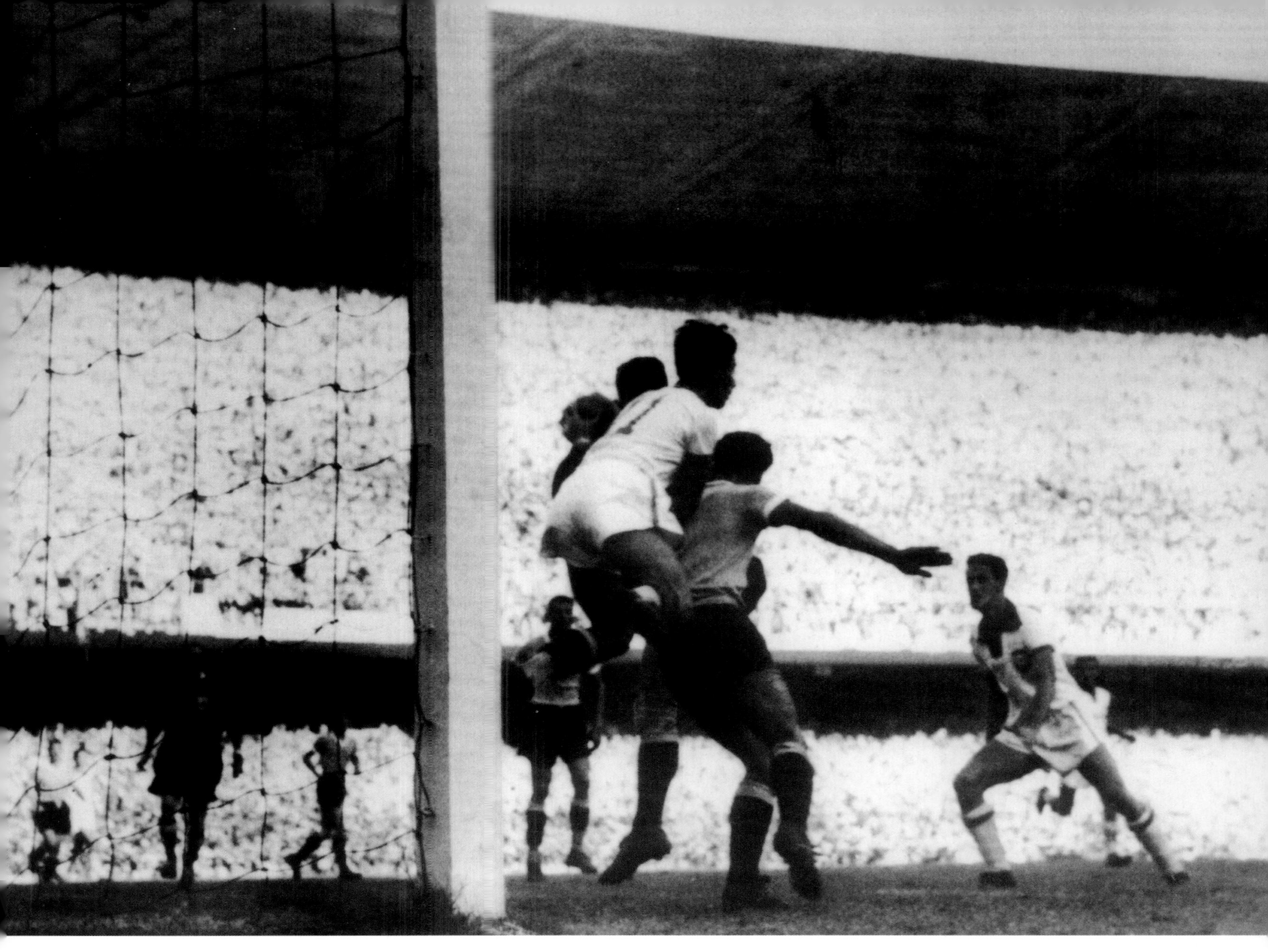

'Only three people have silenced the Maracanã. The Pope, Frank Sinatra… and me.' —ALCIDES GHIGGIA

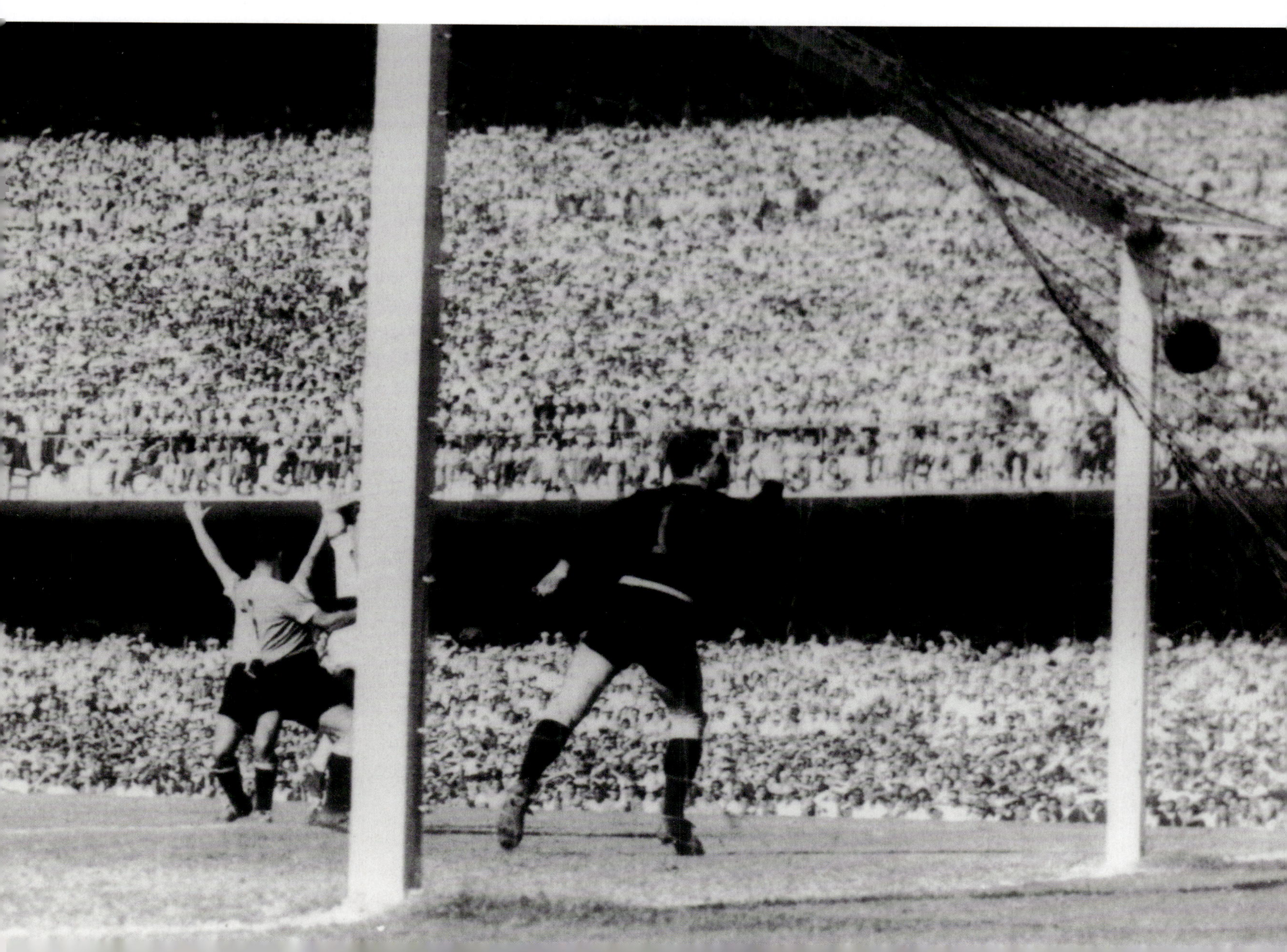

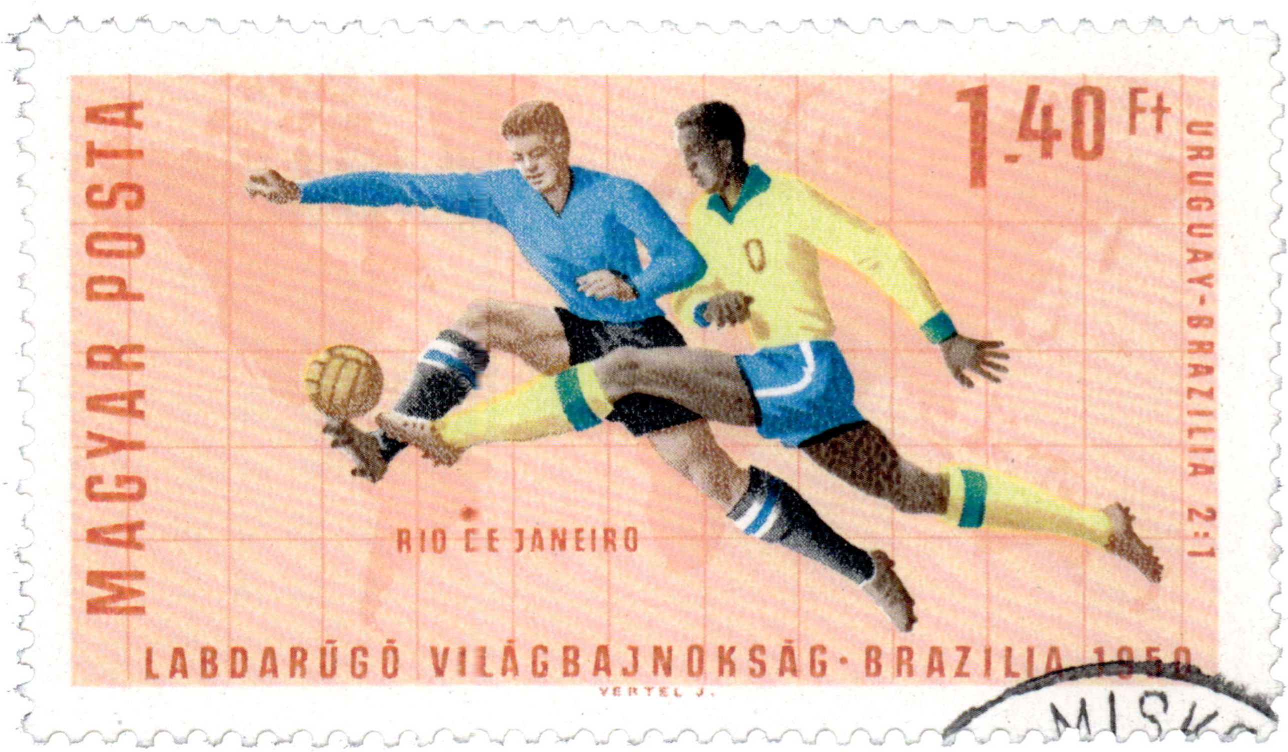



**OPPOSITE** *Uruguay celebrates Ghiggia's winning goal in the seventy-ninth minute.*

**ABOVE** *The 1950 World Cup Final as depicted in a stamp issued by the Hungarian Post, part of a series leading up to the 1966 World Cup.*

# 1954

HOST COUNTRY: **SWITZERLAND**
CHAMPION: **WEST GERMANY**
RUNNER-UP: **HUNGARY**
THIRD PLACE: **AUSTRIA OVER URUGUAY**

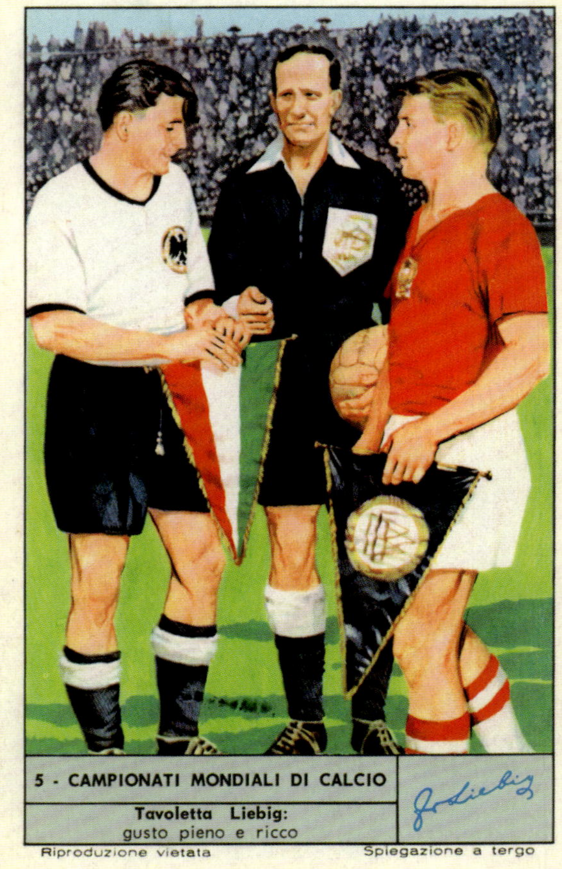



**Capitalising on the incredible success** of the tournament held four years prior, the 1954 World Cup was a high-flying affair featuring dynamic offensive football and an entirely new spectator element — the television. A landmark moment, given how World Cup football has since become the most widely viewed sporting event on the planet. The roots of this intense and enduring international phenomenon could be seen in the wildly enthusiastic response to England's inaugural TV coverage by the European Broadcasting Union (EBU) and the BBC in 1954.

The FIFA Congress had selected Switzerland as host back in July of 1946, on the same day Brazil was awarded the 1950 tournament. As host, the Swiss team qualified automatically, as did the defending-champion Uruguay. Fourteen more teams emerged from continental qualification tournaments. Interestingly, the two teams that played in the previous Cup's third-place game, Sweden and Spain, both failed to qualify. On the other hand, new teams like Scotland, Turkey, and South Korea further expanded the Cup's global reach. And West Germany qualified, bringing in the first German team since the Second World War.

# A QUESTIONABLE FORMAT

**The 1954 tournament used** the familiar opening group stage: sixteen qualifying teams divided into four groups of four. From this, the top-two teams in each group would proceed to a knockout stage. But instead of playing the usual round-robin in this initial stage, the four teams in each group were divided into two seeded teams and two unseeded teams. Seeding was based on recommendations from the Brazilian Federation and a secret ballot by the FIFA Organising Committee, considering factors that included geography, economic means, and sporting interest (such as professional leagues). Only four in-group matches were scheduled, pitting the two seeded teams against each of the two unseeded teams. If two teams tied for second place in their group, they would play an extra playoff game to determine who moved on to the quarter-finals bracket.

Unfortunately, this odd structure meant some interesting in-group pairings didn't get played. For example, Italy never played England in Group 4 but played Switzerland twice! It also led to some inequitable pairings — West Germany got a particularly unfair draw in Group 2. But worse still: If a playoff game for second place ended in a tie, the teams drew lots . . . a truly unsatisfying way to determine a winner. Critics blasted the format and it was never used again in a World Cup tournament.

**OPPOSITE** *An illustration of German and Hungarian captains Fritz Walter (left) and Ferenc Puskás, the 1954 World Cup Finalists, from the 1966 Campionati Mondiali di Calcio ('Football World Cup') series of Liebig trading cards. Between them* *Vincenzo Orlandini, the first Italian to officiate a World Cup Final*

**BELOW** *A 1954-era TV displaying the tournament final at the Deutsches Fußballmuseum ('German Football Museum') in Dortmund.*

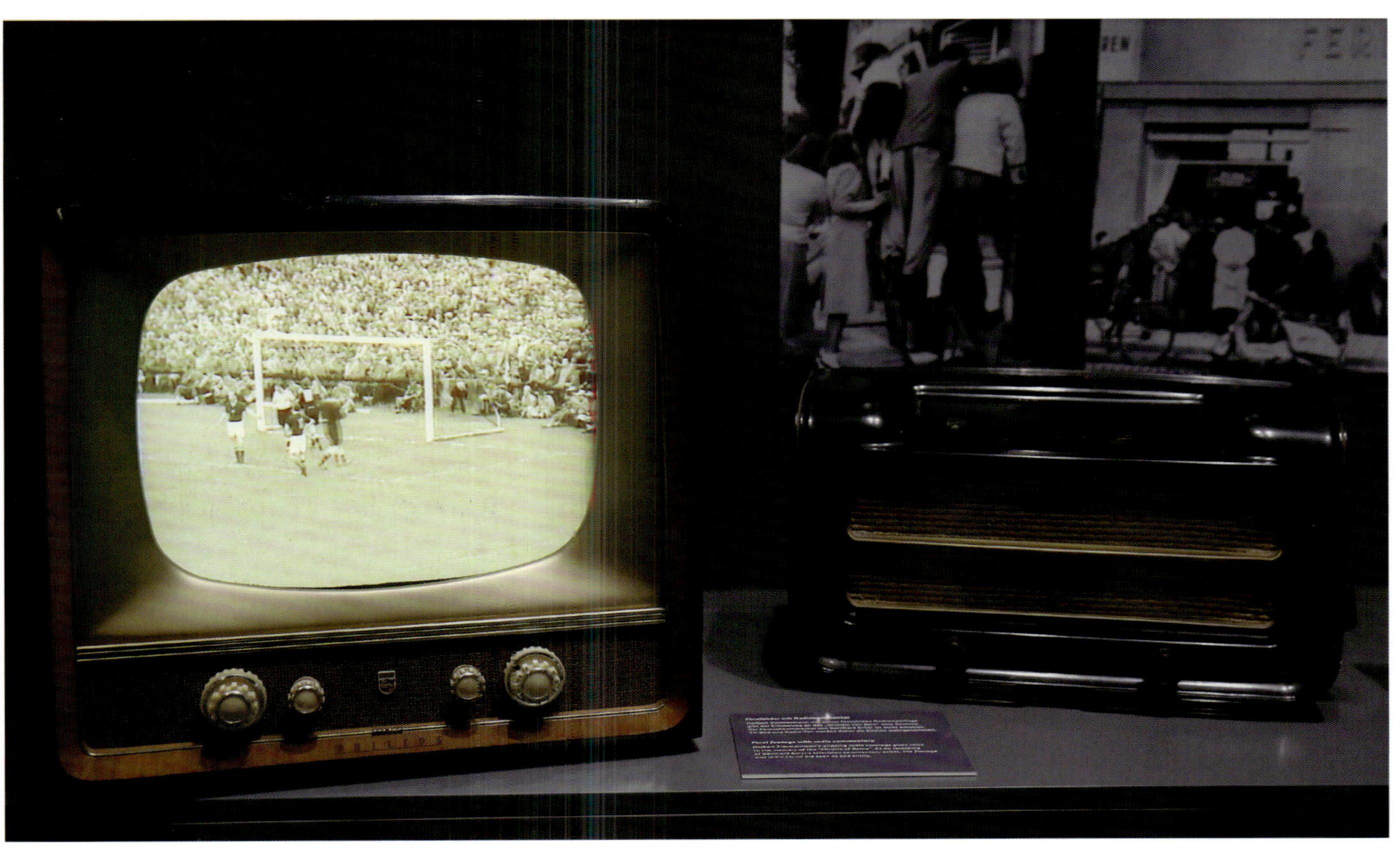

# Tournament: GROUP STAGE

*FIFA-seeded teams*

### GROUP 1: BRAZIL*, FRANCE*, MEXICO, YUGOSLAVIA

| | | |
|---|---|---|
| Brazil 5 | 0 | Mexico |
| Yugoslavia 1 | 0 | France |
| Brazil 1 | 1 | Yugoslavia |
| | | (after extra time) |
| France 3 | 2 | Mexico |

**Advanced to Knockout Stage: Brazil, Yugoslavia**

Mexico's two results gave the country a record of eight losses in eight World Cup games played up to that point.

### GROUP 2: HUNGARY*, TURKEY*, SOUTH KOREA, WEST GERMANY

| | | |
|---|---|---|
| West Germany 4 | 1 | Turkey |
| Hungary 9 | 0 | South Korea |
| Hungary 8 | 3 | West Germany |
| Turkey 7 | 0 | South Korea |
| West Germany 7 | 2 | Turkey |
| | | (Playoff for Second Place) |

**Advanced to Knockout Stage: Hungary, West Germany**

The revolutionary Hungary displayed the full, terrifying extent of their mastery of attacking football, racking up seventeen goals in just two matches. Hungarian forward Sándor Kocsis scored a hat-trick against South Korea and tallied four more goals against the West Germans—seven goals in just two matches!

**BELOW** *German midfielder Horst Eckel in action against Turkish defender Çetin Zeybek and goalkeeper Şükrü Ersoy during the Group 2 playoff.*

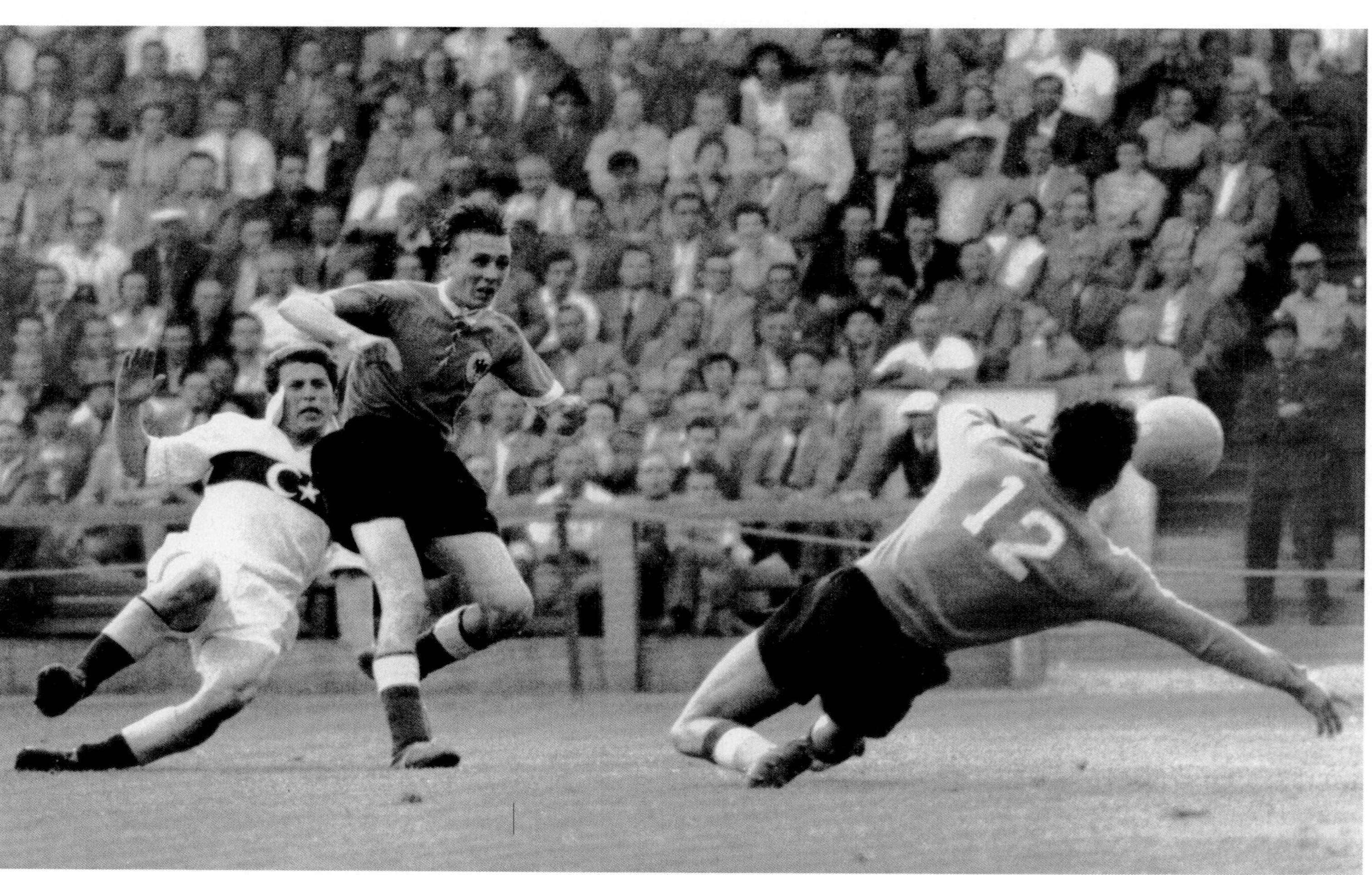

## GROUP 3: AUSTRIA*, URUGUAY*, CZECHOSLOVAKIA, SCOTLAND

| | |
|---|---|
| Uruguay 2 | 0 Czechoslovakia |
| Austria 1 | 0 Scotland |
| Uruguay 7 | 0 Scotland |
| Austria 5 | 0 Czechoslovakia |

**Advanced to Knockout Stage: Uruguay, Austria**

The two unseeded teams in this group, Czechoslovakia and Scotland, failed to score a single goal. Defending-champion Uruguay, featuring seven players from the squad that won the 1950 World Cup, looked very impressive in the group play.

## GROUP 4: ENGLAND*, ITALY*, BELGIUM, SWITZERLAND

| | |
|---|---|
| Switzerland 2 | 1 Italy |
| England 4 | 4 Belgium |
| | (after extra time) |
| Italy 4 | 1 Belgium |
| England 2 | 0 Switzerland |
| Switzerland 4 | 1 Italy |
| | (Playoff for Second Place) |

**Advanced to Knockout Stage: England, Switzerland**

The unseeded host team's initial 2–1 upset of longtime powerhouse Italy was a surprising result…but the 4–1 thrashing in the playoff rematch was downright shocking. Ultimately, it was the great Karl Rappan's return as manager that gave the Swiss team a tactical edge. Meanwhile, England moved on from group play for the first time in a World Cup.

**BELOW** *Switzerland's Jacques Fatton takes a shot on the Italian goal in the Group 4 playoff.*

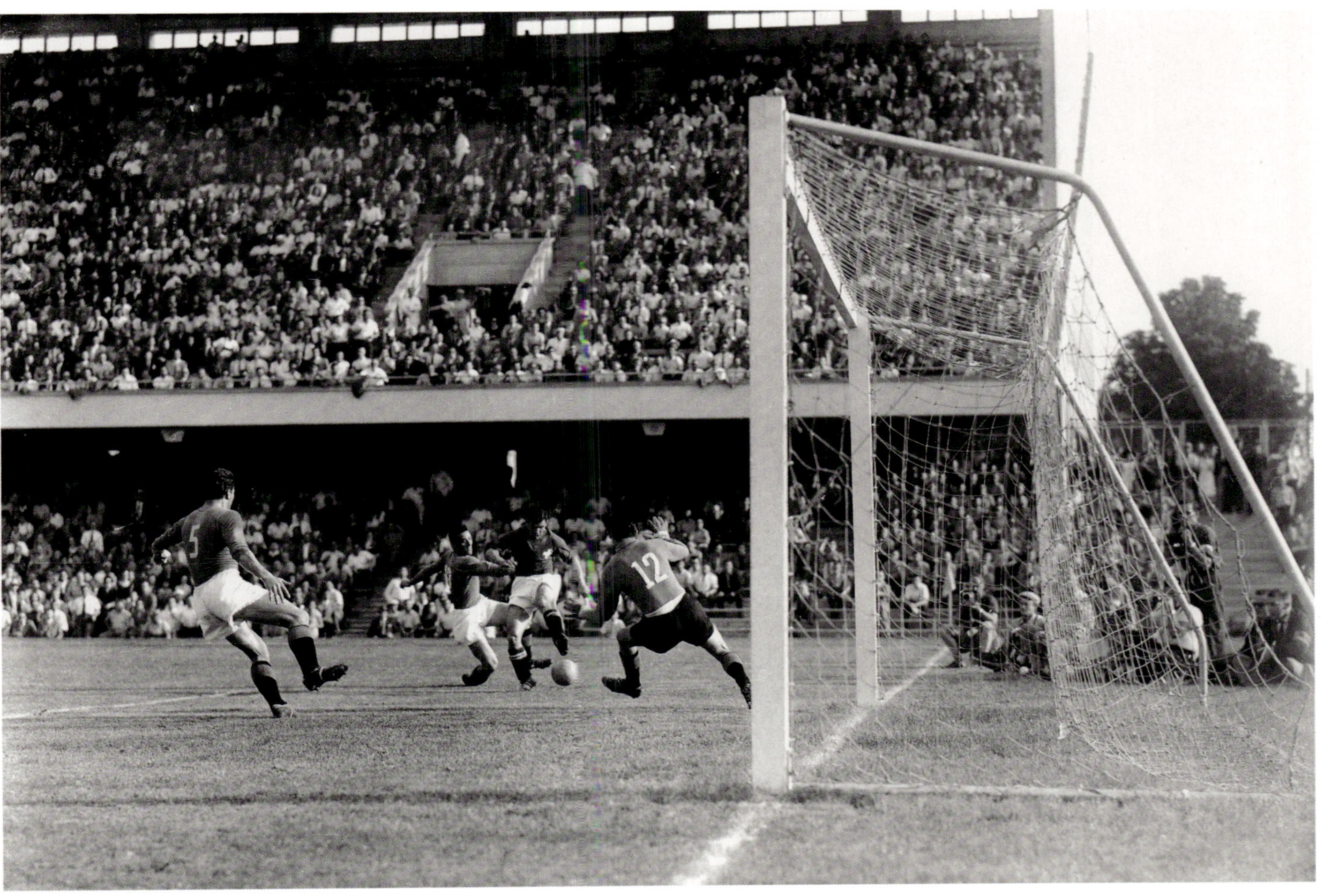

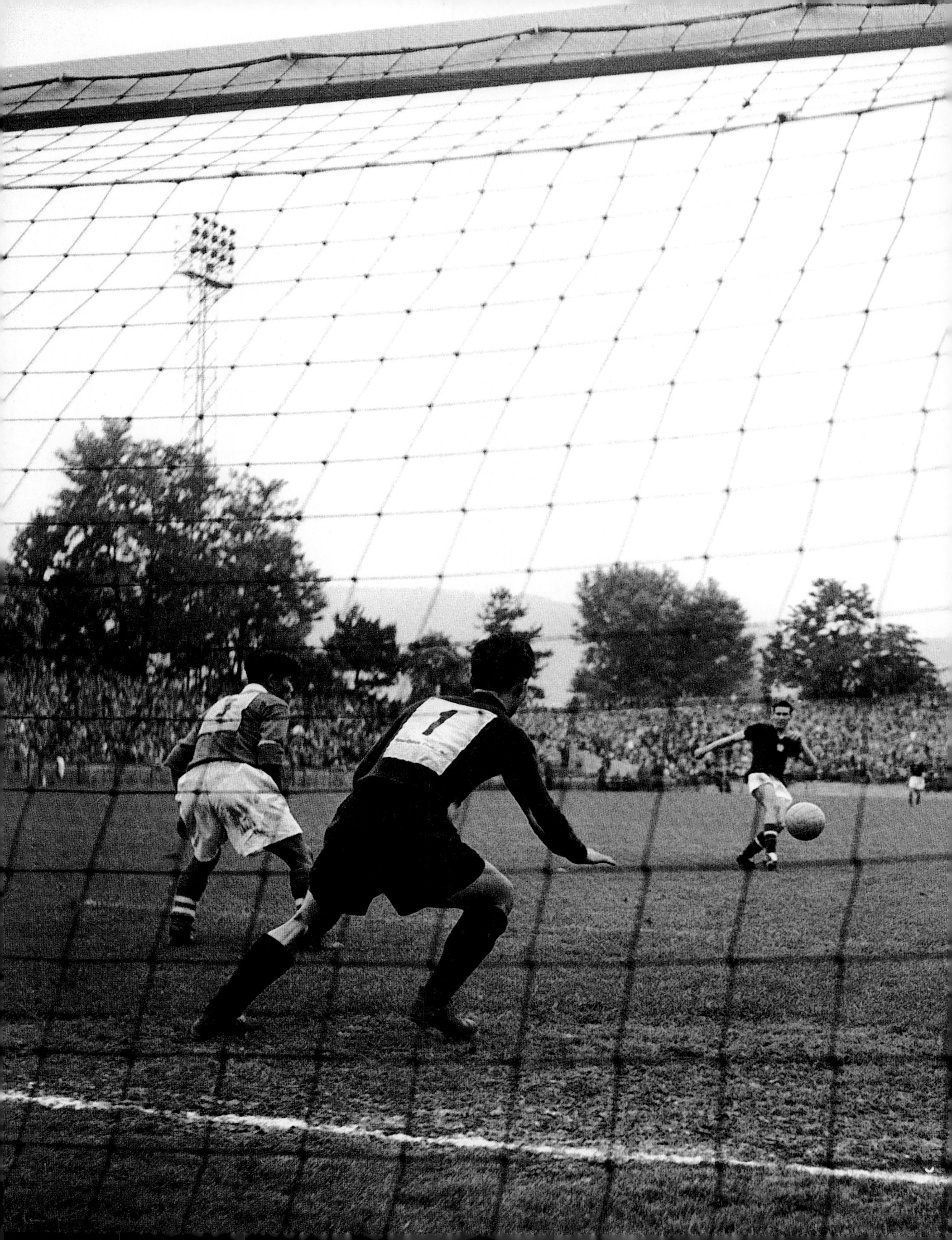

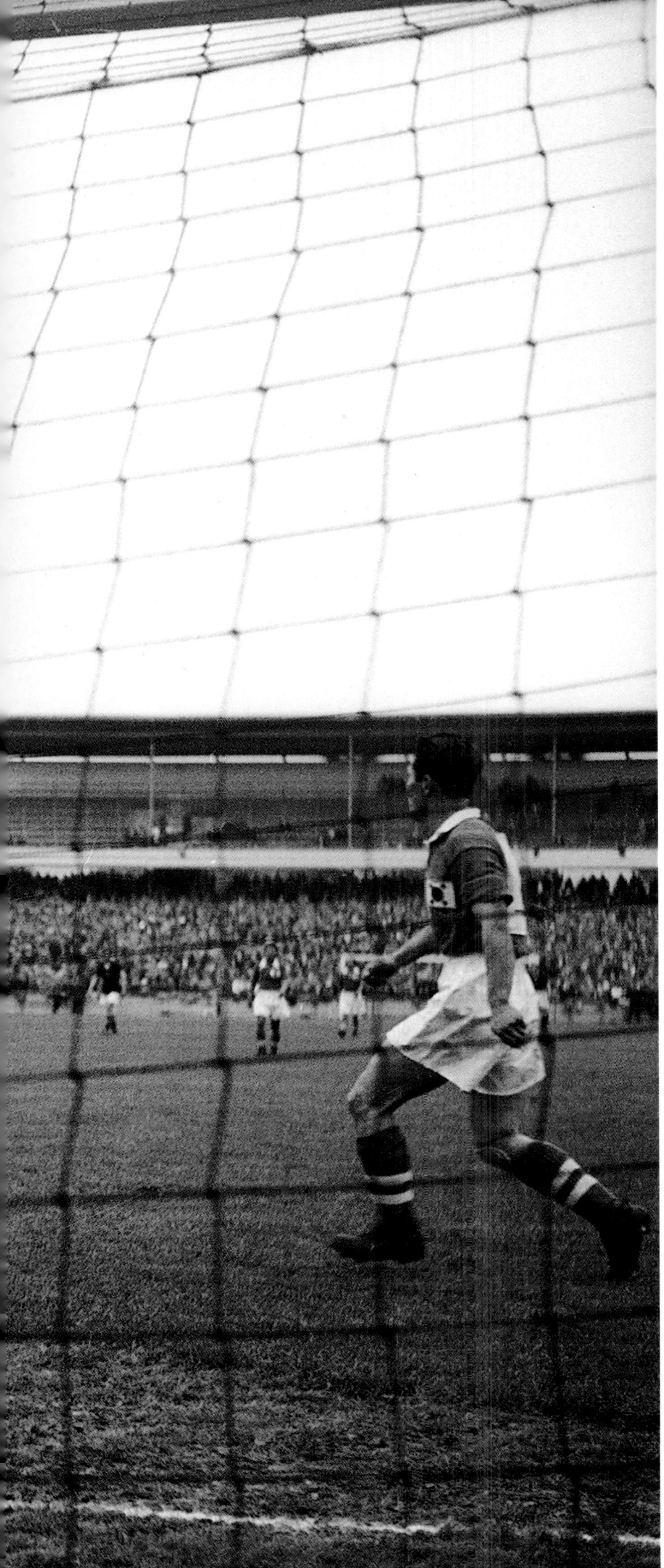

LEFT *The Italian attack attempts to get through the Swiss defence. Switzerland ultimately held them to a −4 goal differential across their two matches.*

## PLAYING THE LINE-UP GAME

**West Germany was thrilled** to be back on football's world stage in 1954, but the country's long suspension from international play led FIFA to leave the Germans unseeded in its assigned group. Due to the tournament's unusual group-play format, West Germany would not play the other unseeded Group 2 team, South Korea, a sure win. Instead, the Germans faced seeded Turkey first — winning easily, 4–1 — and then Hungary, the tournament heavyweight.

Hungary was the reigning Olympic champion and a prohibitive favourite to win the World Cup in 1954. The team's flexible, free-flowing style of play — considered a predecessor to the 'total football' philosophy — had revolutionised tactics in early 1950s Europe. Led by brilliant forward Sándor Kocsis, Hungary's fluid attack terrified opposing defenders. After a 7–1 thrashing in a friendly just a month before the Cup, one English defender said, 'It was like playing people from outer space.' So effective was the Hungarian system that the team hadn't lost in over two years.

As English football legend Sir Stanley Matthews so eloquently put it: '[Hungary's system] was an imaginative combination of exacting ball control, speed of movement, and esoteric vision, knitted together to formulate a style of football that was as innovative as it was productive.'

Given the staggering obstacle before them, the West German coach, Sepp Herberger, decided he didn't want his starting eleven to expend themselves in that match. He played his reserves instead, losing to Hungary 8–3 and leaving West Germany tied with Turkey for second place in the group. Having already beat Turkey in the opener, Herberger knew he'd have the superior side in the playoff, and his starters prevailed easily, to the tune of a 7–2 scoreline, to move into the quarter-finals.

Herberger's squad eventually faced the Hungarians again in the Cup, of course — this time in the final, and with the full German A-team on the pitch.

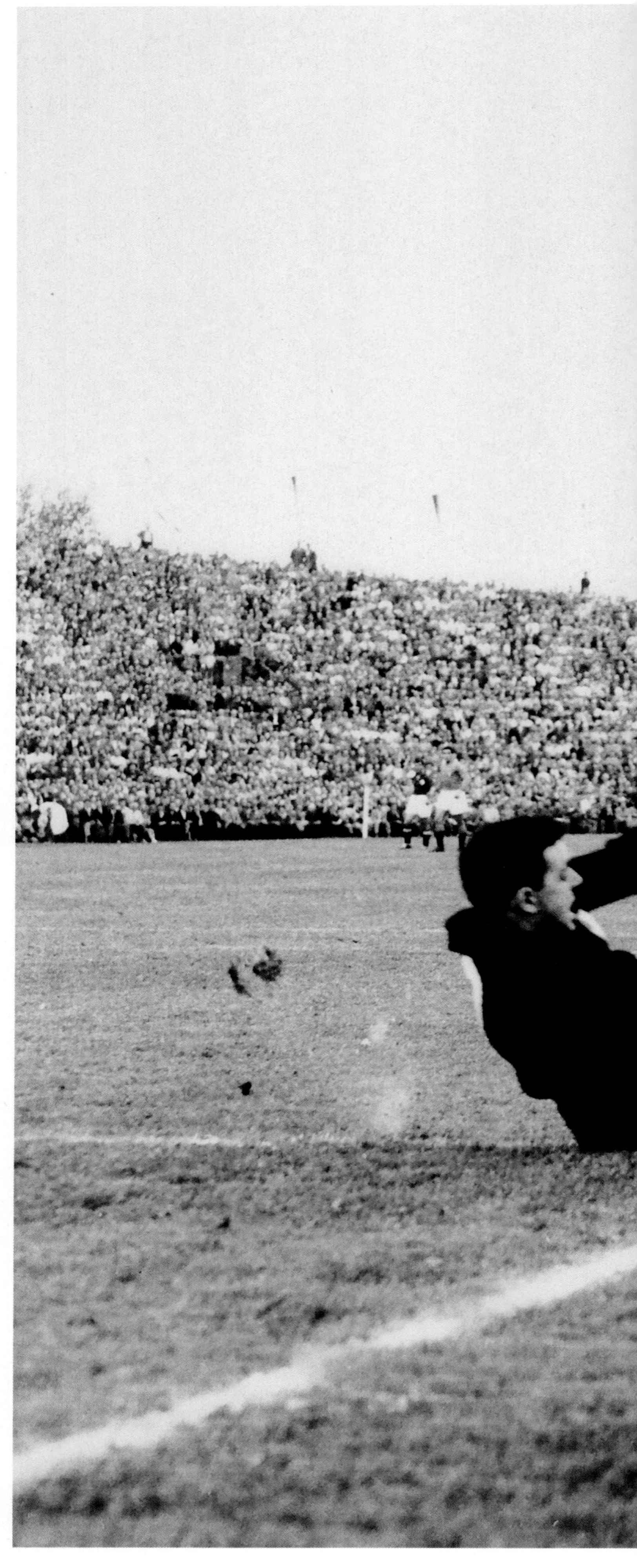

**RIGHT** *The Italian attack attempts to get through the Swiss defence. Switzerland ultimately held them to a −4 goal differential across their two matches.*

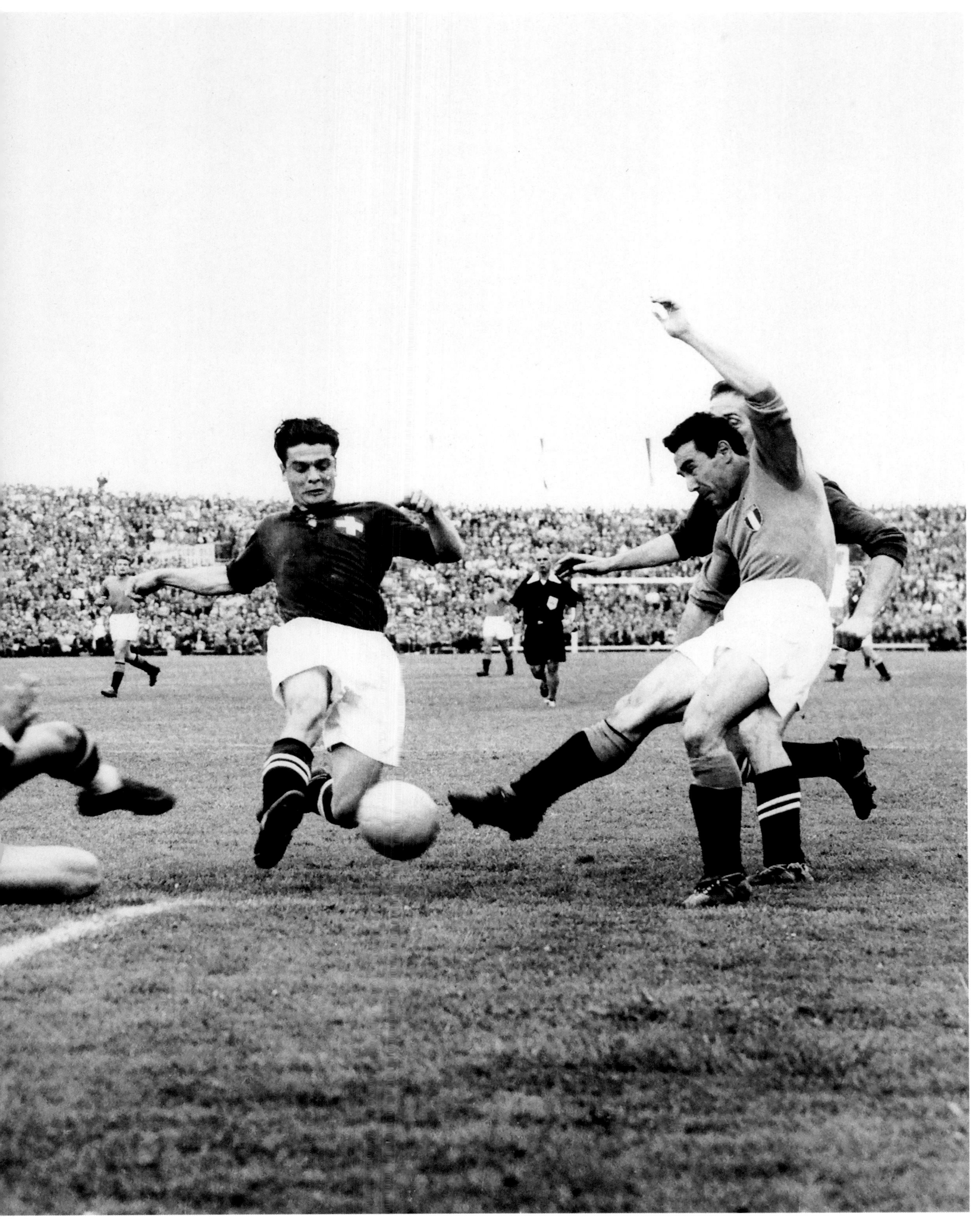

## QUARTER-FINALS

| | |
|---:|:---|
| Austria 7 | 5 Switzerland |
| West Germany 2 | 0 Yugoslavia |
| Hungary 4 | 2 Brazil |
| Uruguay 4 | 2 England |

After defeating England, Uruguay had still never lost a World Cup game in the eleven they'd played since 1930. The twelve goals scored in Austria's 7–5 win over Switzerland is still the highest total in World Cup history (going into the 2026 World Cup). The Swiss newspaper *La Liberté* lauded the Austrians' 'subtle passes that made their opponents go into the void'. The game also featured two hat-tricks: Theodor Wagner for Austria and Josef Hügi for Switzerland.

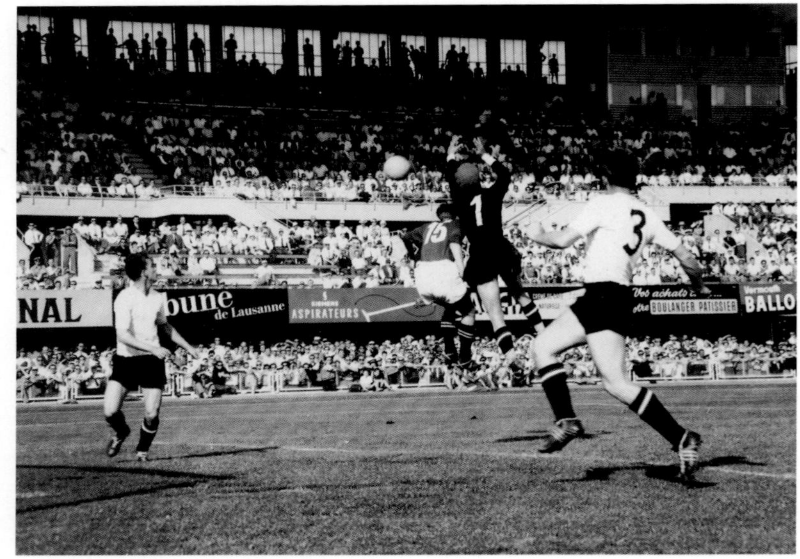

## THE BATTLE OF BERN

**Hungary's quarter-final win over Brazil** was so violently conducted that it became widely known as 'The Battle of Bern', or the dirtiest match in World Cup history... up until that point, at least. Played in a torrential rainfall, the fixture featured a slippery field and a general loss of physical control that led to heinous fouls and red-hot tempers. Hungary took better advantage of the poor footing early on and jumped out to a 2–0 lead within the first seven minutes. A Brazilian penalty kick made it 2–1 at halftime, but tensions were continuing to mount. When Hungary was also awarded a spot-kick in the sixtieth minute, a horde of Brazilian officials and journalists rushed the interlopers off the pitch.

From there, play deteriorated into a succession of increasingly brutal collisions and fighting that eventually sent three players off. As a correspondent for *The Times* reported, 'I have never seen such cruel tackling, cutting down of opponents as if with a scythe.' The game's referee, Arthur Ellis, said, 'They behaved like animals. It was a disgrace.' He awarded forty-two free kicks in the match.

Hungary had converted its penalty kick for a 3–1 lead, but Brazilian forward Julinho slid in a tricky shot in the sixty-fifth minute to make it 3–2. Finally, Hungary salted away the match with a goal in the last two minutes. The final seconds were little more than a running brawl between the two sides. The Hungarian manager, Gusztáv Sebes, needed four stitches to close a cut on his face from a broken bottle in the immediate aftermath of the final whistle. 'This was a battle, a brutal, savage match,' he said later. 'Everyone was having a go — fans, players, and officials.'

Unfortunately, ending the match didn't end the combat. 'Players clashed in the tunnel and a small war broke out in the corridor to the dressing rooms,' said Sebes. It finally ended when Brazil's players broke into Hungary's locker room to escalate the brawl. There, a detachment of Hungary's infamous ÁVH secret police used batons and drawn weapons to drive off the Brazilians.

After the tournament, Brazil lodged a formal protest with FIFA, claiming that the English referee was part of a communist plot to aid Hungary.

**ABOVE** *Austria's Kurt Schmied bobbles the ball due to a challenge from Swiss forward Charles Antenen.*

**OPPOSITE** *Bauer (left) and József Bozsik (right) exchange pennants for Brazil and Hungary, respectively, before the quarter-final bout that would become known as 'The Battle of Bern'.*

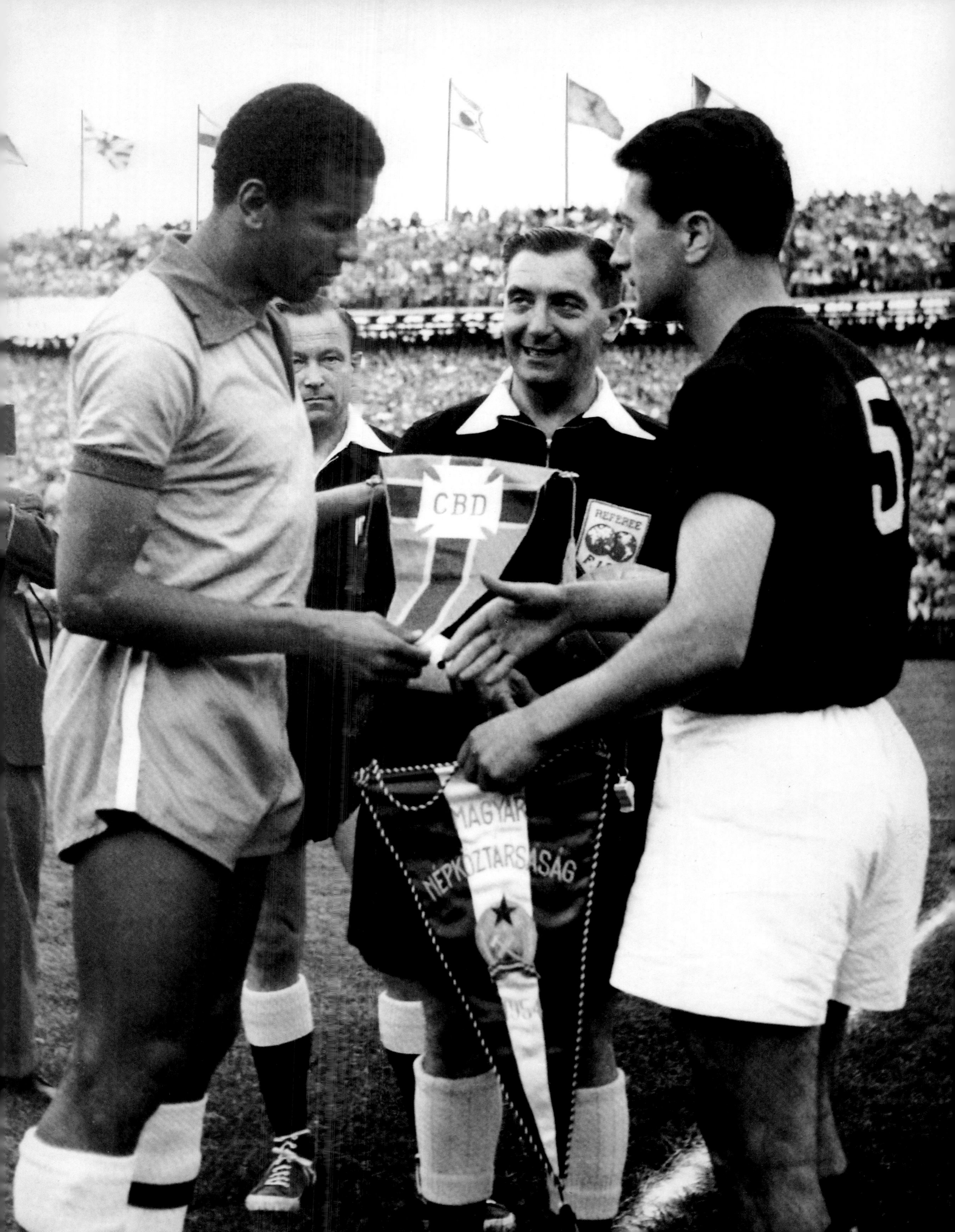
CBD
MAGYAR
NÉPKÖZTÁRSASÁG
REFEREE
FIFA

'*The most beautiful game I've ever seen played—I learned more in those two hours than in twenty years of playing.*'
— **GIANNI BRERA**

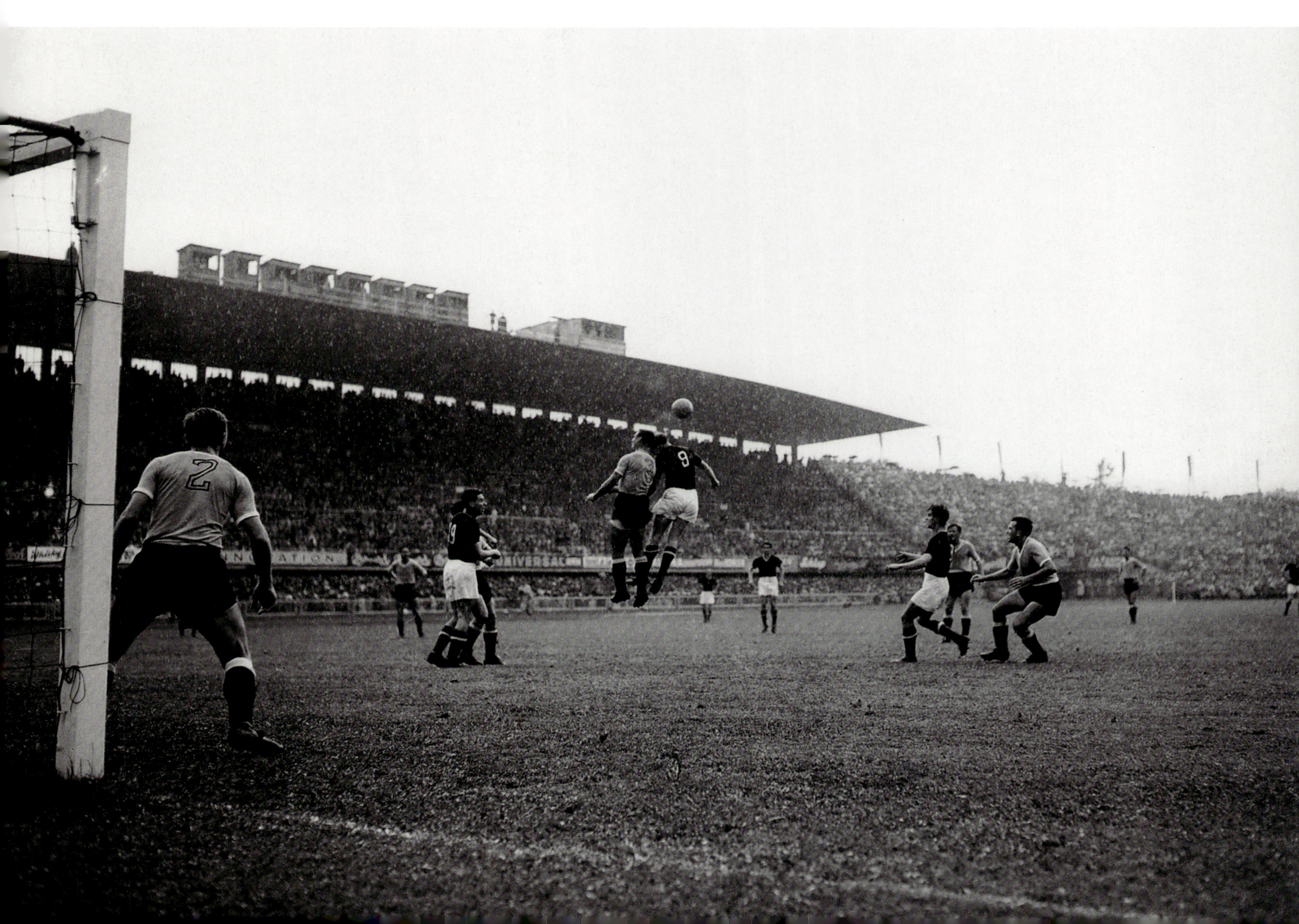

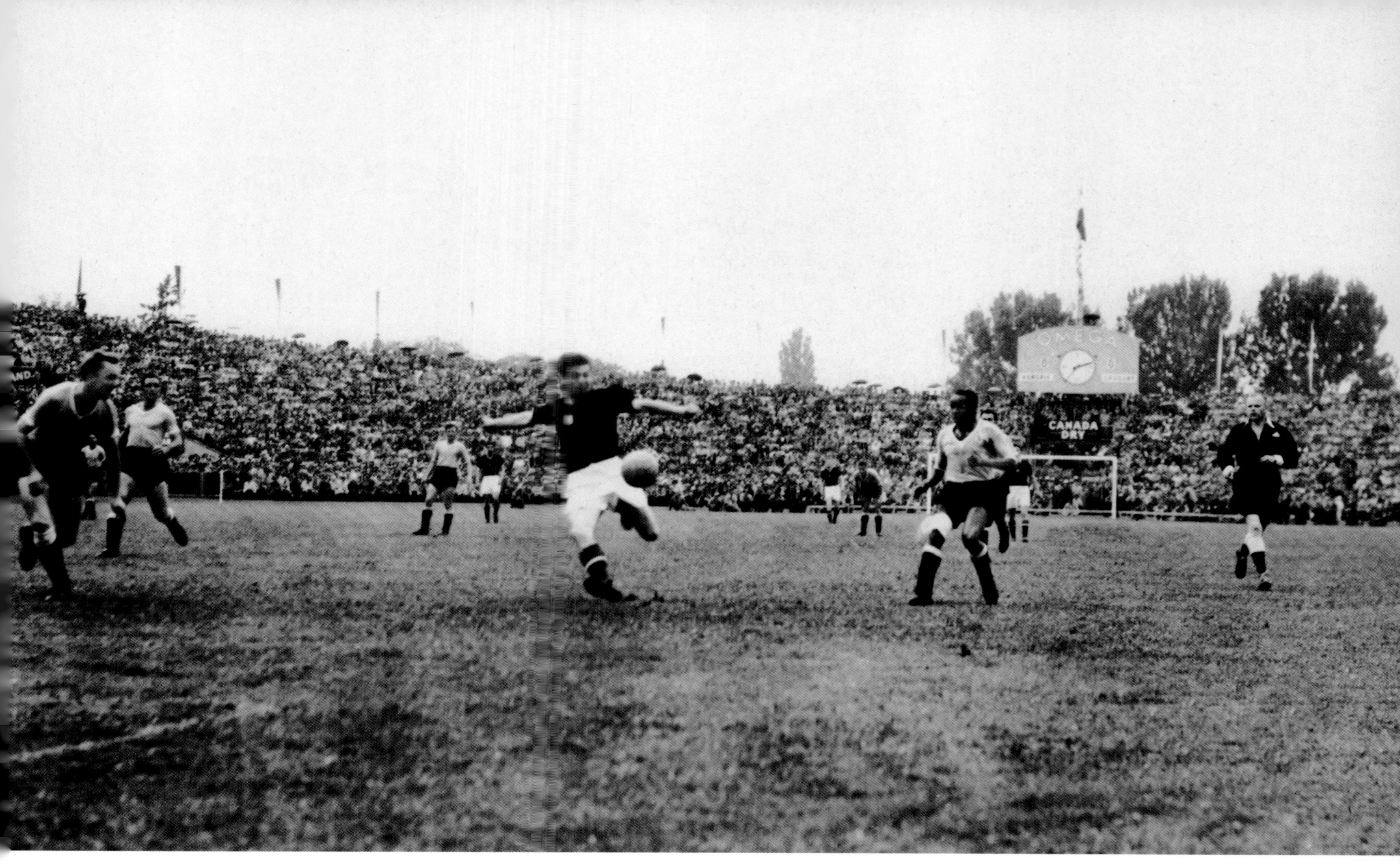

## SEMI-FINALS

West Germany 6 | 1 Austria
Hungary 4 | 2 Uruguay
| (after extra time)

West Germany easily dominated the match against Austria in Basel. Fritz Walter not only assisted on three goals but also slotted home two penalty kicks in the second half to help seal the win for the Germans.

Meanwhile in Lausanne, the fear that Hungary–Uruguay would turn into a reprise of 'The Battle of Bern' led the Swiss authorities to heighten security. But although the match was certainly an intense struggle, it was also a brilliant game of football, fairly played.

Uruguay's Juan Hohberg scored a pair of very fine goals to tie the game 2–2 at the end of regular time. But in overtime, Sándor Kocsis scored his own brace to put Hungary into the final. Afterward, many would call the match one of the greatest ever played. The great football journalist Gianni Brera called it '[t]he most beautiful game I've ever seen played — I learned more in those two hours than in twenty years of playing and being a football critic.'

**OPPOSITE** *William Martínez of Uruguay and Nándor Hidegkuti of Hungary contest the ball in the air. The hard-fought semi-final went to extra time.*

**ABOVE** *Zoltán Czibor of Hungary opens the scoreboard in the semi-final match against Uruguay.*

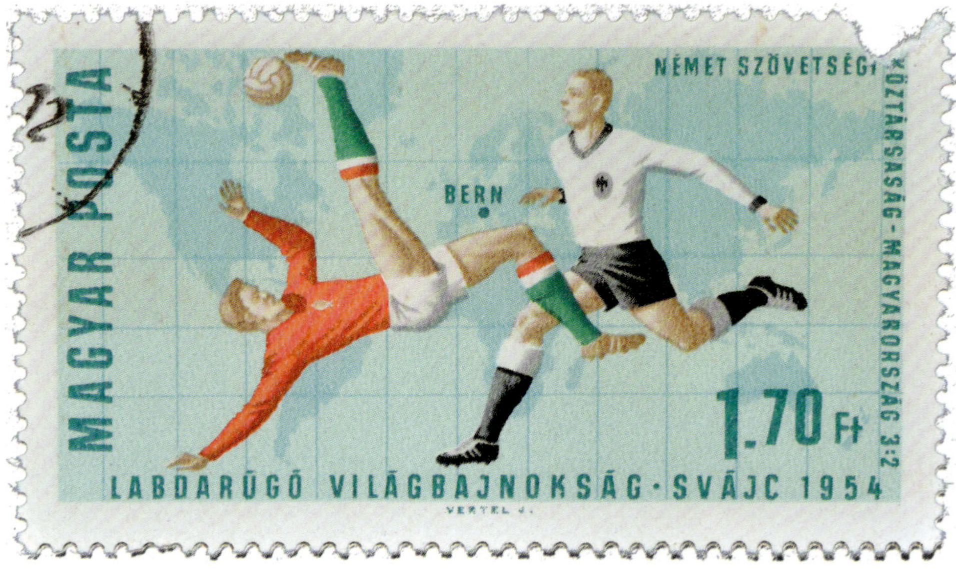




## FINAL

West Germany 3 | 2 Hungary (First Place)
Austria 3 | 1 Uruguay (Third Place)

Austria's solid defeat of Uruguay for a third-place finish capped the country's glorious return to World Cup football after a twenty-year absence due to the 1938 annexation by Nazi Germany and a difficult decade of post-war recovery.

## 'THE MIRACLE OF BERN'

**Wankdorf Stadium in the** Swiss capital of Bern would host the 1954 World Cup Final, pitting Hungary agaisnt West Germany. Although the game was a rematch of an 8–3 Hungarian win in the group stage, a repeat was not likely — the West Germans had rested all their starters in that first contest. Still, Hungary seemed unbeatable, growing stronger the deeper they got into the tournament.

The championship match started in a heavy rain, and scoring happened fast. Hungary struck twice in the first eight minutes, then West Germany got back level with quick goals in the tenth and eighteenth minutes. Not even twenty minutes in, the score was 2–2. The remaining seventy minutes of the match would be a titanic struggle to see which side could score a third goal. Hungary largely controlled the pace, hitting both the post and the crossbar, and forced the West German keeper Toni Turek to make several acrobatic saves.

As regulation time ticked down, the hard-pressing Hungarians seemed to tire a bit, losing half a step as the West Germans began their own press. With just six minutes left, Helmut Rahn buried a shot that gave West Germany the 3–2 lead. Dramatically, just two minutes later, Hungarian captain Ferenc Puskás flicked in a perfect through-pass but was ruled offside. A final point-blank shot was saved by Turek and West Germany clinched their miraculous return to the top of the football world.

Hungary had scored a record twenty-seven goals in the tournament and star forward Sándor Kocsis led all scorers with eleven goals. But it was little consolation for the so-called 'Golden Team' that had seemed destined to hoist the Jules Rimet Trophy. For West Germany, the win had a greater cultural significance, marking a turning point in the nation's rehabilitation from the self-inflicted ravages of the Second World War.

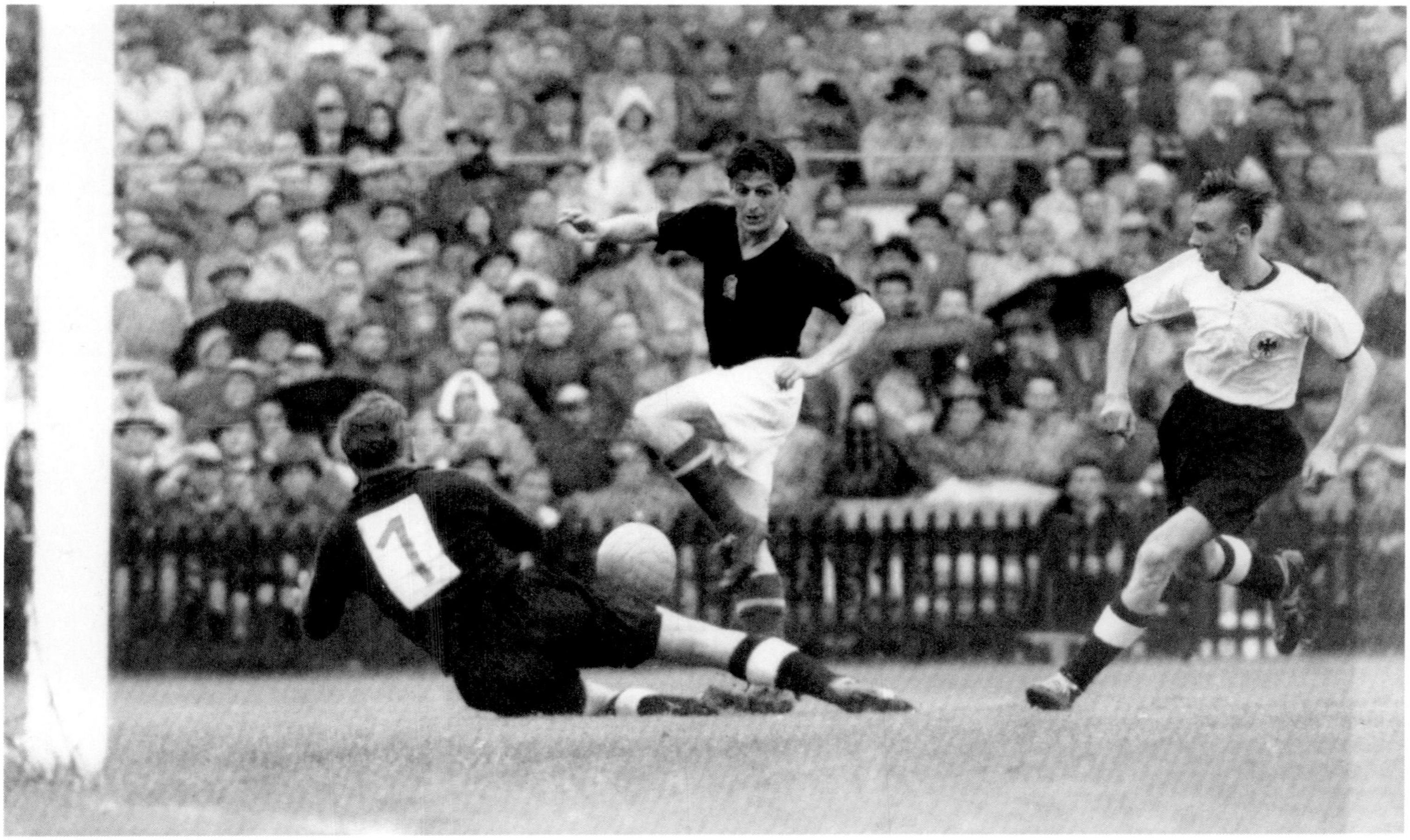

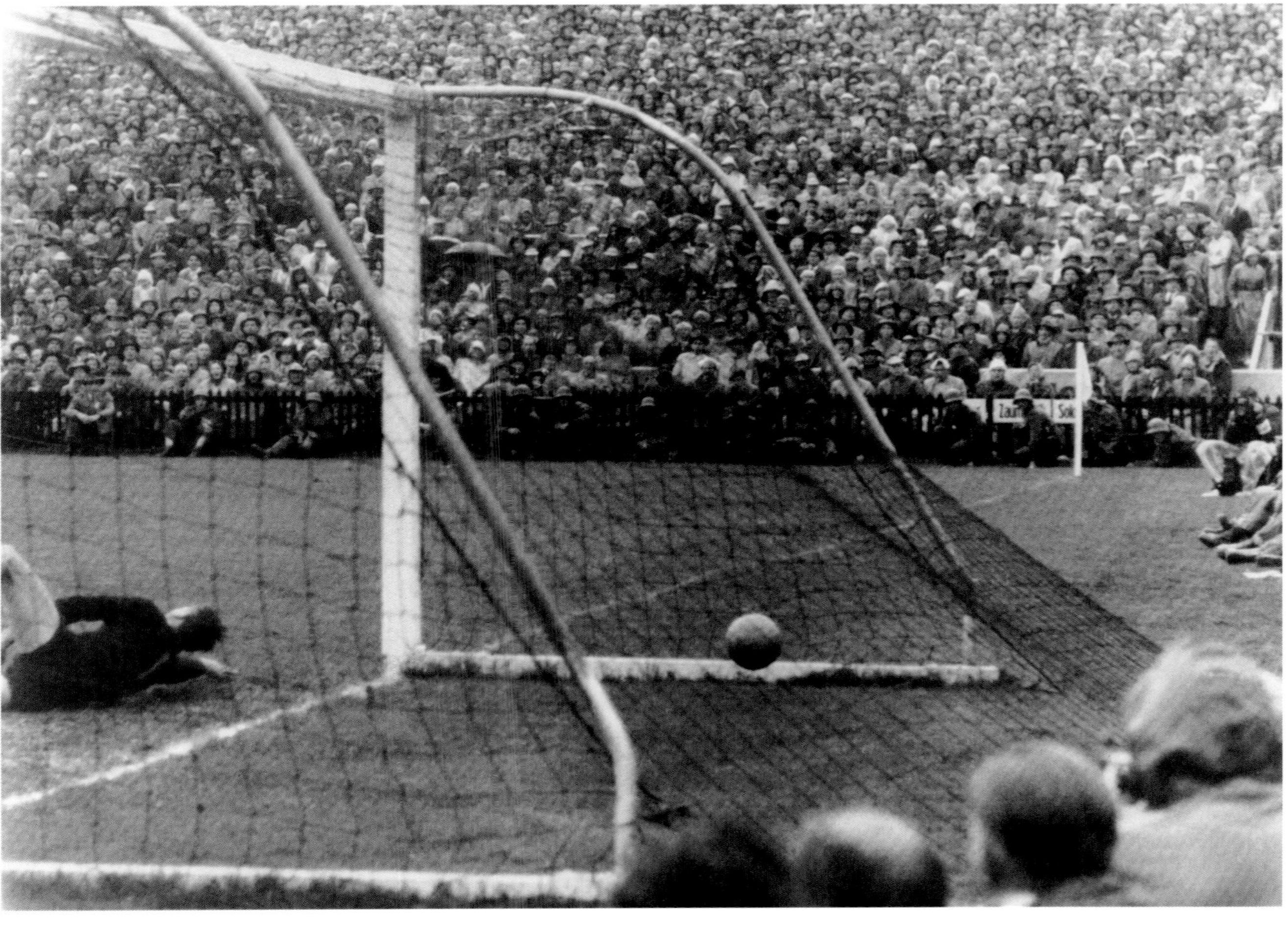

# 1958



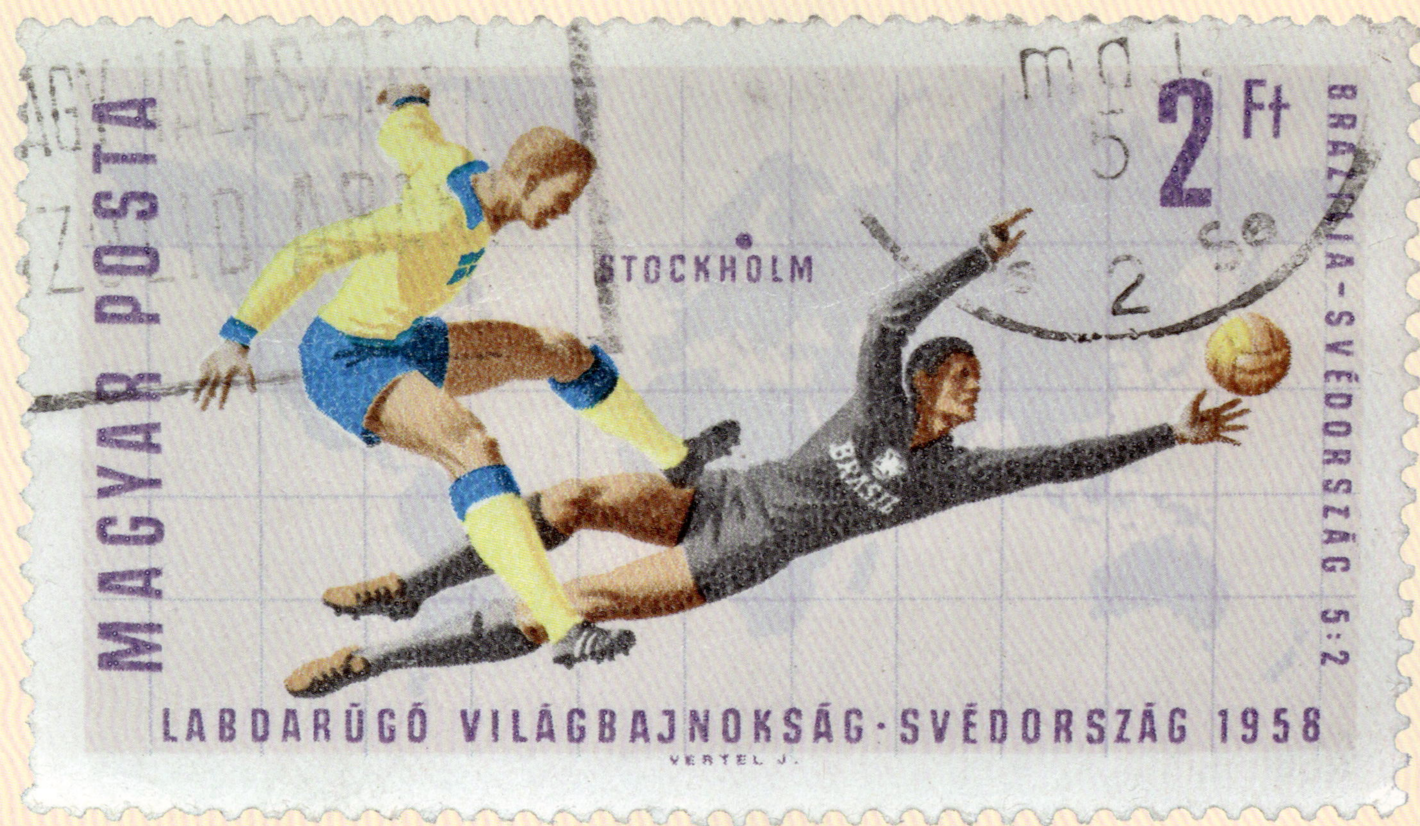


**The 1958 World Cup** offered plenty of compelling story-lines and more than its share of exciting football . . . but two events set this tournament apart in the grand history of the beautiful game. First, it finally saw Brazil atop the winner's podium — a spot that would become a second home for the South American giants. Second, the 1958 World Cup would mark the emergence of a seventeen-year-old player making his World Cup debut. More on Edson Arantes do Nascimento later. For now, let's set the scene.

As the spectacle of a World Cup tournament grew more attractive (and more lucrative) in the post-war era, the competition to host it grew more spirited. In 1950, the FIFA Congress chose Sweden's bid over Argentina, Mexico, and Chile for the 1958 tournament. As a result, Sweden and defending champ West Germany automatically qualified, with the remaining fourteen spots earned in qualification tournaments. A surprising development was that all four of the UK's Home Nations qualified — England, Scotland, Wales, and Northern Ireland — the only time in Cup history this happened. It also marked the first appearance of the Soviet Union in World Cup play. Teams that notably failed to qualify included football powers Italy, Uruguay, Spain, and Belgium.

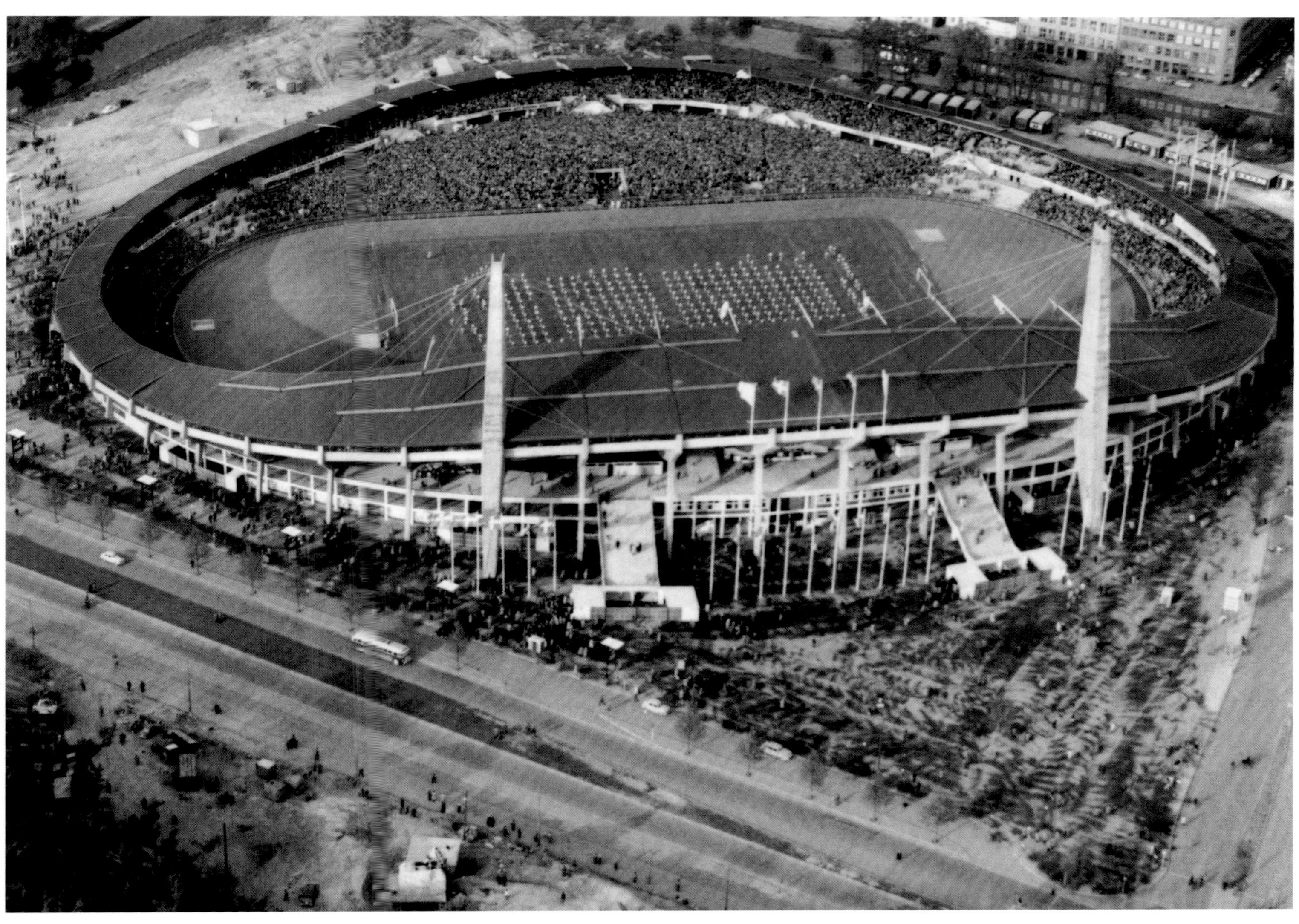



## RETURN OF THE KNOCKOUT

**The 1958 tournament featured** a group stage with sixteen teams divided into groups of four again, but this time each group would play a full round-robin — two points per win, one point for a draw — with the top-two teams moving on to the knockout stage. Thankfully, there was no seeding in these groups. Instead, teams were divided by geography into four pots, then FIFA's Organising Committee selected one team from each pot for each group, ensuring groups with a nice geographical mix. Also of note was the deepening commitment to TV coverage: several matches would be televised across Europe by the European Broadcasting Union.

# Tournament: GROUP STAGE

### GROUP 1: WEST GERMANY, NORTHERN IRELAND, CZECHOSLOVAKIA, ARGENTINA

| | | |
|---|---|---|
| West Germany 3 | 1 | Argentina |
| Northern Ireland 1 | 0 | Czechoslovakia |
| West Germany 2 | 2 | Czechoslovakia |
| Argentina 3 | 1 | Northern Ireland |
| West Germany 2 | 2 | Northern Ireland |
| Czechoslovakia 6 | 1 | Argentina |
| Northern Ireland 2 | 1 | Czechoslovakia |
| | | (Playoff/after extra time) |

***Advanced to Knockout Stage:***
***West Germany, Northern Ireland***

### GROUP 2: FRANCE, YUGOSLAVIA, PARAGUAY, SCOTLAND

| | | |
|---|---|---|
| France 7 | 3 | Paraguay |
| Yugoslavia 1 | 1 | Scotland |
| Yugoslavia 3 | 2 | France |
| Paraguay 3 | 2 | Scotland |
| France 2 | 1 | Scotland |
| Paraguay 3 | 3 | Yugoslavia |

***Advanced to Knockout Stage: France, Yugoslavia***

The biggest surprise of the 1958 World Cup was the qualification and subsequent impressive performance of tiny Northern Ireland. They got in by knocking traditional power Italy out of the qualifying rounds. In group play, the Northern Irish beat a strong Czech squad, drew with defending champ West Germany, tied for second in the group, then played Czechoslovakia again in the playoff…and beat them again. Argentina's last-place finish in the group was another surprise. The team's return to Buenos Aires was met by thousands of irate fans.

Although they both earned four points, France finished in first ahead of Yugoslavia due to goal average. France's Just Fontaine scored a hat-trick against Paraguay, a brace against Yugoslavia, and one more goal against Scotland.

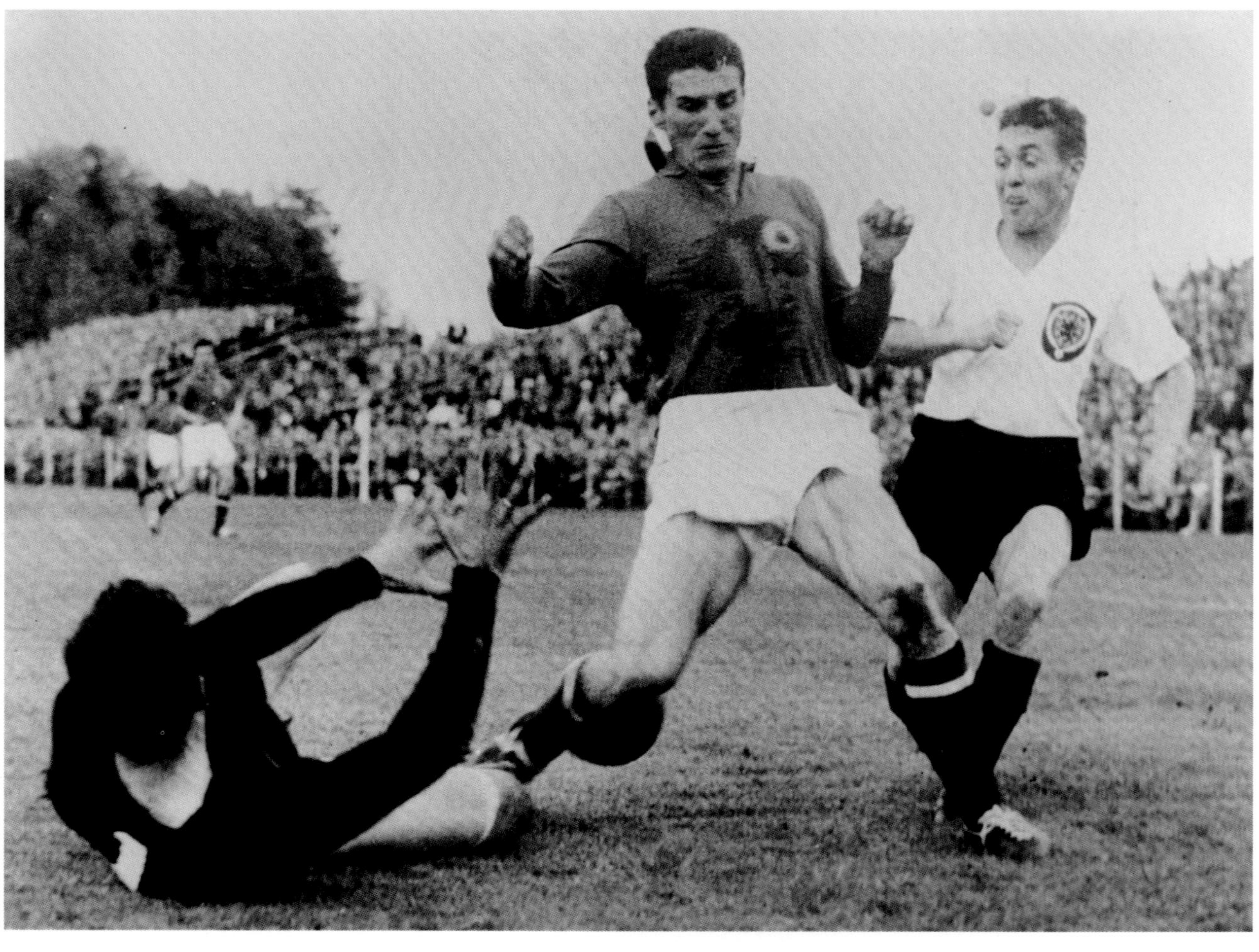

**BELOW** *Yugoslavia's Dobrosav Krstić makes a tackle, and goal-keeper Vladimir Beara goes to the ground to stifle an attempt on goal from Scotland's Bobby Collins.*

## GROUP 3: SWEDEN, WALES, HUNGARY, MEXICO

| | | |
|---|---|---|
| Sweden 3 | 0 | Mexico |
| Hungary 1 | 1 | Wales |
| Mexico 1 | 1 | Wales |
| Sweden 2 | 1 | Hungary |
| Sweden 0 | 0 | Wales |
| Hungary 4 | 0 | Mexico |
| Wales 2 | 1 | Hungary |
| | (Playoff) | |

***Advanced to Knockout Stage: Sweden, Wales***

Host Sweden easily won this group, playing what one observer described as 'powerful, workman-like football'. Meanwhile, just four years after being considered one of the great football sides of all time, Hungary took a shocking nosedive, losing the second-place playoff to Wales. The squad had been depleted after key players fled their homeland after the failed Hungarian Revolution of 1956. And Wales, with its three scrappy draws followed by the playoff win, followed its fellow Home Nations underdog Northern Ireland into the knockout stage. Finally, Mexico earned its first point in World Cup group play after eleven tries!

## GROUP 4: BRAZIL, SOVIET UNION, ENGLAND, AUSTRIA

| | | |
|---|---|---|
| Brazil 3 | 0 | Austria |
| Soviet Union 2 | 2 | England |
| Brazil 0 | 0 | England |
| Soviet Union 2 | 0 | Austria |
| England 2 | 2 | Austria |
| Brazil 2 | 0 | Soviet Union |
| Soviet Union 1 | 0 | England |
| | (Playoff) | |

***Advanced to Knockout Stage: Brazil, Soviet Union***

Brazil's third group match, a 2–0 win over the Soviet Union, marked the first-ever World Cup appearance of the teenage sensation Edson Arantes do Nascimento, better known as Pelé. Meanwhile, the USSR's debut in Cup play came at the expense of England, who lost to the Soviets in the playoff for second place and thus bowed out early yet again.

**BELOW** *Ivor Allchurch of Wales scores in a 1–1 draw with Mexico.*

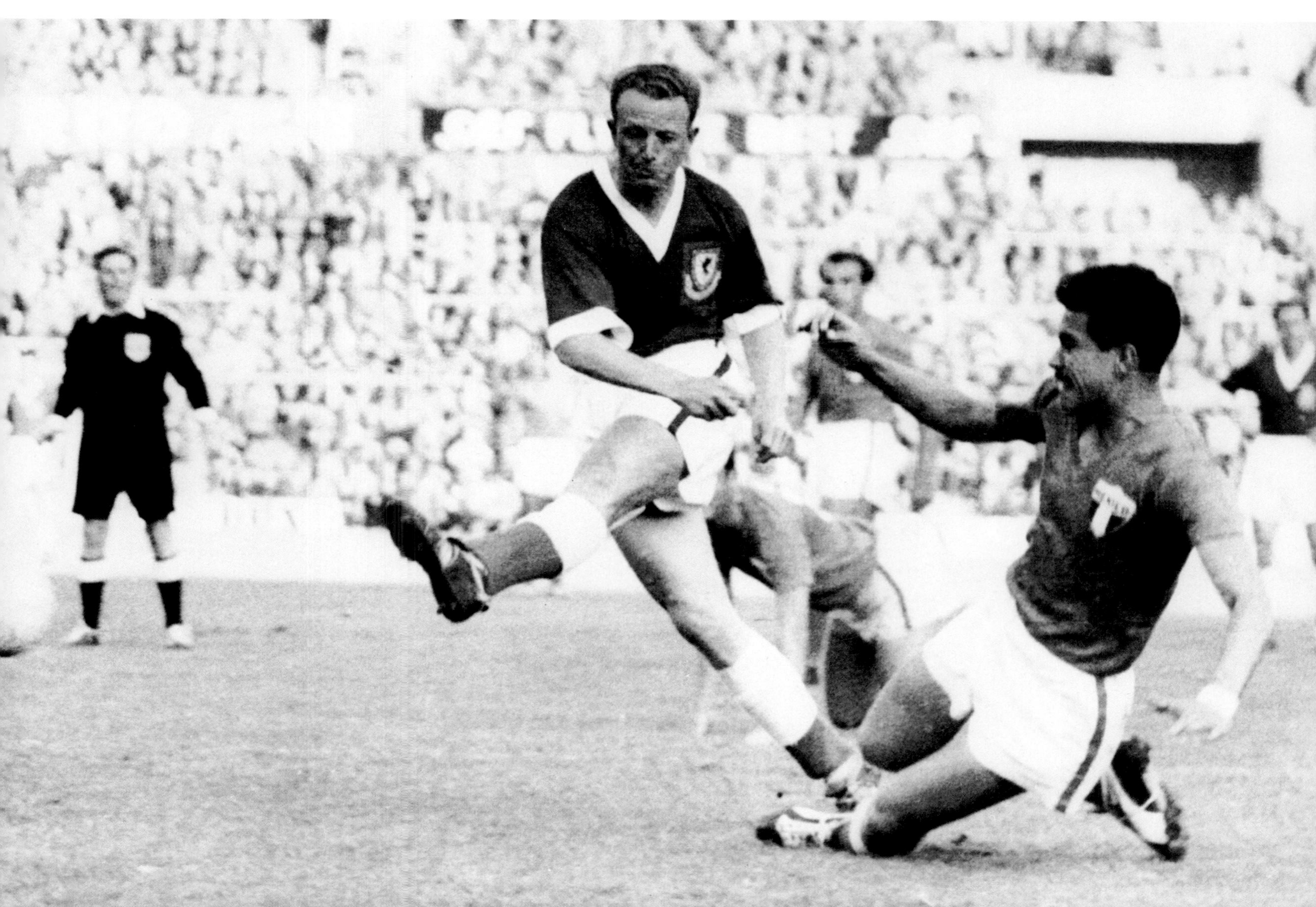

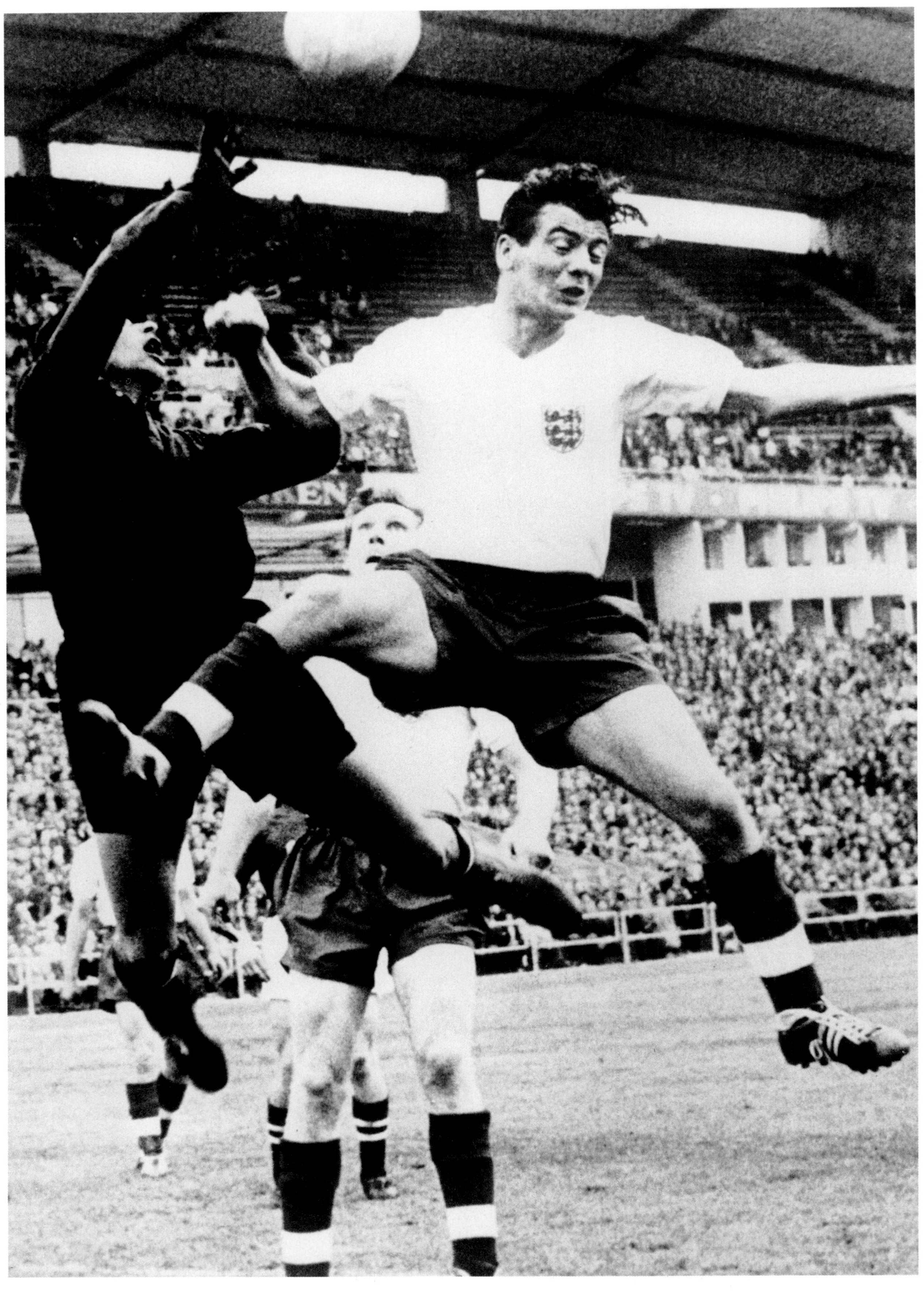

ABOVE *Legendary Soviet goal-keeper Lev 'The Black Spider' Yash-in gets the ball away from English forward Johnny Haynes.*

OPPOSITE *England's Tommy Banks (left) attempts to tackle USSR's Anatoli Ilyin.*

*'The USSR's debut in Cup play came at the expense of England, who lost to the Soviets in the playoff.'*


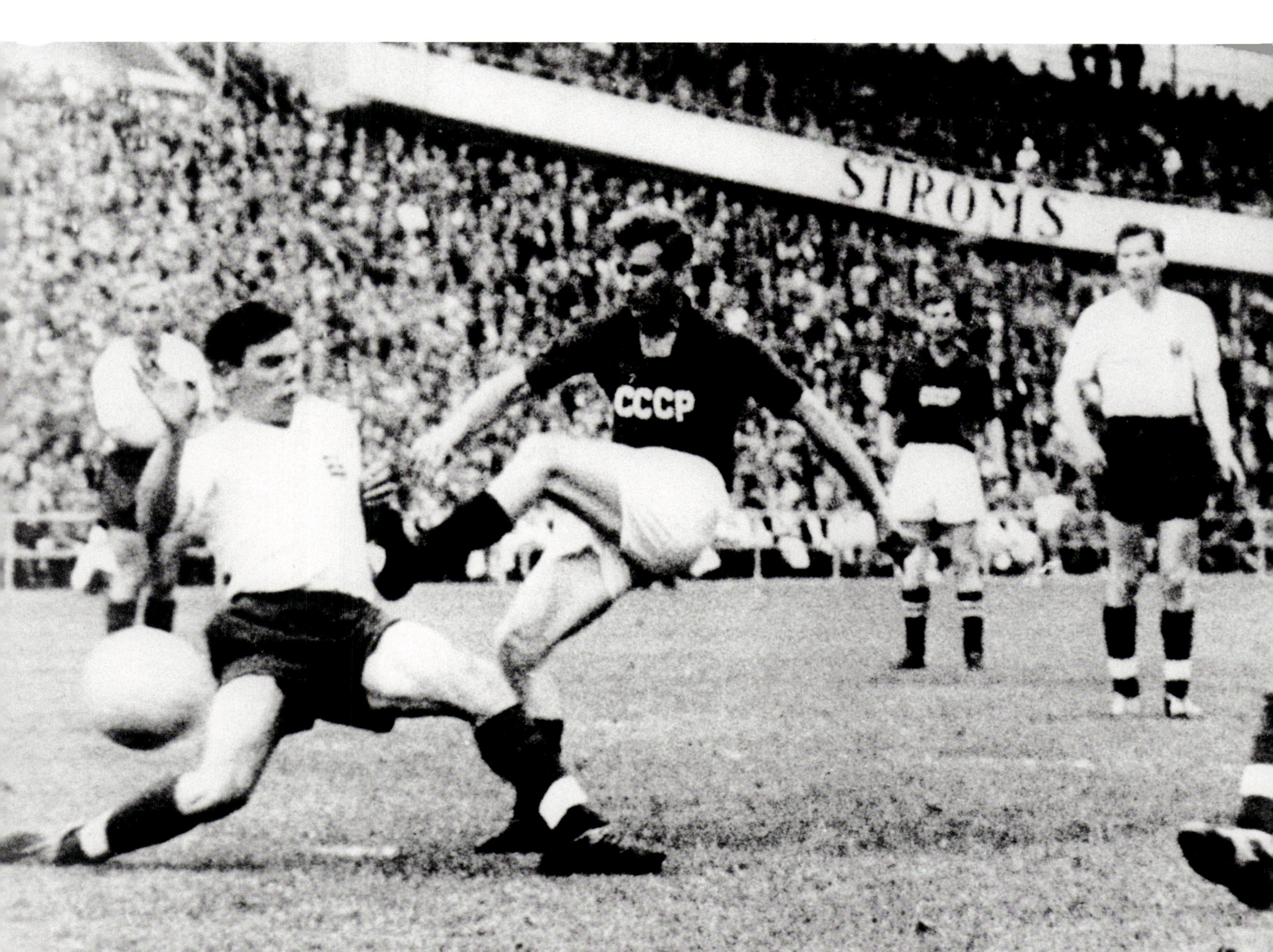

# QUARTER-FINALS

| | |
|---:|:---|
| Brazil 1 | 0 Wales |
| France 4 | 0 Northern Ireland |
| Sweden 2 | 0 Soviet Union |
| West Germany 1 | 0 Yugoslavia |

The two Cinderellas of the tournament, Wales and Northern Ireland, finally bowed out after valiant runs. Home team Sweden moved into the semi-finals along with the defending-champion West Germany. Just Fontaine scored two more goals in France's easy victory over the Northern Irish, bringing his tournament total to an astounding eight... with more to come. And young Pelé scored his first-ever World Cup goal, a game winner for Brazil in the sixty-sixth minute against Wales.



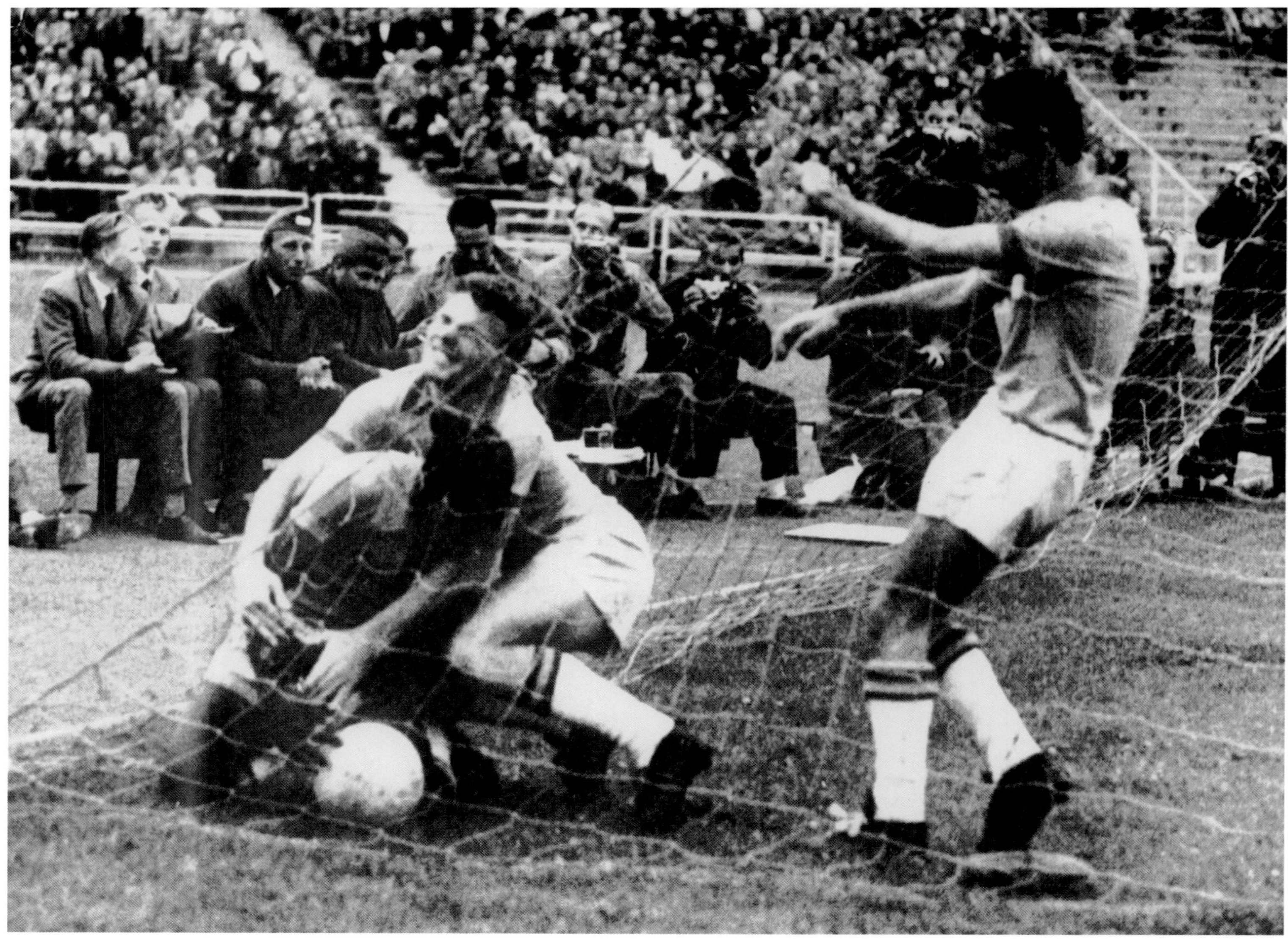

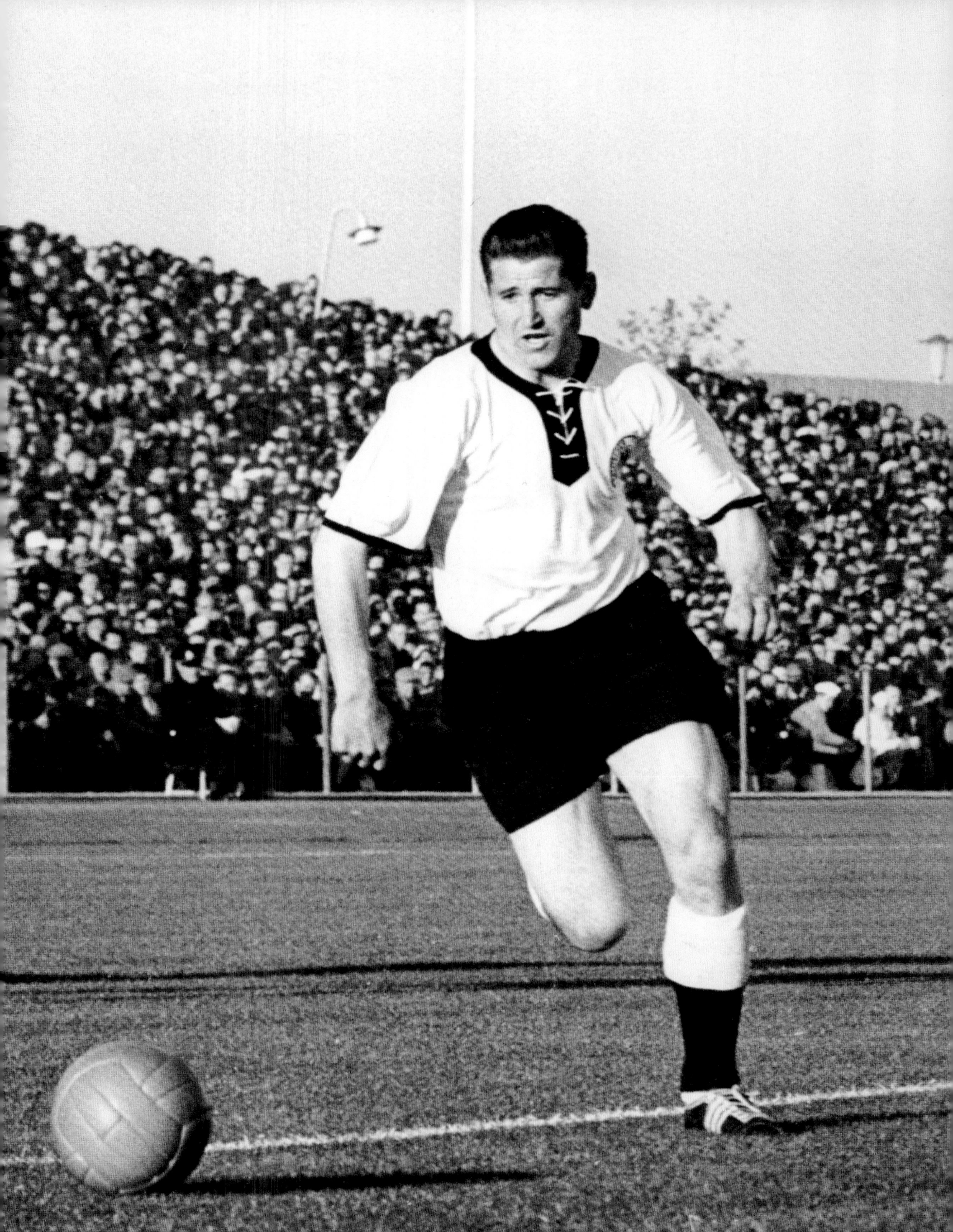

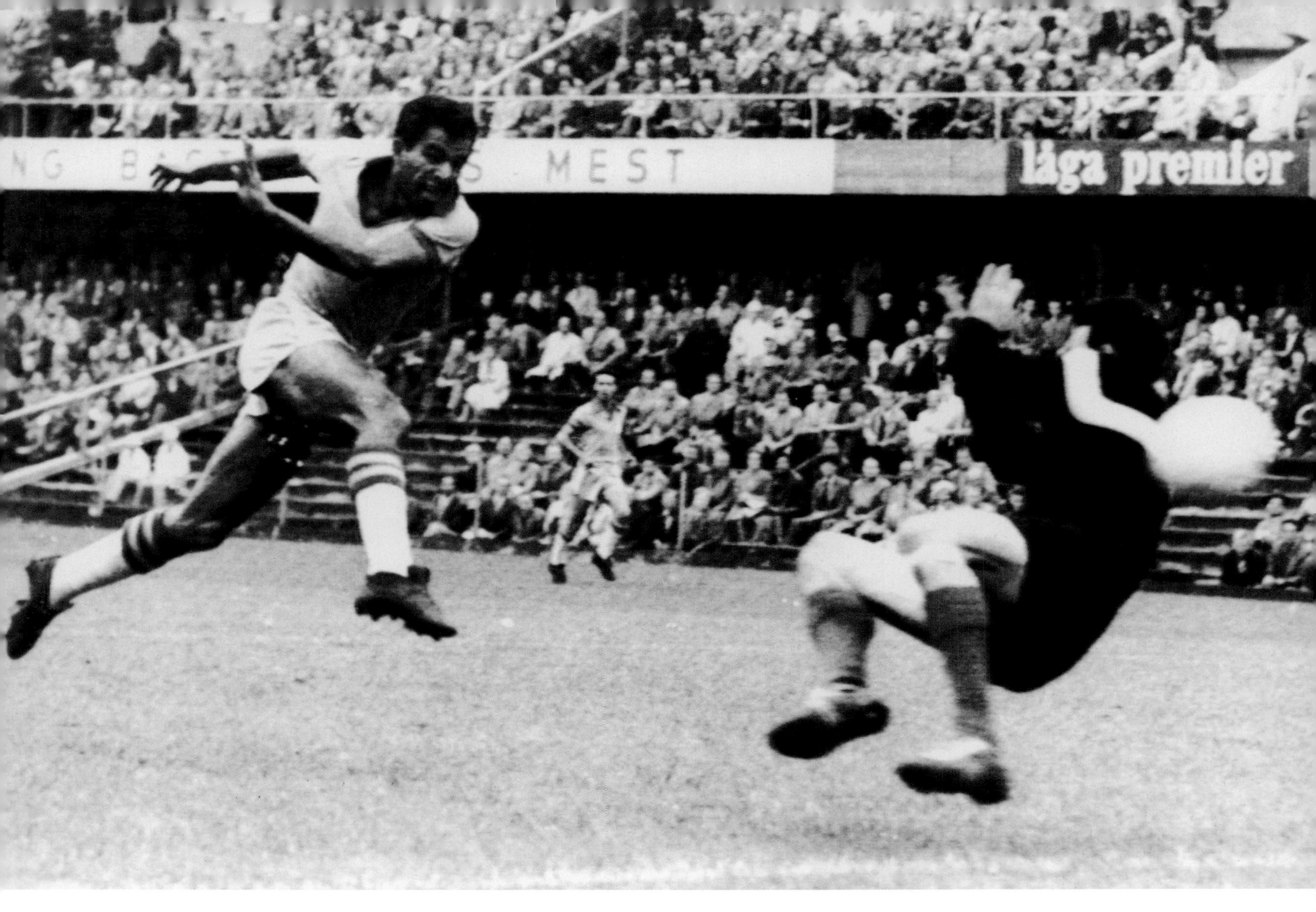



# SEMI-FINALS

Brazil 5 | 2 France
Sweden 3 | 1 West Germany

Just Fontaine scored his ninth goal of the tournament for France, but French captain Robert Jonquet broke his leg in the first half, leaving his side with just ten men, as substitutions were still not allowed in World Cup play. In the second half, Pelé's glorious hat-trick stole the show, giving the world an unmistakable preview of the greatness to come. Sweden's strong play in the other semi-final earned a solid comeback victory for the Scandinavian side, but the match degenerated into a nasty second-half struggle with one West German sent off for violent play and another lost to injury.

**ABOVE** *Brazilian star Vavá's cracking shot gets past French keeper Claude Abbes and finds the back of the net.*

**OPPOSITE** *The physical play between West Germany and Sweden reaches a boiling point in the second half and Erich Juskowiak is sent off in the fifty-eighth minute.*

'Pelé's glorious hat-trick stole the show,
giving the world an unmistakable preview
of the greatness to come.'

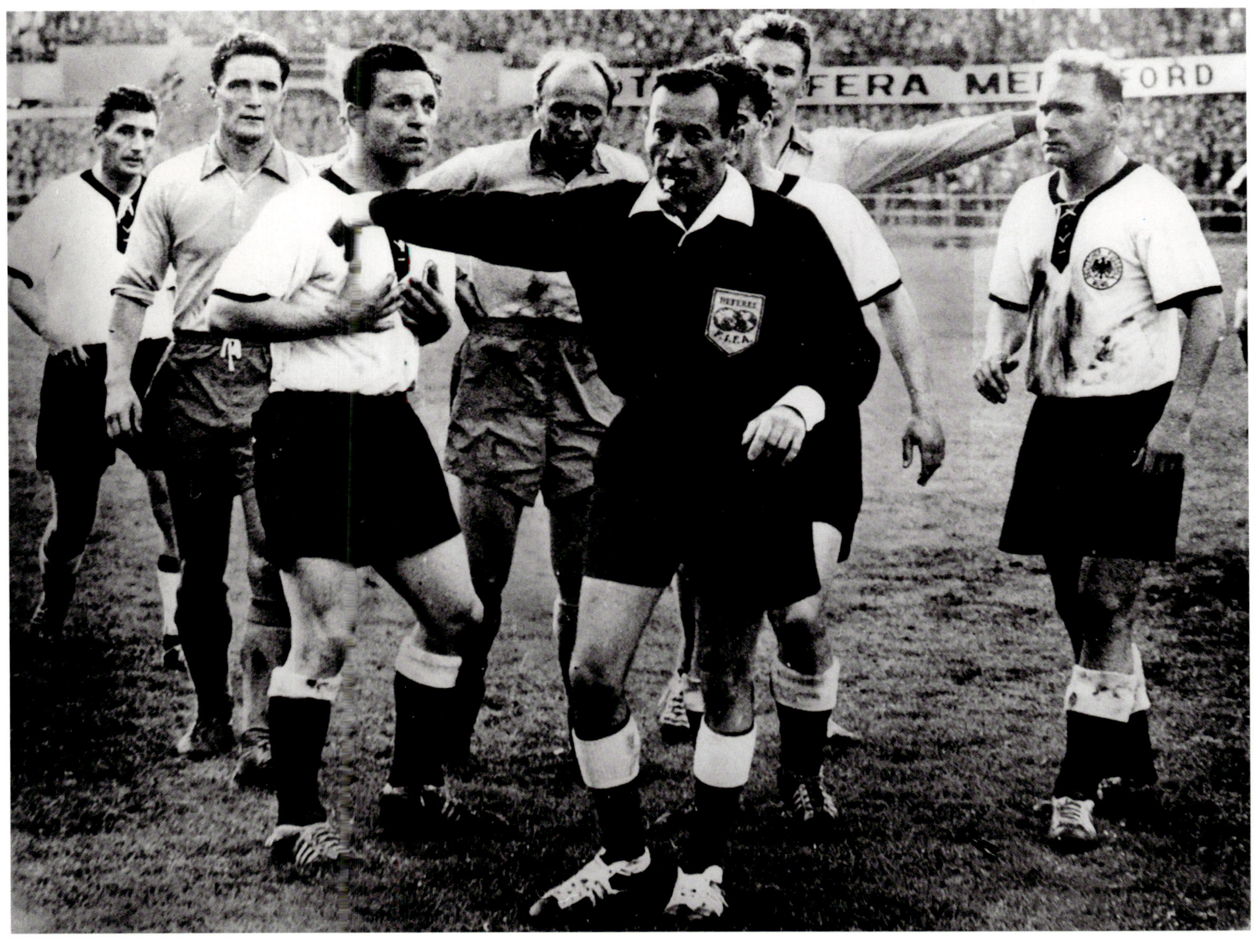

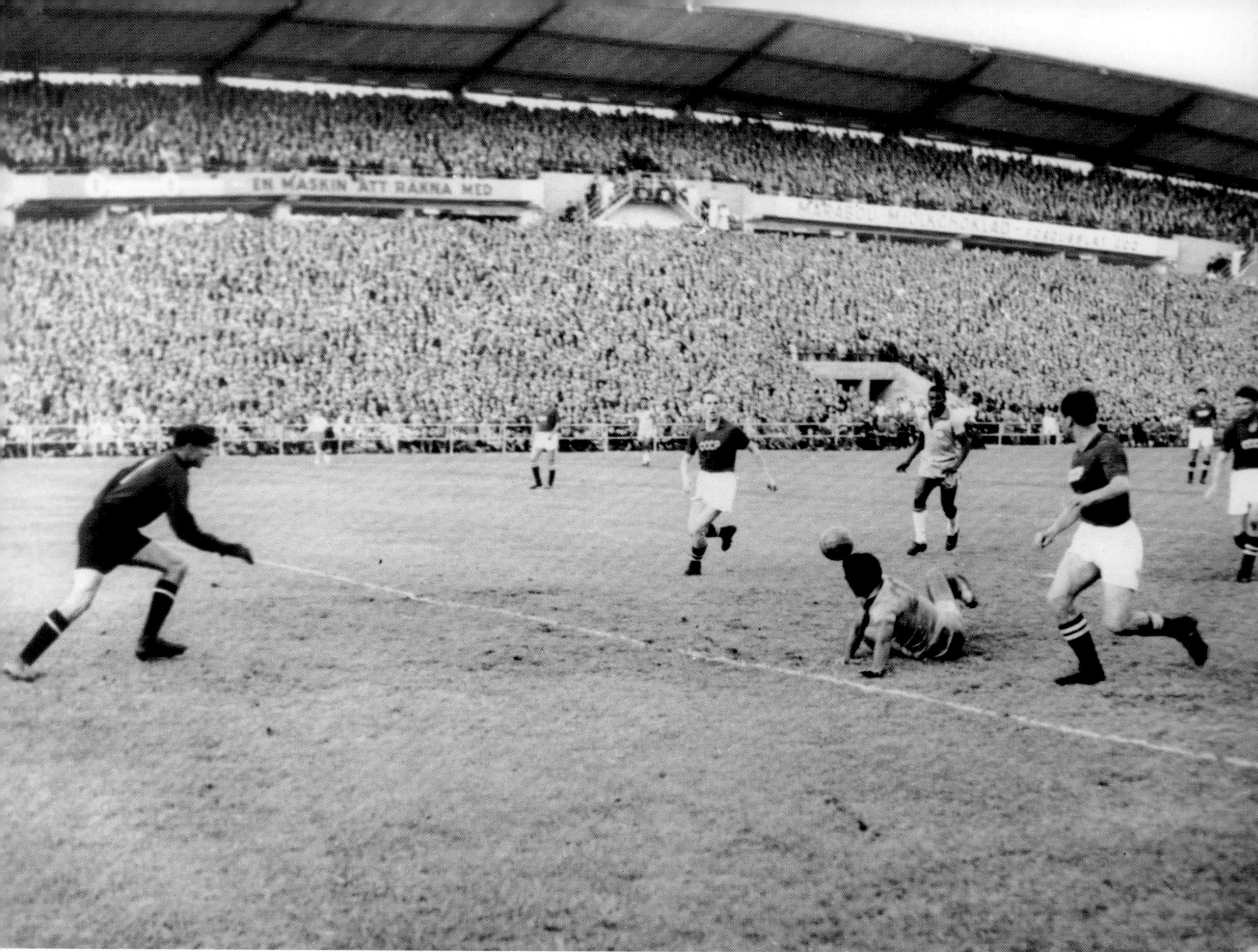

**ABOVE** *Brazil's attacking duo of Pelé and Vavá applied constant pressure to Lev Yashin and the Soviet back line.*

**OPPOSITE** *Pelé in 1961, playing for his club team Santos FC. Even at just twenty-one years of age, many fans and pundits were already crowning him the greatest footballer to ever live.*

# A LEGEND ON THE LAUNCH PAD

**By career's end, Pelé would be** crowned *O Rei* (the King), but Sweden 1958 is where it all began. His debut was about as auspicious as they come. Nursing a knee injury, the young star was held out of Brazil's first two group matches but would see action in the third, when manager Vicente Feola inserted him into the line-up against the Soviet Union. He didn't score, but he assisted star-striker Vavá's second goal and impressed fans and football press alike with his elevated level of play.

In his next appearance, a hard-fought quarter-final matchup versus Wales, the budding phenom scored the game's only goal in the sixty-sixth minute. It was a truly stunning effort — Pelé received the ball on his chest with back to goal, flipped it masterfully past a defender as he spun, and then struck it right-footed off the first bounce, slotting it perfectly into the left corner. The goal not only lifted Brazil into the semi-finals but also made him, at the age of 17 years and 239 days, the youngest player ever to score in a World Cup match. Not surprisingly, that record still holds heading into the 2026 World Cup.

Brazil's semi-final against France turned into Pelé's true breakout performance. With his side clinging to a precarious 2–1 lead in the second half, Pelé went on a veritable rampage, scoring in the fifty-second, sixty-fourth, and seventy-fifth minutes to put Brazil up 5–1. It was a masterful display of cat-quick bursts and quick-touch finishing, first tapping in a pair of loose balls near the goal and then ramming home a full-swinging blast from the top of the box.

Later, the great Frenchman Just Fontaine, a World Cup immortal in his own right, had this to say: 'When I saw Pelé play, it made me feel I should hang up my boots.'

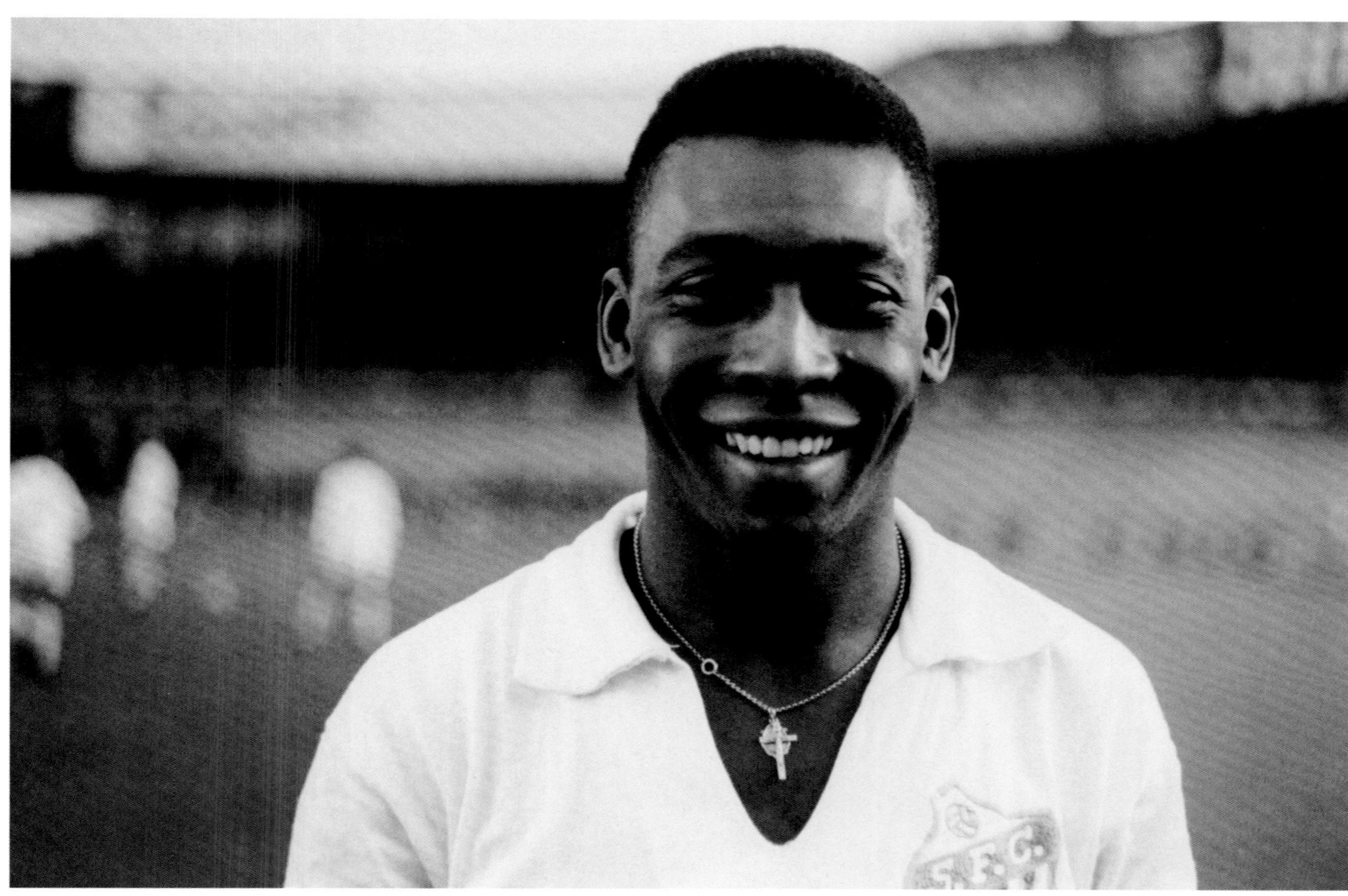

# FINAL

Brazil 5 | 2 Sweden (First Place)
France 6 | 3 West Germany
| (Third Place)

Incredibly, Just Fontaine scored four more goals against West Germany, bringing his grand total to thirteen for the tournament, a record that still stands today. For his part, Pelé scored a brace in Brazil's victory. Ironically, one match would see polar-opposite goal-scoring records: Pelé's goals against Sweden make him the youngest goal-scorer in a World Cup Final (17 years, 249 days), whereas Nils Liedholm's goal against Brazil in the same match makes him the oldest goal scorer in a World Cup Final (35 years, 264 days).

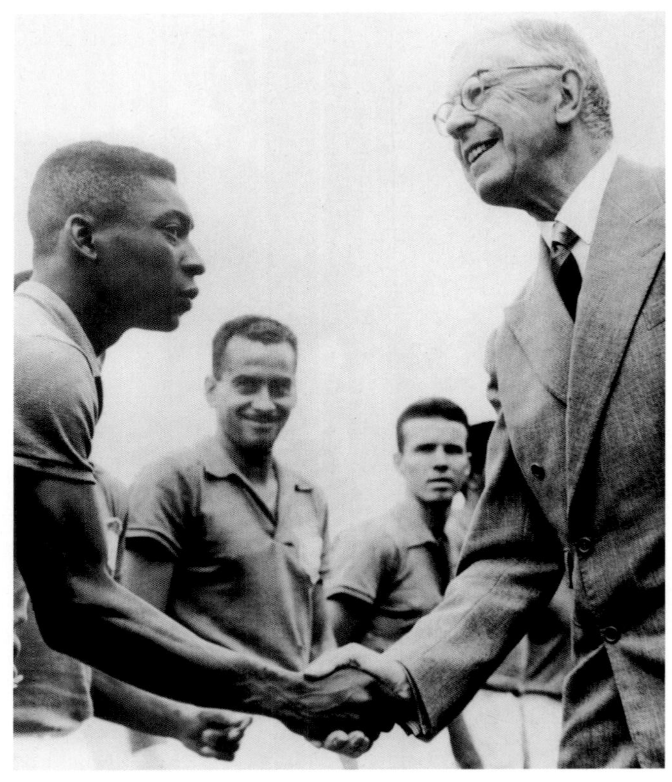

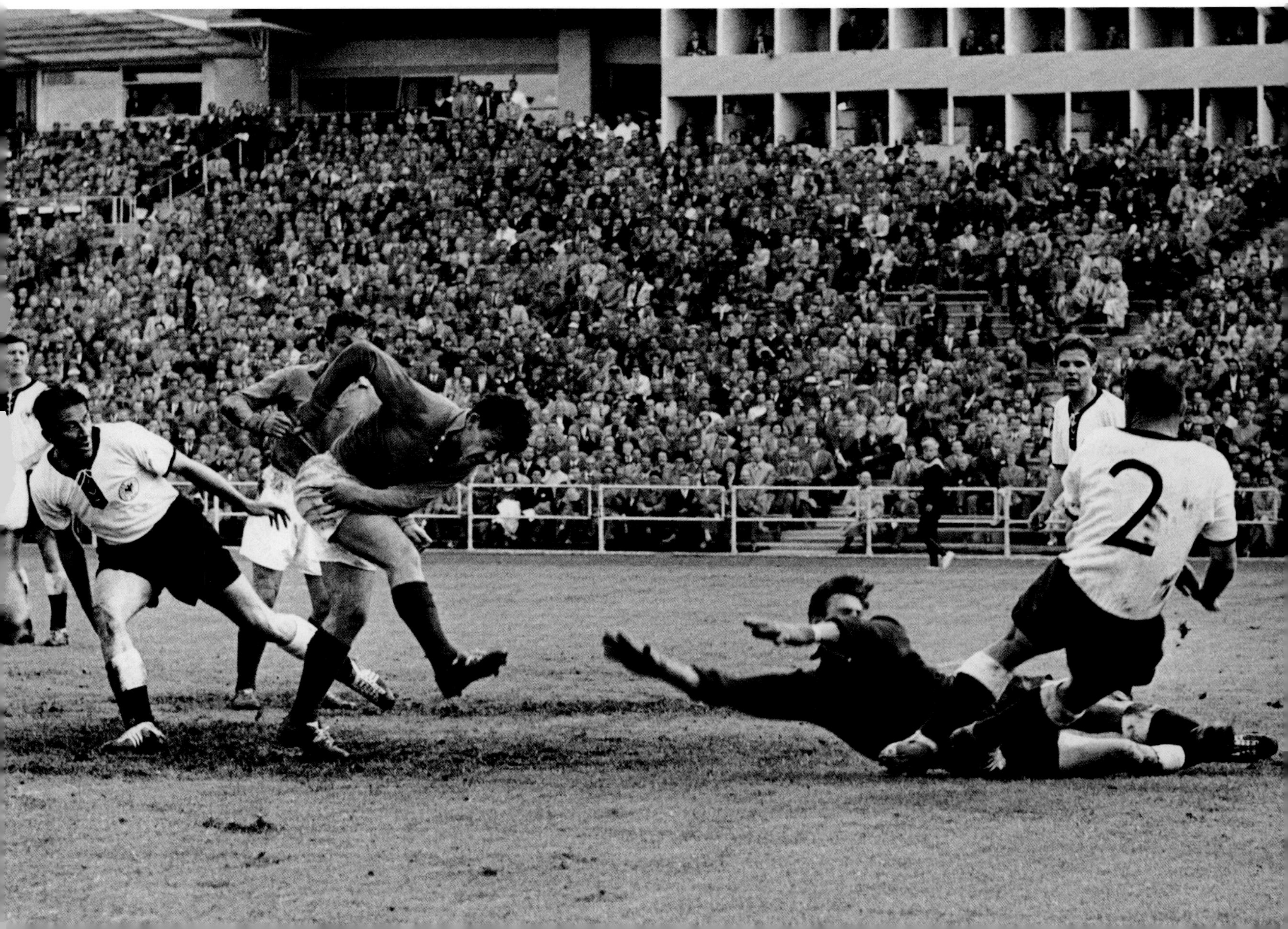

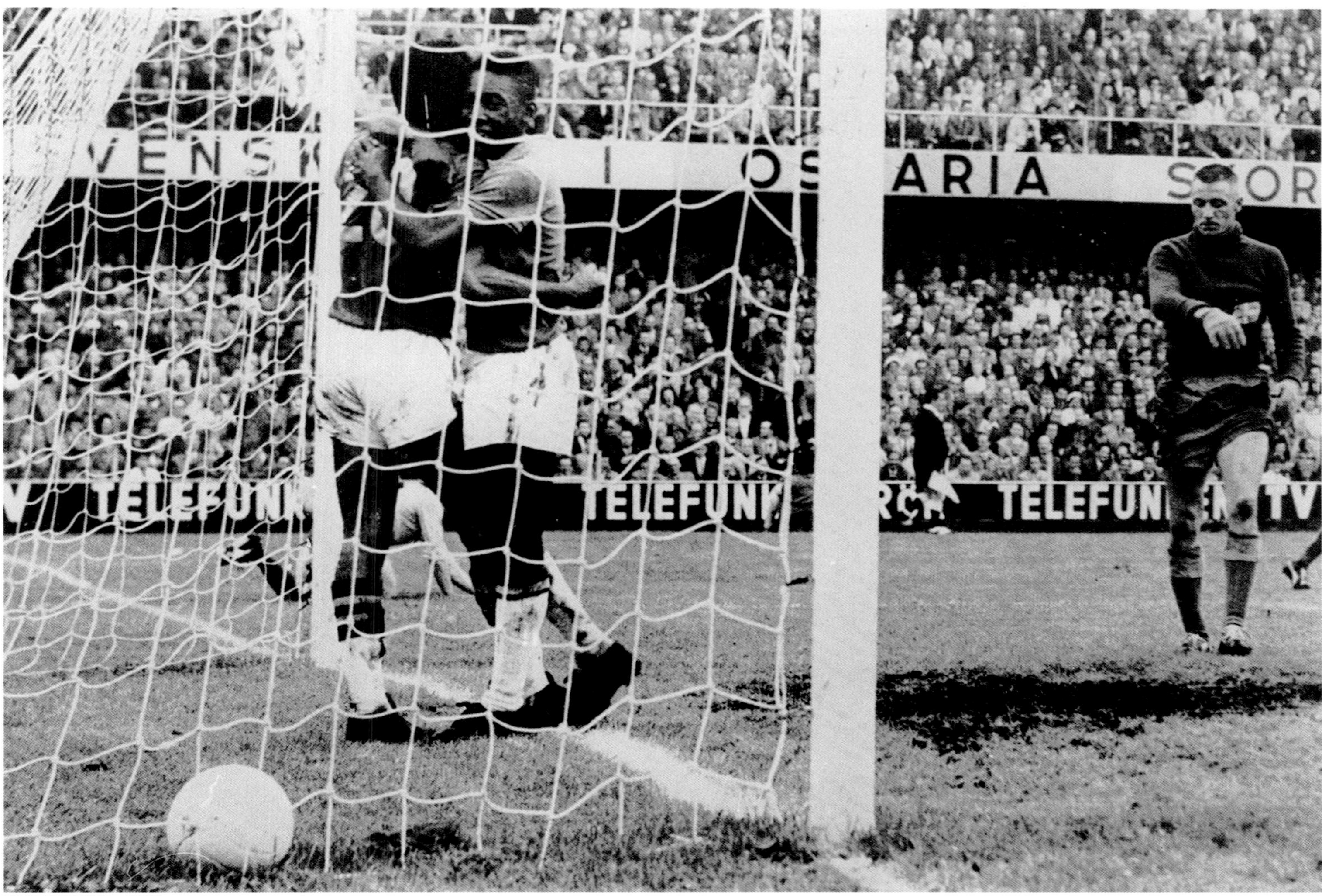

# BRAZIL ASCENDANT AT LAST

**Played in Råsunda Stadium** near Stockholm, the 1958 World Cup Final matched the host team Sweden against Brazil, a rising football power that had finally reached the sport's pinnacle moment. Both teams had yellow kits, but Brazil had no alternate colour to wear. So, after losing the draw for colour choice, Brazil's staff rushed into Stockholm to buy twenty-two blue T-shirts with numbers, then added the Brazilian emblem to each. It seemed like bad luck at first, as Swedish captain Nils Liedholm scored just four minutes into the game and sent the home crowd into joyous hysteria.

But Brazil's centre forward Vavá equalised just five minutes later and struck again before halftime to give his side a 2–1 lead. Then, ten minutes into the second half, young Pelé scored one of the most iconic goals in World Cup history. The Brazilian winger Garrincha sent a long looping cross into the box where Pelé outfought the hulking Swedish defender Sigge Parling to receive the pass on his chest. The ball bounced once on the ground, then Pelé lightly flicked it up and over the head of a second defender crashing on him. He ran around this defender — who kicked him hard in the thigh, a blatant foul that Pelé simply ignored — and calmly volleyed the dropping ball with a rocket past the diving Swedish keeper.

Sweden was essentially finished, but Pelé added to the tally with a header in the final minutes . . . and Brazil hoisted the Jules Rimet Trophy for the first time. After the match, Sigge Parling echoed how everyone felt: 'After the fifth goal, even I wanted to cheer for him.'

**OPPOSITE TOP** *Pelé shakes hands with Swedish King Gustaf VI Adolf.*

**OPPOSITE BOTTOM** *Just Fontaine scores his second goal of the match.*

*As in the rest of the tournament, Fontaine was unplayable in the third-place match — he would score two more before the final whistle.*

**ABOVE** *Pelé and Vavá embrace after one of Vavá's goals in the final against Sweden. They would each score two in the match.*

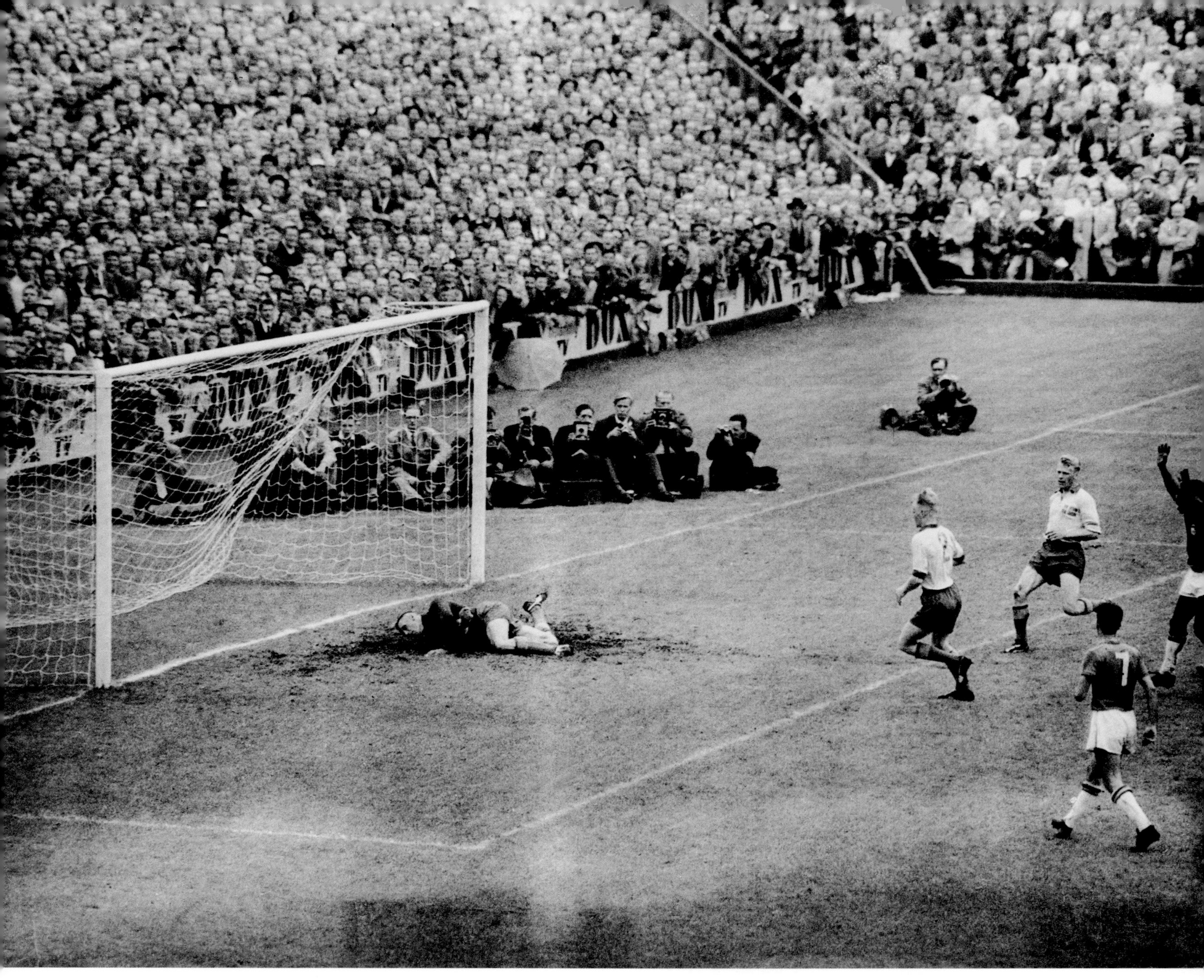

**ABOVE** *Pelé elated after scoring his team's fifth, and final, goal against Sweden.*

**OPPOSITE** *The young Pelé (centre) in an emotional celebration with older teammates Djalma (left) and Gilmar (right).*

*'Brazil atop the winner's podium—
a spot that would become a second
home for the South American giants.'*


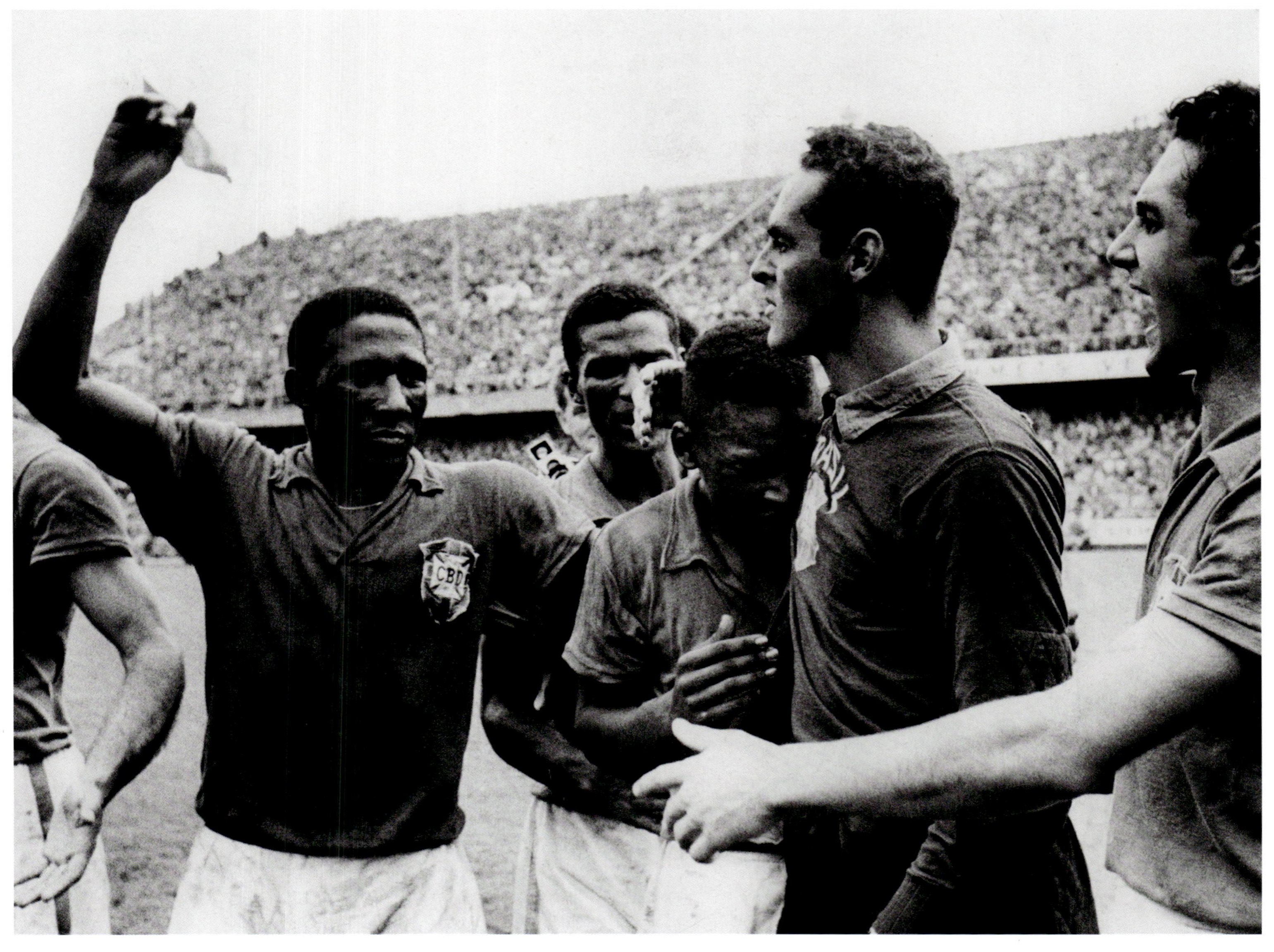

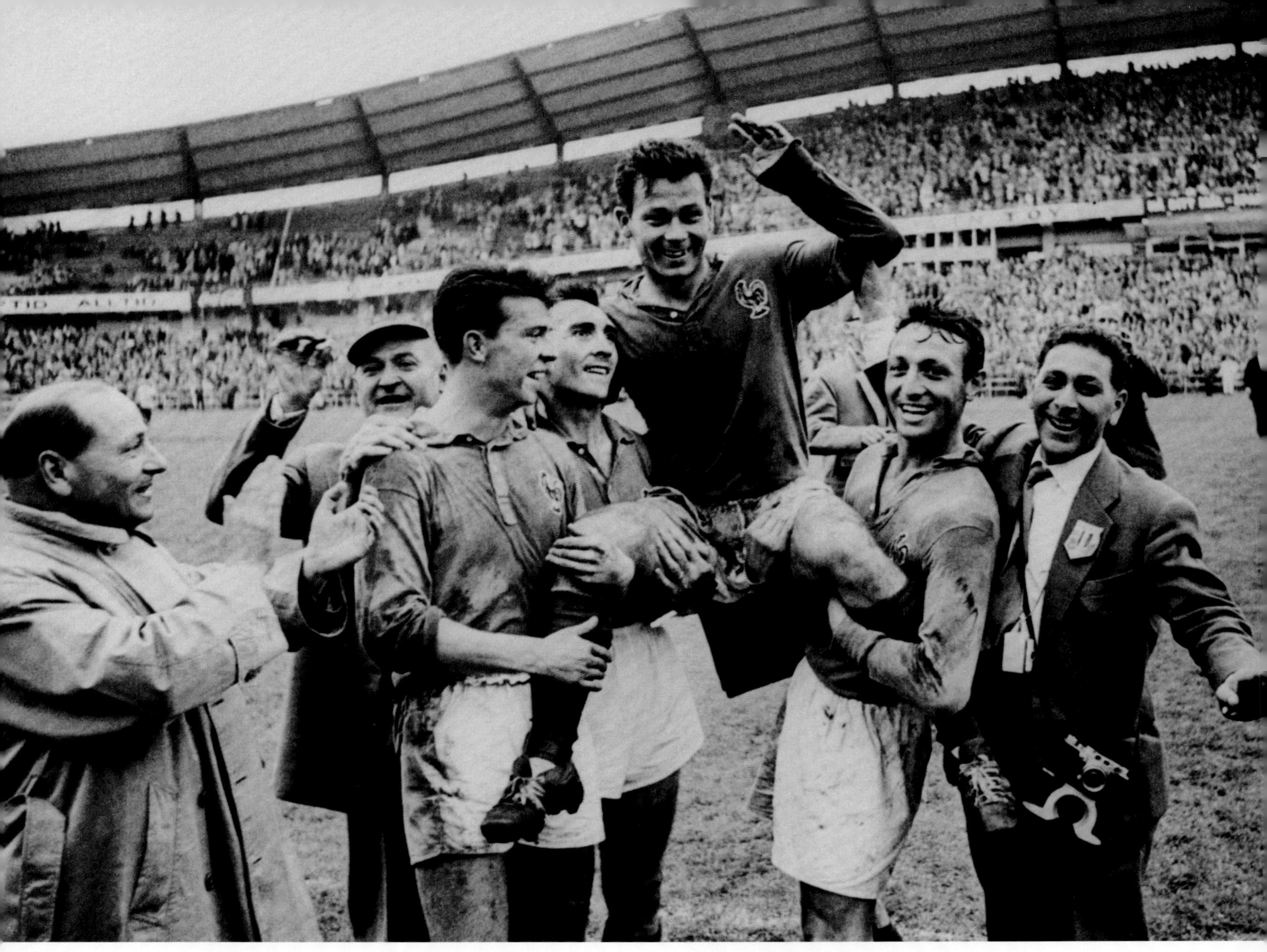

## A RECORD FOR THE AGES

**Prolific French striker Just Fontaine** opened the 1958 World Cup tournament with a blazing performance, serving up a clever hat-trick against Paraguay. He followed that in Group 2 play with a brace against Yugoslavia, and then another goal against Scotland, for a total of six goals in group play. In the quarter-finals, he added *another* brace in a victory over Northern Ireland and tacked on one more goal in France's semi-final loss to Brazil, where he was unfortunately overshadowed by Pelé's brilliant hat-trick.

However, Fontaine saved his best for last. In the third-place match against West Germany, he ended the tournament in glorious fashion with four stunning goals, two in each half, to help give France a 6–3 victory. Paired with his opening hat-trick, the performances made for an exquisite pair of World Cup bookends for the French superstar. And his grand total of thirteen goals still stands as the most ever scored by a player in a single World Cup tournament.

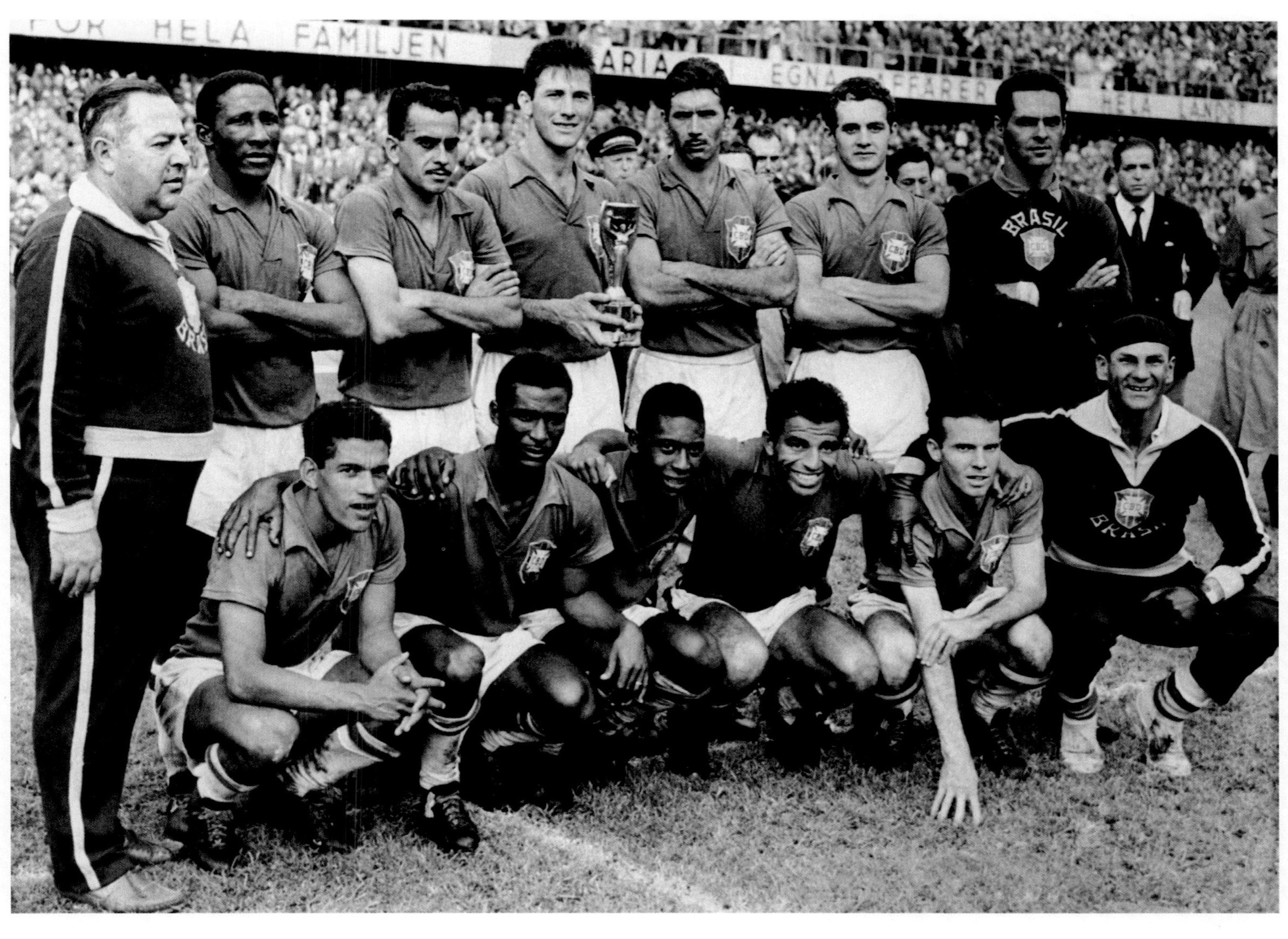



**OPPOSITE** *Just Fontaine lifted by teammates following his record-breaking performance at the 1958 World Cup.*

**ABOVE** *The legendary 1958 squad was Brazil's first to bring home the World Cup Trophy.*

# THE 1960s

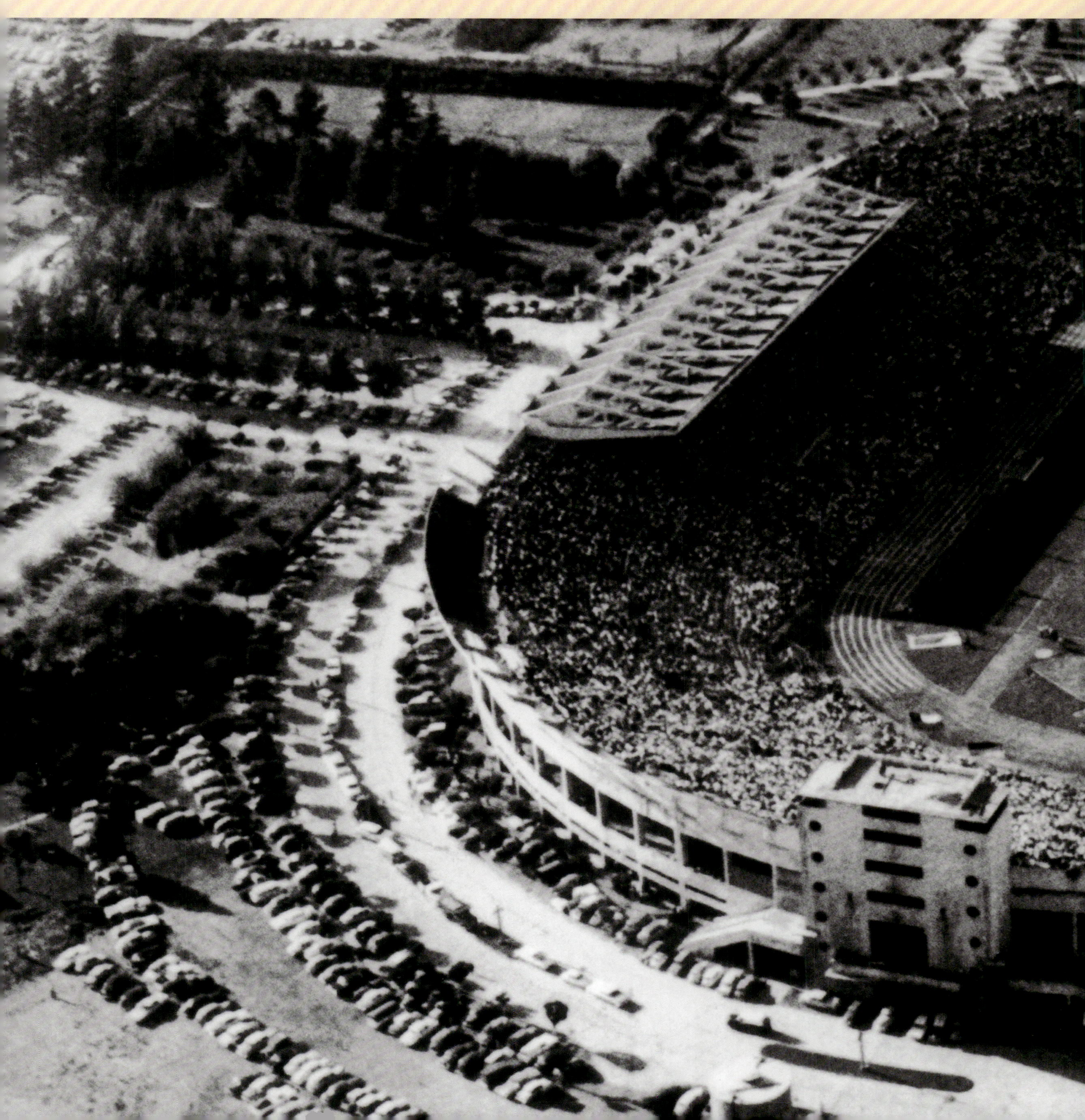

# CHAPTER 4

# The Cup Goes Global

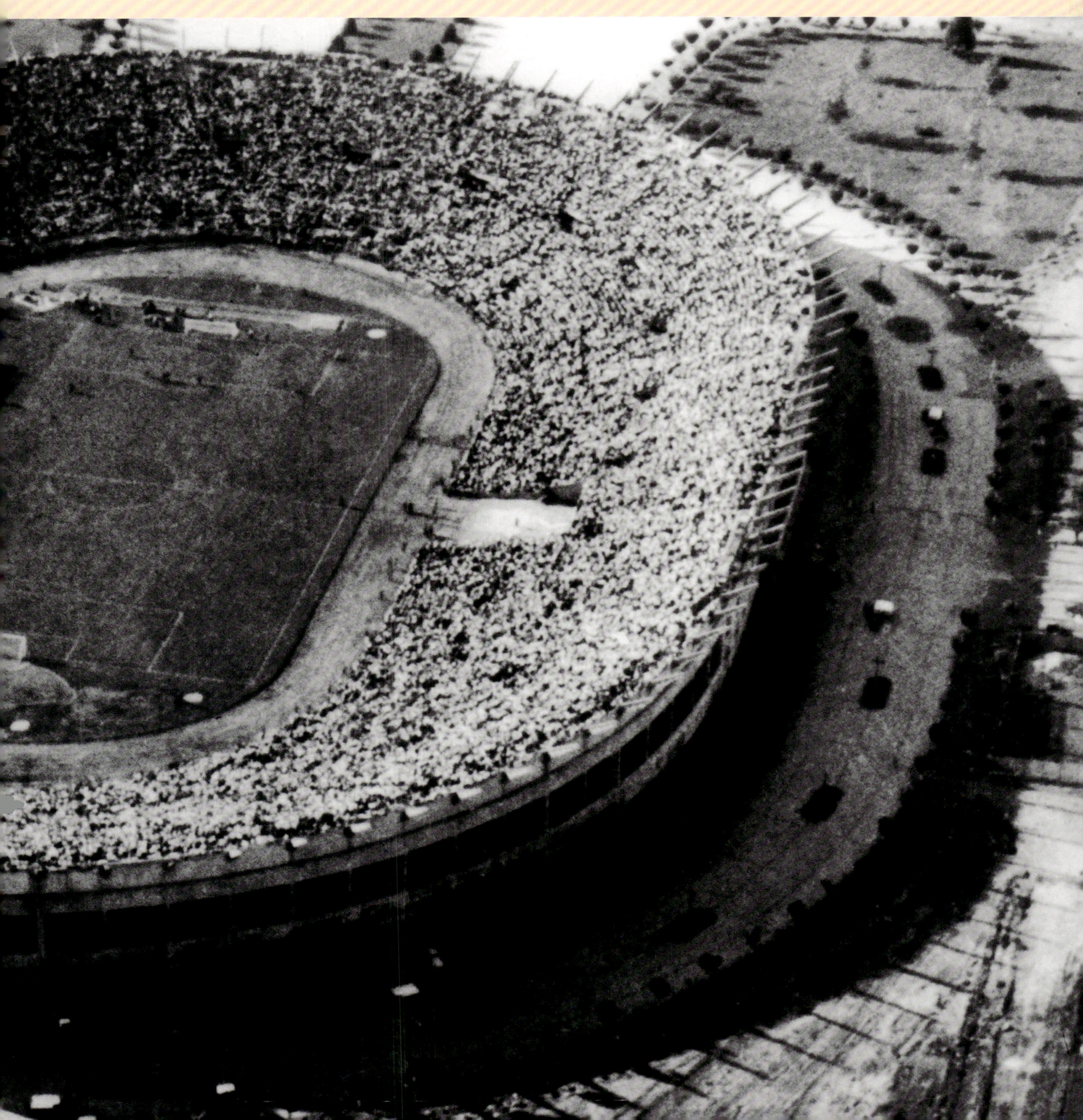

# 1962

HOST COUNTRY:  **CHILE**
CHAMPION:  **BRAZIL**
RUNNER-UP:  **CZECHOSLOVAKIA**
THIRD PLACE:  **CHILE OVER YUGOSLAVIA**

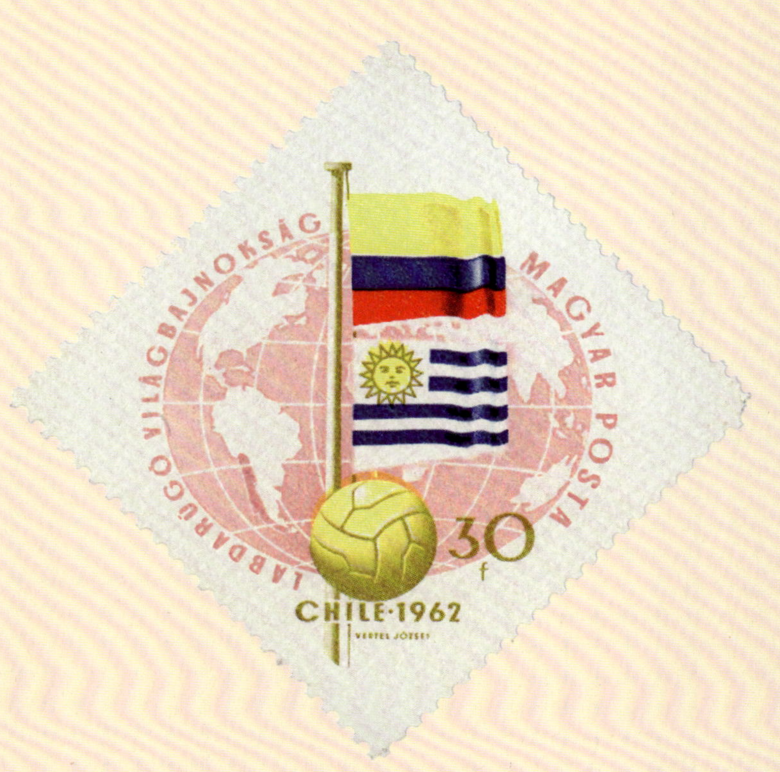
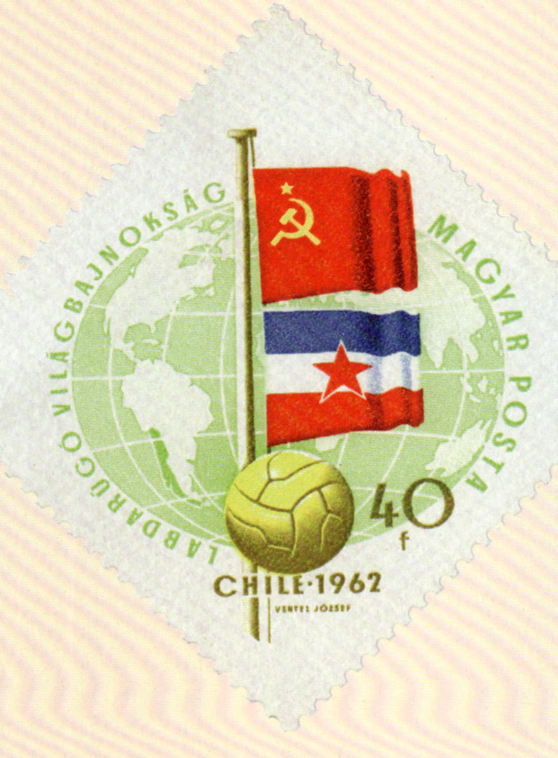

**Politics being politics, even in sports** — and with FIFA's machinations known to rival those of any state — controversies arose once again during the selection process for the 1962 host country. Because Europe had hosted the previous two World Cups, the American football federations threatened a total boycott if the 1962 tournament wasn't held in South America. FIFA certainly appreciated this position and made Argentina the early favourite. But to the great surprise of the Lisbon FIFA Congress, a Chilean delegation presented a remarkably convincing case . . . and the overwhelming majority of voters selected Chile as the 1962 host country.

**PREVIOUS SPREAD** *The Estadio Nacional in Santiago, Chile.*

**ABOVE** *Hungarian stamps for the 1962 World Cup in Chile, designed by József Vertel. The left stamp displays the flags of Colombia and Uruguay. The right stamp displays the flags of the USSR and Yugoslavia.*

**OPPOSITE** *Puerto Montt in June of 1961, one of the many cities devastated by the Great Chilean Earthquake.*

# A SHAKEN HOST

**The initial announcement** of this honour was met with widespread joy in Chile, but the euphoria was shattered on 22 May, 1960. That afternoon, large swaths of Chile—more than 388,000 square kilometres—were devastated by the Valdivia megathrust earthquake and subsequent tsunamis. Measured at 9.4 to 9.6 on the magnitude scale, the *Gran terremoto de Chile* (Great Chilean Earthquake) shook the ground for ten terrifying minutes. This was followed by tsunami waves up to 24 metres high that hammered Chile's southern coastline. Today, the 1960 Valdivia earthquake remains the most powerful ever recorded.

Four of the eight Chilean stadiums originally chosen to host World Cup matches were severely damaged and discarded as venues, even though the tournament was still two years off. The Chilean government, faced with a monumental recovery task, was forced to dial back its support for the tournament logistics. But the Chilean football federation was resolute after determining that the four unaffected stadiums—including flagship Estadio Nacional in Santiago, with its capacity of 75,000—were sufficient to host the thirty-two Cup matches that would be played. Damaged infrastructure was rebuilt with impressive speed over the two years leading up to the opening match kickoff: Chile versus Switzerland.

Amazingly, Chile's World Cup tournament proceeded on schedule, marked by first-rate organisation and warm hospitality. Unfortunately, the host's heroic resilience was occasionally overshadowed by a few unruly teams and their undisciplined on-field antics.

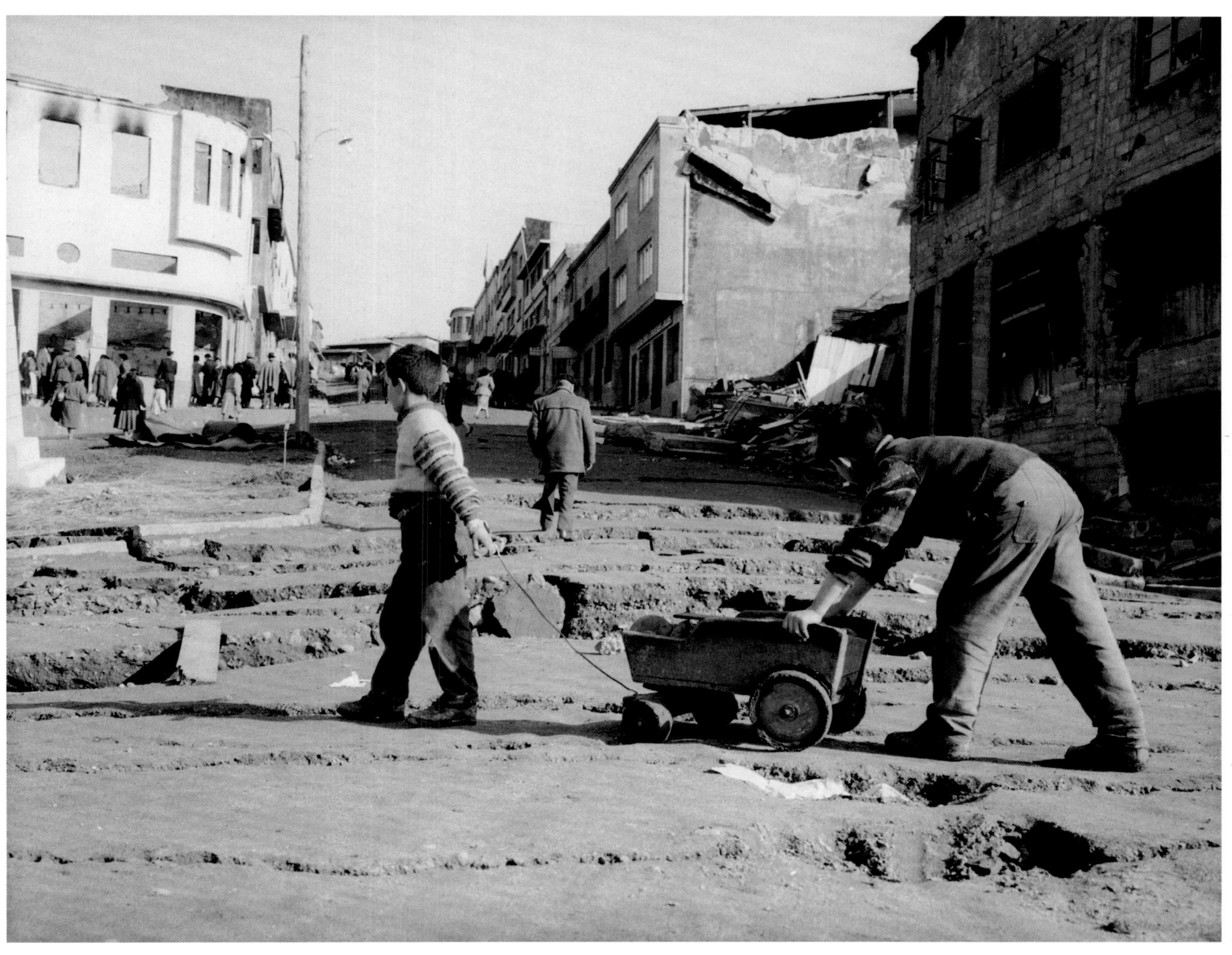

# Tournament: GROUP STAGE

### GROUP 1: SOVIET UNION, YUGOSLAVIA, URUGUAY, COLOMBIA

| | | |
|---|---|---|
| Uruguay 2 | 1 | Colombia |
| Soviet Union 2 | 0 | Yugoslavia |
| Yugoslavia 3 | 1 | Uruguay |
| Soviet Union 4 | 4 | Colombia |
| Soviet Union 2 | 1 | Uruguay |
| Yugoslavia 5 | 0 | Colombia |

**Advanced to Knockout Stage: Soviet Union, Yugoslavia**

The 1962 tournament marked a distinctive shift in tactics, with an emphasis on defensively oriented football growing in prominence. Goal totals were still moderate in Group 1, but the scores in the other groups were historically low. The Soviets, led by now-legendary goalkeeper Lev Yashin, won the group with decisive performances.

### GROUP 2: WEST GERMANY, CHILE, ITALY, SWITZERLAND

| | | |
|---|---|---|
| Chile 3 | 1 | Switzerland |
| West Germany 0 | 0 | Italy |
| Chile 2 | 0 | Italy |
| West Germany 2 | 1 | Switzerland |
| West Germany 2 | 0 | Chile |
| Italy 3 | 0 | Switzerland |

**Advanced to Knockout Stage: West Germany, Chile**

As bad as the infamous 'Battle of Bern' was back in 1954—when Brazilian and Hungarian players, officials, and fans fought on the pitch and in the locker-room tunnels—the clash between Italy and host Chile in Santiago may have been even worse. And Italy's matches against West Germany and Switzerland were hardly any better.

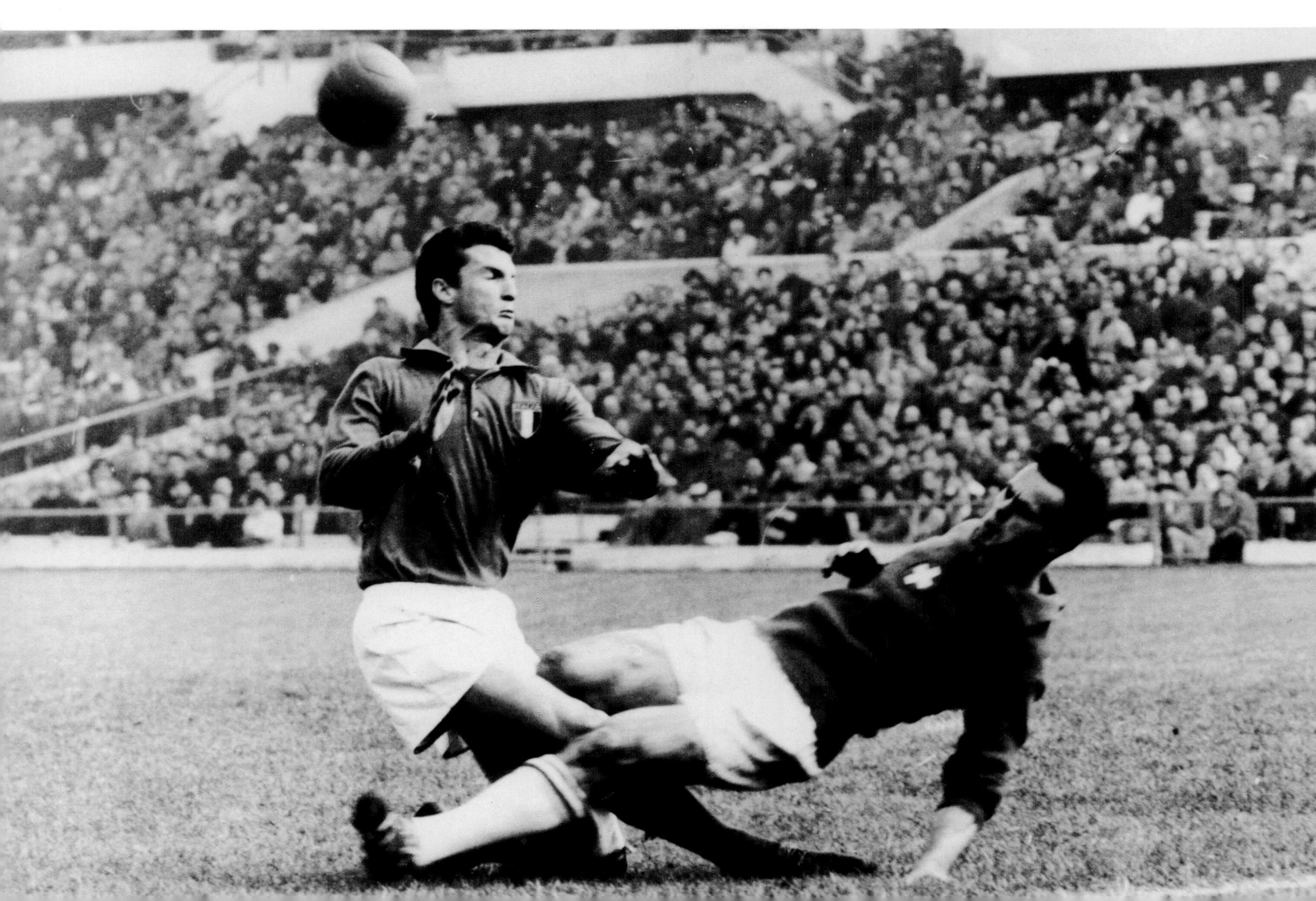

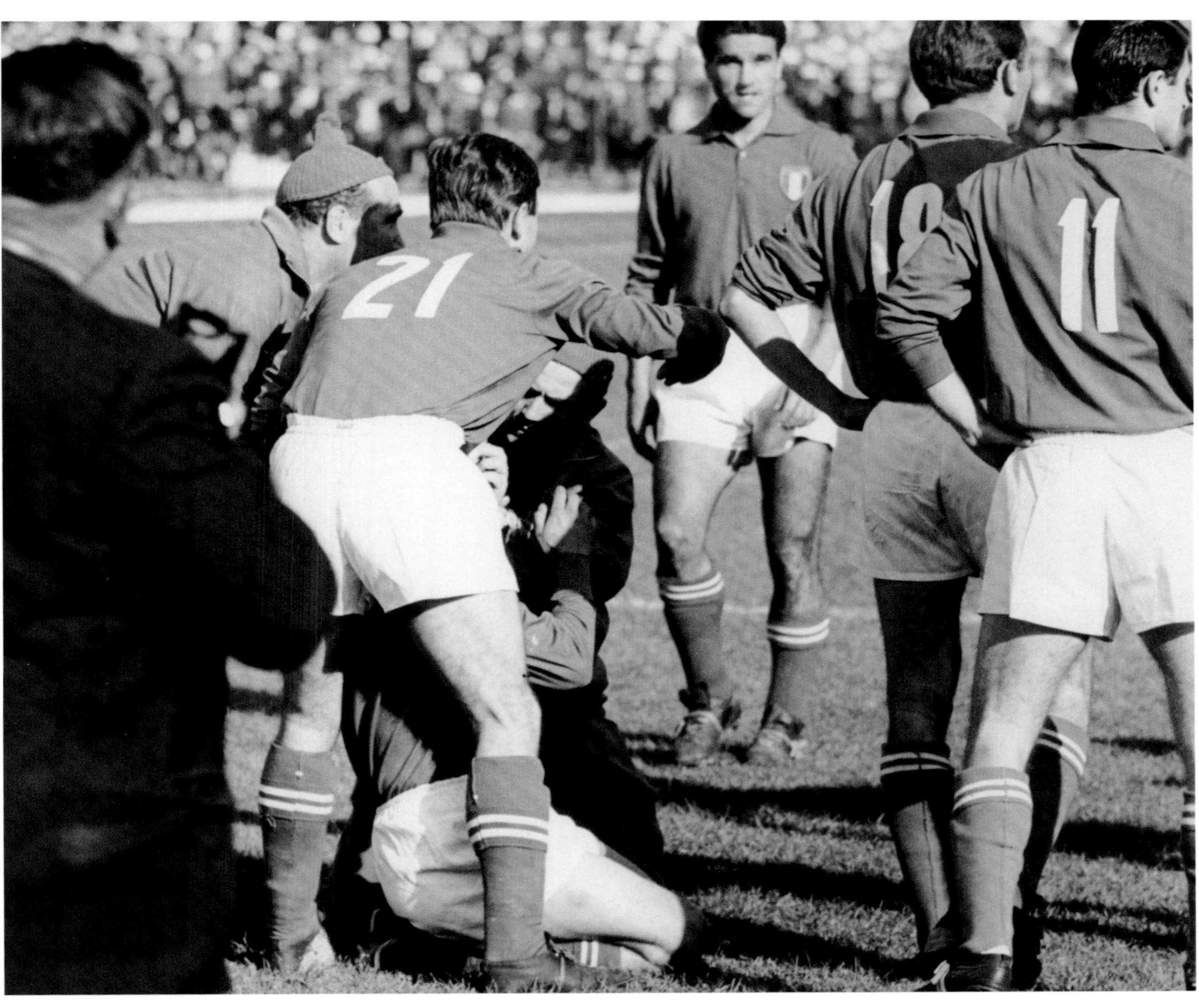



**OPPOSITE** *A rough challenge between Angelo Sormani of Italy (left) and Heinz Schneiter of Switzerland (right). Italy's 1962 squad became known for its physicality and, arguably, reckless play.*

**ABOVE** *La Batalla de Santiago between Italy and Chile. Here, Italian players check on a teammate who seems to have been injured.*

**FOLLOWING SPREAD, LEFT** *Germany's Willi Schulz lies on the ground after a tackle from an opposing player on the Italian side.*

**FOLLOWING SPREAD, RIGHT** *England's 1962 squad.*

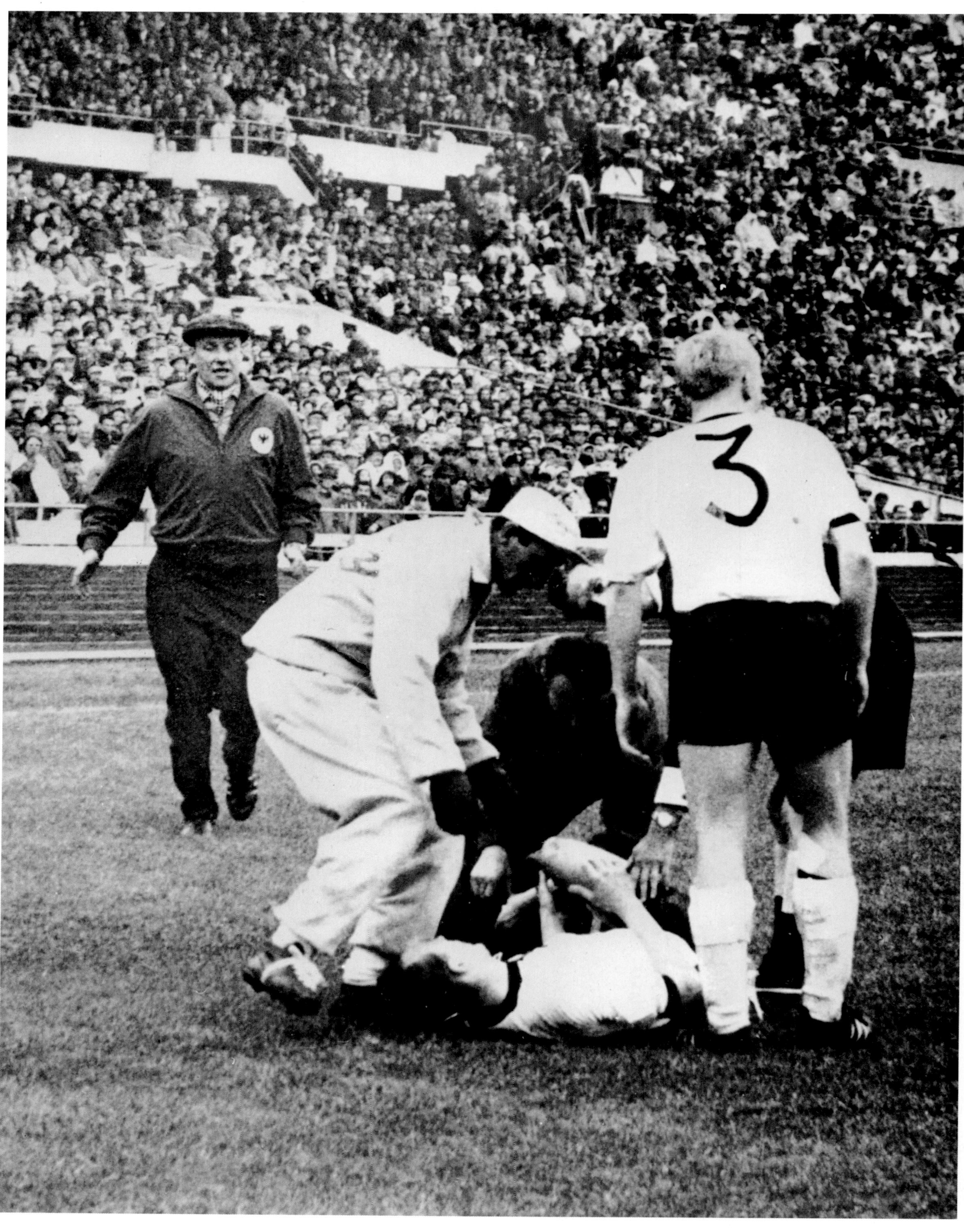

### GROUP 3: BRAZIL, CZECHOSLOVAKIA, MEXICO, SPAIN

| | | |
|---|---|---|
| Brazil 2 | 0 | Mexico |
| Czechoslovakia 1 | 0 | Spain |
| Brazil 0 | 0 | Czechoslovakia |
| Spain 1 | 0 | Mexico |
| Brazil 2 | 1 | Spain |
| Mexico 3 | 1 | Czechoslovakia |

**Advanced to Knockout Stage: Brazil, Czechoslovakia**

Just 1.83 goals per game for this group! Even more significant, or so it seemed at the time, was the tourney-ending thigh injury suffered by Brazil's twenty-one-year-old superstar Pelé against Czechoslovakia. It was a huge blow, as Pelé had already gotten off to a hot start by scoring against Mexico in the first game. In the end, however, other Brazilian players like Garrincha, Vavá, and Amarildo (the latter just twenty-three years old himself) rose up to guide their talented side through the tournament. Indeed, after a superlative performance, Garrincha emerged from the Cup as a super-star in his own right—the French newspaper *L'Équipe* described him as '[the] most extraordinary right winger football has known'. But in their final group-stage match, it was young Amarildo's second-half brace that rescued Brazil after falling behind Spain.

Also notable: Brazil never lost an international match when fielding both Pelé and Garrincha.

### GROUP 4: HUNGARY, ENGLAND, ARGENTINA, BULGARIA

| | | |
|---|---|---|
| Argentina 1 | 0 | Bulgaria |
| Hungary 2 | 1 | England |
| England 3 | 1 | Argentina |
| Hungary 6 | 1 | Bulgaria |
| Hungary 0 | 0 | Argentina |
| England 0 | 0 | Bulgaria |

**Advanced to Knockout Stage: Hungary, England**

With stalwart defence on the rise, Hungary's 6–1 thrashing of Bulgaria was a major outlier, as the rest of the matches averaged 1.6 goals. The last round of the round-robin saw the teams clamp down even more: the four teams produced exactly zero goals.

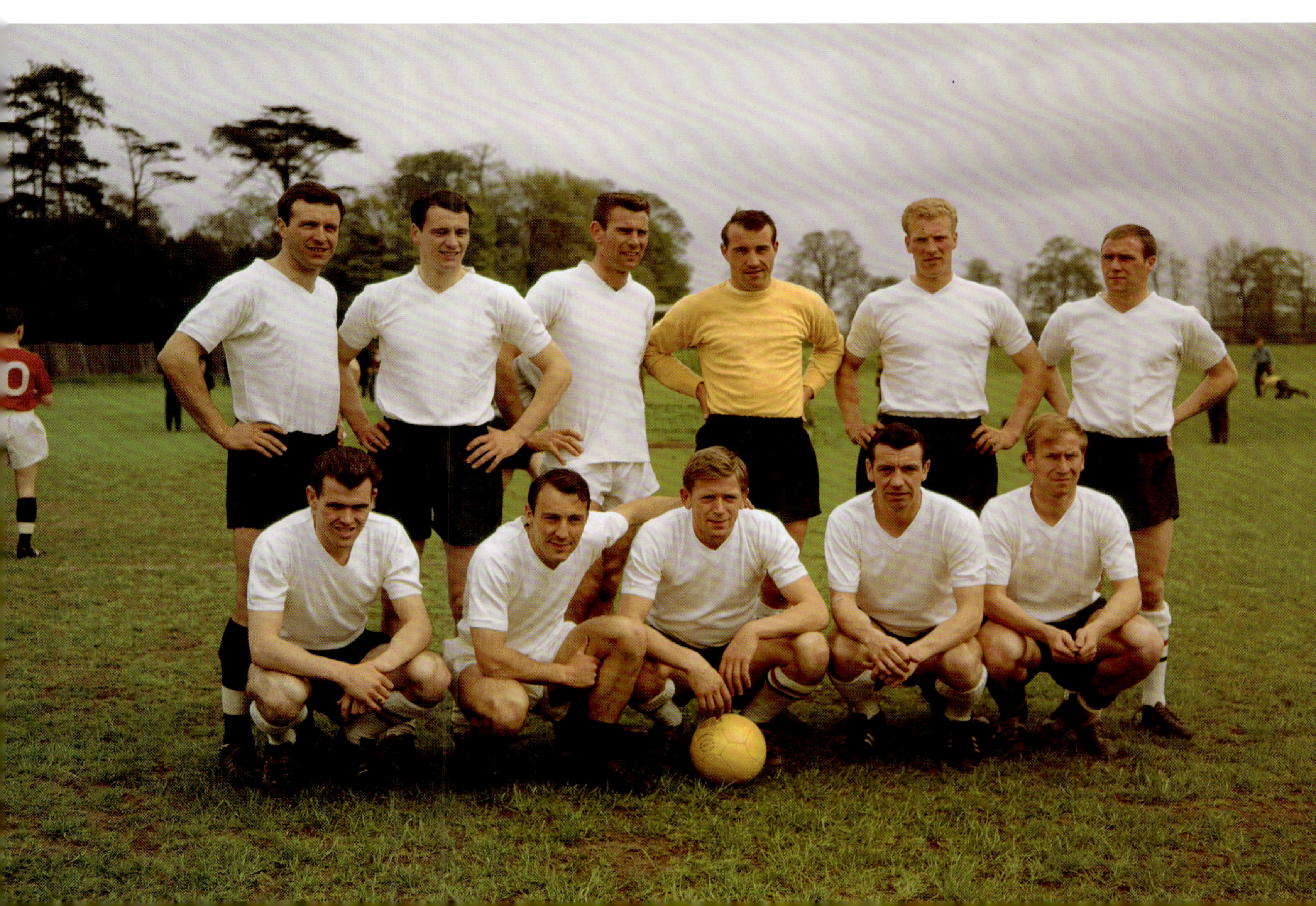

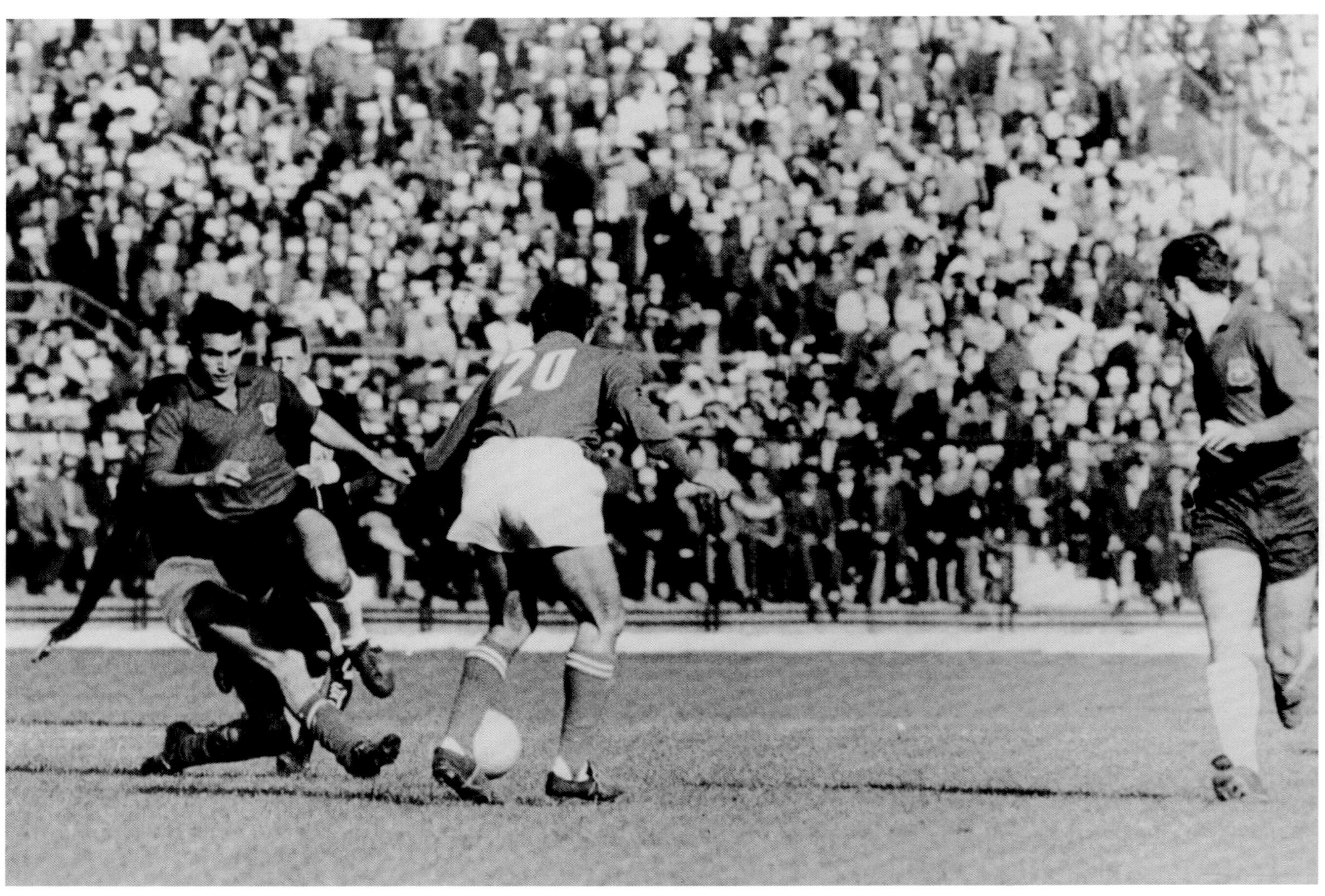

# WRESTLING AND WARFARE

**The pregame buildup** to the group-stage pairing of Chile versus Italy included some nasty, insulting commentary by the Italian media. Most distastefully, the journalist Corrado Pizzinelli described the host country as a backwater dump whose citizens were prone to illiteracy, poverty, prostitution, and crime. Chilean media hit back hard, with the tabloids *El Mercurio* and *Clarín de Santiago* reprinting the inflammatory Italian articles, trolling the Italians as fascist pigs whose players were cheaters caught up in a doping scandal and hyping the upcoming match as a 'World War' in their headlines. By game time, the rivalry was a powder keg that needed just the tiniest of sparks to ignite.

To the surprise of no one, the game started out bad and only got worse. The first brutal foul was called just twelve seconds into the match. The first ejection came at the eight-minute mark, but the Italian player Giorgio Ferrini refused to leave. A phalanx of police officers had to literally drag him off the pitch. As the match continued, play was regularly interrupted by fistfights, and multiple players ended up with facial contusions and broken noses. Police were forced to intervene on-field four separate times. Another Italian player, Mario David, was ejected later. Ultimately, Chile won the game 2–0 — and the match was instantly dubbed 'The Battle of Santiago'. Fittingly, Italy's team needed a police escort.

Sadly, the mayhem continued in Italy's next matchup. As the *London Express* put it: 'The tournament shows every sign of developing into a violent bloodbath. Reports read like battlefield dispatches; the Italy vs West Germany match was described as "wrestling and warfare".'

**ABOVE** *An Italian defender tackles a Chilean player from behind.*

**OPPOSITE** *Italy's Mario David is sent off.*

'The tournament shows every sign of
developing into a violent bloodbath.'
—THE LONDON EXPRESS

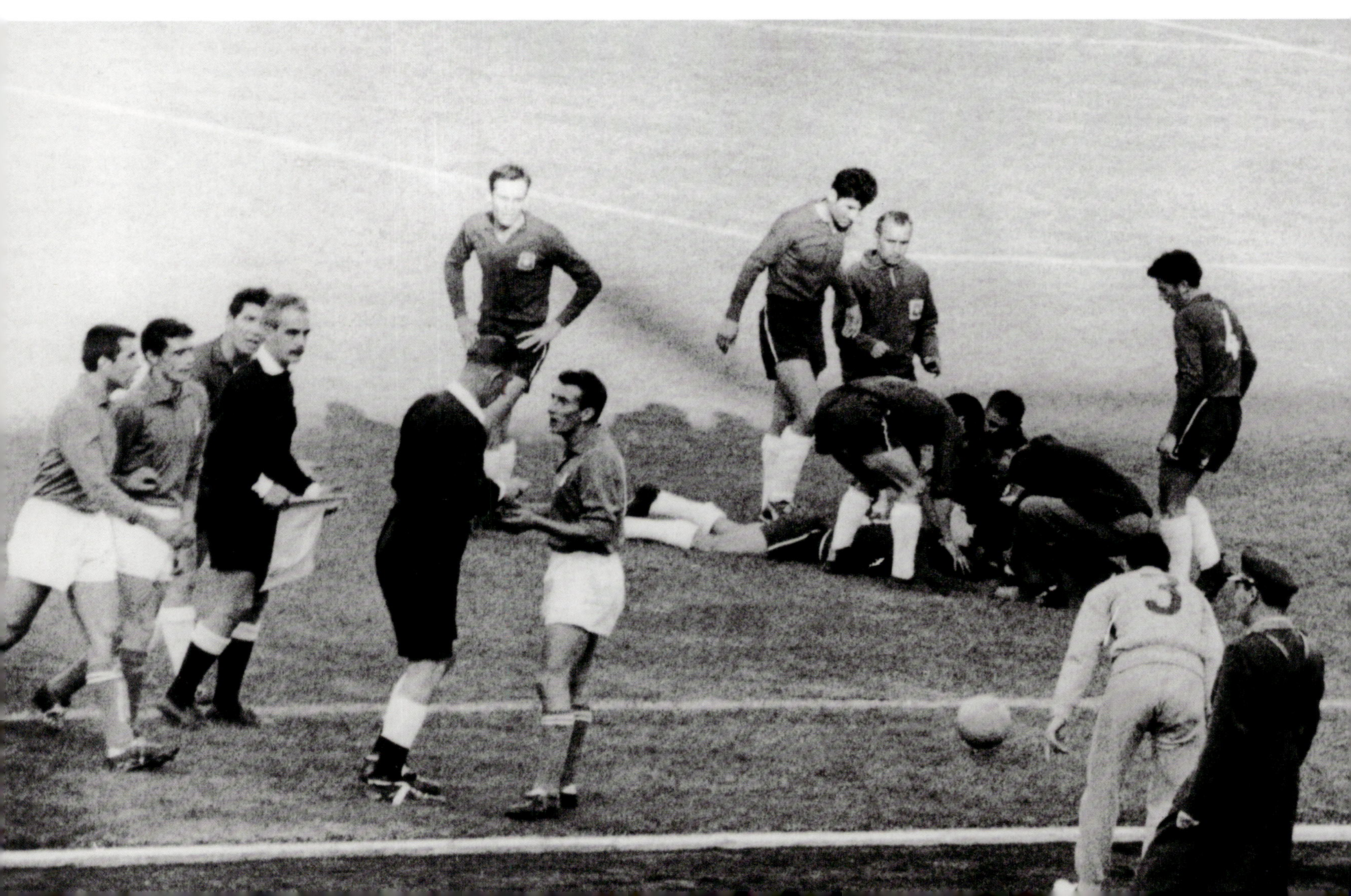

# QUARTER-FINALS

Chile 2 | 1 Soviet Union
Brazil 3 | 1 England
Yugoslavia 1 | 0 West Germany
Czechoslovakia 1 | 0 Hungary

In a highly anticipated matchup that lived up to its billing, Garrincha scored a brilliant brace and added an assist to lead Brazil over England, 3–1. An unstoppable flash down Brazil's right wing, Garrincha continued to emerge as the revelation of the tournament—the British press called him a 'snake charmer'. But the big excitement was home team Chile's 2–1 win over the Soviets to earn a semi-final matchup against the defending Cup champions.

On the other side of the draw, the two Slavic teams each won a tense, 1–0 defensive struggle against a tough European foe. The Czechs scored their goal early then went into a defensive shell (so common in this Cup). Hungary dominated the rest of the game but couldn't break through to score. Meanwhile, the Yugoslavs scored their winning goal with just five minutes left to grind past the disappointed West Germans, who had largely controlled the pace of play.

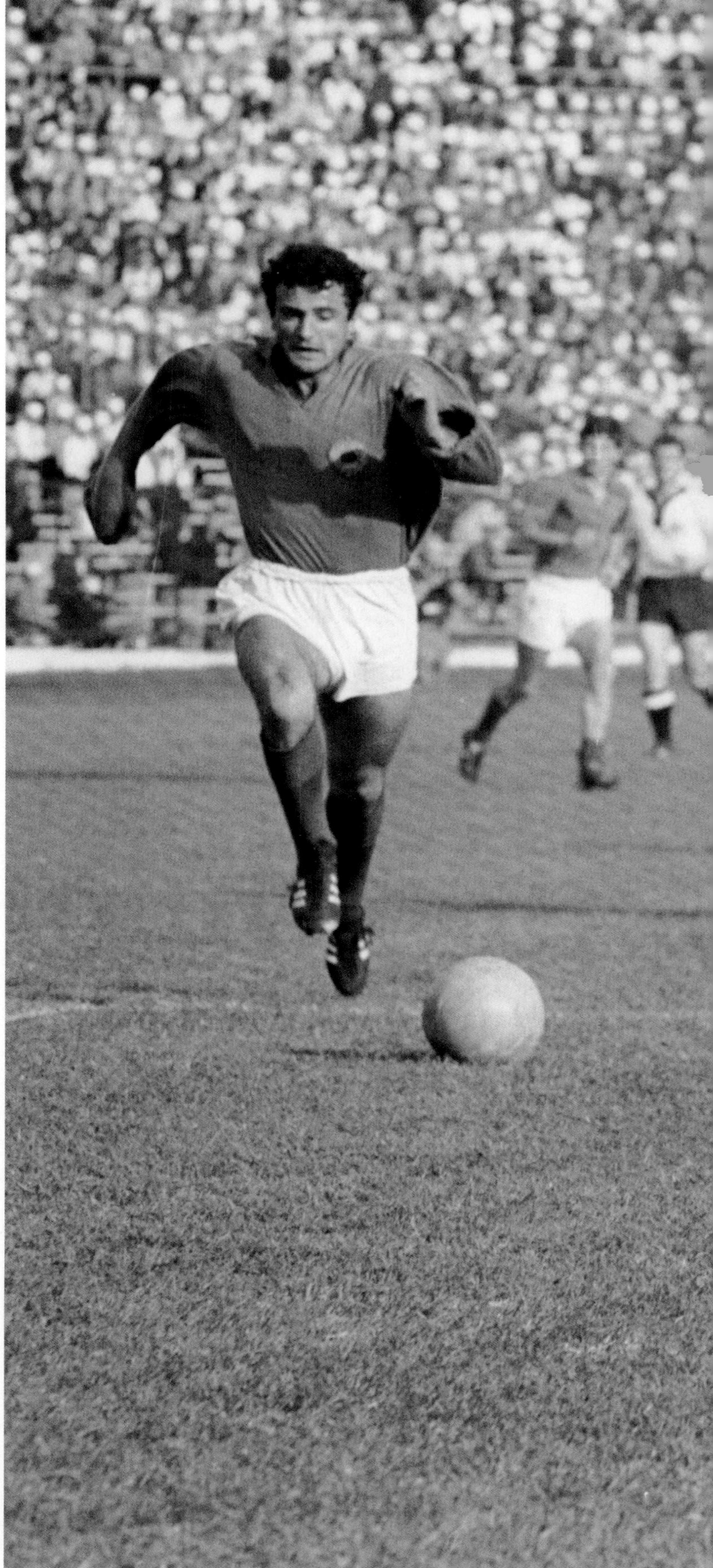

**OPPOSITE** *Yugoslavia's Milan Galić making a dynamic run on the ball as German defender Herbert Erhardt attempts to chase him down.*

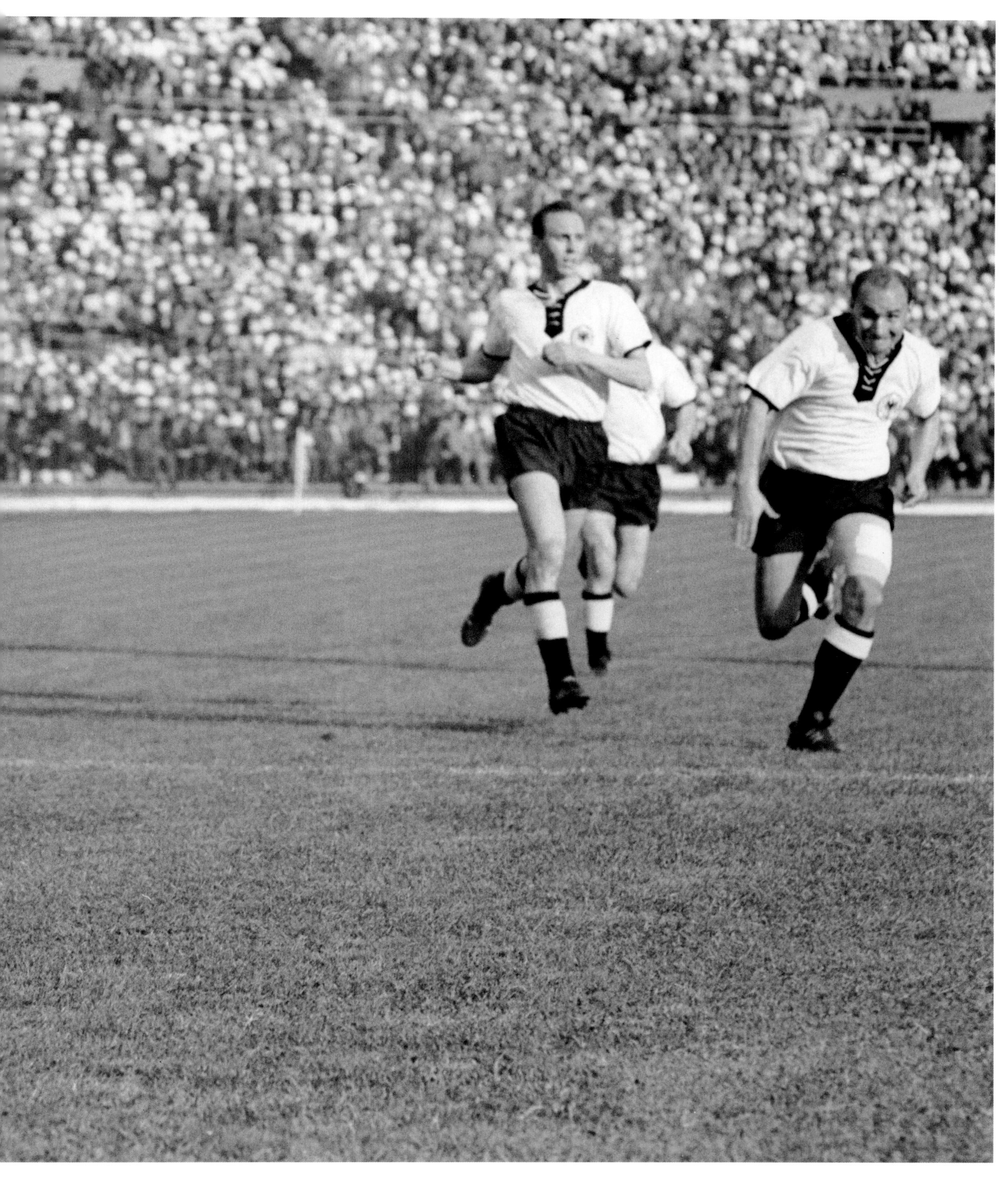

# SEMI-FINALS

Brazil 4 | 2 Chile
Czechoslovakia 3 | 1 Yugoslavia

In the first semi-final, both European teams started cautiously, leading to a 0–0 halftime score. The second half proved more engaging, as the Czechs scored right away and Yugoslavia equalised twenty-one minutes later. But Czech striker Adolf Scherer notched two goals in the final ten minutes to put Czechoslovakia in a World Cup Final for the second time.

In Santiago, the South American side of the draw was feisty, wide open, and quite entertaining. Chile tried to neutralise Brazil's superior talent with physicality, but it didn't work. Garrincha broke free with a first-half brace for the Brazilians and then Vavá did the same in the second half to wrap up an impressive 4–2 win over the host team and its large, enthusiastic home crowd at Estadio Nacional.

**BELOW** *Brazilian star Garrincha (far left) exits the pitch after being sent off by Peruvian referee Arturo Yamasaki (far right).*

**OPPOSITE** *Zito scores Brazil's second goal in the final with an acrobatic header over Czechoslovakian keeper Viliam Schrojf.*

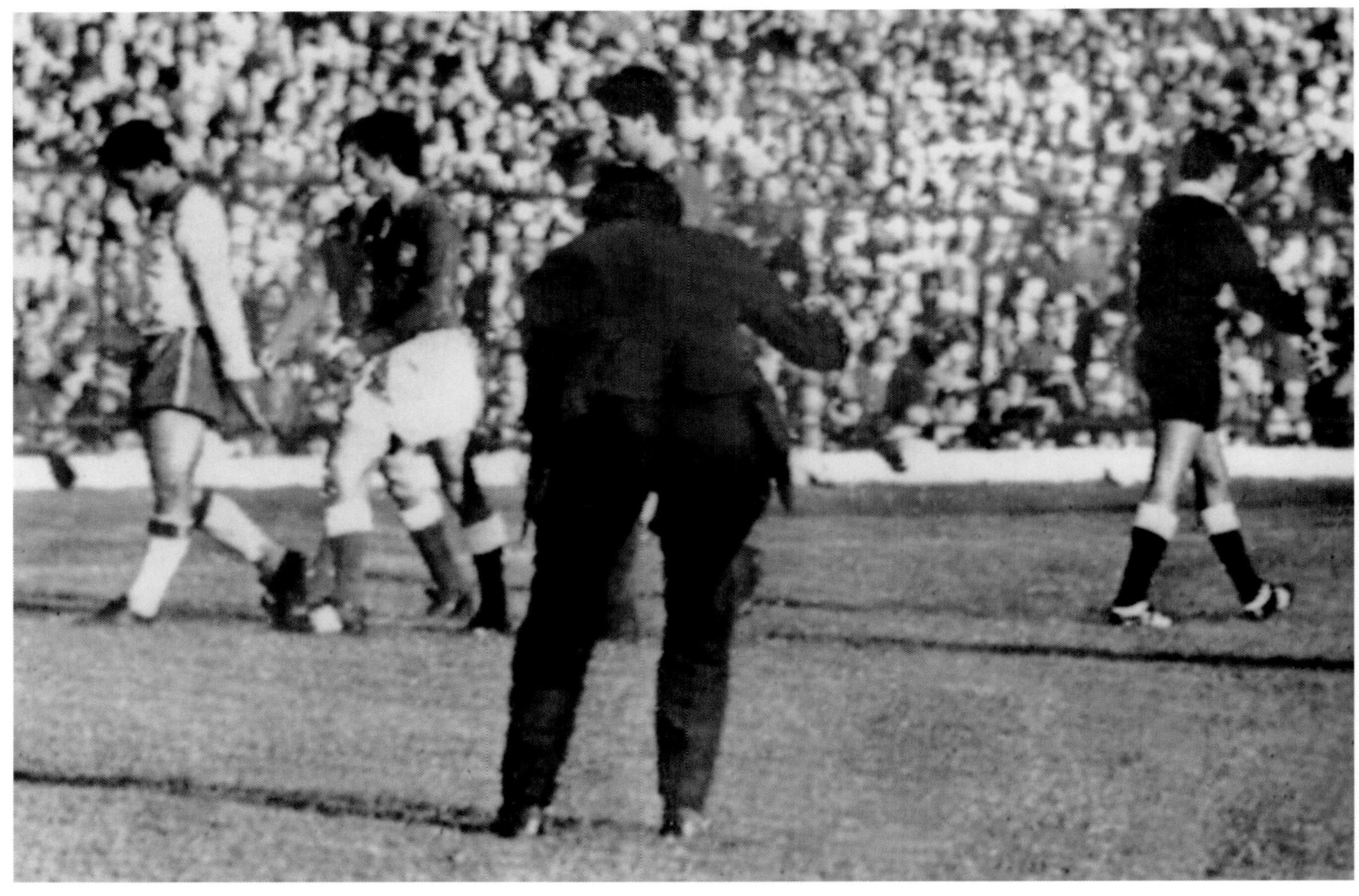

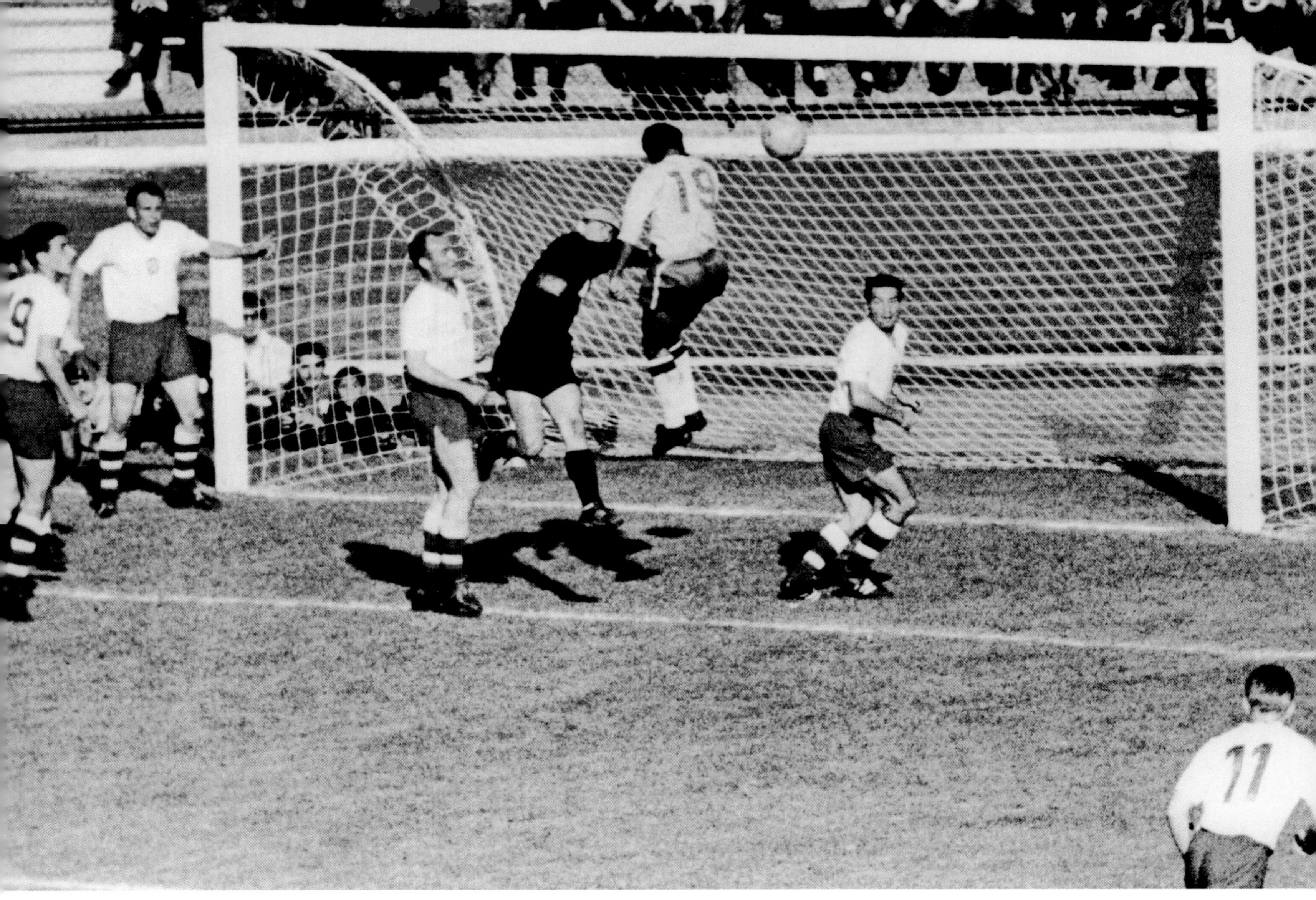

## FINAL

| | |
|---|---|
| Brazil 3 | 1 Czechoslovakia |
| | (First Place) |
| Chile 1 | 0 Yugoslavia |
| | (Third Place) |

Chile gave its loyal fans a truly thrilling experience in the third-place match against Yugoslavia. A tight, hard-fought game was deadlocked at 0–0 until the very final seconds when Chilean midfielder Eladio Rojas netted a shot that absolutely rocked the stadium. The victory triggered a joyous all-night celebration in Santiago.

The next day, 17 June, featured a Brazil–Czechoslovakia final that would be a rematch of their lacklustre 0–0 tie in group play two weeks earlier. The Czechs jumped out front after just fifteen minutes when Adolf Scherer slotted a perfect long pass through the Brazilian defence to mid-fielder Josef Masopust (later named the 1962 European Footballer of the Year), who beat the goalkeeper for a 1–0 lead. But Brazil struck back just two minutes later when Amarildo poked in a ball mishandled by the Czech keeper, Viliam Schrojf.

The teams went into the half tied 1–1, but the second half belonged to Brazil. A sharp header from Zito seized the lead and then Vavá's adroit pounce on another Czech keeper error wrapped up Brazil's second consecutive World Cup Final victory, 3–1. Garrincha, who tied with five other players (including his teammate Vavá) for top scorer, was named Player of the Tournament. And the Brazilian dynastic flag was firmly planted in World Cup soil.

'The Brazilian dynastic flag was firmly
planted in World Cup soil.'


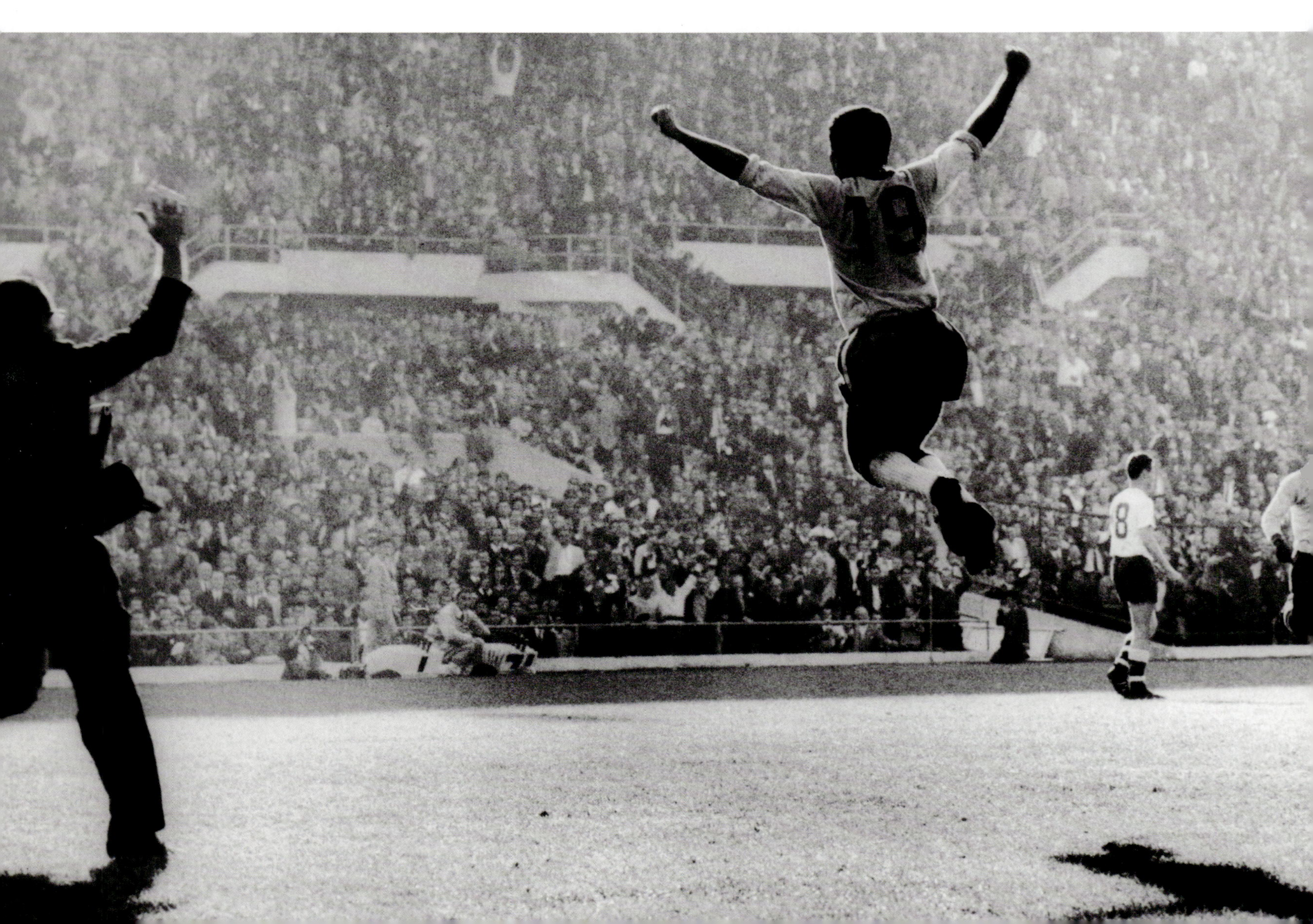

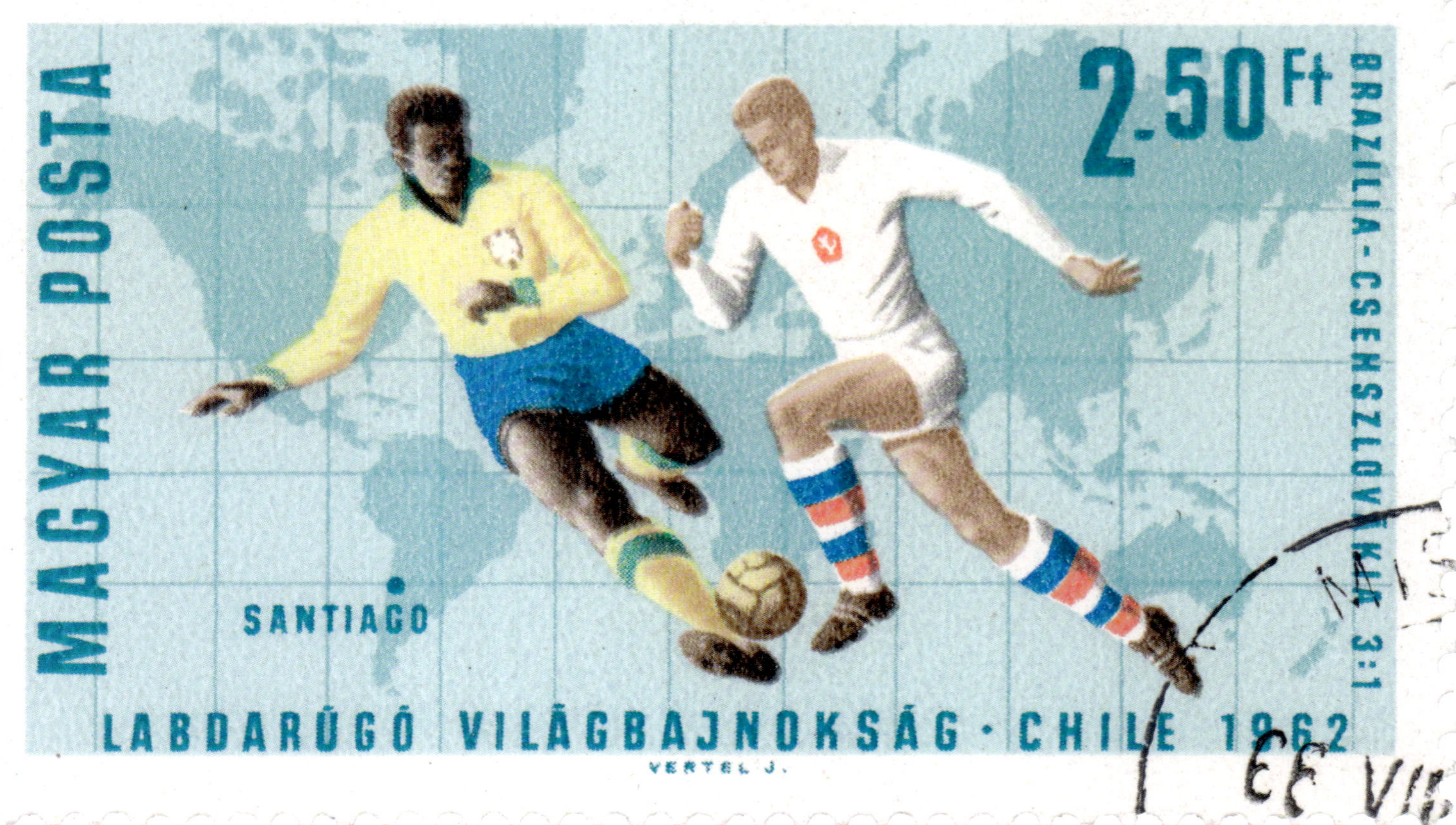


**OPPOSITE** *Vavá leaps in celebration after scoring Brazil's third and final goal.*

**ABOVE** *The 1962 World Cup Final as depicted in a stamp issued by the Hungarian Post, part of a series leading up to the 1966 World Cup.*

# 1966

HOST COUNTRY: **ENGLAND**
CHAMPION: **ENGLAND**
RUNNER-UP: **WEST GERMANY**
THIRD PLACE: **PORTUGAL OVER SOVIET UNION**

**FIFA believed that the 1966** edition of the World Cup would be a break-out year for the true globalisation of football due to one main reason: TV broadcast technology had made significant leaps in the early 1960s. The 1962 launch of the Telstar satellite made live events transmissible to all corners of the world. Live coverage of extraordinary cultural events such as the JFK assassination in 1963 and The Beatles' 1964 appearance on the *Ed Sullivan Show* had driven an almost exponential growth in TV ownership worldwide. Although the Chilean-hosted Cup in 1962 had modest TV coverage — FIFA sold the broadcast rights to the European Broadcasting Union for an almost comically low bid of $75,000 — all parties recognised that a World Cup hosted by England had immense global viewership potential. England had the world's best TV facilities, outside of the United States, and TV transmission infrastructure was spreading rapidly across the rest of Europe. FIFA's bet proved to be a sage one: the final match in 1966 between England and West Germany drew an astronomical global TV audience estimated at *400 million viewers.*

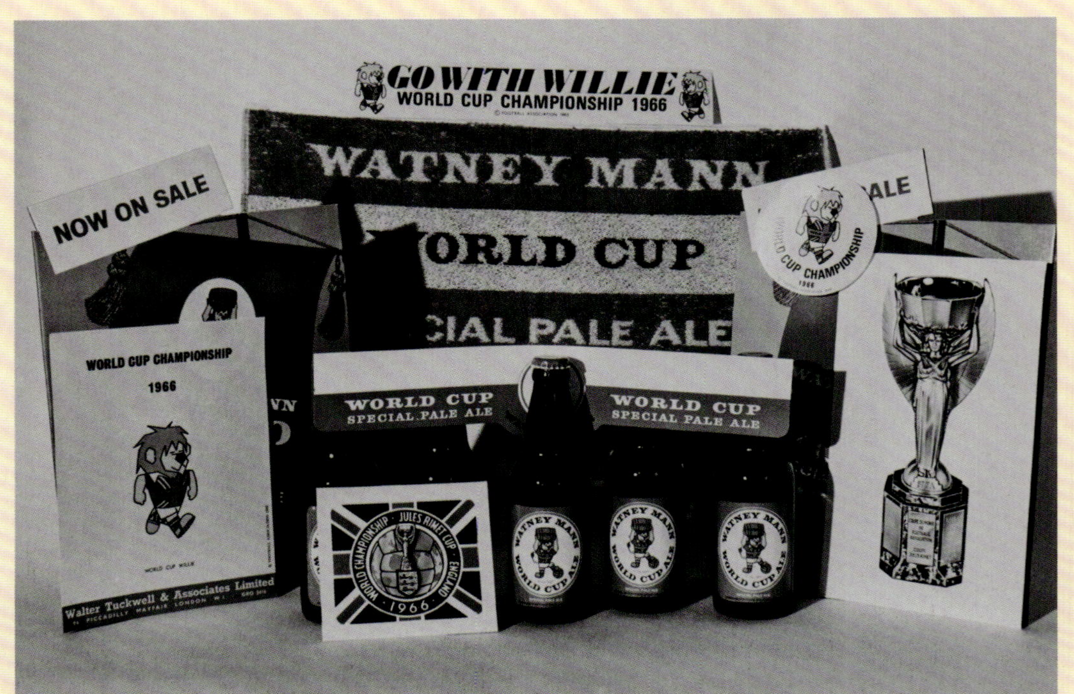


**LEFT** *Promotional merchandise for the 1966 World Cutp in England.*

**OPPOSITE TOP** *Pickles the collie dog with his owners David and Jeanne Corbett. David holds the £5,000 reward check for Pickles having found the stolen Jules Rimet Trophy.*

**OPPOSITE BOTTOM** *The London chief superintendent (right) displays the recovered Jules Rimet Trophy. To his left is District Commander John Lawlor.*

## PICKLES AND THE JULES RIMET

**With young Baby Boomers** coming of age in a surge of social extroversion after many years of post-war austerity, England proved the perfect hosts for the 1966 World Cup. 'Swinging London' was a global centre of culture, music, and fashion. Given their incredible impact on the global stage, the first-ever English-speaking Cup hosts felt an overwhelming sense that their time had arrived in the arena of football, too. The so-called 'Creators of Football' firmly believed that the sporting gods owed them their due after years of disappointing underachievement.

Things didn't start out well, though. In the build-up to the tournament, the Jules Rimet Trophy was stolen from its 'secure' display case in Westminster City Hall. After six days of panic and outrage, the missing item was found under a southeast London hedge by . . . a dog out for a stroll. Pickles, a photogenic mixed-breed collie, became a hero and overnight celebrity, stealing the World Cup's early spotlight. His owner, David Corbett, also became 5,000 pounds richer.

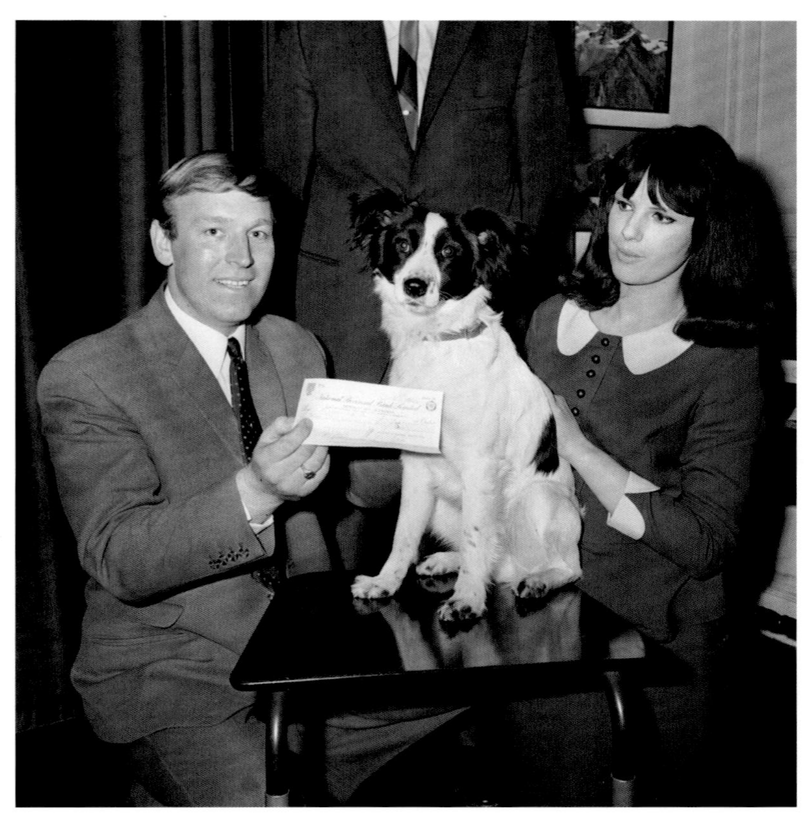

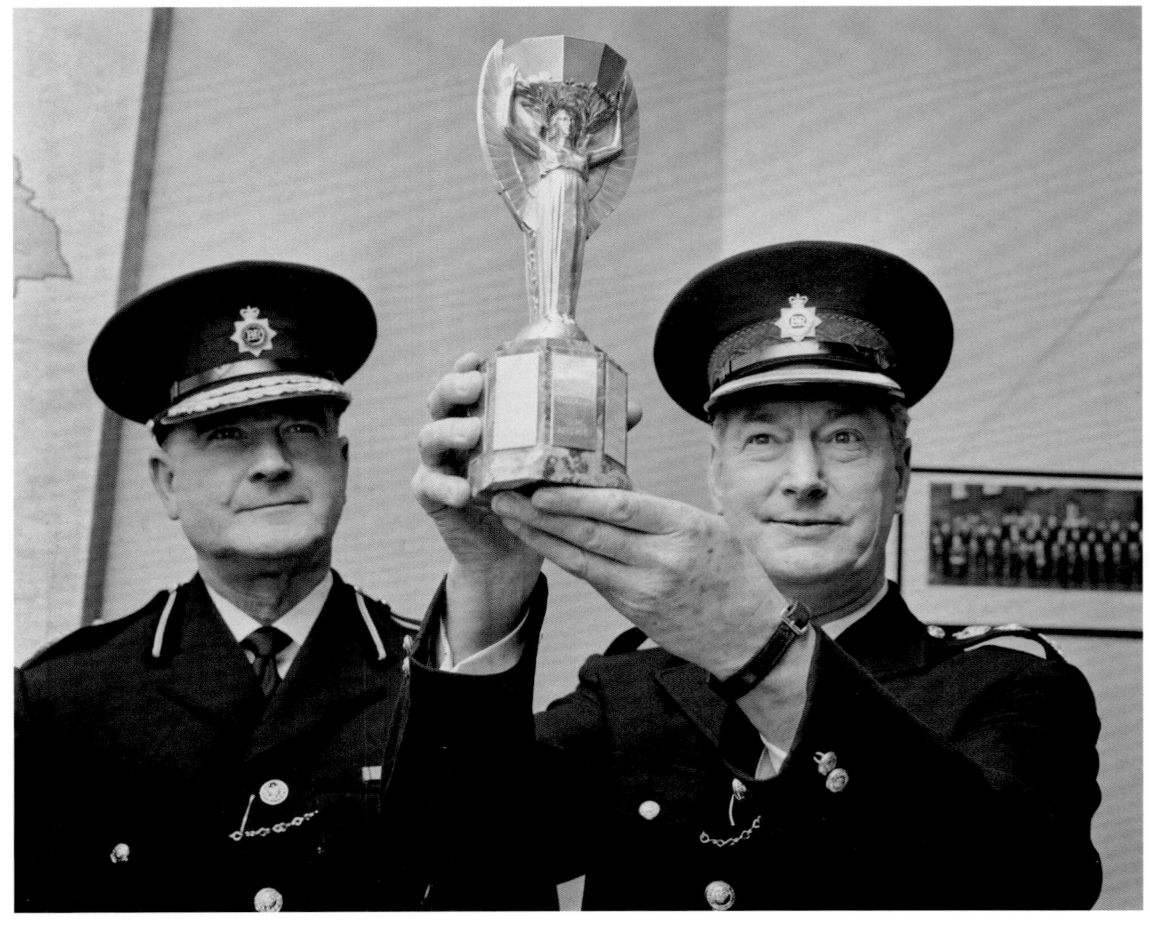

# Tournament: GROUP STAGE

### GROUP 1: ENGLAND, URUGUAY, MEXICO, FRANCE

| | |
|---:|:---|
| England 0 | 0 Uruguay |
| France 1 | 1 Mexico |
| Uruguay 2 | 1 France |
| England 2 | 0 Mexico |
| Mexico 0 | 0 Uruguay |
| England 2 | 0 France |

**Advanced to Knockout Stage: England, Uruguay**

Most of the Group 1 matches were played in the original Wembley Stadium in London, a venerable venue. England got off to a less-than-scintillating start in a cagey 0–0 tie with Uruguay but finally got its attack into gear with a pair of dominating 2–0 wins versus Mexico and France to finish first in the group. Under manager Alf Ramsey, England played an unconventionally narrow (for the time) 4-4-2 formation. Given that the 4-4-2 employed no designated wingers, the English were dubbed the 'wingless wonders'. Uruguay snagged the group's second quarter-finals spot.

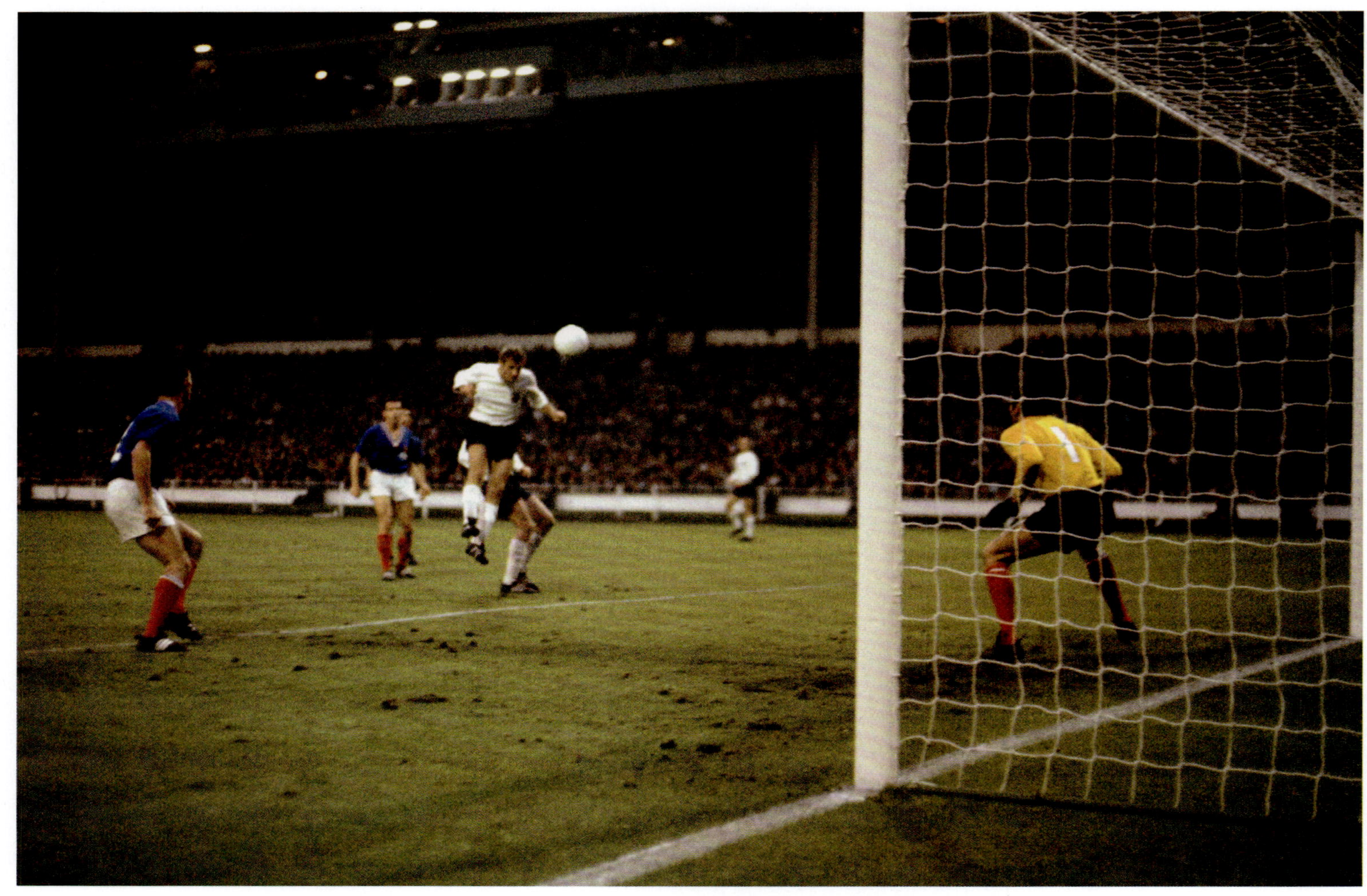

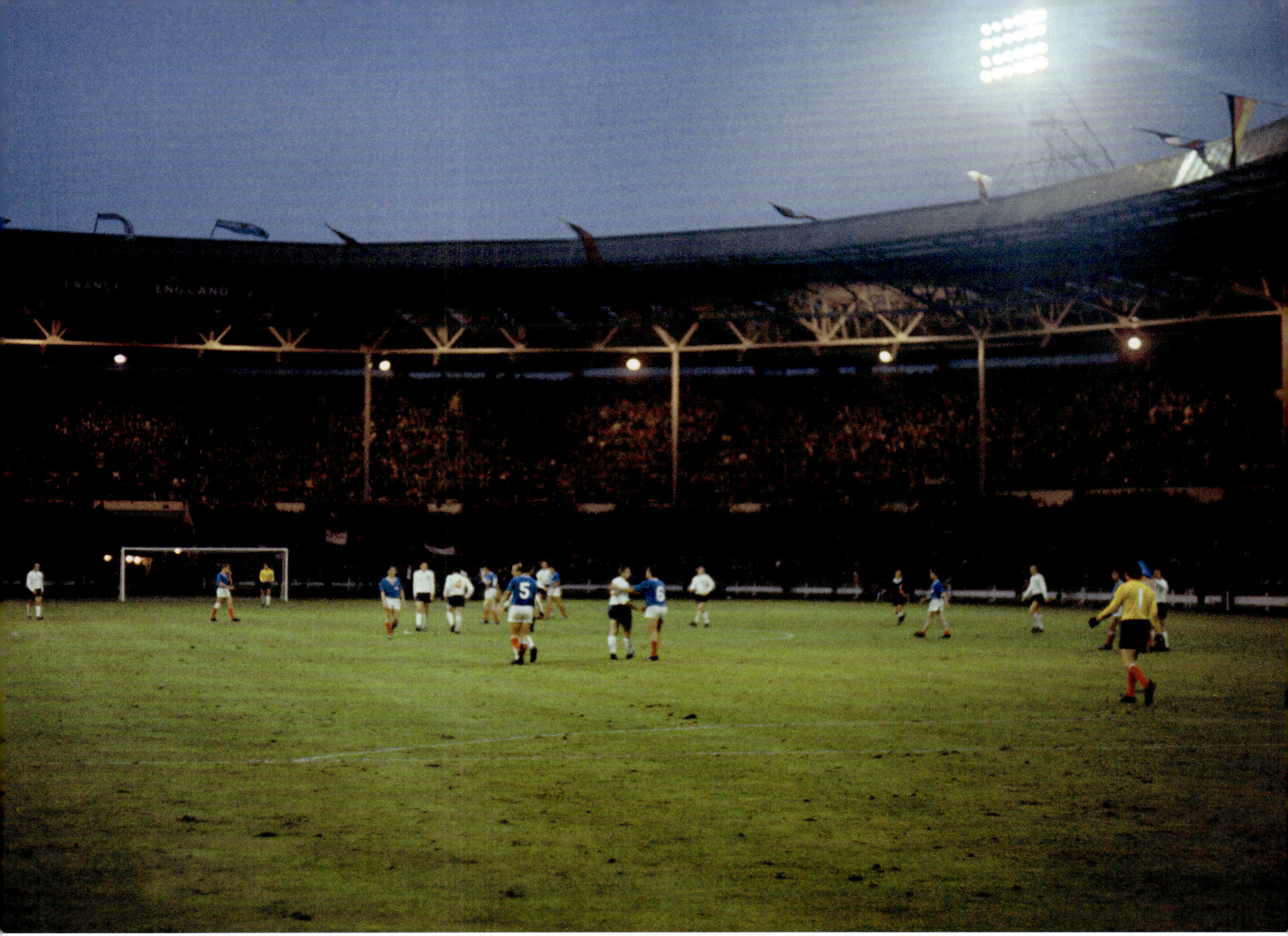

**OPPOSITE** *Roger Hunt launches a powerful header at French keeper Marcel Aubour for England's second goal of the match.*

**ABOVE** *English and French players shake hands after the final whistle.*

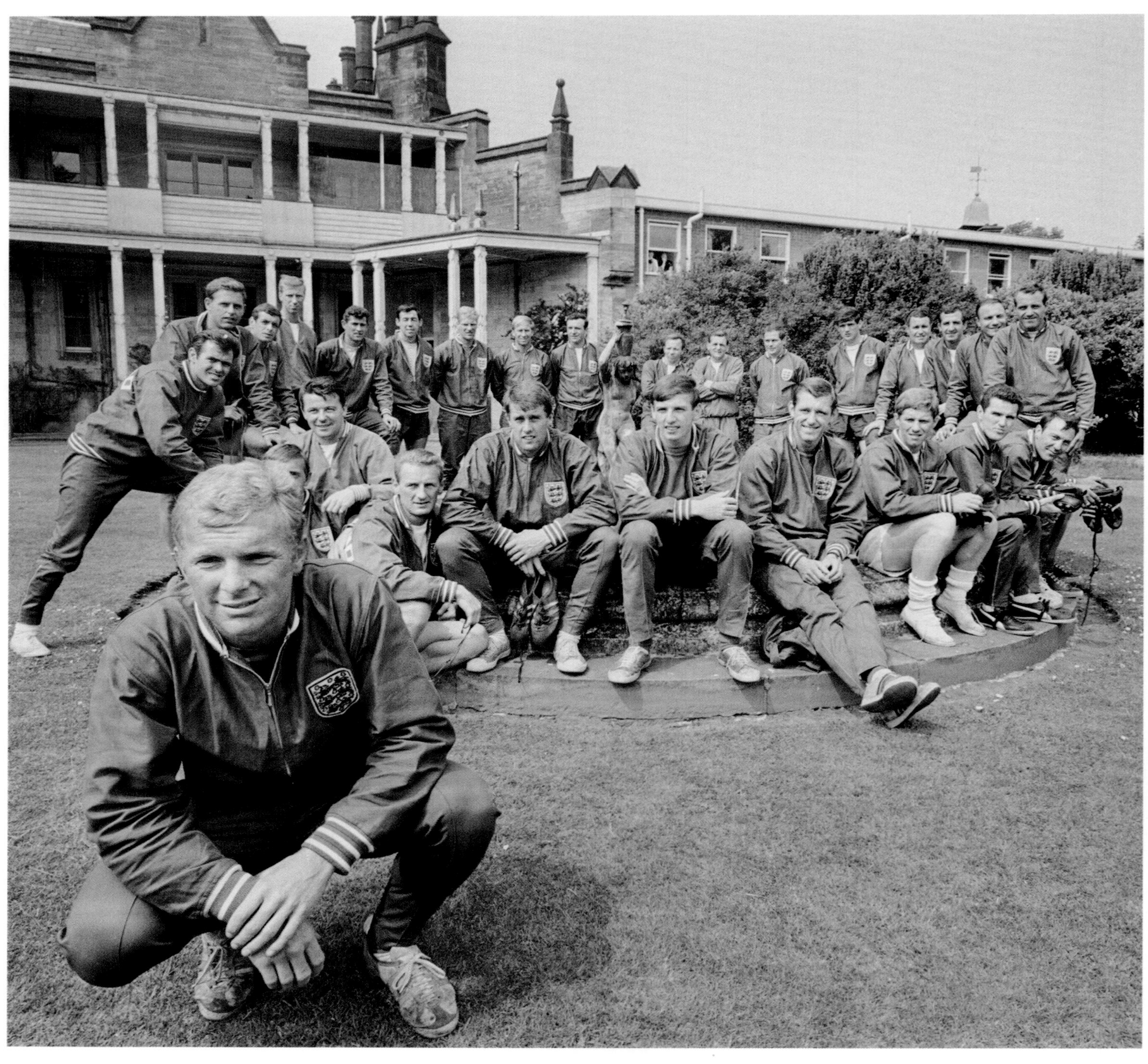

**ABOVE** *The England squad, with captain Bobby Moore in the front, during preparatory training for the 1966 World Cup — the tournament that would see them make national history.*

**OPPOSITE** *England's Jimmy Greaves carries the ball forward in the group-stage match against Uruguay, in a dynamic colour photograph that showcases the iconic all-white kits and the Three Lions crest.*

'The English were dubbed the
"wingless wonders".'

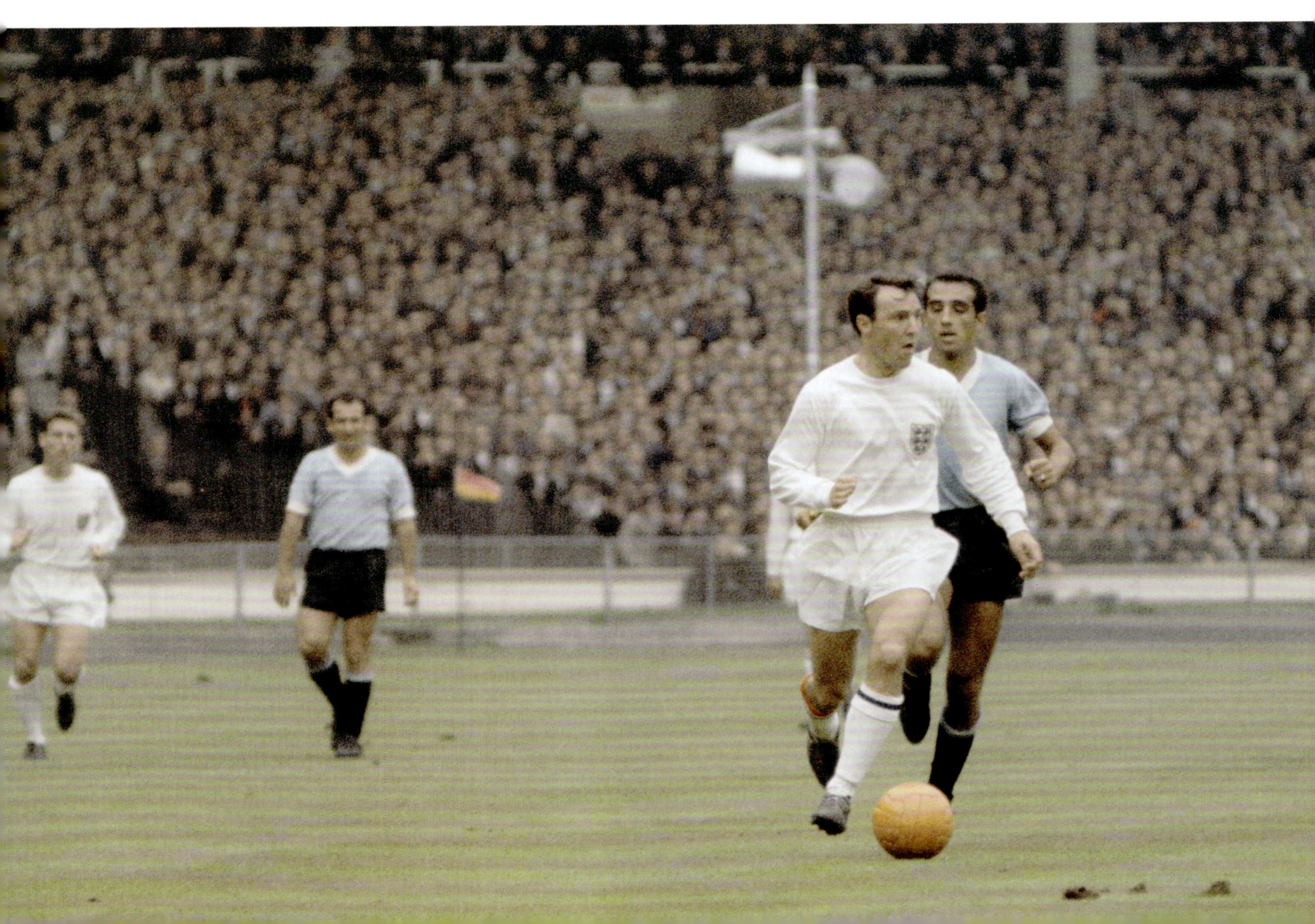

West Germany was the class of this group, but scrappy Argentina gave them a physical fight in their 0–0 match, despite finishing with only ten players. Both teams easily moved on to the knockout stage.



Defending-champion Brazil struggled with key injuries, including the loss of Pelé during its first game, and suffered a crushing elimination loss to a Portugal squad led by the brilliant Eusébio, who scored a remarkable brace. With three group wins, Portugal joined England as the two best-looking teams in the stage.

**BELOW** *Eusébio celebrates after scoring Portugal's second goal against Brazil.*

**OPPOSITE TOP** *Lev Yashin, the legendary Soviet goalkeeper, arrives to a training session, 1962.*

**OPPOSITE BOTTOM** *In Brazil's final group-stage match, Pelé exits the pitch early with a knee injury brought about by several violent Portuguese tackles. He had been previously injured in Brazil's opener against Bulgaria and forced to sit out their second match against Hungary.*

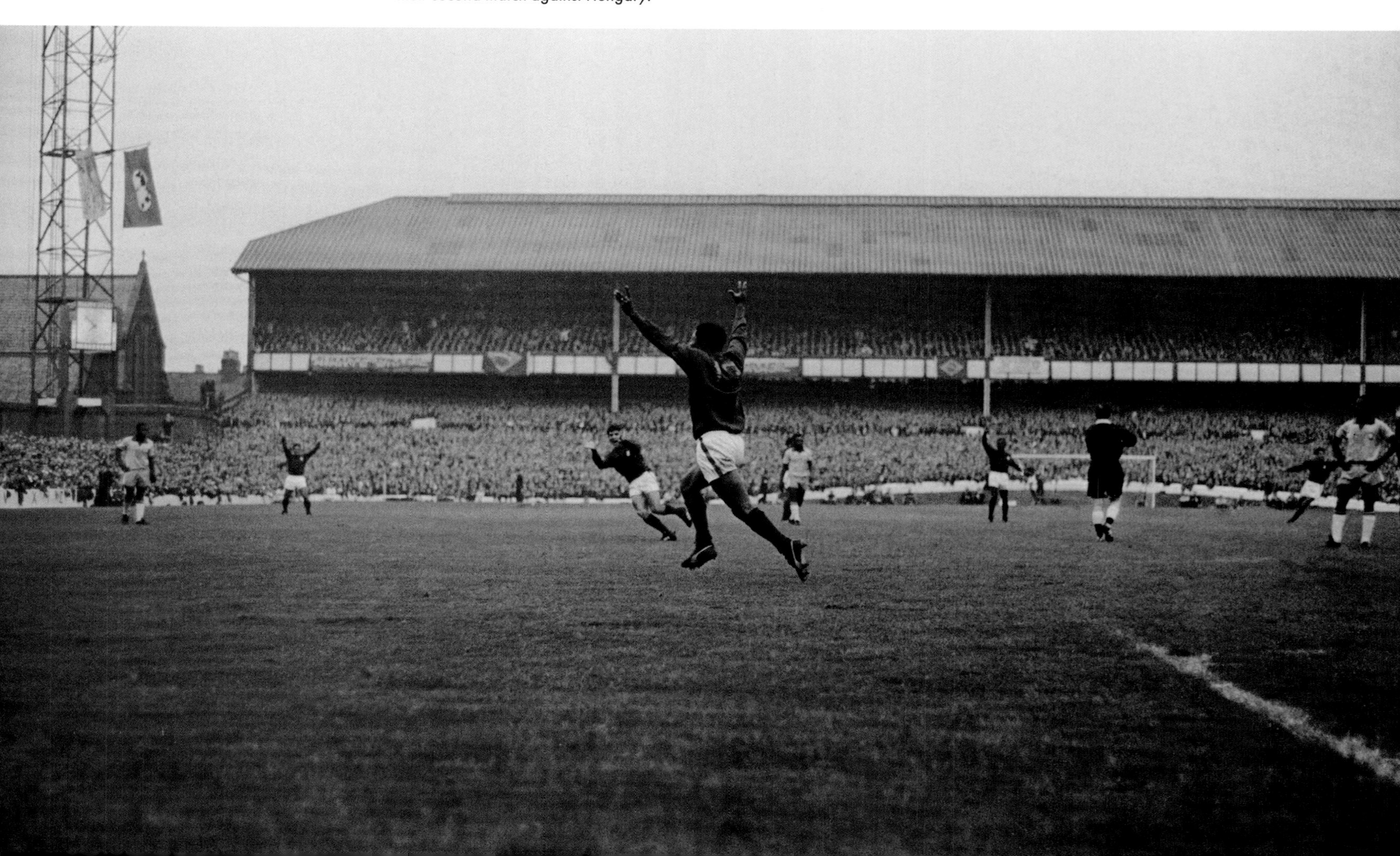

| | | |
|---:|:---:|:---|
| Soviet Union 3 | 0 | North Korea |
| Italy 2 | 0 | Chile |
| Chile 1 | 1 | North Korea |
| Soviet Union 1 | 0 | Italy |
| North Korea 1 | 0 | Italy |
| Soviet Union 2 | 1 | Chile |

**Advanced to Knockout Stage: Soviet Union, North Korea**

North Korea arrived in England as a completely unknown entity and, after its 3–0 loss to a strong Soviet squad, most observers discounted them as overmatched. But a shocking win over a complacent Italy—North Korea scored the lone goal with just three minutes left—put them in the quarter-finals.

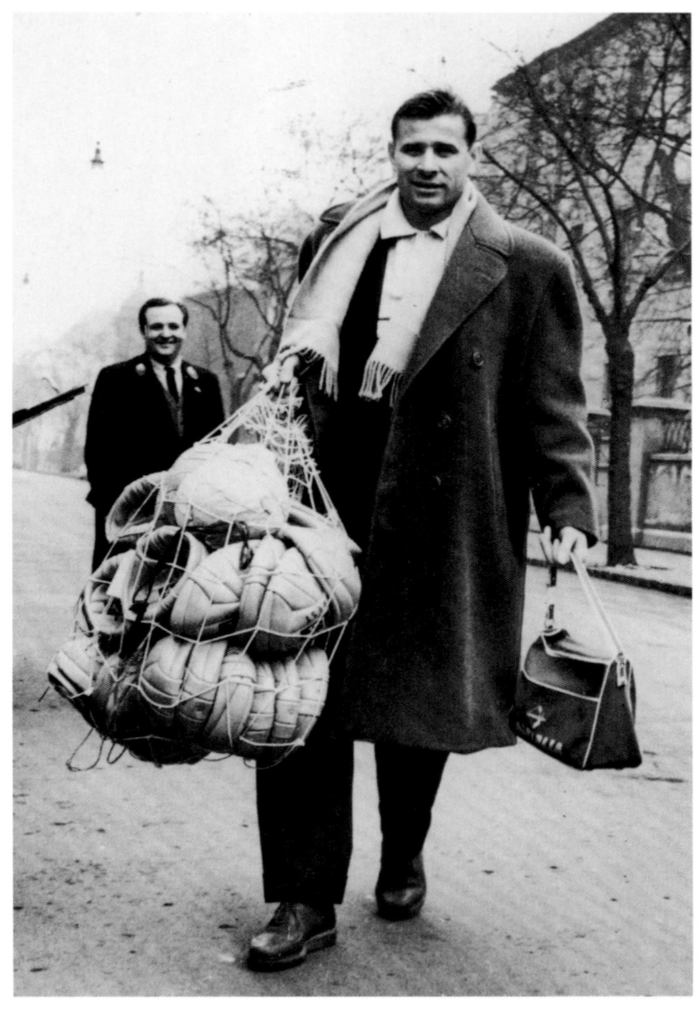

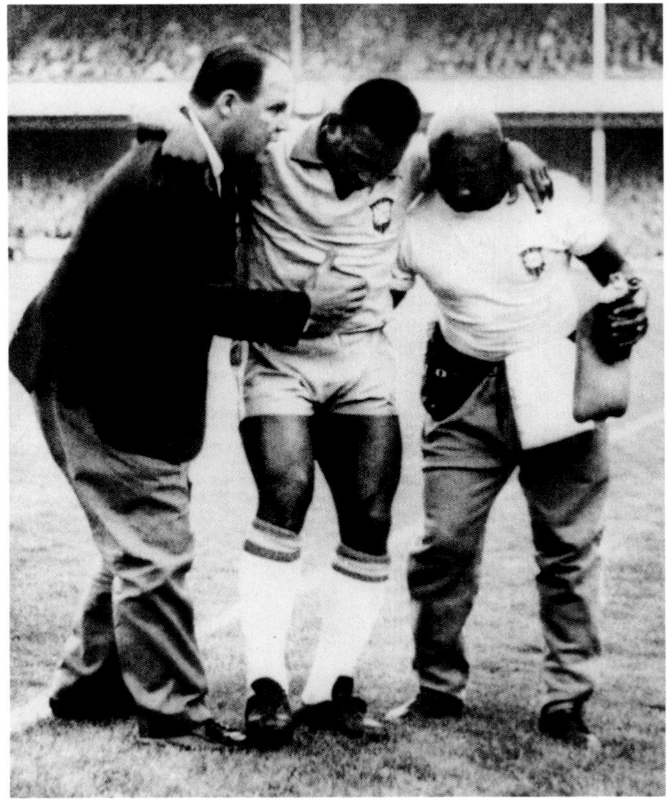

# THE BLACK SPIDER OF MOSCOW

**Imposing, athletic Soviet goalkeeper** Lev Yashin is universally considered one of the greatest at his position in the history of football. Known as the 'Black Spider' for his signature all-dark uniform and unparalleled agility, Yashin revolutionised goalkeeping with his acrobatic saves and aggressive, highly vocal presence in the box. He was never afraid to charge off his line to intercept crosses, cut off shot angles, or challenge attackers.

Yashin led the Soviets to a gold medal at the 1956 Olympic Games and first place at the 1960 European Nations Cup. His performance in the 1962 World Cup wasn't quite up to his lofty standards, but he still helped the Soviet Union finish first in a very difficult group and reach the quarter-finals. The next year, Yashin was awarded the Ballon d'Or as European player of the year (still the only goalkeeper to win the prestigious honour) and 1966 would see him continue his strong form and lead the Soviet Union to its best-ever finish at the World Cup.

# QUARTER-FINALS

| | | |
|---:|:---|:---|
| England 1 | 0 | Argentina |
| Portugal 5 | 3 | North Korea |
| West Germany 4 | 0 | Uruguay |
| Soviet Union 2 | 1 | Hungary |

England had conceded zero goals in group play and its stellar defence continued in a 1–0 elimination of Argentina. But the controversial first-half sendoff of Argentine captain Antonio Rattín triggered a turmoil of bad feelings. Rattín refused to leave, halting the game for nearly ten minutes, and for a time it appeared the entire Argentina side would walk off in protest. Englishman Geoff Hurst headed home the match's only goal in the seventy-eighth minute to secure the win.

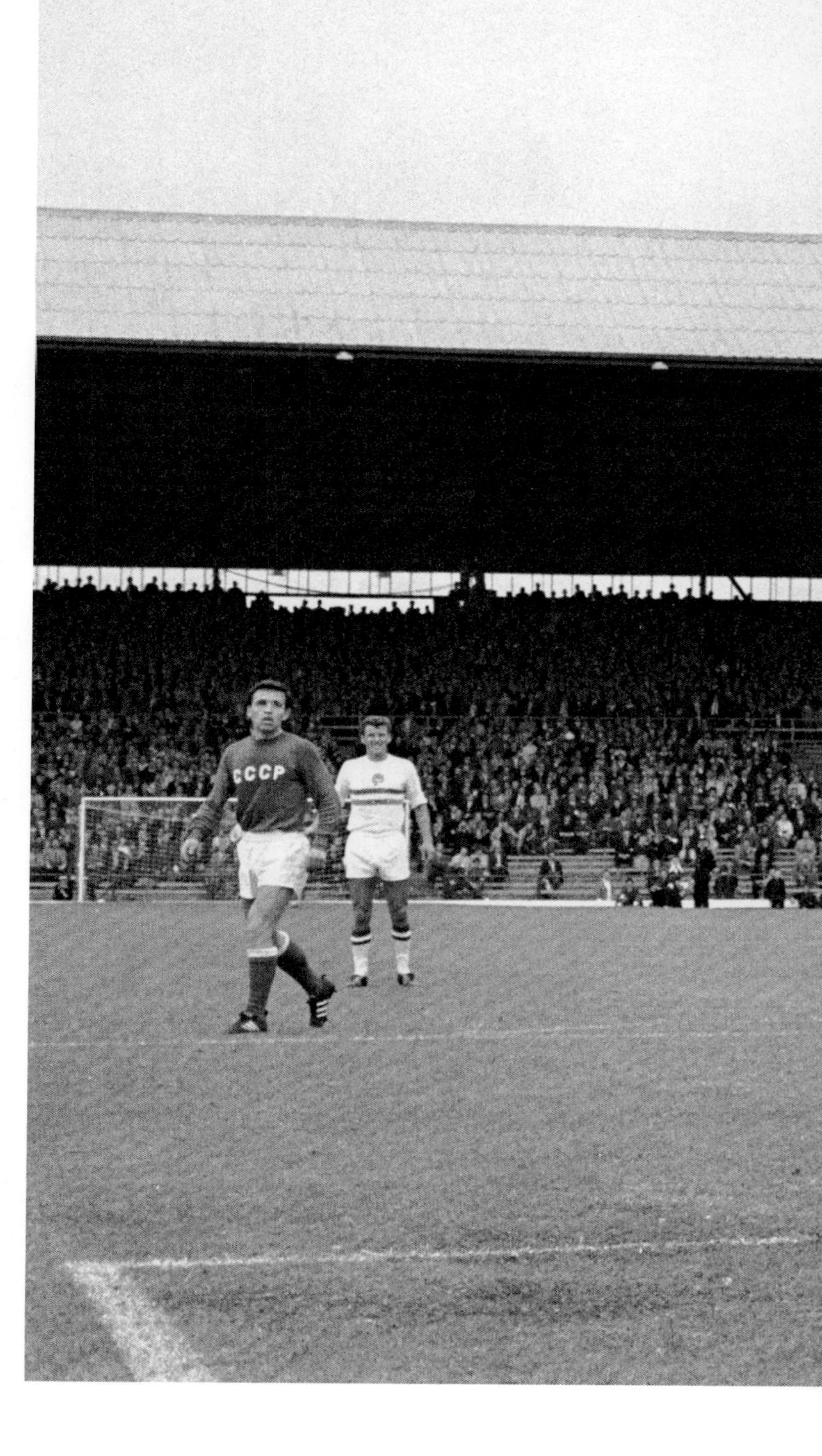

**RIGHT** *The Black Spider in rare form at the 1966 World Cup, reaching around his own team-mate's head to collect the ball in the quarter-final bout with Hungary.*

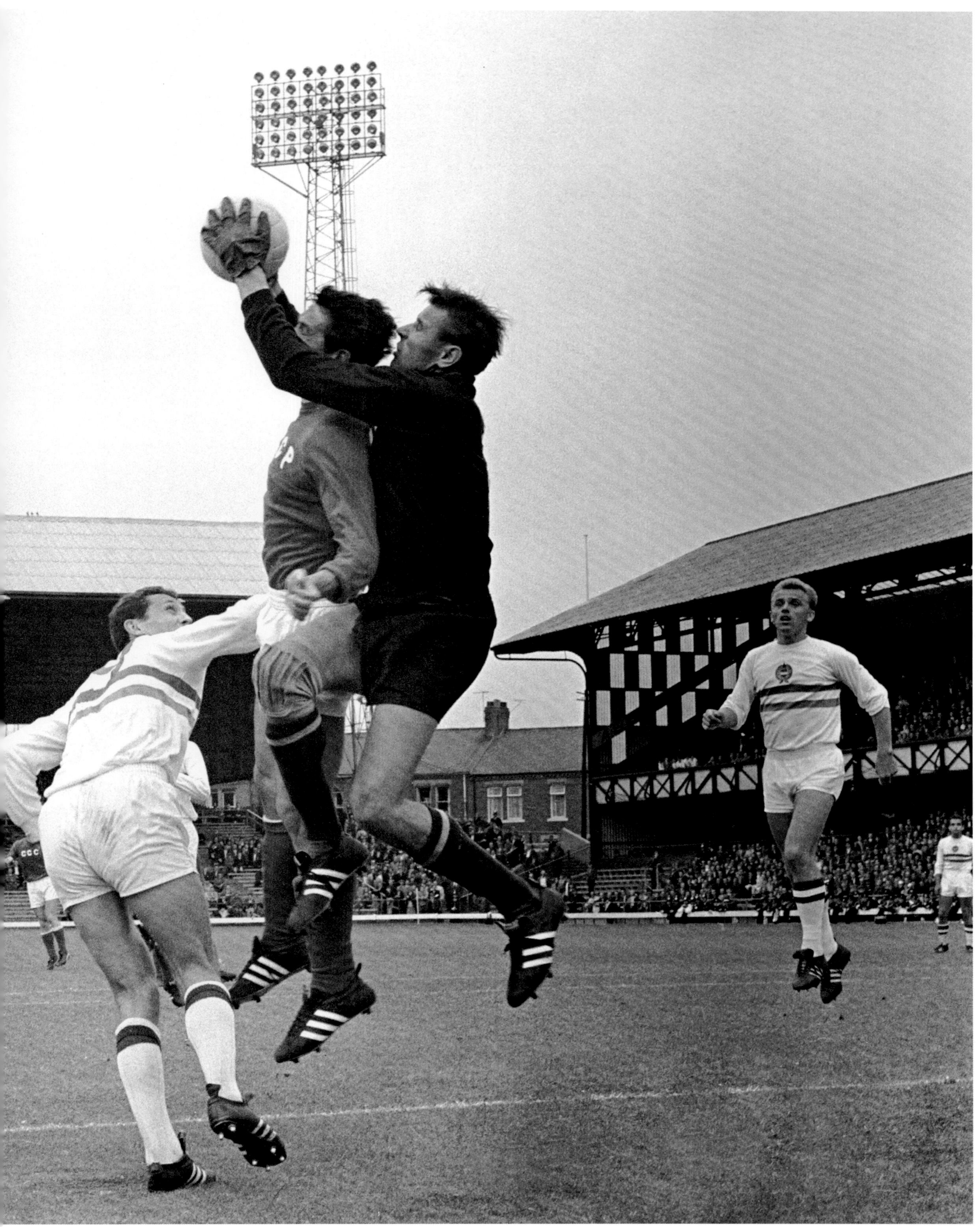

# EUSÉBIO'S MAGNIFICENT COMEBACK

**North Korea was the Cinderella** team of the 1966 tournament. After a tough initial loss to the Soviet Union, they managed a tie versus Chile and knocked out Italy to slide into the knockout stage. Then, in an astonishing quarter-final match, the North Koreans had Portugal, one of the pretournament favourites, down 3–0 after just twenty-five minutes. A massive upset was brewing.

Then the majestic Eusébio took over the match. Today considered one of the greatest of all time, the 'Black Panther' had had enough of North Korea's joy at Portugal's expense. 'He simply took the game by the scruff of the neck', as one observer put it. Over the next thirty-two minutes, Eusébio was relentless and unstoppable, scoring four straight goals to thrust Portugal into the lead by sheer will.

Memorably, after each successful finish he'd rush into the net, snag the ball, and sprint to the centre spot as his team-mates ran with him. To cap the bravura performance, he lofted a perfect corner kick to assist in a final goal (5–3) and lock up Portugal's slot in the semi-finals. Eusébio's performance in that match has become a cornerstone of World Cup lore, and along with Pelé, he became one of the most recognizable and respected faces in the history of the tournament.

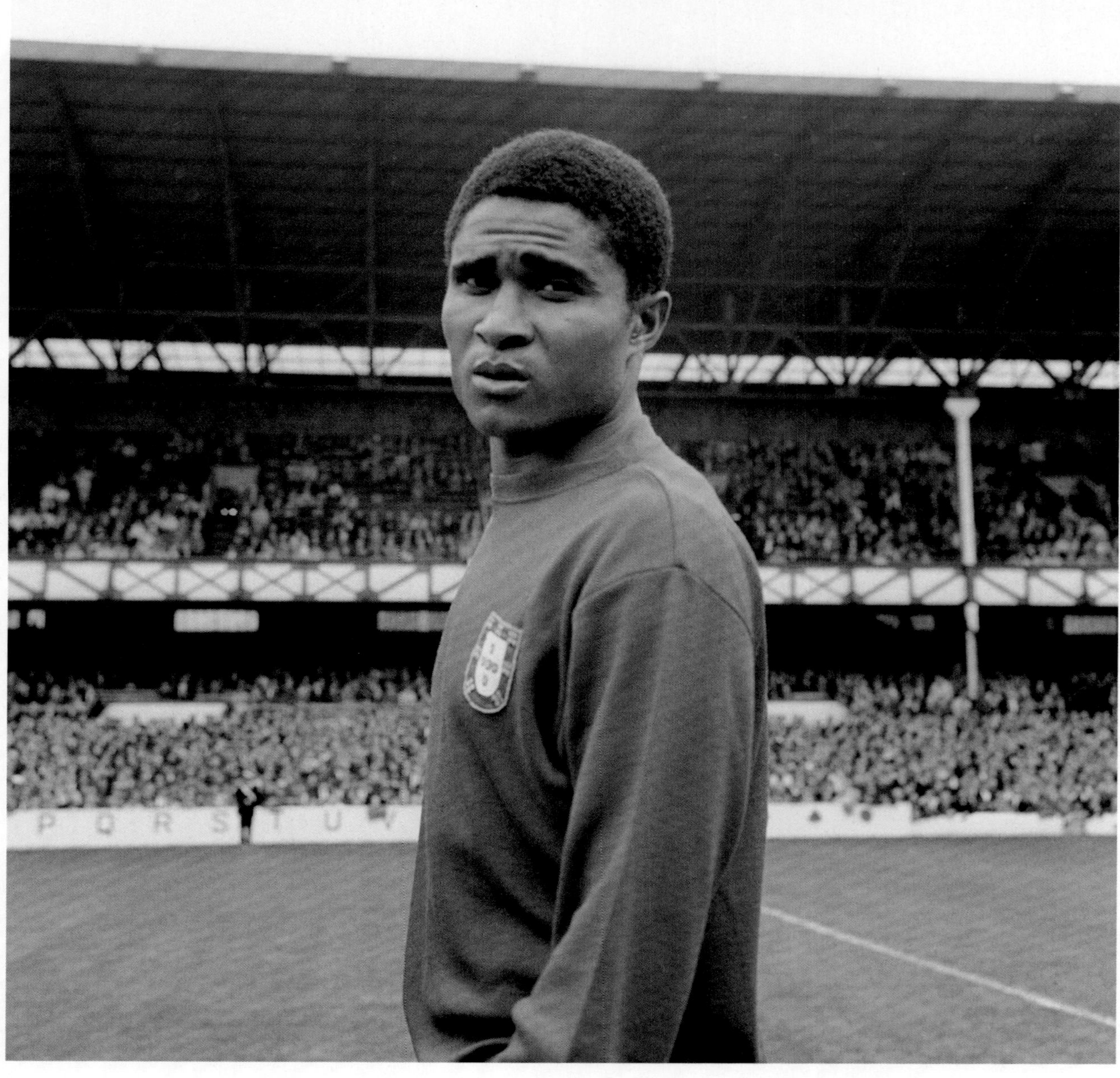

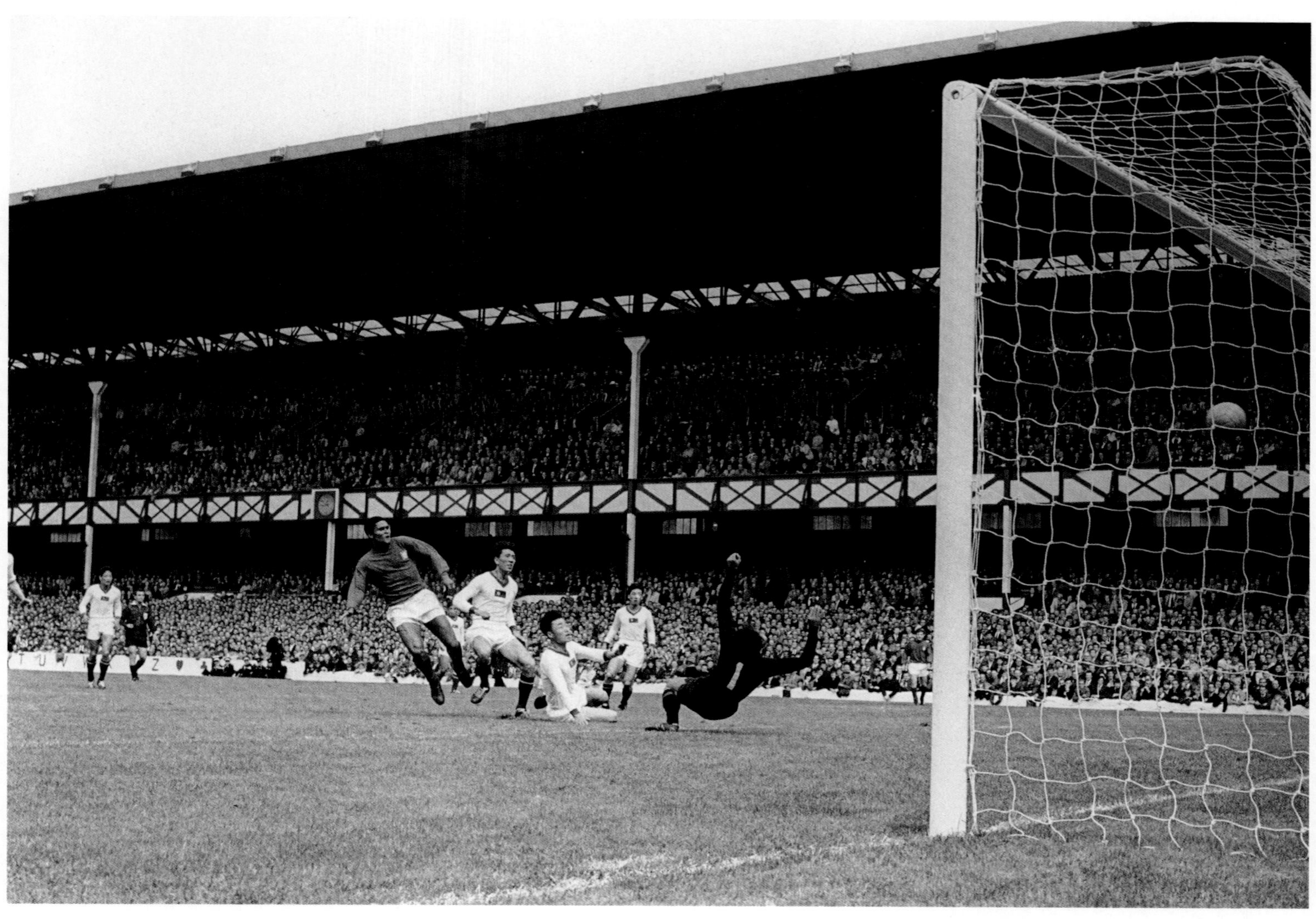

OPPOSITE Eusébio before
facing off against North Korea
in the quarter-finals.

ABOVE Eusébio watches his first
goal of the match beat North
Korean keeper Li Chan-myung on
its way to the back of the net. This
goal would spark Eusébio's masterclass performance and jump-start
Portugal's comeback.

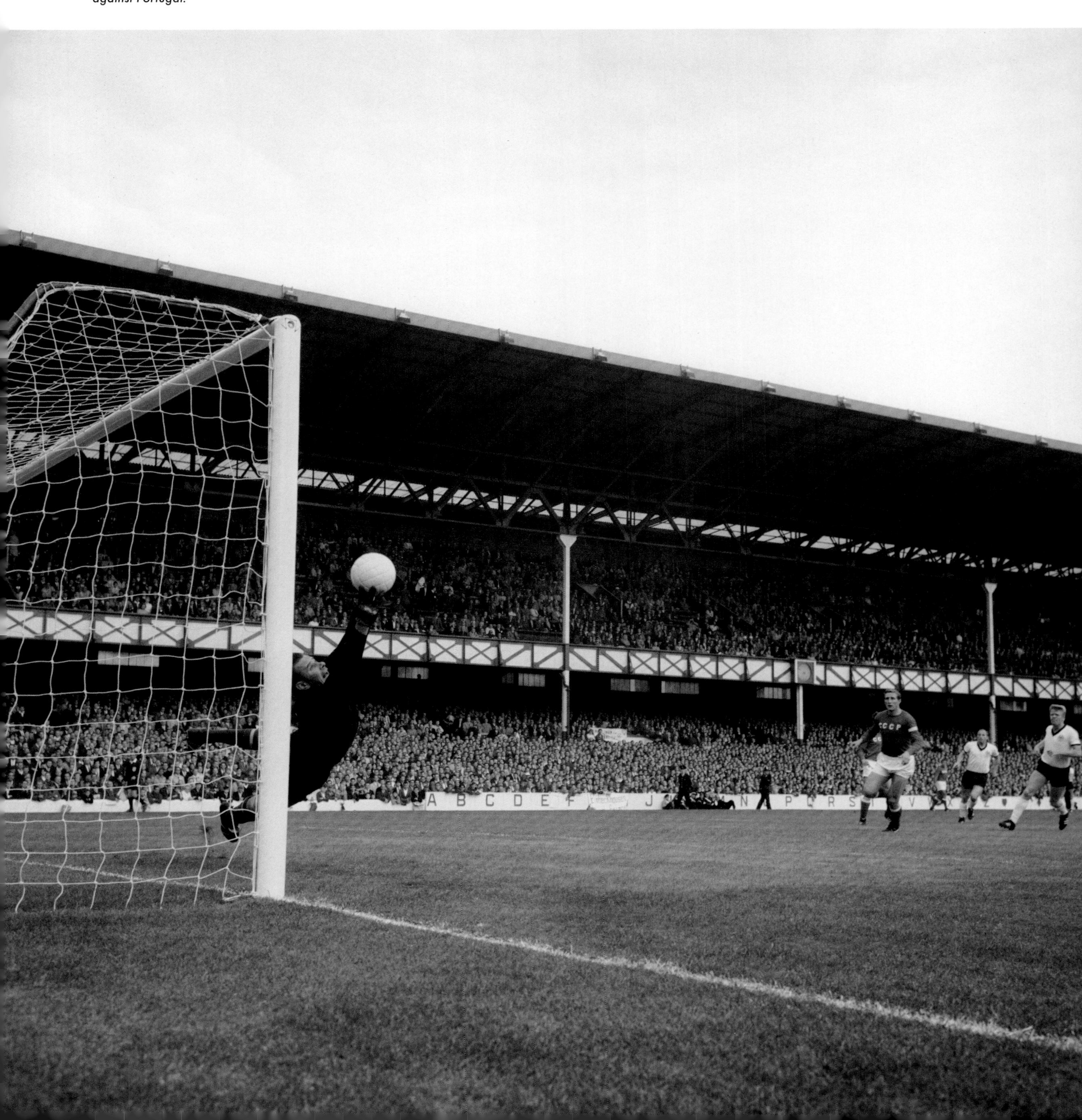



**BELOW** *'The Black Spider'
Lev Yashin with an acrobatic
save against West Germany
in the semi-final.*

**OPPOSITE** *Bobby Charlton's
low-driven strike to the bottom-
right corner for England's
second goal in the semi-final
against Portugal.*

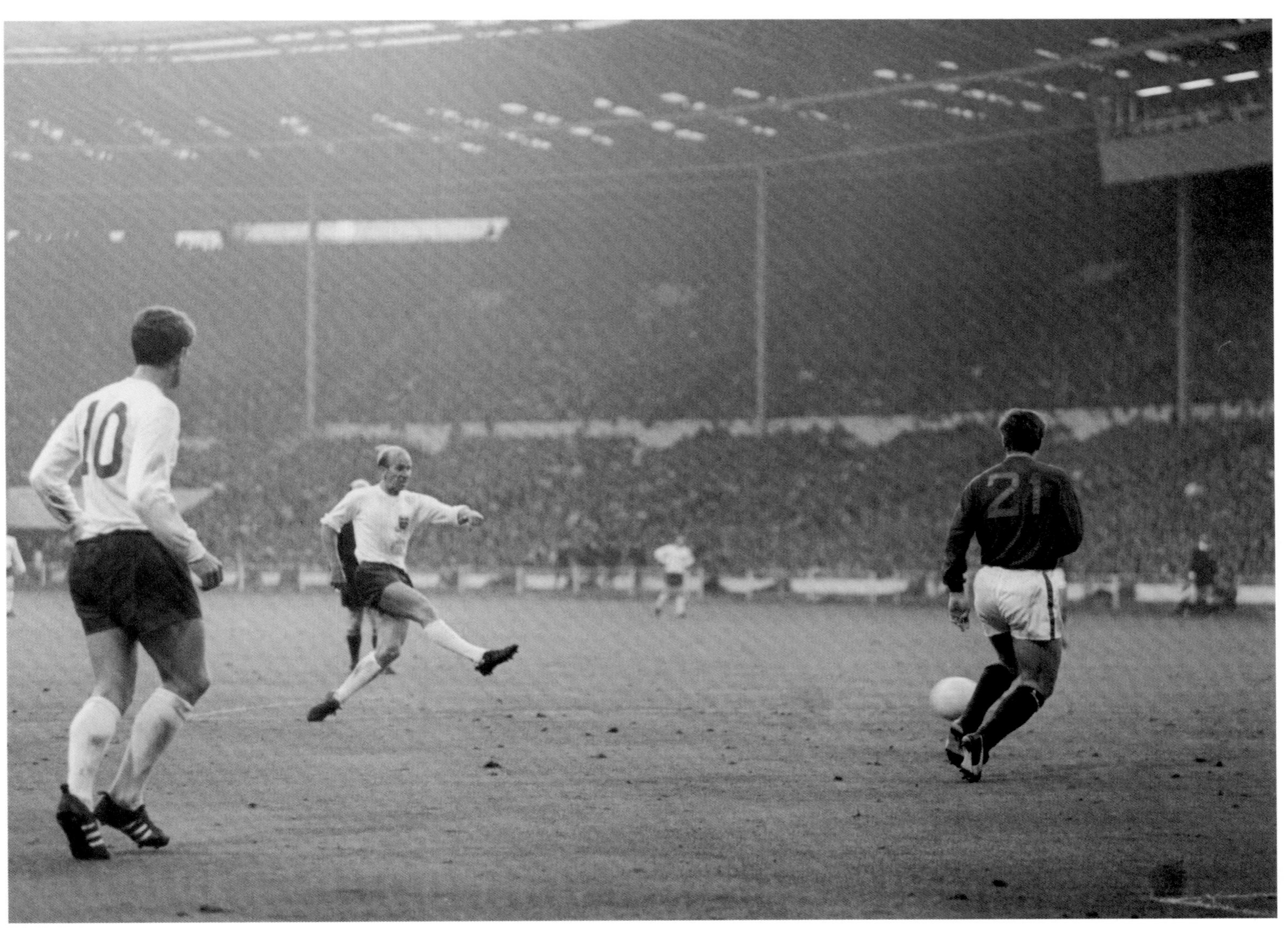

## SEMI-FINALS

England 2 | 1 Portugal
West Germany 2 | 1 Soviet Union

The Soviet winger Igor Chislenko was kicked out in the first half just after the West Germans scored the first goal. Playing against ten, the Germans took firm control to earn their place in the Cup Final—rising central defender Franz Beckenbauer blasted a long shot past the Soviets' great goalkeeper Lev Yashin for a 2–0 lead. A very late Soviet goal made things briefly interesting, but West Germany thwarted any last-second comeback.

On the other side, England took a skilful 2–0 lead, thanks to the brilliant work of Bobby Charlton, but finally conceded its first goal of the tournament when Portugal was awarded a penalty kick that Eusébio calmly buried in the net at the eighty-two-minute mark. The final eight minutes were dramatic and entertaining, but England held on to reach the final.

# FINAL

England 4 | 2 West Germany
| (after extra time)
| (First Place)
Portugal 2 | 1 Soviet Union
| (Third Place)

The solid Soviets played well, but Portugal earned a thrilling third-place finish thanks to an early goal from Eusébio and a last-minute tally from José Torres. Impressive play throughout the tournament made Portugal's final standing a well-deserved reward. Eusébio easily won top scorer of the tournament with a total of nine goals.

In the final at Wembley Stadium, West Germany jumped out to a 1–0 lead after a passing flurry was finished off by the prolific forward Helmut Haller. Geoff Hurst equalised just six minutes later. The 1–1 stalemate held for sixty full minutes until England scored after a corner and deflection. But as the final seconds counted down, a West German free kick caromed across the English goal and Wolfgang Weber banged it home to trigger extra time.

Next came the game's one truly controversial call. A hard Hurst rocket in the 101st minute hammered the crossbar, ricochetted straight down, and bounced back out into play. But the Soviet linesman ruled the ball had hit the ground *behind* the goal line, so the Swiss referee awarded England a goal. That very crossbar is now on display at the new Wembley Stadium. The West Germans pressed hard for the equaliser and in the last minute pushed their entire defensive line forward into the attack, but Hurst broke free on a counter to score in the final seconds and seal a 4–2 victory for England on its home soil. Until 2022, Hurst's hat-trick was the only one scored in a FIFA World Cup Final.

Again, an estimated 400 million viewers watched the World Cup Final match live on TV, including well over half the population of the UK. Amusingly, the final strides of Hurst's game-ending scoring jaunt were accompanied by spectators who'd burst onto the field from the stands. As the BBC commentator famously called it: 'And here comes Hurst! He's got…some people are on the pitch, they think it's all over! [Here, Hurst shoots and scores.] *It is now! It's four!'*

Along with Queen Elizabeth handing the trophy found by Pickles the dog to English captain Bobby Moore, Hurst's blistering final shot (with the wild fan escort just off screen) was an enduring image of the 1966 World Cup, the first sporting event fully experienced live on a global scale.

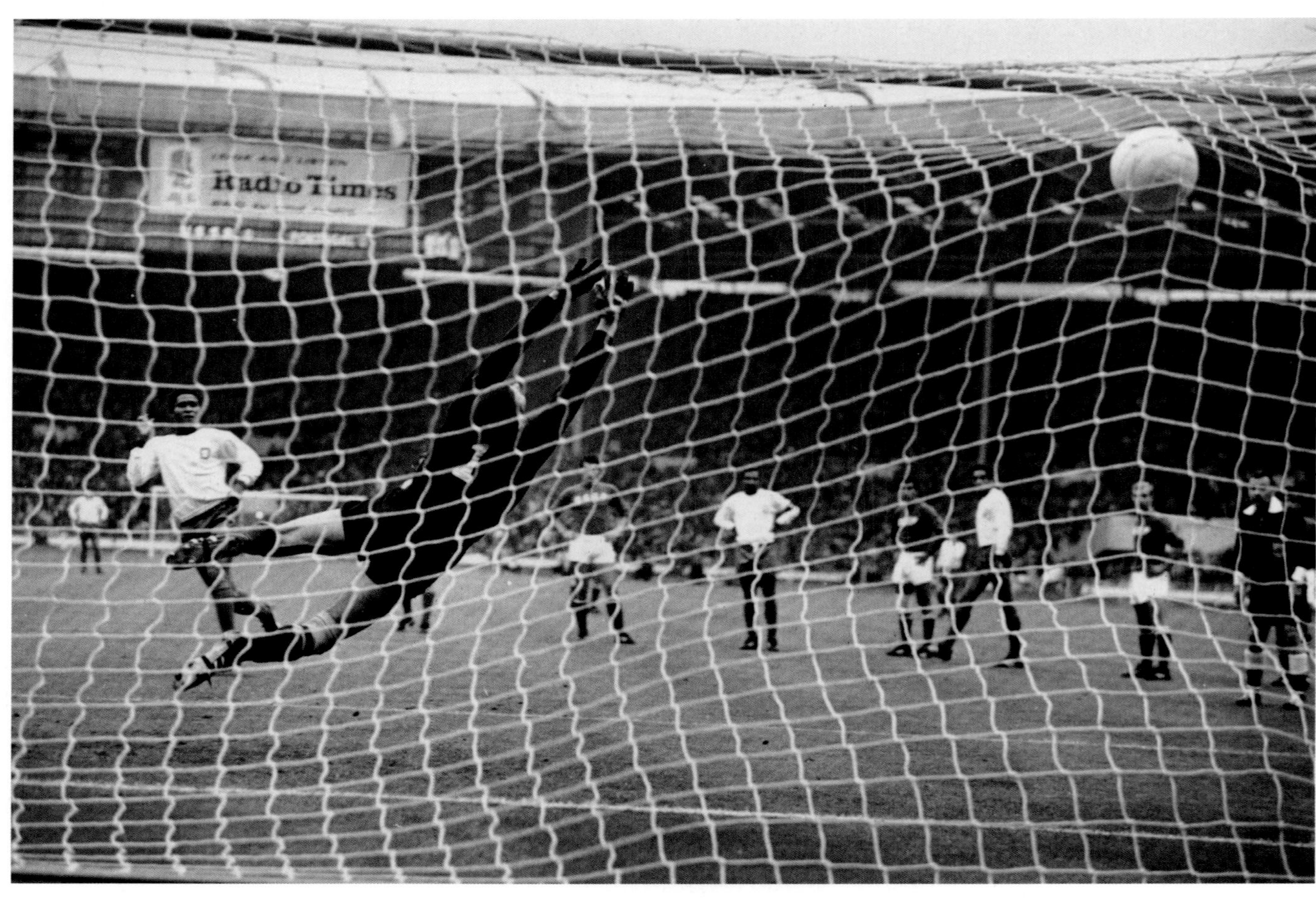

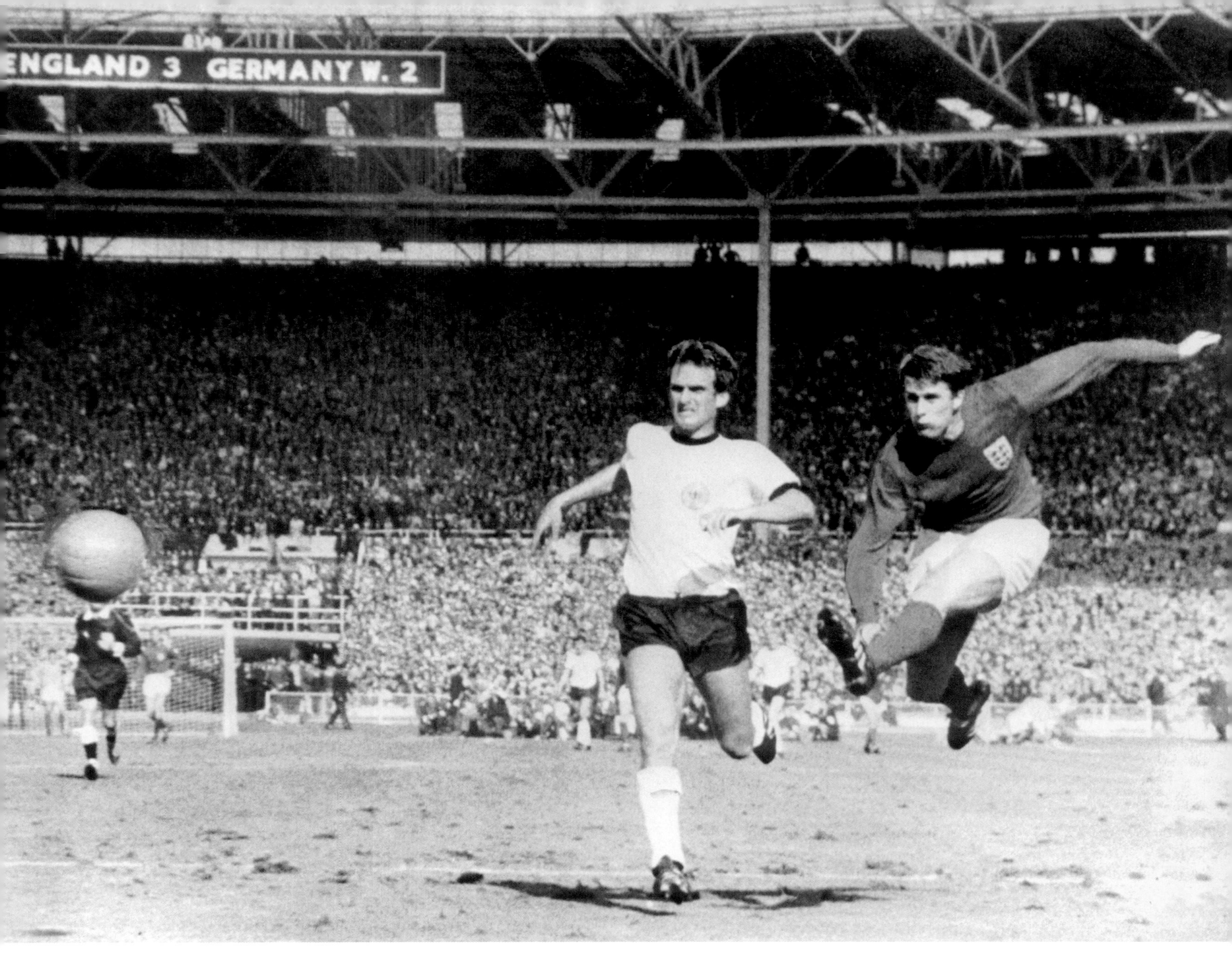


**OPPOSITE** *Eusébio converts Portugal's penalty against Lev Yashin and the Soviets in the third-place match, possibly the two most brilliant individual performers of the tournament.*

**ABOVE** *Geoff Hurst completes his hat-trick in the final moments of extra time and seals England's World Cup victory on home soil.*

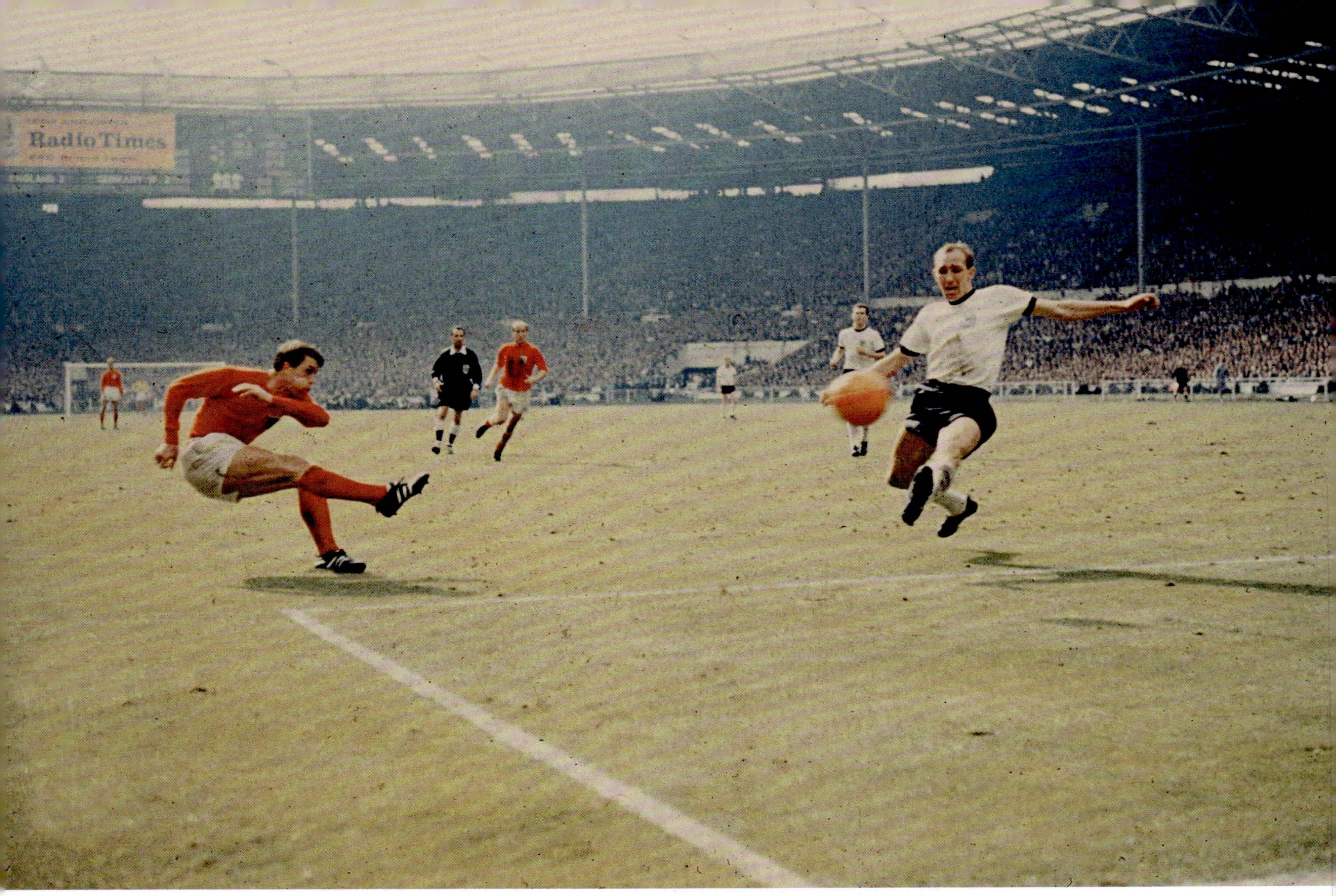



**ABOVE** *Geoff Hurst's second goal (which put England up 3–2 in extra time) remains one of the most controversial in World Cup history. Most experts agree that the entirety of the ball did not cross the goal line.*

**OPPOSITE** *English captain Bobby Moore lifts the trophy after defeating West Germany in the final.*

'The 1966 World Cup, the first
sporting event fully experienced
live on a global scale.'

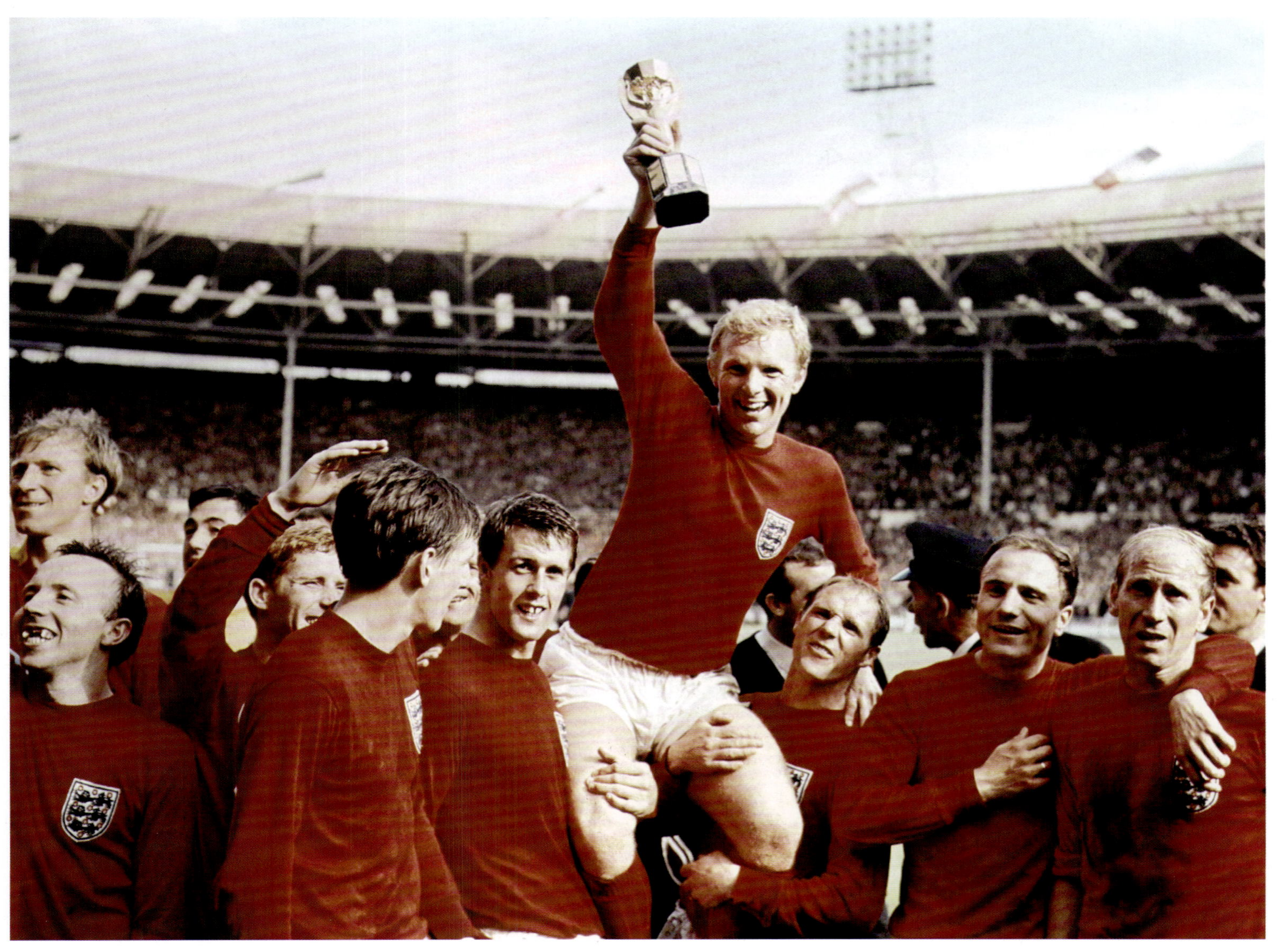

# THE 1970s

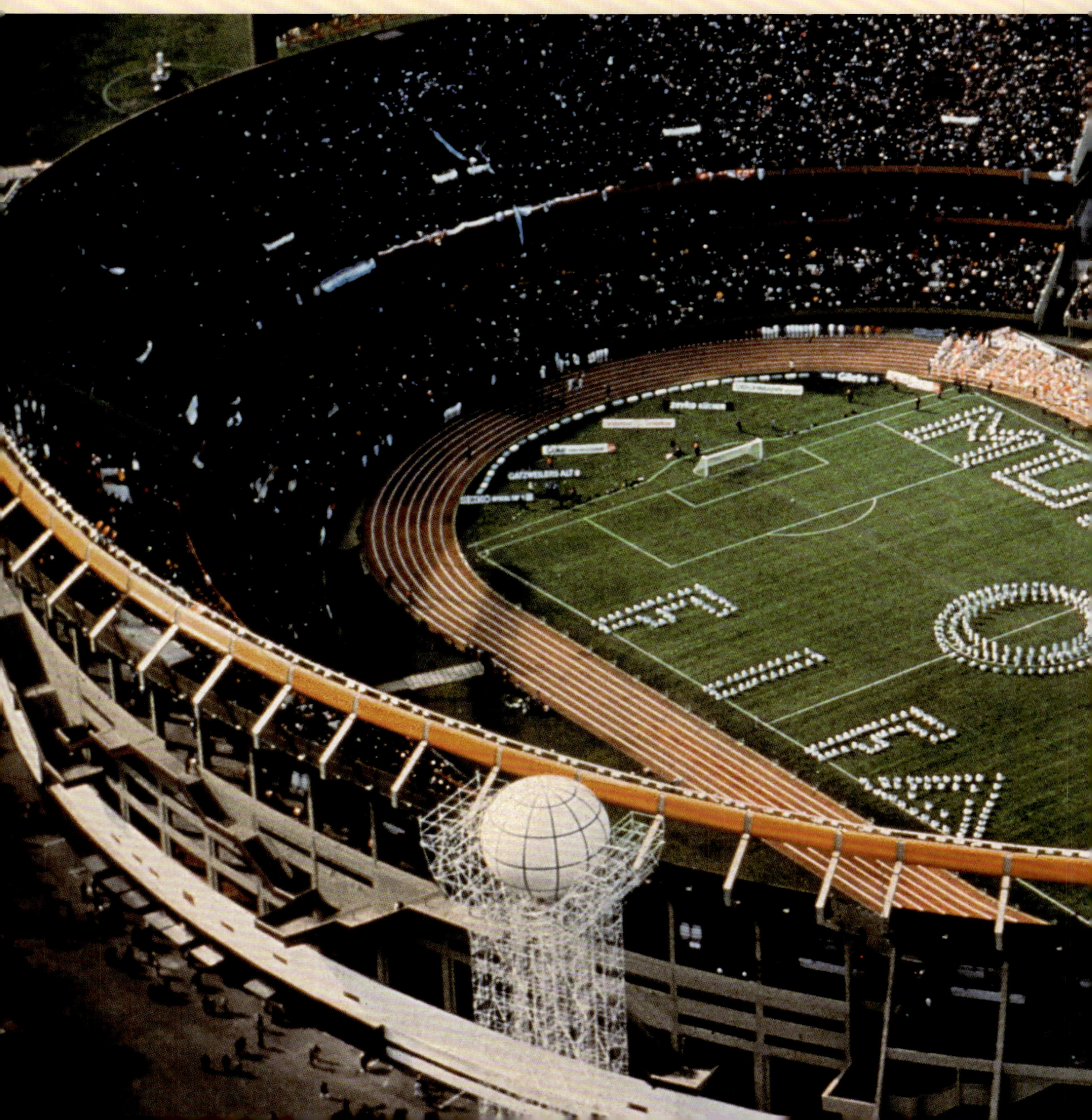

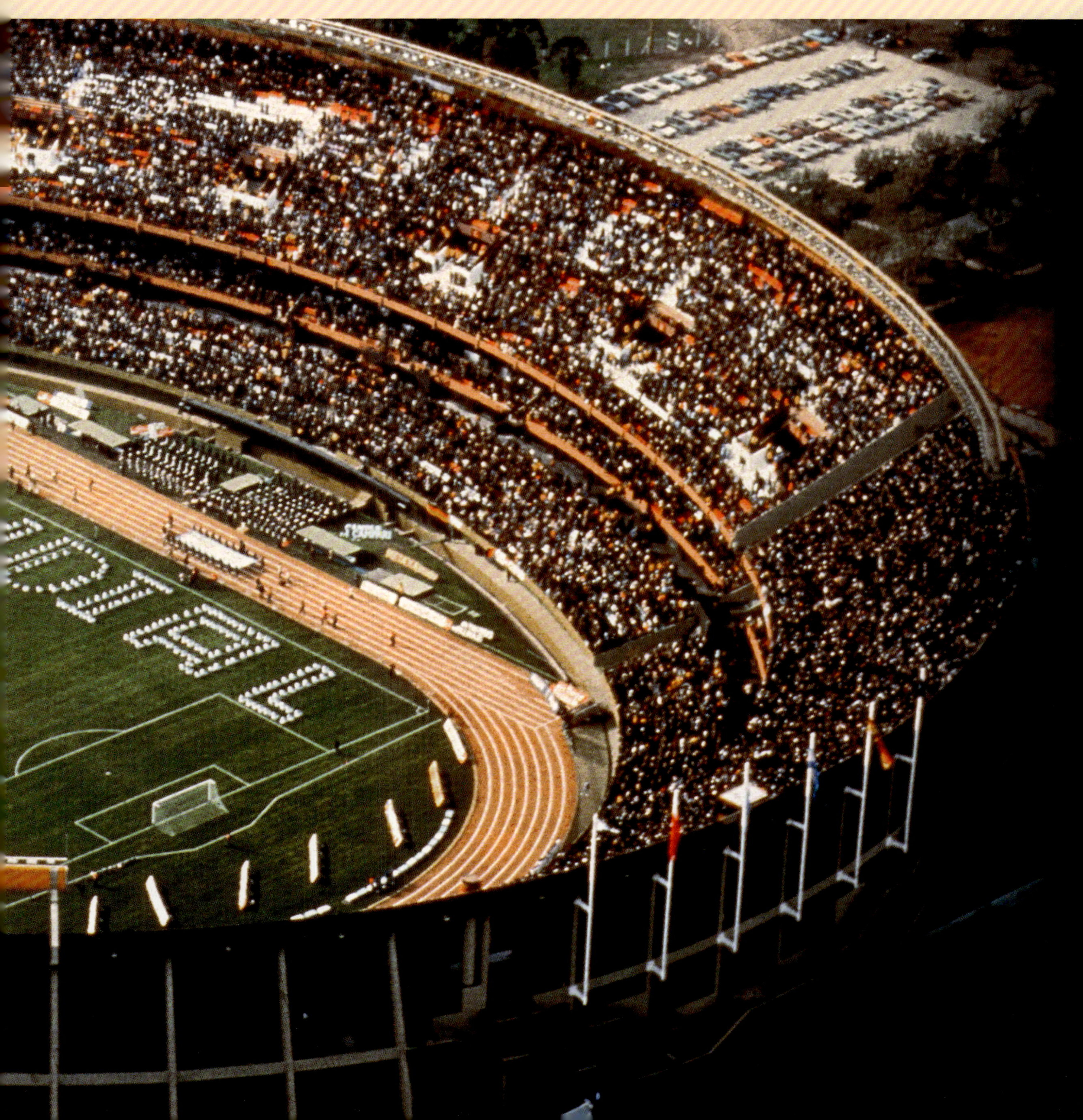

# 1970

HOST COUNTRY: **MEXICO**
CHAMPION: **BRAZIL**
RUNNER-UP: **ITALY**
THIRD PLACE: **WEST GERMANY OVER URUGUAY**

**In 1964, FIFA selected** Mexico City to host the 1970 World Cup, knowing full well that the altitude and hot, rainy summer weather at most venues would add new challenges to training regimens and preparation efforts for most teams. This would be the first Cup tournament held outside of Europe or South America, and the first with a guaranteed qualification spot for a team from the African confederation. As it turned out, Mexico 1970 would feature several firsts.

An extremely popular change — one *long* overdue — was each team's ability to substitute up to two players per match. This would be welcome in any tournament, but especially one likely to experience a punishing combo of heat and thin air. Another smart addition was the introduction of red and yellow penalty cards to help clarify calls and overcome language barriers between players and centre referees. This Cup would also debut the iconic thirty-two-panel Adidas Telstar as the official match ball, with its visually striking black-and-white alternating 'Buckminster' design — a big aesthetic improvement over the old brown ball made of leather strip panels sewn up with laces.

Finally, it would also be the first World Cup broadcast live in colour around the world, a landmark moment in the history of TV sports. The TV coverage would also deploy multiple camera angles and slow-motion replays to enhance dramatic moments — novelties that we take for granted today.

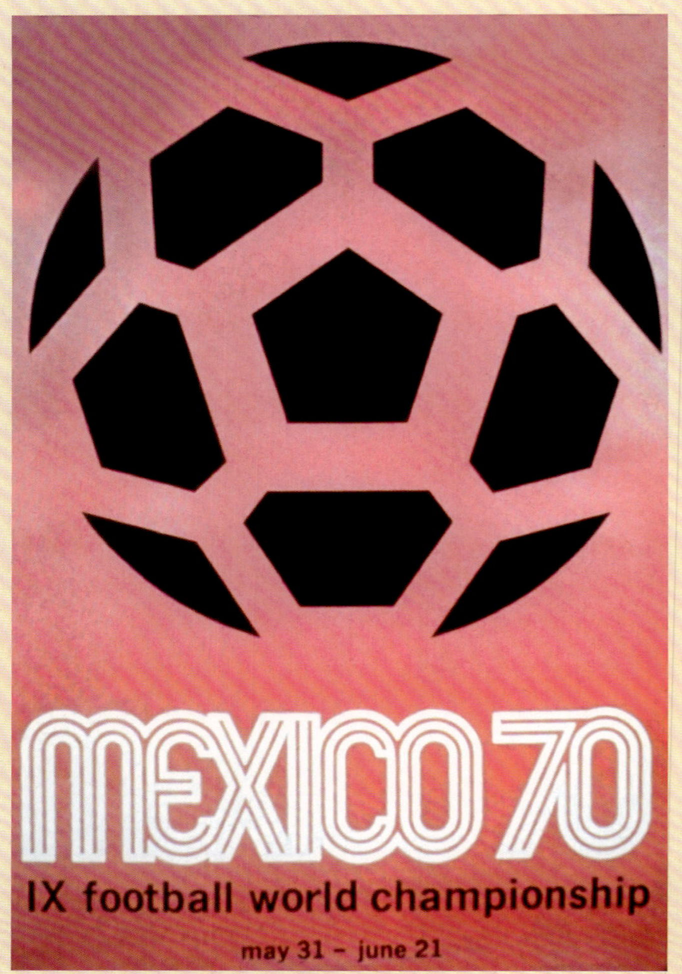

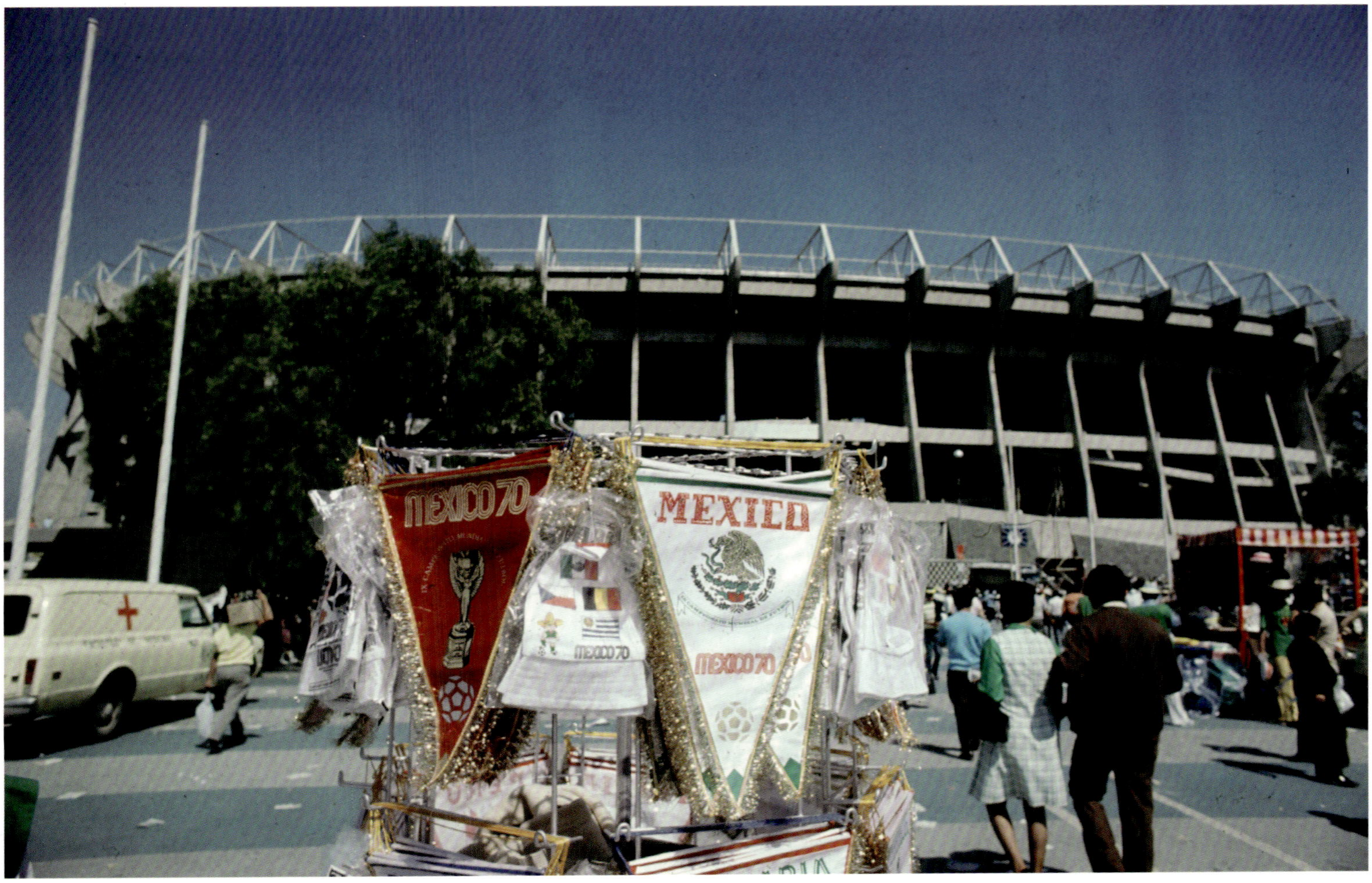

**PREVIOUS SPREAD** *An aerial view of the opening ceremony at the Estadio Monumental in Buenos Aires.*

**OPPOSITE** *The official poster of the 1970 World Cup, vibrant and minimalist, was issued in several colours and designed by American graphic designer Lance Wyman. Wyman had previously worked on promotional materials for the 1968 Summer Olympics.*

**ABOVE** *Souvenirs and pennants outside the Estadio Azteca in Mexico City.*

**RIGHT** *The iconic Adidas Telstar, official match ball of the 1970 World Cup. Its black-and-white panel design took inspiration from Eigil Nielsen, the founder of Select Sport and a former Danish goal-keeper. The Telstar has become a universally recognised symbol.*

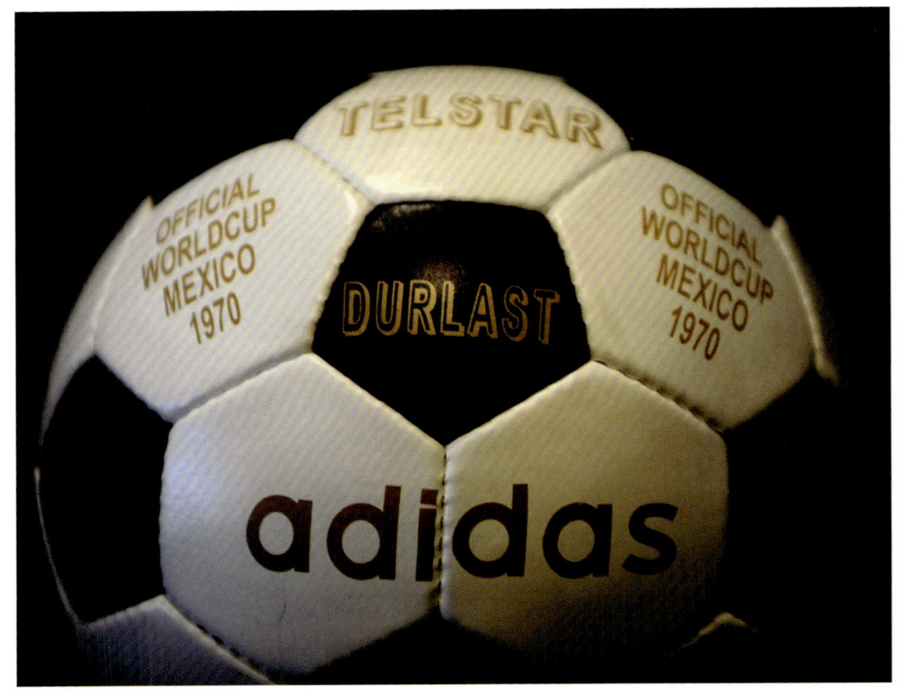

# Tournament: GROUP STAGE

### GROUP 1: SOVIET UNION, MEXICO, BELGIUM, EL SALVADOR

| | | |
|---:|---|---|
| Mexico 0 | 0 | Soviet Union |
| Belgium 3 | 1 | El Salvador |
| Soviet Union 4 | 1 | Belgium |
| Mexico 4 | 0 | El Salvador |
| Soviet Union 2 | 0 | El Salvador |
| Mexico 1 | 0 | Belgium |

**Advanced to Knockout Stage: Soviet Union, Mexico**

Played in Mexico City's grand new Azteca Stadium, these matches drew immense crowds for the home team. At the end, with Mexico and the Soviet Union tied on points and goal difference, the group 'winner' was determined by a draw of lots. But even though the Soviets won the draw, an ecstatic second-place Mexico moved into the knockout stage for the first time in its footballing history. Another historical first: in the tournament's kickoff match between the two teams, Soviet forward Anatoliy Puzach became the first-ever substitute player in a FIFA World Cup match when he came on to start the second half.

### GROUP 2: ITALY, URUGUAY, SWEDEN, ISRAEL

| | | |
|---:|---|---|
| Uruguay 2 | 0 | Israel |
| Italy 1 | 0 | Sweden |
| Uruguay 0 | 0 | Italy |
| Sweden 1 | 1 | Israel |
| Sweden 1 | 0 | Uruguay |
| Italy 0 | 0 | Israel |

**Advanced to Knockout Stage: Italy, Uruguay**

The defensive tactics that dominated the previous two Cup certainly influenced this group's play—six total goals in six games. Incredibly, Italy finished first in the group while scoring just a single goal in its three matches. The Italy–Sweden game, played in Toluca at 2,650 metres above sea level, was a grim display of energy conservation by both sides.

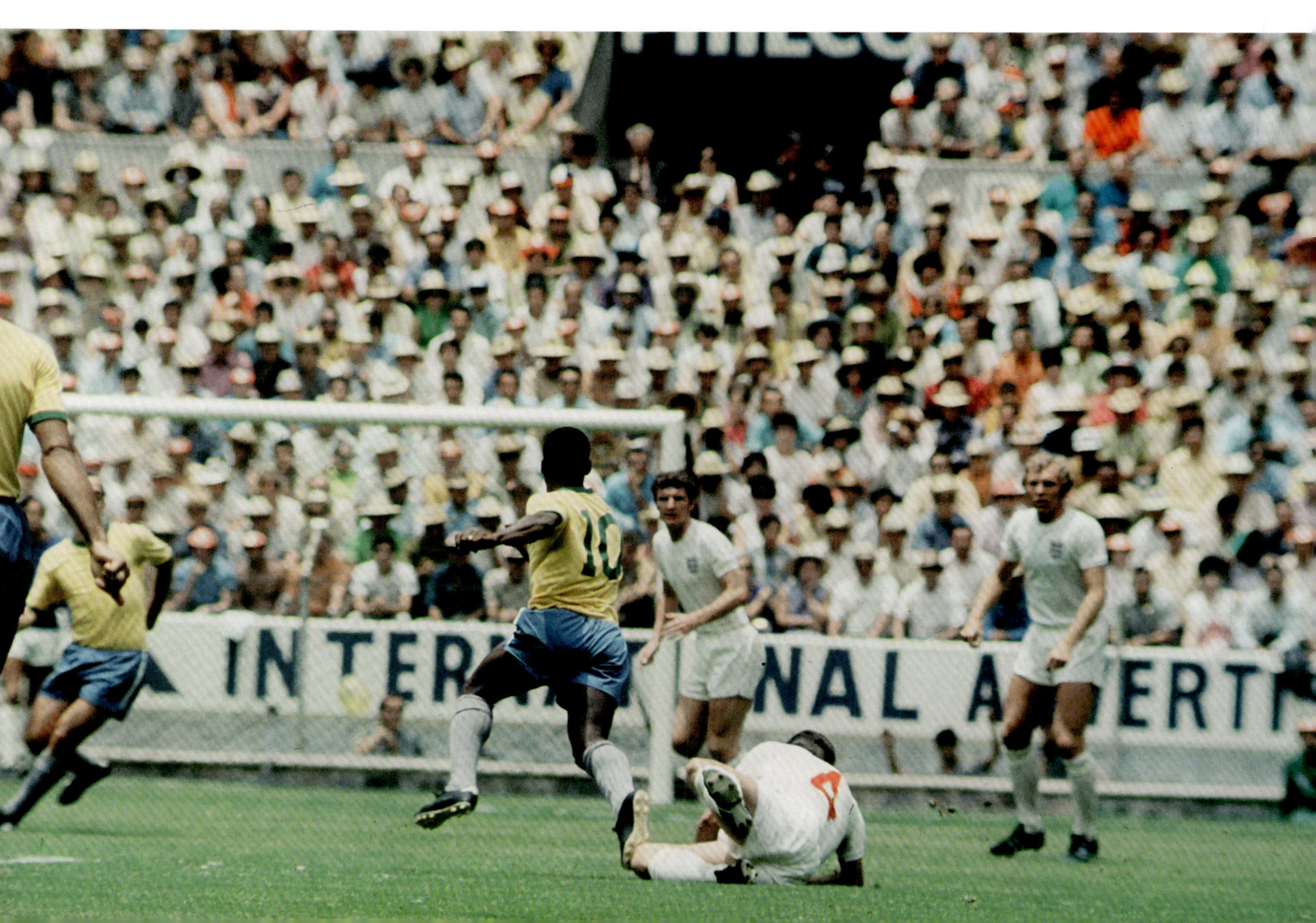

### GROUP 3: BRAZIL, ENGLAND, ROMANIA, CZECHOSLOVAKIA

| | | |
|---:|:---:|:---|
| England 1 | 0 | Romania |
| Brazil 4 | 1 | Czechoslovakia |
| Romania 2 | 1 | Czechoslovakia |
| Brazil 1 | 0 | England |
| Brazil 3 | 2 | Romania |
| England 1 | 0 | Czechoslovakia |

**_Advanced to Knockout Stage: Brazil, England_**

The champions of the previous two World Cups, Brazil and England, were drawn into this 'Group of Death' but both managed to advance to the quarter-finals. Overall, the English defence kept up its stellar play, allowing only one goal, but the English attack only produced two goals (of which one was a penalty kick). Meanwhile, Brazil's offence ran wild, scoring eight times, with four by Jairzinho and two by Pelé. The England–Brazil match proved to be an epic, with plenty of tough, hard-nosed play. Brazilian head coach Mário Zagallo called it 'a game for adults'. Indeed, a consensus of observers fully expected to see the two play again in the final.

**OPPOSITE** *Pelé glides around English defender Alan Mullery's tackle.*

**BELOW** *Mexico's José Vantolrá with a hard challenge on Evgeny Lovchev of the Soviet Union. A physical 0–0 draw that featured the first yellow card in World Cup history — shown to the Soviet Union's Kakhi Asatiani in the thirtieth minute.*

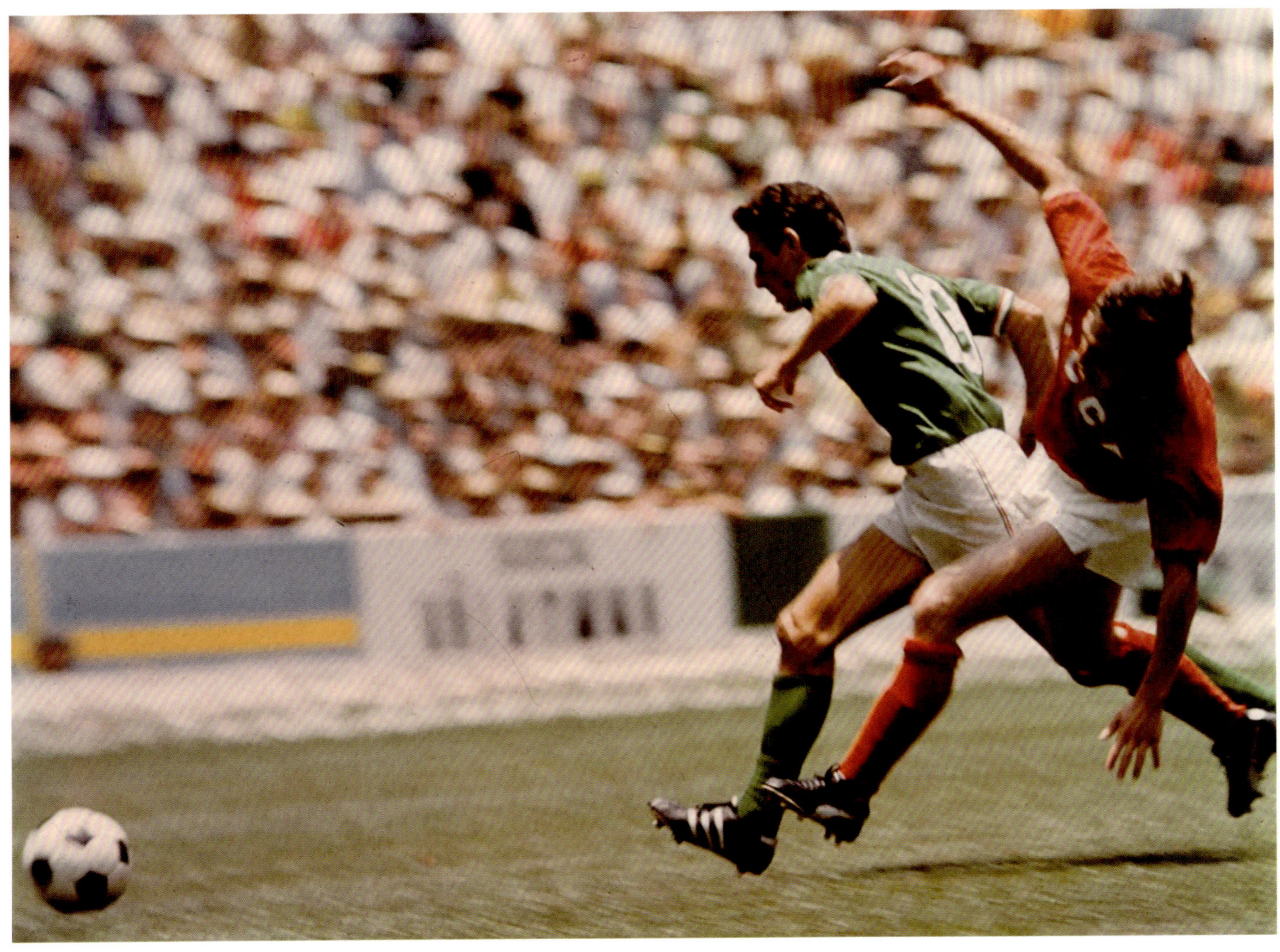

| | | |
|---:|:---:|:---|
| Peru 3 | 2 | Bulgaria |
| West Germany 2 | 1 | Morocco |
| Peru 3 | 0 | Morocco |
| West Germany 5 | 2 | Bulgaria |
| West Germany 3 | 1 | Peru |
| Bulgaria 1 | 1 | Morocco |

**Advanced to Knockout Stage: West Germany, Peru**

Gerd Müller exploded onto the international scene in the flashiest way possible, notching *two* hat-tricks in group play. Just two days before Peru's opening match against Bulgaria, the powerful Ancash earthquake off the Peruvian coast triggered massive debris-flow avalanches across the country, obliterating villages and killing 100,000 people. Stunned by the event, Peru played its opener in black armbands... but after trailing 2–0 early, the team made a spectacular comeback to win 3–2.

Peru went on to surprise the group by playing a relentless attacking style with flair, creativity, and an emphasis on one-touch passing influenced by their Brazilian coach, Didi, and exemplified by their catalyst and all-time great, Teófilo Cubillas. Not only was the system entertaining but it also worked, winning two games and advancing the Peruvians to the knockout stage.

Cubillas would notch five goals in the tournament, scoring at least once in all four of Peru's matches, including one against Brazil in Peru's 4–2 quarter-final loss. After Brazil won the 1970 Cup Final, Pelé reportedly said, 'Don't worry, I already have a successor, and it is Teófilo Cubillas.'

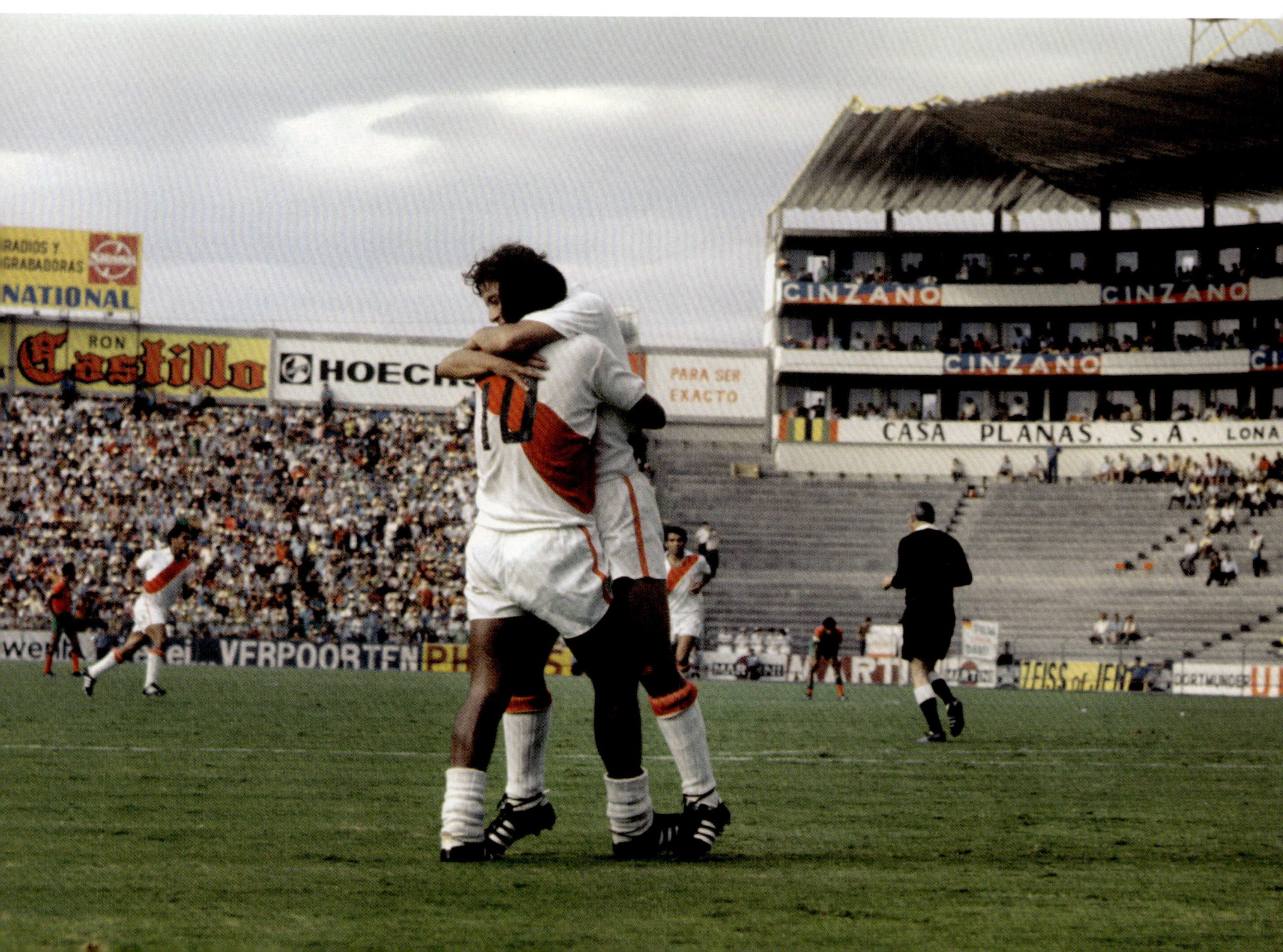

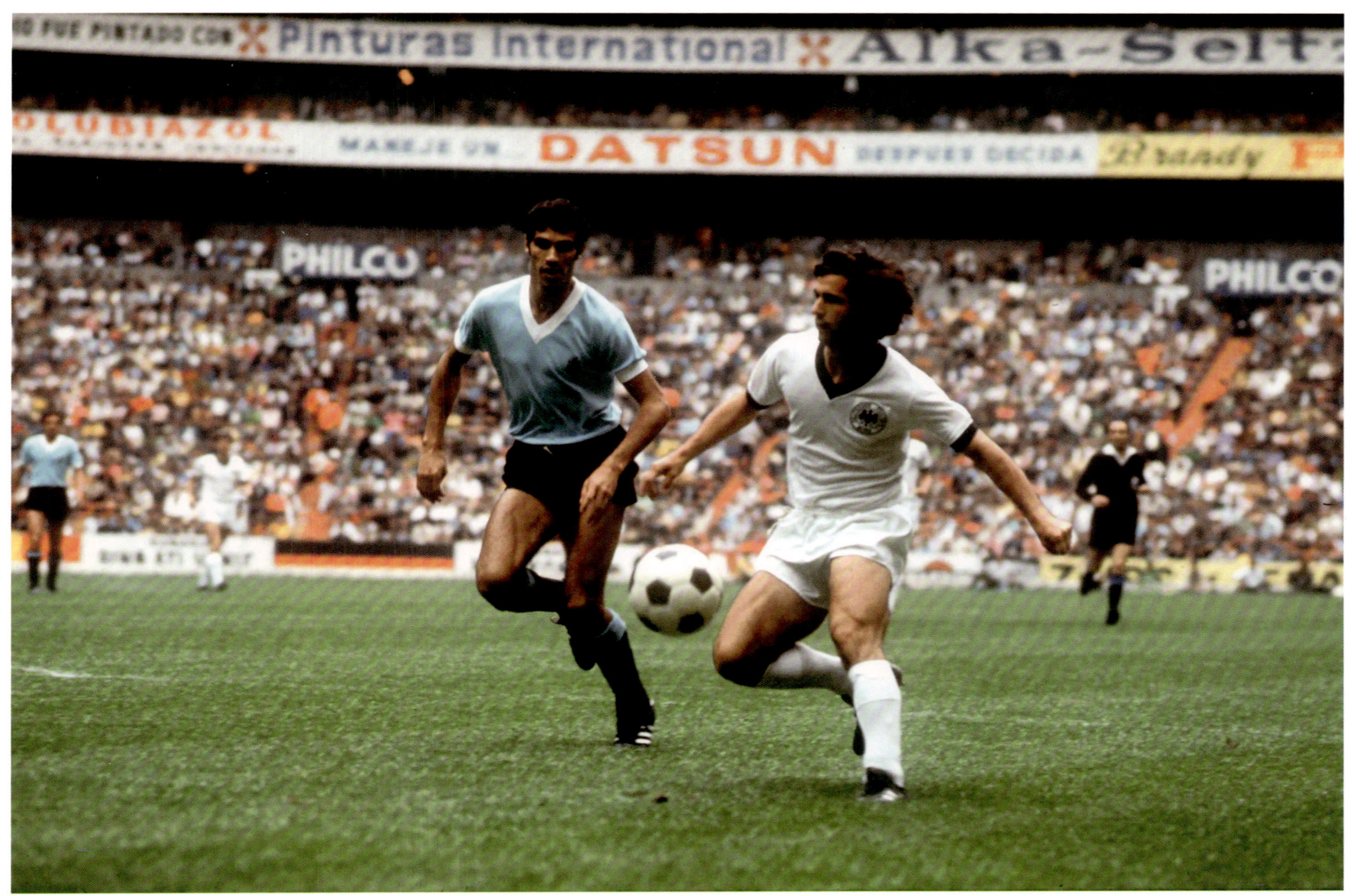

## 'THE ULTIMATE GOAL POACHER'

**That backhanded compliment from** Gary Lineker, an elite goal scorer himself, sums up the complicated brilliance of Gerd Müller, the greatest scorer of his generation. Müller's clinical finishing around the six-yard goal box was almost mythic in quality. The journalist David Winner captured its essence, calling Müller 'short, squat, awkward-looking and not notably fast . . . but he had a lethal acceleration over short distances, a remarkable aerial game, and uncanny goal scoring instincts.' His teammate, the peerless centre-back Franz Beckenbauer, said of being matched against Müller in training practises: 'I never had a chance.'

Müller was perhaps the greatest revelation of a 1970 World Cup that was otherwise dominated by Brazil's greatest team ever and its line-up of superstars like Pelé, Carlos Alberto, and Jairzinho. Hat-tricks in back-to-back group games, plus a brace in the semi-finals? Ten goals for the tournament? It was a transcendent performance by a twenty-four-year-old striker on a team full of its own stars, too, like Beckenbauer, captain Uwe Seeler, and the great Sepp Maier in goal. Müller's 1970 coming-out party in Mexico has rarely been matched in football history, but there was more to come from the legendary goal poacher.

**OPPOSITE** *Number 10 Teófilo Cubillas, retroactively awarded the tournament's FIFA Young Player Award, embraces teammate Roberto Chale after scoring against Morocco in a 3–0 victory.*

**ABOVE** *West Germany's talismanic striker Gerd Müller prepares to take on Uruguayan defender Atilio Ancheta in the third-place match.*

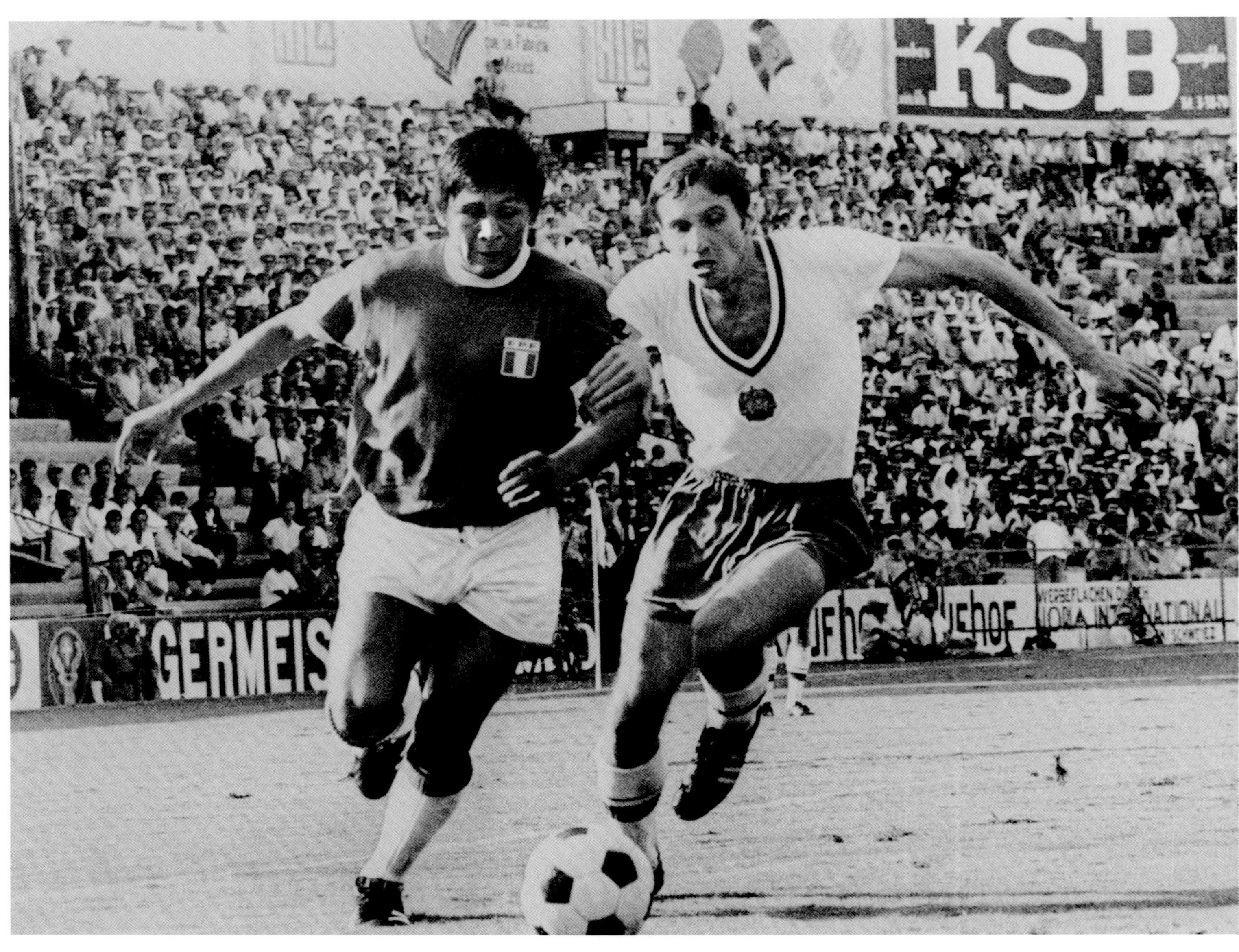

**ABOVE** *Peru's Hugo Sotil dribbles past Bulgaria's Ivan Davidov in the Group 4 opener.*

**OPPOSITE** *Wolfgang Overath of West Germany is challenged by Héctor Chumpitaz (nicknamed El Capitán de América) of Peru. West Germany ended Peru's surprising hot streak with a 3–1 victory.*

*'The first World Cup broadcast live in colour around the world, a landmark moment in the history of TV sports.'*

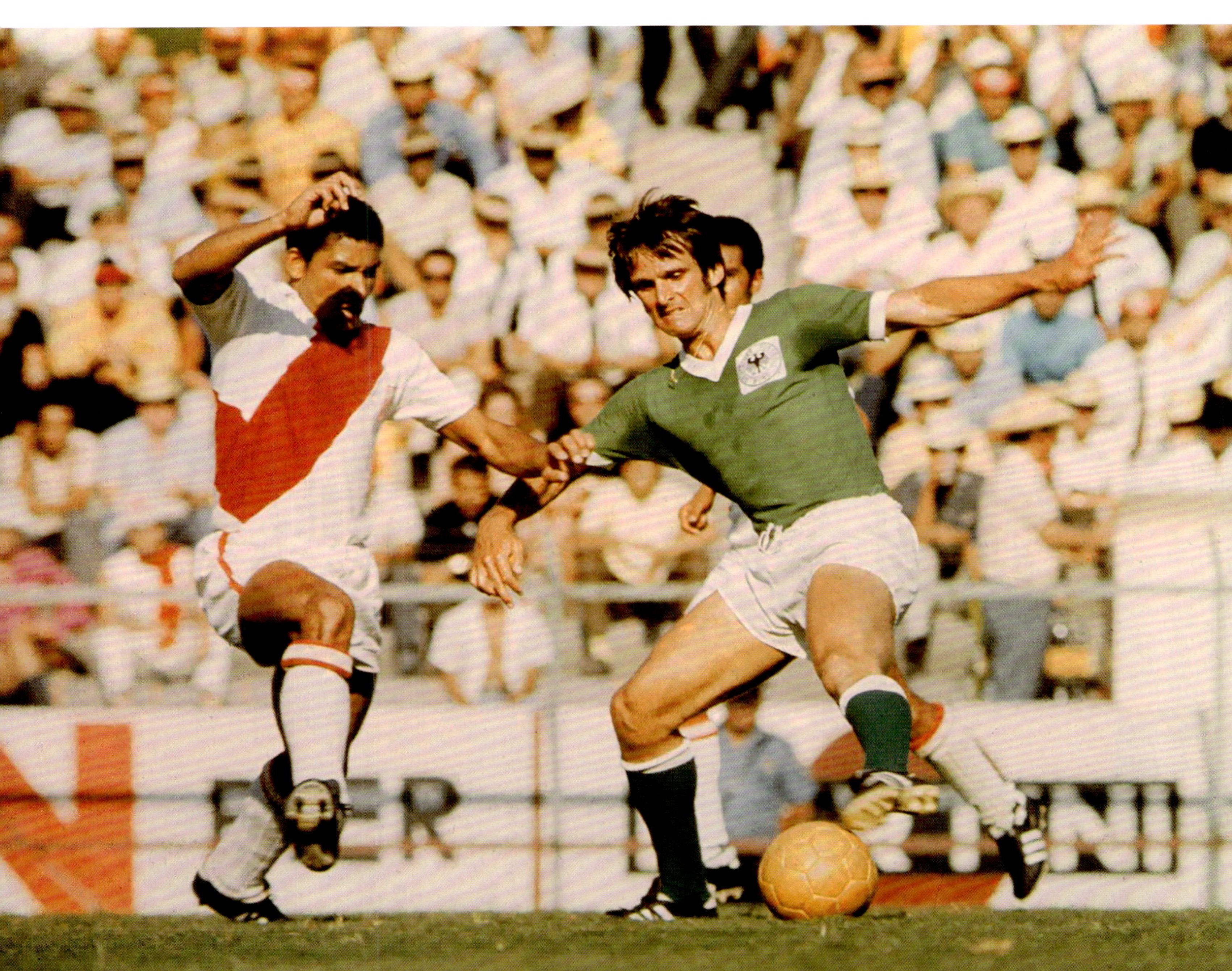

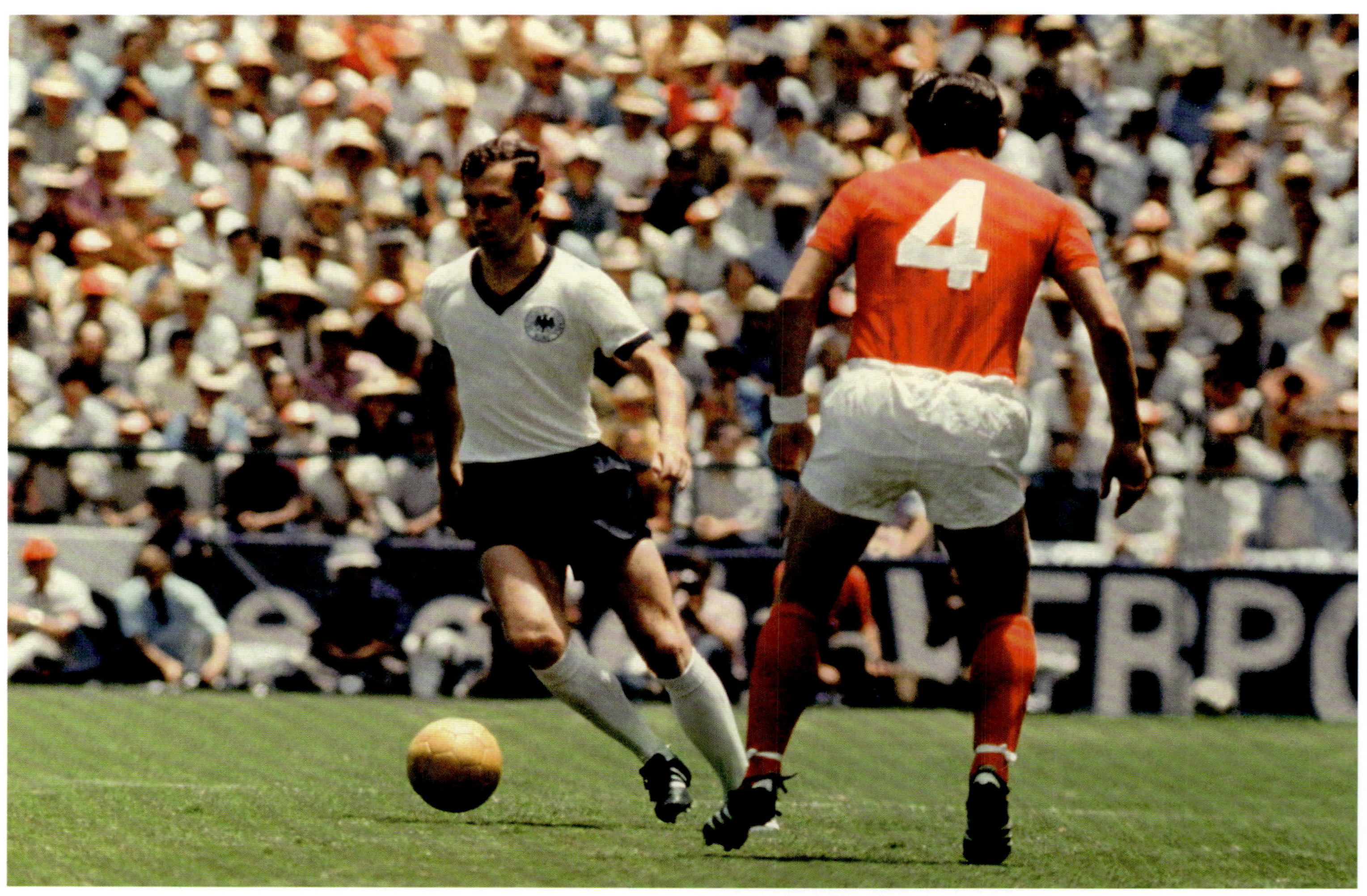

## QUARTER-FINALS

| | | |
|---:|---|---|
| Uruguay 1 | 0 | Soviet Union |
| | | (after extra time) |
| Brazil 4 | 2 | Peru |
| Italy 4 | 1 | Mexico |
| West Germany 3 | 2 | England |
| | | (after extra time) |

England blew a 2–0 lead in its loss, with the inexorable Müller volleying home the winner in extra time for West Germany. Mexico thrilled the home crowd in Toluca by taking the early lead against Italy, but an unfortunate own goal tied the score. The cohesive Italian attack broke down the Mexican defence for three more goals in the second half.

Brazil versus Peru was an eagerly anticipated matchup of two high-flying offences committed to all-out attack. Brazil scored two early, but a dangerous Peru side fought back to make it 2–1 (Gallardo) and then 3–2 (Cubillas). Finally, a late Jairzinho capper locked the win for Brazil. By contrast, the Soviet Union versus Uruguay was described as a 'dull and dirty match', closely contested, with the lone goal scored in extra time. The Soviets complained that the ball had rolled out of play before the goal action, but TV replays—an exciting and helpful new addition for live TV viewers—showed that it had not.

**ABOVE** *Franz Beckenbauer (left), nicknamed Der Kaiser (The Emperor). The defensive anchor of an ascending West Germany, he frequently stepped forward to support the midfield and contributed the first goal in his side's quarter-final victory over England.*

**OPPOSITE** *Italy legend Gianni Rivera (far left, partially obscured by teammate Angelo Domenghini, wearing the number 13) watches the path of his strike. The ball would find the back of the net and eliminate West Germany. It was the fifth goal to be scored during extra time.*

# SEMI-FINALS

Brazil 3 | 1 Uruguay
Italy 4 | 3 West Germany
| (after extra time)

The semi-finals saw two monumental matches played simultaneously on 17 June. One was the rematch of *El Maracanazo*, Brazil's heartbreaking 1950 loss to Uruguay. As was their habit, Brazil conceded the first goal to Uruguay but equalised just before halftime. The second half was a back-and-forth affair until Jairzinho, who scored the deciding goal in several contests during this Cup, put his side ahead at the seventy-six-minute mark. Brazil added an insurance goal in the final minute, completing their redemption.

The other semifinal, pitting Italy against West Germany, was equally remarkable—so remarkable that a plaque placed at Estadio Azteca where the match was played commemorates it as '*Partido del Siglo*'—'The Game of the Century'. Italy scored early and eighty minutes later sat on the very edge of a 1–0 victory until a miraculous goal by Karl-Heinz Schnellinger, a defender who pushed forward in the desperate final seconds. As it unfolded, the German TV commentator Ernst Huberty famously shouted, '*Schnellinger! Of all people!*' It was the only goal he ever scored in his forty-seven caps for the national team.

Extra time turned into an extraordinary flurry of tit-for-tat drama, with an outrageous five more goals scored. Gerd Müller gave West Germany its first lead, but two swift Italian goals pushed them back ahead, 3–2. Then Müller scored yet again at 110' (his tenth of the tournament) to knot the score. But just one minute later, Gianni Rivera drove home a heroic winner for Italy, sending them to the final.

On the topic of heroism: Franz Beckenbauer fractured his clavicle in the seventieth minute, but West Germany had already used up its two allotted substitutions. So 'der Kaiser' stayed on the pitch…and played the rest of the match, plus extra time, with his arm in a tight sling.

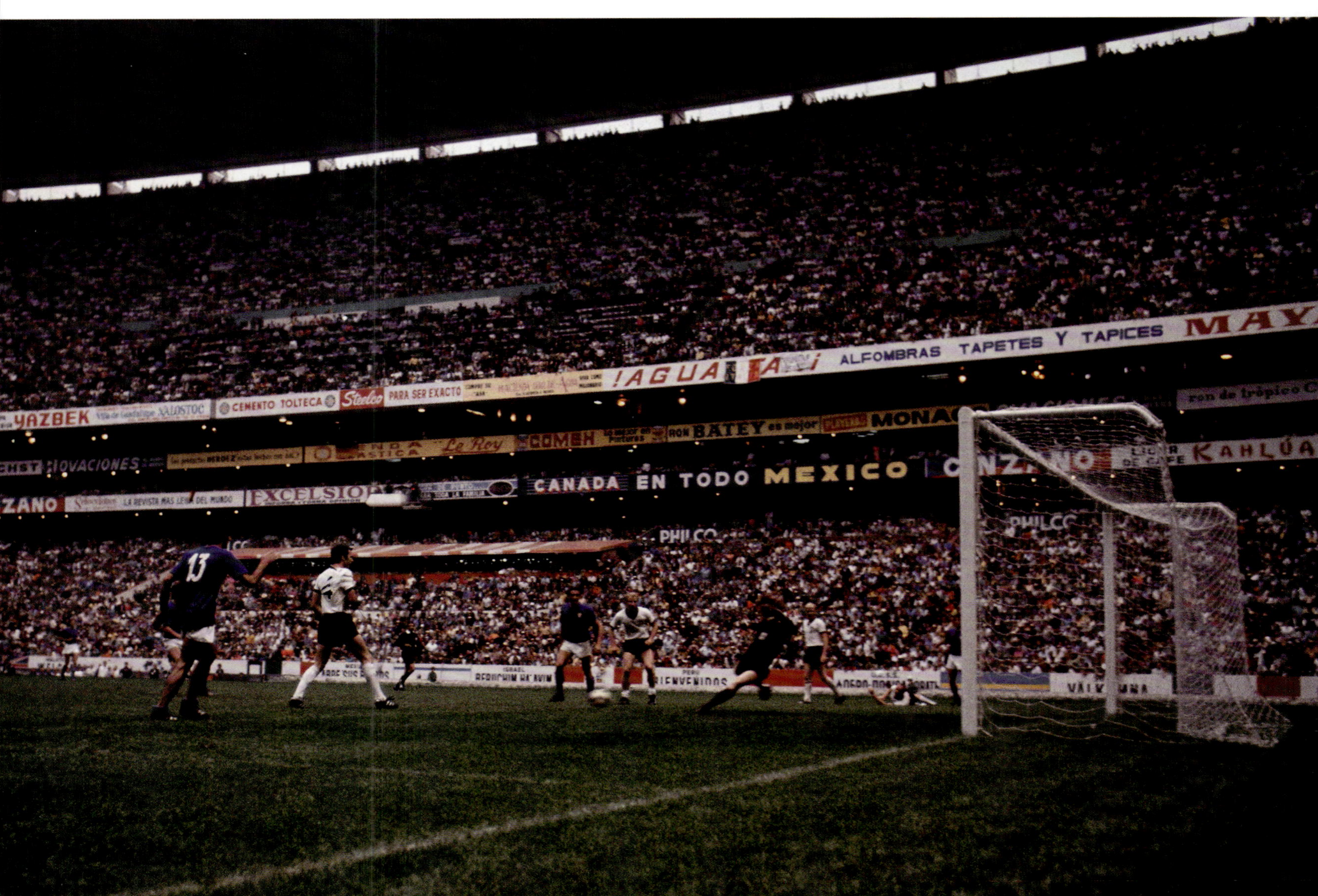

## PELÉ'S AUDACIOUS MISS

**The 1970 Brazil–Uruguay semi-final** was an epic clash made even more memorable by Pelé's legendary 'runaround' move in the second half — often called the most skilful miss in World Cup history. With the score tied 1–1, Brazilian forward Tostão slid a through ball in front of Pelé as he burst behind the defence. Pelé reached the ball before the charging Uruguayan goalkeeper, Ladislao Mazurkiewicz, but faked a touch, freezing Mazurkiewicz and letting the ball roll past the keeper on the outside.

In a flash, Pelé burst around the keeper's other side, reaching the rolling ball just to the right of the now-untended goal. Unfortunately, the angle was too sharp, and Pelé's shot slid a few inches wide left . . . but observers were still stunned by the brilliant creativity, soon to become a permanent piece of football folklore. Sportswriters dubbed it the 'magical miss' and a confirmation of Pelé's consummate skill. *The Indian Express* called it 'stripping football to its most rarified essence'.

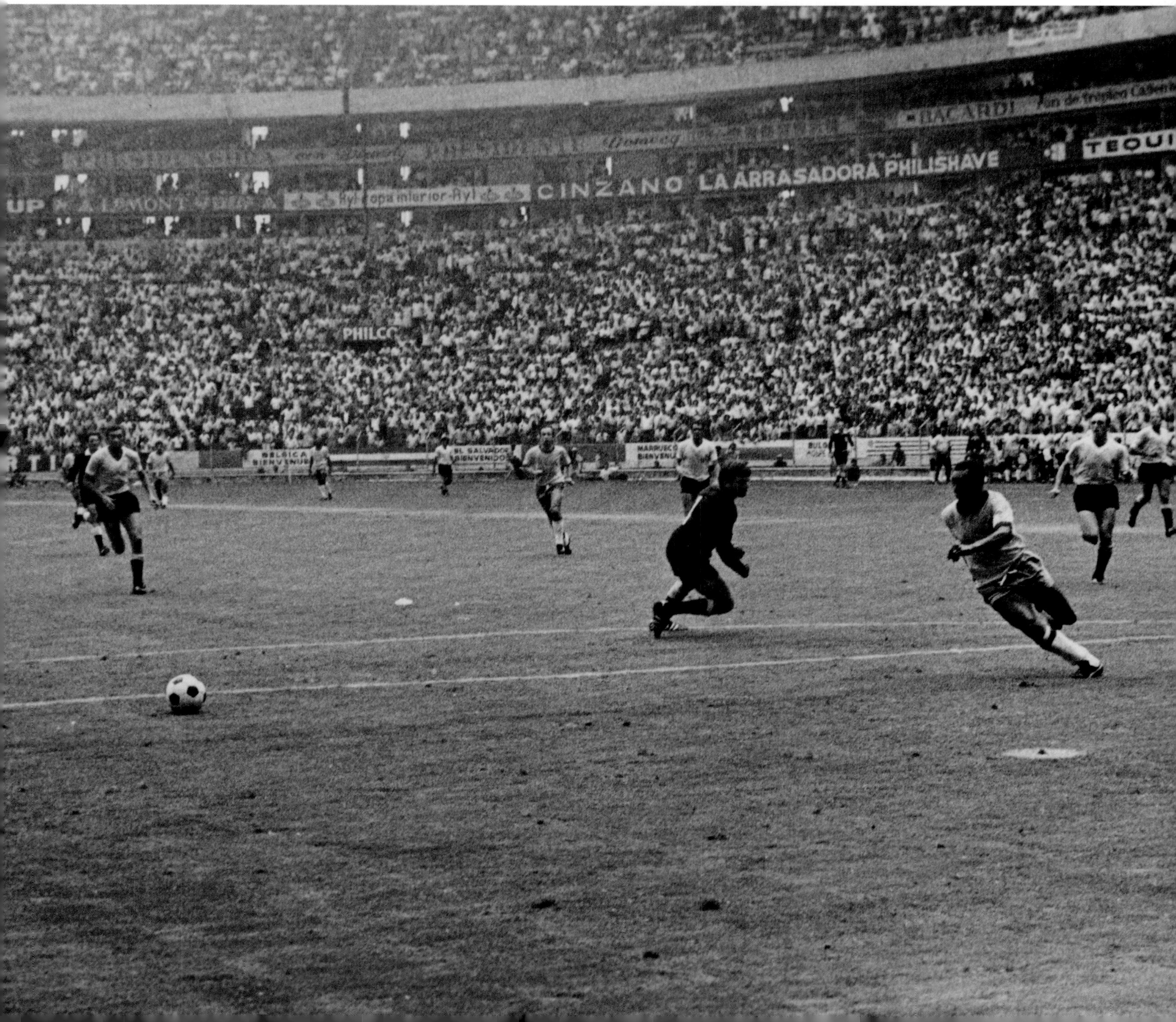

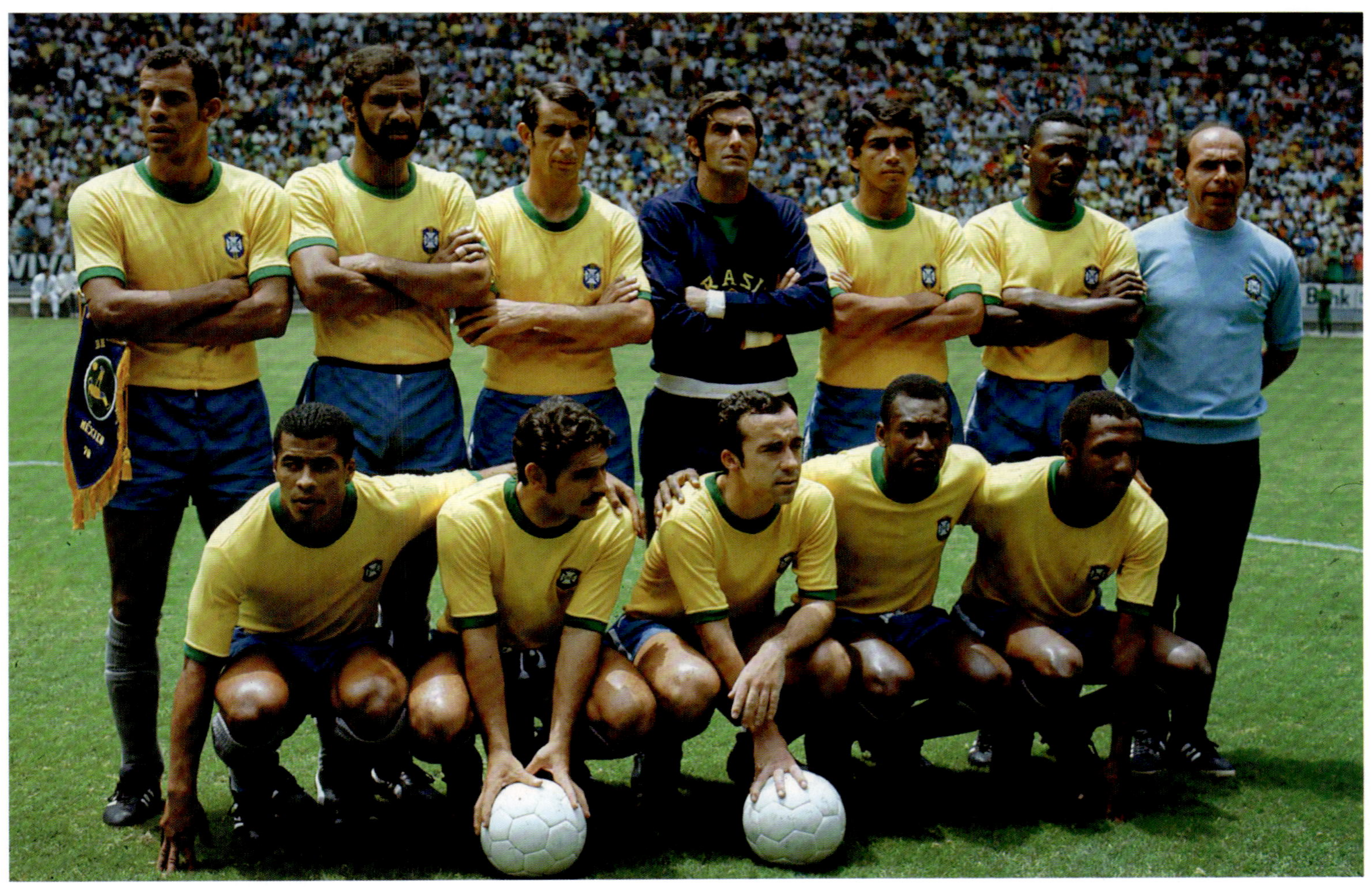

**OPPOSITE** *Pelé successfully rounds Uruguayan Ladislao Mazurkiewicz, but his shot would go just wide.*

**ABOVE** *Brazil's 1970 squad, widely considered among the very best World Cup teams ever assembled. They became permanent keepers of the Jules Rimet Trophy for winning Brazil its third title.*

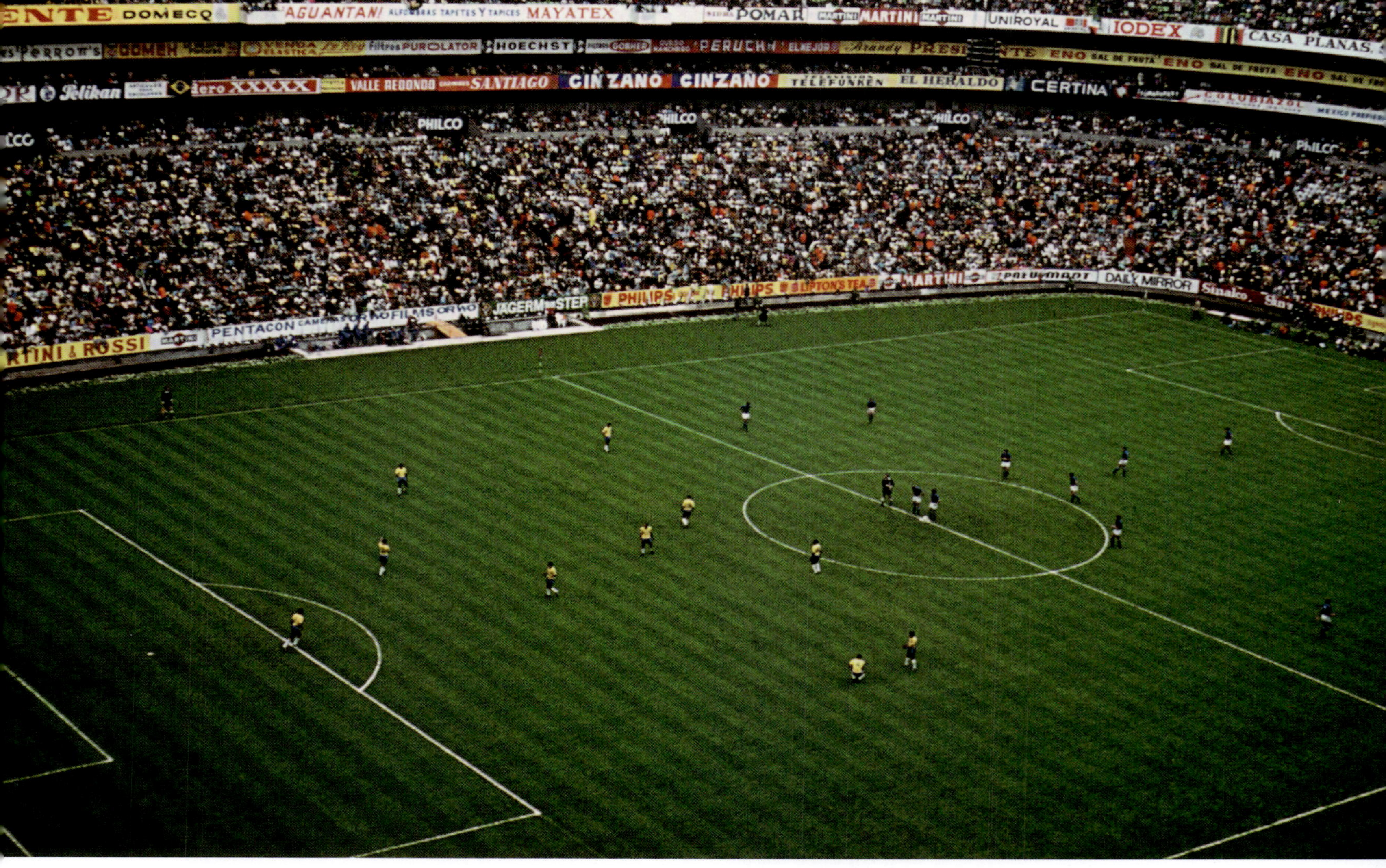

## FINAL

| Brazil 4 | 1 Italy (First Place) |
|---|---|
| West Germany 1 | 0 Uruguay (Third Place) |

The third-place match drew an appreciative 100,000 fans to Estadio Azteca in Mexico City. Uruguay played aggressive attacking football, and even though Wolfgang Overath tallied first for the Germans in the twenty-sixth minute, few thought it would be the end of scoring. But West Germany had become adept at soaking up pressure and defusing seemingly lethal attacks, and the frustrated Uruguayans couldn't convert on their chances. Their only consolation was being the only team in the tournament to stop Gerd Müller from scoring, as Müller had also scored in all six pre-Cup qualifiers that West Germany played, a remarkable string of offensive production for a single striker.

The next day, the Cup Final turned into a perfect culmination of the generally exciting, fast-paced tournament. Brazil's 'Golden Team' was too much to handle, although Italy played a stout first half and equalised after Pelé's early goal, going into halftime tied at 1–1. In the second half, however, the Brazilian attack simply overwhelmed the chasing Italians with three lovely scores down the stretch, capped by another glorious moment— the iconic 'Nine Pass Goal'.

And with that, Brazil finished an undefeated run by what many consider the greatest team in World Cup history. With transcendent players like Pelé, Jairzinho, Rivellino, Carlos Alberto, and Tostão, Brazil had mastered a creative attacking style that relied as much on clever sequential connections as on individual talent. Brazil's 1970 run to the title would also cement the great Pelé's status as the first global sports legend. As team captain Carlos Alberto put it, 'Playing with Pelé felt like you had God on your side.'

By winning their third World Cup championship, Brazil was awarded the Jules Rimet Trophy to keep in perpetuity, as stipulated by Rimet himself back in 1930.

# THE FLOWING NINE-MAN MOVE

***The Guardian* called** the final goal of the 1970 World Cup Final 'a goal that has come to embody the apotheosis of team sport'. Starting from its defensive half, Brazil linked nine consecutive passes, including Pelé's perfectly weighted final ball into space, before Carlos Alberto's thundering strike into the far-left corner made the score 4–1. To the rest of the world, the sequence epitomised the joyful spontaneity of 'The Beautiful Game' as played by the Brazilians.

**OPPOSITE** *The Estadio Azteca as Brazil and Italy await the starting whistle of the final.*

**BELOW** *Tostão and Pelé run toward goal scorer Carlos Alberto (behind the net), celebrating one of the most brilliant team goals in football history.*

**FOLLOWING PAGE, LEFT** *Pelé during the 1970 World Cup.*

**FOLLOWING PAGE, RIGHT** *Pelé immortalised following Brazil's triumph and, in the eyes of many, assumes the throne as football's greatest-ever exponent.*

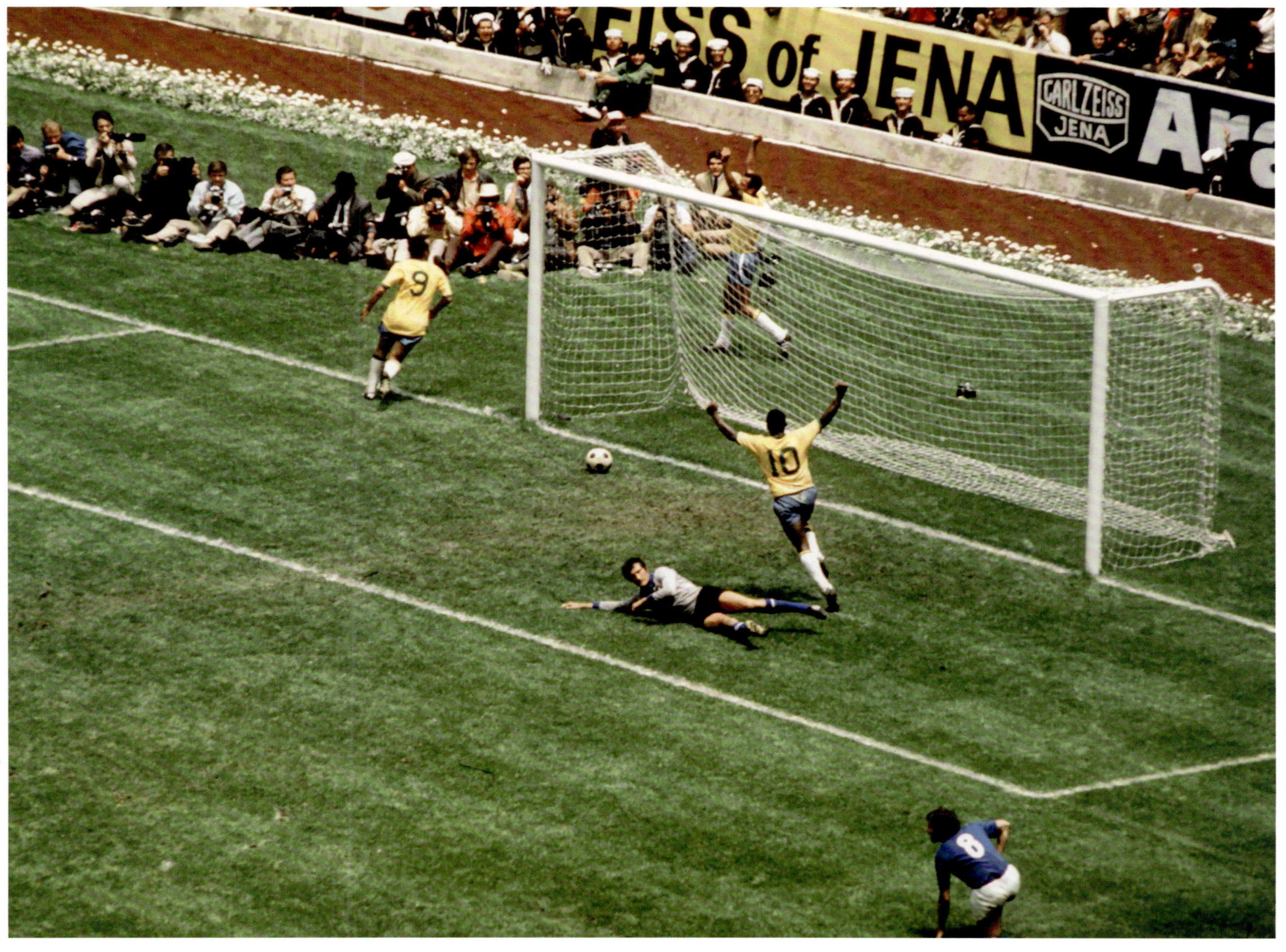

## PELÉ ELEVATED

**When the final whistle** of the 1970 World Cup signified Brazil's return to the throne, the squad instinctively hoisted its reigning king into the air. Clearly the team's leader and talisman, Pelé was the spearpoint of what *The Times* so poetically called 'the relentless menace of Brazil's magnificent attackers [who] preoccupied the opposition with worries about survival'.

Esteemed football analyst and writer John Giles provided a perfect benediction for Pelé's performance in that 1970 Cup, and for his overall brilliance: 'Pele's greatest gift is humility. If the most effective thing he can do on the field is roll the ball six yards to the nearest man, that is what he does. Nobody is better at doing the impossible when it's needed, but he has no inclination to indulge in unnecessary miracles.'

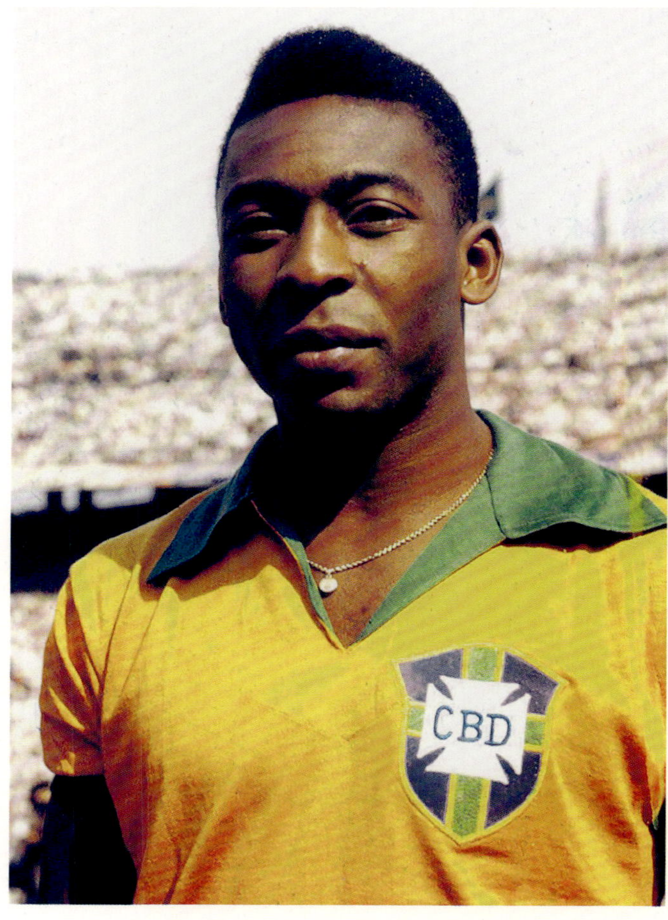

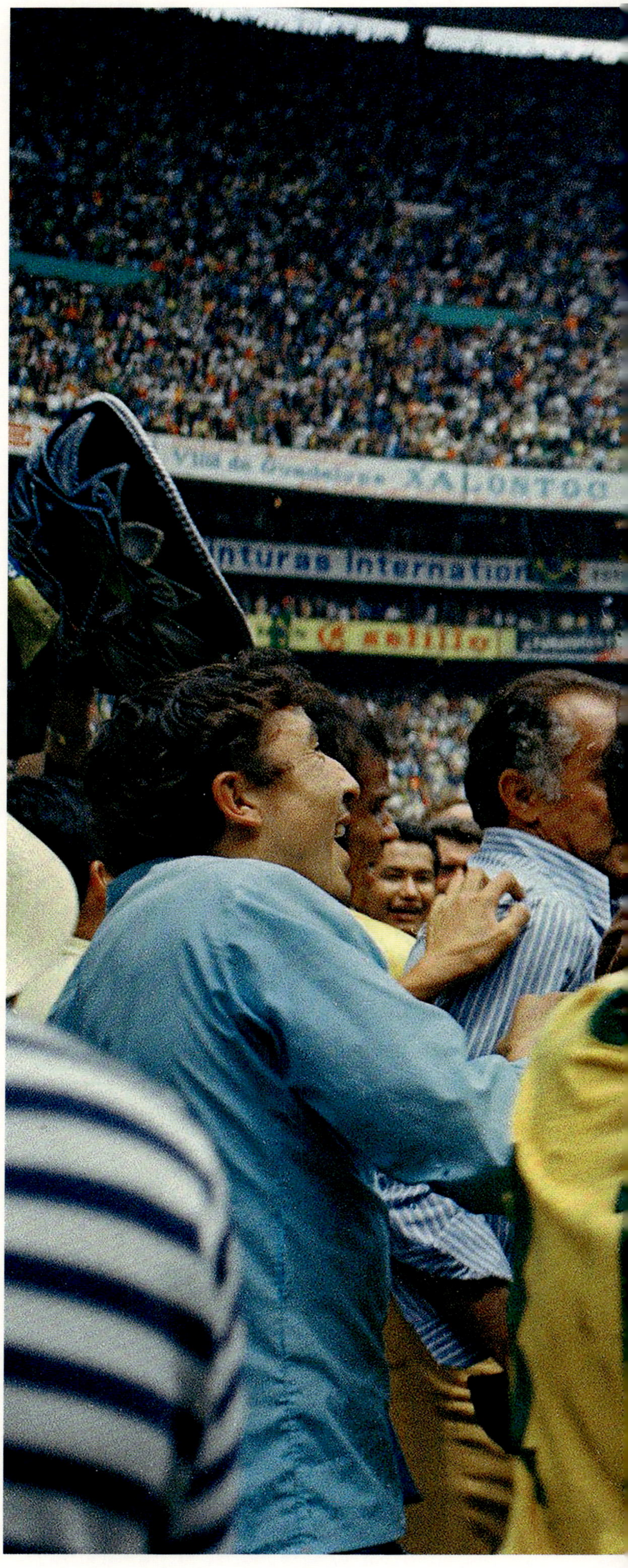

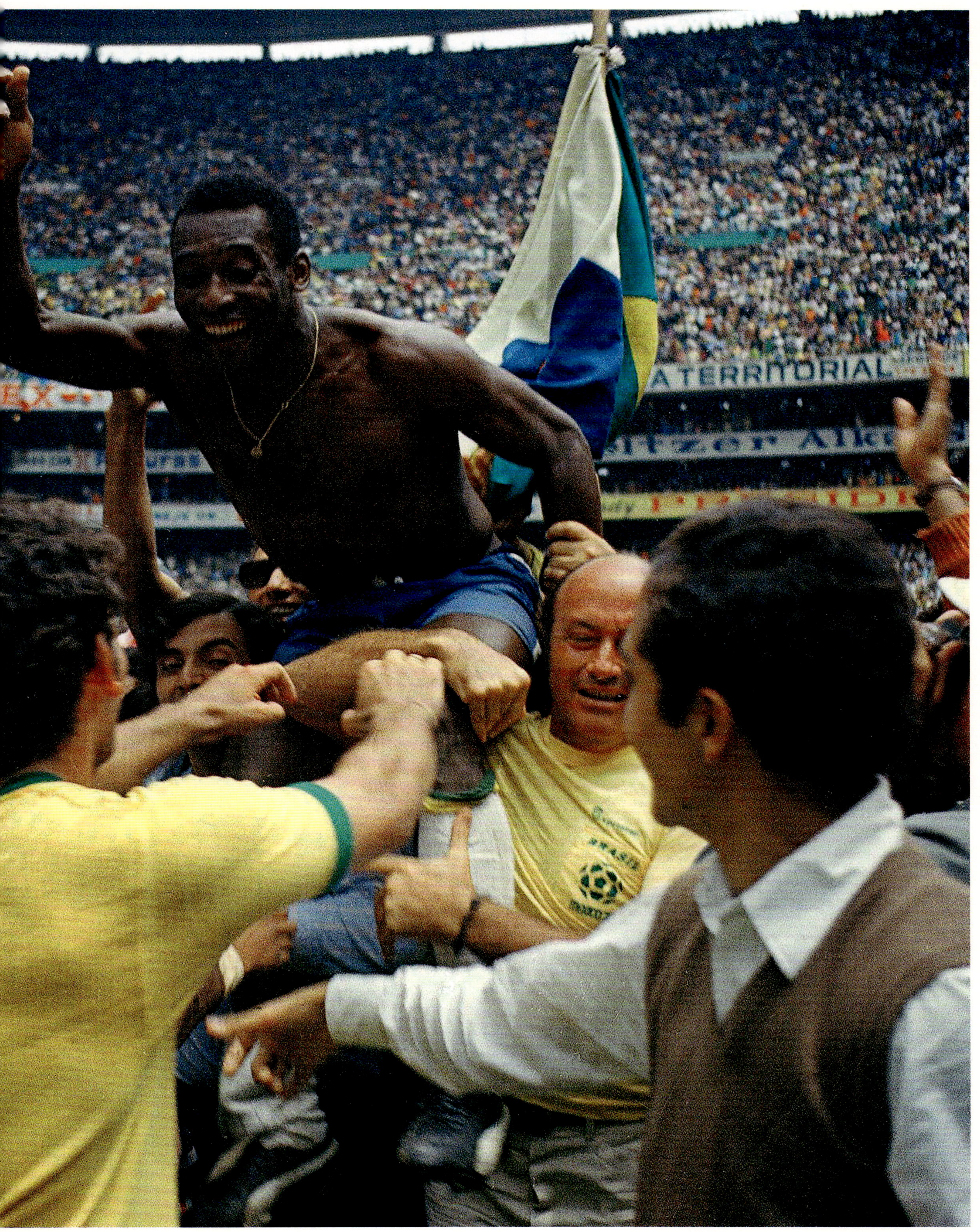

# 1974

HOST COUNTRY: **WEST GERMANY**
CHAMPION: **WEST GERMANY**
RUNNER-UP: **NETHERLANDS**
THIRD PLACE: **POLAND OVER BRAZIL**

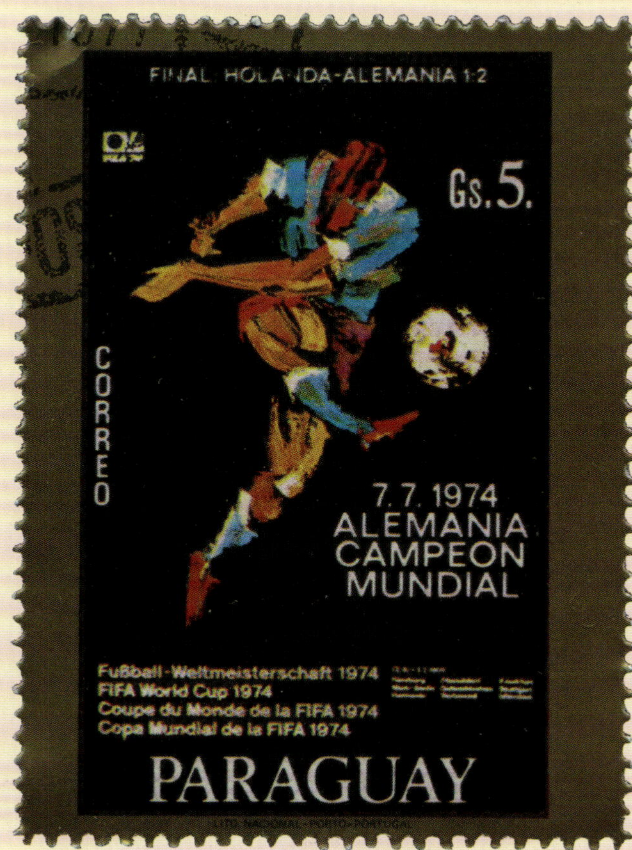



**World events put a heavy stamp** on the 1974 World Cup hosted by West Germany. Just two years earlier, a murderous terrorist attack on Israeli athletes had shattered the Munich Summer Olympics so, as a result, security for the World Cup tournament was heavy and expansive, with tactical police units guarding team hotels. And with West Berlin chosen as a co-host — a walled-in West German urban island surrounded by Soviet-controlled East German territory — the spectre of the ongoing Cold War loomed over the Cup, too.

*LEFT A Paraguayan stamp displays the official 1974 World Cup poster, designed by German artist Horst Schäfer, an abstract, impressionistic interpretation of a footballer's form and movement.*

# A NEW FORMAT

**Despite international turmoil,** the essence of goodwill inspired by World Cup competition remained strong. Because Brazil had been gifted the Jules Rimet Trophy after winning its third championship in 1970, FIFA sponsored a design contest for a new trophy and received fifty-three submissions from seven countries. The winning design came from Italian sculptor Silvio Gazzaniga: two stylised human figures holding up a golden Earth. Thus, the Cup itself now reflected the international spirit of co-operation. Called the 'FIFA World Cup Trophy', it was cast of 18-karat gold with two bands of malachite on its base.

The 1974 Cup also featured a new scheduling plan. The initial group stage kept the now-customary round-robin format (four groups of four), but instead of moving into a knockout stage, the eight advancing teams were sorted into two more groups of four, with each group playing another round-robin. The two group winners of that second stage met in the final, with the respective runners-up playing in a third-place match. If either of those two matches ended in a tie after extra time, FIFA introduced the penalty shootout to determine the winner — a skill-based method that proved much better, and much more popular, than drawing lots.

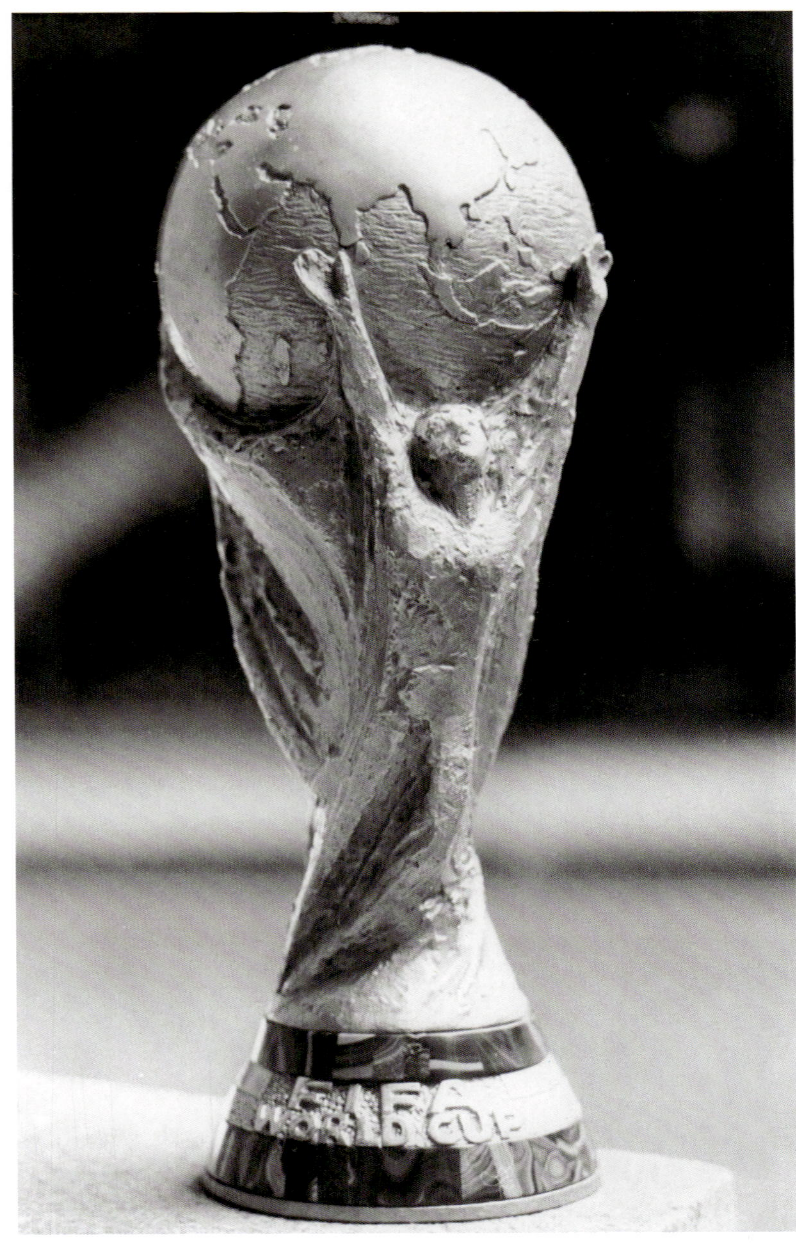

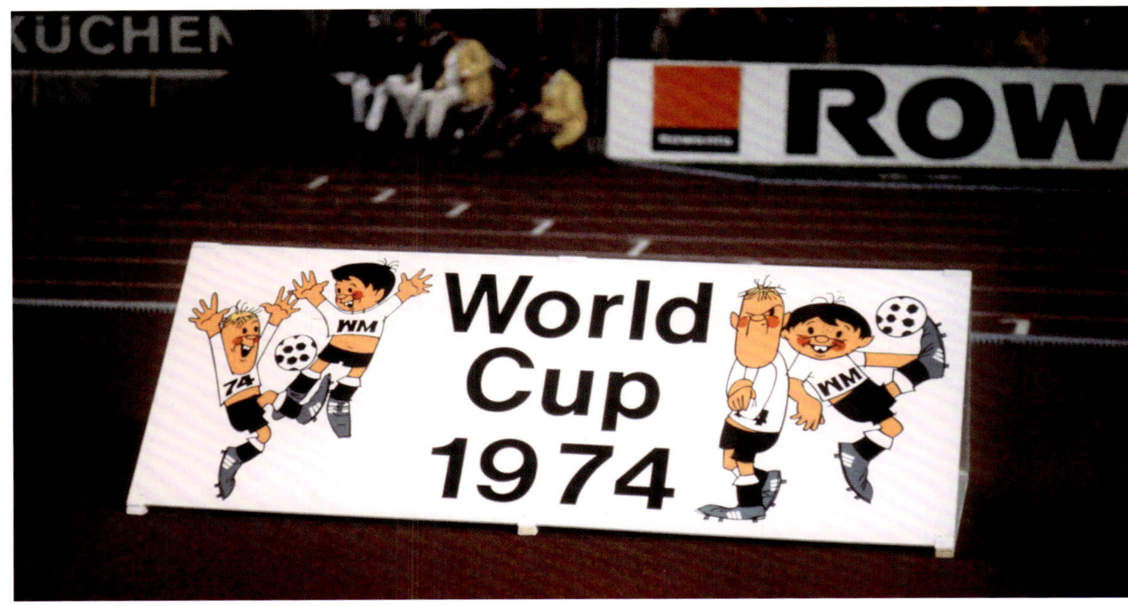



**LEFT** *A billboard featuring Tip and Tap, the official mascots of the 1974 World Cup.*

**ABOVE** *The new FIFA World Cup Trophy, introduced in 1974 and still in use as of the 2026 World Cup.*

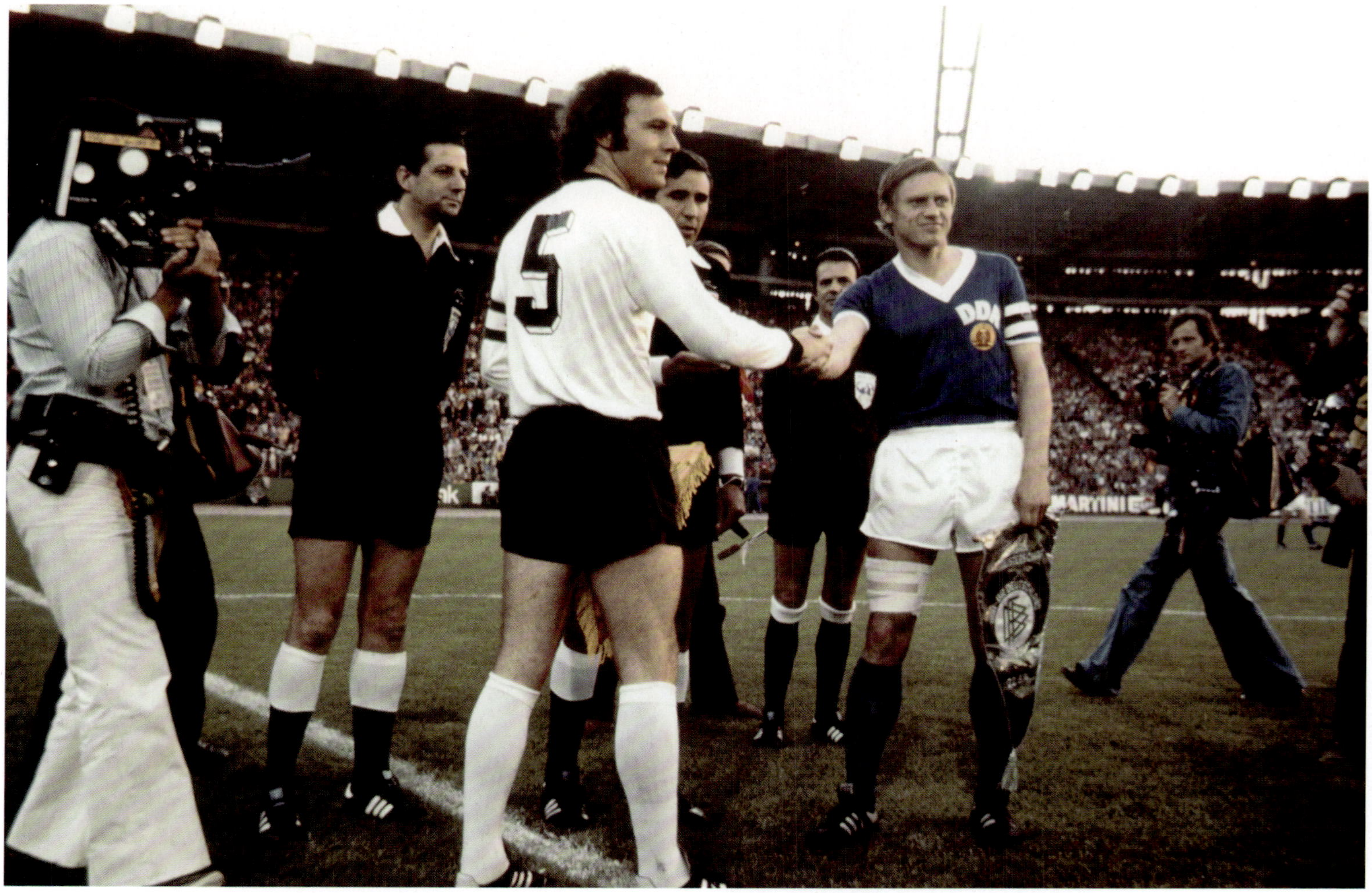

## EAST vs WEST

**Group 1 featured the** slightly uncomfortable pairing of West and East Germany, the first and only time their senior national teams would ever play. (Their amateur squads did meet three times in the Olympics, however.) The East's 1–0 victory was a true shocker, considering West Germany was a tournament favourite and this was East Germany's first-ever Cup. Many consider it one of the biggest upsets in Cup history, even though both teams had already qualified for the next stage thanks to their respective results through the first two matches.

As you might expect, the politically charged match drew intense interest and an enormous TV audience across the two Germanys. The forward who scored, Jürgen Sparwasser, became such a hero in East Germany that 'The Sparwasser Goal', as it was simply known, became an emblem of national pride. Ironically, by winning the group, the East Germans ended up in the tougher second-round group (with powerhouses Brazil, Argentina, and the Netherlands) while the West Germans went on to win the tournament.

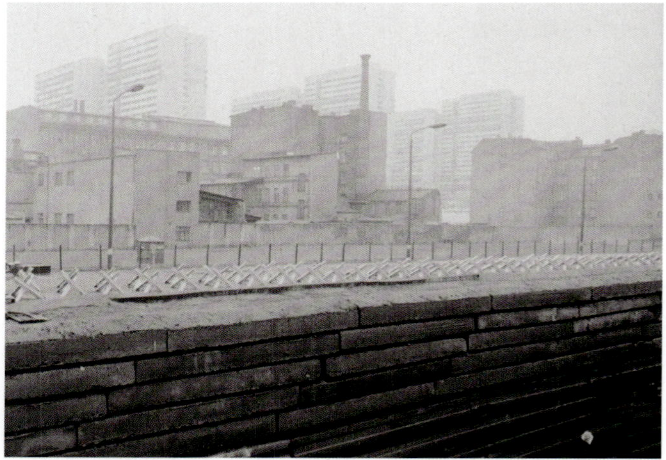

**TOP** West German captain Franz Beckenbauer and East German captain Bernd Bransch exchange pennants and shake hands before their politically charged Group 1 matchup. A profound chapter in World Cup history.

**ABOVE** The Berlin Wall from the side of West Berlin, looking out at East Berlin. With football's uniquely potent international significance, political tension often casts a shadow over the World Cup. The 1974 tournament is one of the starkest examples — hosted by a nation divided by the Cold War.

**OPPOSITE** Joachim Streich (far left) scores the winning goal for East Germany. His strike beat Horst-Dieter Höttges (centre left), Hans-Hubert 'Berti' Vogts (centre right), and Sepp Maier (far right).

# Tournament: FIRST GROUP STAGE

**GROUP 1: EAST GERMANY, WEST GERMANY, CHILE, AUSTRALIA**

| | | |
|---|---|---|
| West Germany 1 | 0 | Chile |
| East Germany 2 | 0 | Australia |
| West Germany 3 | 0 | Australia |
| Chile 1 | 1 | East Germany |
| Australia 0 | 0 | Chile |
| East Germany 1 | 0 | West Germany |

**Advanced to Second Group Stage:**

**East Germany, West Germany**

The big upset was East Germany's politically super-charged victory over its neighbour West Germany, made even more exciting by both teams moving on to the next stage. The East German government, fearing mass defections, had severely restricted travel by its citizens to World Cup matches in West Germany, allowing only 1,500 East Germans—*The Independent* labelled them 'hand-picked apparatchiks' that included a number of Stasi secret security agents—to travel to Hamburg for the East–West match.

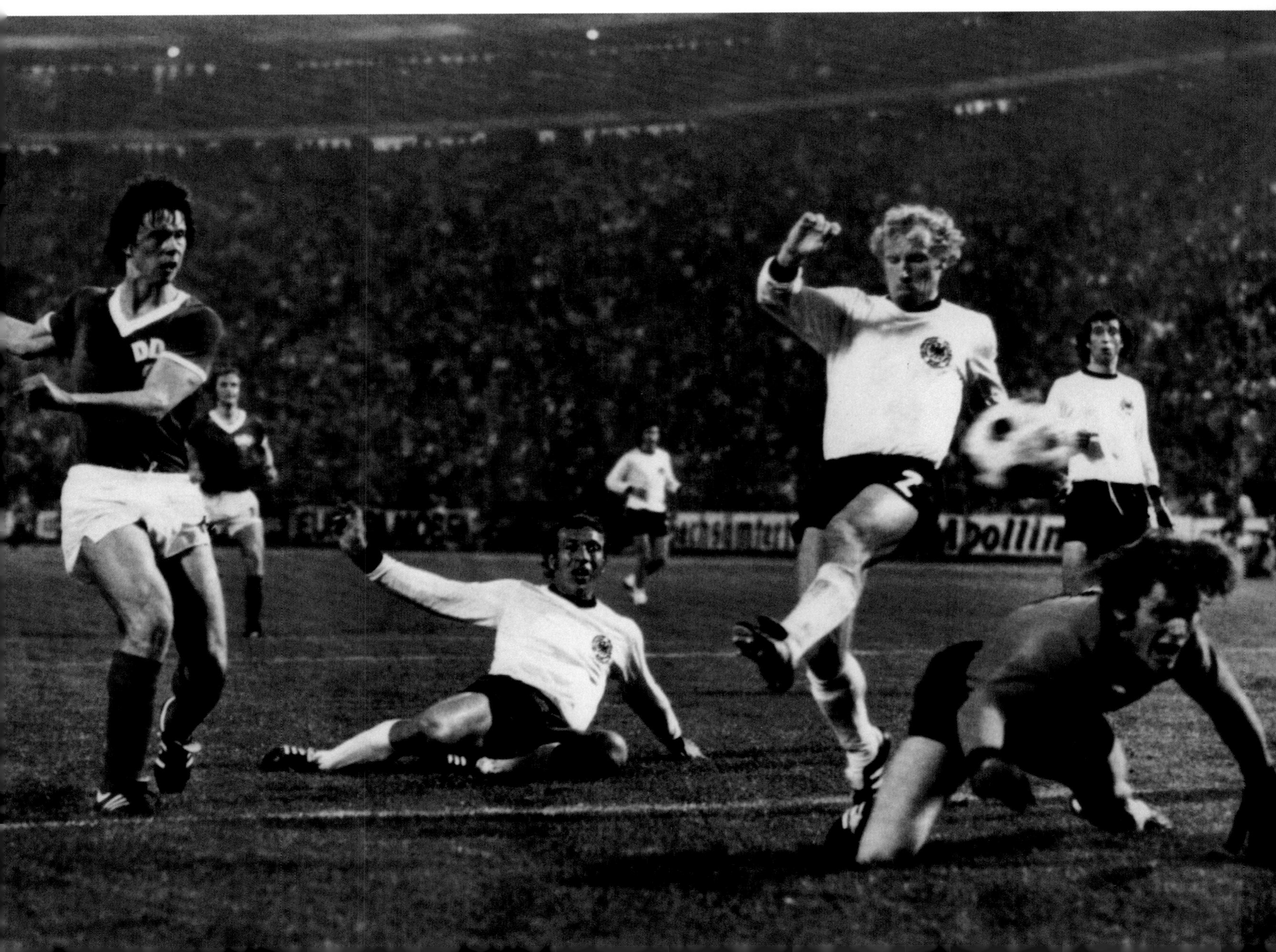

### GROUP 2: YUGOSLAVIA, BRAZIL, SCOTLAND, ZAIRE

| | | |
|---|---|---|
| Brazil 0 | | 0 Yugoslavia |
| Scotland 2 | | 0 Zaire |
| Yugoslavia 9 | | 0 Zaire |
| Scotland 0 | | 0 Brazil |
| Scotland 1 | | 1 Yugoslavia |
| Brazil 3 | | 0 Zaire |

**Advanced to Second Group Stage: Yugoslavia, Brazil**

Every match in Group 2 that did not include Zaire ended up in a tie, whereas the three other teams all crushed Zaire easily. As a result, Yugoslavia, Brazil, and Scotland all tied on points, but the Slavs took first place thanks to the goal-differential advantage they gained from routing Zaire 9–0. Brazil barely edged Scotland for second in the standings by beating Zaire 3–0 compared to Scotland's 2–0. Thus, Scotland never lost a match…but still went home after the first round.

### GROUP 3: NETHERLANDS, SWEDEN, BULGARIA, URUGUAY

| | | |
|---|---|---|
| Netherlands 2 | | 0 Uruguay |
| Sweden 0 | | 0 Bulgaria |
| Bulgaria 1 | | 1 Uruguay |
| Netherlands 0 | | 0 Sweden |
| Netherlands 4 | | 1 Bulgaria |
| Sweden 3 | | 0 Uruguay |

**Advanced to Second Group Stage: Netherlands, Sweden**

Dutch football in the early 1970s was in the thrall of an innovative tactical system dubbed 'Total Football', made famous by the Dutch professional club Ajax and its rising superstar Johan Cruyff. The Netherlands overcame a frustrating 0–0 tie with Sweden in group play to win the group and move into the next round.

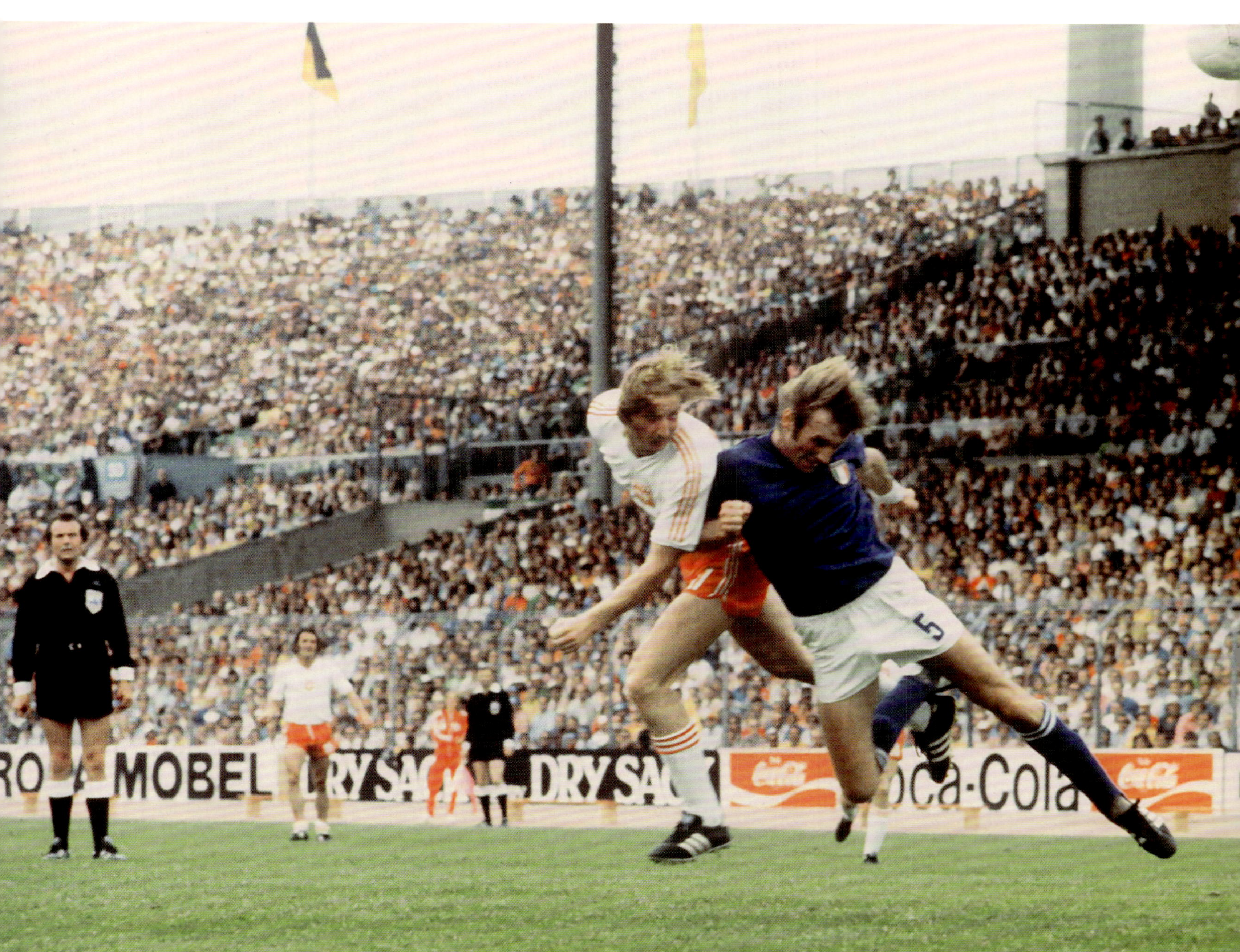

**GROUP 4: POLAND, ARGENTINA, ITALY, HAITI**

| | | |
|---:|:--|:--|
| Italy 3 | 1 | Haiti |
| Poland 3 | 2 | Argentina |
| Argentina 1 | 1 | Italy |
| Poland 7 | 0 | Haiti |
| Argentina 4 | 1 | Haiti |
| Poland 2 | 1 | Italy |

**Advanced to Second Group Stage: Poland, Argentina**

The reigning Olympic champion Poland stunned both Argentina and Italy, finishing first in Group 4 with three impressive wins. Argentina narrowly slid into second place over Italy on goal differential.

**OPPOSITE** *Andrzej Szarmach fights through Italian defender Francesco Morini's powerful tackle to get a header on the ball for Poland's first goal.*

**BELOW** *Three frames from a fuzzy television broadcast show Cruyff's ingenious turn.*

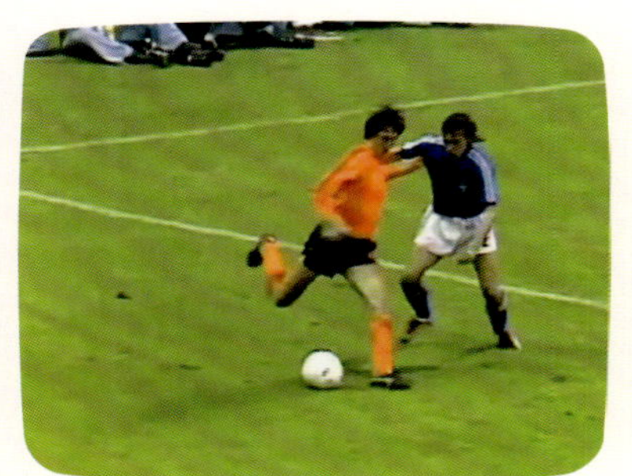 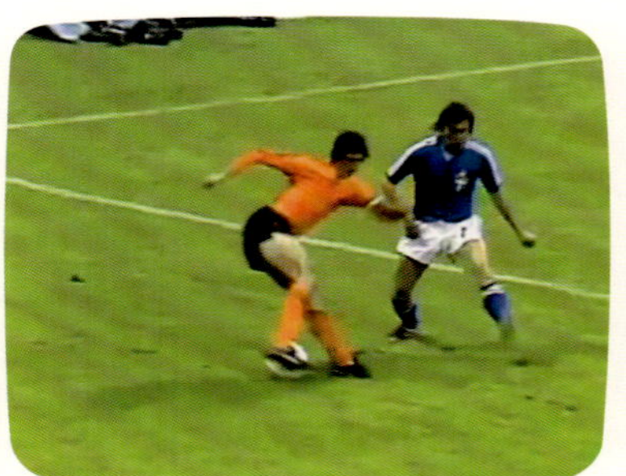 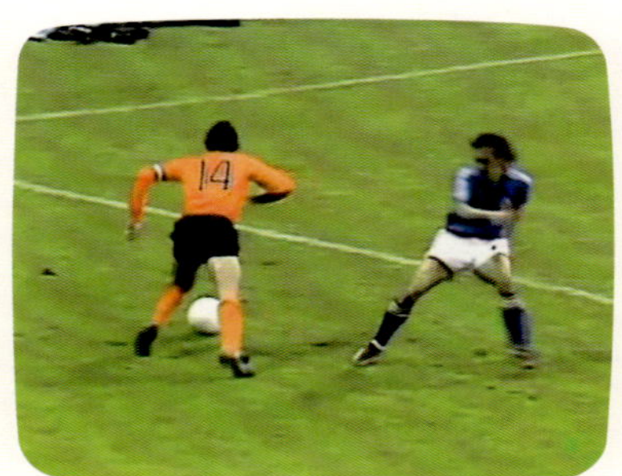 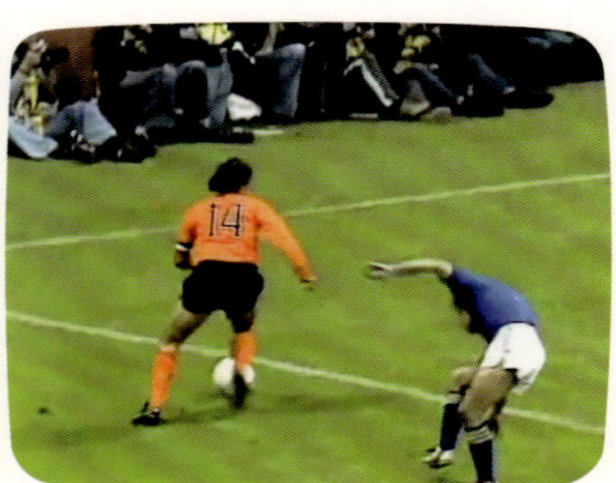

## THE CRUYFF TURN

**In the twenty-second minute** of an otherwise-unremarkable 0–0 tie with Sweden in Group 3 play, the brilliant Dutch superstar Johan Cruyff made technical history with the debut of his legendary 'Cruyff Turn'— a mesmerising, lightning-quick move that fakes a shot or pass and then pulls the ball behind the planted foot so that the player can quickly burst in the new direction. FIFA's official website has an entire page that commemorates the manoeuvre, calling it the 'supersonic swivel that dropped jaws across the planet'.

Today, of course, millions of kids around the globe practise 'the Cruyff' every day: there can be no greater testament to its ingenuity than the fact that one of the greatest manoeuvres in the history of sports is now considered a necessary staple in any aspiring footballer's arsenal. Amazingly, the inventor admitted that he'd never practised the move before trying it at that moment. 'I never practised tricks in training,' said Cruyff. 'It was spontaneous. I was in a difficult position, [and] I needed a solution. And then the whole world seemed to be talking about it.'

The move's victim, Swedish defender Jan Olsson, called it 'a moment of absolute genius' and always considered it an honour to have participated in its lore, even as the bamboozled dupe. With a laugh, Olsson noted that for years, people would approach him with a ball and 'ask if I'd let them do the move on me.' He added, 'I still don't know how he did it.'

# SECOND GROUP STAGE

## GROUP A: NETHERLANDS, BRAZIL, EAST GERMANY, ARGENTINA

| | | |
|---:|:---|:---|
| Netherlands 4 | 0 | Argentina |
| Brazil 1 | 0 | East Germany |
| Brazil 2 | 1 | Argentina |
| Netherlands 2 | 0 | East Germany |
| Argentina 1 | 1 | East Germany |
| Netherlands 2 | 0 | Brazil |

**Advanced to Final: Netherlands**

**Advanced to Third-Place Playoff: Brazil**

## GROUP B: WEST GERMANY, POLAND, SWEDEN, YUGOSLAVIA

| | | |
|---:|:---|:---|
| West Germany 2 | 0 | Yugoslavia |
| Poland 1 | 0 | Sweden |
| Poland 2 | 1 | Yugoslavia |
| West Germany 4 | 2 | Sweden |
| West Germany 1 | 0 | Poland |
| Sweden 2 | 1 | Yugoslavia |

**Advanced to Final: West Germany**

**Advanced to Third-Place Playoff: Poland**

The Netherlands laid waste to Group A with three convincing victories, starting with a 4–0 romp over Argentina that saw Johan Cruyff score a brace. The Netherlands–Brazil matchup was the headliner, though. Neither team scored in the first half, but Johan Neeskens broke the ice just five minutes after the break and Cruyff sealed the 2–0 win fifteen minutes later.

The Group B finalist came down to a gritty match in Frankfurt between West Germany and Poland. As usual in key West German contests, the winning goal came from the irrepressible Gerd Müller, this time in the seventy-sixth minute. Müller scored only four goals in 1974, compared to the amazing ten he netted during the 1970 World Cup, but all four were critical to West Germany's successful march through this tournament.

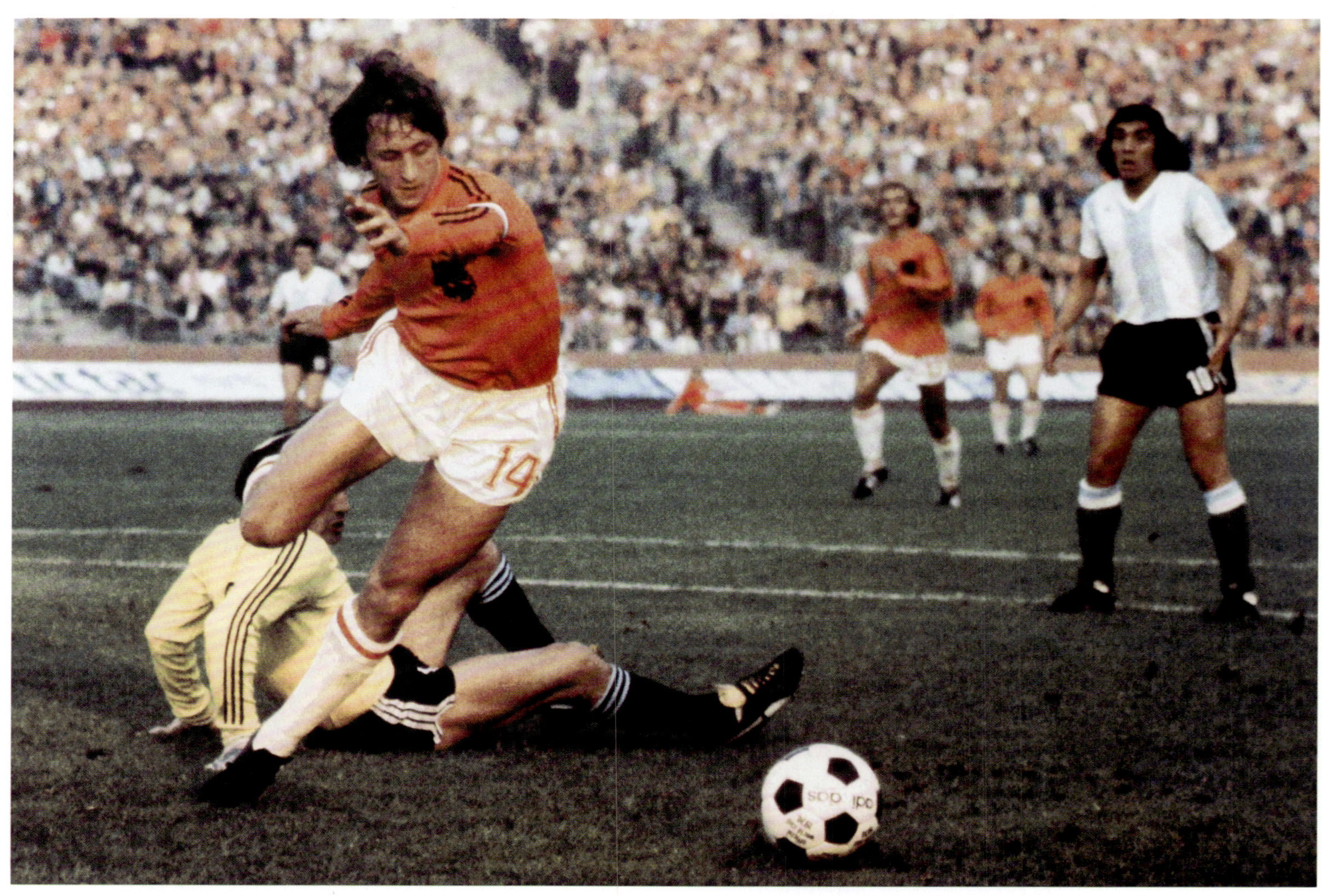

# THE ADVENT OF TOTAL FOOTBALL

**The Netherlands burst onto** the international scene in the early 1970s by adopting the 'Total Football' concept, a revolutionary tactical system that had begun to dominate the European game. Developed by the Dutch club Ajax under manager Rinus Michels, the system asked players to switch roles freely according to the ever-changing tactical situations that could unfold throughout the course of ninety minutes. Thus, its success relied on players who possessed not only superior field awareness but also an individual skill-set versatile enough for all aspects of the game — attacking, defending, possessing, and moving off the ball — from one end of the pitch to the other. It also demanded great fitness and relentless, high-intensity pressure.

To be fair, various teams had been playing different versions of this system for decades. But it was the 'Dutch Whirl', as some called it, that pushed the versatility of interchangeable positions to thrilling, gorgeous extremes. Fielding a squad of talented technicians, led by the brilliant Johan Cruyff, the Netherlands played a fluid style that emphasised possession of the ball. This prodigious possession was enabled by the players forming a never-ending series of triangles (thus, always two options open) for quick, short passes. Defenders would 'whirl' forward up the wing, adding width and numerical superiority to the point of attack, while opposite side midfielders and even forwards might rotate back to fill vacated spaces.

Overall, Total Football sought to mesh individual talent with a sense of collective responsibility in all phases of the game. Though the system's tactical concepts were not complex, they required everyone's unwavering attunement to the game's flow. Cruyff, as always, put it best. 'Playing football is simple,' he said. 'But playing simple football is the hardest thing there is.'

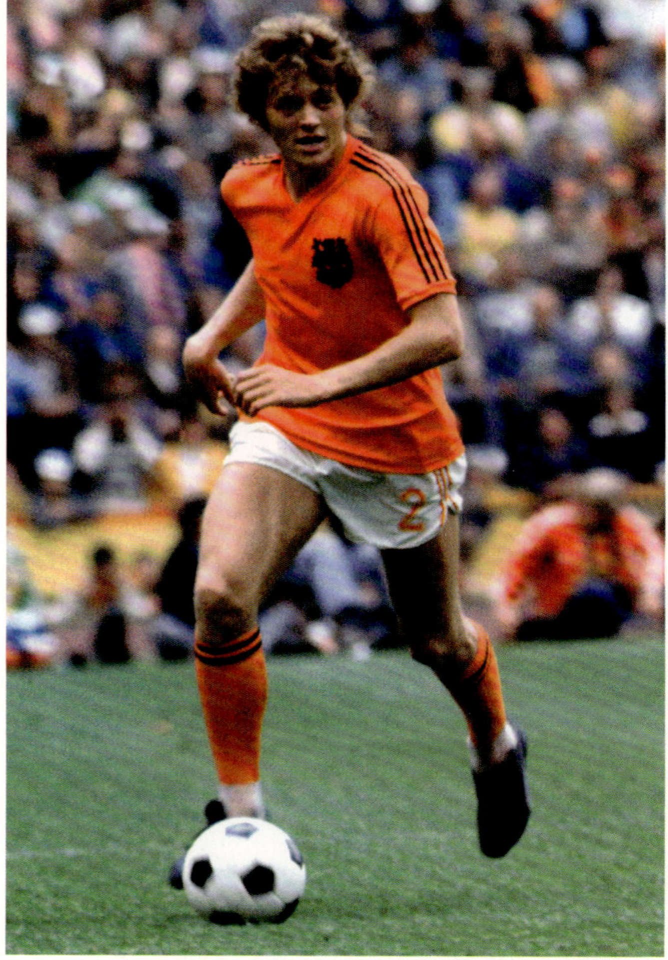

**OPPOSITE** *Johan Cruyff drops Argentine keeper Daniel Carnevali to the grass before putting the ball in the net for a 1–0 Dutch lead in the second group stage.*

**RIGHT** *Wim Suurbier (top right) and Arie Haan (bottom right), two key defenders in the Dutch 'Total Football' line-up. Both were described as quick, hardworking, and capable of contributing in the attack.*

# FINAL

| West Germany 2 | 1 Netherlands |
|---|---|
| | (First Place) |
| Poland 1 | 0 Brazil |
| | (Third Place) |

Poland finished a strong tournament with a well-deserved victory against the still-potent Brazilians. En route to a third-place finish, the Polish winger Grzegorz Lato netted the only goal and finished with a total of seven on the tournament, leading all goal scorers.

In the Final, contrasting styles made for fascinating football. The Netherlands held the ball beautifully for almost two minutes from the opening kickoff and, before a single West German had touched the ball, Johan Cruyff made a slashing dribble into the penalty box where he was cut down. Johan Neeskens converted the penalty kick for a quick 1–0 lead.

But in the end, it was Franz Beckenbauer's steady leadership and Gerd Müller's preternatural nose for the goal that made the difference for West Germany. Midway through the half, West Germany scored a penalty kick of their own to draw even at 1–1. Then Müller, dubbed '*Der Bomber*' by the Munich press, scrambled to receive a pass just outside the goal box that bounced behind him, forcing an awkward swivel to shoot. But he struck the shot perfectly into the far corner for a 2–1 lead that held up through a tense second half.

For the distraught Dutch and Johan Cruyff, the only consolation was that their thrilling and innovative performances throughout the tournament became legendary, forever changing the way that football would be played.

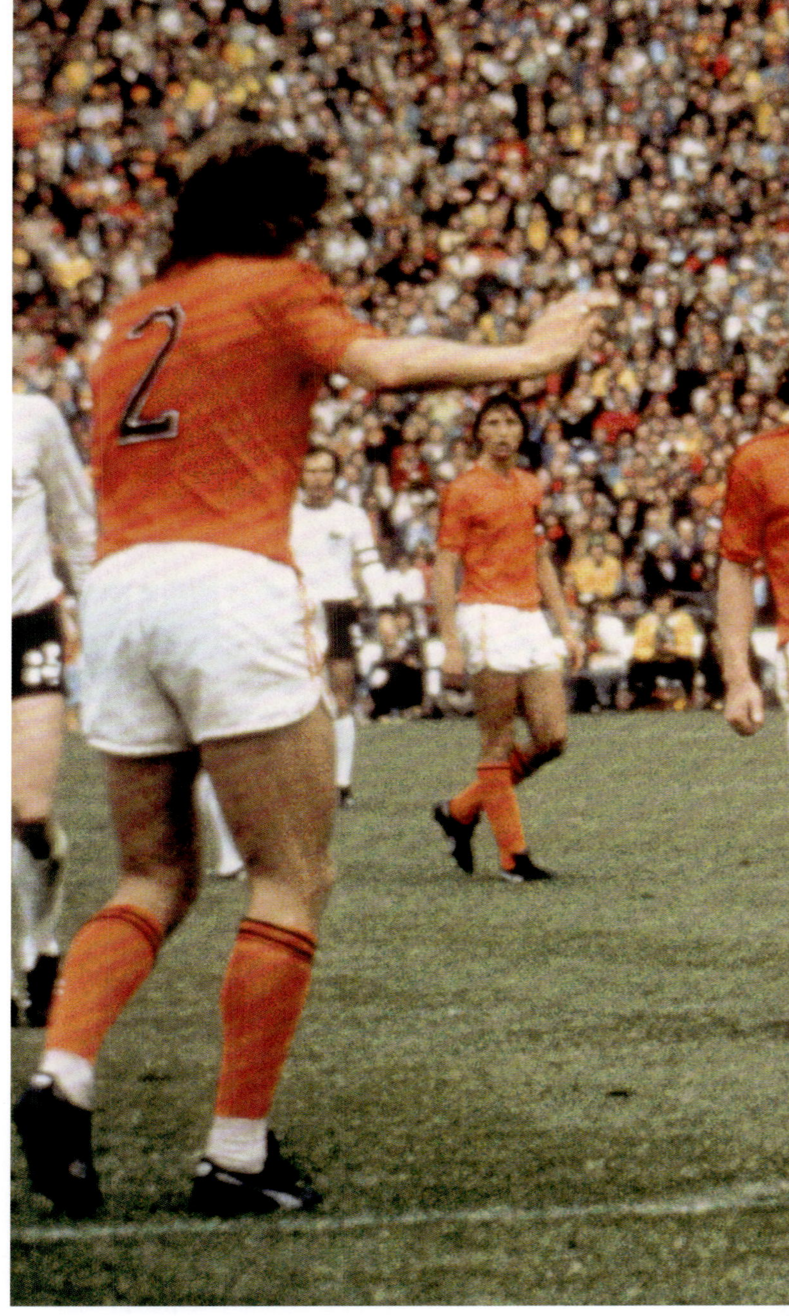

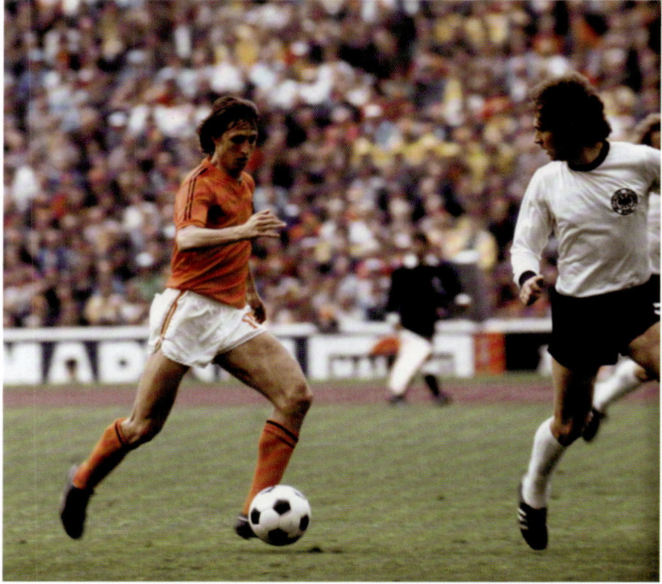

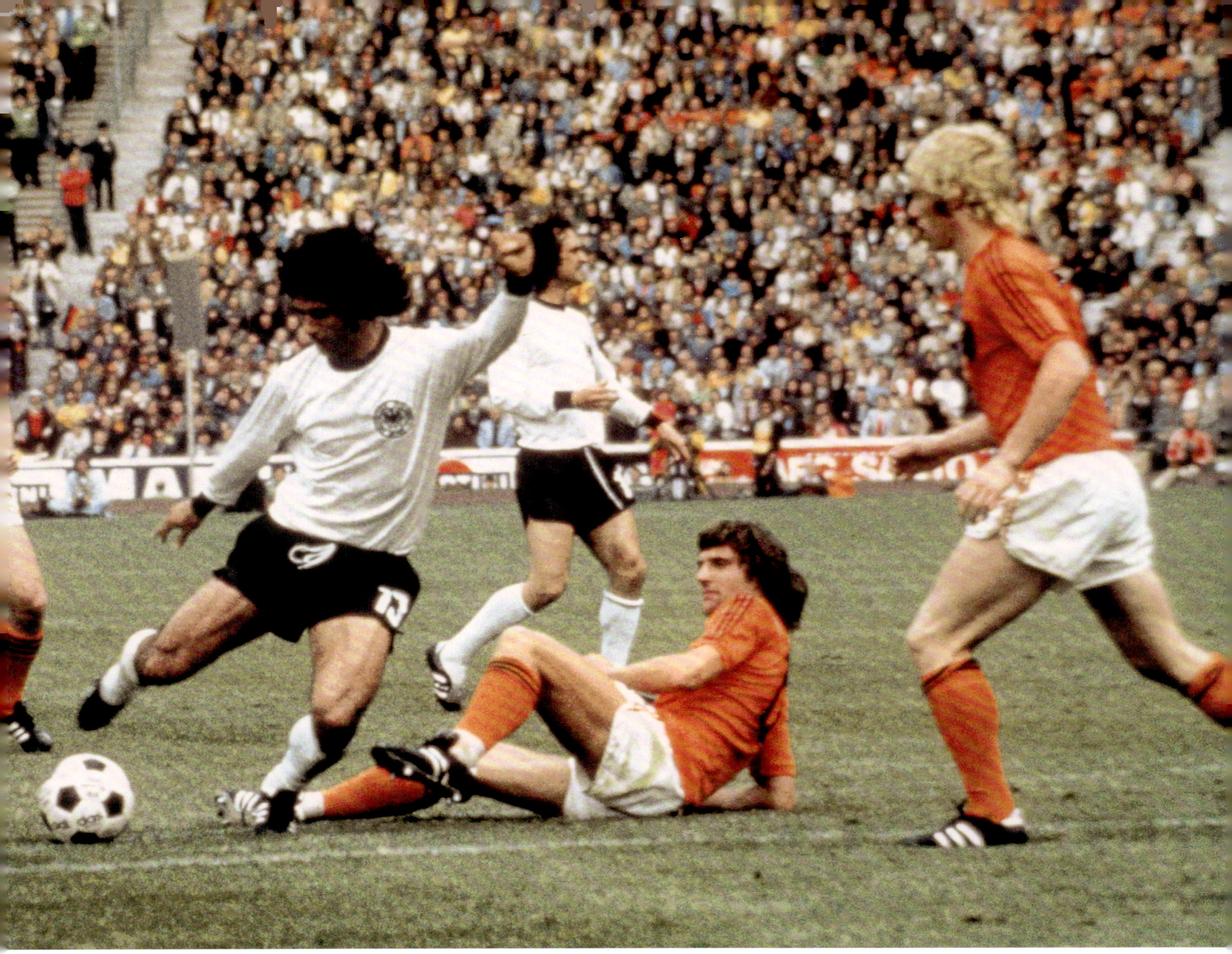

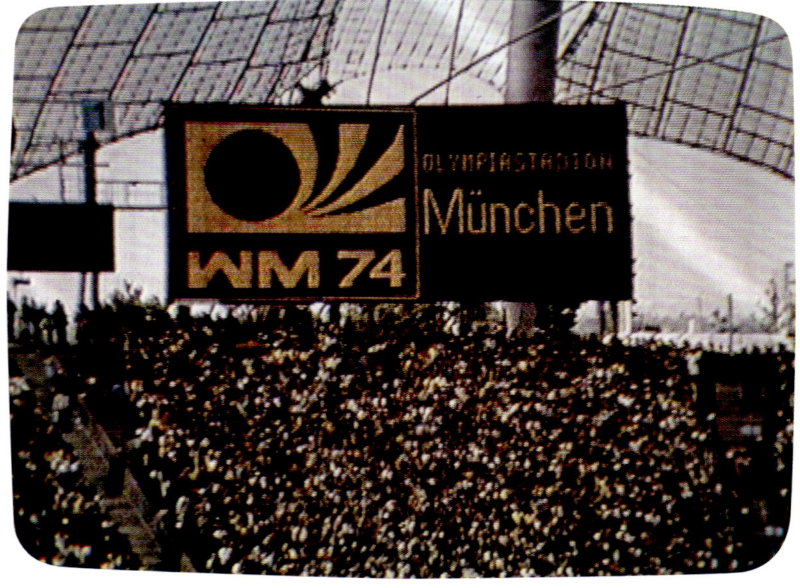

**OPPOSITE** *Johan Cruyff attempts to take on Franz Beckenbauer.*

**ABOVE** *Gerd Müller scores the winner against the Netherlands in the final.*

**RIGHT** *An electric billboard displays the 1974 World Cup logo and Olympiastadion München ('Munich Olympic Stadium') before the final.*

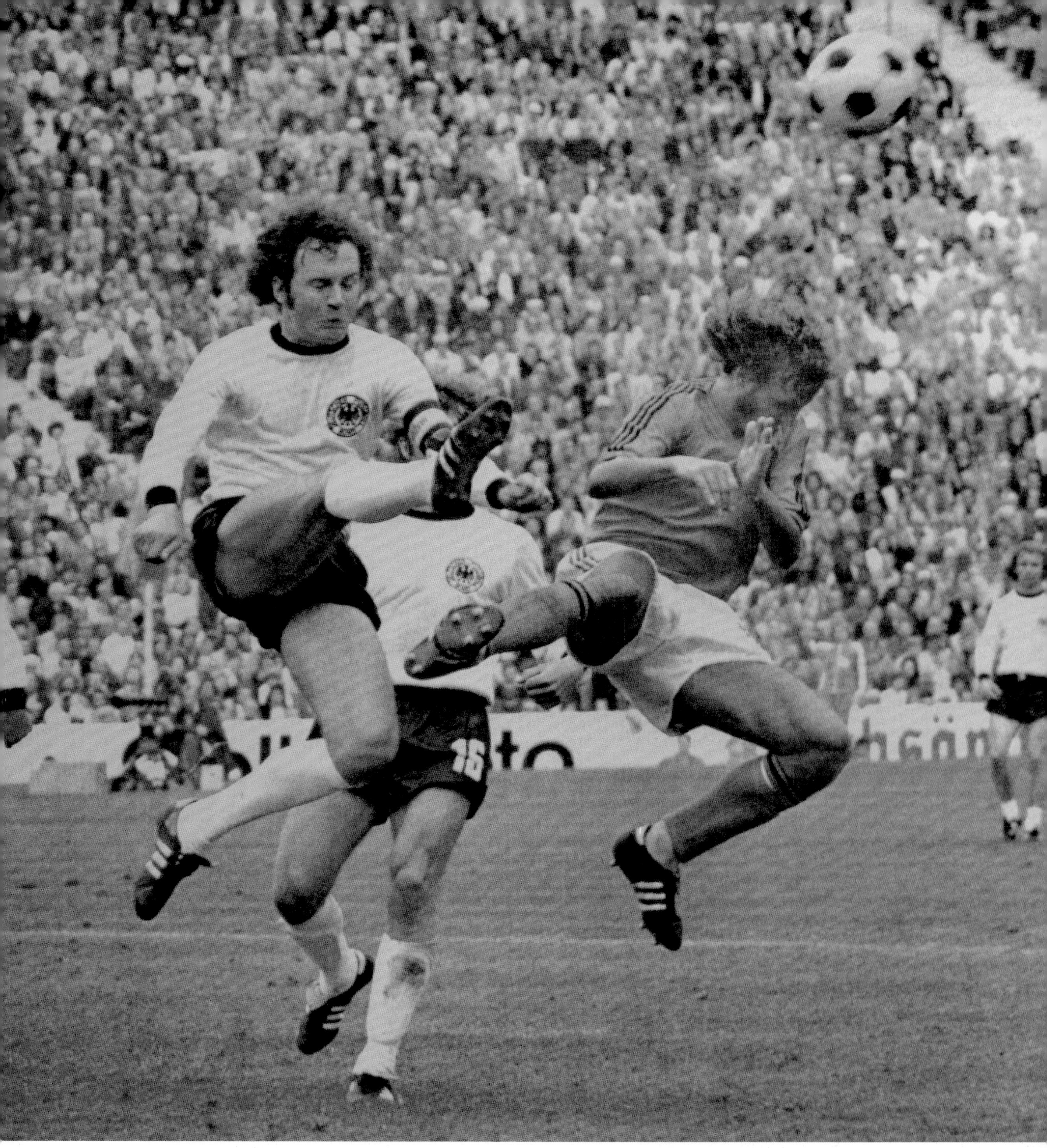

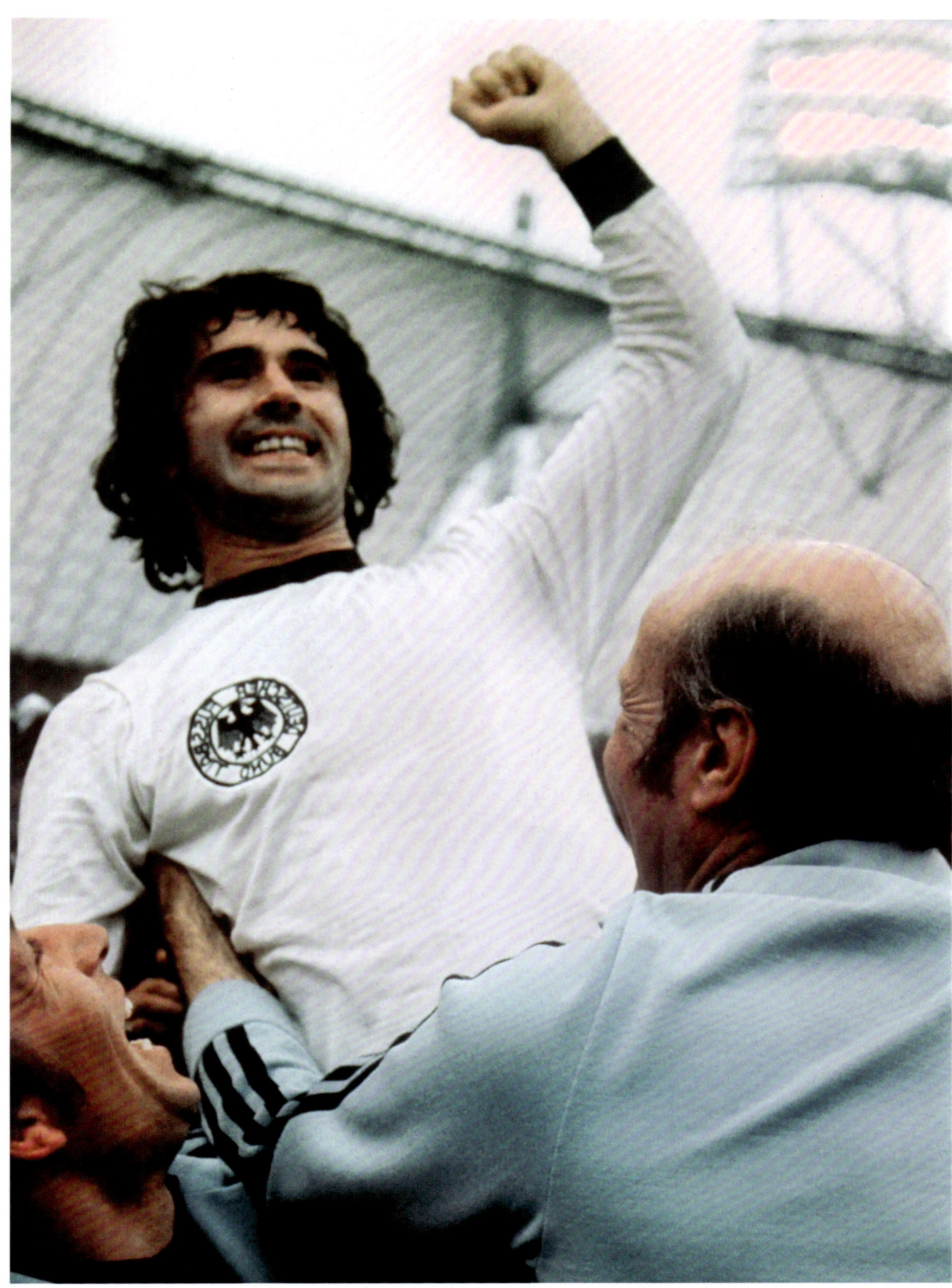

**OPPOSITE** *Germany's Franz Beckenbauer (left), putting in a defensive performance for the ages, shuts down Dutch midfielder Johan Neeskens (right).*

**RIGHT** *Gerd 'Der Bomber' Müller lifts his fists triumphantly after his tenth goal leads West Germany to ultimate victory on home soil.*

# THE NEW LORDS OF FOOTBALL

**The 1974 World Cup Final** matched the two players vying to succeed the great Pelé as the pre-eminent player in the world: Dutch superstar Johan Cruyff and the inimitable West German captain Franz Beckenbauer. As the BBC so blithely put it, 'The 1974 final was an examination of character. Cruyff led the more gifted team, but Beckenbauer the stronger-willed one.' In many ways, the match played out exactly like that, with moments of fluid Dutch brilliance surrounded by stretches of relentless West German pressure, tactical discipline, and sturdy defence.

In the end, the rock-steady Beckenbauer won the game, whereas Cruyff's artistry won the hearts of football purists. But the two great men were anything but antagonists. Their high mutual regard was evident even in the game-opening handshake. In subsequent years, Cruyff openly acknowledged his rival as a significant influence on his career and a valued confidante. 'We instinctively had a great respect for each other,' he said, 'and that grew organically into a great friendship.' And when Cruyff passed away in 2016, Beckenbauer admitted that 'Johan . . . was a brother to me.'

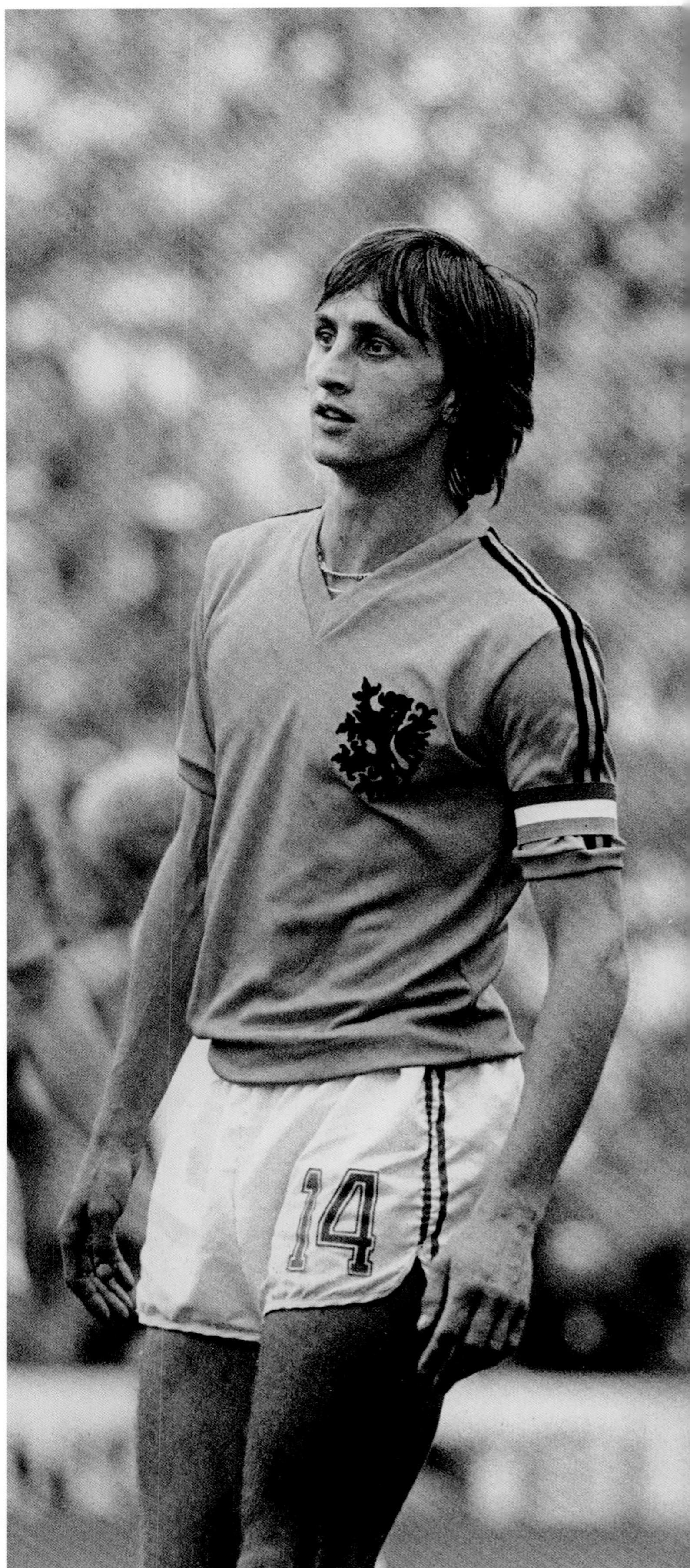

**OPPOSITE** *Johan Cruyff (left) and Franz Beckenbauer (right).*

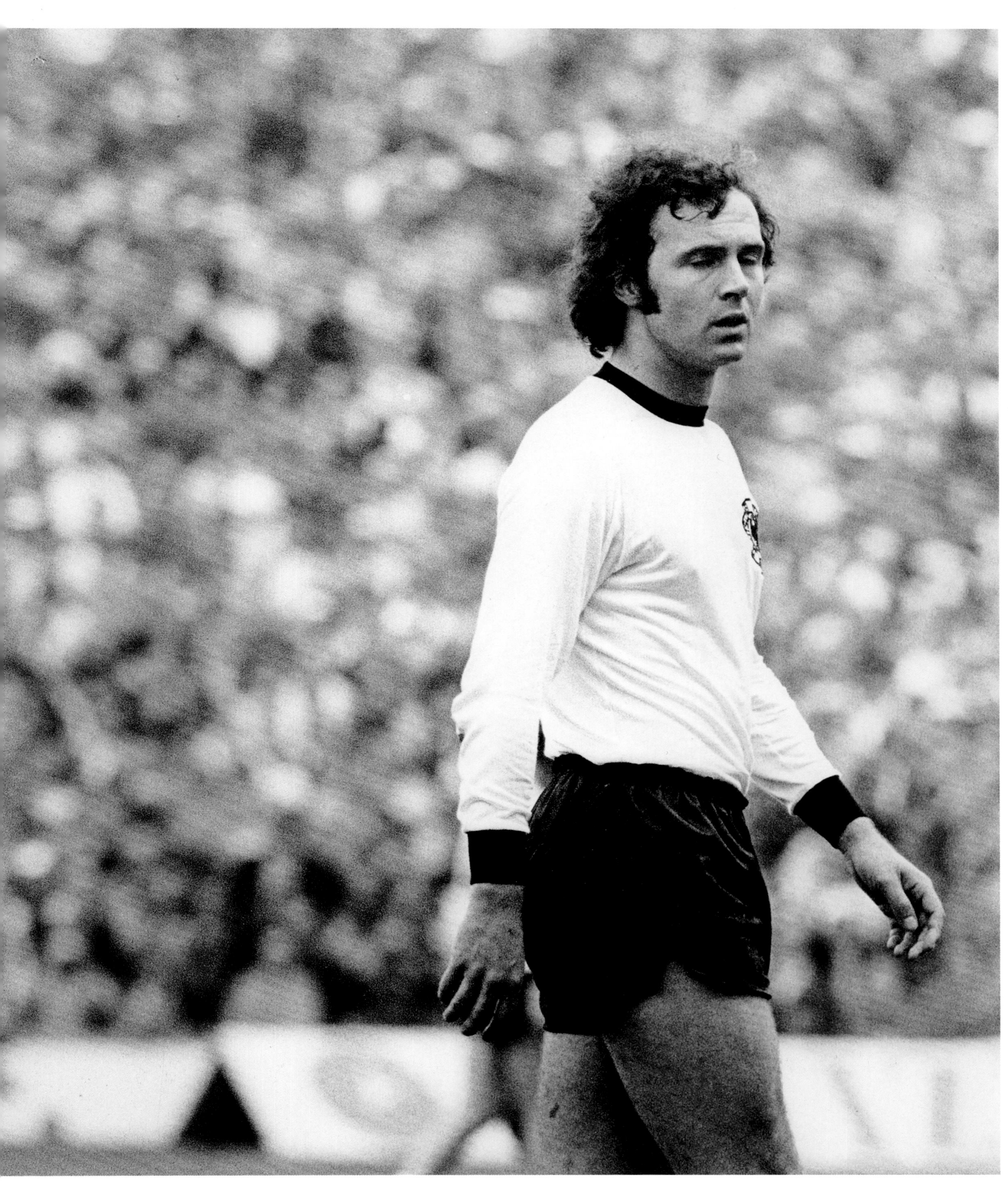

# 1978

HOST COUNTRY: **ARGENTINA**
CHAMPION: **ARGENTINA**
RUNNER-UP: **NETHERLANDS**
THIRD PLACE: **BRAZIL OVER ITALY**

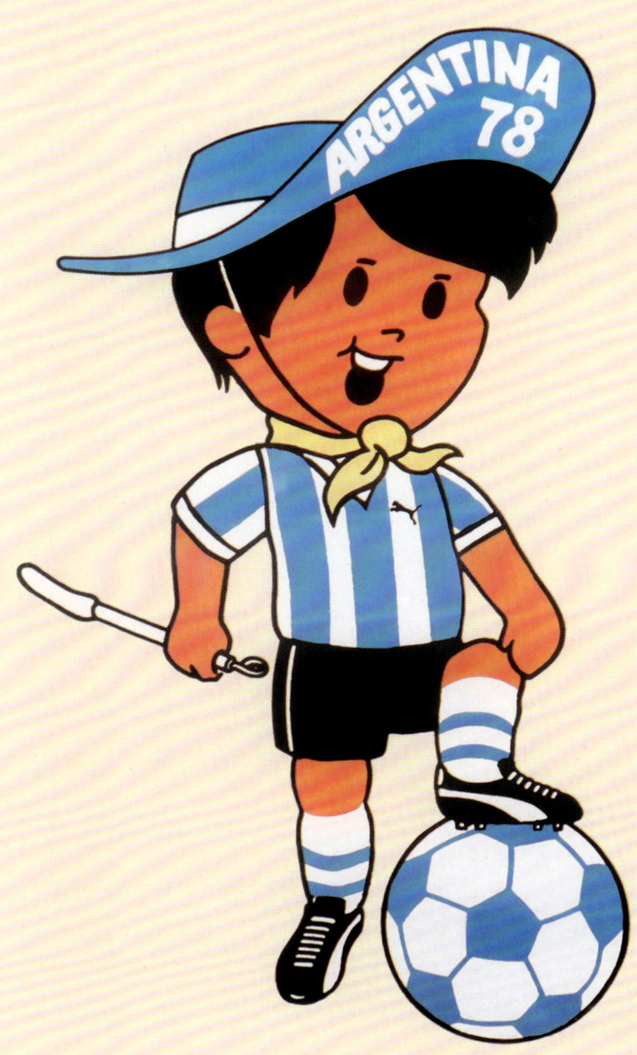

**An all-too-usual cloud** of controversy surrounded the 1978 World Cup. FIFA had selected Argentina as host back in 1966, but ten years later, a right-wing military junta staged a successful coup to overthrow Argentina's democratically elected government, prompting several national football federations to consider boycotting the upcoming tournament. In the end, none did, and Argentina spent an estimated $700 million to prepare for it, including the construction of three brand-new stadiums, extensive transport upgrades in its host cities, and the installation of a new communications infrastructure that cost a staggering $100 million alone.

But the Argentine military junta's authoritarian practises and censorship efforts brought back sour memories of Mussolini's fascist showcase at the 1934 World Cup in Italy. The journalist Jimmy Burns called it 'the most highly politicised sporting circus since Berlin 1936,' referring to Hitler's cynical attempts to propagandise the Olympics. Meanwhile, Montoneros guerrillas and other opposition forces sought to make the Cup a referendum on the regime's brutal repression of dissent. The corrosive politics cast a dark shadow on the tournament and rumours of match-fixing and other scandals plagued the media coverage leading up to the first kickoff.

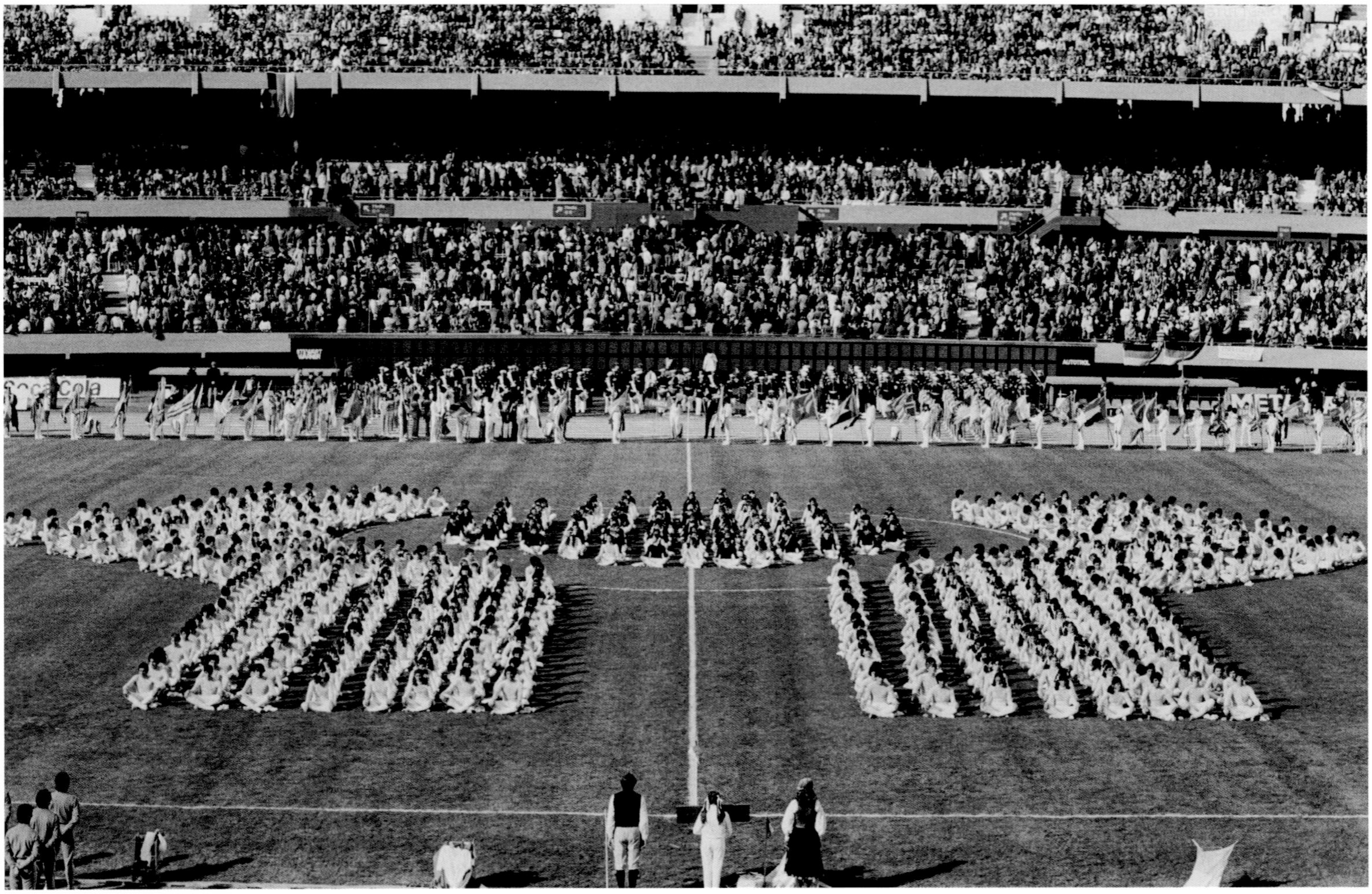

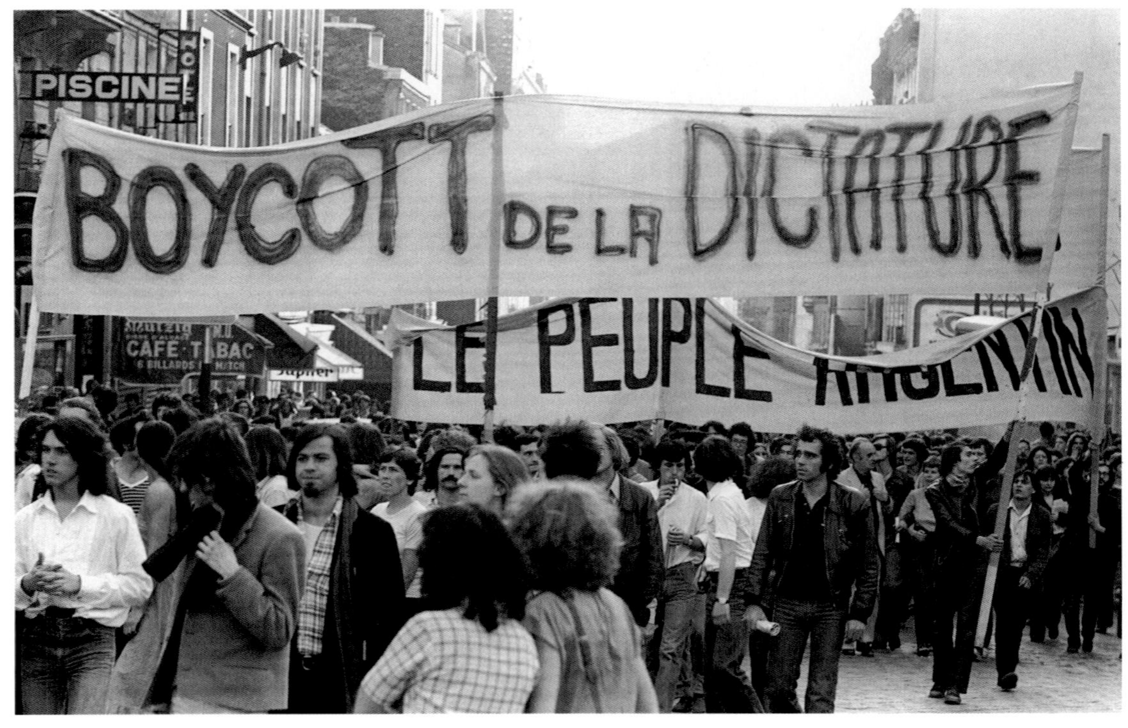

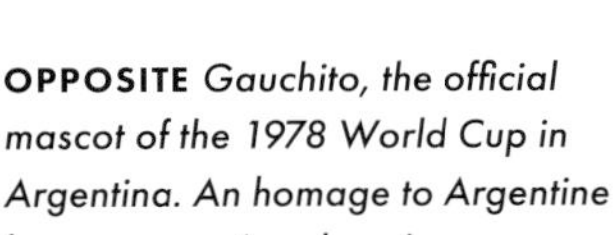

OPPOSITE *Gauchito, the official mascot of the 1978 World Cup in Argentina. An homage to Argentine horsemen, or 'cowboys'.*

ABOVE *The opening ceremony of the 1978 World Cup.*

RIGHT *Protesters in Paris calling for a boycott of the World Cup due to Argentina's oppressive military junta.*

# Tournament: FIRST GROUP STAGE

### GROUP 1: ITALY, ARGENTINA, FRANCE, HUNGARY

| | | |
|---:|:---:|:---|
| Italy 2 | 1 | France |
| Argentina 2 | 1 | Hungary |
| Italy 3 | 1 | Hungary |
| Argentina 2 | 1 | France |
| France 3 | 1 | Hungary |
| Italy 1 | 0 | Argentina |

**_Advanced to Second Group Stage: Italy, Argentina_**

### GROUP 2: POLAND, WEST GERMANY, TUNISIA, MEXICO

| | | |
|---:|:---:|:---|
| West Germany 0 | 0 | Poland |
| Tunisia 3 | 1 | Mexico |
| West Germany 6 | 0 | Mexico |
| Poland 1 | 0 | Tunisia |
| West Germany 0 | 0 | Tunisia |
| Poland 3 | 0 | Mexico |

**_Advanced to Second Group Stage: Poland, West Germany_**

The selection committee put Argentina in a very tough group against three traditionally powerful European squads. Italy swept through with three victories, including a 1–0 win over the hosts, to place first. But Argentina managed two narrow 2–1 wins over France and Hungary to snag second place and move on to the next stage.

Poland continued the strong play of its third-place finish in the 1974 World Cup by finishing first in Group 2. They started off with a draw against defending-champion West Germany and followed it up with two solid wins. The West Germans also moved on after overcoming a surprisingly dreary 0–0 draw with underdog Tunisia. The West German squad clearly missed Franz Beckenbauer's leadership and Gerd Müller's timely goals. Tunisia's win over Mexico was the first ever by an African nation in a World Cup.

**BELOW** *The Frenchman Henri Michel (centre) attempts a strike from distance against an ever-staunch Italian defence.*

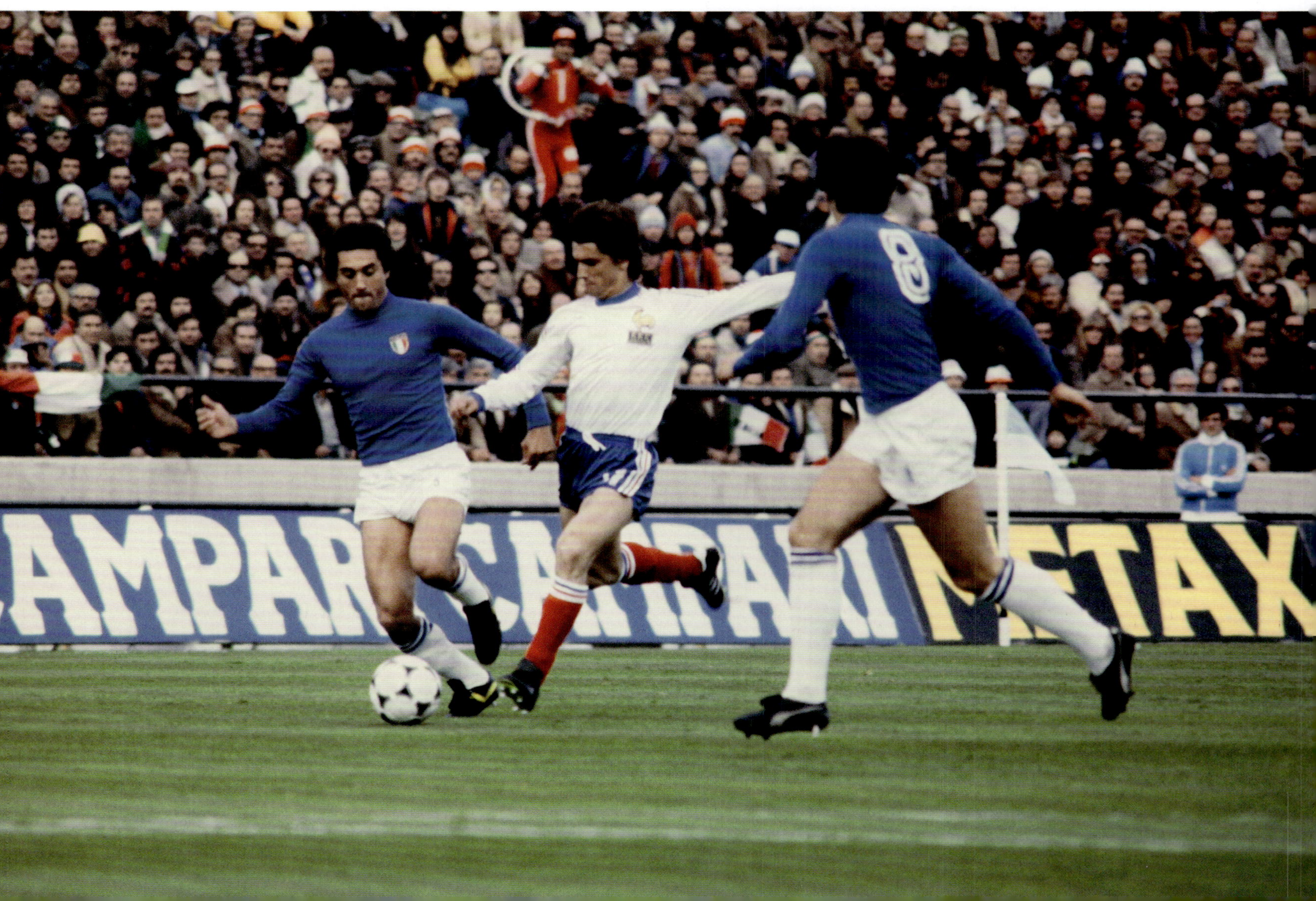

**GROUP 3: AUSTRIA, BRAZIL, SPAIN, SWEDEN**

| Austria 2 | 1 Spain |
|---|---|
| Brazil 1 | 1 Sweden |
| Austria 1 | 0 Sweden |
| Brazil 0 | 0 Spain |
| Spain 1 | 0 Sweden |
| Brazil 1 | 0 Austria |

***Advanced to Second Group Stage: Austria, Brazil***

Austria finished first in Group 3 despite losing 1–0 to Brazil and matching the Brazilians in both points (four each) and goal differential (+1 each). The tie-breaker: Austria scored more overall goals than Brazil (3–2).

**GROUP 4: PERU, NETHERLANDS, SCOTLAND, IRAN**

| Peru 3 | 1 Scotland |
|---|---|
| Netherlands 3 | 0 Iran |
| Scotland 1 | 1 Iran |
| Netherlands 0 | 0 Peru |
| Peru 4 | 1 Iran |
| Scotland 3 | 2 Netherlands |

***Advanced to Second Group Stage: Peru, Netherlands***

Peru finished unbeaten to win Group 4, a result that included a 0–0 tie with the Netherlands, a Cup favourite despite the loss of retired Johan Cruyff. A shocking loss to Scotland left the Netherlands tied in points with the Scots, but a +3 lead in goal differential sent the Dutch through to the next group stage in second place.

**BELOW** *A kit mix-up forced France to wear the green-and-white-striped shirt of local second-division club Kimberley de Mar del Plata in their Group 1 match with Hungary.*

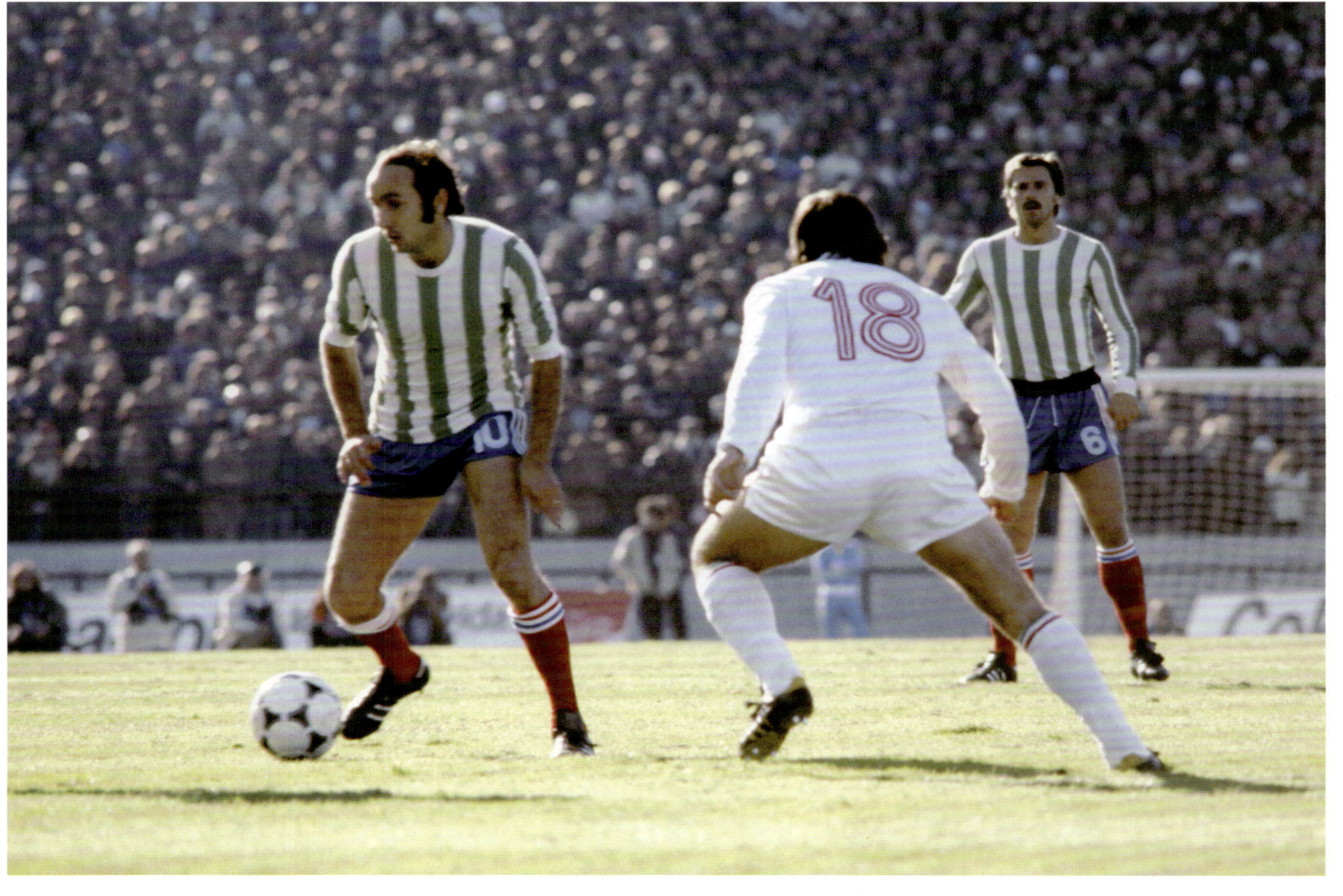

# SECOND GROUP STAGE

**GROUP A: NETHERLANDS, ITALY,
WEST GERMANY, AUSTRIA**

| Netherlands 5 | 1 Austria |
| Italy 0 | 0 West Germany |
| Netherlands 2 | 2 West Germany |
| Italy 1 | 0 Austria |
| Austria 3 | 2 West Germany |
| Netherlands 2 | 1 Italy |

**Advanced to Final: Netherlands**

**Advanced to Third-Place Playoff: Italy**

**GROUP B: ARGENTINA, BRAZIL, POLAND, PERU**

| Brazil 3 | 0 Peru |
| Argentina 2 | 0 Poland |
| Poland 1 | 0 Peru |
| Argentina 0 | 0 Brazil |
| Brazil 3 | 1 Poland |
| Argentina 6 | 0 Peru |

**Advanced to Final: Argentina**

**Advanced to Third-Place Playoff: Brazil**

The second group stage featured an all-European Group A and a mostly South American Group B, virtually ensuring that an exciting final would pit the two pre-eminent football continents against one another. The Netherlands would make up for their disappointing start in the first group stage by scoring solid victories over two very good teams in Austria and Italy, followed by a thrilling 2–2 draw with their 1974 nemesis, defending champion West Germany. The impressive performances sent the Dutch on to the final as favourites.

This stage boiled down to a goal-differential controversy, with accusations of behind-the-scenes manipulation by the home junta. Brazil and Argentina both beat their respective first opponents and then played each other to a tense, somewhat violent 0–0 draw. Thus, the last day's matches turned into a race for goals, with both Argentina and Brazil trying to run up the score on their overmatched opponents.

In what seemed a finality, Brazil earned a solid 3–1 win over Poland. As a result, Argentina needed to make up a four-goal deficit in the differential tally…which they did easily?

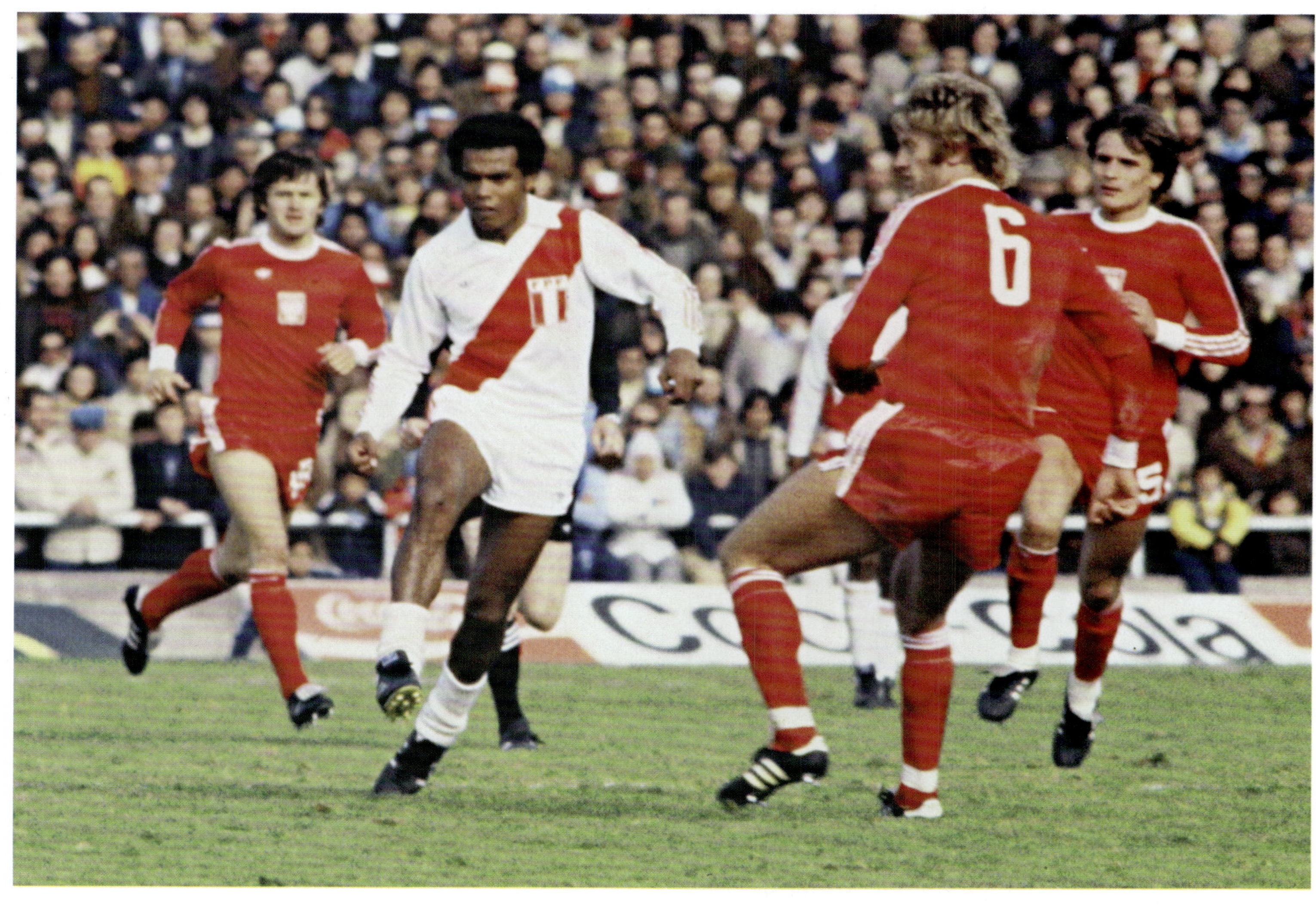

Perhaps far too easily. Argentina beat a solid Peru side 6–0. Critics responded with outrage and open accusations that Peru had been threatened or bribed to collapse so badly that Argentina would be allowed to progress.

Additional reports came out alleging that Argentina's fascist dictator, Jorge Rafael Videla, had entered the Peruvian dressing room, just minutes before the team was set to enter the pitch, to deliver a message. And, to cap it off, he was accompanied by no less than the former US Secretary of State Henry Kissinger, whose meddling in South American governance was well-known even then. In any case, the big win was an extraordinary (shocking) result that bumped the home team into the Cup Final and dropped an angry Brazil into the third-place match.

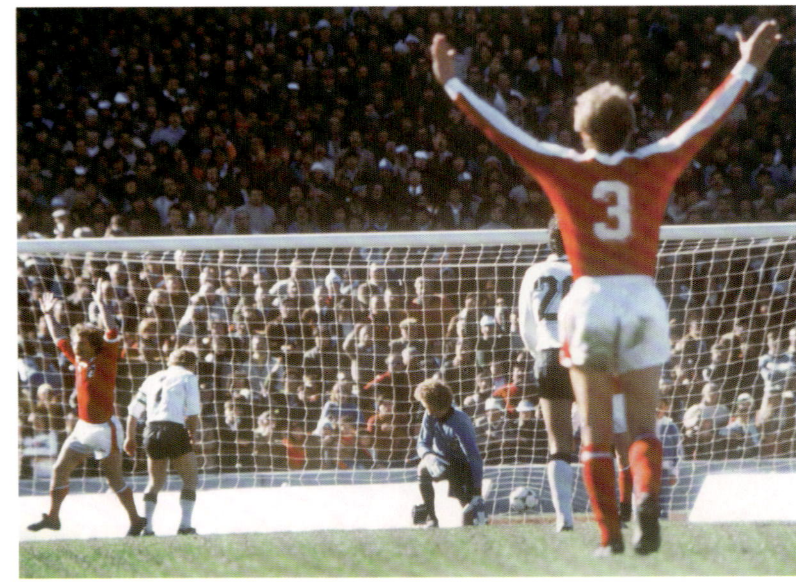

**OPPOSITE** *Peru's Teófilo Cubillas (centre left) sends a pass with the outside of his foot past Polish defender Jerzy Gorgoń. Poland would ultimately win 1–0.*

**ABOVE** *Austria's Erich Obermayer (right) celebrates after West Germany's captain Berti Vogts scores an own goal to tie the game at 1–1. The own goal would end up making the difference for Austria in their 3–2 victory.*

**BELOW** *Argentina's fourth goal in their controversial and infamous victory over Peru. For the conspiracy theorists, clues abound. Argentine-born Peruvian keeper Ramón Quiroga stands out of position to a suspicious degree, defender Héctor Chumpitaz lifts his arm in protest of Leopoldo Luque's offside position, and the goal scorer himself was likely surprised to be left totally unmarked in his opponent's penalty box.*

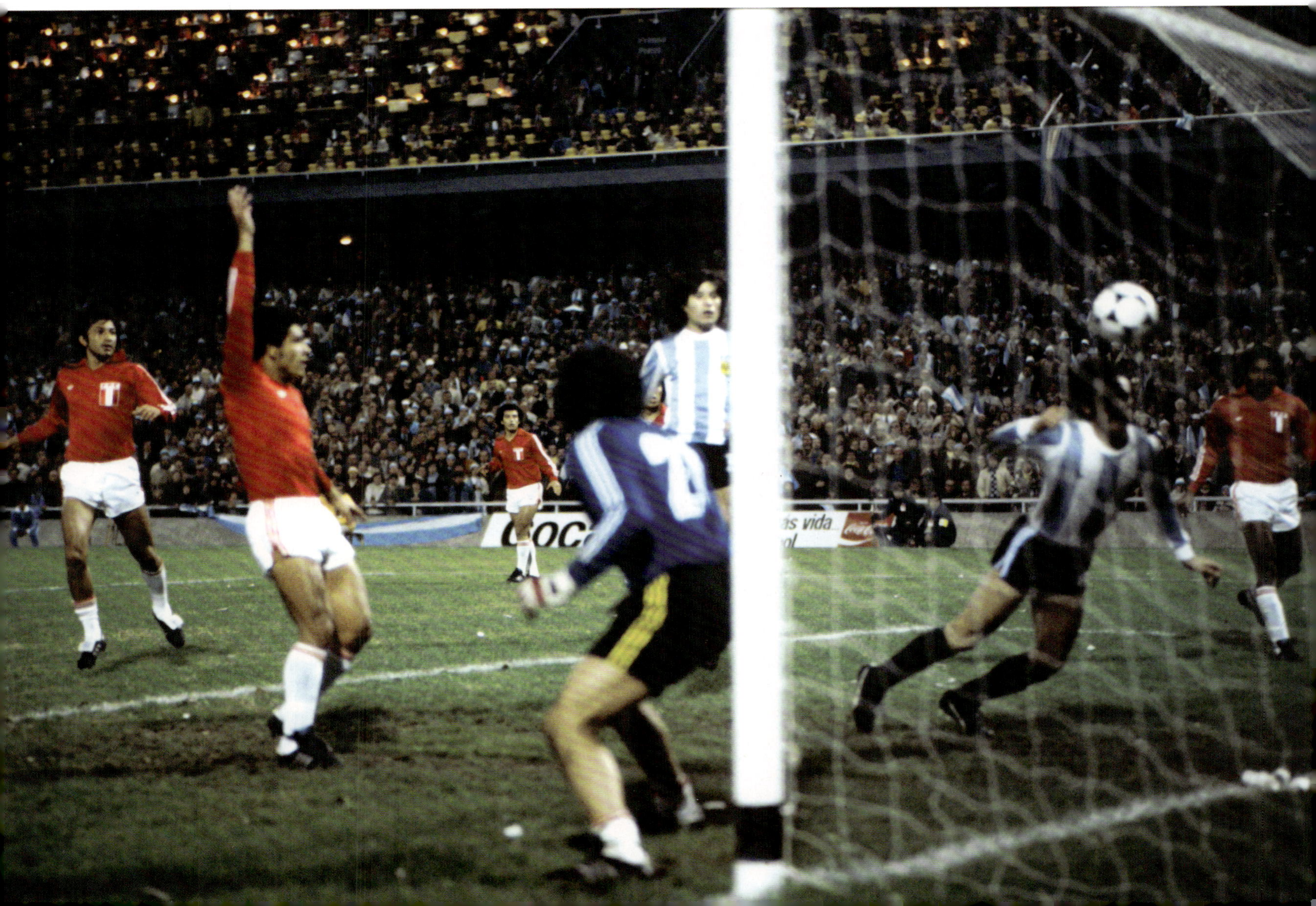

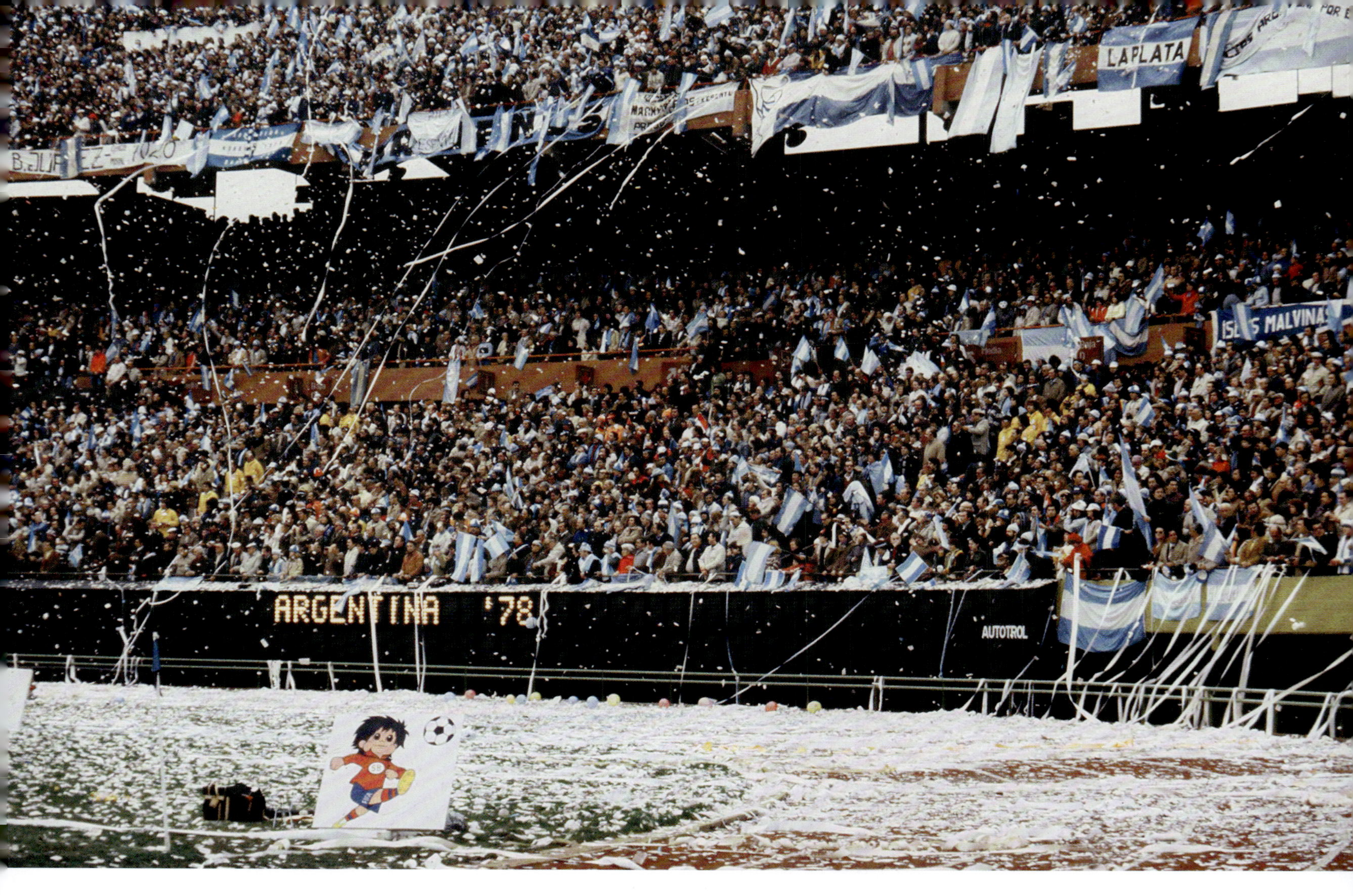



**ABOVE** *Argentinian fans celebrating their country's victory on home soil? Not quite, as the match was still yet to kick off.*

**OPPOSITE** *Mario Kempes of Argentina led all scorers with six goals in the 1978 World Cup.*

# FINAL

Argentina 3 | 1 Netherlands
(First Place)
Brazil 2 | 1 Italy
(Third Place)

Brazil's third-place victory over a very good Italian squad (who had beaten Argentina 1–0 in the first group stage) meant they finished as the only undefeated team in the tournament, with three wins, three draws, and zero losses. Meanwhile, both teams in the championship match, Argentina and the Netherlands, had one tournament loss apiece. As a result, the Brazilian coach Cláudio Coutinho declared his side the 'moral champions' of the 1978 World Cup.

The Netherlands didn't have Cruyff this time, but their side still featured plenty of world-class players, including seven returning starters from the 1974 World Cup Finalist squad. On the other side, all the military hijinks and match-fixing controversy tended to obscure the fact that Argentina fielded a remarkably talented squad, too. Striker/attacking midfielder Mario Kempes was an emerging international star and prolific goal scorer who ended up leading the tournament with six goals, while forward Leopoldo Luque added four more to form a deadly one-two punch up front.

On the morning of the final, David Miller, the chief sportswriter for *The Daily Express*, wrote that tension hung in the air 'like the thunderstorms which have rumbled round Buenos Aires for the last week' and the cavernous Estadio Monumental in Buenos Aires filled up with 'perhaps the most hostile and frenzied crowd in the history of football'. Military units lined the grounds with a hint of menace as a snowstorm of white ticker tape blew across the stadium.

The contest itself was indeed rough and hostile, starting with some pre-match gamesmanship and stalling and followed by numerous jabs and swipes and stomps from both sides during play. Fouls that today would earn instant red cards went unpunished. Kempes gave Argentina an early lead with a strike in the thirty-eighth minute, but the Dutch finally equalised with a powerful header in the eighty-second. And the match went into extra time.

This is where Argentina proved themselves the more persistent side, buoyed perhaps by the home crowd's rising energy. As described by the writer Tim Pears: 'Now, socks rolled down around ankles, the Argentina players began once again to stampede forward, galloping towards their destiny.' Kempes stabbed home his second goal at the 105' mark and then Daniel Bertoni knocked in another to seal the Argentine victory. The stadium erupted like an Andean super volcano.

It's hard to say exactly how hosting and winning the World Cup affected the nation's rocky political climate… but Argentina's head coach César Luis Menotti found an angle that he would often repeat in the years afterward: 'Football is always a beautiful pretext for being happy.'

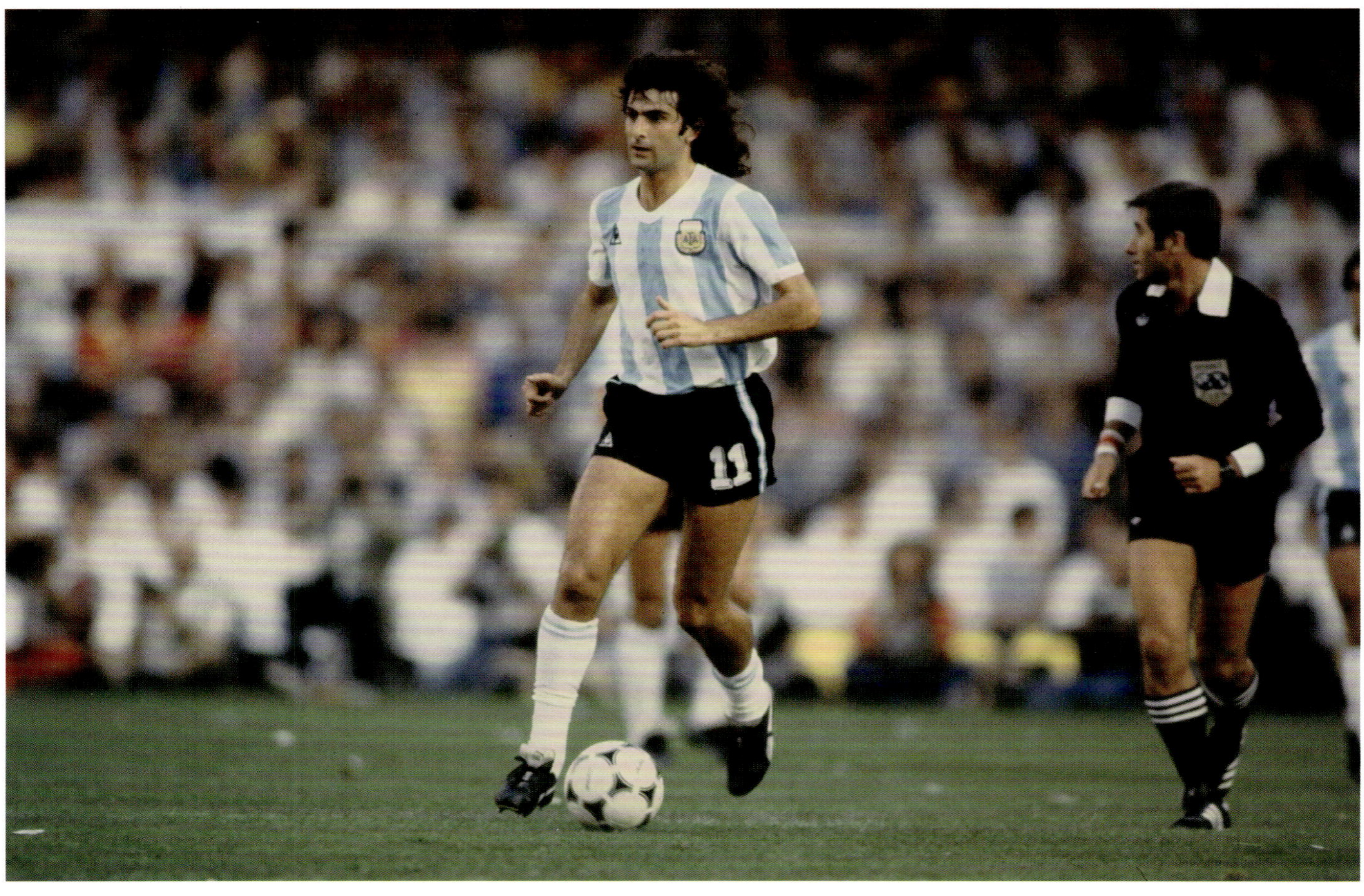

*'Now, socks rolled down around ankles,
the Argentina players began once again
to stampede forward, galloping towards
their destiny.'* — **TIM PEARS**

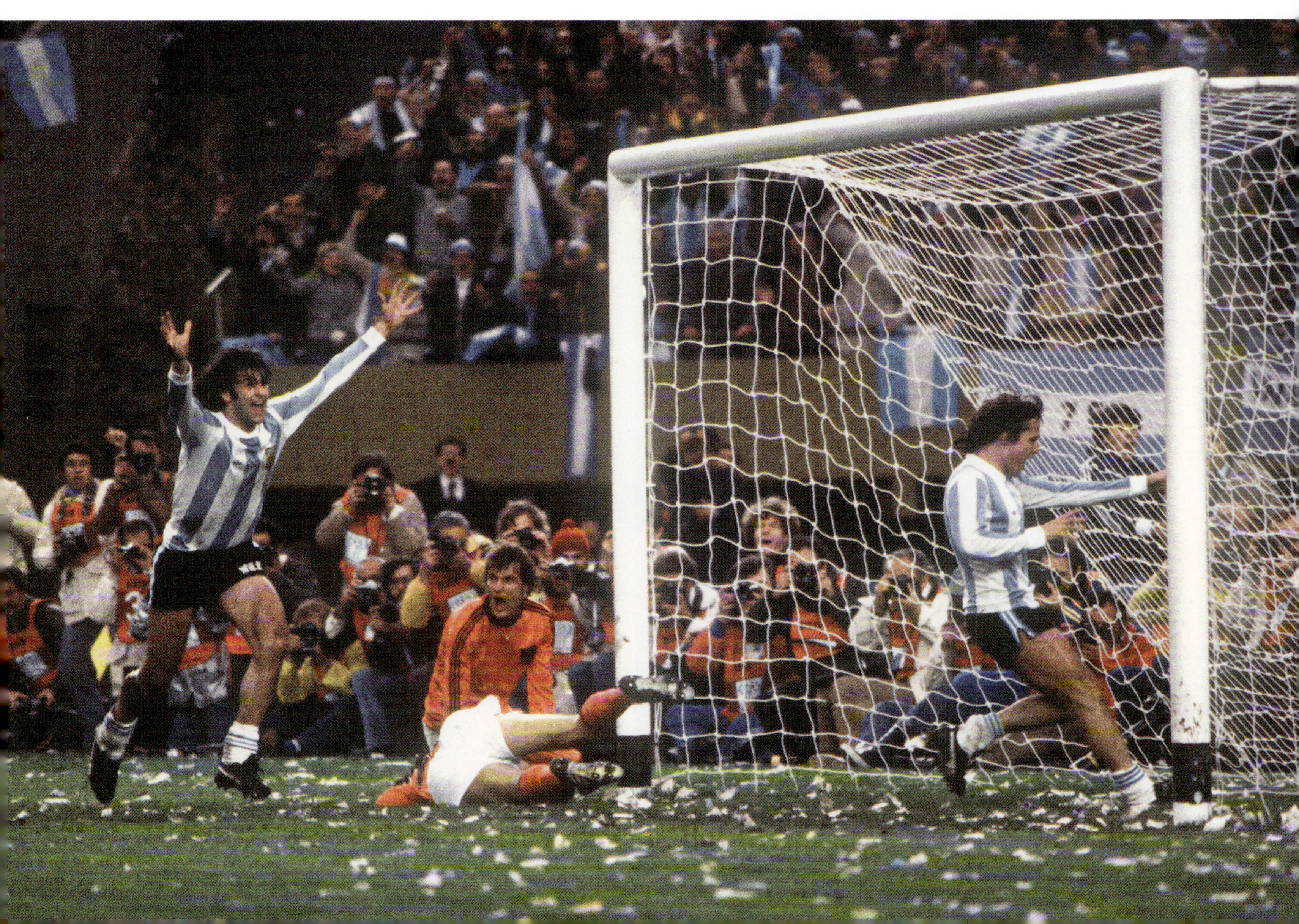

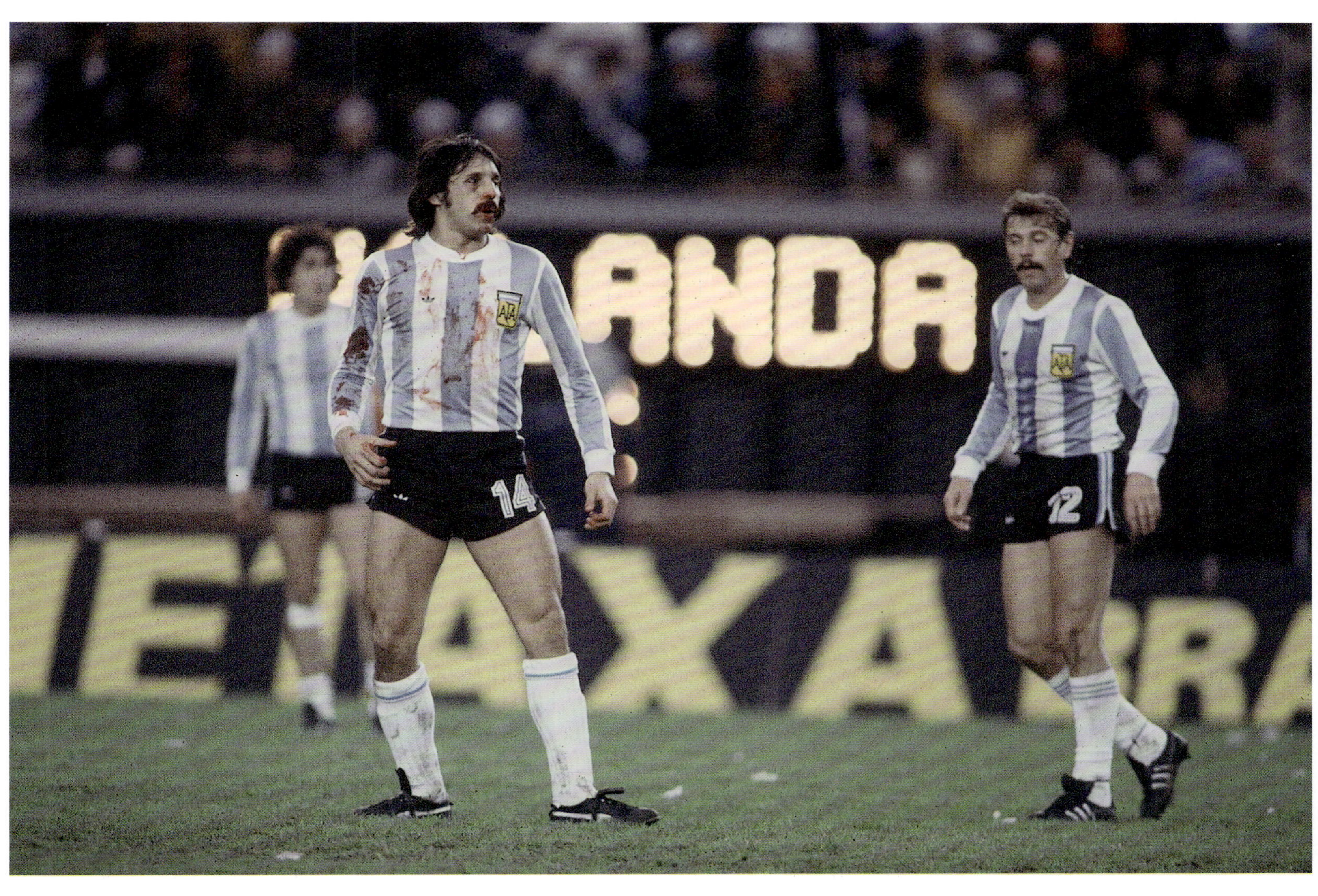

OPPOSITE *Mario Kempes (far left) celebrates after scoring in extra time of the final. Dutch defenders Wim Suurbier (centre, face down) and Jan Poortvliet (centre, facing Kempes) in agony.*

ABOVE *Argentina's Leopoldo Luque (centre) with a surprising amount of red on his celeste-and-white jersey after sustaining a nose injury.*

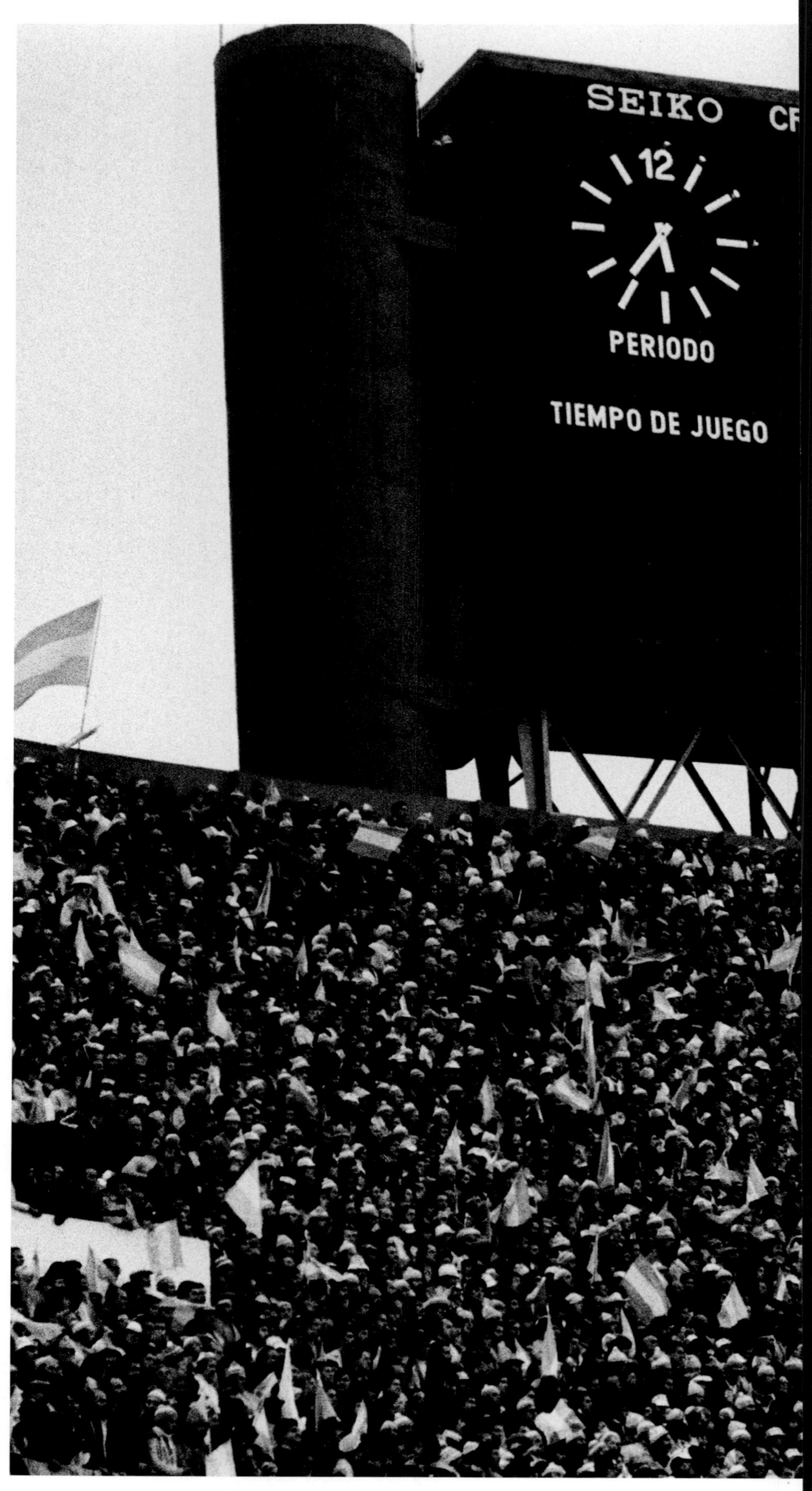



**RIGHT** *Argentina Champion!*

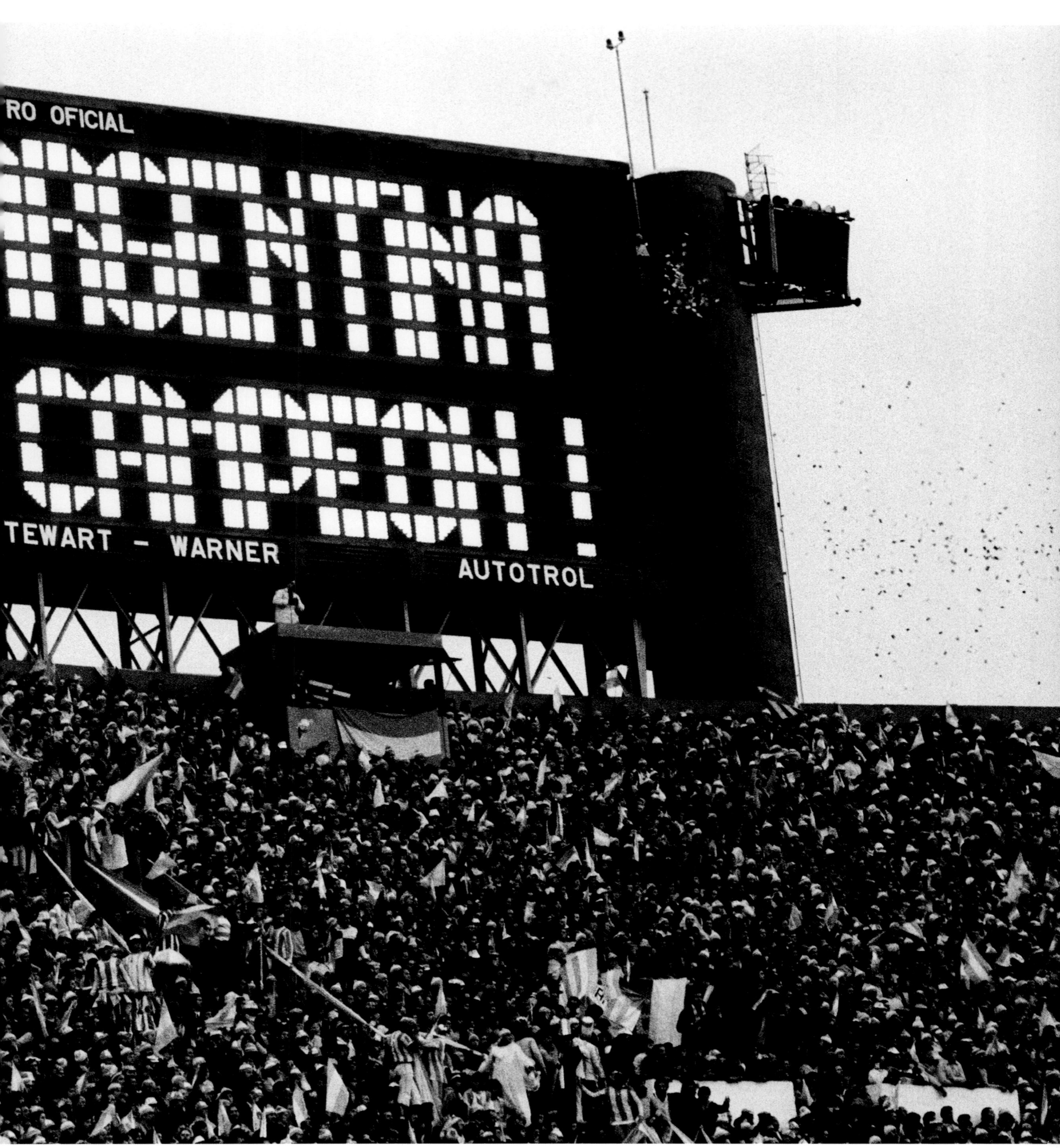
RO OFICIAL
ARGENTINA
CAMPEON !
TEWART — WARNER
AUTOTROL

# THE 1980s

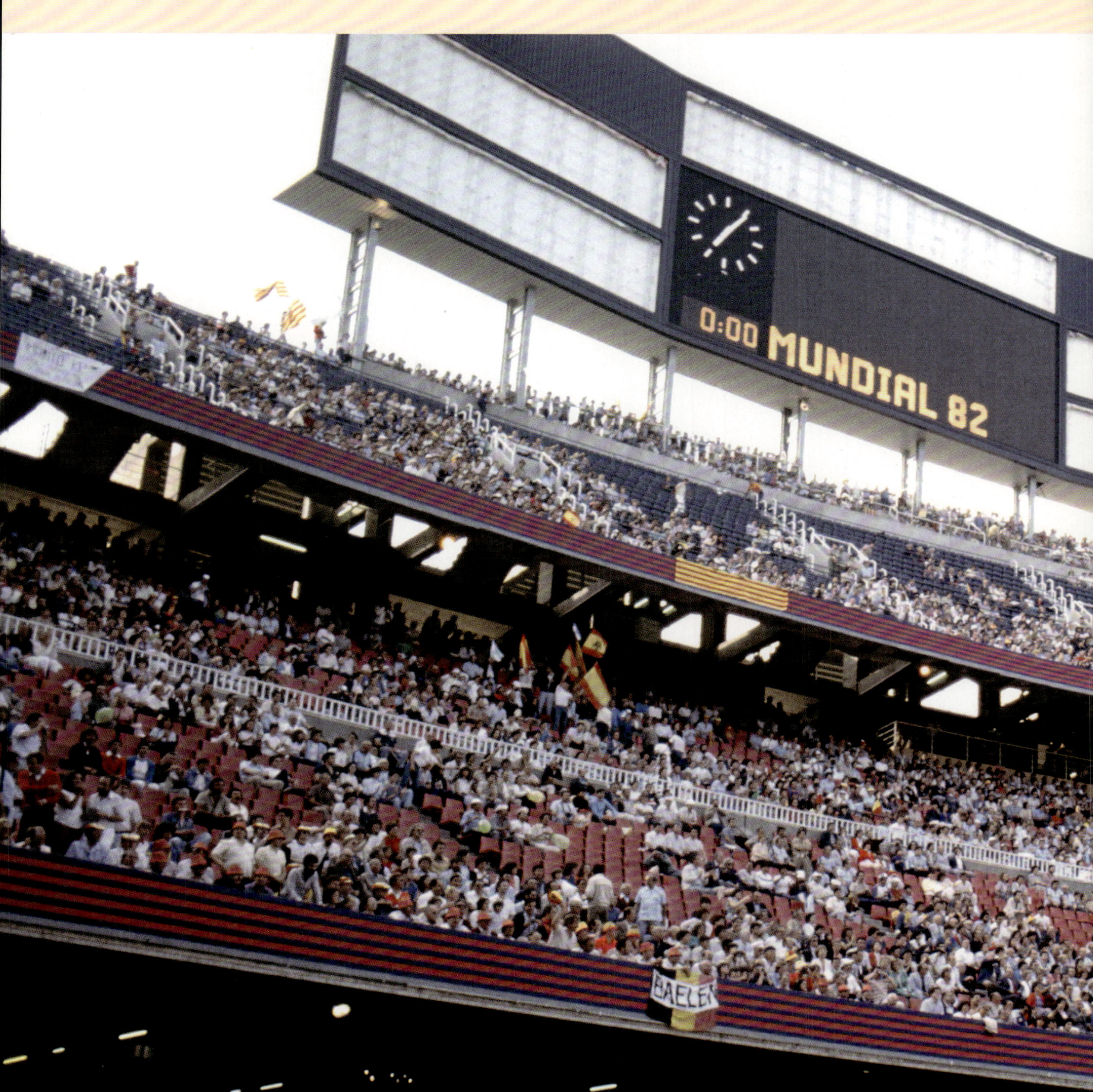

# CHAPTER 6

# *Italy's Class and the Hand of God*

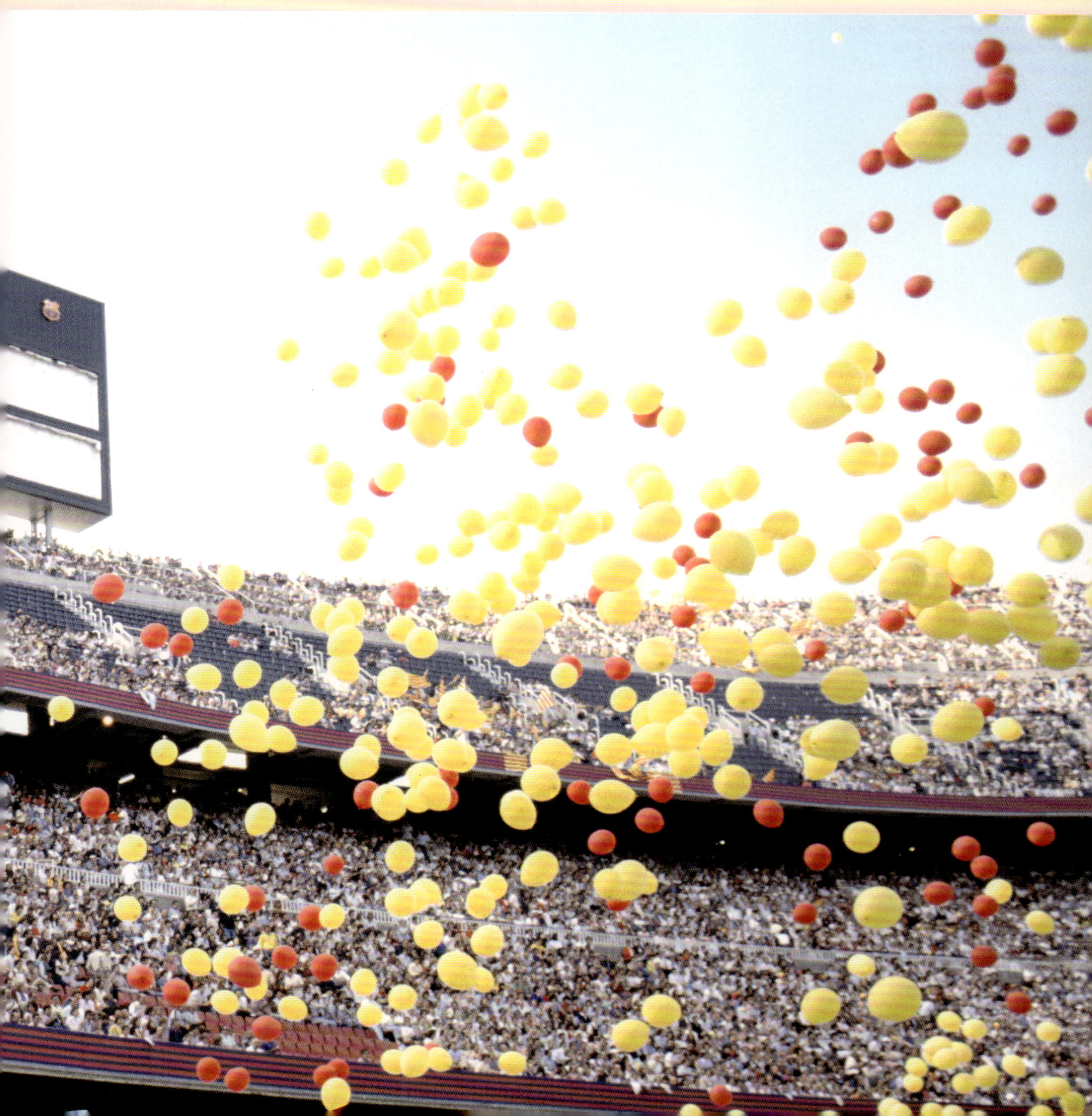

# 1982



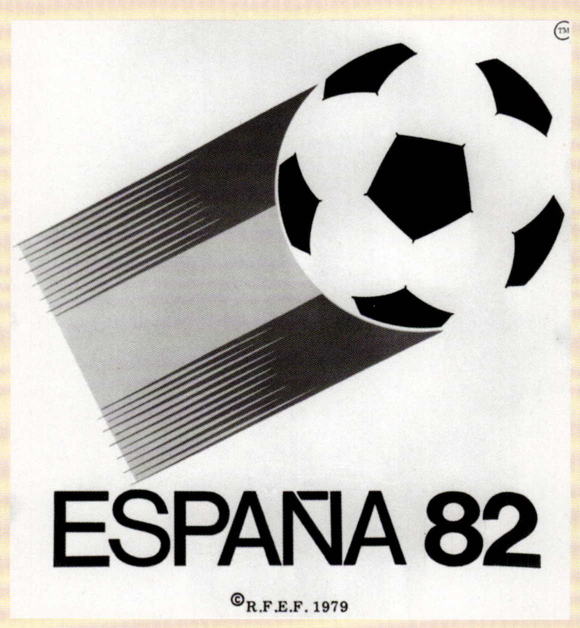


**Spain's selection as the** 1982 World Cup host was, surprisingly, free of controversy. When the choice was originally made back in 1966, Spain was still ruled by a military dictatorship under Francisco Franco. But when Franco died in 1975, his regime was succeeded by a constitutional monarchy that transitioned to a democratic system under the new King of Spain, Juan Carlos I. It was fortunate that, given the World Cup's historical weight and political influence, hosting the tournament would help open Spanish society further, strengthening connections to other countries and cultures. The only political tensions were between the United Kingdom and Argentina, which had just ended a deadly, though undeclared, ten-week war over the Falkland Islands — with hundreds of military personnel killed on both sides.

**PREVIOUS SPREAD** *Red and yellow balloons are released during the 1982 World Cup opening ceremony at the Camp Nou in Barcelona, Spain.*

**ABOVE** *The official logo of the 1982 World Cup in Spain.*

**OPPOSITE** *Cameroonian defender Elie Onana gets around Italy's Paolo Rossi.*

## 24 TEAMS, 17 FIELDS, THREE STAGES

**With the 1982 edition,** FIFA expanded the tournament to twenty-four teams, allowing for more countries from outside of Europe and South America to take part. Squads from Kuwait, Algeria, Cameroon, New Zealand, and Honduras made their World Cup debuts. The committee also devised a unique new format to accommodate the wider field. The first round featured six groups of four, played in the usual round-robin style, with the top-two teams in each group moving on to a second group stage. This second stage featured four groups of three teams, again round-robin, with each group winner moving on to the semi-finals. Spain's expansive sports infrastructure also let FIFA distribute matches to seventeen different stadiums in fourteen cities.

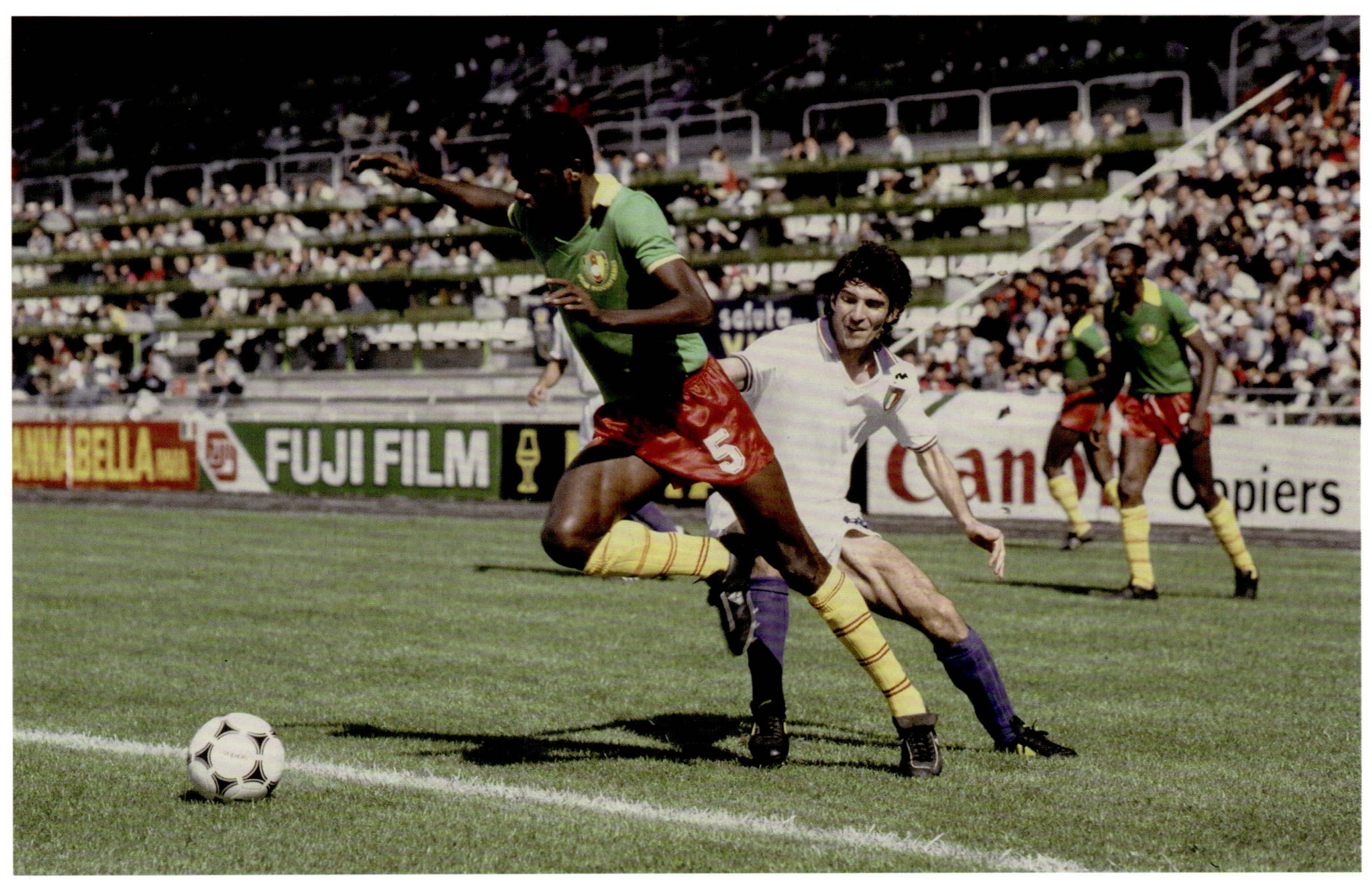

# Tournament: GROUP STAGE

### GROUP 1: POLAND, ITALY, CAMEROON, PERU

| | |
|---:|:---|
| Italy 0 | 0 Poland |
| Peru 0 | 0 Cameroon |
| Italy 1 | 1 Peru |
| Poland 0 | 0 Cameroon |
| Poland 5 | 1 Peru |
| Italy 1 | 1 Cameroon |

**Advanced to Second Group Stage: Poland, Italy**

### GROUP 2: WEST GERMANY, AUSTRIA, ALGERIA, CHILE

| | |
|---:|:---|
| Algeria 2 | 1 West Germany |
| Austria 1 | 0 Chile |
| West Germany 4 | 1 Chile |
| Austria 2 | 0 Algeria |
| Algeria 3 | 2 Chile |
| West Germany 1 | 0 Austria |

**Advanced to Second Group Stage: West Germany, Austria**

Italy's three ties, especially against newcomer Cameroon, were roundly criticised by the Italian press and seen as a gloomy harbinger of bad things to come—ironic, given the Cup's outcome. Poland's strong play caught the football world's attention, and they suddenly became a side to watch.

Algeria's astounding debut, a 2–1 win over defending-champion West Germany, is still considered one of the great World Cup upsets. Like Italy in Group 1, West Germany was underwhelming in this first group stage. And even though losing to Algeria wouldn't be the full story, it wouldn't be their lowest moment, either. West Germany's final group-stage match against Austria has been labelled 'The Disgrace of Gijón' because, after an early West German goal assured that both sides would advance ahead of Algeria, the game devolved into aimless passing in the second half. The incensed crowd jeered and chanted '*Fuera! Fuera!*' ('Get out! Get out!') at the corrupt scene before them.

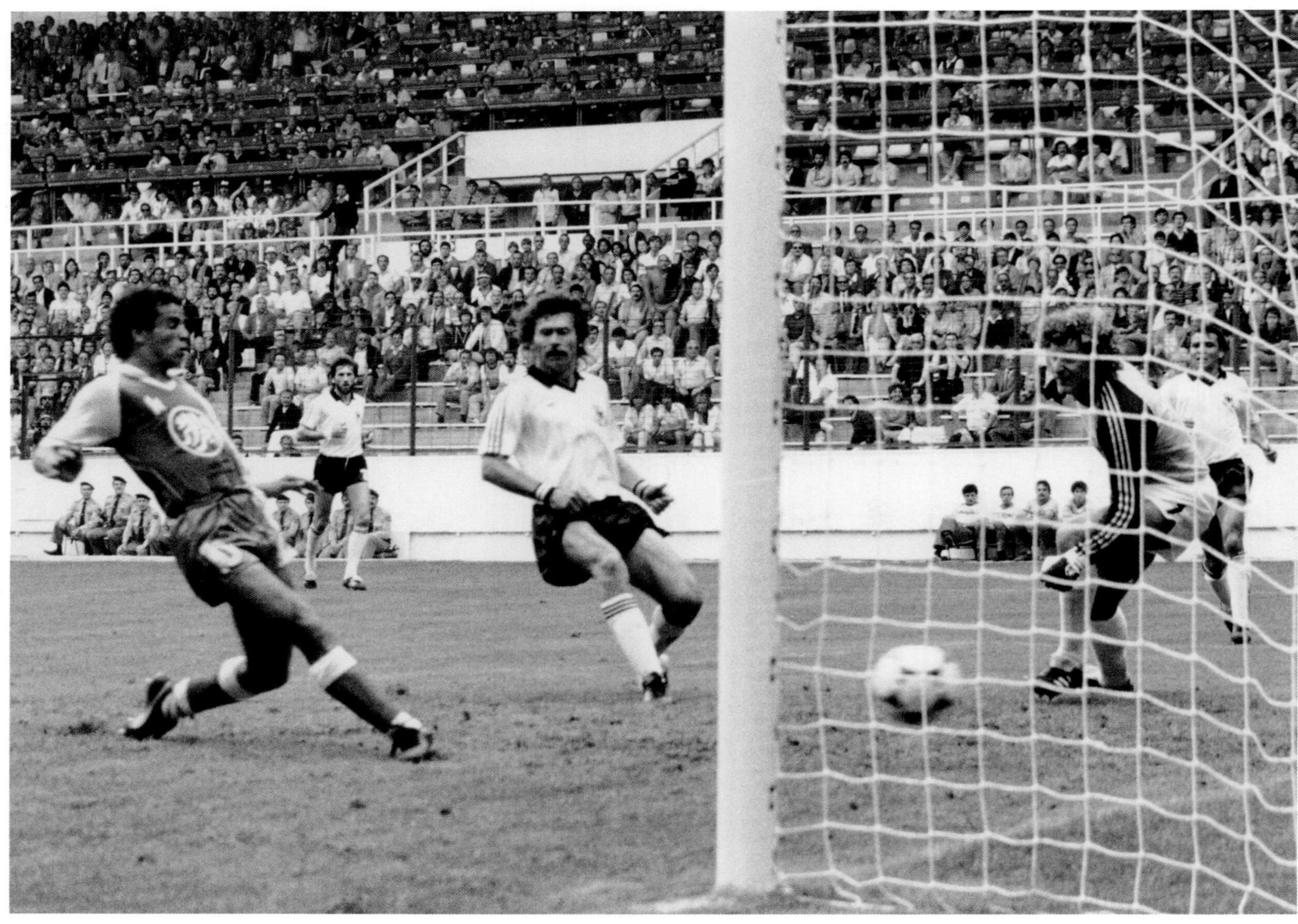

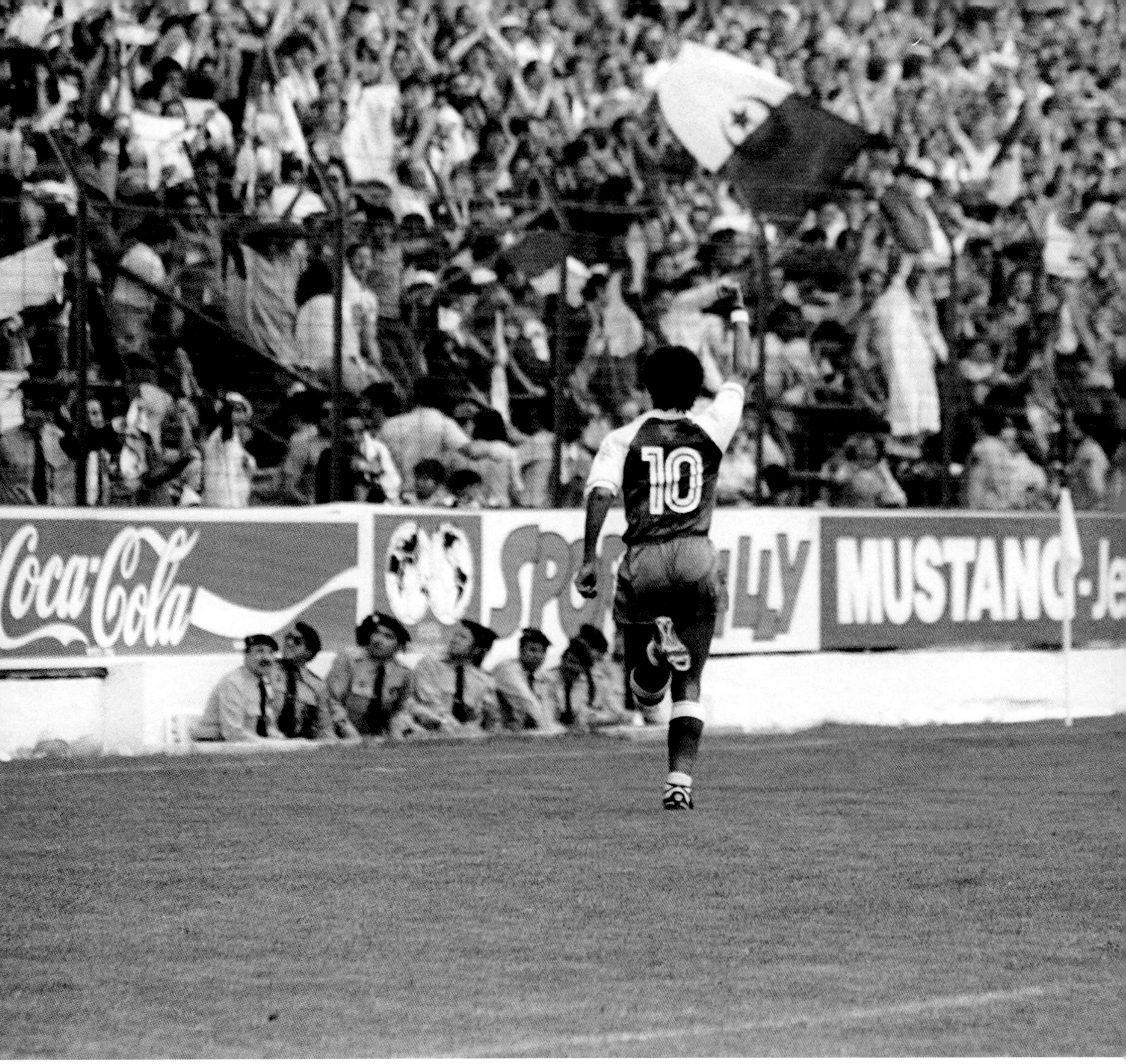



**OPPOSITE** *Lakhdar Belloumi
scores the winning goal for
Algeria's shocking 2–1 victory
over West Germany.*

**ABOVE** *Belloumi runs to the
stands to celebrate with the
Algerian supporters.*

## GROUP 3: BELGIUM, ARGENTINA, HUNGARY, EL SALVADOR

| | | |
|---|---|---|
| Belgium 1 | 0 | Argentina |
| Hungary 10 | 1 | El Salvador |
| Argentina 4 | 1 | Hungary |
| Belgium 1 | 0 | El Salvador |
| Belgium 1 | 1 | Hungary |
| Argentina 2 | 0 | El Salvador |

***Advanced to Second Group Stage: Belgium, Argentina***

The Spanish crowds were particularly excited to see a young Argentine in his first World Cup: Diego Maradona had just signed with Spain's pre-eminent professional club, FC Barcelona, for a then-record fee of $7.6 million. The budding star had a rough tournament, suffering considerable physical punishment in a series of very loosely officiated matches. He did score twice against Hungary, however, in a sign of things to come.

## GROUP 4: ENGLAND, FRANCE, CZECHOSLOVAKIA, KUWAIT

| | | |
|---|---|---|
| England 3 | 1 | France |
| Czechoslovakia 1 | 1 | Kuwait |
| England 2 | 0 | Czechoslovakia |
| France 4 | 1 | Kuwait |
| France 1 | 1 | Czechoslovakia |
| England 1 | 0 | Kuwait |

***Advanced to Second Group Stage: England, France***

England scored just twenty-seven seconds into its match with France. Both teams advanced to the second group stage with ease.

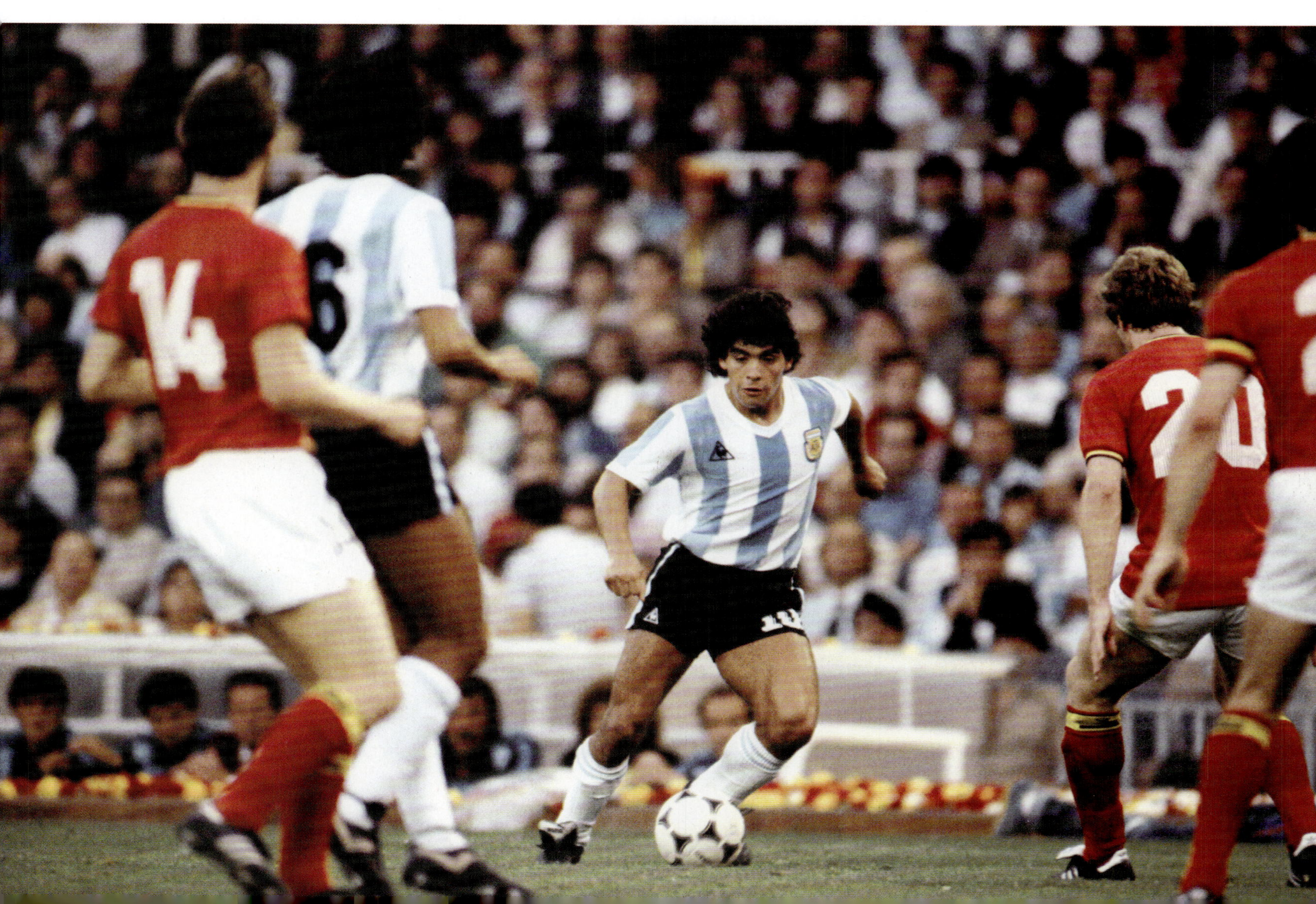

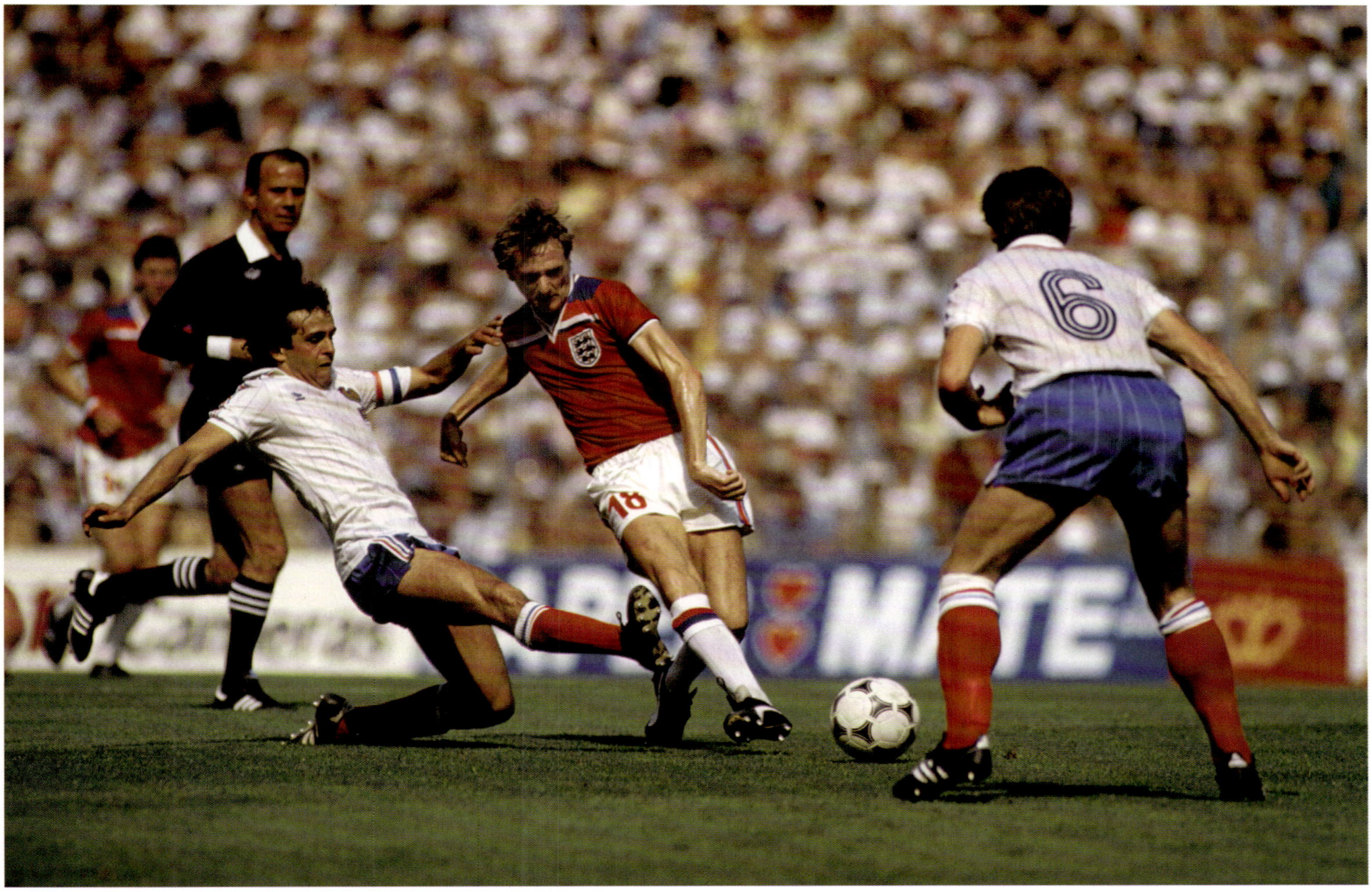

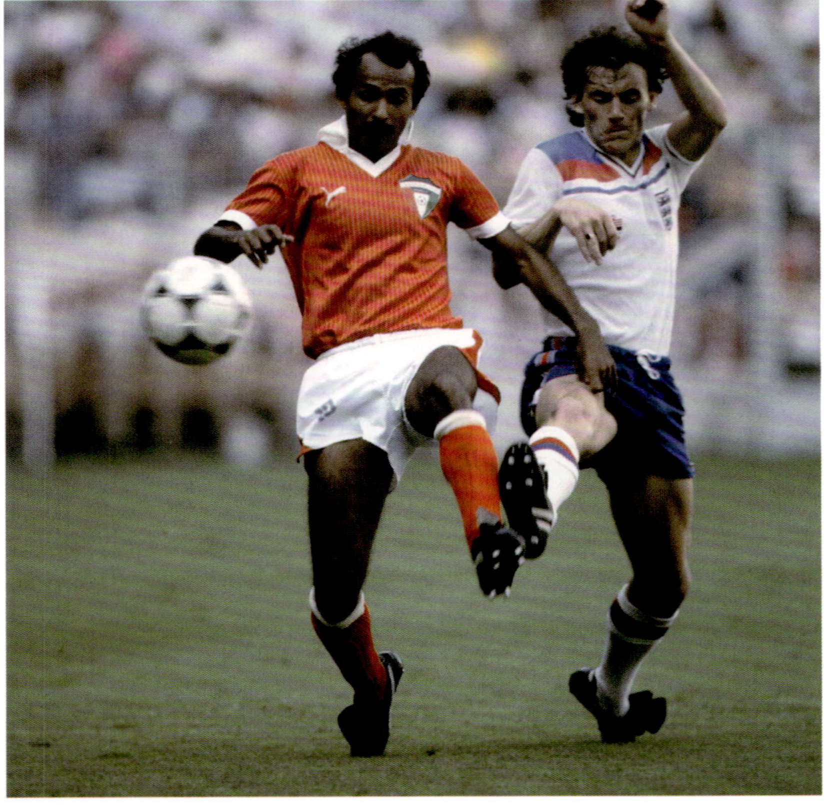

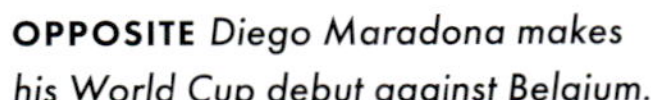

**OPPOSITE** *Diego Maradona makes his World Cup debut against Belgium.*

**ABOVE** *France's Michel Platini (left) with a sliding challenge on English-man Phil Thompson (centre).*

**RIGHT** *Abdulaziz Al-Anberi of Kuawit (left) beats England's Steve Coppell to the ball.*

| | |
|---|---|
| Spain 1 | 1 Honduras |
| Yugoslavia 0 | 0 Northern Ireland |
| Spain 2 | 1 Yugoslavia |
| Honduras 1 | 1 Northern Ireland |
| Yugoslavia 1 | 0 Honduras |
| Northern Ireland 1 | 0 Spain |

***Advanced to Second Group Stage: Northern Ireland, Spain***

Scrappy Northern Ireland won this evenly matched group that featured three draws and three one-goal games. The host team Spain advanced by edging out Yugoslavia on goals scored, 3–2.

### GROUP 6: BRAZIL, SOVIET UNION, SCOTLAND, NEW ZEALAND

| | |
|---|---|
| Brazil 2 | 1 Soviet Union |
| Scotland 5 | 2 New Zealand |
| Brazil 4 | 1 Scotland |
| Soviet Union 3 | 0 New Zealand |
| Soviet Union 2 | 2 Scotland |
| Brazil 4 | 2 New Zealand |

***Advanced to Second Group Stage: Brazil, Soviet Union***

Brazil's talented attack, seemingly as potent as ever, helped them sweep through group play with three impressive wins and the Soviet Union slipped into the second spot over Scotland on goal differential. By tournament's end, this Brazilian squad would be considered one of the greatest sides that didn't win their World Cup. Following a 4–1 dismantling at the hands of Brazil, Scotland's manager Jock Stein, whose team was solid in its own right, admitted: 'It will be good for soccer if they win it. It's never easy to accept defeat, but this one is different.'

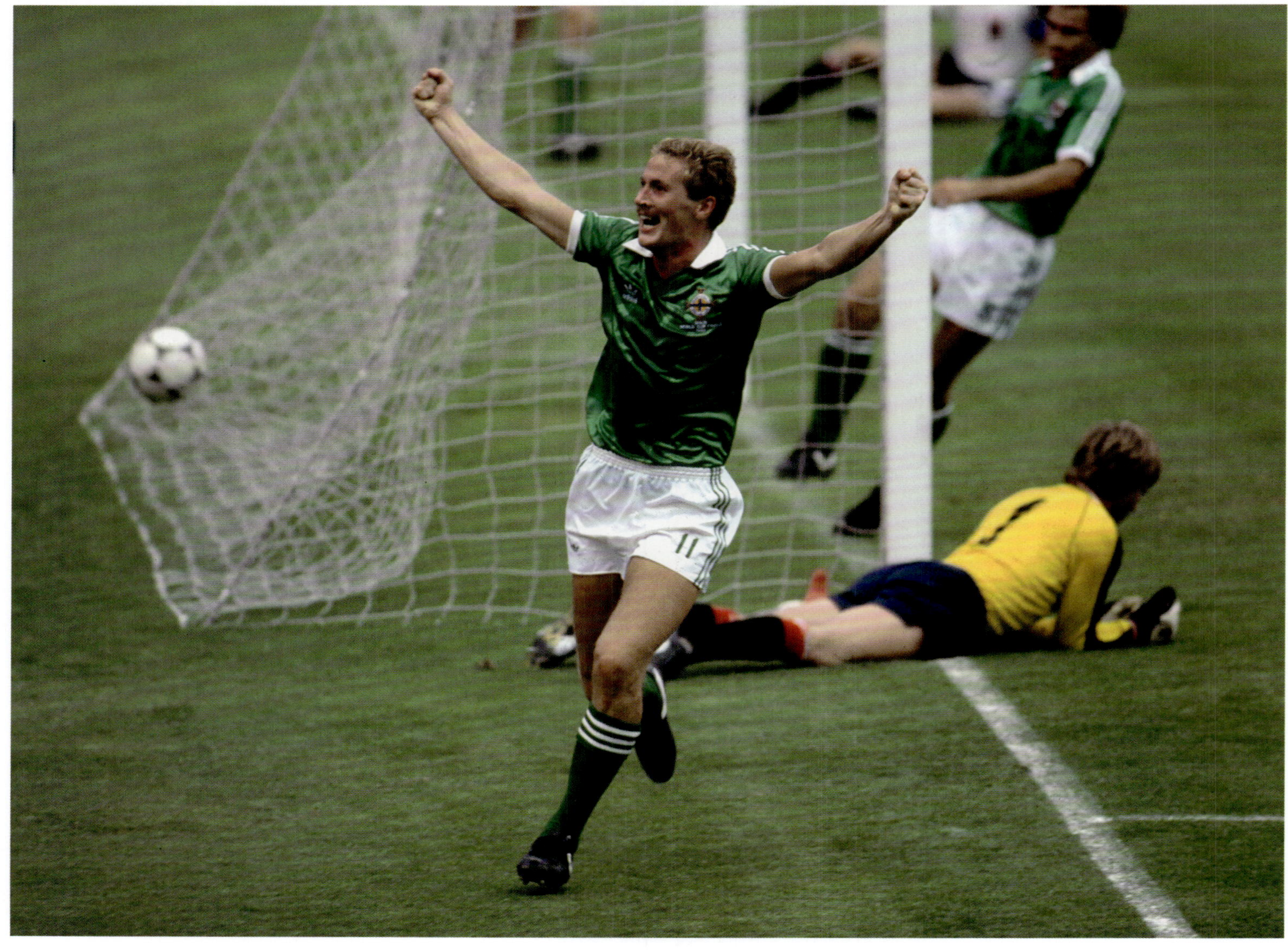

# THE SHEIKH'S REVERSED WHISTLE

**Perhaps the most interesting moment** of the first round came in Group 4's France–Kuwait match. When a piercing whistle from the stands was mistaken for the referee's, Kuwait's entire team halted to wait for the call which never came. French midfielder Alain Giresse kept advancing and deposited the ball in the Kuwait net as everyone else stood watching. At first, the centre referee called it a goal, but the high-ranking Kuwaiti Sheikh Fahad rushed onto the field to protest, and the ref reversed his decision.

**OPPOSITE** *Billy Hamilton of Northern Ireland celebrates his opening goal against Austria (match results Second Group Stage, Group D).*

**BELOW** *Sheikh Ahmad Al-Fahad Al-Sabah, the brother of the Emir of Kuwait, after rushing the field to protest a call in the match against France.*

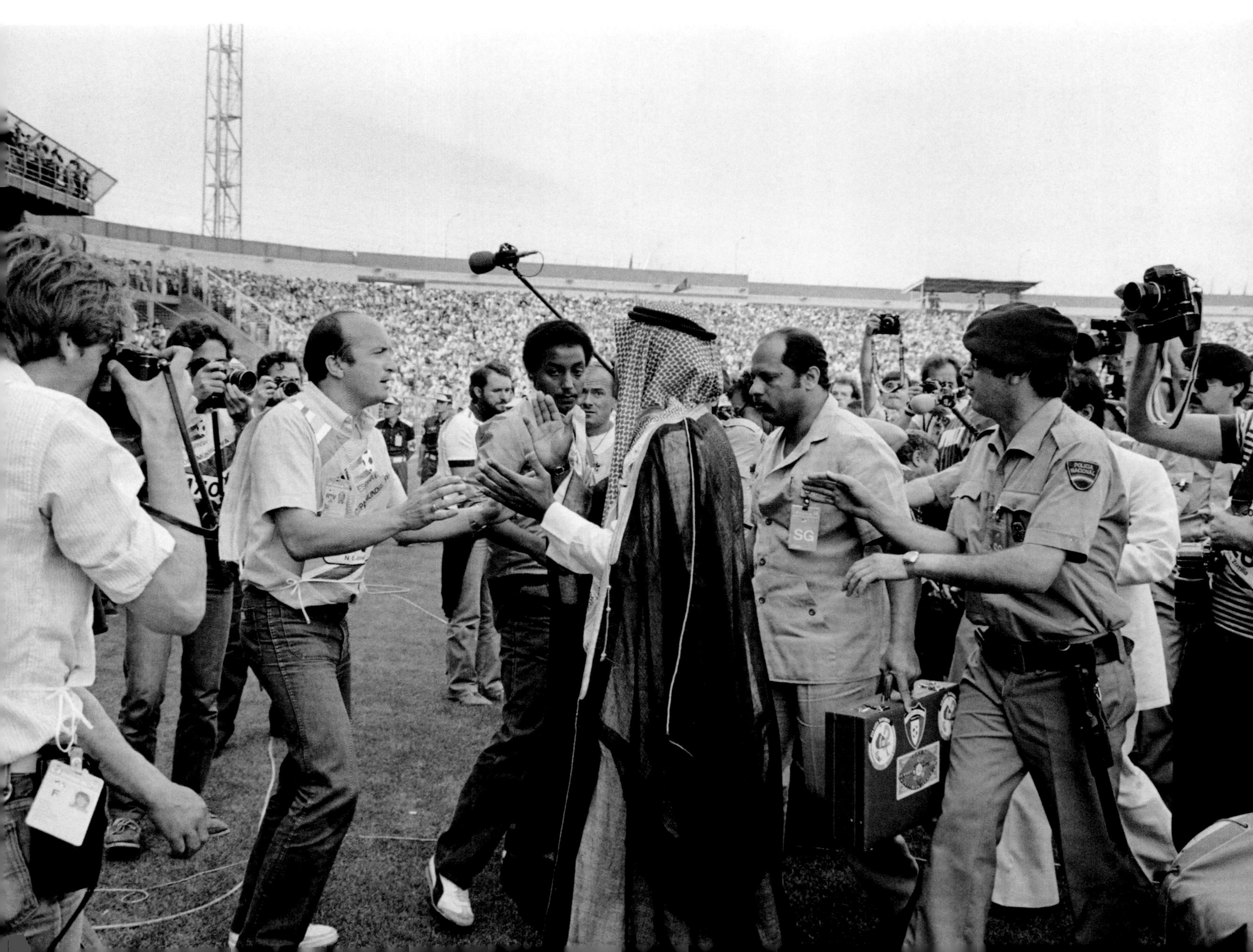

# SECOND GROUP STAGE

### GROUP A: POLAND, SOVIET UNION, BELGIUM

| | | |
|---|---|---|
| Poland 3 | 0 | Belgium |
| Soviet Union 1 | 0 | Belgium |
| Soviet Union 0 | 0 | Poland |

**Advanced to Knockout Stage: Poland**

Poland continued its strong run through the tournament, advancing to the knockout stage via a 0–0 draw with the Soviets that locked in a higher goal differential for 'The White Eagles'. The difference was a stellar hat-trick by Zbigniew Boniek in Poland's opening 3–0 win over Belgium.

### GROUP B: WEST GERMANY, ENGLAND, SPAIN

| | | |
|---|---|---|
| West Germany 0 | 0 | England |
| West Germany 2 | 1 | Spain |
| Spain 0 | 0 | England |

**Advanced to Knockout Stage: West Germany**

In a tightly contested round-robin, England managed stout 0–0 draws against both West Germany and Spain. Thus, the difference was West Germany's close 2–1 win over the Spanish hosts, which sent them on to the knockouts.

**BELOW** *Belgium's Gerard Plessers with an unsuccessful slide tackle on Poland's Zbigniew Boniek in the second group stage.*

**OPPOSITE** *Italian striker Paolo Rossi (far right) immediately gets started on his hat-trick against Brazil, scoring his first goal just five minutes into the match.*

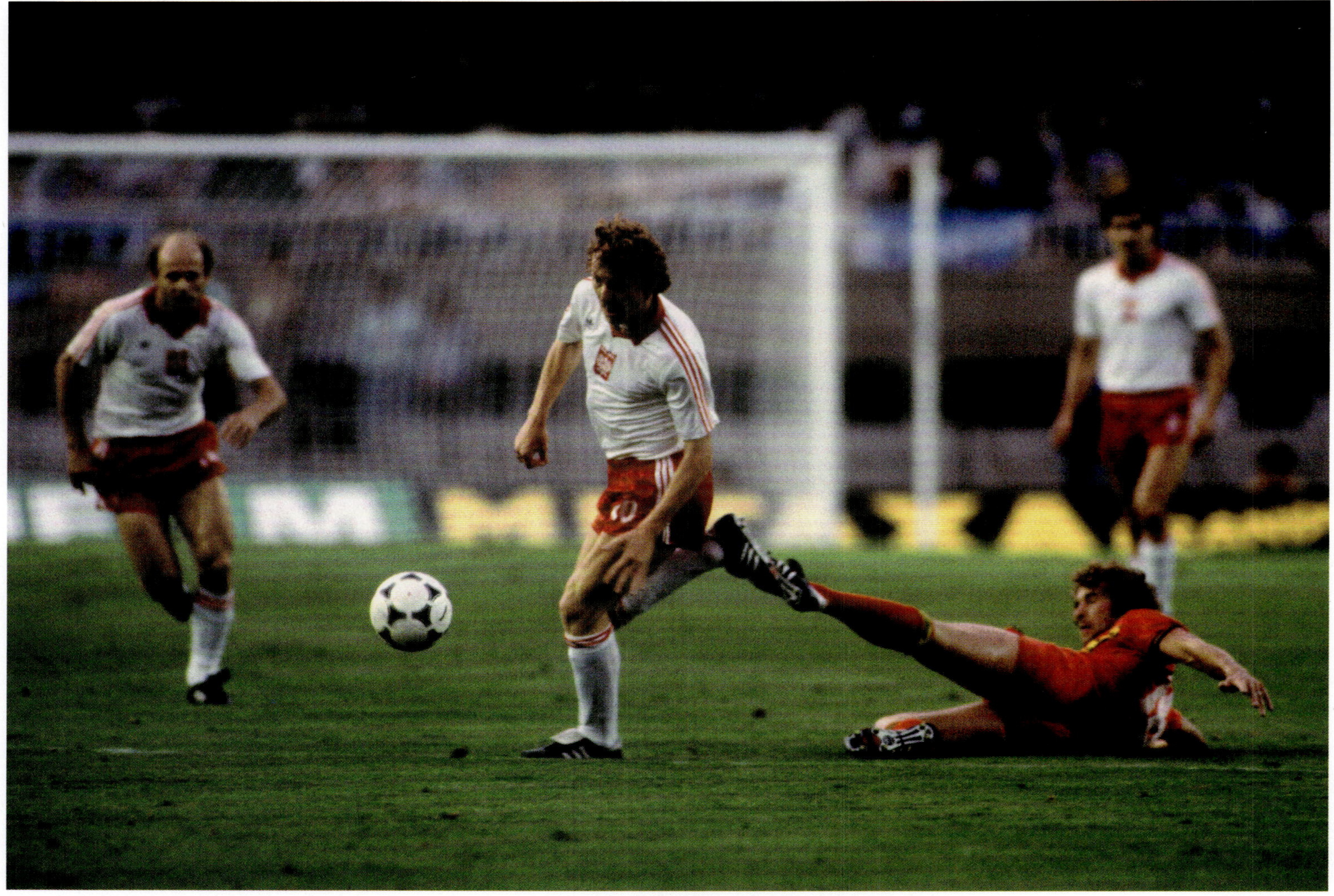

| | | |
|---|---|---|
| Italy 2 | 1 | Argentina |
| Brazil 3 | 1 | Argentina |
| Italy 3 | 2 | Brazil |

***Advanced to Knockout Stage: Italy***

Italy and Brazil both dispensed with Argentina by building multi-goal leads that proved insurmountable. This set up a classic final match in Barcelona—the Italy–Brazil Group C decider is now widely considered one of the greatest in football history. Known as 'The Sarrià Tragedy' in Brazil, it ousted one of the most fearsome attacking squads ever seen in World Cup play.



| | | |
|---|---|---|
| France 1 | 0 | Austria |
| Austria 2 | 2 | Northern Ireland |
| France 4 | 1 | Northern Ireland |

***Advanced to Knockout Stage: France***

When Northern Ireland tied Austria, it set up the possibility of a fairy-tale trip to the semi-finals for the underdogs. But France slammed that storybook shut with a dominating 4–1 win in the group's last game. With its two solid victories, France won the group and advanced to a history-making (and notorious) matchup with West Germany.

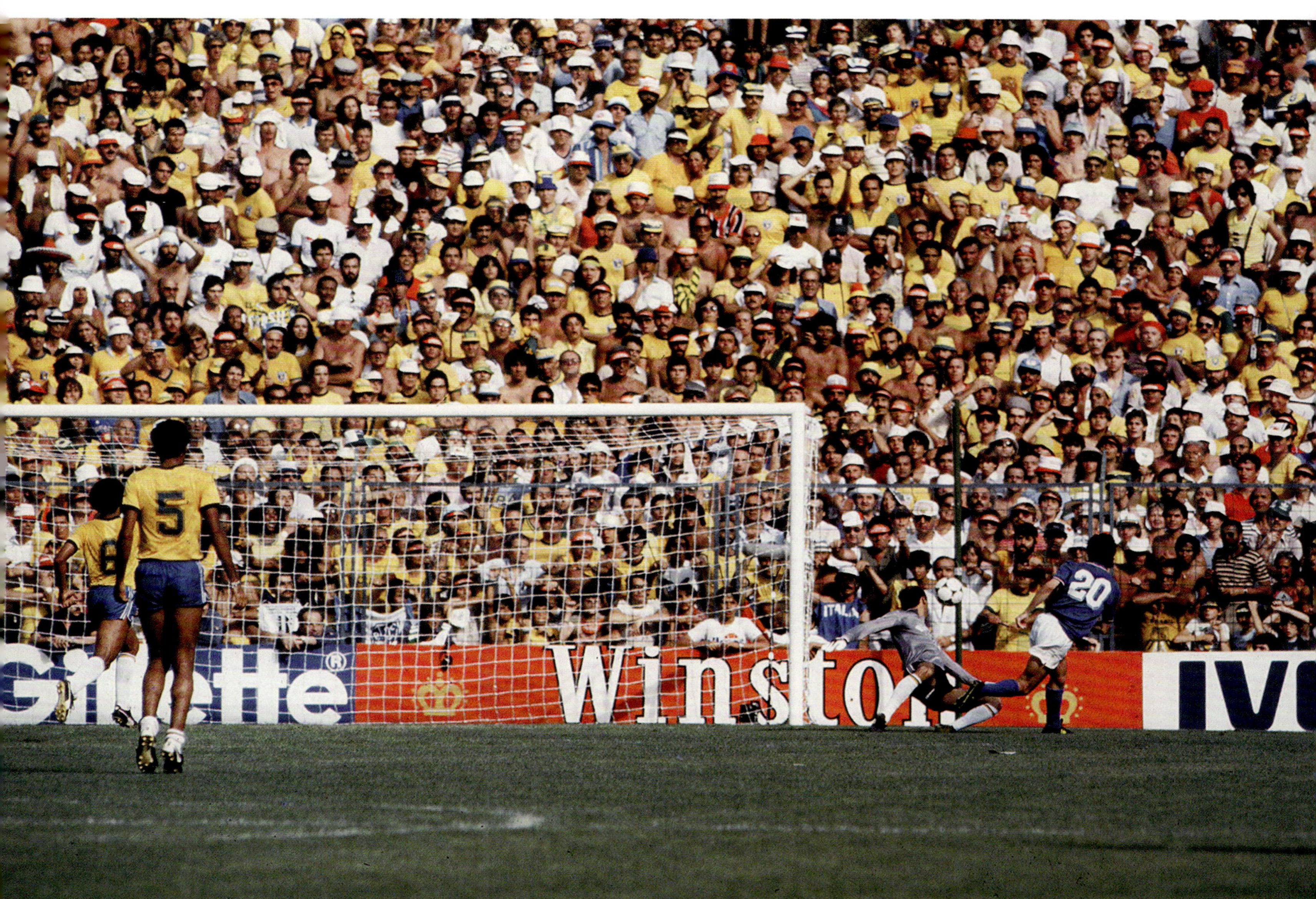

# THE SARRIÀ TRAGEDY

**When Brazil met Italy** on 5 July, 1982, in Barcelona's Sarrià Stadium, it was a classic clash of opposing styles — irresistible force meets immovable object. Under manager Telê Santana, Brazil's capacity for brilliant attacking panache — embodied in the free-form playmaking of its star midfielders, the flamboyant Zico and the elegant Sócrates — had charmed the football world. 'Shunning pragmatism and the demands of creating a rigid system,' wrote the sports journalist Tom Adams, 'Santana instead entrusted his creative players with a freedom to express themselves' and broke free from tactical constraints imposed by his predecessor. Sócrates himself called the team's style 'irreverent, joyful, creative, free-flowing'.

The Italian side, on the other hand, was more limited in its creative flow but far better organised under the guidance of manager Enzo Bearzot. Noted for its fierce tactical discipline on defence, Bearzot's system was also built to generate swift transitions to counterattack. Defender Claudio Gentile displayed remarkable man-marking tenacity in neutralising brilliant attackers like Argentina's Diego Maradona and Brazil's Zico, whereas Gaetano Scirea played a refined libero whose savvy sense of shape and support kept his defence well aligned. Ahead of them roamed a dangerous counter-weapon in forward Paolo Rossi.

As expected, the match was largely played in the Italian half. But despite the constant pressure from Brazil, Rossi broke loose on counters to score in the fifth and twenty-fifth minutes, exploiting Brazil's lax defending in the box for the first goal and a crucially misplaced pass from defensive midfielder Toninho Cerezo for the second. Brazil's killer attack was able to equalise twice and even seemed on the front foot before Rossi capped his hat-trick at 74' for a 3–2 lead. From there, the densely layered Italian defence protected the lead for the win, with Dino Zoff, Italy's brilliant forty-year-old goalkeeper, making a phenomenal save in the final seconds.

And so, despite playing some of the most thrilling football ever seen, Brazil's collection of artists didn't even make it to the knockout stage. The Brazilian press labelled it the 'Sarrià Tragedy' and the demoralising result led future Brazilian coaches to favour a less flashy and more direct style of physical, counterattacking football. Many considered Brazil's pivot away from '*joga bonito*' to be a great loss to the game's beauty, but future squads would bring back the flair and prodigious talent that Brazil was most known, and most loved, for.

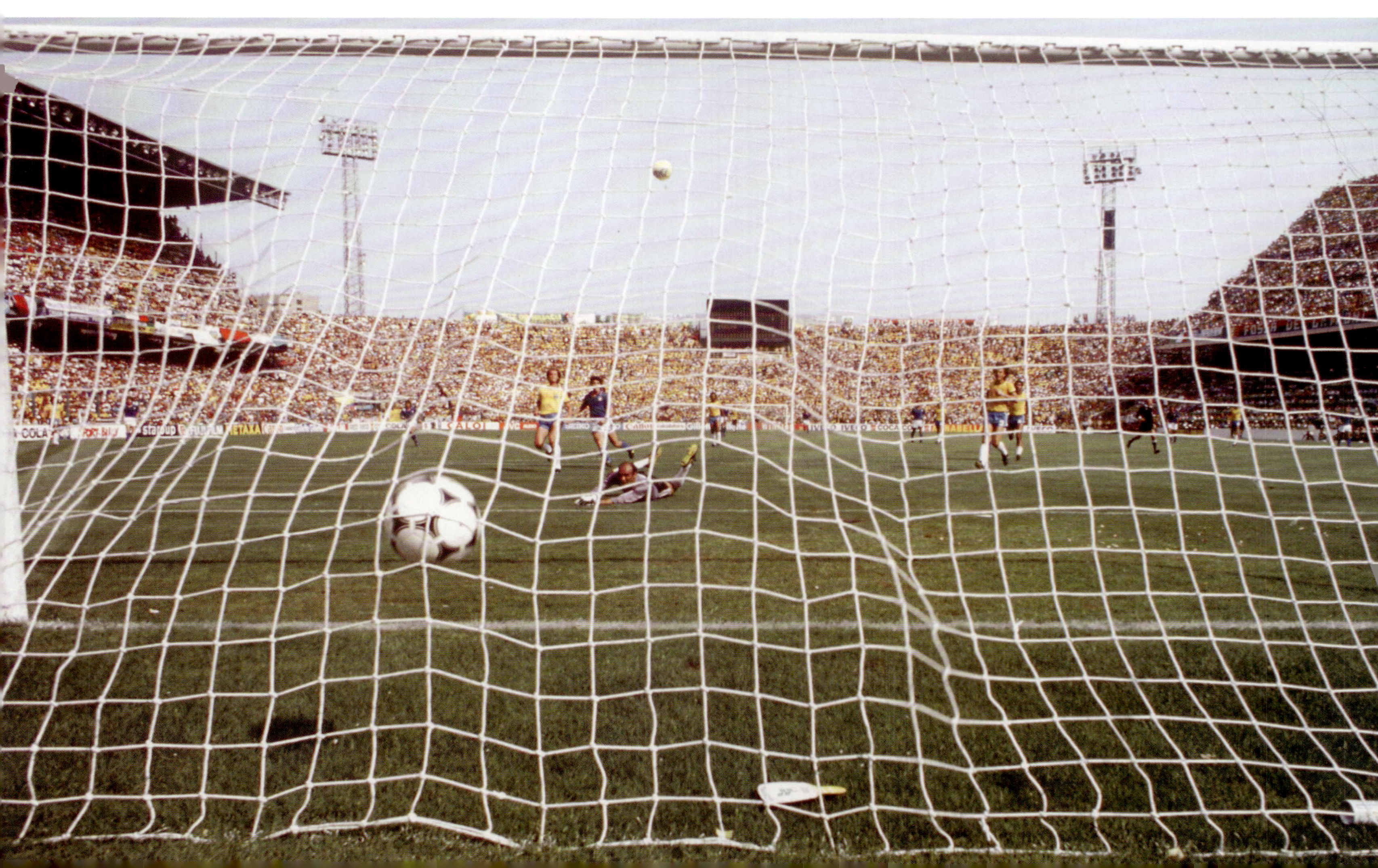

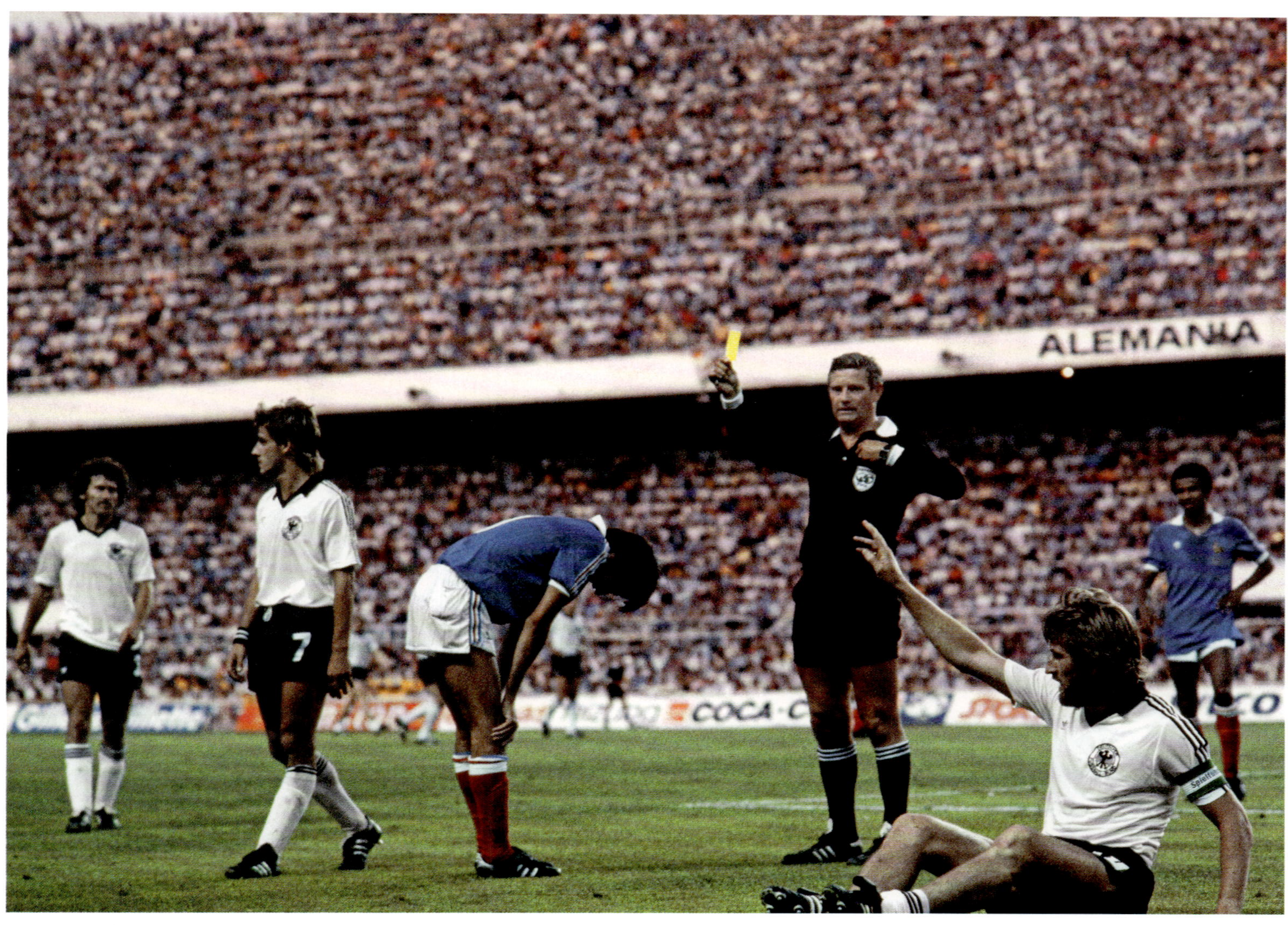

# SEMI-FINALS

Italy 2 | 0 Poland
West Germany 3 | 3 France
(West Germany wins 5–4 on penalty kicks)

In the first semi-final, Italy's newest protagonist Paolo Rossi uncorked a savoury brace and his vaunted defensive mates shut down the Polish attack for a 2–0 victory. The second semi-final, pitting France against West Germany, was the first World Cup match to be decided by a penalty-kick shootout. And the 120 minutes leading up to it were laden with drama, too.

**OPPOSITE** *Brazil's goalkeeper Waldir Peres watches hopelessly from the ground as Paolo Rossi's second goal for Italy hits the back of the net.*

**ABOVE** *Dutch referee Charles Corver awards a yellow card to Frenchman Alain Giresse in the infamous* Noche en Sevilla *semi-final bout between West Germany and France.*

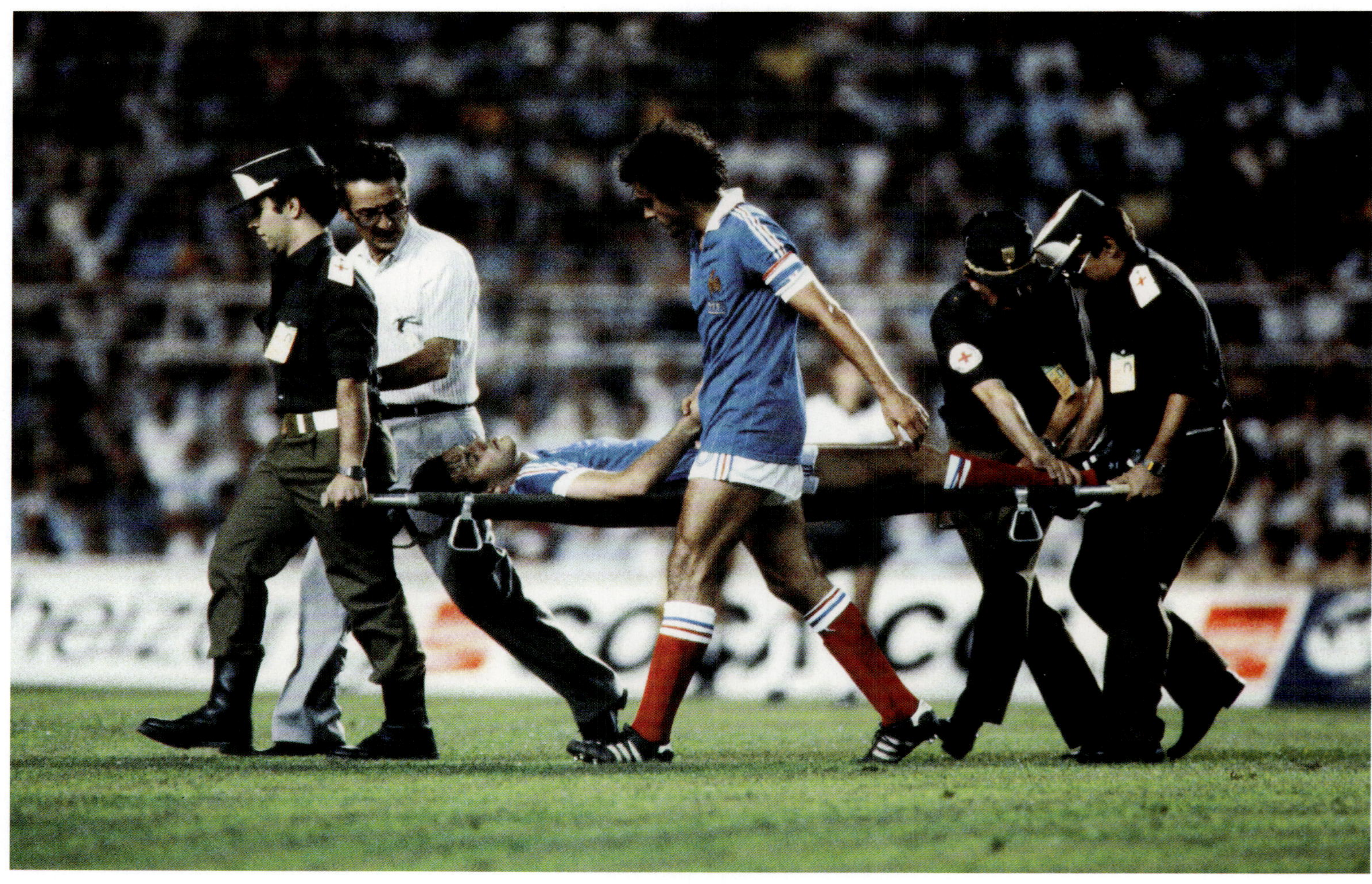

## THE NIGHT IN SEVILLE

**The West Germany versus France** semi-final match on 8 July, 1982, was a particularly dazzling, dramatic, and controversial affair. Known afterwards in both nations as 'The Night in Seville', it saw a tactically superior performance from both sides marred by a single moment of infamously rough play — a particularly ugly moment that one writer called 'the most horrific challenge in World Cup history'.

Defender Patrick Battiston, who had just subbed into the match for France, found himself breaking free behind the West German defence. Receiving a wonderful pass from magisterial attacking midfielder Michel Platini, Battiston flicked a shot just centimetres wide of the post as goalkeeper Toni Schumacher charged at him and leapt. Completely missing the ball, Schumacher swivelled sideways and slammed his hip full force into Battiston's head, a terrifying collision. The Frenchman was knocked out cold, lost three teeth, cracked three ribs, and damaged a vertebra. He was carried off the pitch on a stretcher, given oxygen, and rushed to a hospital. No foul was called, and regulation time ended in a tense 1–1 tie. The French daily *L'Équipe* called it 'a story of unpunished violence . . . a morality tale we'll tell our children'.

But even after ninety minutes, the Sevillian night was just getting started. A magnificently frantic extra time saw France score twice in the first eight minutes to pull ahead 3–1, only to have the West Germans draw level in the second fifteen-minute period, their third goal a spectacular bicycle kick by forward Klaus Fischer. *The Guardian* called it 'a back-and-forth, six-goal, bona fide thriller between two teams packed with top-drawer talent performing at full pelt'. Extra time ended 3–3, triggering the World Cup's first-ever penalty-kick shootout.

Unfortunately for France and their hopes of karmic retribution, the hero of the shootout was, in fact, the villain: Schumacher. His two gymnastic saves were enough to push West Germany through to the Cup Final.

'A particularly dazzling, dramatic, and controversial affair.'



**OPPOSITE** *French captain Michel Platini holds teammate Patrick Battiston's hand as the latter is stretchered off the pitch with a serious injury from German goalkeeper Toni Schumacher.*

**RIGHT** *The French squad prepares for extra time.*

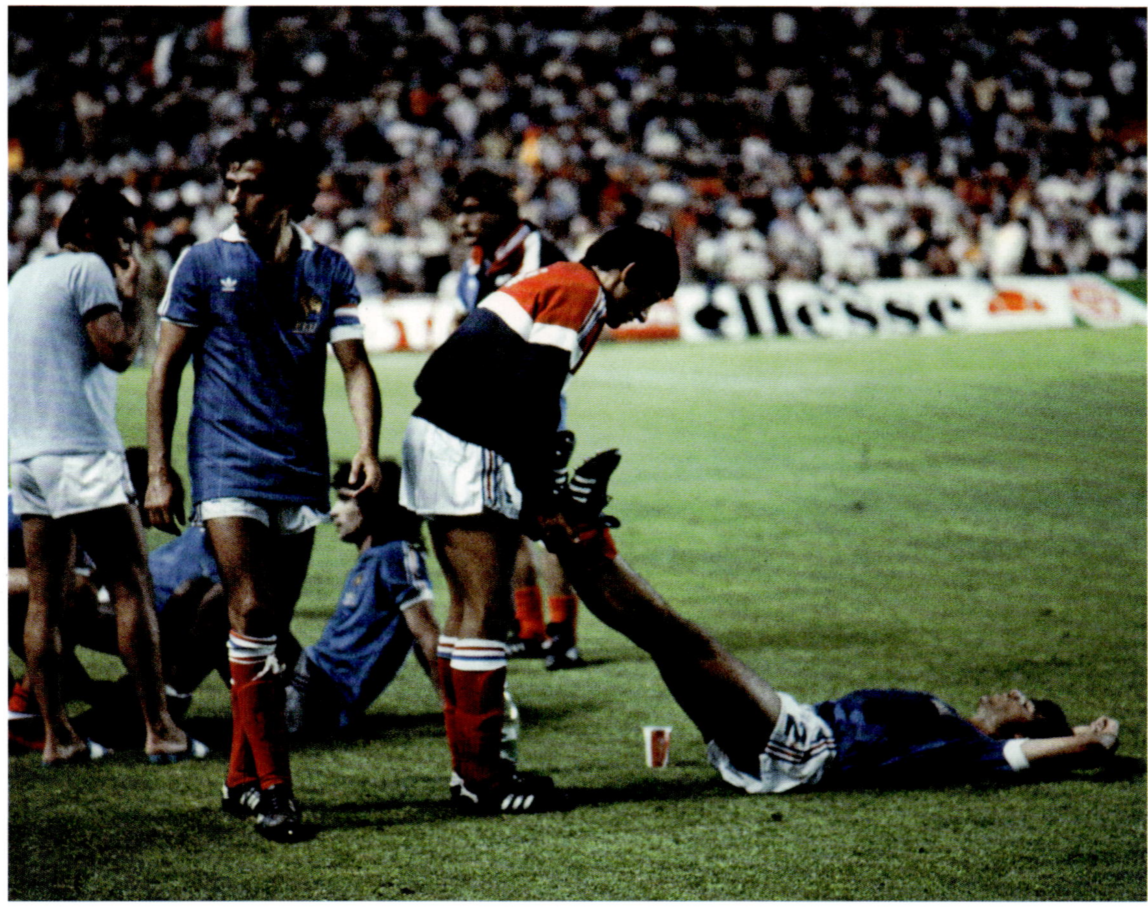

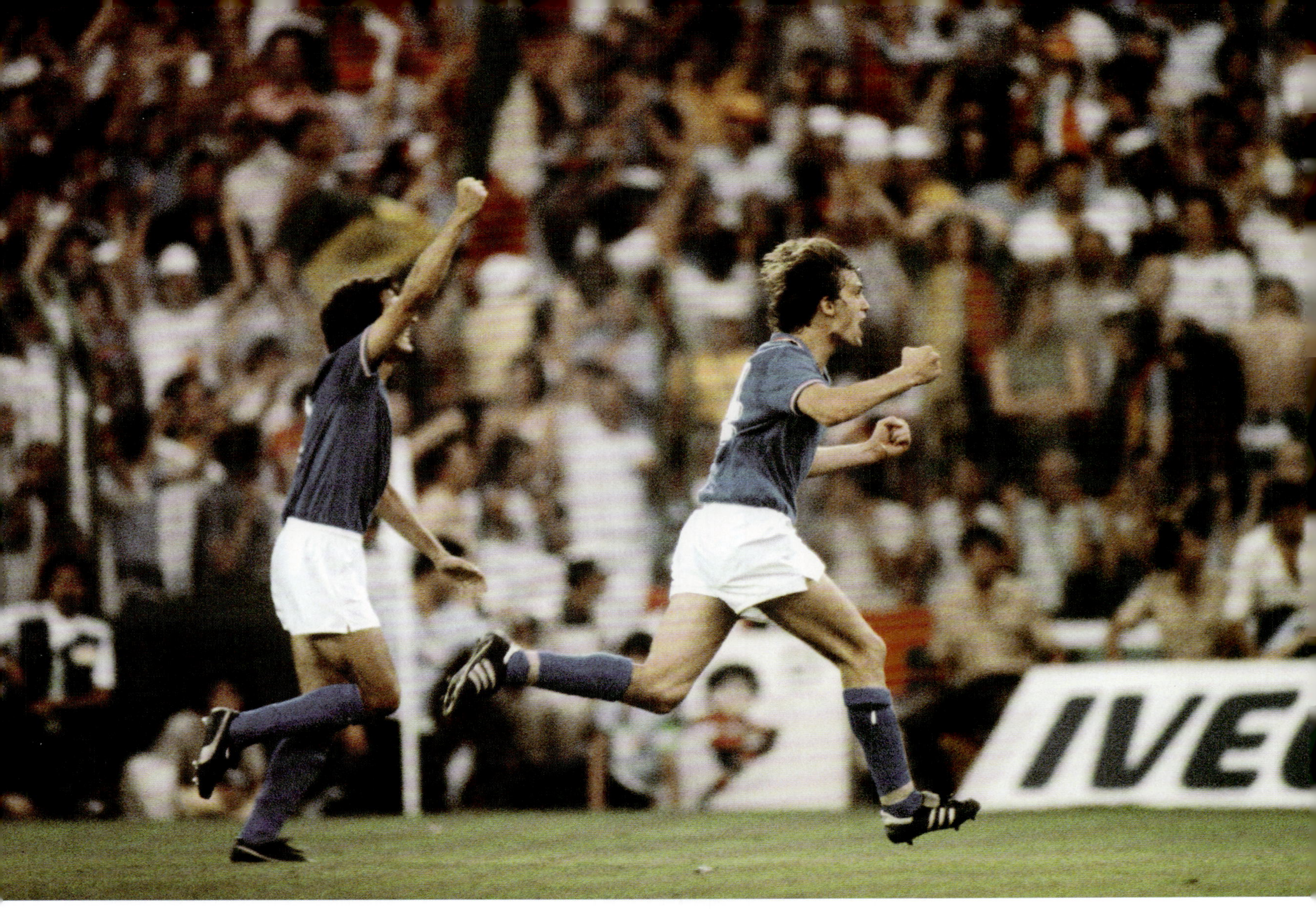


## FINAL

| | | |
|---|---|---|
| Italy 3 | 1 West Germany | (First Place) |
| Poland 3 | 2 France | (Third Place) |

Poland added another chapter to France's painful Cup-ending dramas with a close but solid 3–2 victory in the third-place match. After France scored early, the relentless Polish pressure produced three straight goals within just six minutes on the game clock. A goal at 72' raised French hopes a bit, but Poland slammed the door shut with disciplined defending in the closing minutes.

Italy entered the championship matchup with impressive momentum, rallying from a dull series of three draws (with only two goals scored) in the first group stage to beat Argentina, Brazil, and Poland in succession. Meanwhile, the West Germans appeared somewhat drained after their long and intense semi-final against France. The first half was scoreless, with the best chance an Italian penalty shot missed wide, but Italy took firm control in the second half. The Azzurri scored three unanswered goals, out of which were born two immortal moments of World Cup joy.

Italy's Paolo Rossi, who ended as the top scorer of the tournament, with six goals, was awarded the newly introduced 'Golden Shoe' trophy (renamed the 'Golden Boot' in 2010). And with their victory, Italy joined Brazil as the only countries with three World Cup championships.

# THE SCREAM AND THE WAG

**When Marco Tardelli scored** the second of Italy's three second-half goals in the 1982 World Cup Final, he sprinted wildly towards the Italian bench, fists clenched and head shaking, screaming *'Gol! Gol! Gol!'* as tears streamed down his face. Known afterwards as the 'Tardelli Scream', his unforgettable celebration became one of the most iconic images of sheer joy in World Cup lore. Afterwards, he said, 'I was born with that scream inside of me. That was just the moment it came out.' The BBC has heralded it one of the five greatest World Cup moments of all time.

Italy's third goal in the match, a left-footed blast by Alessandro Altobelli, triggered a more measured but equally iconic image of celebration. As the stands around him exploded with joy, a grinning Italian President Sandro Pertini turned to the cameras trained on him and, with a politician's savvy sense of timing, wagged his finger playfully toward the German delegation and King Juan Carlos I of Spain, saying, 'They won't catch us now.' Another beloved image in Italy is Pertini on the flight home, playing cards with team members — the World Cup Trophy sitting on the table.

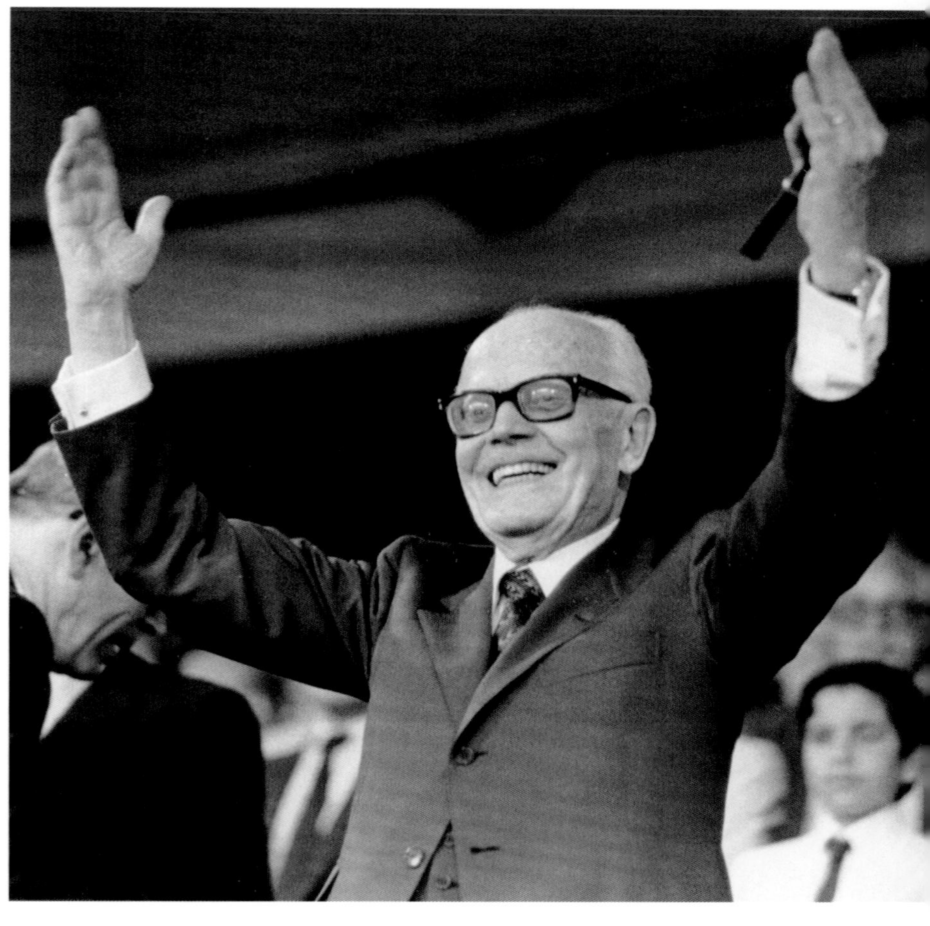

**OPPOSITE** *Marco Tardelli (right) celebrates his goal for Italy in the Final.*

**ABOVE** *Italian President Sandro Pertini, jubilant as his country triumphs at the 1982 World Cup.*

# 1986



**Back in 1974, FIFA had selected** Colombia to host the 1986 World Cup. But eight years later, in 1982, the new Colombian president withdrew, saying his country couldn't afford to stage a twenty-four-team tournament. So, FIFA's executive committee selected Mexico as replacement host, making them the first two-time hosts in World Cup history. This tournament featured plenty of dramatic lore, but it will always be known as Maradona's Cup. The Argentine legend created some of the most legendary moments in World Cup history . . . and led his team to ultimate victory.

Off the pitch, one other memorable phenomenon, one that every fan of every sport played in a stadium will recognise and appreciate, would rise to prominence at the 1986 tournament: The Wave. Originally known as 'the Mexican wave', it added a new element of kinetic energy to large stadium crowds.

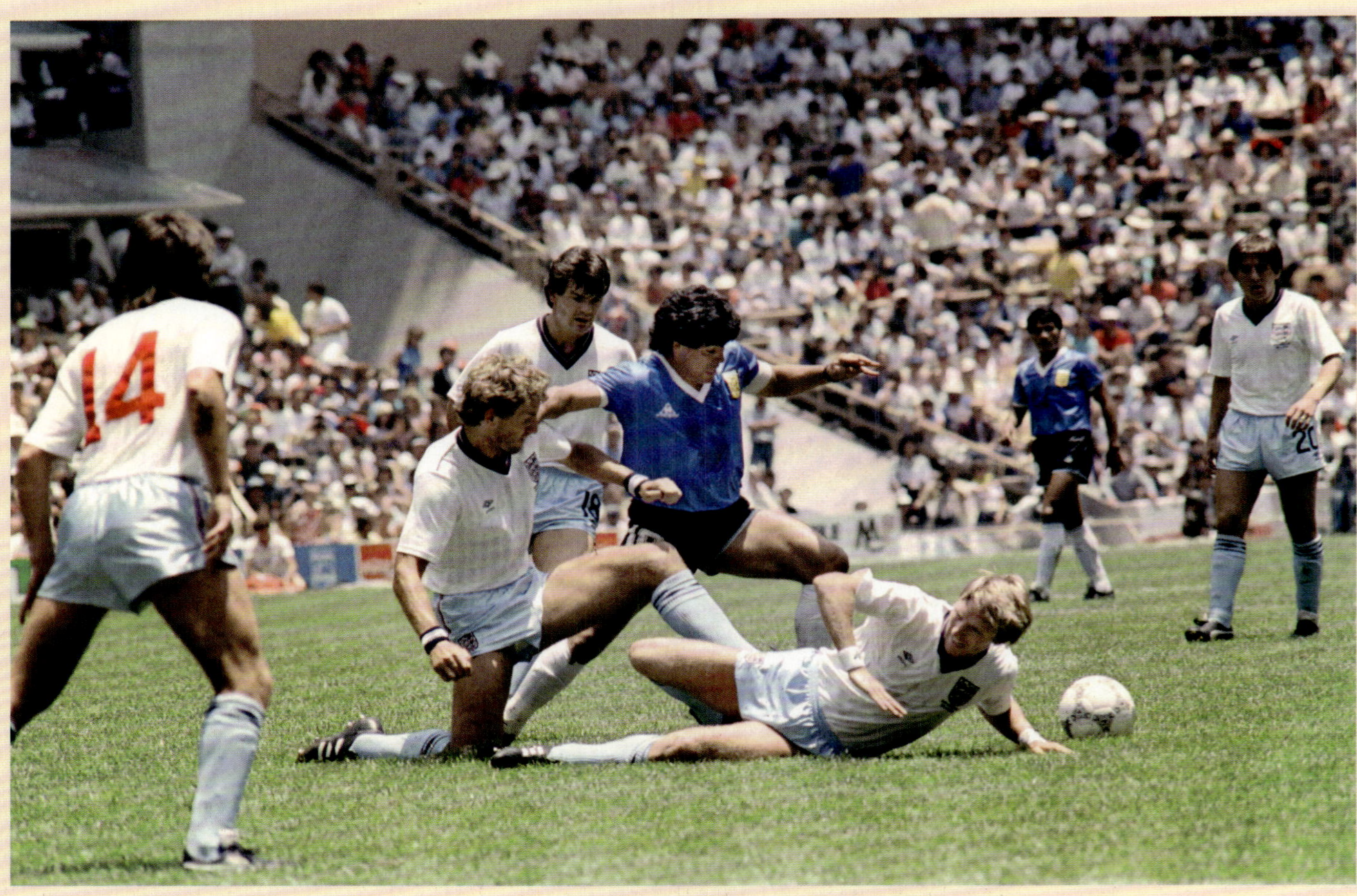

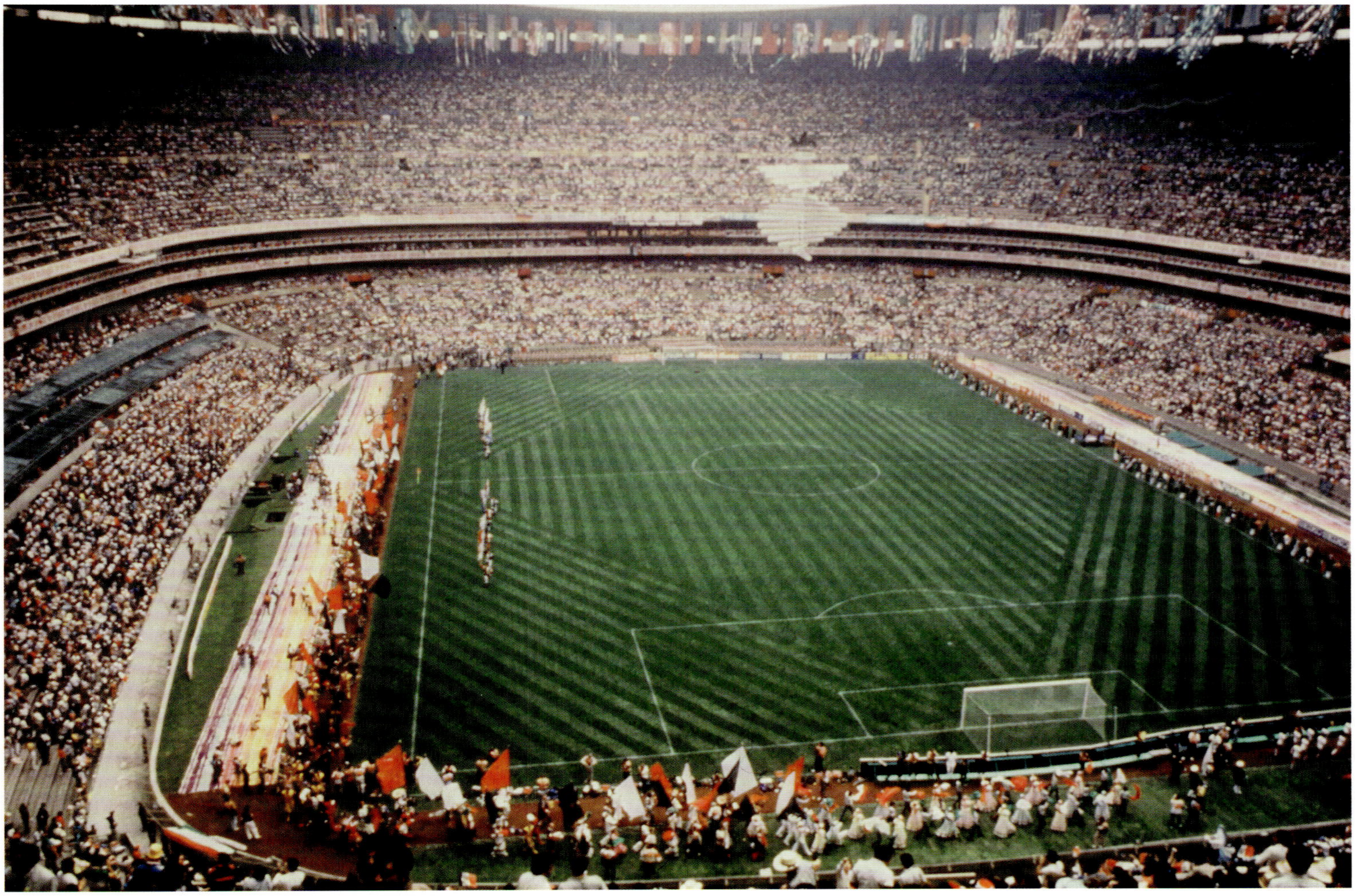

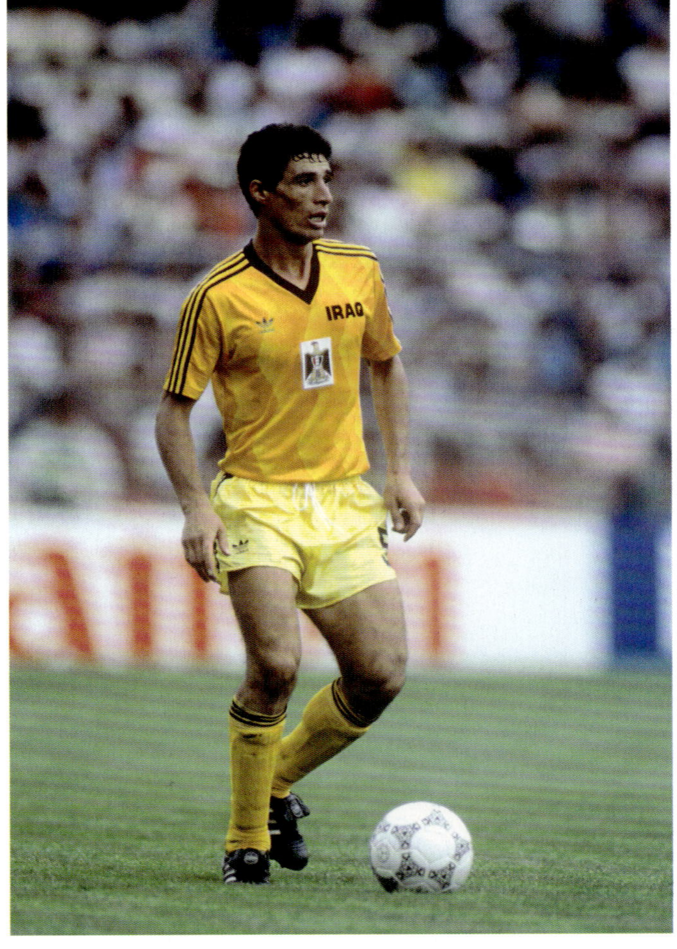



**OPPOSITE** *Three Englishmen are not enough to stop Argentina's Diego Maradona on this fateful quarter-final.*

**ABOVE** *The World Cup returns to Mexico City's Estadio Azteca.*

**RIGHT** *Samir Shaker of Iraq, one of the three nations (alongside Denmark and Canada) to make its World Cup debut in 1986.*

# Tournament: GROUP STAGE

**The 1986 tournament saw** further tweaks to the playoff format. After the first group stage, the top-two finishers in each group (twelve teams), plus the four highest-ranked third-place finishers, would move into the Round of 16, kicking off the knockout stage.

### GROUP A: ARGENTINA, ITALY, BULGARIA, SOUTH KOREA

| | |
|---|---|
| Bulgaria 1 | 1 Italy |
| Argentina 3 | 1 South Korea |
| Italy 1 | 1 Argentina |
| South Korea 1 | 1 Bulgaria |
| Italy 3 | 2 South Korea |
| Argentina 2 | 0 Bulgaria |

**Advanced to Knockout Stage: Argentina, Italy, Bulgaria**

The two heavyweights in Group A were clearly Argentina and the defending champions, Italy. Maradona's first goal of the tournament leveled their 1–1 showdown match, and the Argentines would go on to claim first place with a 2–0 victory over Bulgaria.

### GROUP B: MEXICO, PARAGUAY, BELGIUM, IRAQ

| | |
|---|---|
| Mexico 2 | 1 Belgium |
| Paraguay 1 | 0 Iraq |
| Mexico 1 | 1 Paraguay |
| Belgium 2 | 1 Iraq |
| Paraguay 2 | 2 Belgium |
| Mexico 1 | 0 Iraq |

**Advanced to Knockout Stage: Mexico, Paraguay, Belgium**

Host Mexico, led by their superstar forward Hugo Sánchez, thrilled the home crowds with a first-place finish in Group B that included wins over Belgium and Iraq, plus a hard-fought draw with second-place Paraguay. Sánchez, a La Liga star with Real Madrid, scored only one tournament goal but his presence inspired the team and fired up the fans. Belgium also advanced to the knockout stage as the top-ranked third-place finisher in group play.

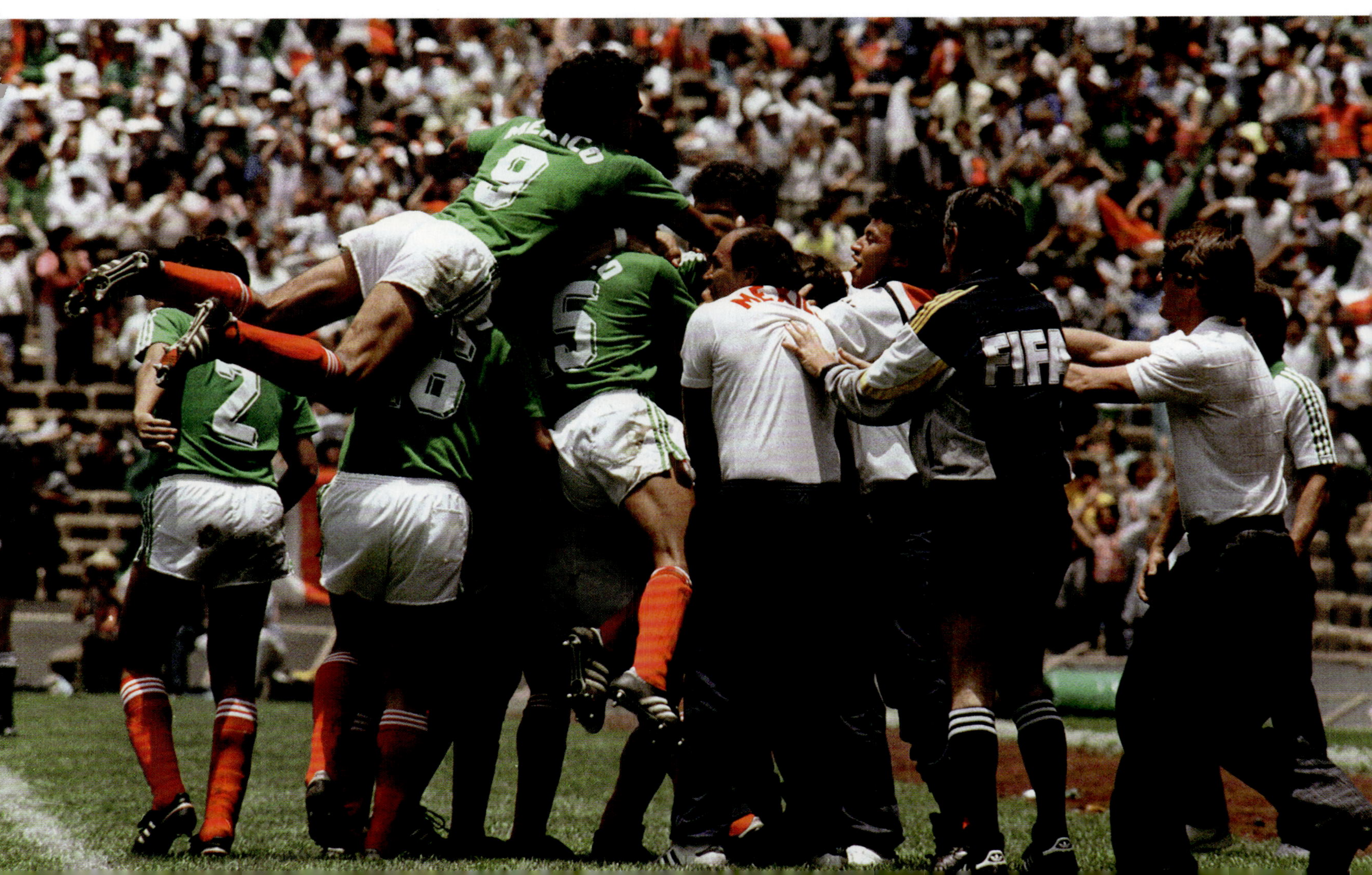

| France 1 | 0 Canada |
|---|---|
| Soviet Union 6 | 1 Hungary |
| France 1 | 1 Soviet Union |
| Hungary 2 | 0 Canada |
| France 3 | 0 Hungary |
| Soviet Union 2 | 0 Canada |

**Advanced to Knockout Stage: Soviet Union, France**

The Soviets and the reigning European champion France drew 1–1 and both easily brushed aside the others to move on to the knockouts. Russia's 6–0 obliteration of Hungary, including two goals in the opening four minutes, showed just how far Hungarian football had fallen from its 1950s glory days. Meanwhile, Canada's World Cup debut produced exactly zero goals but plenty of pride back home as they gave the French a good run in a spirited 1–0 loss.

**OPPOSITE** *The Mexican team celebrating Fernando Quirarte's opening goal against Belgium. Striker Hugo Sánchez, famous at the time for his goal scoring exploits with Real Madrid, leaps on top.*

**BELOW** *Soviet midfielder Pavlo Yakovenko with a sliding tackle onto France's Alain Giresse.*

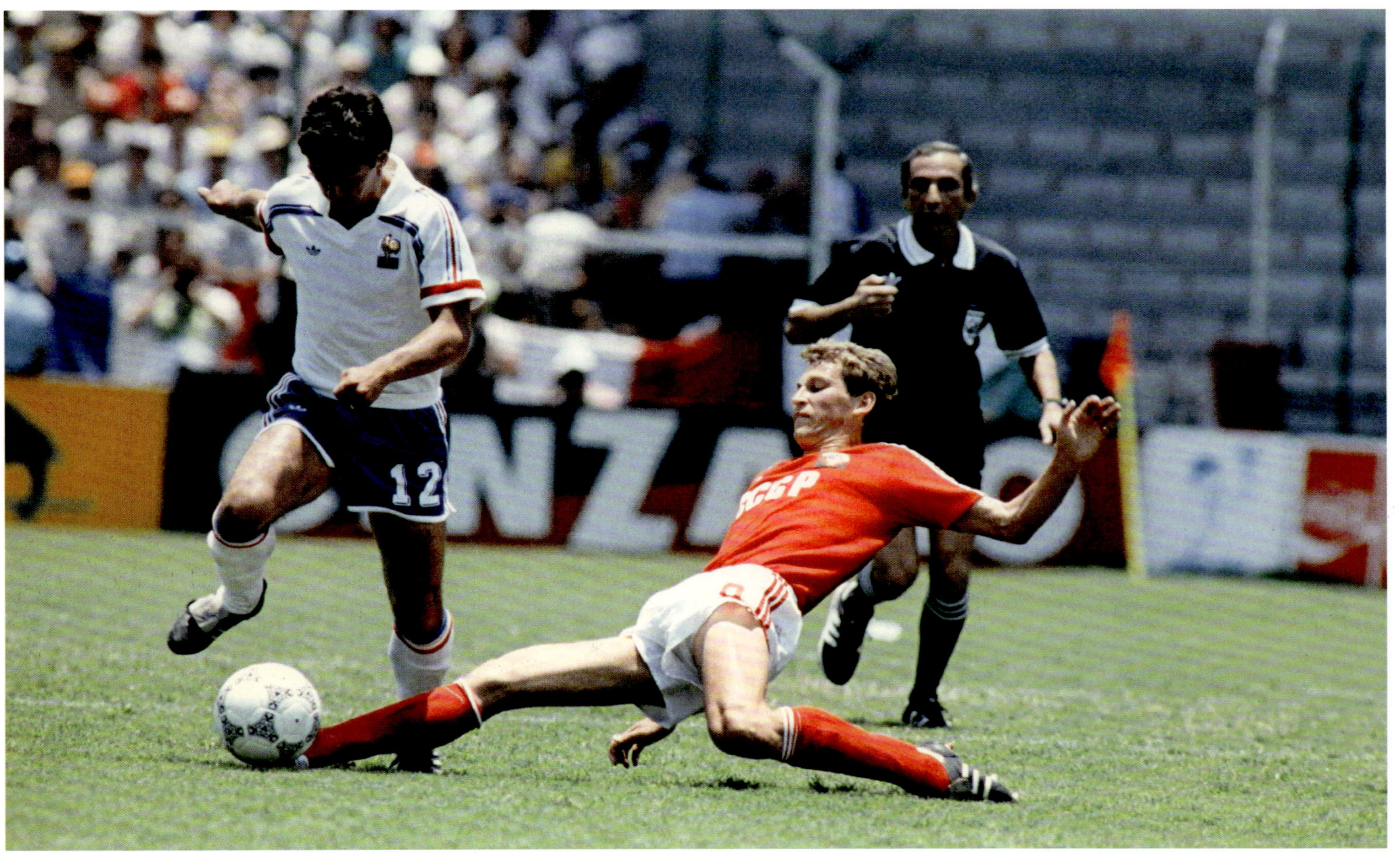

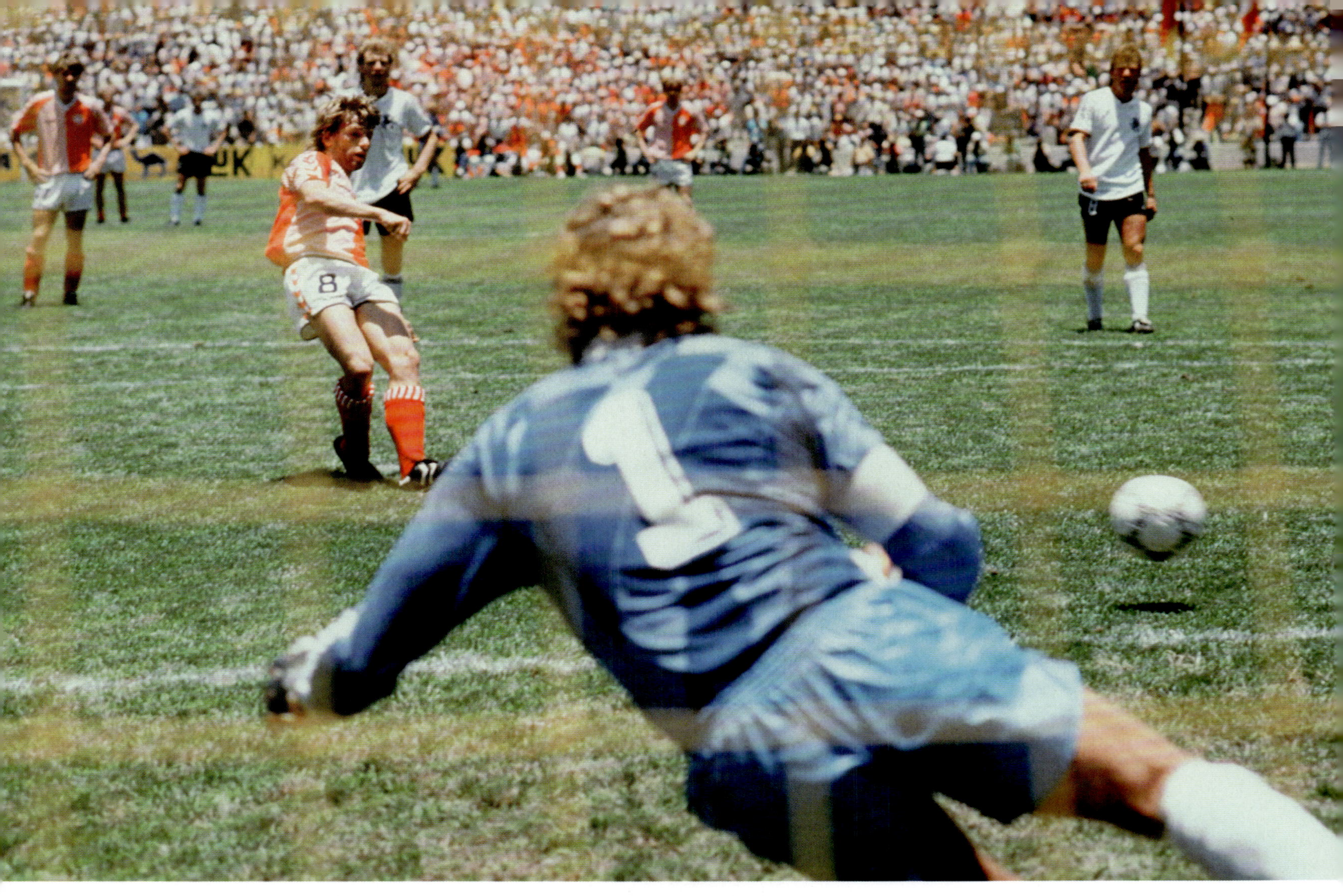

**GROUP D: BRAZIL, SPAIN,
NORTHERN IRELAND, ALGERIA**

| | | |
|---|---|---|
| Brazil 1 | 0 | Spain |
| Algeria 1 | 1 | Northern Ireland |
| Brazil 1 | 0 | Algeria |
| Spain 2 | 1 | Northern Ireland |
| Brazil 3 | 0 | Northern Ireland |
| Spain 3 | 0 | Algeria |

***Advanced to Knockout Stage: Brazil, Spain***

**GROUP E: DENMARK, WEST GERMANY,
URUGUAY, SCOTLAND**

| | | |
|---|---|---|
| Uruguay 1 | 1 | West Germany |
| Denmark 1 | 0 | Scotland |
| West Germany 2 | 1 | Scotland |
| Denmark 6 | 1 | Uruguay |
| Denmark 2 | 0 | West Germany |
| Scotland 0 | 0 | Uruguay |

***Advanced to Knockout Stage: Denmark,
West Germany, Uruguay***

As in the previous Cup, Brazil blew through the group stage looking as dangerous as ever on the attack, although Spain looked solid, too. Their group-opening contest was exciting football, well-played and evenly matched—but featured two dubious crossbar calls. A wicked Spanish volley by Míchel struck the bar, ricochetted downward inside the line, then bounced out. Replays showed a clear goal, but the linesman said no. Then, at the sixty-second minute, a Brazilian shot also struck the bar and bounced directly to Sócrates for a dramatic header into the net. This time, replays showed that he was in an offside position when the first shot was taken, but again no call was made. Thus, Brazil won a thrilling 1–0 clash of titans.

Denmark became the early sensation of the Cup by claiming three victories in three games—and against a very tough group. Dubbed the 'Danish Dynamite' for their relentless attacking style, they burst onto the international stage with a stunning 6–1 dispatch of storied Uruguay, led by a skilful hat-trick from forward Preben Elkjær. The Danes followed that performance with an impressive 2–0 shutdown of West Germany.

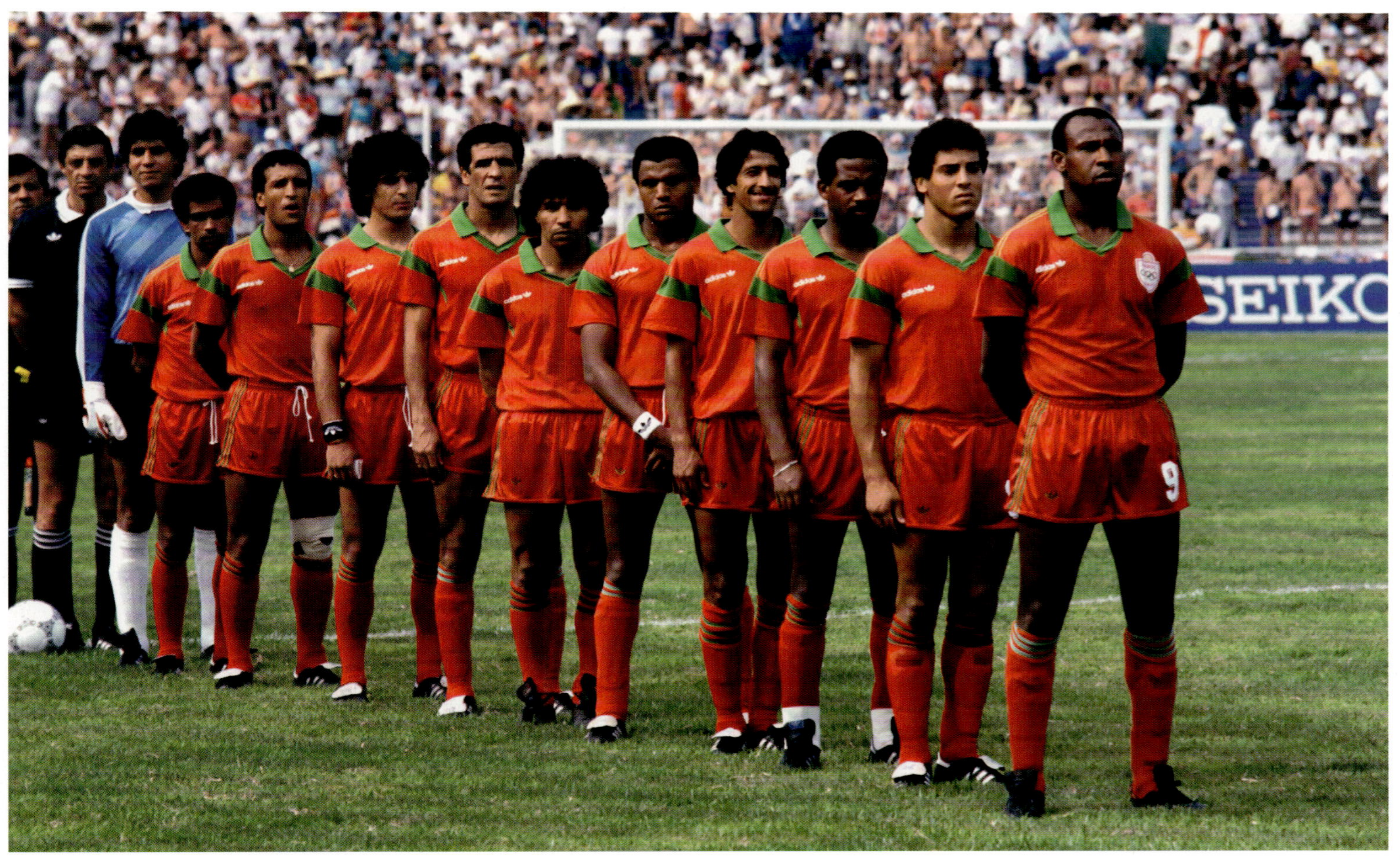



### GROUP F: MOROCCO, ENGLAND, POLAND, PORTUGAL

| | |
|---|---|
| Morocco 0 | 0 Poland |
| Portugal 1 | 0 England |
| England 0 | 0 Morocco |
| Poland 1 | 0 Portugal |
| England 2 | 1 Poland |
| Morocco 3 | 1 Portugal |

**Advanced to Knockout Stage: Morocco, England, Poland**

In a shocking upend of tradition, Morocco finished in first place ahead of European powers England, Poland, and Portugal. In doing so, The Atlas Lions became the first African team in World Cup history to ever progress beyond the first round. It wasn't always spectacular—two matches were solid, somewhat uneventful, 0–0 draws—but a decisive 3–1 win over a Portugal squad that was enmeshed in a bitter dispute with its football federation saw Morocco surge into first place.

**OPPOSITE** *Denmark's Jesper Olsen converts the penalty against West German keeper Toni Schumacher.*

**ABOVE** *The Morocco line-up ahead of its Group F match with England.*

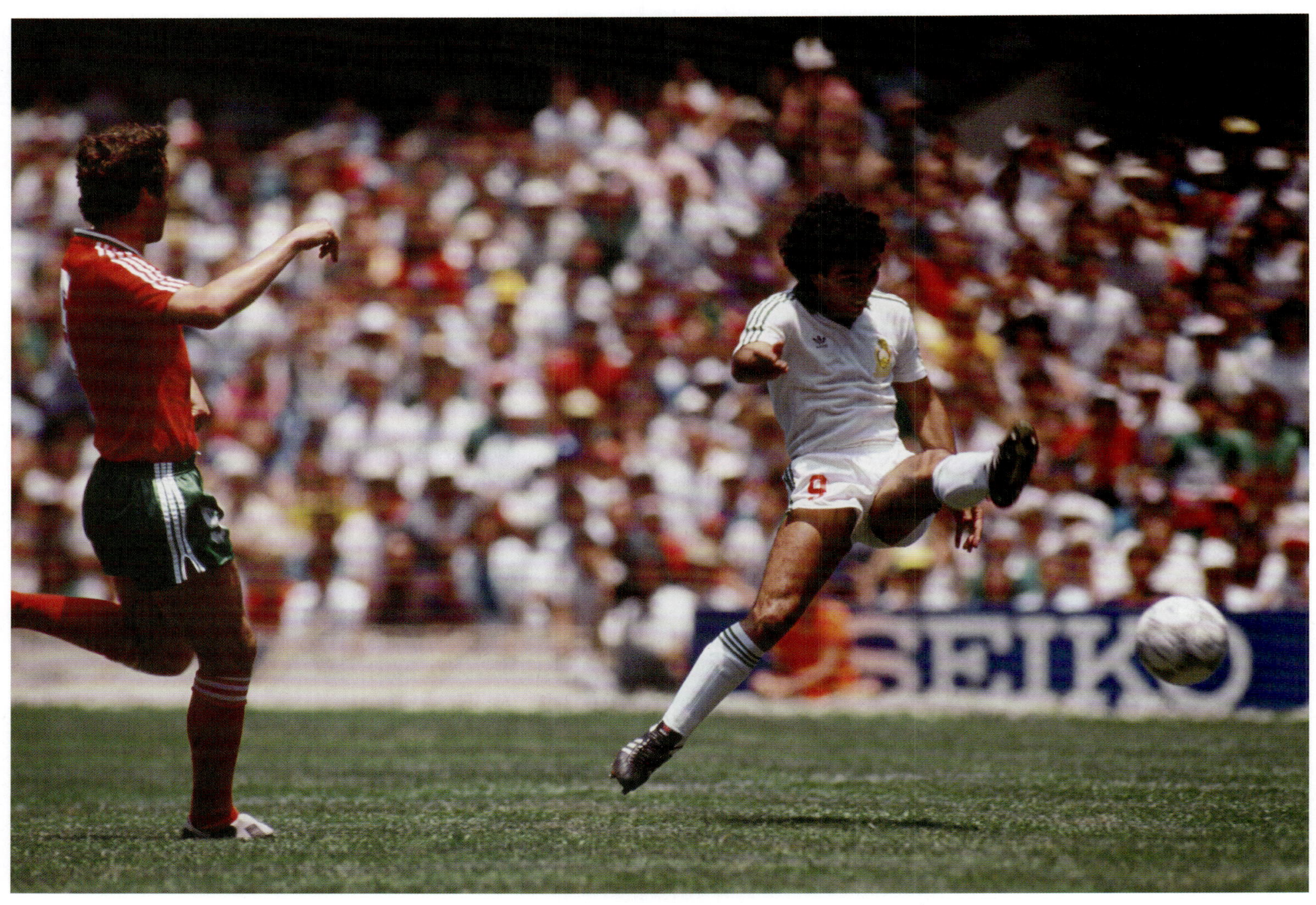

## KNOCKOUT STAGE

**The expanded bracket** of sixteen teams brought an exciting new measure of drama to the tournament, adding eight more gripping, single-elimination contests to the schedule. No more draws, no more strategic manoeuvreing for points — just win and move on . . . or lose and go home.

**ABOVE** *Hugo Sánchez (right) show-casing alacrity against Bulgaria in the Round of 16.*

**OPPOSITE** *In the Round of 16, Gary Lineker scores his second goal for England against Paraguay.*

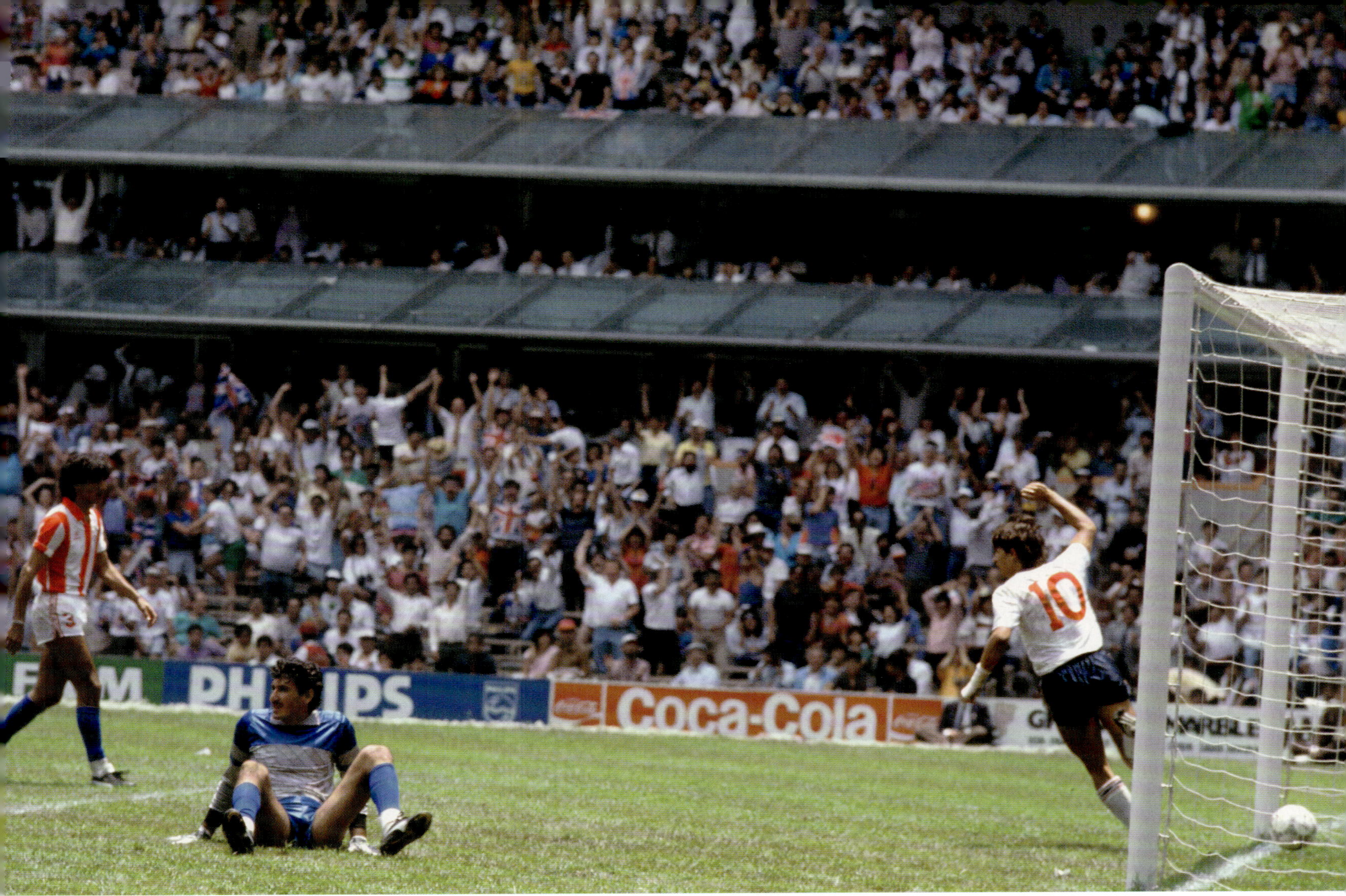

## ROUND OF 16

| | | |
|---:|:---|:---|
| Argentina | 1 | 0 Uruguay |
| England | 3 | 0 Paraguay |
| Spain | 5 | 1 Denmark |
| Belgium | 4 | 3 Soviet Union |
| | | (after extra time) |
| Brazil | 4 | 0 Poland |
| France | 2 | 0 Italy |
| West Germany | 1 | 0 Morocco |
| Mexico | 2 | 0 Bulgaria |

Mexico continued to thrill its home fans with an easy win over Bulgaria, and Brazil looked unstoppable in a 4–0 thrashing of Poland. After taking an early lead against Spain, the exciting Danes drowned in a Spanish tsunami of five straight goals, including four by young forward Emilio Butragueño. Upstart Morocco put up a spirited fight against heavyweight West Germany, but tragedy would strike with just two minutes left in the match. A free-kick missile from Lothar Matthäus saw the back of the net…and the Moroccans out of the tournament.

England's Gary Lineker—still considered one of the very best strikers in English football history—scored a brace to help his side knock out Paraguay and reach the quarter-finals. With six total goals, Lineker would go on to win the Golden Shoe. France decisively ended Italy's championship defence, while Argentina eked out a slim win over Uruguay. The round's true thriller was the match between Belgium and the Soviet Union, tied at 2–2 after regulation. The Belgians knocked in two in extra time for a 4–2 lead before the Soviets responded with a penalty at 111'. With the scoreline at 4–3, the final nine minutes were frantic…and gloriously entertaining.

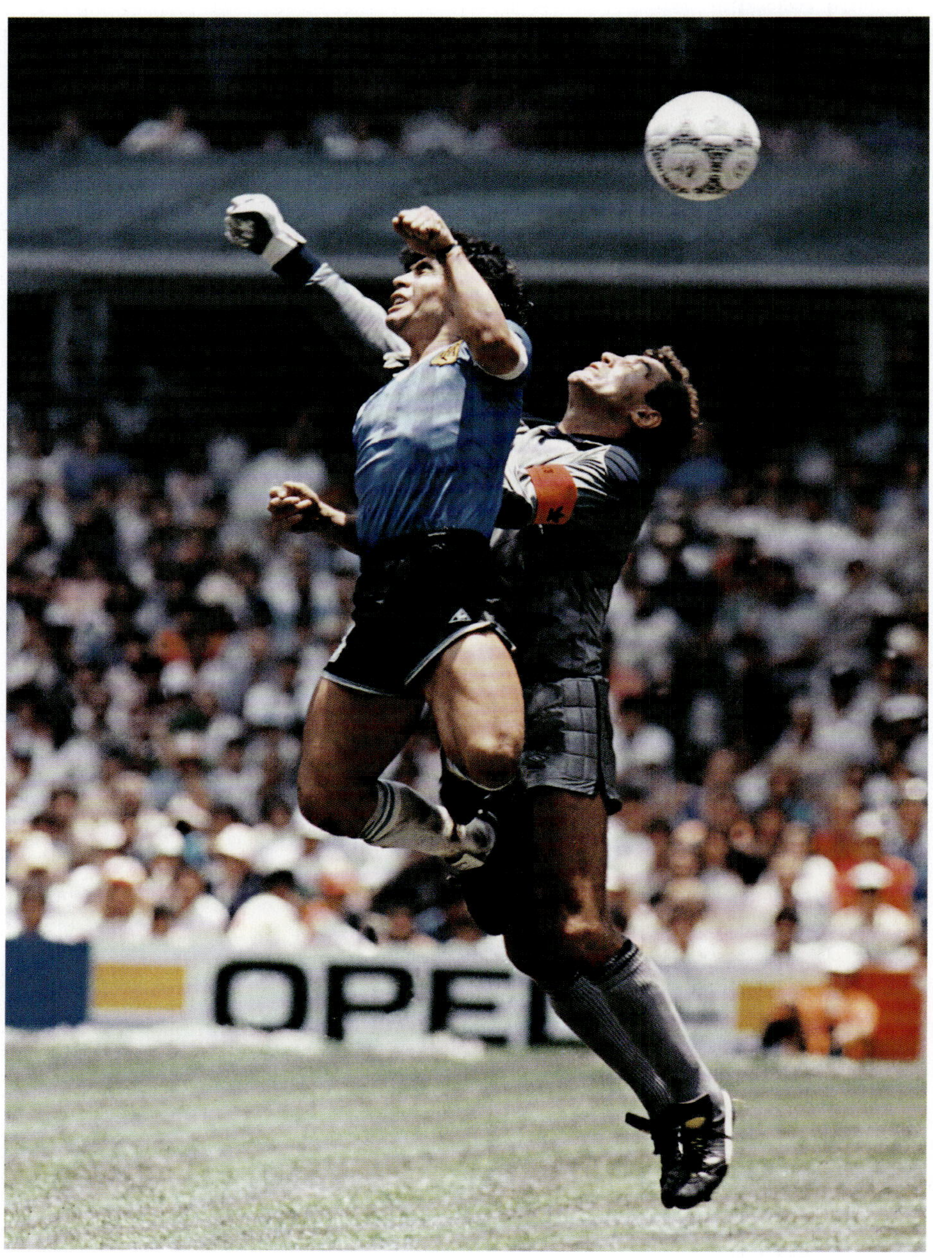

## QUARTER-FINALS

| | |
|---|---|
| Argentina 2 | 1 England |
| Belgium 1 | 1 Spain |
| | (5–4 on penalty kicks) |
| France 1 | 1 Brazil |
| | (4–3 on penalty kicks) |
| West Germany 0 | 0 Mexico |
| | (4–1 on penalty kicks) |

The quarter-final round produced three gut-wrenching penalty shootouts in its four matches. The first shootout came after Brazil dominated in regulation time but missed a second-half penalty kick and at least two other prime goal opportunities, whereas France showed great resilience in extra time but could not score again either. Then France outshot Brazil 4–3 in the shootout.

The other two quarter-finals featured evenly matched sides. First, Mexico nearly rewarded the throngs packing Estadio Universitario in Monterrey with a late goal that was disallowed. But in the shootout, West Germany's masterful goalkeeper Toni Schumacher parried away two of Mexico's first three kicks (diving hard right on all three tries), while his own shooters converted all four of theirs for the win. The Belgians and Spanish also put in an equitable showing, with Belgium winning a white-knuckle shootout 5–4 by banging home all five of their penalty shots.

But the lone contest decided in regulation time, England versus Argentina, would produce two of the most legendary goals in World Cup history.

# MARADONA'S MYTHIC BRACE

**Two of the most famous goals** in World Cup history were scored by the same man, and just four minutes apart. One goal wrapped in controversy, the other in pure majesty.

### 'La Mano de Dios' ('The Hand of God')

**The first meeting between these** two nations since the short but bloody Falklands War in 1982, political tensions were running hot and national pride was on the line heading into this quarter-final bout between England and Argentina in Mexico City.

Tied at 0–0 early in the second half, England's vaunted defence, which had allowed only one goal in their four prior matches, was valiantly fending off Argentina's attack. Despite several imaginative chances created by Argentine playmaker and superstar Diego Maradona, the gridlock showed no signs of opening up.

And then, in the fifty-first minute, a misplayed ball by an English midfielder looped into the penalty area where Maradona had burst toward the goal. England's goal-keeper, Peter Shilton, moved off his line to punch the ball, but Maradona got there first. The much smaller Argentine jumped, trying to flick the ball with his head. Instead, he nudged it subtly past Shilton into the net with his outstretched left fist.

The referee ruled it a legitimate header, and as no VAR replay check was available at that time, Argentina was ahead 1–0. At the postgame press conference, Maradona said the goal was scored 'a little with the head of Maradona and a little with the hand of God'. Hence, it was immortalised in football lore as the 'Hand of God'.

**THIS SPREAD** *Front and rear angles of Maradona's La mano de Dios.*

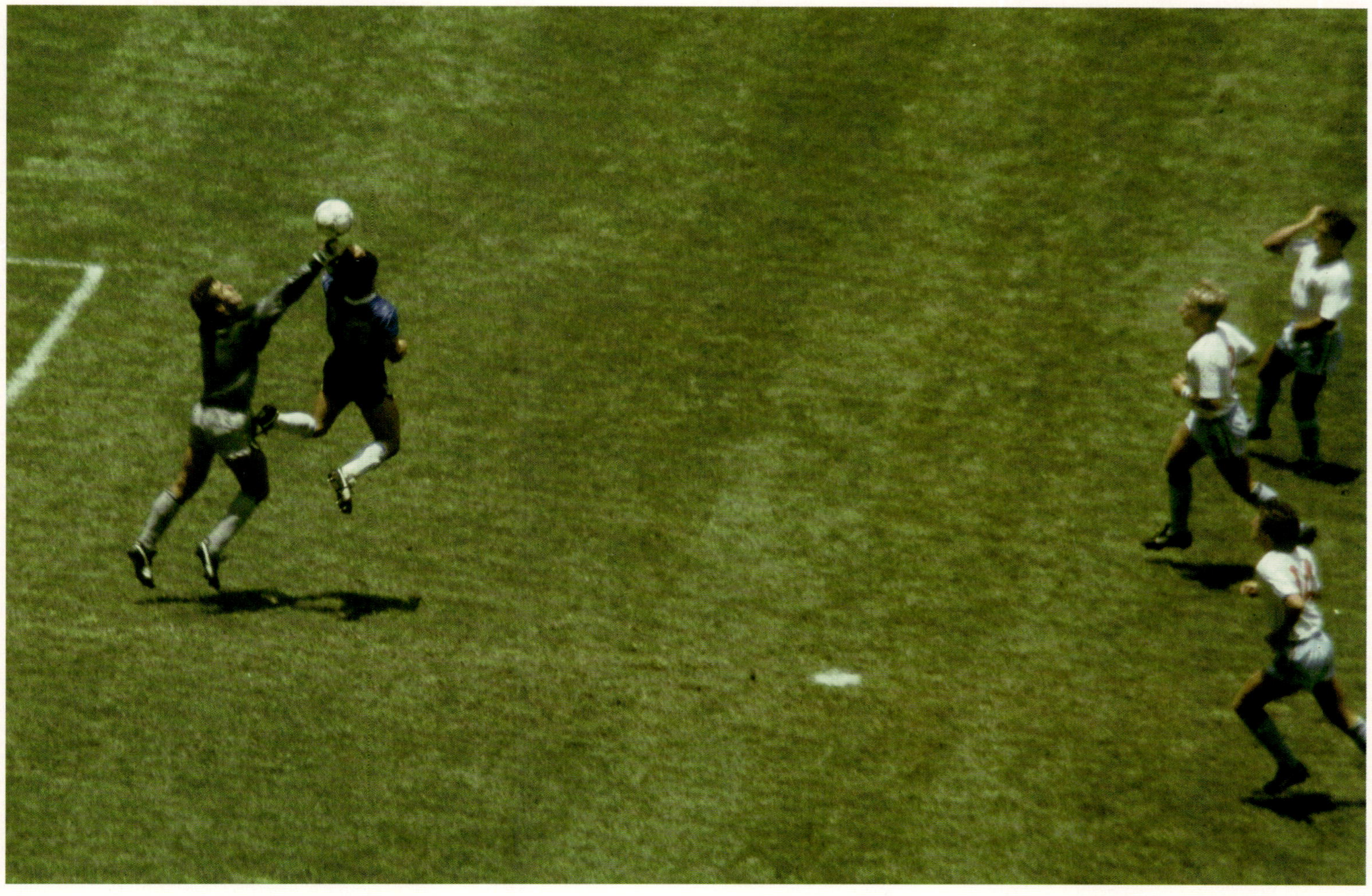

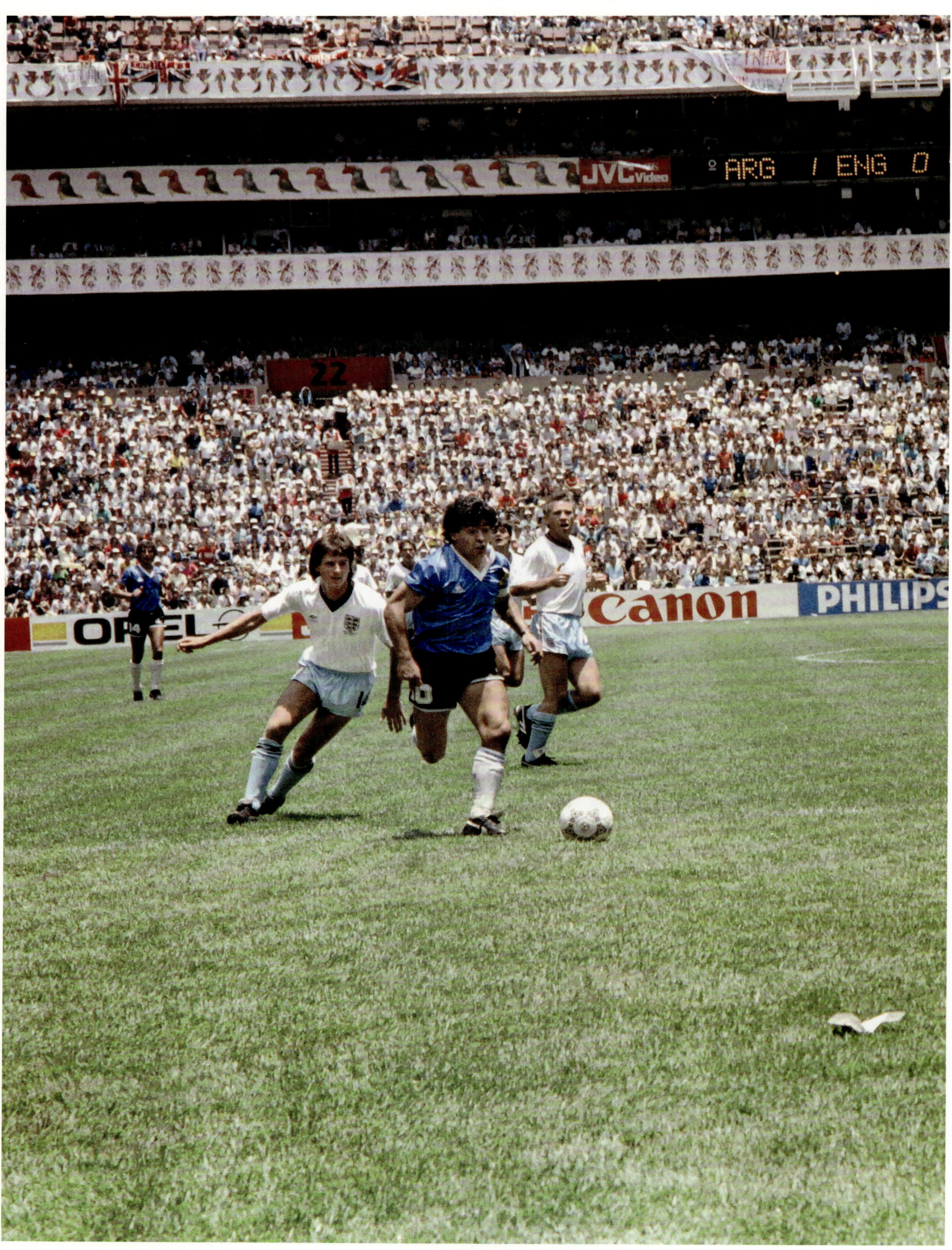

JVC Video
ARG 1 ENG 0
Canon
PHILIPS
OPEL

## 'The Goal of the Century'

**Four minutes later,** Maradona received a pass at mid-field under heavy pressure. He juked and swivelled around two English players crashing onto him and then exploded down the sideline, accelerating away from a third Englishman who had arrived to provide support. He cut left past a flailing fourth defender, cut right past a fifth, faked the English keeper Shilton to the ground, and then rapped the ball into the empty net as one of the chasing defenders finally chopped him down. Eleven magic touches in eleven seconds, a seventy-five-yard run, and five defenders, plus the keeper, defeated off the dribble. In 2002, FIFA voted it the Goal of the Century.

Maradona's incomparable run to glory inspired a live TV call for the ages by Uruguayan commentator Víctor Hugo Morales, who, overcome by emotion, howled:

*Goooooooaaaal! I want to cry! Holy God, long live football! What a goal! Die-gol! Maradona! Forgive me, it's enough to make you cry! What an unforgettable run in the play of all time! Cosmic kite, what planet did you come from, to leave so many Englishmen behind, so that the whole country is a clenched fist shouting for Argentina?...Thank you, God: for football, for Maradona, for these tears!* [translated from Spanish]

England made a late push that produced a goal in the eighty-first minute by the great Gary Lineker, his sixth of the tournament, but Argentina held on to win, 2–1, and Maradona's run of greatness was not yet over. In the semi-final matchup versus Belgium, the 'cosmic kite' would score yet another cunning brace, thus producing all four of Argentina's goals in the team's decisive march into the Final.

**THIS SPREAD** *The closing sequence of Maradona's Goal of the Century.*

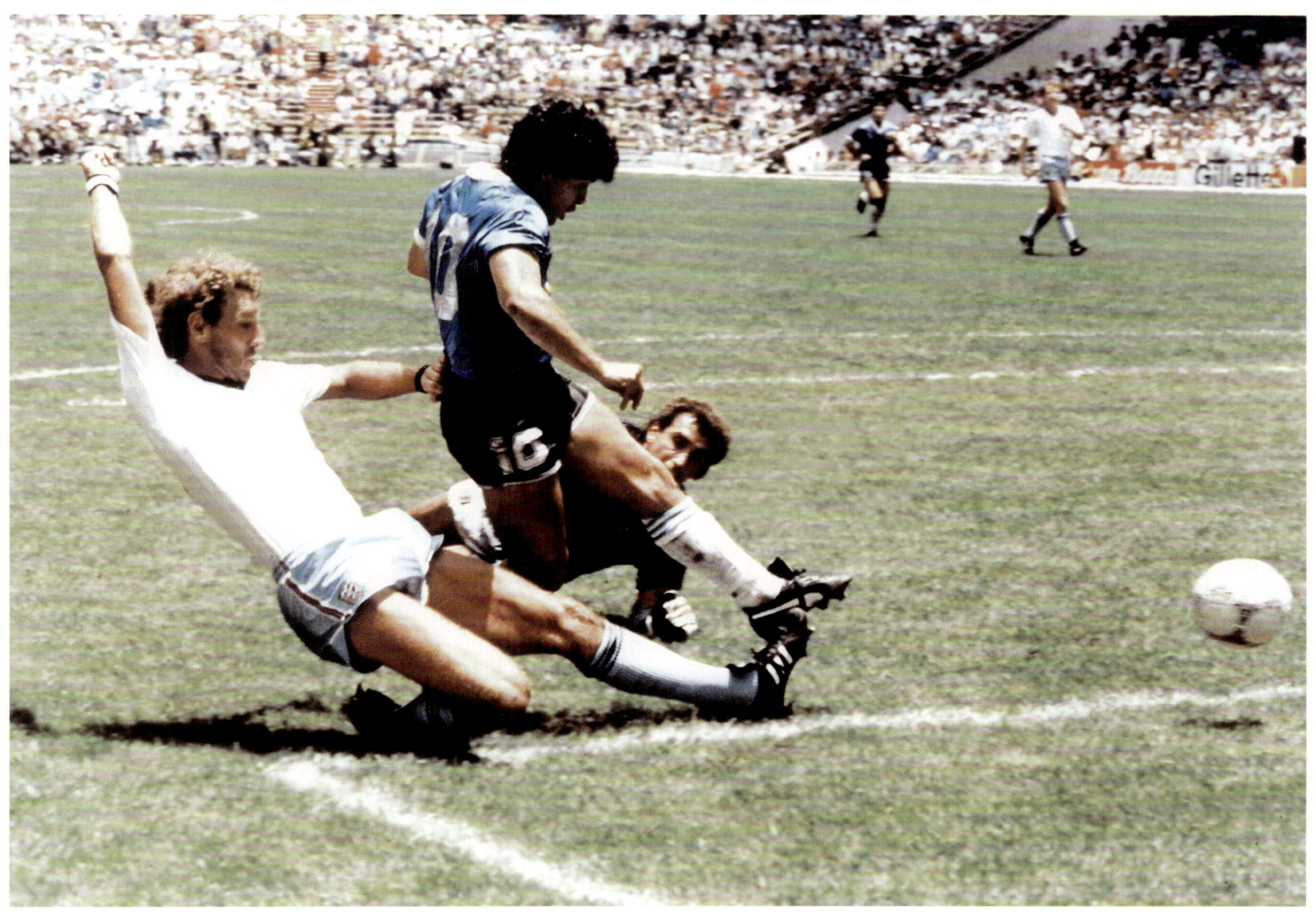

# SEMI-FINALS

Argentina 2 | 0 Belgium
West Germany 2 | 0 France

The two semi-final matchups lacked some of the drama of previous contests, as the victors allowed no scoring by their opponents. Maradona continued his wizardry with two second-half goals to lift Argentina to a comfortable win over Belgium. On the other side, West Germany scored early, played disciplined defence, and then locked in its second consecutive berth in a World Cup Final with a Rudi Völler goal in the eighty-eighth minute to beat France 2–0.

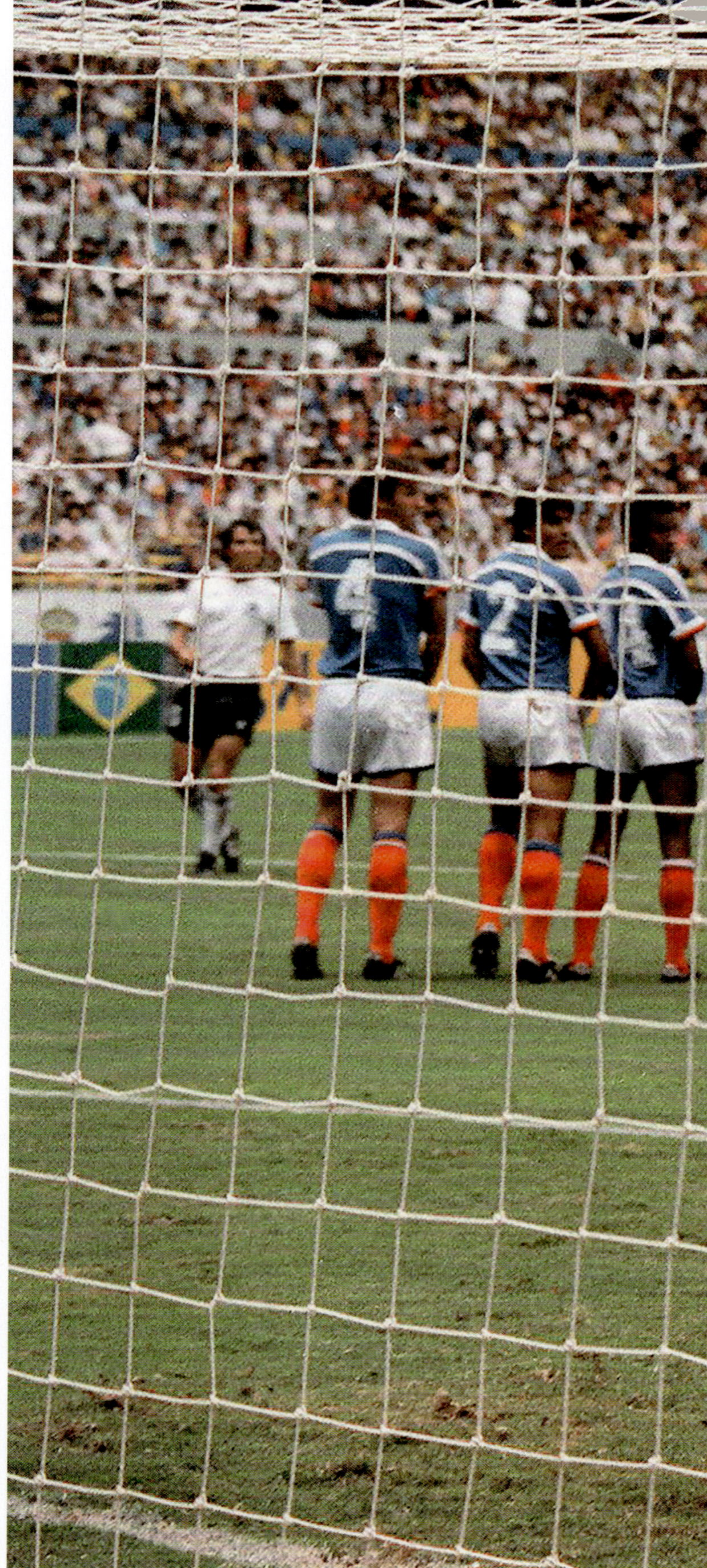

**OPPOSITE** *French keeper Joël Bats is unable to contain the powerful free kick from Andreas Brehme, and West Germany goes up 1–0 in the semi-final.*

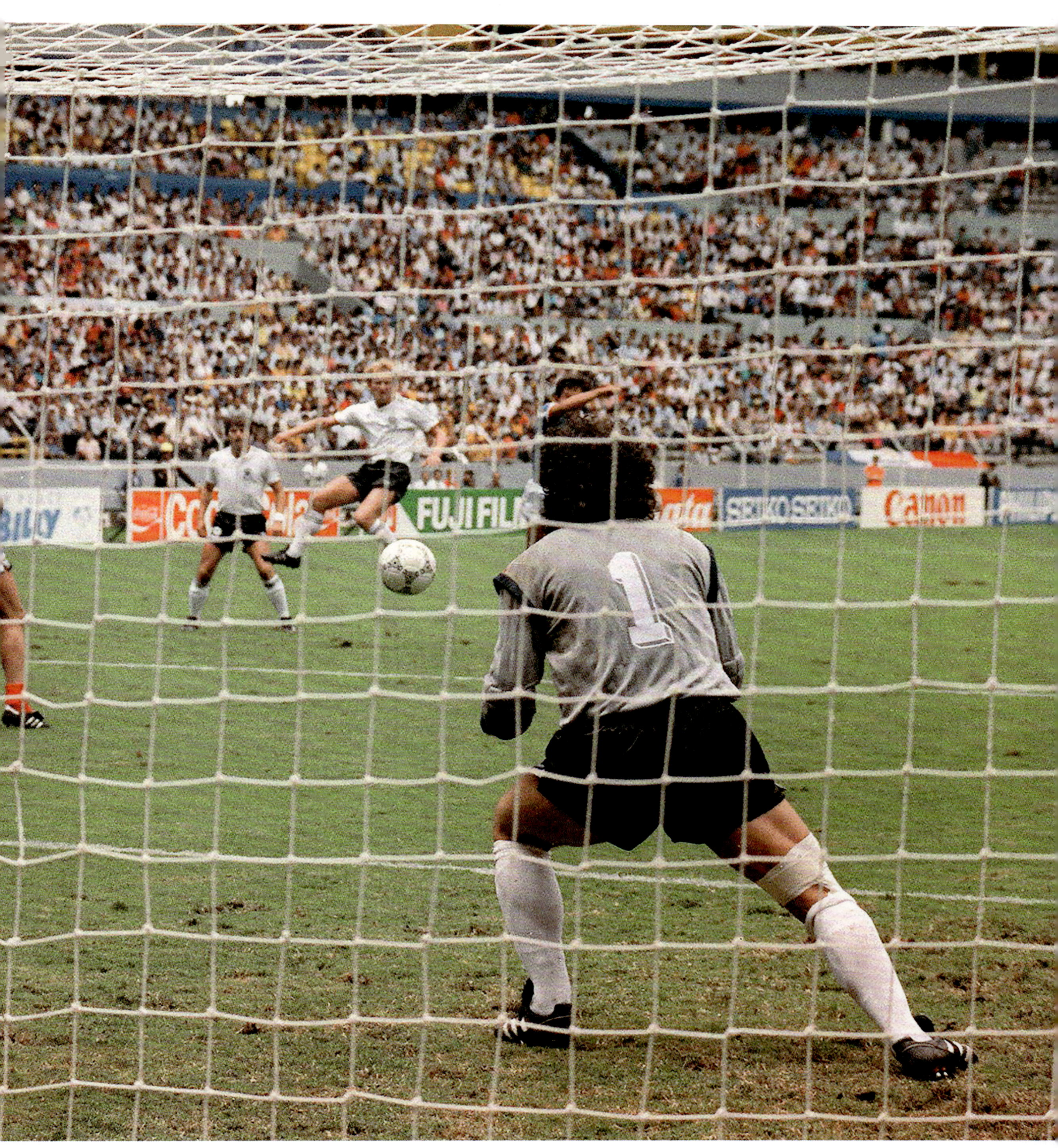

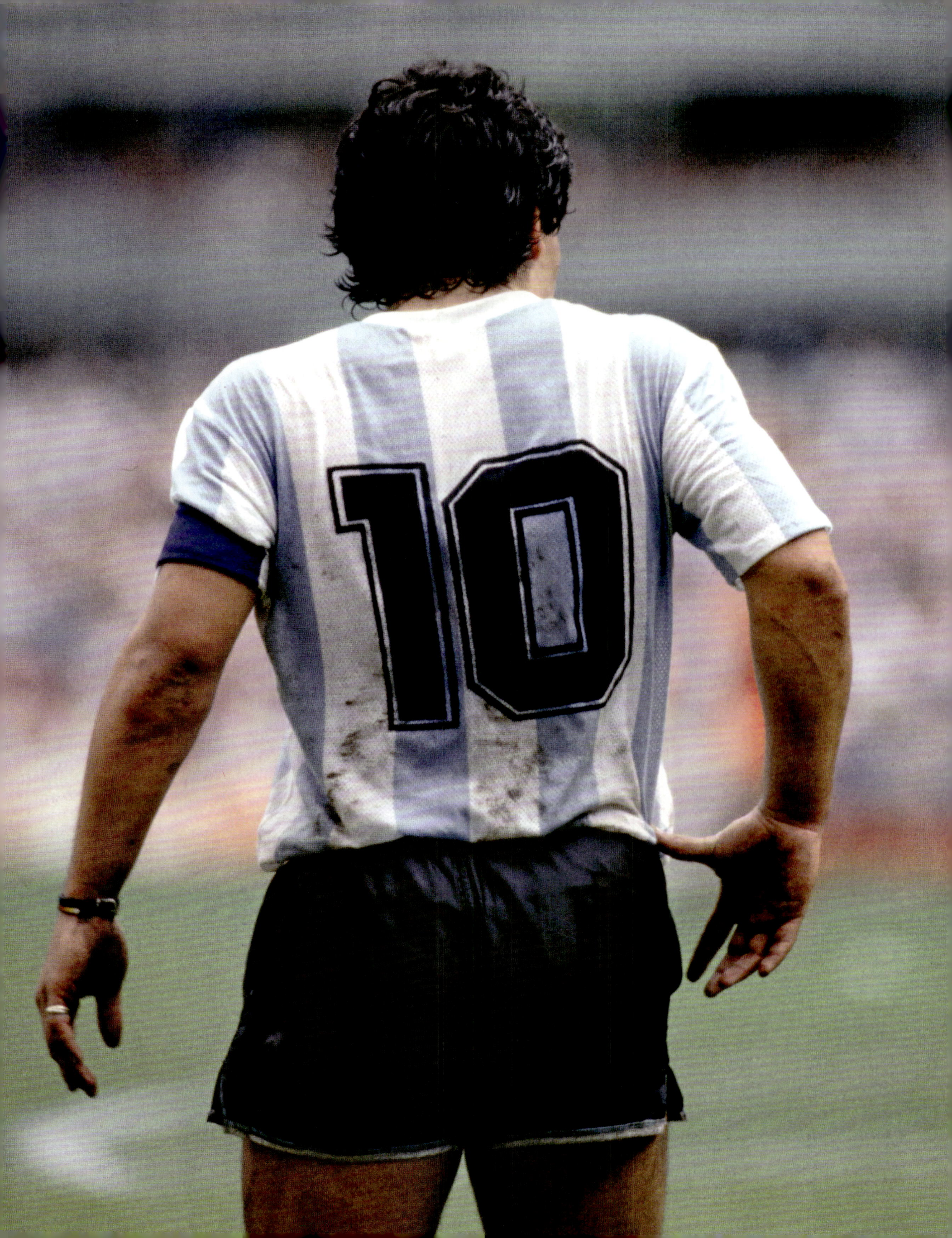

# FINAL

| | |
|---|---|
| Argentina 3 | 2 West Germany |
| | (First Place) |
| France 4 | 2 Belgium |
| | (after extra time) |
| | (Third Place) |

The third-place match was a well-played 2–2 draw at the end of regulation time. France would seize the momentum in the extra minutes, scoring twice for the victory. In the Cup Final, before a crowd of 115,000 in Mexico City's Estadio Azteca, West Germany tried to neutralise the electric Maradona with tight, physical marking. However, the heavy attention needed to contain Maradona created channels of space for his talented teammates. By the fifty-sixth minute, Argentina had fashioned a 2–0 lead and seemed to be cruising to an easy victory in the second half.

Refusing to go down without a fight, the gritty West Germans mounted one of their patented, seemingly inevitable comebacks with a pair of gorgeous, powerful headers scored off corner kicks just seven minutes apart, including one from Rudi Völler that leveled things with just ten minutes to play. It seemed like extra time, and possibly another shootout, loomed. But a mere three minutes after Völler's goal, Maradona made his final golden mark on the tournament when he slid a perfect pass out to an unmarked Jorge Burruchaga on the right flank, who outraced a German defender and calmly slotted the shot past the charging Schumacher (always a fearsome sight) for the winning goal. And, as with Pelé sixteen years prior, the World Cup was once again the stage upon which a king would be crowned.

**OPPOSITE** *Like Pelé before him, Diego Maradona was immortalised in the number 10 jersey at the Estadio Azteca.*

**RIGHT** *After arguably the definitive World Cup performance of the twentieth century, Maradona hoists the trophy.*

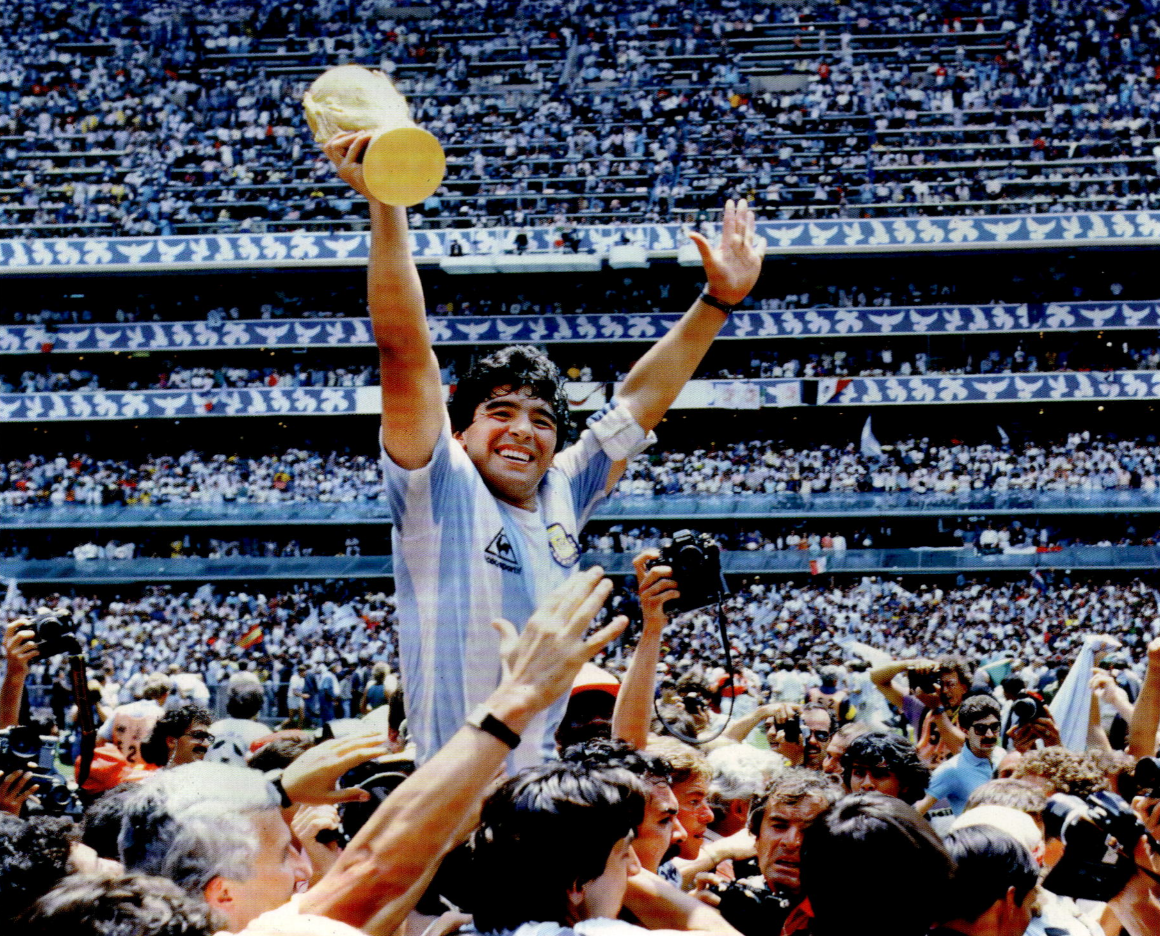

# THE 1990s

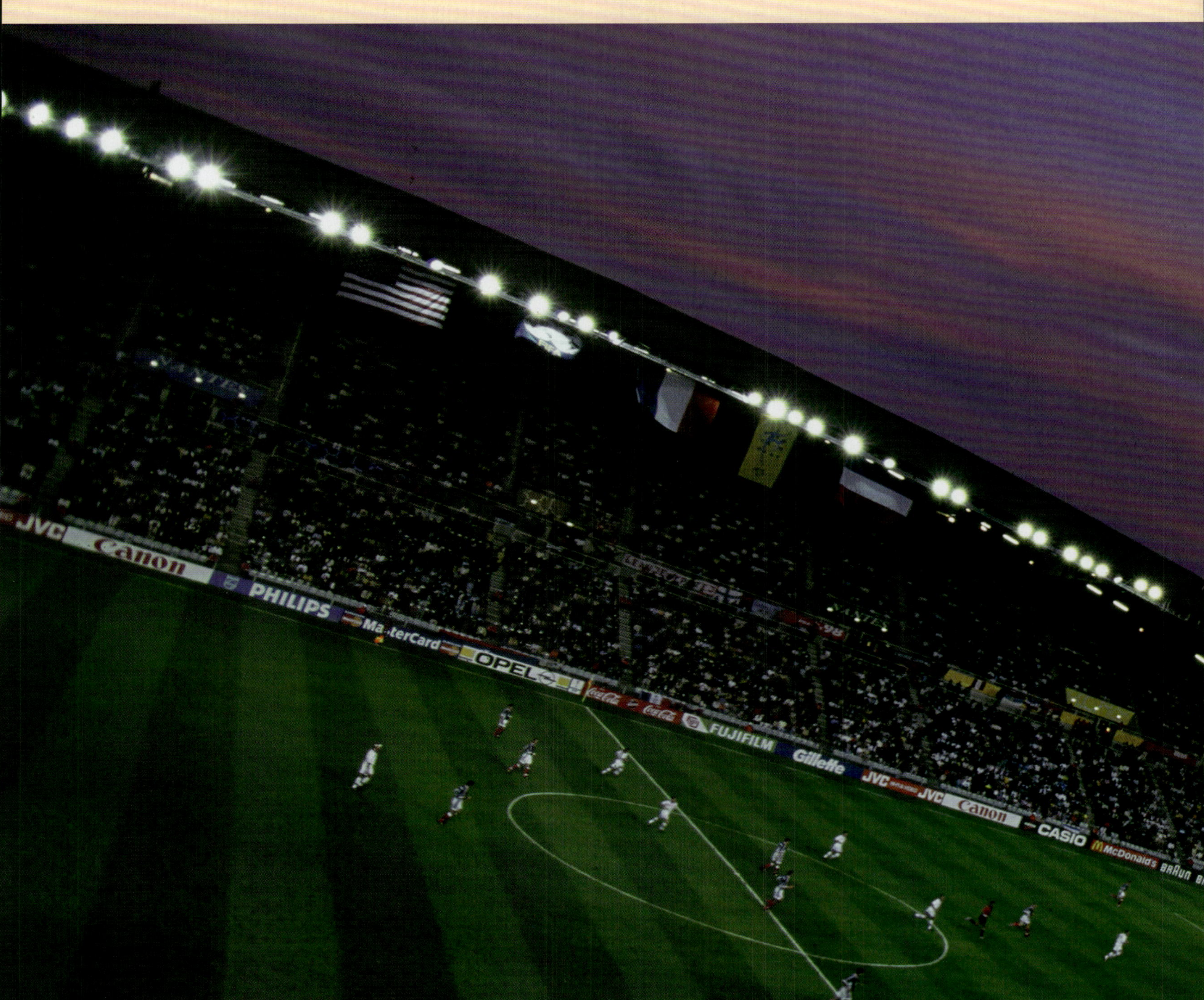

# CHAPTER 7

# The Cup Conquers North America

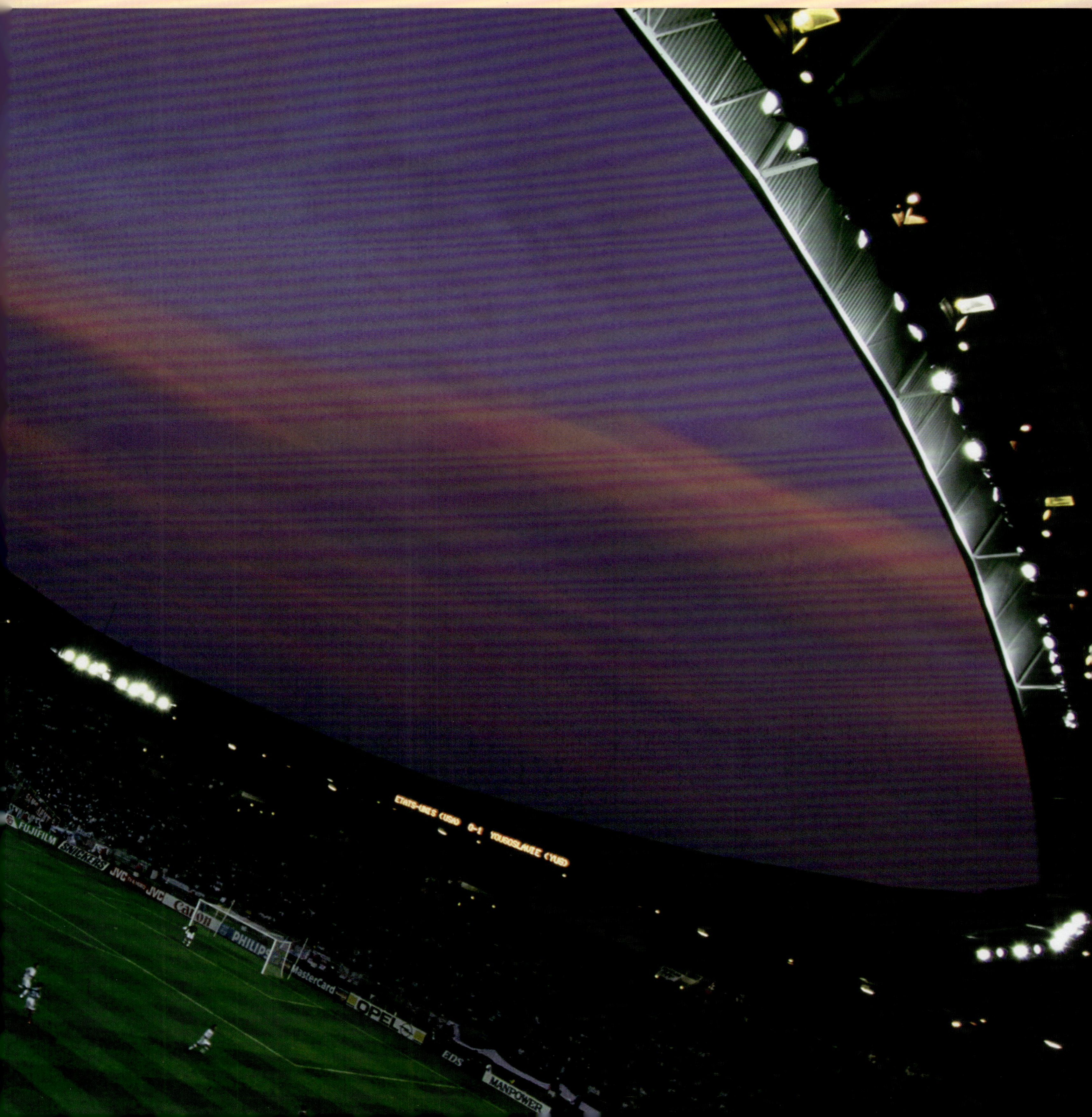

# 1990

HOST COUNTRY: **ITALY**
CHAMPION: **WEST GERMANY**
RUNNER-UP: **ARGENTINA**
THIRD PLACE: **ITALY OVER ENGLAND**

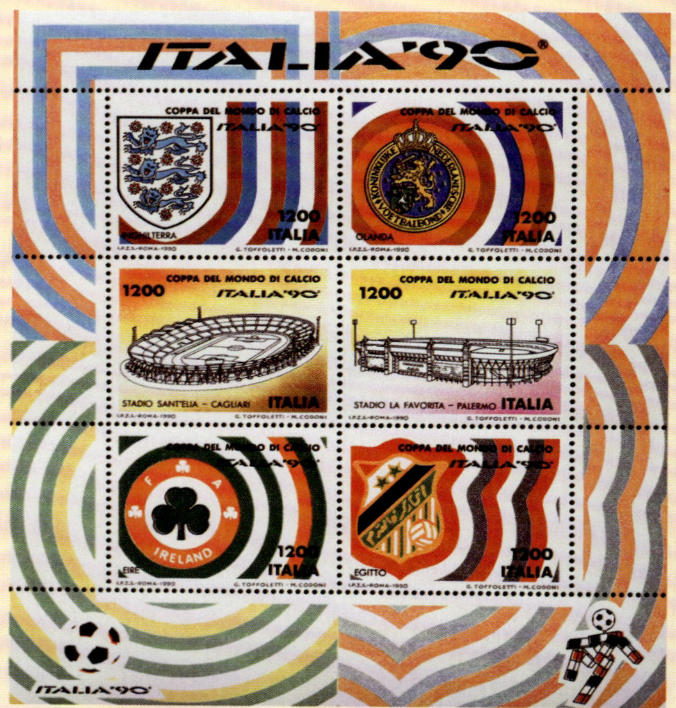


**Italy hosted its second** World Cup Finals tournament (and first since 1934) in a sprawling, celebratory, month-long affair that featured two brand-new stadiums in Turin and Bari plus ten extensively refurbished ones, a project that reportedly cost a billion dollars. Cup fever was real, and staging a first-rate tournament was now an international showcase event for any host country. Back in 1987, the European TV rights to the next three World Cups had been sold for a whopping $440 million — a key milestone in FIFA's transformation into a multibillion-dollar enterprise. In 1990, Italy's World Cup would reach a record 27 billion TV viewers. It was also the first Cup broadcast in HDTV, which provided the perfect conduit for pomp and ceremony, joy and athletic drama. The beautiful game, up close and personal.

**PREVIOUS SPREAD** *A picturesque view of the Stade de la Beaujoire in Nantes, France, during the 1998 World Cup. The match is a Group F bout between Yugoslavia and USA.*

**ABOVE** *Official stamps for the 1990 tournament. Inspiration was drawn from the Italian stadium venues and the flags of participating nations.*

**OPPOSITE** *The 1990 World Cup opening ceremony at the San Siro in Milan.*

## NONE SHALL SLEEP!

**If you're a World Cup fan,** you likely know this piece well because it's become part of the Cup's de facto soundtrack. In 1990, the BBC used Luciano Pavarotti's 1972 recording of the 'Nessun Dorma' aria from Puccini's opera *Turandot* as the theme song for its television coverage of Italy's World Cup. But it was the legendary tenor's live performance of that aria, at the Baths of Caracalla in Rome, on the eve of the 1990 Cup Final that mesmerised a massive global football audience . . . and made the piece synonymous with World Cup pageantry.

Pavarotti was joined that night by fellow legends Plácido Domingo and José Carreras in the first of their famous 'Three Tenors' concerts. The trio would go on to sing 'Nessun Dorma' (which translates to 'None shall sleep') live before the three subsequent Cup Finals in 1994, 1998, and 2002.

## BEAUTIFUL GAME NO MORE?

**Stylistically, the 1990 Cup** featured a general style of play that many felt was hurting what Pelé had once called 'the beautiful game'. For most, the defensive bunkering, rough play, and time-wasting tactics led to too many injuries, too many dull, low-scoring affairs, and too many penalty-kick shootouts. To this day, Italy 1990 remains the lowest-scoring World Cup in history. This motivated FIFA's rules committees to make decisive changes to counter football's drift towards the conservative, cynical tactics that stymied a creative, open flow of play.

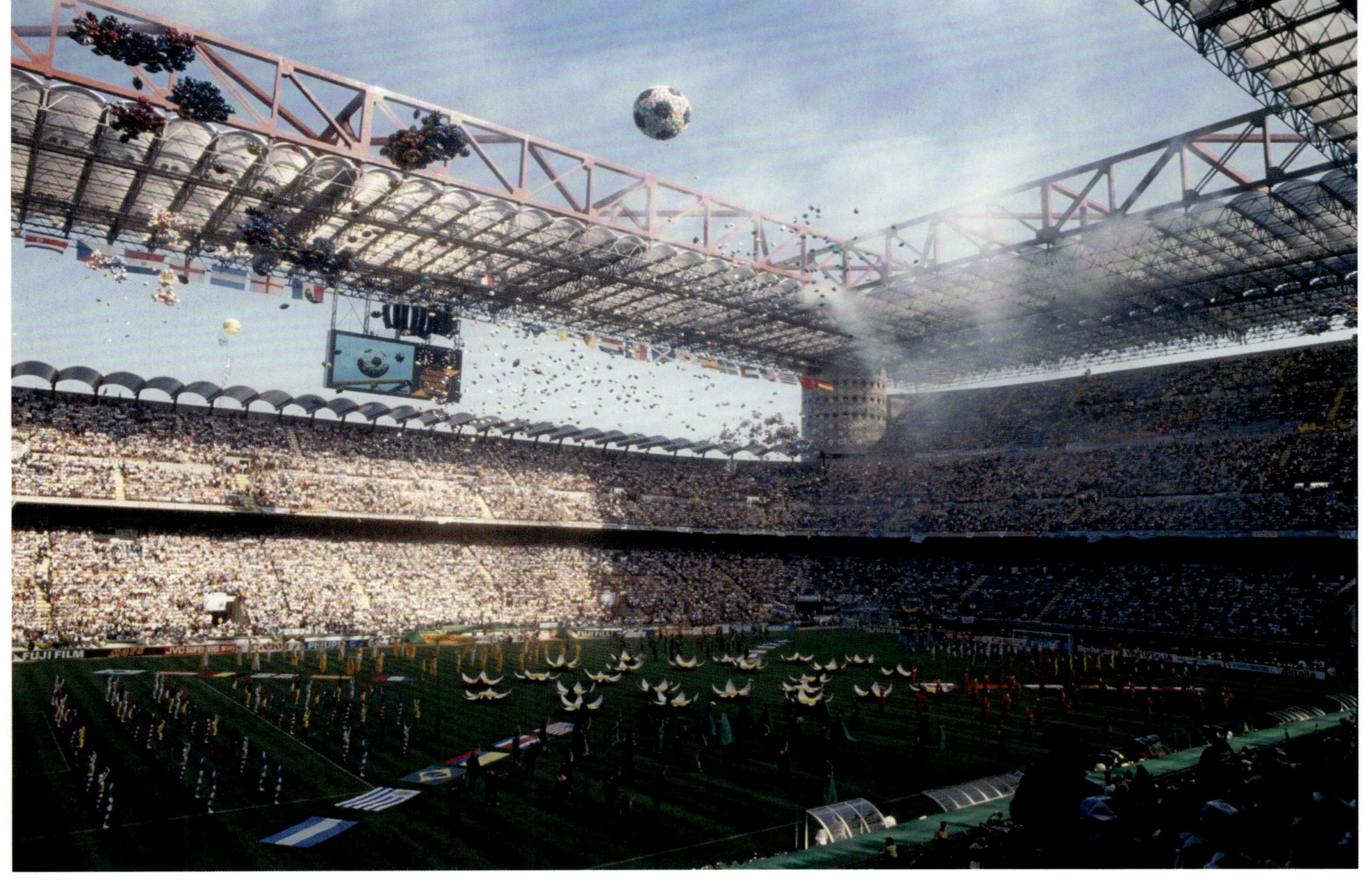

# Tournament: GROUP STAGE

**Having finally found a format** that was popular and successful, Italy 1990 followed the same format as the previous Cup. It would also end with a rematch of the previous Cup Final, Argentina versus West Germany.

### GROUP A: ITALY, CZECHOSLOVAKIA, AUSTRIA, USA

| | | |
|---:|---|---|
| Italy 1 | 0 | Austria |
| Czechoslovakia 5 | 1 | USA |
| Italy 1 | 0 | USA |
| Czechoslovakia 1 | 0 | Austria |
| Italy 2 | 0 | Czechoslovakia |
| Austria 2 | 1 | USA |

***Advanced to Knockout Stage: Italy, Czechoslovakia***

Italy swept all three group matches with stifling defence and emerged as a favourite to win the tournament, especially given the home-soil advantage. The USA fielded a team of mostly college players and part-timers, as evidenced by the hard lesson they received in their opener with Czechoslovakia. The team's following two matches were a different story: gritty one-goal losses to Italy and Austria that seemed to foretell future growth into a more competitive national side.

### GROUP B: CAMEROON, ROMANIA, ARGENTINA, SOVIET UNION

| | | |
|---:|---|---|
| Cameroon 1 | 0 | Argentina |
| Romania 2 | 0 | Soviet Union |
| Argentina 2 | 0 | Soviet Union |
| Cameroon 2 | 1 | Romania |
| Argentina 1 | 1 | Romania |
| Soviet Union 4 | 0 | Cameroon |

***Advanced to Knockout Stage: Cameroon, Romania, Argentina***

First-place Cameroon was the revelation of Group B. The Indomitable Lions' remarkable victory over reigning-champion Argentina came despite ending the match with only nine men on the field. Meanwhile, Argentina barely made it out of the group stage with their third-place finish. At this point, it wasn't easy to picture them making another final.

**BELOW** *Andrea Carnevale of Italy takes a hard challenge in the Group A match against Austria.*

**OPPOSITE** *Cameroon's François Omam-Biyik with a stunning header to shock reigning-champions Argentina at the San Siro. On the following page, his now-iconic celebration of joy and disbelief.*

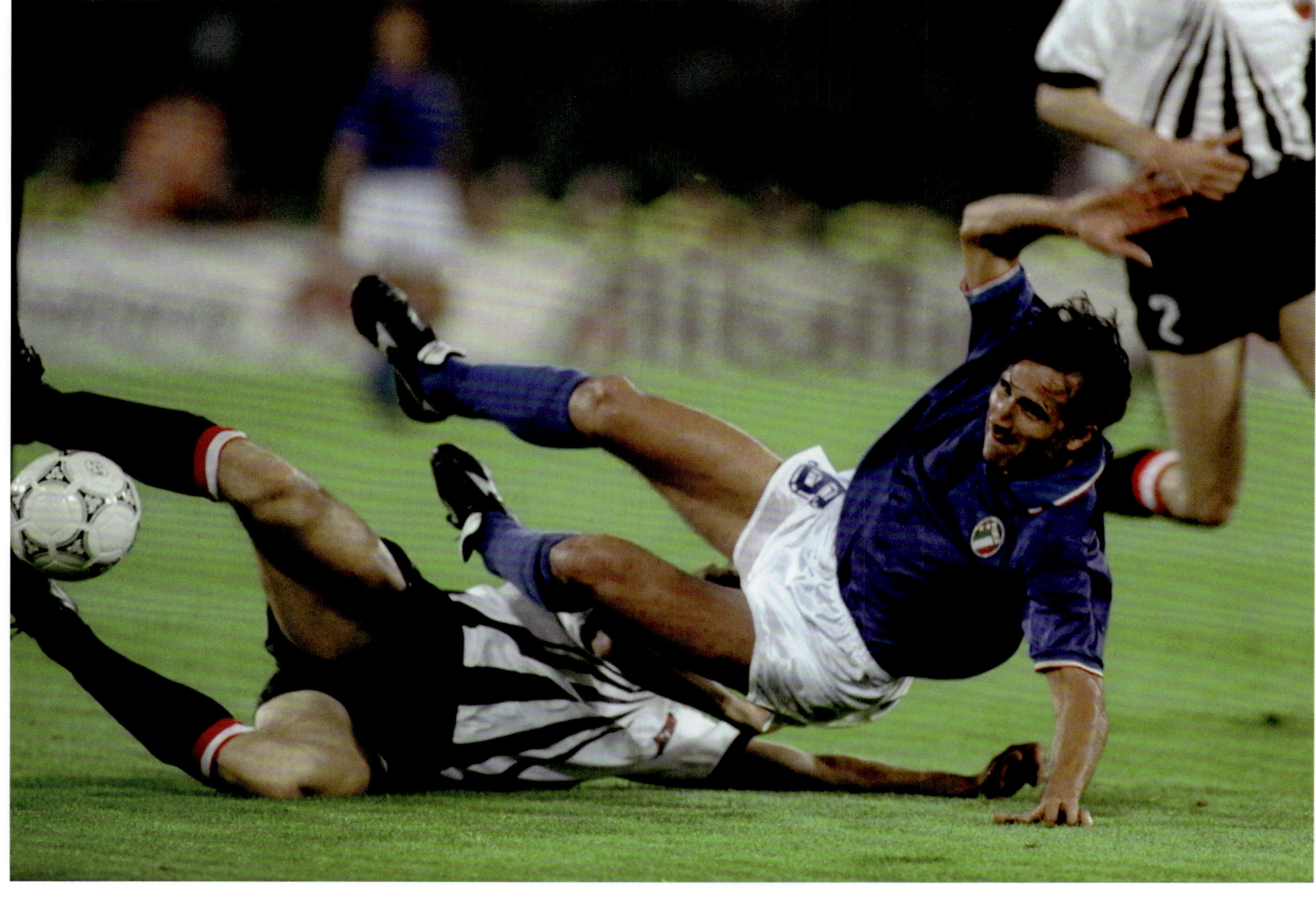

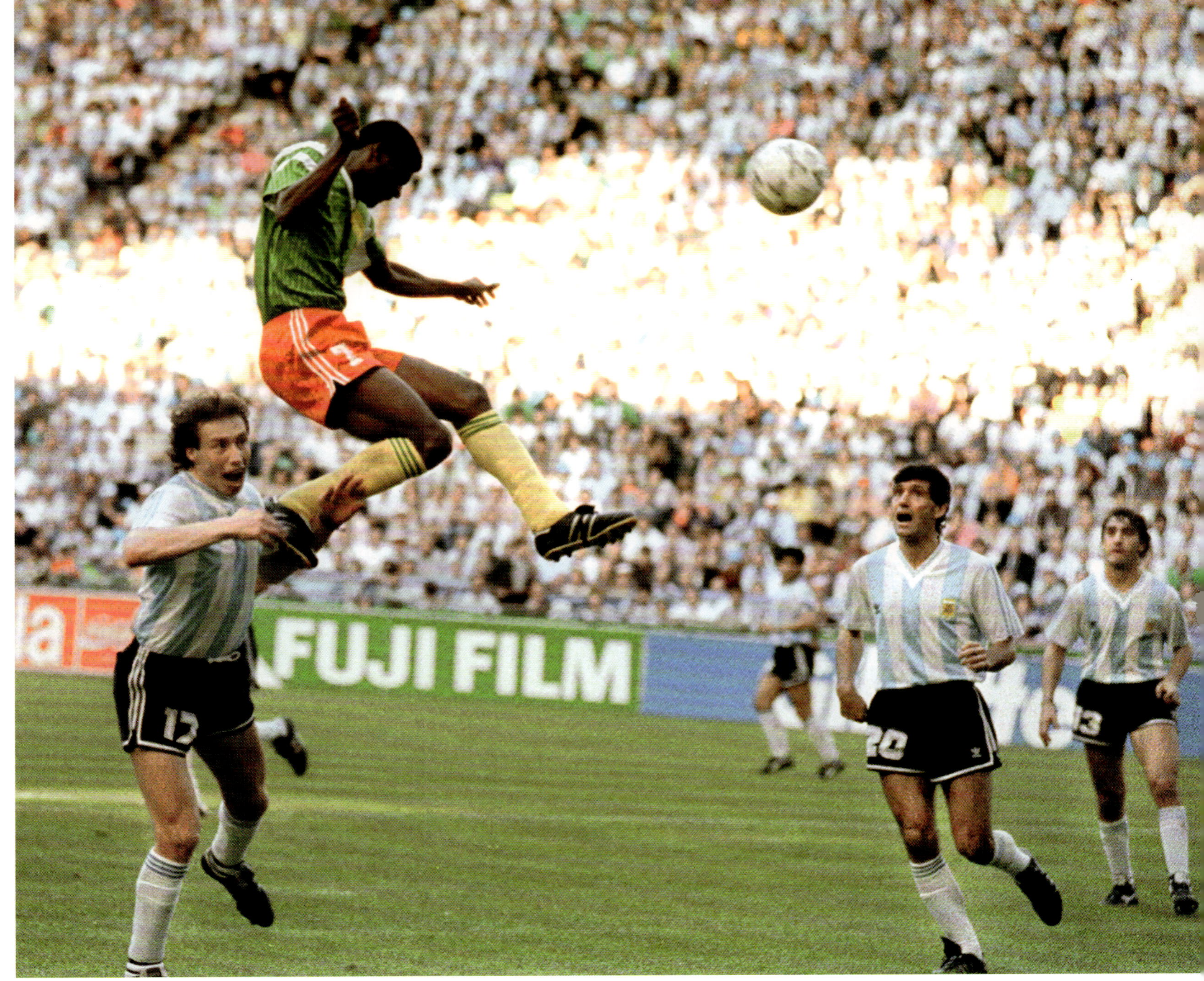

<table>
<tr><td colspan="2">GROUP C: BRAZIL, COSTA RICA,<br>SCOTLAND, SWEDEN</td></tr>
<tr><td align="right">Brazil 2</td><td>1 Sweden</td></tr>
<tr><td align="right">Costa Rica 1</td><td>0 Scotland</td></tr>
<tr><td align="right">Brazil 1</td><td>0 Costa Rica</td></tr>
<tr><td align="right">Scotland 2</td><td>1 Sweden</td></tr>
<tr><td align="right">Brazil 1</td><td>0 Scotland</td></tr>
<tr><td align="right">Costa Rica 2</td><td>1 Sweden</td></tr>
</table>

***Advanced to Knockout Stage: Brazil, Costa Rica***

Brazil went unbeaten but didn't have its usual scoring explosion, instead playing a more defensive style and eking out three narrow, low-scoring wins. Costa Rica surprised with wins over Scotland and Sweden, advancing to the knockout stage in its first World Cup.

<table>
<tr><td colspan="2">GROUP D: WEST GERMANY, YUGOSLAVIA,<br>COLOMBIA, UNITED ARAB EMIRATES</td></tr>
<tr><td align="right">Colombia 2</td><td>0 UAE</td></tr>
<tr><td align="right">West Germany 4</td><td>1 Yugoslavia</td></tr>
<tr><td align="right">Yugoslavia 1</td><td>0 Colombia</td></tr>
<tr><td align="right">West Germany 5</td><td>1 UAE</td></tr>
<tr><td align="right">West Germany 1</td><td>1 Colombia</td></tr>
<tr><td align="right">Yugoslavia 4</td><td>1 UAE</td></tr>
</table>

***Advanced to Knockout Stage:***

***West Germany, Yugoslavia, Colombia***

West Germany crushed its first two foes and then tied a Colombian squad led by talented attacking midfielder and captain, Carlos Valderrama. Managed now by the great Franz Beckenbauer, captained by Lothar Matthäus, and spearheaded by two dynamic forwards in Jürgen Klinsmann and Rudi Völler, the West Germans looked like a formidable force.

| | | |
|---|---|---|
| Belgium 2 | 0 | South Korea |
| Uruguay 0 | 0 | Spain |
| Belgium 3 | 1 | Uruguay |
| Spain 3 | 1 | South Korea |
| Spain 2 | 1 | Belgium |
| Uruguay 1 | 0 | South Korea |

**Advanced to Knockout Stage: Spain, Belgium, Uruguay**

A hat-trick from Míchel against South Korea highlighted unbeaten Spain's first-place finish in this group. Belgium's two wins put them in second, whereas Uruguay needed a stoppage-time goal against South Korea to barely advance into the knockout stage as the weakest of the four third-place teams in group play that qualified.



| | | |
|---|---|---|
| England 1 | 1 | Republic of Ireland |
| Netherlands 1 | 1 | Egypt |
| England 0 | 0 | Netherlands |
| Republic of Ireland 0 | 0 | Egypt |
| England 1 | 0 | Egypt |
| Republic of Ireland 1 | 1 | Netherlands |

**Advanced to Knockout Stage: England,
Republic of Ireland, Netherlands**

One of the lowest-scoring groups in World Cup history, all six games ended with neither team scoring more than one goal. Only one match, England's 1–0 win over Egypt, produced an actual winner and loser. This group, more than any other, exemplified the overall pattern emerging in the 1990 tournament: conservative tactics and stacked defences. Football writer Alex Keble points specifically to the scoreless Ireland–Egypt snoozefest as 'a game so painfully bad the International Football Association Board (IFAB) changed the laws of football to stop it happening again'. Egypt's ultra-defensive strategy involved repeatedly passing the ball back to their goalkeeper, who would pick it up (legal back then), stroll around the box as long as he could, and then punt it away. After a while, Ireland, who only needed a draw, followed suit. The time-wasting was so boring and egregious that the IFAB decided to limit the foot back-pass by making it an infraction for the keeper to handle it. 'This made football faster and more entertaining overnight,' said Keble.

**OPPOSITE** *Ireland's Kevin Sheedy fires off a volley that is contested midair by Egypt's Hany Ramzy.*

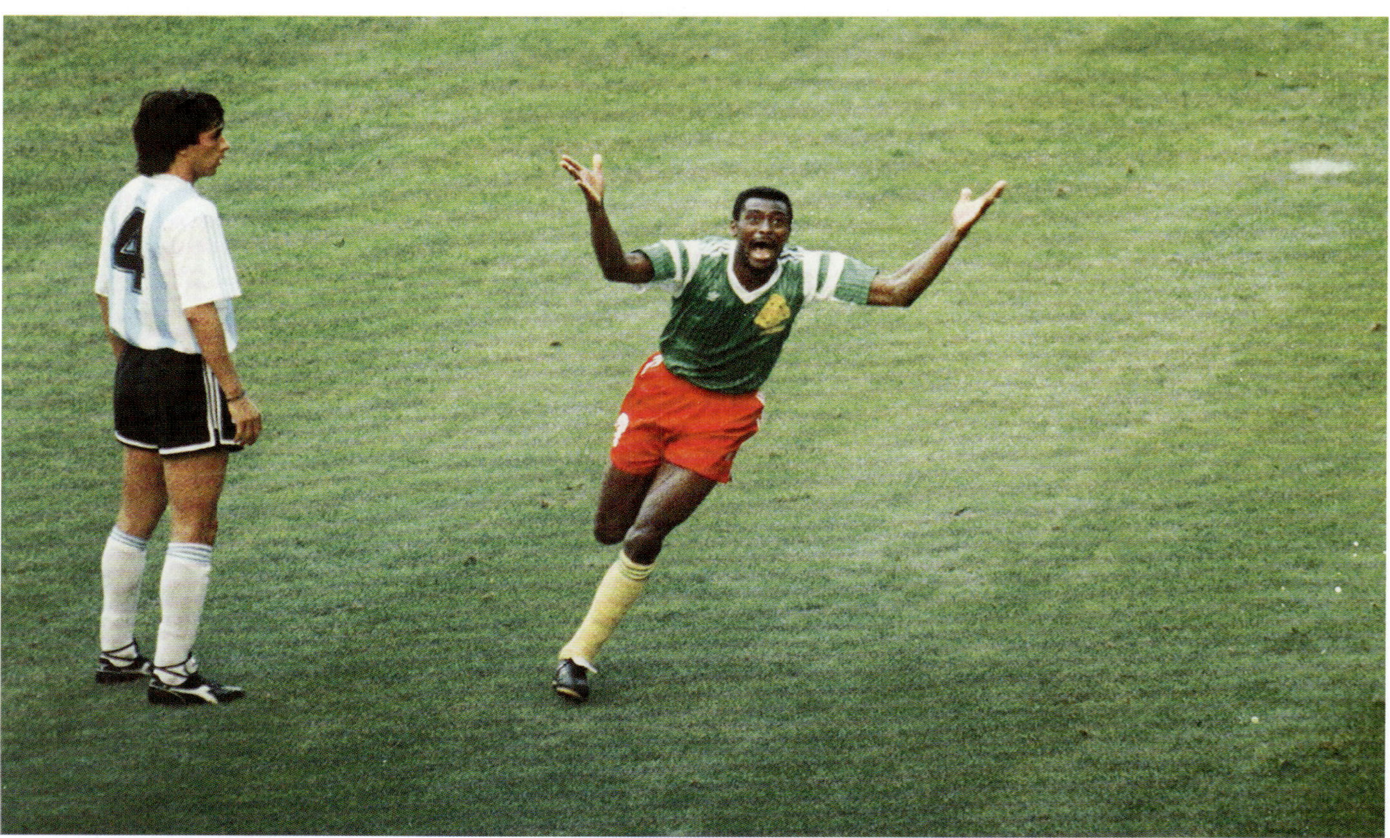

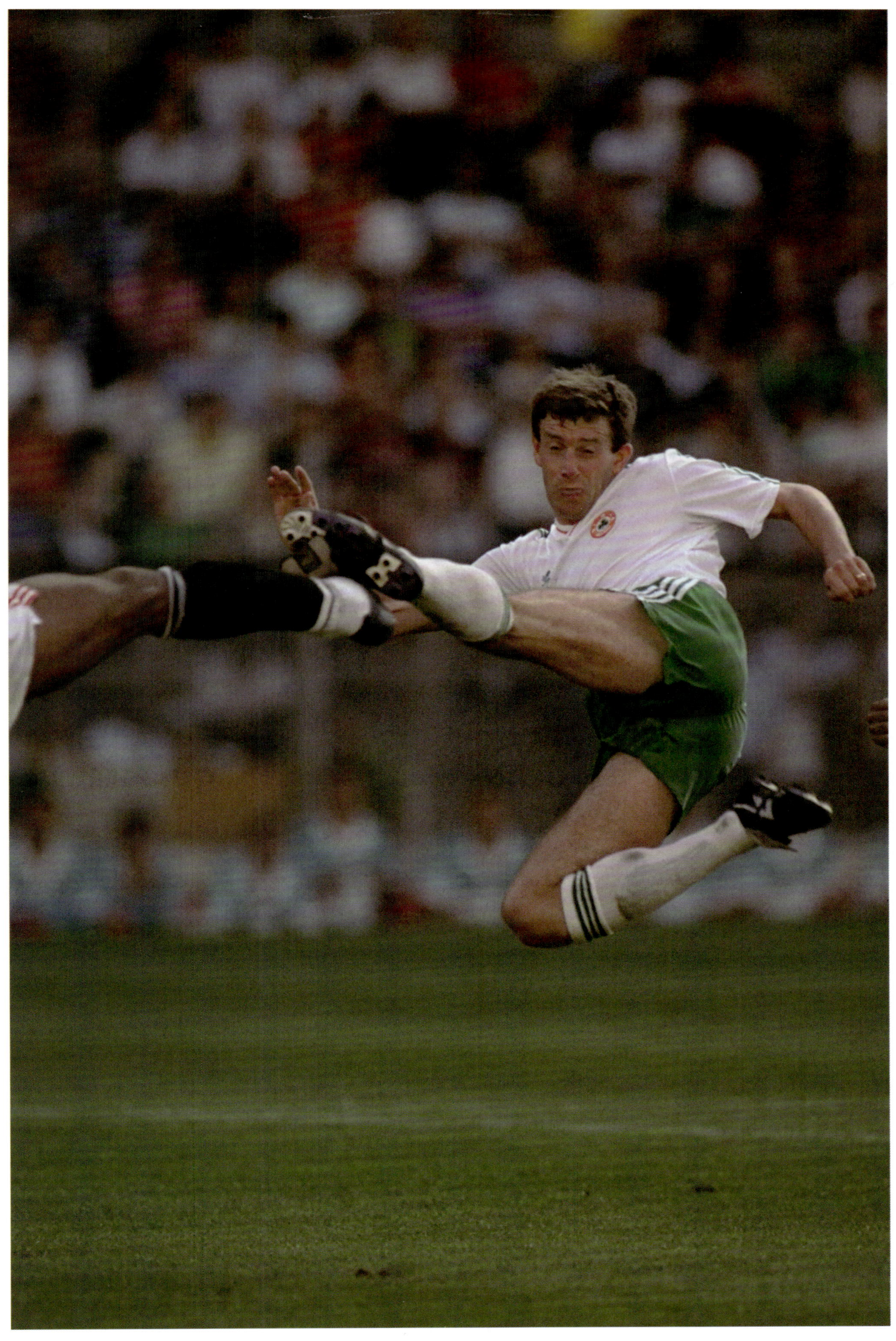

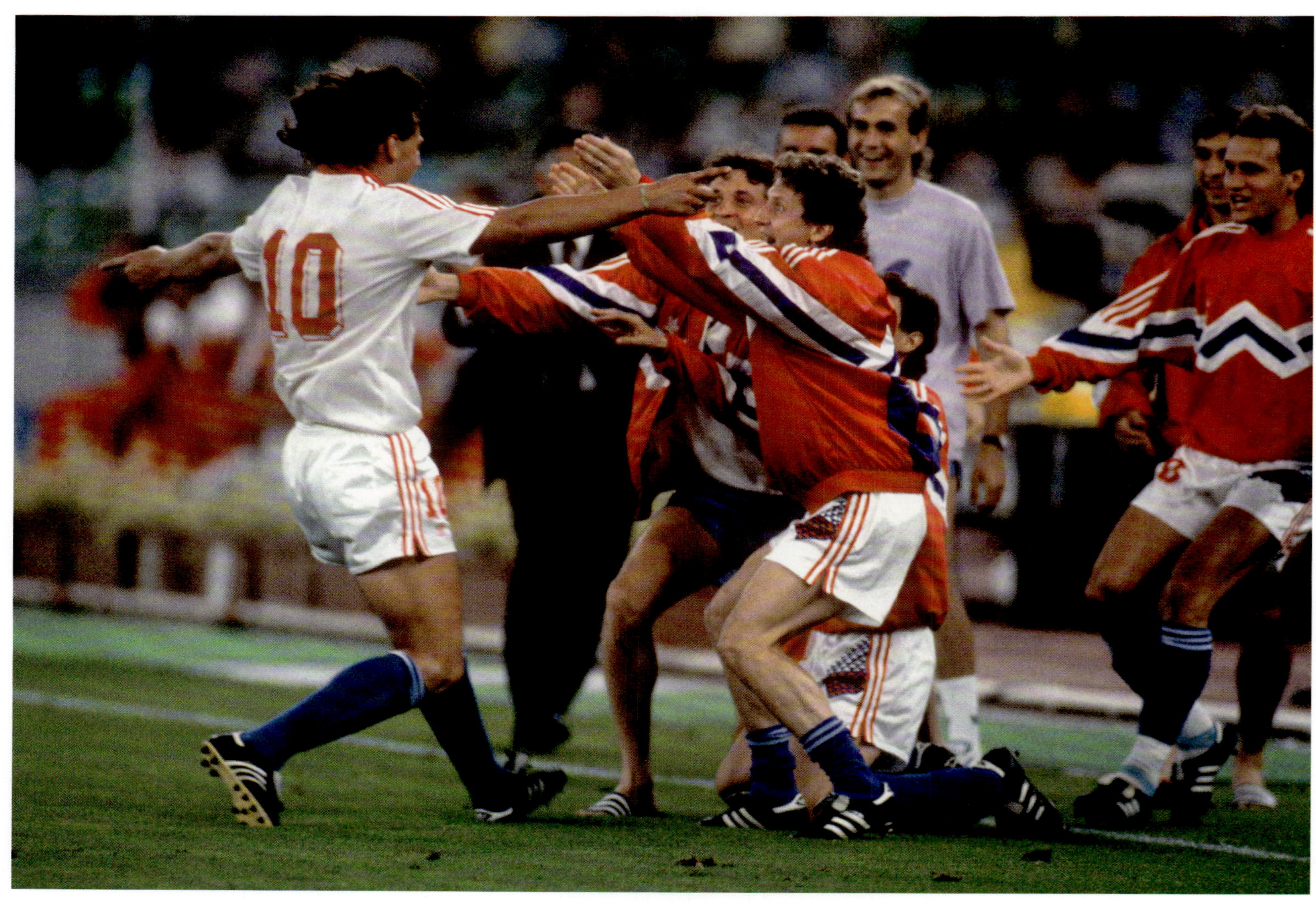

## KNOCKOUT STAGE
## ROUND OF 16

| | |
|---:|:---|
| Argentina 1 | 0 Brazil |
| Yugoslavia 2 | 1 Spain |
| Republic of Ireland 0 | 0 Romania |
| | (5–4 on penalty kicks) |
| Italy 2 | 0 Uruguay |
| Czechoslovakia 4 | 1 Costa Rica |
| West Germany 2 | 1 Netherlands |
| Cameroon 2 | 1 Colombia |
| England 1 | 0 Belgium |

Cautious play continued to predominate, and goal totals stayed low outside of Czechoslovakia's rout of Costa Rica. And yet, despite the close scorelines, only one match went to penalty kicks. Argentina's late goal to beat Brazil was probably the most decisive moment in this round, although the West Germany–Netherlands match also featured strong play in a highly anticipated rematch of their intense semi-final in the previous European Championship. Roger Milla scored twice in extra time to power Cameroon's 2–0 win over Colombia—and lead an African team to a World Cup quarter-final for the first time.

## QUARTER-FINALS

| | |
|---:|:---|
| Argentina 0 | 0 Yugoslavia |
| | (3–2 on penalty kicks) |
| Italy 1 | 0 Republic of Ireland |
| West Germany 1 | 0 Czechoslovakia |
| England 3 | 2 Cameroon |

All four quarter-finals were tense, tight contests. There were only two goals scored (one a penalty) in regular time in the first three matches. The fourth match was a considerable departure, though no less intense; three of the five goals were penalty kicks. Clearly, standard goals were devilishly hard to come by. Italy, long known for its defensive prowess, was looking especially strong. Their shutout of Ireland, in fact, ensured a clean sheet through the first five matches. And when the quarter-finals were all said and done, the four star-studded semi-finalists who emerged—Argentina, Italy, West Germany, and England—were all former champions. Together, they had won eight of the thirteen World Cups.

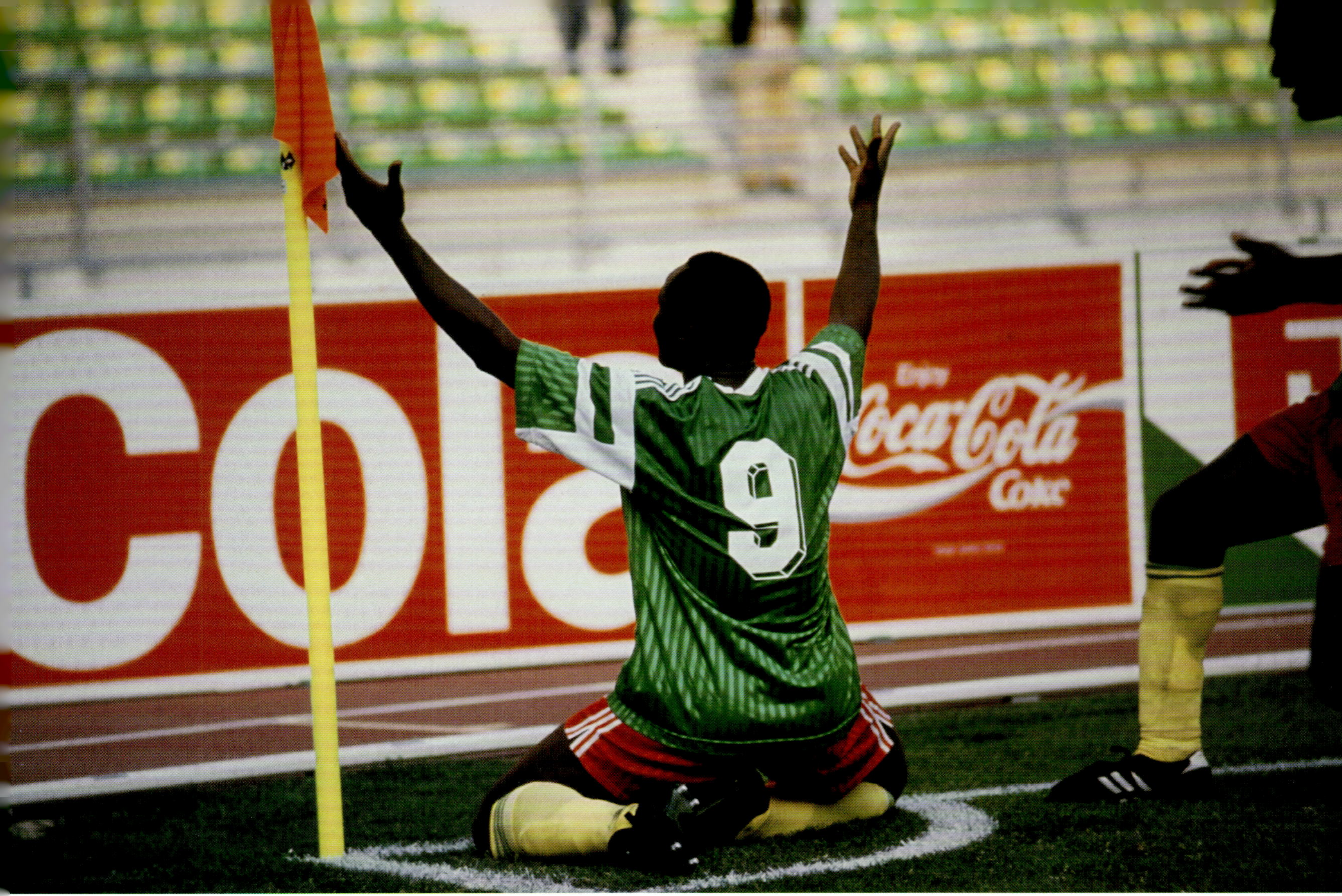

## CAMEROON TO THE CORNER!

**Led by the four goals** and joyous corner-flag celebrations of thirty-eight-year-old forward Roger Milla — who'd come out of retirement at the personal request of his country's president, Paul Biya — the Indomitable Lions of Cameroon made a huge impression on football fans across the globe. They were no fluke. Starting with an earth-shattering win over defending-champion Argentina, the Lions went on to defeat Romania to qualify for the knockout stage and then top Colombia 2–1 in extra time in the Round of 16 — all building up to a thrilling quarter-final match against England.

Much of Cameroon's squad played in Ligue 1, France's highest-level football league, and they were well prepared to take on England's crisp professionalism. The Indomitable Lions scored twice in four minutes to take a 2–1 lead after eighty-two minutes, looking poised to stun the world yet again. But Gary Lineker's penalty kick tied the match, and yet another Lineker penalty came in extra time to win it for England — the other 'Lions'. In the end, Cameroon's success became an enduring image of Africa's emergence onto the international scene.

**OPPOSITE** *Czechoslovakia's Tomáš Skuhravý celebrates his hat-trick against Costa Rica.*

**ABOVE** *Roger Milla at the corner flag after scoring against Romania.*

# SEMI-FINALS

Argentina 1 | 1 Italy
  | (4–3 on penalty kicks)
West Germany 1 | 1 England
  | (4–3 on penalty kicks)

Again, the semi-final results reflected the tournament trends—two 1–1 draws decided by penalty-kick shootouts.

In the first match, Italy took a commanding position early and opened the marker with a goal at the seventeenth minute. Despite looking as sturdy as ever, Argentina struck back with an equaliser in the second half—and became the first team to score against Italy in the tournament. In extra time, the first fifteen-minute period went eight minutes longer than scheduled because, in the intensity of the moment, the referee simply forgot to check his watch. In the end, despite conceding only a single goal in six matches, and never once trailing in open play, the Italians would fall in the penalty-kick shootout.

In the other semi-final, the emotional moment that reverberated with fans worldwide was the moment in extra time when the gifted Englishman Paul 'Gazza' Gascoigne was shown his second yellow card of the tournament—which, by rule, meant he had to sit out the next match. Even if England won, he'd have to miss the Cup Final. On the TV close-up, the world could see the moment this realisation struck Gazza. Ultimately, England would end up falling to West Germany anyway, but Gazza's tears became an indelible symbol of Italy 1990 and the undying passion of World Cup football.

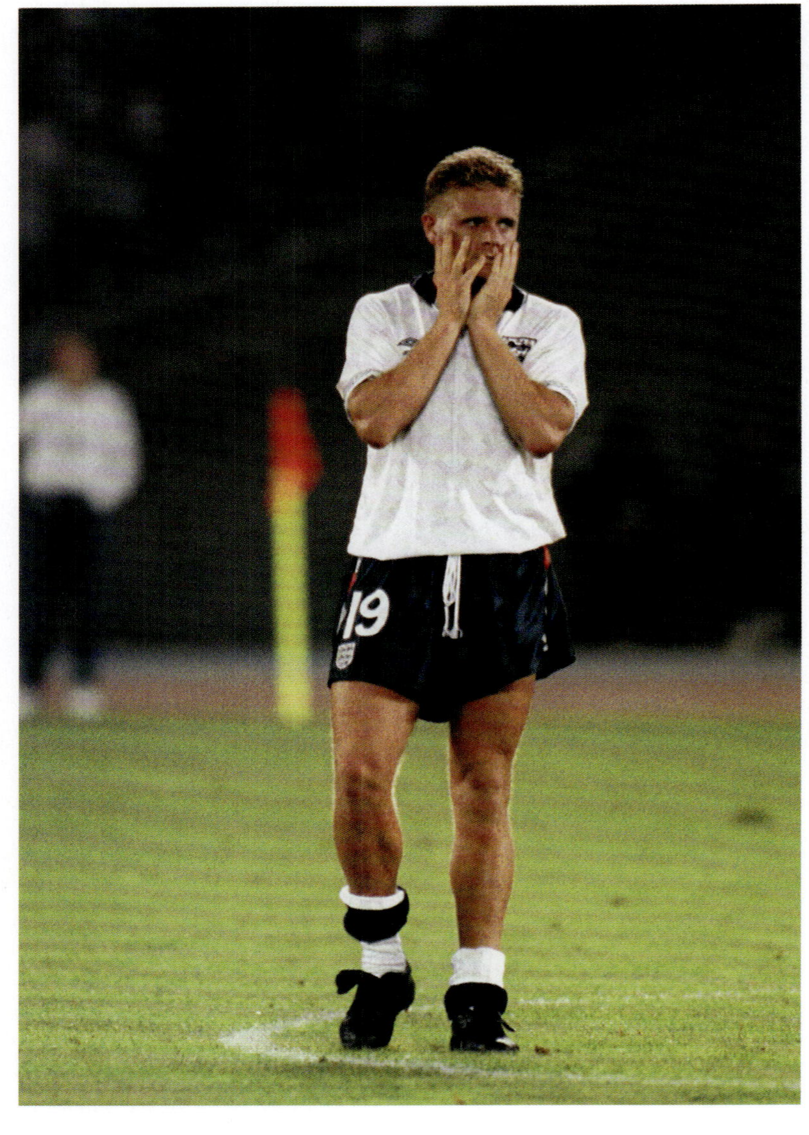

**ABOVE** *Defeat: Paul Gascoigne of England holds his face, and tears, after falling to West Germany.*

**OPPOSITE** *Triumph: West Germans Andreas Brehme (left) and Klaus Augenthaler (right) embrace after defeating England in the semi-final.*

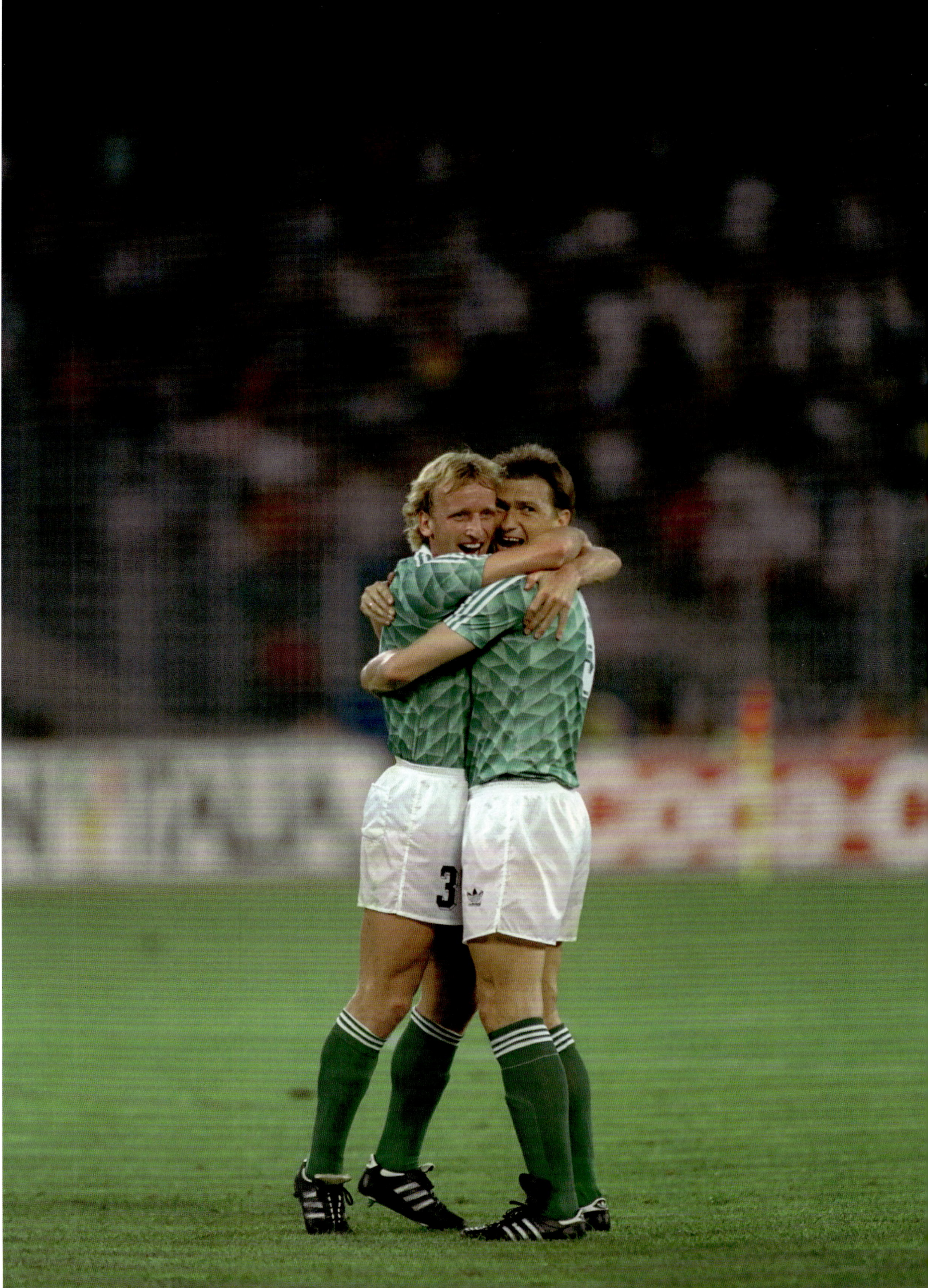

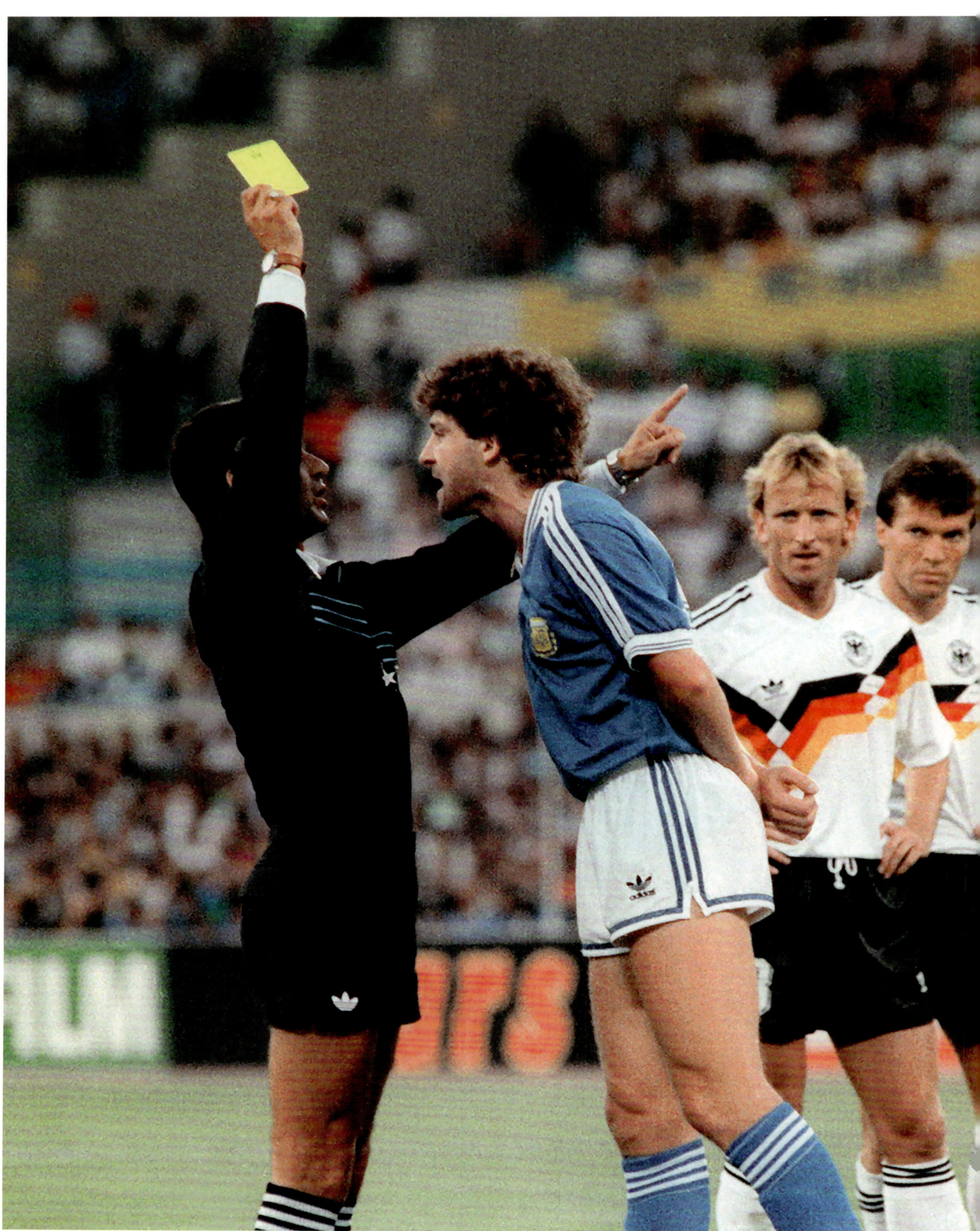

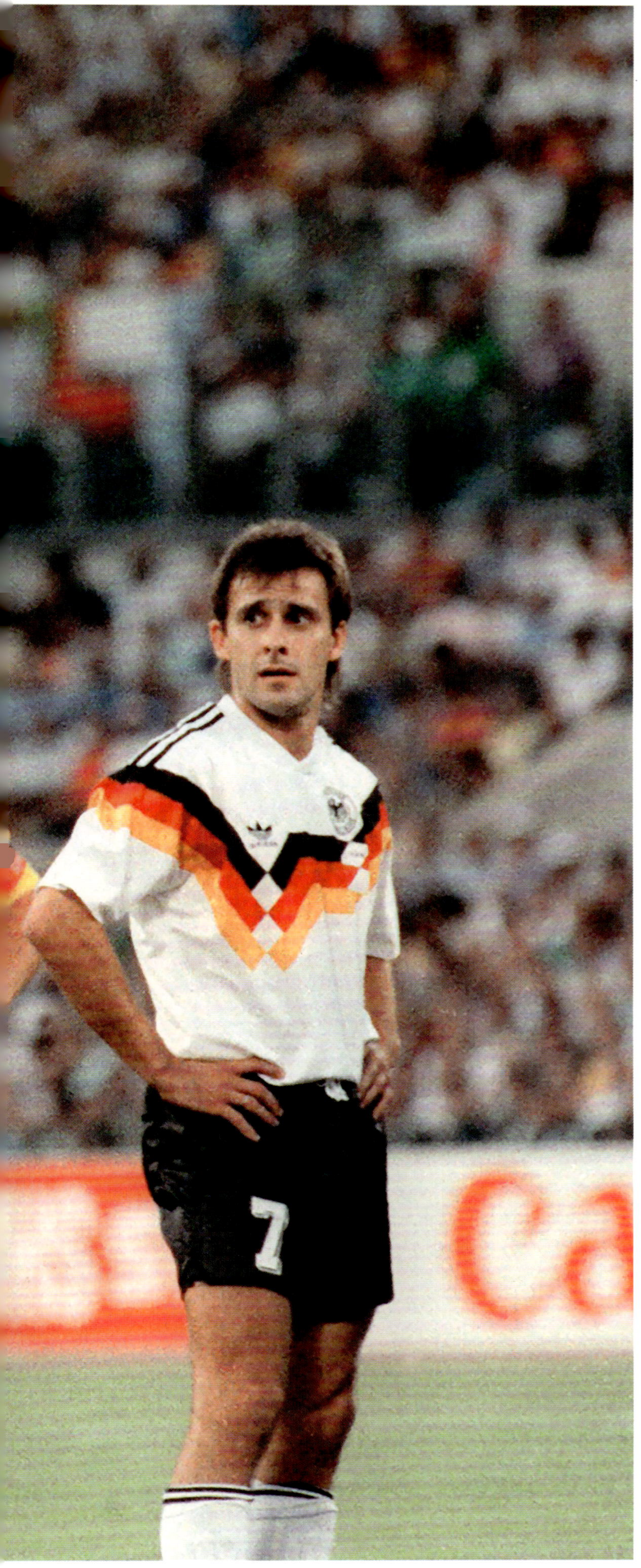

**OPPOSITE** *Argentina's Gustavo
Dezotti, possibly in disagreement
with Mexican referee Edgardo
Codesal's decision to give him a
yellow card in the fifth minute.*

# FINAL

West Germany 1 | 0 Argentina (First Place)

Italy 2 | 1 England (Third Place)

The third-place game turned out to be one of the most entertaining of Italia '90. With no elimination at stake, both sides played wide-open football. Three goals in the final twenty minutes provided an explosive, festive finish. Unfortunately, the final was much the opposite: the BBC called it 'negative, defensive, cynical football…probably the worst in World Cup history'. When Argentina's Pedro Monzón was red-carded in the sixty-fifth minute, he earned the dubious honour of being the first player to ever be sent off during a World Cup Final.

Argentina, riddled with injuries, could muster little offence throughout the match and spent much of the second half bunkered into a defensive formation, hoping for a shoot-out. Questionable refereeing led to flaring tensions on both sides: an obvious foul in the box by Argentine goalkeeper Goycochea went uncalled; an erroneous corner was given to Argentina at the seventy-eighth minute; another uncalled foul in the box at 79' favoured West Germany; and finally, in the eighty-fifth minute, a questionable call against Argentina for a challenge on Rudi Völler led to a penalty kick that produced the game's only goal.

*The New York Times* described the game's frenzied final moments: 'With time running out for Argentina, the frustration was evident, reaching its worst point when Gustavo Dezotti…lassoed Jürgen Kohler around the neck with his arm and threw him down.' As a result, the South Americans finished with nine on the pitch and a 1–0 deficit on the scoreboard.

Thus, in truly chaotic fashion, West Germany won its third World Cup title. Already a legend, Franz Beckenbauer became the second man (after Mário Zagallo of Brazil) to lead his nation to World Cup glory as a player and then a coach.

# 1994

HOST COUNTRY: **UNITED STATES**
CHAMPION: **BRAZIL**
RUNNER-UP: **ITALY**
THIRD PLACE: **SWEDEN OVER BULGARIA**

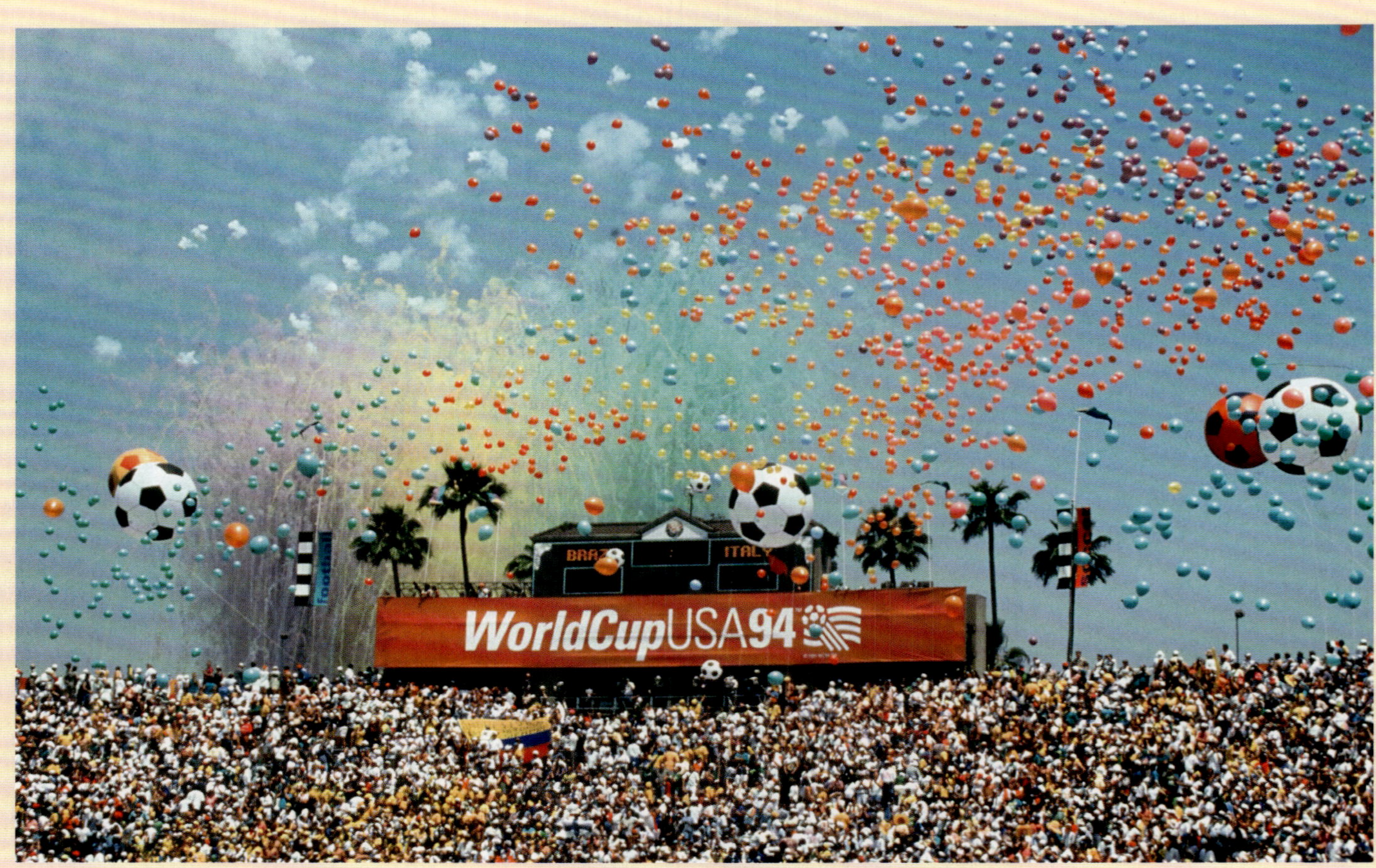


**Sometimes a smart bet** can pay off big. On 4 July, 1988, when FIFA selected the United States to host the 1994 FIFA World Cup tournament, it seemed a strange choice. The United States didn't even have a professional football league, as the North American Soccer League (NASL) had folded in 1985. Yes, American youth leagues were booming in the 1980s and the college scene was flourishing, too, but association football (soccer, as it is called in the United States) was clearly a second-class citizen in the world of American sports.

Still, FIFA chose to make a calculated gamble. The United States was easily the biggest sports market in the world and had a massive infrastructure of sporting venues. The 1984 Summer Olympic Games in Los Angeles, for example, had been a smashing success — and FIFA took special note of the surprising popularity of the Olympic football competition, which drew an eye-popping 1.4 million spectators. That, along with the grass-roots growth of the sport across the country, convinced FIFA to invest in the future of association football by exposing its most sublime manifestation, the quadrennial World Cup, to 250 million Americans, more than 70 percent of whom considered themselves 'sports fans'.

# HOW FOOTBALL BECAME 'SOCCER'

**If you're a typical American** sports fan, you refer to the sport played at the FIFA World Cup as 'soccer'. Even casual international sports fans know that in the United States the term *football* is almost exclusively associated with American football, the well-padded, gladiatorial game played at universities like Alabama, Michigan, University of Southern California, and Nebraska. NFL football is not only big business in America but a massive cultural entity as well, so sharing the sport's name wasn't really an option for fans and promoters of global football.

But where did the term soccer come from? One would assume it to be an American invention, but this is not so. Back in the nineteenth century, the original name for that sport in England was 'association football'. Association got shortened into the slang term *assoc* and then further shortened by students at Cambridge and Oxford to *soccer*. As they would often refer to someone who plays rugby football as a 'rugger', someone who plays 'assoc' football became a 'soccer'. Before long, the term became a nickname for the sport itself.

So, even though the English invented the game as it's known today, they must also take credit (or blame) for the term that's dominant in other English-speaking countries like the United States, Canada, and Australia . . . even though the British still prefer the term football.

And with the national behemoth gridiron football already laying claim to the 'football' nickname in the United States, 'soccer' was transformed into the formal designation of association football, where the premier professional league is officially named Major League Soccer (MLS).

# THE BIRTH OF MLS

**One condition FIFA imposed** when approving the US bid to host the 1994 World Cup was a contractual agreement to start a new professional soccer league in the United States. Thus, Major League Soccer was founded in 1993 and started play in 1996 with ten teams. The new league struggled some at first, but by the mid-2010s, its franchises had become more profitable and its fan bases had widened considerably. This growth was, in part, thanks to a wave of sleek new soccer-specific stadiums and the signing of higher-level players from abroad (like David Beckham, Thierry Henry, Kaká, Wayne Rooney, and David Villa) to mix in with budding American stars. In 2023, MLS's profile exploded to even further heights when Lionel Messi, fresh off the crowning achievement of his career, signed with the brand-new Inter Miami CF.

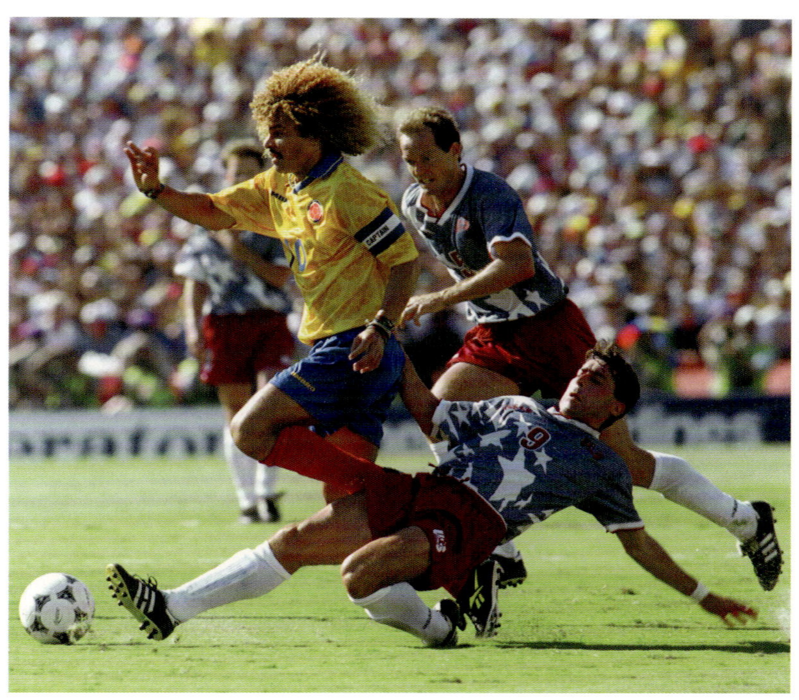

| | |
|---|---|
| USA 1 | 1 Switzerland |
| Romania 3 | 1 Colombia |
| Switzerland 4 | 1 Romania |
| USA 2 | 1 Colombia |
| Colombia 2 | 0 Switzerland |
| Romania 1 | 0 USA |

***Advanced to Knockout Stage: Romania, Switzerland, USA***

Home-crowd excitement for the USA in group play was exceptional. The team rewarded its fans by tying a solid Switzerland side in the Pontiac Silverdome (the first-ever Cup match played in an indoor stadium) and then beating a strong South American team (aided by a now-infamous Colombian own-goal error) en route to the Round of 16.



| | |
|---|---|
| Cameroon 2 | 2 Sweden |
| Brazil 2 | 0 Russia |
| Brazil 3 | 0 Cameroon |
| Sweden 3 | 1 Russia |
| Russia 6 | 1 Cameroon |
| Brazil 1 | 1 Sweden |

***Advanced to Knockout Stage: Brazil, Sweden***

Appearing as 'Russia' for the first time in its history (following the dissolution of the Soviet Union in 1991), the Russian side mostly struggled and failed to advance, despite a 6–1 thumping of Cameroon. In that match, Oleg Salenko became the only man (to date) to score five goals in a single World Cup game. Brazil led the group with two convincing wins and a strategically played draw with Sweden, who also advanced. Both squads would go on to be tournament semi-finalists.

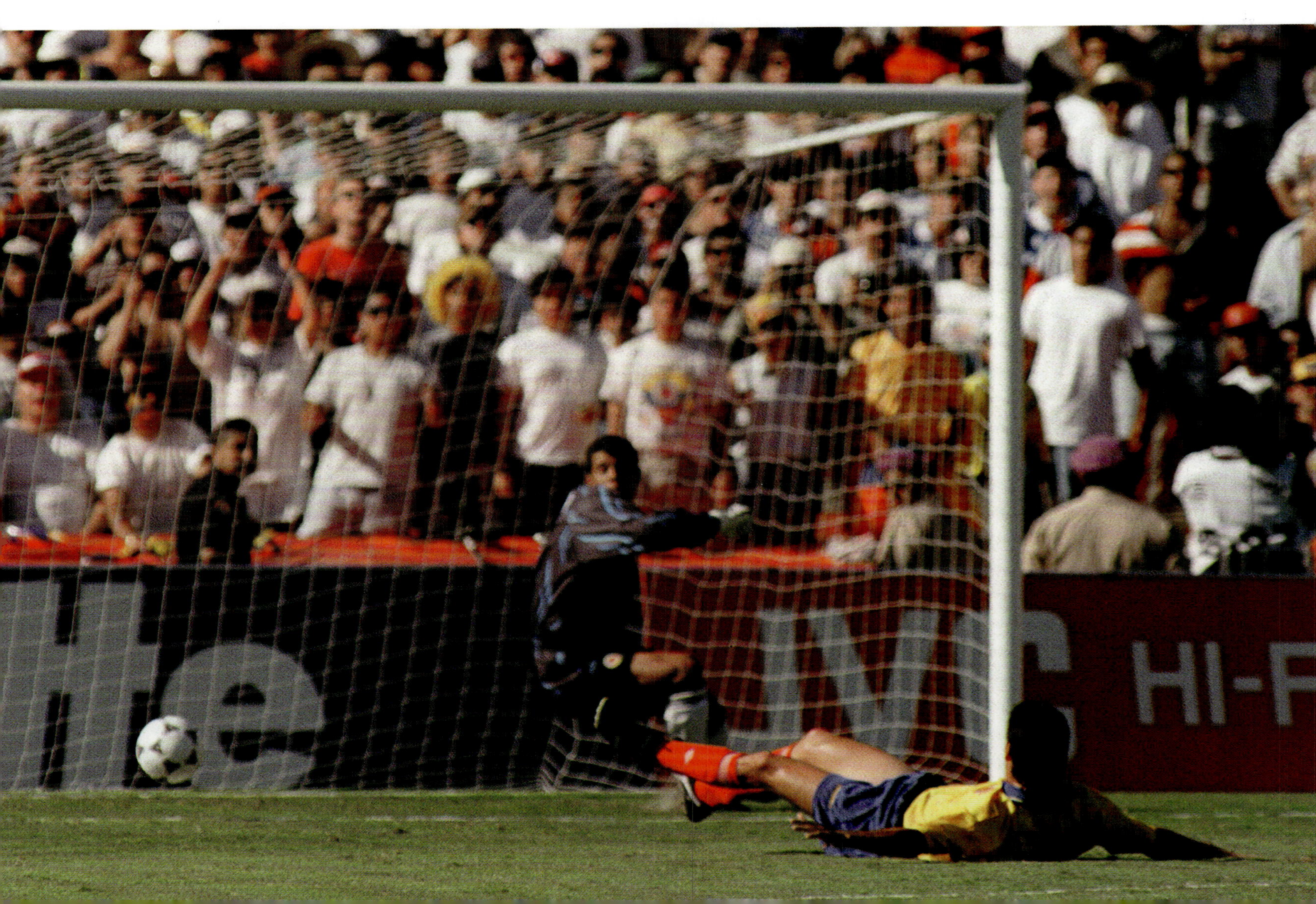

## GROUP C: GERMANY, SPAIN, SOUTH KOREA, BOLIVIA

| | | |
|---|---|---|
| Germany 1 | 0 | Bolivia |
| Spain 2 | 2 | South Korea |
| Germany 1 | 1 | Spain |
| South Korea 0 | 0 | Bolivia |
| Spain 3 | 1 | Bolivia |
| Germany 3 | 2 | South Korea |

***Advanced to Knockout Stage: Germany, Spain***

Germany's strong national team, once again unified under one flag, moved undefeated through the group, as did Spain. South Korea was the surprise team, starting with two goals in the final four minutes to earn a rousing 2–2 draw with Spain. Then, after trailing 3–0 at halftime to Germany, the resilient Koreans fought back to 3–2 and nearly got a late equaliser.

## GROUP D: NIGERIA, BULGARIA, ARGENTINA, GREECE

| | | |
|---|---|---|
| Argentina 4 | 0 | Greece |
| Nigeria 3 | 0 | Bulgaria |
| Argentina 2 | 1 | Nigeria |
| Bulgaria 4 | 0 | Greece |
| Bulgaria 2 | 0 | Argentina |
| Nigeria 2 | 0 | Greece |

***Advanced to Knockout Stage: Nigeria, Bulgaria, Argentina***

Argentina, led by Diego Maradona, won its first two matches before suffering a tough 2–0 loss to Bulgaria. In a sad development, Maradona tested positive for ephedrine, a banned weight-loss drug, and was banished from the tournament. His goal versus Greece would be his last ever at the World Cup. On the other end, the World Cup debut of Nigeria was a rousing success. Despite a close loss to the Argentines, the African side managed to win the group on goal differential after two solid victories over Bulgaria and Greece.

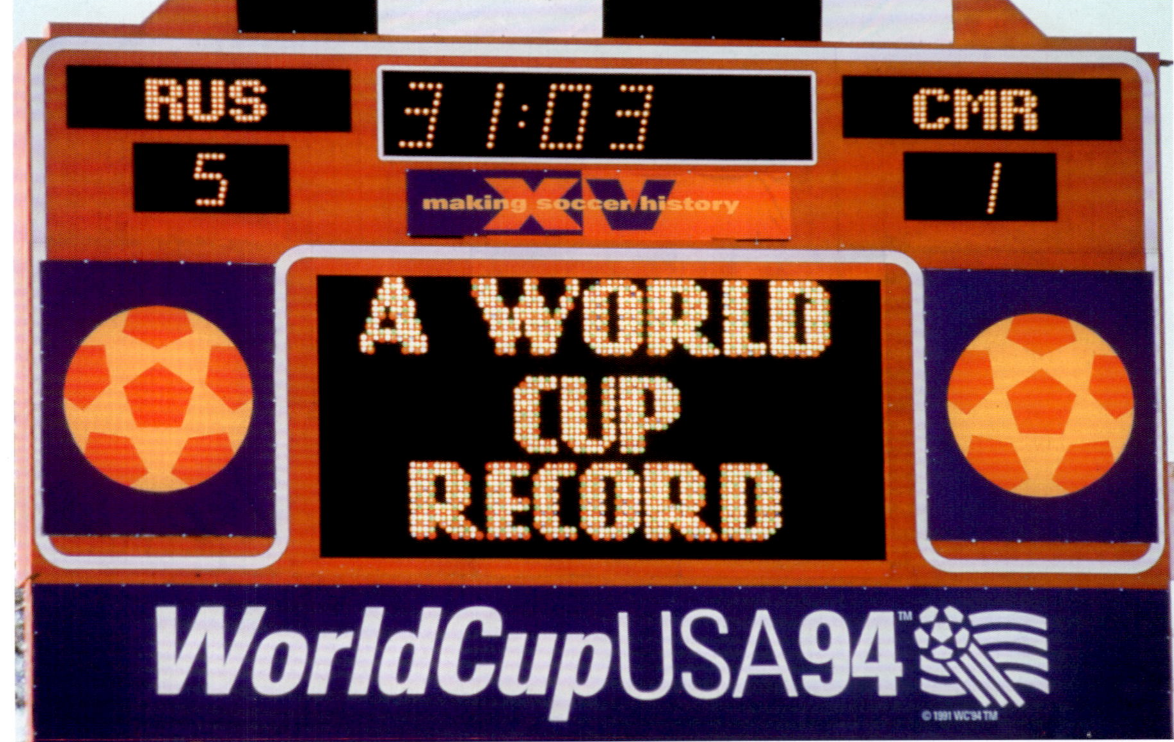


**OPPOSITE** *Andrés Escobar of Colombia scores an own goal against USA. His side would ultimately lose the match 1–2, and many believe that Escobar's tragic assassination was in retaliation for this blunder.*

**RIGHT** *The scoreboard displays a 5–1 victory for Russia over Cameroon. All five of Russia's goals were scored by Oleg Salenko, a single-game record which still stands through the 2022 World Cup.*

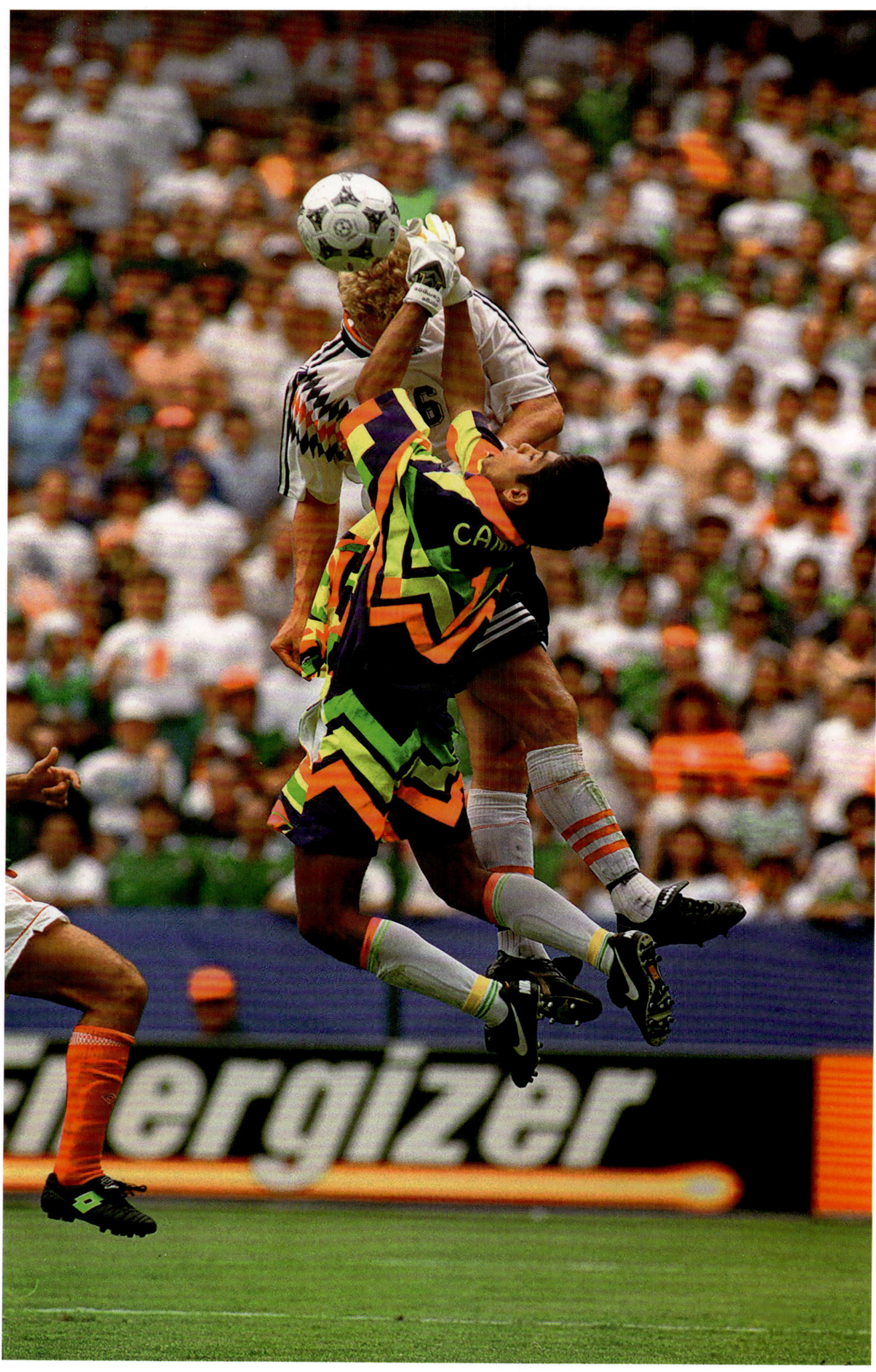

energizer

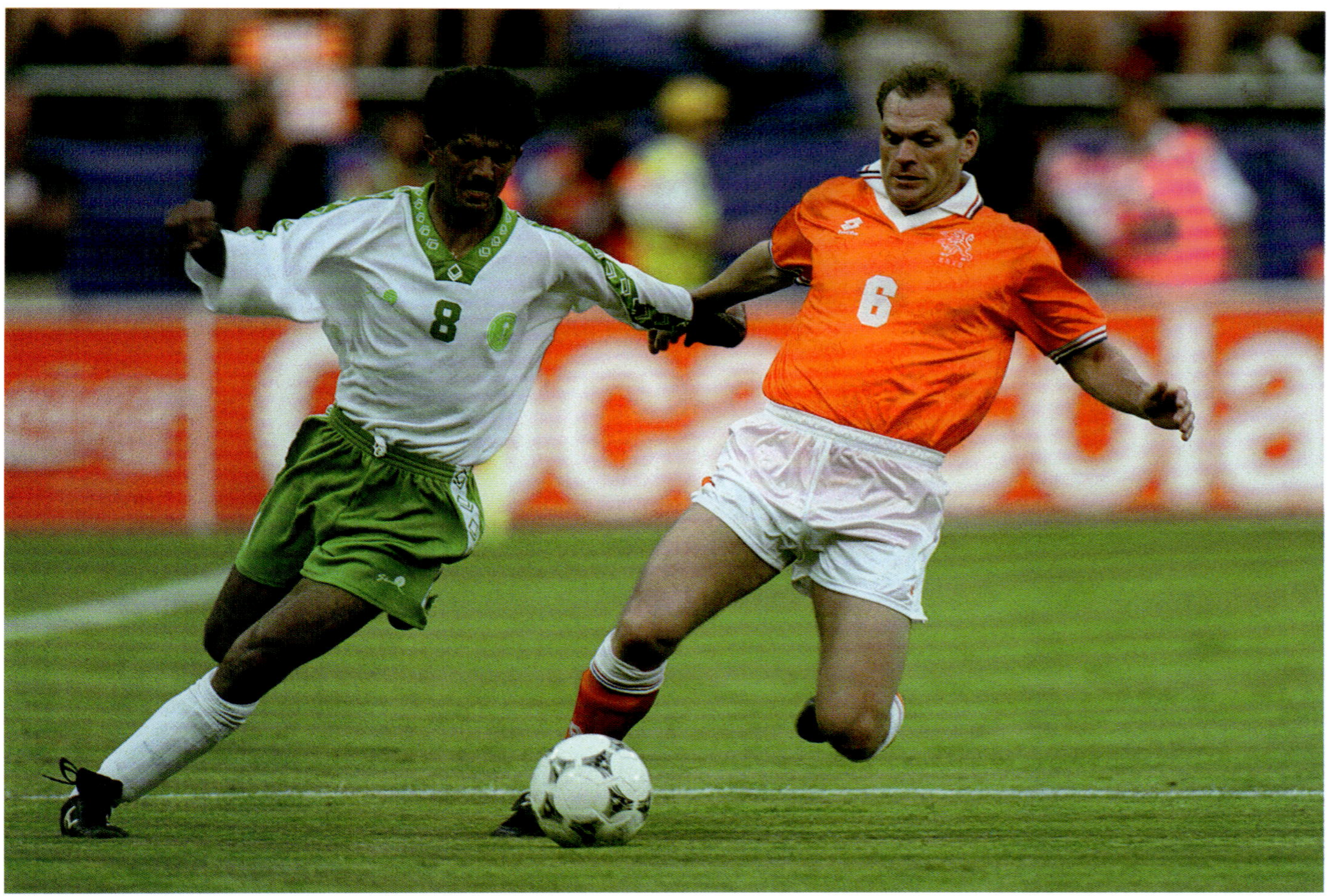

## GROUP E: MEXICO, REPUBLIC OF IRELAND, ITALY, NORWAY

| | |
|---|---|
| Republic of Ireland 1 | 0 Italy |
| Norway 1 | 0 Mexico |
| Italy 1 | 0 Norway |
| Mexico 2 | 1 Republic of Ireland |
| Italy 1 | 1 Mexico |
| Republic of Ireland 0 | 0 Norway |

***Advanced to Knockout Stage: Mexico, Republic of Ireland, Italy***

## GROUP F: NETHERLANDS, SAUDI ARABIA, BELGIUM, MOROCCO

| | |
|---|---|
| Belgium 1 | 0 Morocco |
| Netherlands 2 | 1 Saudi Arabia |
| Belgium 1 | 0 Netherlands |
| Saudi Arabia 2 | 1 Morocco |
| Saudi Arabia 1 | 0 Belgium |
| Netherlands 2 | 1 Morocco |

***Advanced to Knockout Stage: Netherlands, Saudi Arabia, Belgium***

The first group in World Cup history where all four teams finished with the same point total. Even more amazingly, all had the same goal differential of zero as well. Italy's upset loss to an inspired Ireland (led by the nearly superhuman defence of Irish centre-back Paul McGrath) in the opener nearly cost them dearly, but the odd group results let the Italians slip through to the next round as one of the top third-place teams. The least fortunate were Norway. Perhaps unjustly, their favouring of defence over attack ended up their undoing: though they only conceded a single goal (the lowest in the group), they also only scored a single goal. The 'goals for' tie-breaker meant that they were the lone Group E side to be sent home after the round-robin.

Saudi Arabia's 1–0 upset of Belgium included one of the most spectacular goals of the Cup: Saeed Al-Owairan received a ball deep in the Saudi half and unleashed a wild solo run, cutting through much of the Belgian team before reaching the corner of the six-yard box and ripping a shot over the diving goalkeeper.

**OPPOSITE** *Mexican keeper Jorge Campos, sporting a colourful uniform, makes the save on Jostein Flo's header. Norway would eventually find an eighty-fourth-minute winner for a 1–0 victory.*

**ABOVE** *Fahad Al-Bishi of Saudi Arabia and Jan Wouters of the Netherlands compete for the ball.*

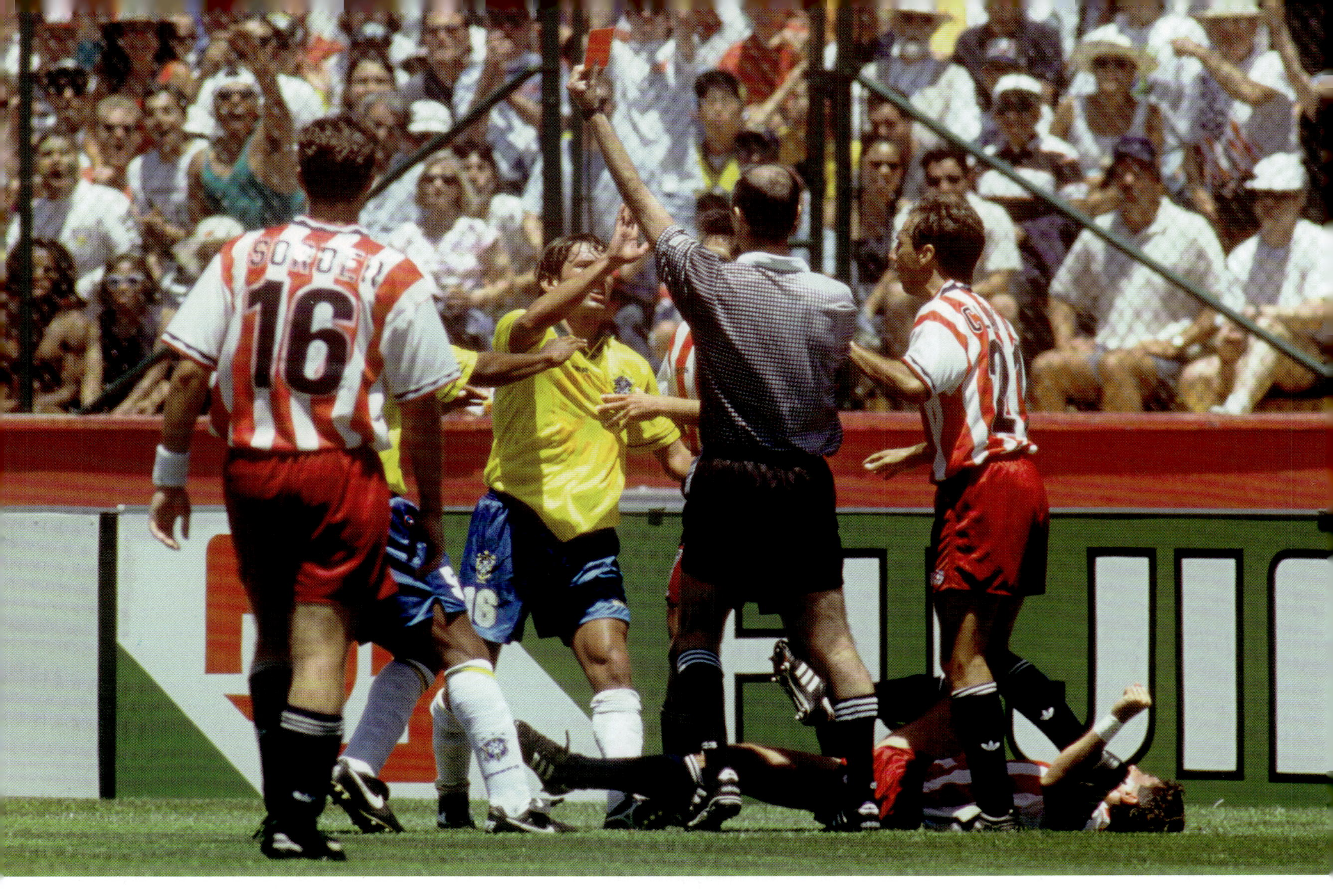

## KNOCKOUT STAGE
## ROUND OF 16

| | | |
|---|---|---|
| Romania 3 | 2 Argentina | |
| Sweden 3 | 1 Saudi Arabia | |
| Netherlands 2 | 0 Republic of Ireland | |
| Brazil 1 | 0 USA | |
| Bulgaria 1 | 1 Mexico | |
| | (3–1 on penalty kicks) | |
| Germany 3 | 2 Belgium | |
| Italy 2 | 1 Nigeria | |
| Spain 3 | 0 Switzerland | |

Brazil easily dominated possession versus the USA but lost left-back Leonardo when his vicious elbow swipe broke the jaw of American Tab Ramos. Despite playing a man down, the Brazilians kept up the pressure and finally broke through with a goal in the seventy-second minute. In the bottom half of the draw, the Italians trailed dynamic Nigeria 1–0 with just two minutes left when Italian star Roberto Baggio finally bagged his first goal of the tournament. Then, in extra time, Baggio slotted home a penalty kick to send Italy to the quarter-finals.

# QUARTER-FINALS

| | |
|---|---|
| Sweden 2 | 2 Romania |
| | (5–4 on penalty kicks) |
| Brazil 3 | 2 Netherlands |
| Bulgaria 2 | 1 Germany |
| Italy 2 | 1 Spain |

The Bulgarians became the Cup Cinderella team after reaching the semi-finals with impressive wins over Argentina, Mexico, and Germany, the latter a stirring come-from-behind quarter-final victory over the defending champions. For Italy, Roberto Baggio once again played the hero, scoring the winner against Spain with just two minutes left. In an exhilarating match, Brazil jumped ahead of the Netherlands 2–0 only to have the Dutch level the score with fourteen minutes to go. Five minutes later, Brazil's Branco launched a free-kick rocket from long range that sliced through a gap in the Dutch wall and whizzed just inside the far post for the win.

**OPPOSITE** *Brazil's Leonardo pleads against a red card after breaking the jaw of American defender Tab Ramos. Leonardo was suspended for an additional four games, meaning he could not return for the remainder of the Cup.*

**BELOW** *Daniel Prodan of Romania covers his eyes with his hands (and boots) after being eliminated by Sweden in a penalty shootout.*

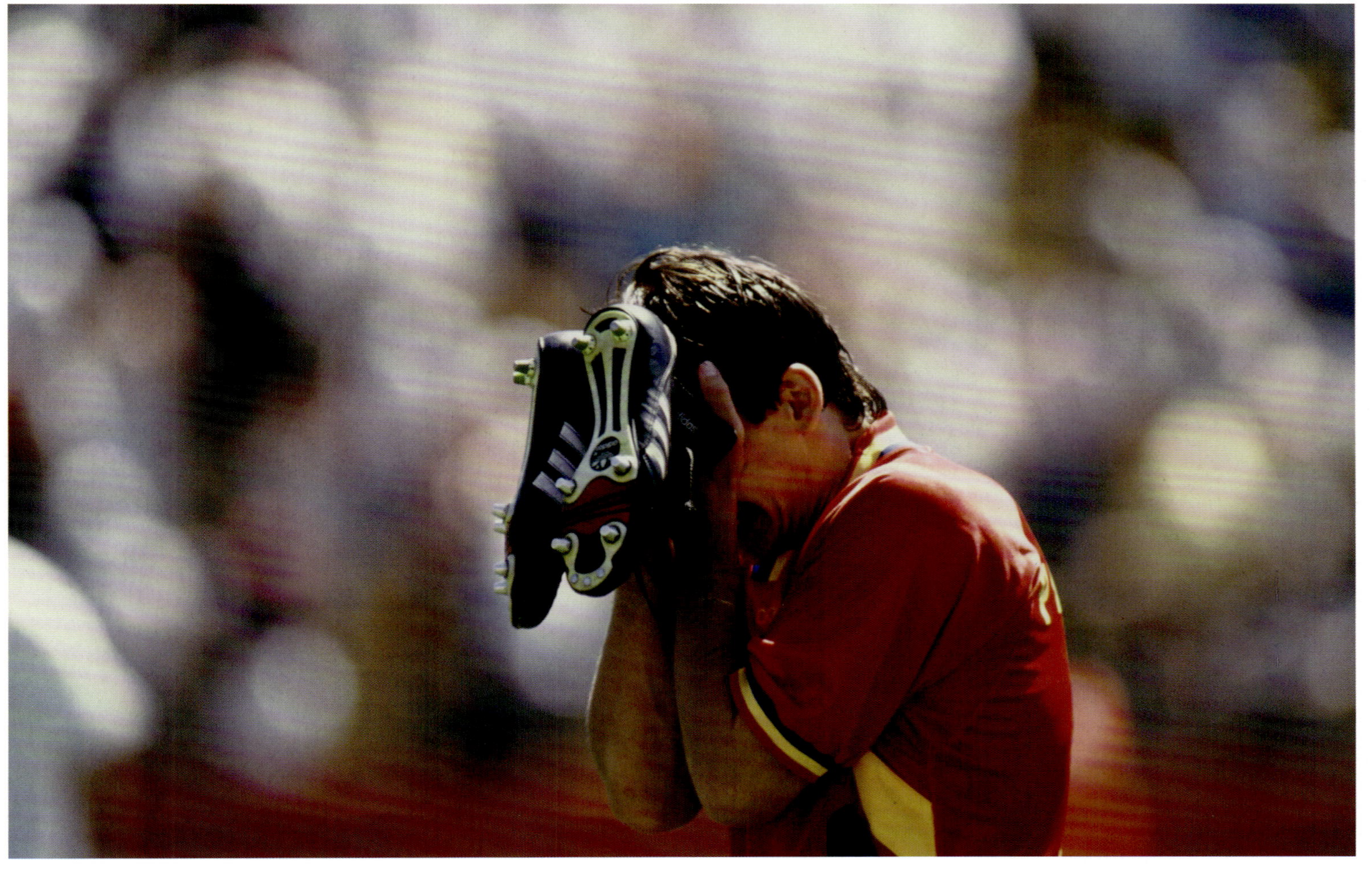

# SEMI-FINALS

Brazil 1 | 0 Sweden
Italy 2 | 1 Bulgaria

Roberto Baggio continued his mastery with two gorgeous goals in a four-minute span of the first half. Bulgaria scored a penalty, but the second half was another Italian defensive masterclass: its back line clinically defanged the Bulgarian attack to protect its 2–1 victory margin.

In the other semi-final, Sweden's captain Jonas Thern was sent off with a red card in the sixty-third minute of a scoreless struggle, leaving the Swedes with only ten on the pitch. This slight advantage was enough for the magnificent new Brazilian star Romário to penetrate with a brilliant dribbling run, cap it off with a lightning-quick jab to the far corner, and deliver a 1–0 win.

**BELOW** *Italy protagonist Roberto Baggio skilfully evades Bulgaria's Trifon Ivanov in the semi-finals.*

**OPPOSITE** *Iconic Italian defender Paolo Maldini dispossesses Brazilian striker Romário, who had five goals on the tournament.*

**FOLLOWING SPREAD** *An aerial view of the 1994 World Cup Final at the Rose Bowl in Pasadena, California. The match boasted an attendance of 94,194.*

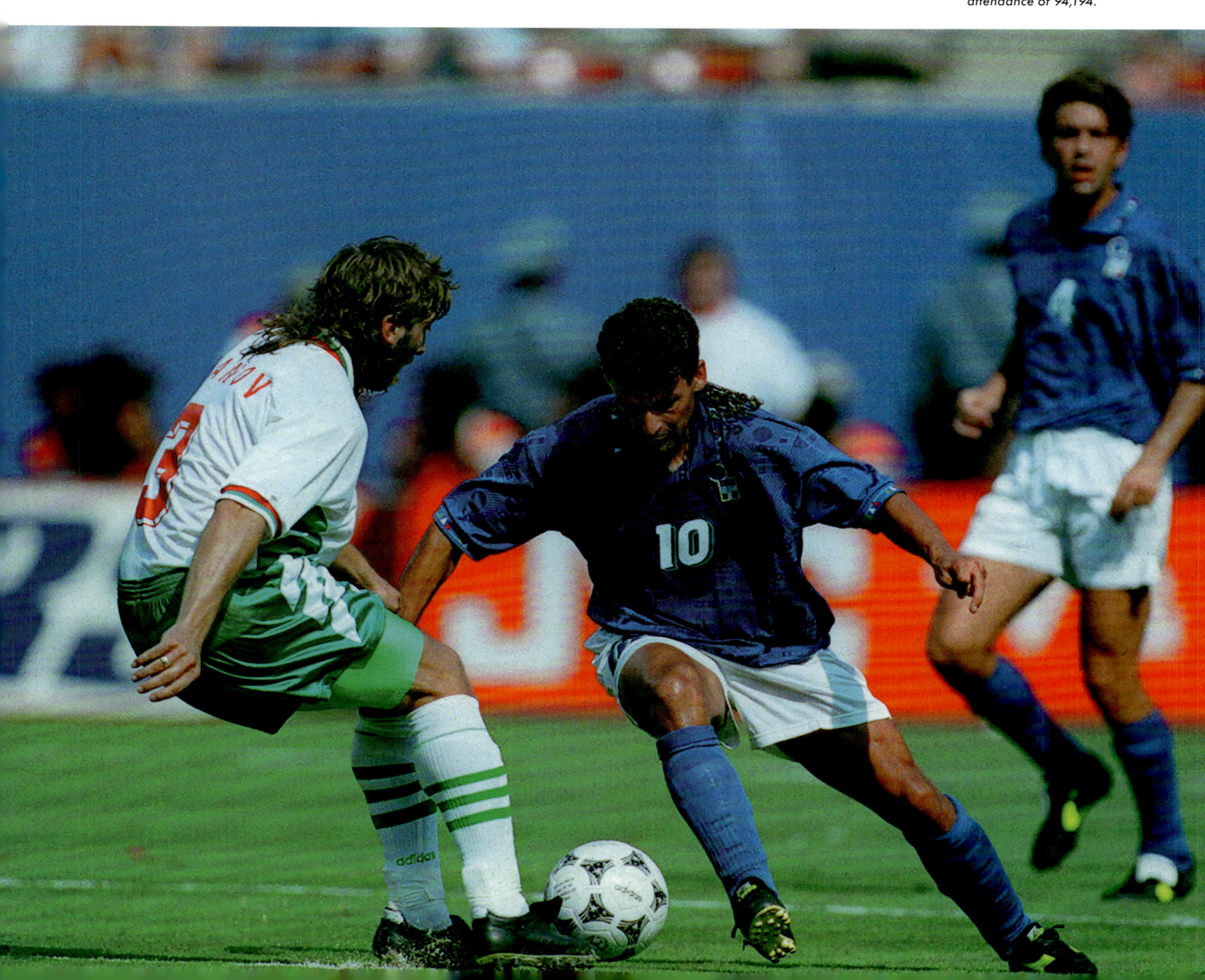

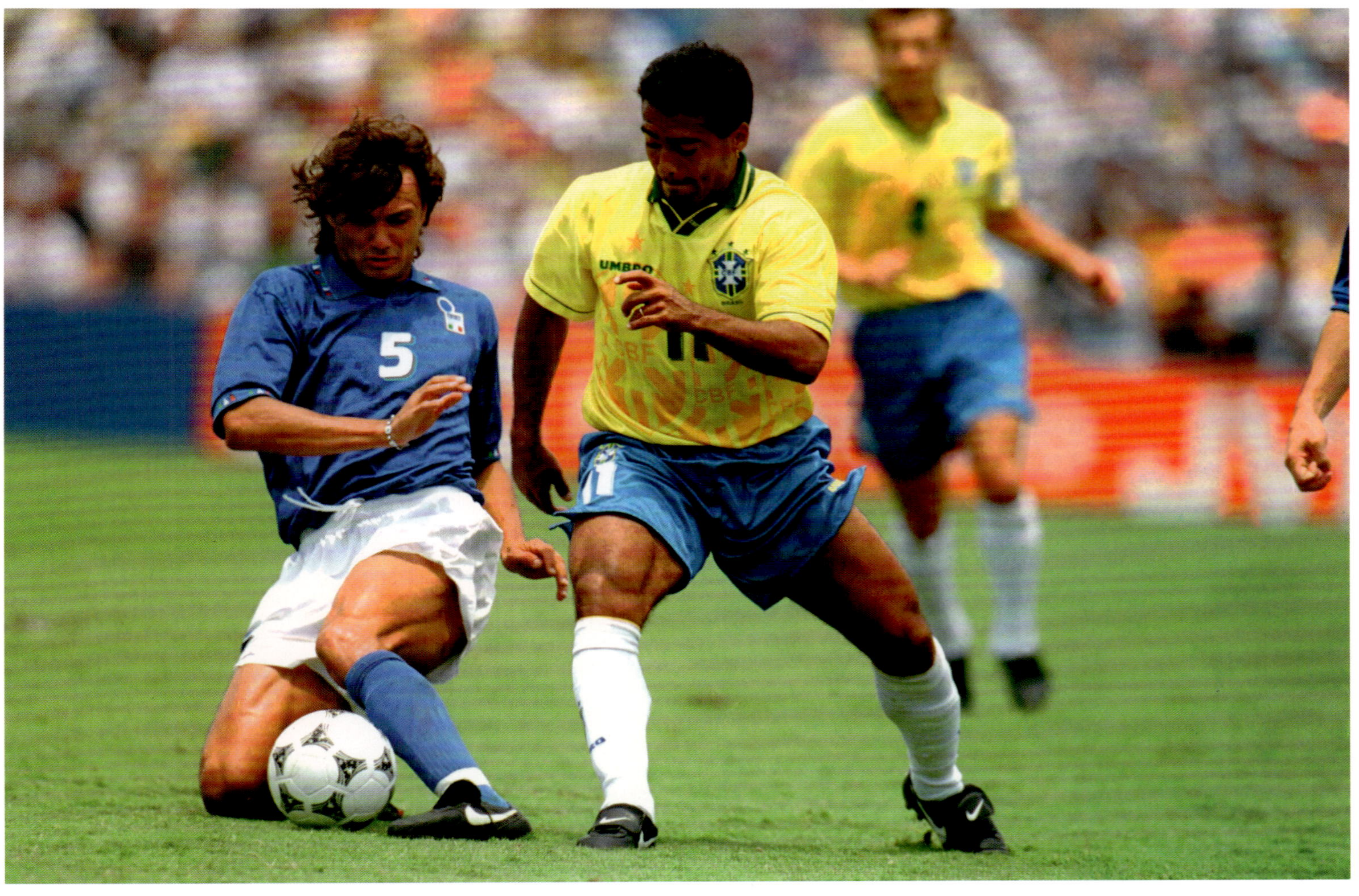

## FINAL

Brazil 0 | 0 Italy
| (3–2 on penalty kicks)
| (First Place)
Sweden 4 | 0 Bulgaria
| (Third Place)

Impressive Sweden made quick work of the third-place match, scoring three goals in just the first ten minutes of the match and ending the enchanted Bulgarian run on a bit of a sour note. In the Cup Final, football bluebloods Brazil and Italy met on the pitch at the epic Rose Bowl in Pasadena, California, though the Final itself was a bit less awe-inspiring. One commentator called it 'a tedious match devoid of chances'. Both sides played conservatively, nobody scored, and after regulation and extra time, the two under-delivering giants stumbled into the first penalty-kick shootout in World Cup Final history.

The dramatic tension of a shootout in front of 90,000 spectators and a live worldwide TV audience of two billion with nothing less than the World Cup hanging in the balance?

Well, it was certainly immense, and quite unprecedented in the history of global sports. Of course, it came down to the last kick. Unfortunately for Italy, Roberto Baggio, the man whose marvellous goals in the knockouts had lifted his team into the Final, missed Italy's final shot and handed Brazil a 3–2 victory in the shootout.

By almost any measure, FIFA's experiment with American hosting was a grand success. New rules boosting offence and faster play bumped the per-game scoring average from the dismal 2.21 four years earlier to a much more satisfying and entertaining 2.71. America's marketing juggernaut produced posters, apparel, and other themed merchandise that helped imprint iconic images of the World Cup in the global zeitgeist and 'spread the fever'.

And to this day, the 1994 tournament's total attendance of almost 3.6 million (average of 70,000 per match) remains the most in World Cup history—even with FIFA expanding the number of teams from twenty-four to thirty-six in 1998, boosting the number of matches played from fifty-two to sixty-four.

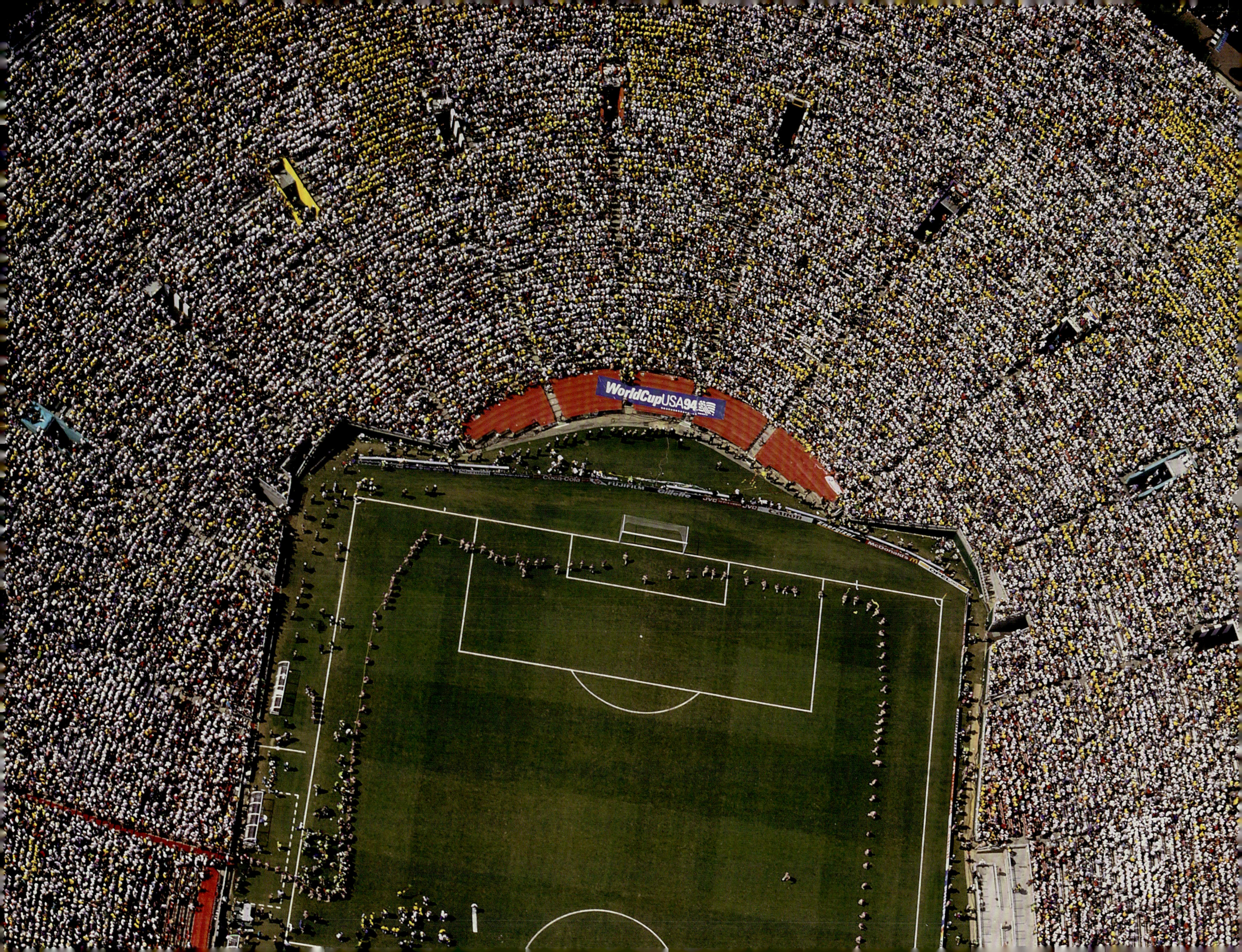

WorldCupUSA94

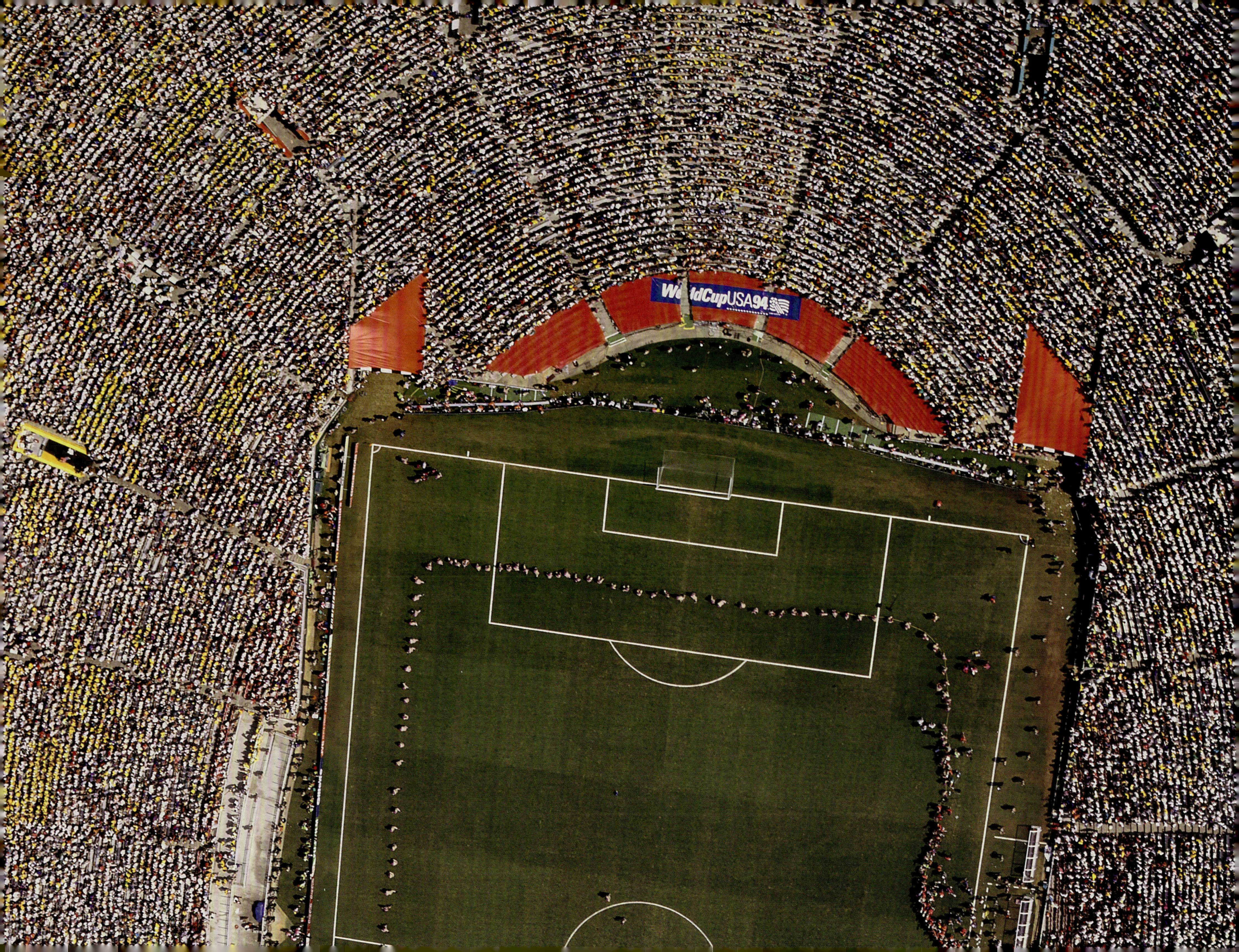

WorldCupUSA94

# THE MAN WHO DIED STANDING

**Nobody had a better** individual tournament performance in USA '94 than Roberto Baggio. Clinically, and with brilliant flair, he scored the game-winning goals in *all three* of Italy's knockout-stage matches leading up to the final. Baggio knocked in five of his team's six goals in that trio of high-pressure contests: both of Italy's goals against Nigeria in the Round of 16, the game winner against Spain in the quarter-final, and then both of Italy's goals against Bulgaria in the semi-final. By any measure, Baggio's dazzling championship run was among the very best the World Cup has ever seen, before or since.

Unfortunately, he'll also be remembered for his demeanor at the very last moment of the tournament — the last shot of the Cup Final shootout. After four rounds of the shootout, Brazil had converted three and missed one, whereas Italy had converted two and missed two. Thus, Brazil was up 3–2 as Roberto Baggio stepped up to take Italy's fifth round shot, which he needed to convert to keep Italy alive. He looked calm, took a breath, stepped to the ball . . . and launched it high over the crossbar. Game over.

Baggio stood at the spot for eight long minutes after the miss, stoic and unmoving. That moment became iconic, and he was soon dubbed 'The Man Who Died Standing'. It's unclear who first coined the phrase, but it soon became a universal designation. To his credit, Baggio handled the moment with grace, made no excuses, and went on to play several more years of top-level football for both club and country.

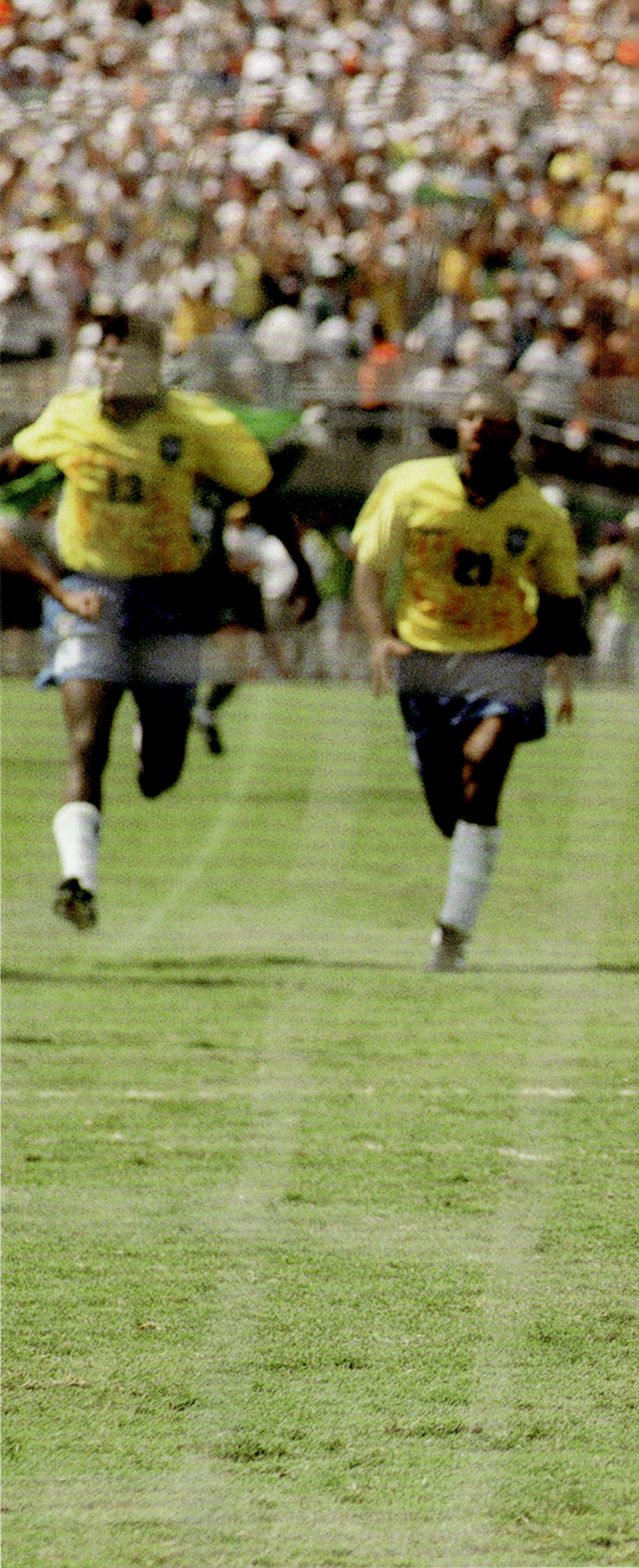

**OPPOSITE** *Roberto Baggio (far right), the man who died standing after missing his crucial penalty kick in the final. Behind him, victorious Brazilians leap with exuberance.*

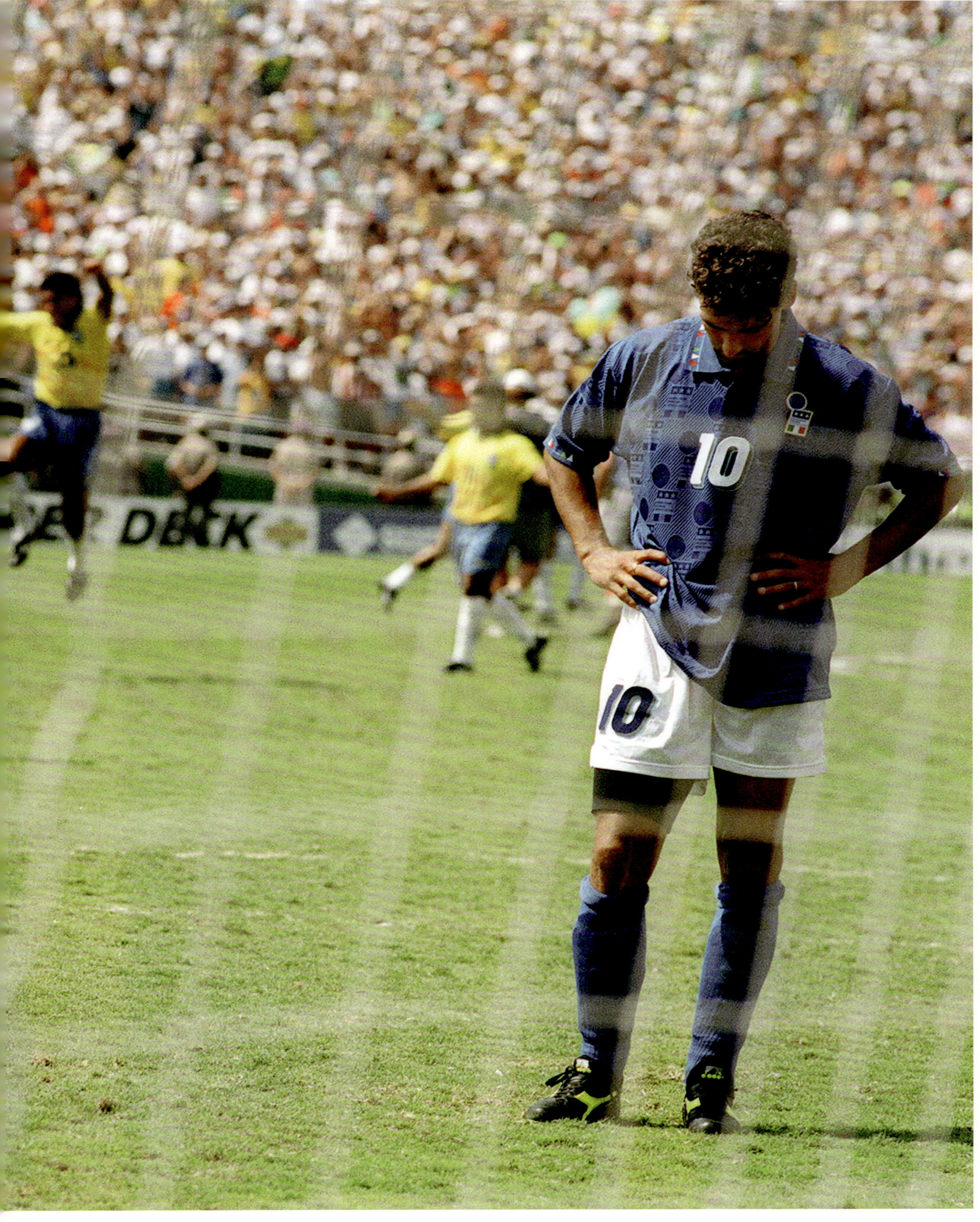

# 1998



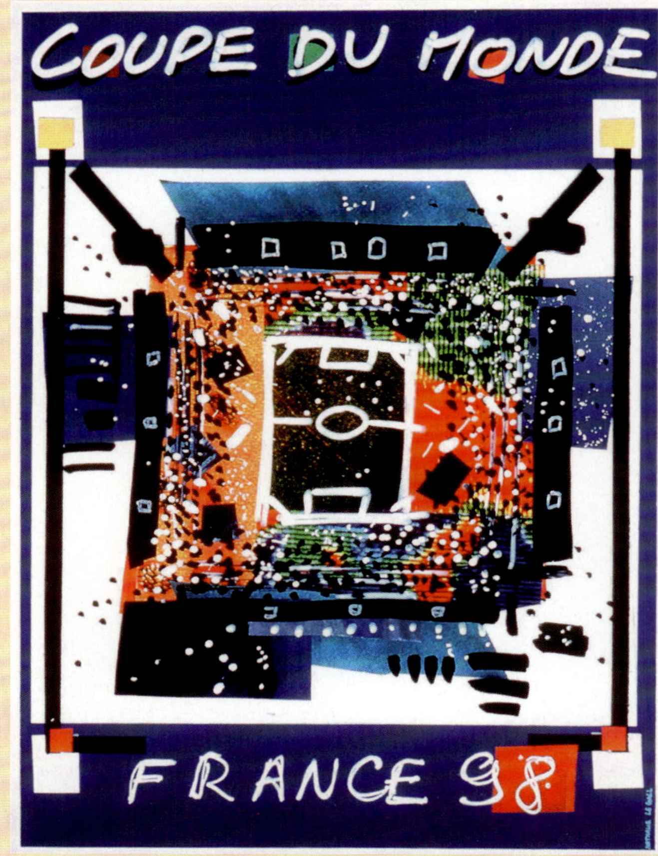


**The World Cup came back** to French soil in 1998, exactly sixty years after the country's first stint as tournament host. This time, of course, France (and the world at large) faced far less uncertain circumstances. Back in 1938, France was barely two years away from Nazi invasion and occupation. The centrepiece of the new French bid was a pledge to build a brand-new national stadium, and so the flagship Stade de France, with a capacity of over 80,000, was erected in the Parisian suburb of Saint-Denis. The Cup's founding father, Jules Rimet, would have been thrilled to see his home country erect such a magnificent edifice, organise such a widely praised international event, and, best of all, finally achieve such a sublime result.

**ABOVE** *Paris native Nathalie Le Gall's design for the official 1998 World Cup poster.*

**OPPOSITE** *Filip De Wilde, Belgium's goalkeeper, stretches out in a fruitless attempt to save Alberto García Aspe's penalty for Mexico.*

## MORE TEAMS, MORE 'FAIR PLAY'

**FIFA expanded the field** from twenty-four to thirty-two teams, assigned to eight groups of four in the group stage, which helped widen the geographic representation. As for style of play, FIFA's rules committees were still concerned about gamesmanship and reserved tactics that rewarded rough and physical teams. The new 'back-pass rule' added in 1992 had helped reduce stalling tactics, but for France '98, FIFA's Sports Medical Committee wanted to address player safety. As such, a new tool was created for referees to employ: aggressive tackles from behind were now outright banned and eligible for an immediate red-card expulsion. And to reduce the possibility of teams playing short-handed due to injuries, FIFA increased the number of substitutions allowed per match from two to three. One other interesting experiment was the introduction of a sudden-death format for all knockout matches called the 'golden goal rule'. Under the old rules, teams tied after regular time would play two full fifteen-minute periods of extra time, regardless of how many goals were scored. But under the new rule, the first goal scored in extra time would instantly win the match for the scoring team and end the game. Though thrilling, the 'golden goal' would be discontinued after the 2002 tournament due to concerns over fairness.

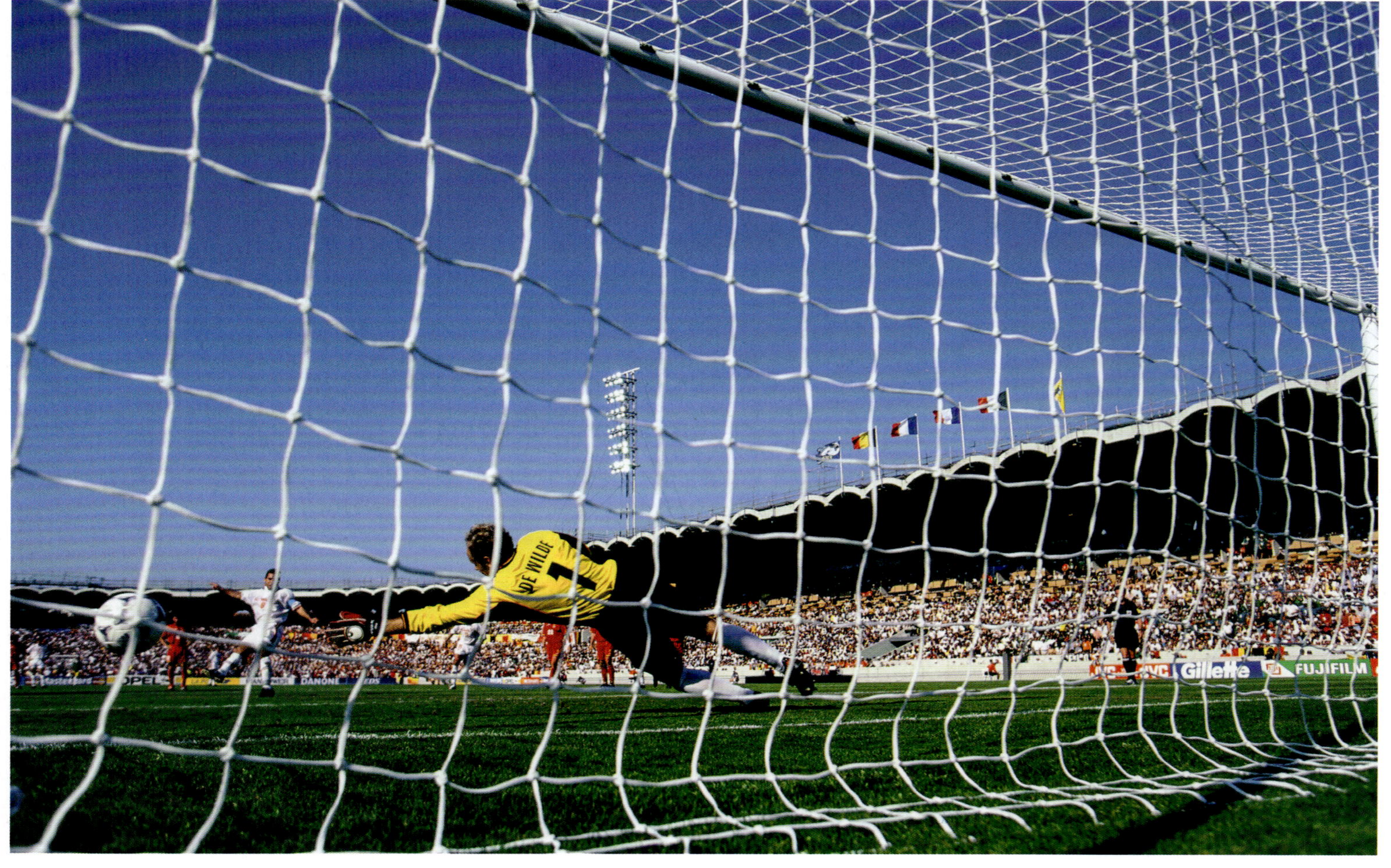

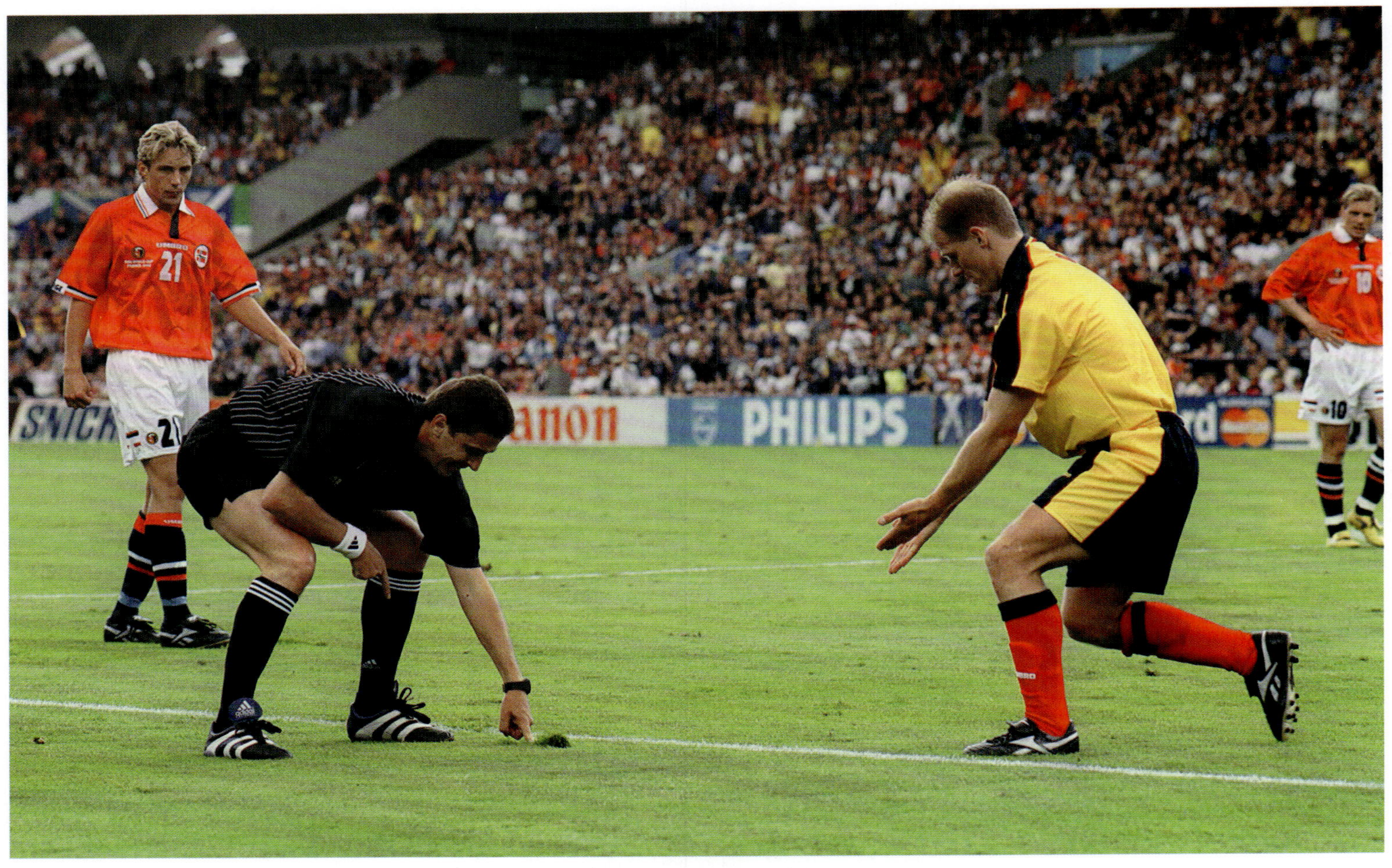

## Tournament: GROUP STAGE

**Having finally found a format** that was both popular and successful, Italy 1990 followed the same format as the previous Cup. It would also end with a rematch of the previous Cup Final, Argentina versus West Germany.



| | | |
|---:|---|---|
| Brazil 2 | 1 | Scotland |
| Morocco 2 | 2 | Norway |
| Scotland 1 | 1 | Norway |
| Brazil 3 | 0 | Morocco |
| Morocco 3 | 0 | Scotland |
| Norway 2 | 1 | Brazil |

***Advanced to Knockout Stage: Brazil, Norway***

Reigning-champion Brazil, featuring a new rising superstar in twenty-one-year-old Ronaldo. The Seleção started off strong with two solid wins (including a 3–0 rout of Morocco that saw goals from all three of Ronaldo, Rivaldo, and Bebeto) but ended group play with a surprising 2–1 loss to Norway, who in turn finished in second behind the Brazilians.

**ABOVE** *Scotland's Gordon Durie protests referee Lázsló Vágner's decision to place the foul just outside Norway's penalty box.*

**OPPOSITE** *French wunderkind and future legend, Thierry Henry attempts to beat Saudi Arabia's Abdullah Zubromawi in an aerial challenge. Henry would notch two goals in the match.*

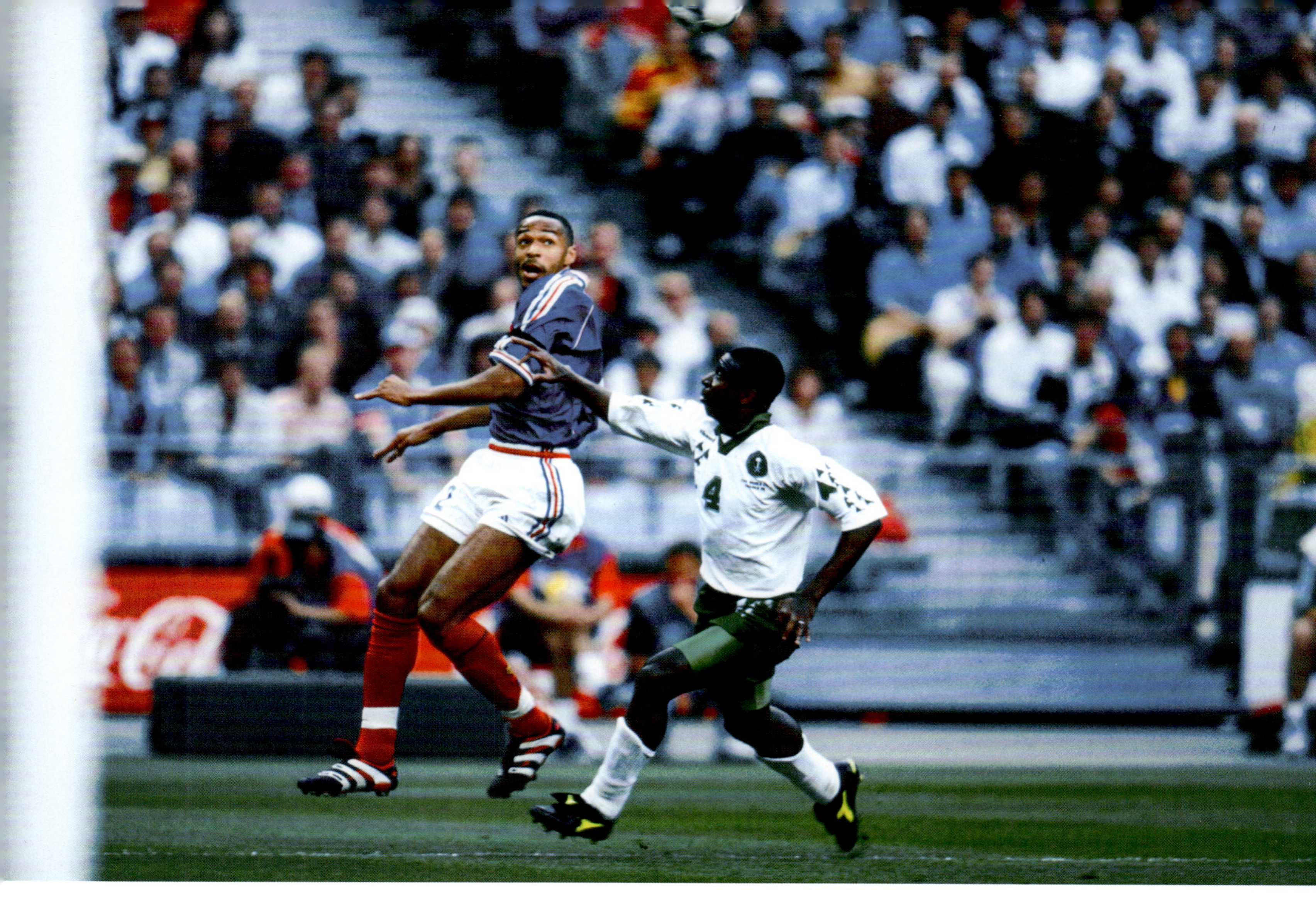

## GROUP B: ITALY, CHILE, AUSTRIA, CAMEROON

| | | |
|---:|:---|:---|
| Italy | 2 | 2 Chile |
| Cameroon | 1 | 1 Austria |
| Chile | 1 | 1 Austria |
| Italy | 3 | 0 Cameroon |
| Italy | 2 | 1 Austria |
| Chile | 1 | 1 Cameroon |

***Advanced to Knockout Stage: Italy, Chile***

Italy swept through undefeated to win the group. Their closest match was a 2–2 draw with Chile that included a late penalty strike from Roberto Baggio, allowing him to atone (somewhat) for his miss in the 1994 Cup Final. Three straight draws boosted Chile into second place and the knockout stage.

## GROUP C: FRANCE, DENMARK, SOUTH AFRICA, SAUDI ARABIA

| | | |
|---:|:---|:---|
| Denmark | 1 | 0 Saudi Arabia |
| France | 3 | 0 South Africa |
| South Africa | 1 | 1 Denmark |
| France | 4 | 0 Saudi Arabia |
| France | 2 | 1 Denmark |
| South Africa | 2 | 2 Saudi Arabia |

***Advanced to Knockout Stage: France, Denmark***

Led by three Thierry Henry goals, France delighted the home crowds with two easy victories and a close win over sturdy Denmark, who also advanced. A red card and two-game suspension to the brilliant but incendiary star Zinedine Zidane in the 4–0 thrashing of Saudi Arabia was the only French setback. South Africa, readmitted to FIFA in 1992 after finally ending apartheid, made a solid World Cup debut with two ties and a loss to the eventual champion.

### GROUP D: NIGERIA, PARAGUAY, SPAIN, BULGARIA

| | | |
|---|---|---|
| Paraguay 0 | 0 | Bulgaria |
| Nigeria 3 | 2 | Spain |
| Nigeria 1 | 0 | Bulgaria |
| Spain 0 | 0 | Paraguay |
| Paraguay 3 | 1 | Nigeria |
| Spain 6 | 1 | Bulgaria |

**Advanced to Knockout Stage: Nigeria, Paraguay**

Nigeria continued its string of strong World Cup showings, earning six points with victories over Spain, the top seed in the group, and Bulgaria. Paraguay beat the Nigerians but draws in the other two fixtures put Los Guaraníes in second place. Spain washed out, once again failing to live up to pre-tourney expectations.

### GROUP E: NETHERLANDS, MEXICO, BELGIUM, SOUTH KOREA

| | | |
|---|---|---|
| Mexico 3 | 1 | South Korea |
| Netherlands 0 | 0 | Belgium |
| Belgium 2 | 2 | Mexico |
| Netherlands 5 | 0 | South Korea |
| Netherlands 2 | 2 | Mexico |
| Belgium 1 | 1 | South Korea |

**Advanced to Knockout Stage: Netherlands, Mexico**

The Netherlands and Mexico tied their match 2–2 and their point totals at 5. The Dutch won the group due on goal differential, but a resilient Mexico moved on, too. Extremely resilient, in fact: both of Mexico's draws saw them recover from 2–0 deficits.

### GROUP F: GERMANY, FR YUGOSLAVIA, IRAN, USA

| | | |
|---|---|---|
| FR Yugoslavia 1 | 0 | Iran |
| Germany 2 | 0 | USA |
| Germany 2 | 2 | FR Yugoslavia |
| Iran 2 | 1 | USA |
| Germany 2 | 0 | Iran |
| FR Yugoslavia 1 | 0 | USA |

**Advanced to Knockout Stage: Germany, FR Yugoslavia**

Germany and FR Yugoslavia dominated the group and finished tied on points, with Germany getting the top slot on goal differential. In their heated head-to-head matchup, the Yugoslavs grabbed a 2–0 lead but gave up an own goal at 72' followed by a German equaliser just six minutes later for the 2–2 draw. The USA came into the tournament with high hopes but suffered three losses and managed only one goal.

### GROUP G: ROMANIA, ENGLAND, COLOMBIA, TUNISIA

| | | |
|---|---|---|
| England 2 | 0 | Tunisia |
| Romania 1 | 0 | Colombia |
| Colombia 1 | 0 | Tunisia |
| Romania 2 | 1 | England |
| England 2 | 0 | Colombia |
| Romania 1 | 1 | Tunisia |

**Advanced to Knockout Stage: Romania, England**

Fielding a balanced team led by the veteran Alan Shearer and powered by the young core of Paul Scholes, David Beckham, Gary Neville, and the even younger Michael Owen (just eighteen years old), England played well in a pair of 2–0 wins. Most expected them to win all three matches…but Romania's Dan Petrescu had other ideas. The outside midfielder stole their showdown match with a dramatic ninetieth-minute goal to win the game and top the group.

### GROUP H: ARGENTINA, CROATIA, JAMAICA, JAPAN

| | | |
|---|---|---|
| Argentina 1 | 0 | Japan |
| Croatia 3 | 1 | Jamaica |
| Croatia 1 | 0 | Japan |
| Argentina 5 | 0 | Jamaica |
| Argentina 1 | 0 | Croatia |
| Jamaica 2 | 1 | Japan |

**Advanced to Knockout Stage: Argentina, Croatia**

Argentina won every match, delighting crowds with a return to their old brand of attacking football, and cruised past three opponents making first-ever World Cup appearances. Argentine forward Gabriel Batistuta got off to a blazing start with four goals, including a hat-trick against Jamaica. Croatia looked strong, though, and gave the Argentines a good challenge to finish second in the group.

**OPPOSITE TOP** Nigeria's Daniel Amokachi throws his arms upwards after Victor Ikpeba scores for a 1–0 lead over Bulgaria.

**OPPOSITE BOTTOM** Viorel Moldovan of Romania (centre) elated after scoring against a highly favoured England side. His teammate Dan Petrescu would later net a ninetieth-minute winner for a stunning 2–1 victory.

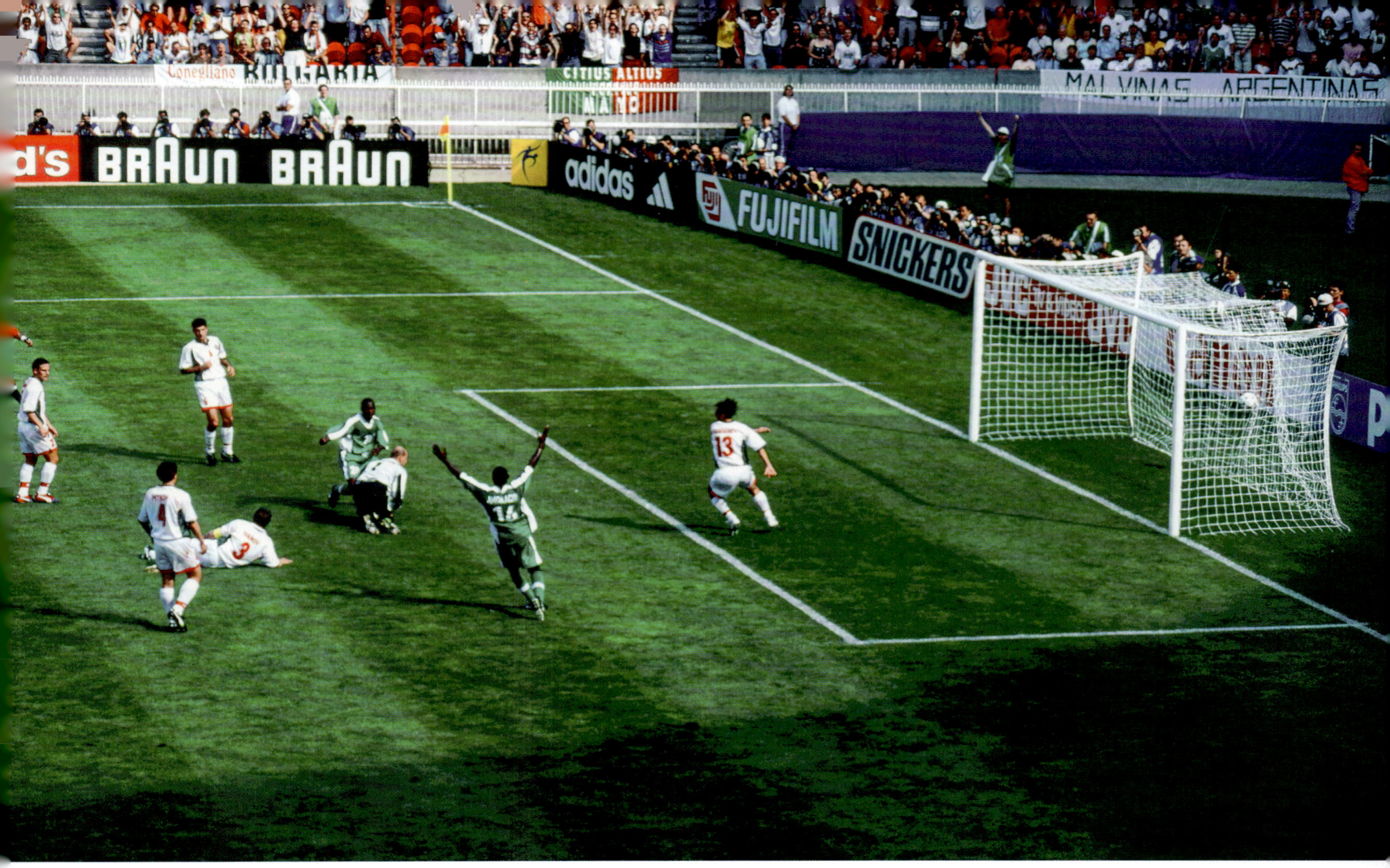
BULGARIA
CITIUS ALTIUS
MALVINAS ARGENTINAS
BRAUN BRAUN
adidas
FUJIFILM
SNICKERS

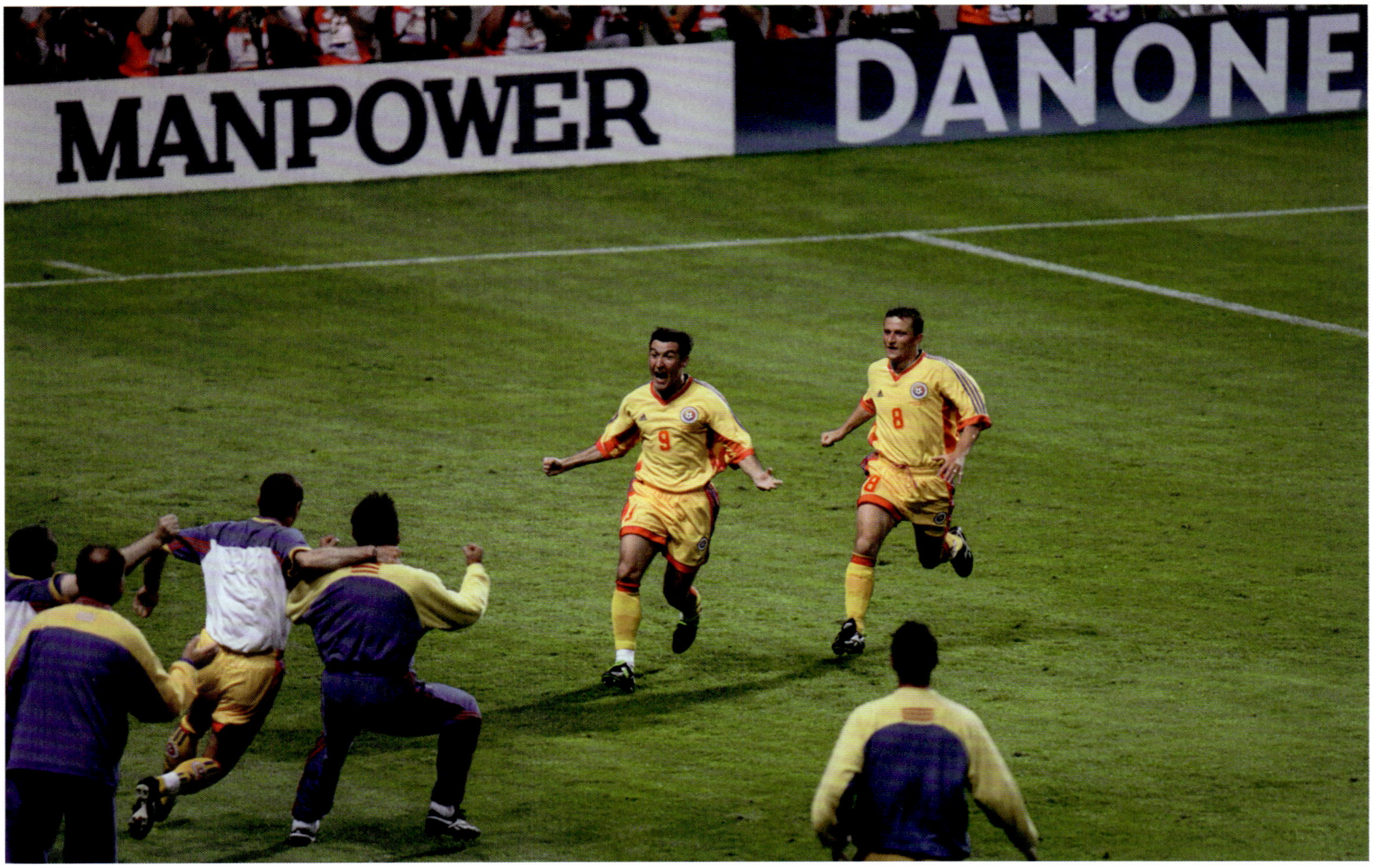
MANPOWER
DANONE

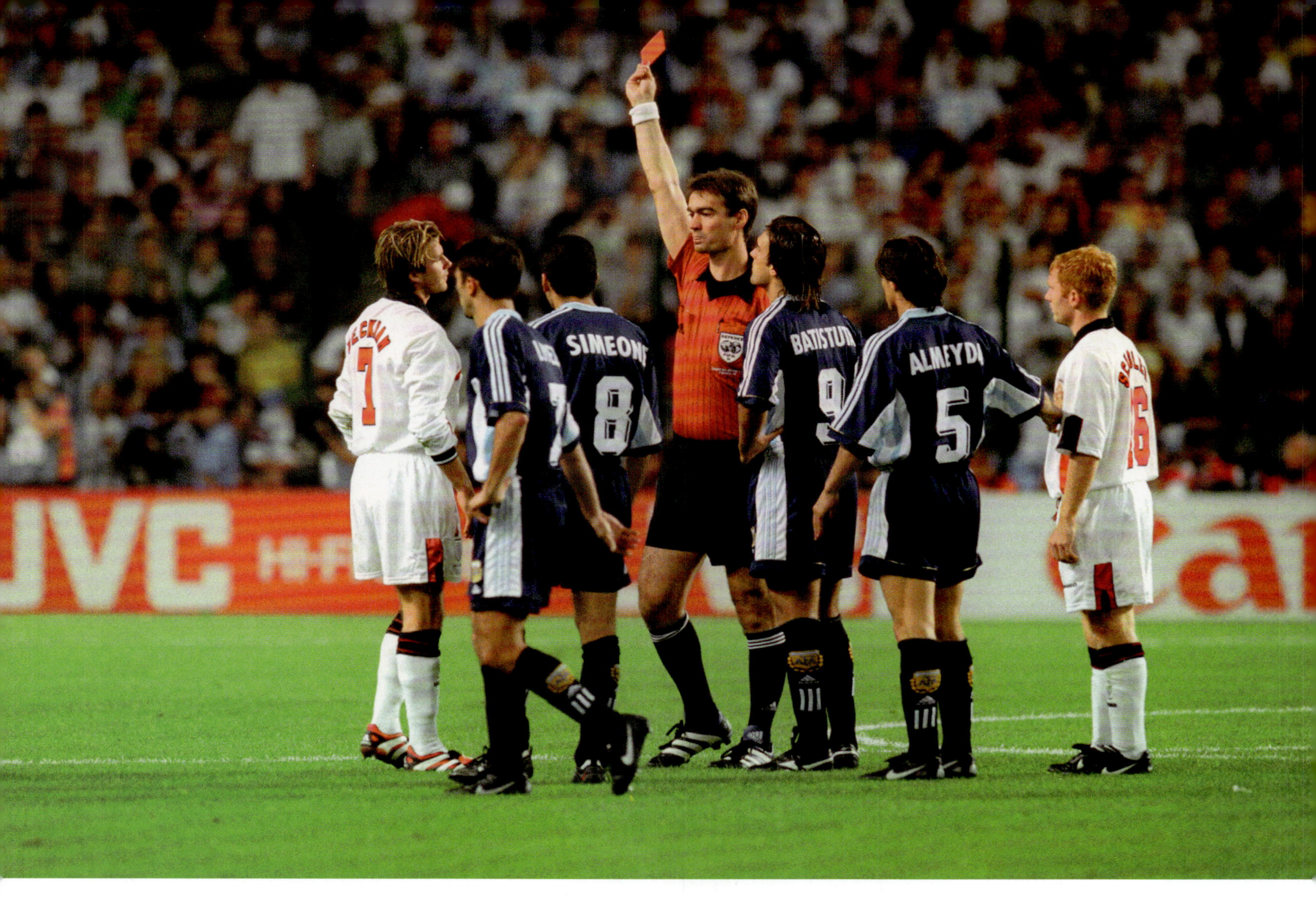

## KNOCKOUT STAGE
## ROUND OF 16

| | |
|---|---|
| Brazil 4 | 1 Chile |
| Denmark 4 | 1 Nigeria |
| Netherlands 2 | 1 FR Yugoslavia |
| Argentina 2 | 2 England |
| | (4–3 on penalty kicks) |
| Italy 1 | 0 Norway |
| France 1 | 0 Paraguay |
| | (after sudden-death extra time) |
| Germany 2 | 1 Mexico |
| Croatia 1 | 0 Romania |

Italian forward Christian Vieri scored his fifth goal of the tournament to give his side the 1–0 win over Norway, Ronaldo scored a brace to pace Brazil's 4–1 thrashing of Chile, and Denmark easily brushed aside Nigeria by the same score. England, despite a brilliant solo run by the young Michael Owen in the sixteenth minute, came up short in a nail-biter penalty shootout, losing to Argentina on the final kick. England's star David Beckham was red-carded early in the second half for a foolish retaliation, forcing his team to play with ten all the way to the shootout. Back home, Beckham effigies were angrily burned.

Germany had to claw back late after falling behind Mexico and the Netherlands needed a stoppage-time goal to beat Yugoslavia. But perhaps the round's most nerve-racking match was France's deadly duel with Paraguay. With the score tied 0–0 in the second extra-time period, French defender Laurent Blanc finally scored the World Cup's first-ever golden goal to end the match and give the Cup hosts a hard-earned 1–0 victory.

# QUARTER-FINALS

| | |
|---|---|
| France 0 | 0 Italy |
| | (4–3 on penalty kicks) |
| Brazil 3 | 2 Denmark |
| Netherlands 2 | 1 Argentina |
| Croatia 3 | 0 Germany |

A tense 0–0 tie sent Italy and France to a shootout. With France leading 4–3 going to the tenth kick, Italy's Luigi Di Biagio banged his shot off the crossbar and the hosts moved on. Croatia provided the biggest surprise of the round, dismantling Germany 3–0. An eighty-fifth-minute goal by Davor Šuker was his fourth of the tournament. Denmark and Brazil fought a seesaw battle, but Rivaldo's spectacular brace was the difference in Brazil's 3–2 victory.

And in perhaps the best and most dramatic finish of the entire tournament, Netherlands captain Frank de Boer lofted a towering sixty-yard pass deep into the box in the ninetieth minute of a 1–1 tie with Argentina. There, Dutch striker Dennis Bergkamp set the ball down with a perfect feathered touch while in full sprint, tapped inside the last defender, and pushed a precise shot past the keeper to send his team into the semi-finals.

**OPPOSITE** *Danish referee Kim Milton Nielsen shows English star David Beckham a red card in the forty-seventh minute against Argentina.*

**BELOW** *Croatian players celebrate after scoring in their upset 3–0 demolition of Germany.*

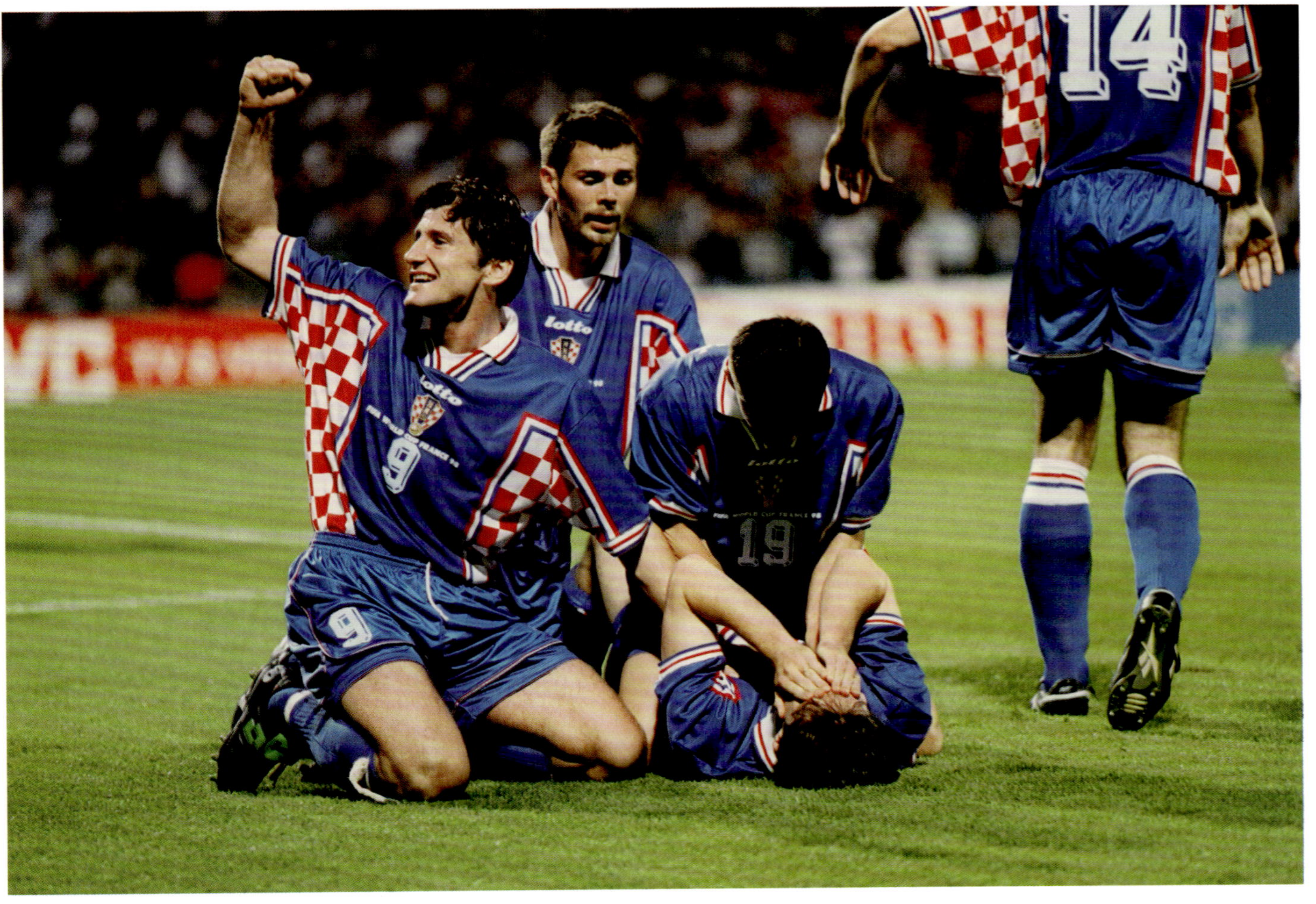

## SEMI-FINALS

Brazil 1 | 1 Netherlands
(4–2 on penalty kicks)
France 2 | 1 Croatia

The Netherlands and Brazil punched and counterpunched
to a 1–1 draw at the end of extra time. In the shootout, Brazil
displayed surgical precision, netting all four of its penalty
shots, whereas the Dutch missed their last two. In the other
semi-final, Croatia drew first blood—courtesy of Davor Šuker,
of course, his fifth tournament goal—but just one minute
later, French outside-back Lilian Thuram made a run into
the Croatia box, received a perfect through-pass, and slotted
it past the diving keeper. Then in the sixty-ninth minute,
Thuram made another wide run, pounced on a misplayed
ball just outside the box, and hammered home a left-footed
shot for the lead. The French held on and advanced to their
first-ever Cup Final.

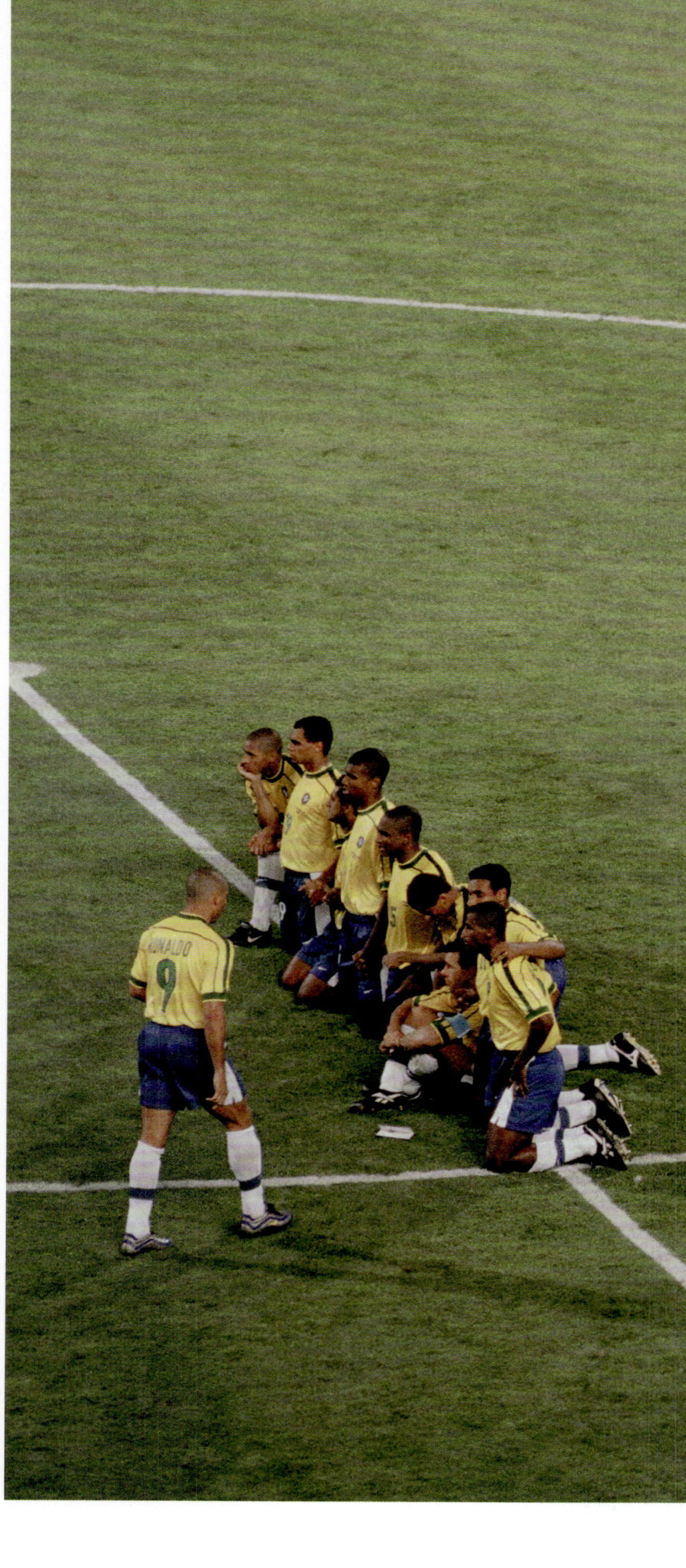

**RIGHT** *Brazil (left) and the
Netherlands (right) during the
semi-final penalty shootout.*

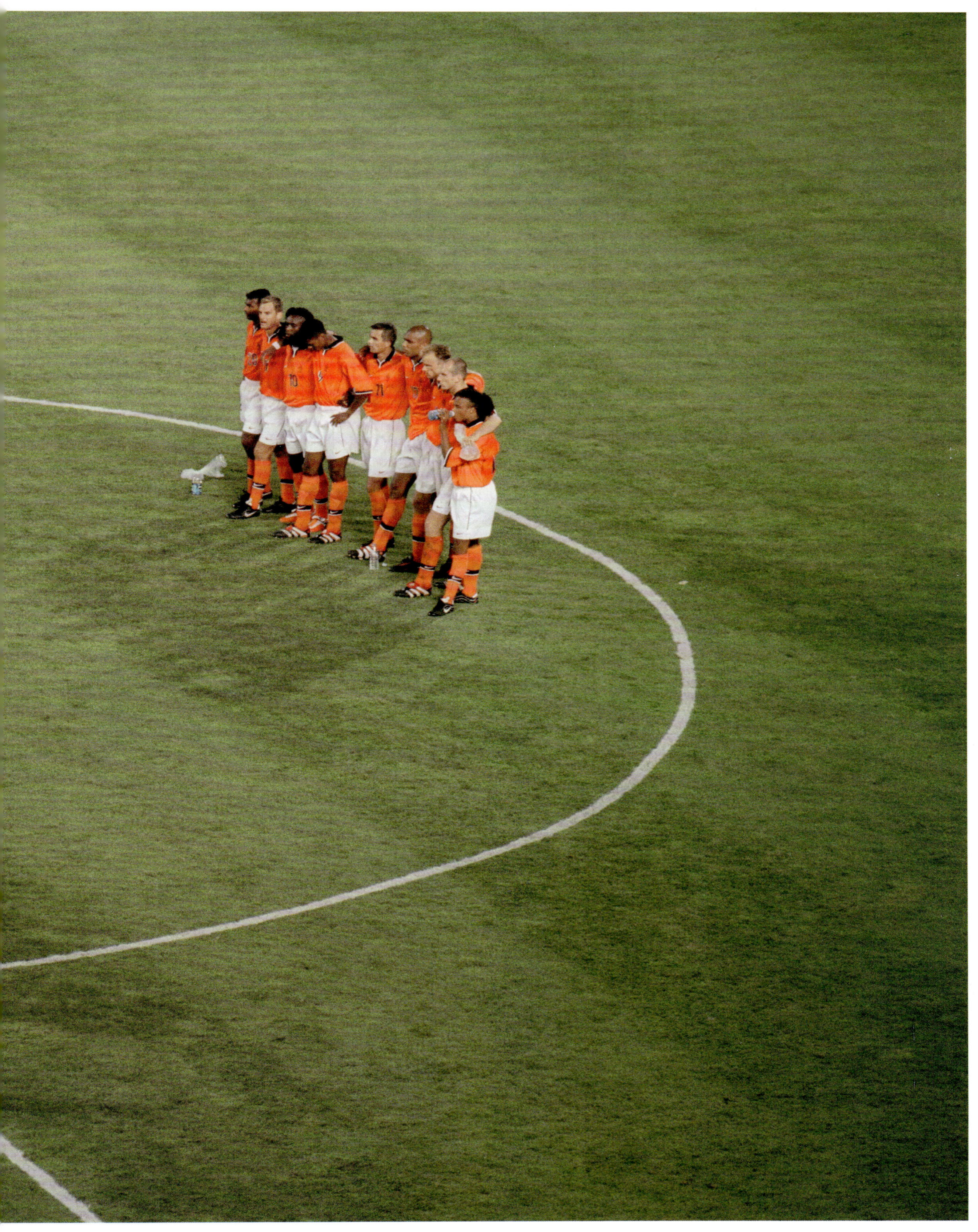

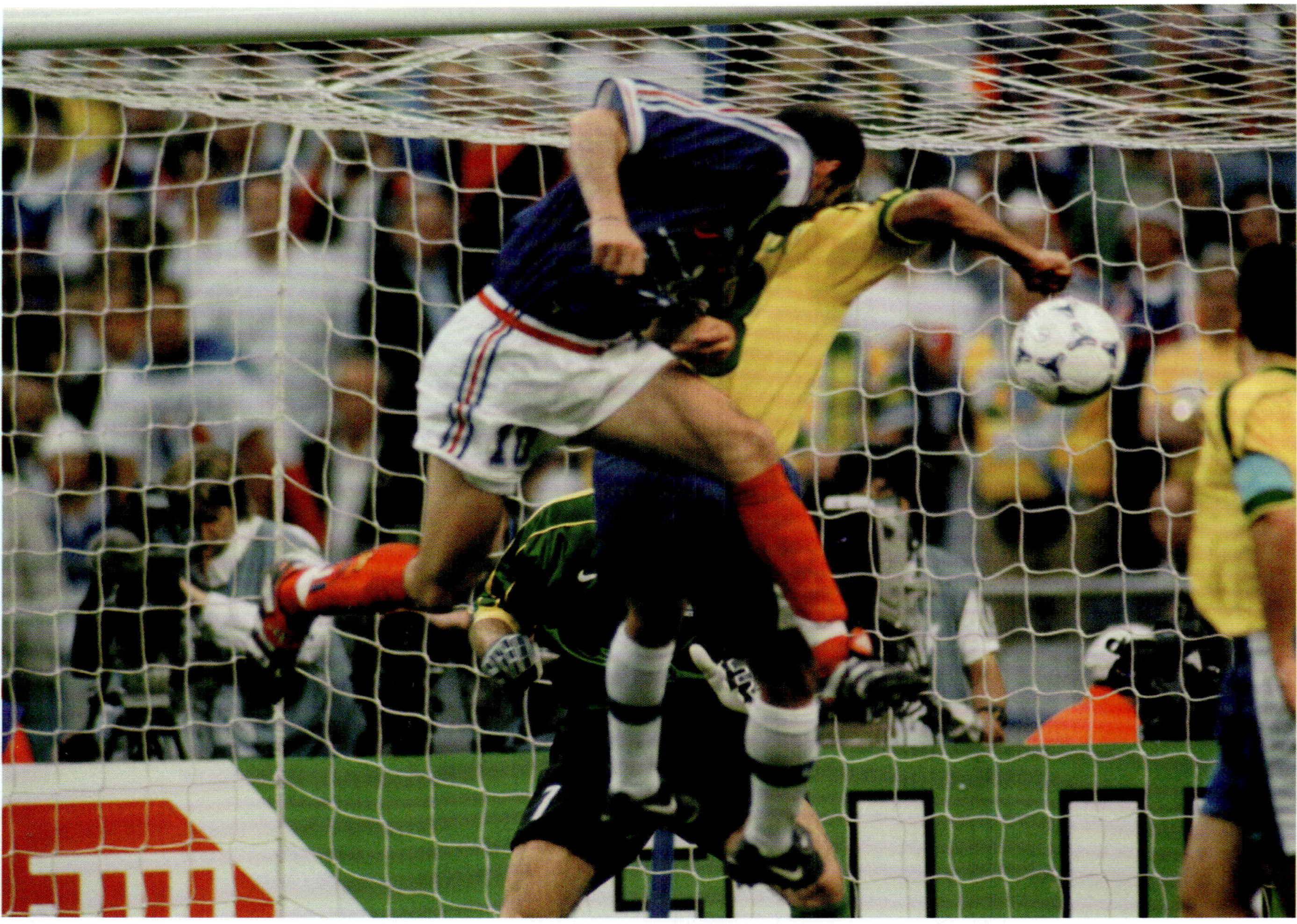

## MASTER OF THE AIR

**Zinedine Zidane's unique combination** of flair, vision, and power made him one of the greatest attacking mid-fielders in football history. Throughout the 1998 World Cup, he dominated the central third of the pitch, helping France control the pace of every match. With Zidane on the prowl, the French gave up just a single goal in group play and then conceded only one more goal in all four knockout matches combined.

But for as superlative as Zidane was with the ball at his feet, his path to victory against Brazil's mighty 1998 squad came through the air. In the first half of the Cup Final, his two scoring headers off corner kicks were near clones of each other, one from each side. In both cases, the tenacious Zidane simply outmuscled the defenders and banged home a vicious header just inside the near post that left the Brazilian keeper flat-footed.

## FINAL

| France 3 | 0 Brazil |
| --- | --- |
| | (First Place) |
| Croatia 2 | 1 Netherlands |
| | (Third Place) |

In the third-place game, Croatia's winning goal was, once again, scored by Davor Šuker, earning him the Golden Shoe Award as top scorer. The World Cup Final, played in the magnificent Stade de France, ended up an iconic aerial clinic by the hard-headed French superstar Zinedine Zidane. Twice in the first half, Zidane nailed perfect headers to give his country the lead. In the end, France added one more, overwhelming Brazil 3–0 for France's first title. A stunning, overdue triumph for the host nation.

**THIS SPREAD** *The final in which Zinedine Zidane entered the French pantheon. His first header goal (above) was nearly identical to his second (opposite), save that it came from the opposite corner.*

'Zidane's unique combination of flair, vision, and power made him one of the greatest attacking midfielders in football history.'

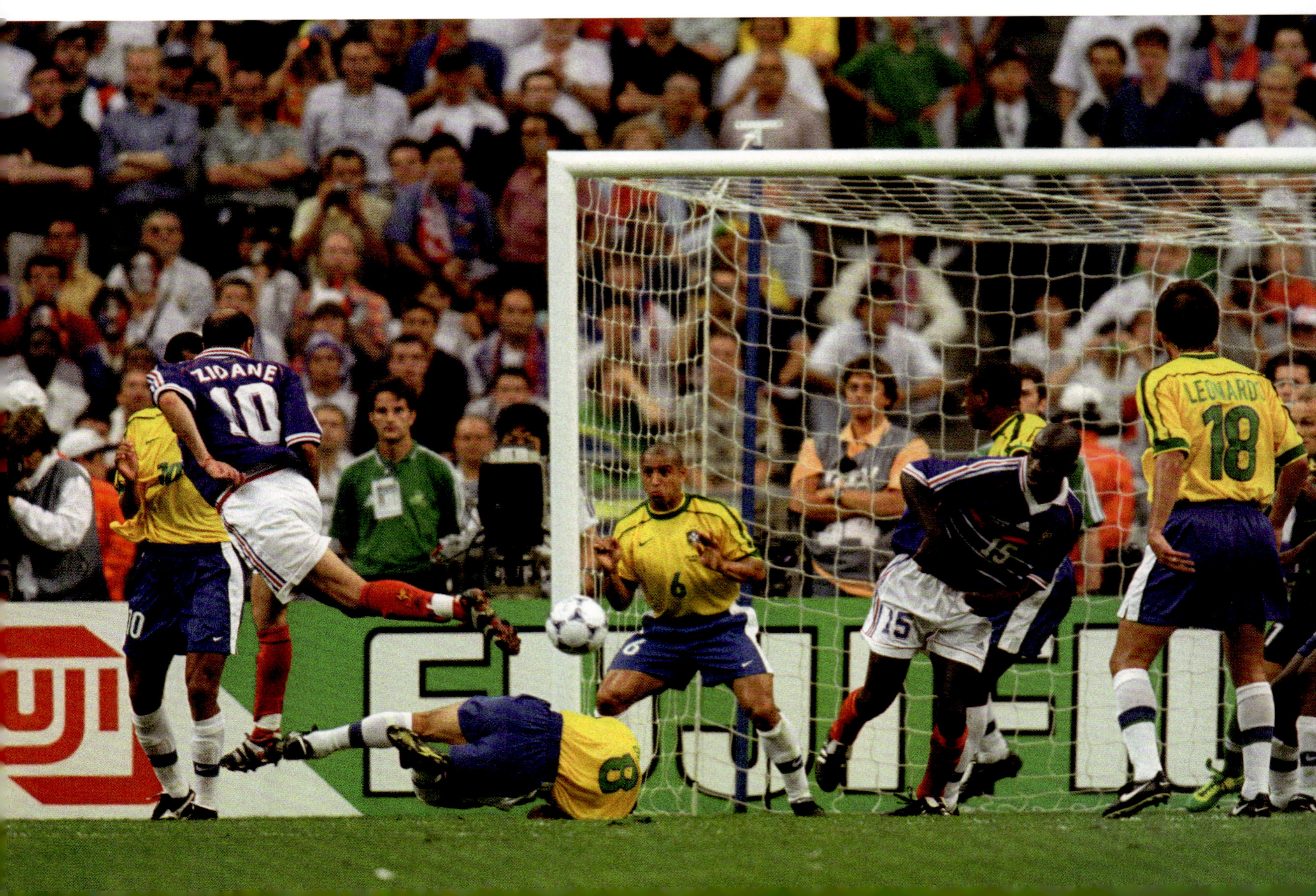

# THE 2000s

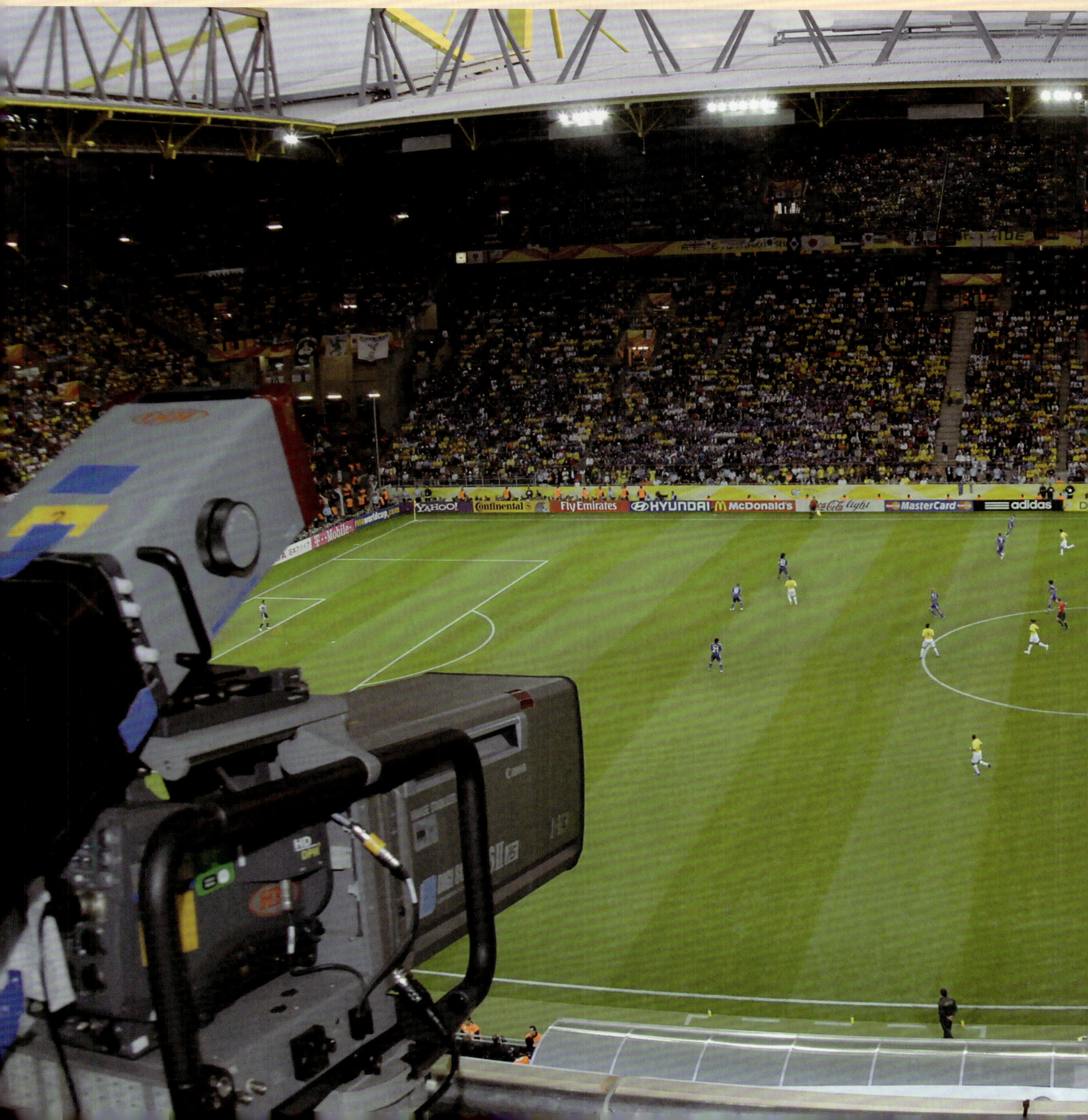

# CHAPTER 8

# *Brazil Five, Italy Four*

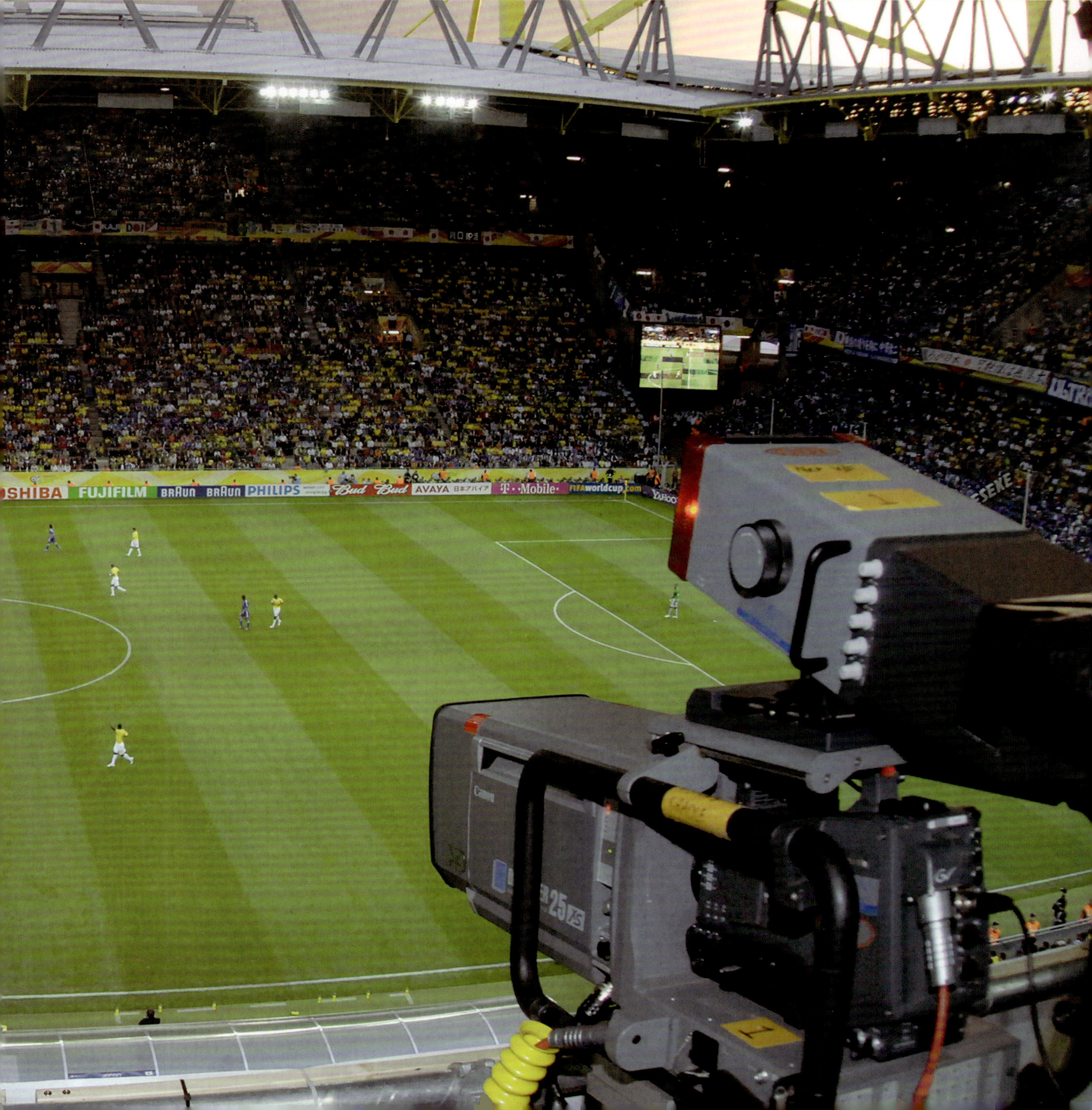

# 2002



**With the dawn** of a new millennium, FIFA bolstered its never-ending efforts to spread World Cup fever around the world by selecting Japan and South Korea as co-hosts of the 2002 tournament. The two countries had originally submitted separate bids but in May 1996 they combined them into a single proposal, a bold and brilliant move that won unanimous support in the FIFA Congress. To prepare for this first Cup competition to be held in Asia, the two co-hosts truly went all out: each built ten brand-new stadiums, twenty total, from the ground up.

With thirty-two teams now in the tournament, only the top-two teams from each of the eight groups would advance to the knockout stage's Round of 16. Japan and South Korea automatically qualified, as did defending-champion France, although this was the last time FIFA granted a free pass to the current trophy holder. New countries making their debut in World Cup play included China, Slovenia, Ecuador, and Senegal, and excitement ran high as new energy flowed into the great global spectacle — five different football federations were represented in the 2002 Cup quarter-finals!

But in the end . . . well, who better to showcase football excellence in this first World Cup Final of the twenty-first century (and the new millennium) than Brazil and Germany, the two most successful nations in the history of the competition?

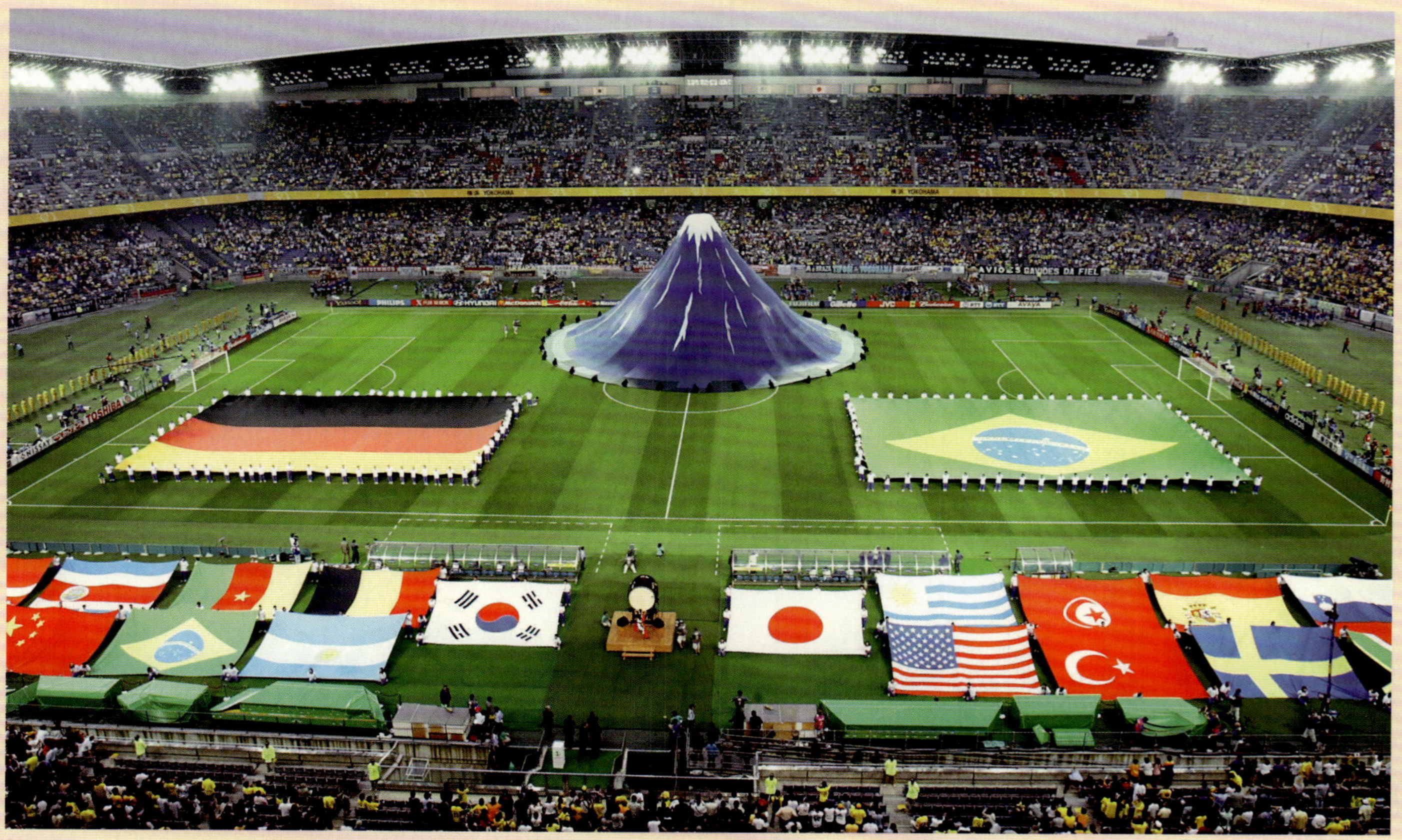

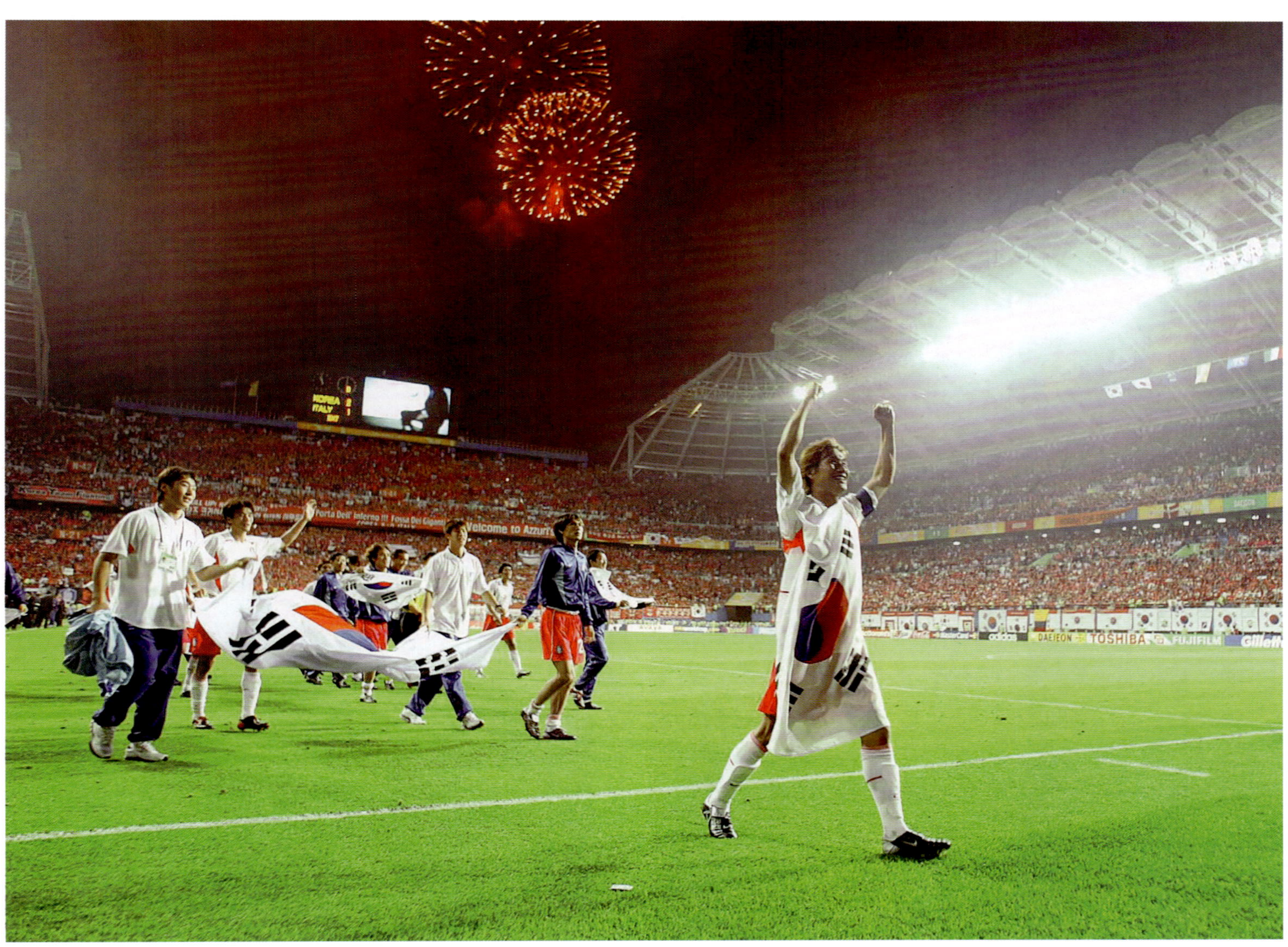





**PREVIOUS SPREAD** *A look ahead at Germany 2006, where Brazil and Japan face off at the Westfalenstadion in Dortmund.*

**OPPOSITE** *The ceremony for the 2002 World Cup Final between Germany and Brazil, at the International Stadium Yokohama. On prominent display, a replica of co-host Japan's Mt. Fuji.*

**ABOVE** *Co-host South Korea celebrates at the Daejeon World Cup Stadium after Ahn Jung-hwan's golden goal against Italy.*

# Tournament: GROUP STAGE

### GROUP A: DENMARK, SENEGAL, URUGUAY, FRANCE

| | | |
|---|---|---|
| Senegal 1 | 0 | France |
| Denmark 2 | 1 | Uruguay |
| Denmark 1 | 1 | Senegal |
| France 0 | 0 | Uruguay |
| Denmark 2 | 0 | France |
| Senegal 3 | 3 | Uruguay |

***Advanced to Knockout Stage: Denmark, Senegal***

### GROUP B: SPAIN, PARAGUAY, SOUTH AFRICA, SLOVENIA

| | | |
|---|---|---|
| Paraguay 2 | 2 | South Africa |
| Spain 3 | 1 | Slovenia |
| Spain 3 | 1 | Paraguay |
| South Africa 1 | 0 | Slovenia |
| Spain 3 | 2 | South Africa |
| Paraguay 3 | 1 | Slovenia |

***Advanced to Knockout Stage: Spain, Paraguay***

In as shocking a result as can be imagined, defending-champion France, unbeatable just four years earlier, failed to score a single goal and finished dead last in the group. The French downfall started with a 1–0 loss to a surprising Senegal squad led by a brilliant midfielder with the wonderfully rhythmic name of Papa Bouba Diop, who scored three times in group play; the Senegalese also forged draws with world powers Uruguay and Denmark. Denmark, who had shared a group with France in the previous Cup as well, got their 2–0 revenge for 1998, looked formidable on the whole, and won the group.

Spain seemed ready to live up to its billing at last, scoring three goals in all three victories and storming through group play. Paraguay just barely edged out evenly matched South Africa for advancement as it came down to goals scored.

**BELOW** *Paraguay's Jorge Campos with a dynamite shot against Slovenia for the 3–1 victory. The ball would hit the bottom of the top goalpost and deflect straight down for a stunning finish.*

**OPPOSITE** *The three Rs of Brazil: Rivaldo, Ronaldinho (on top), and Ronaldo (centre). The trio is pictured after Ronaldo scored a fiftieth-minute equaliser against Turkey, assisted by Rivaldo.*

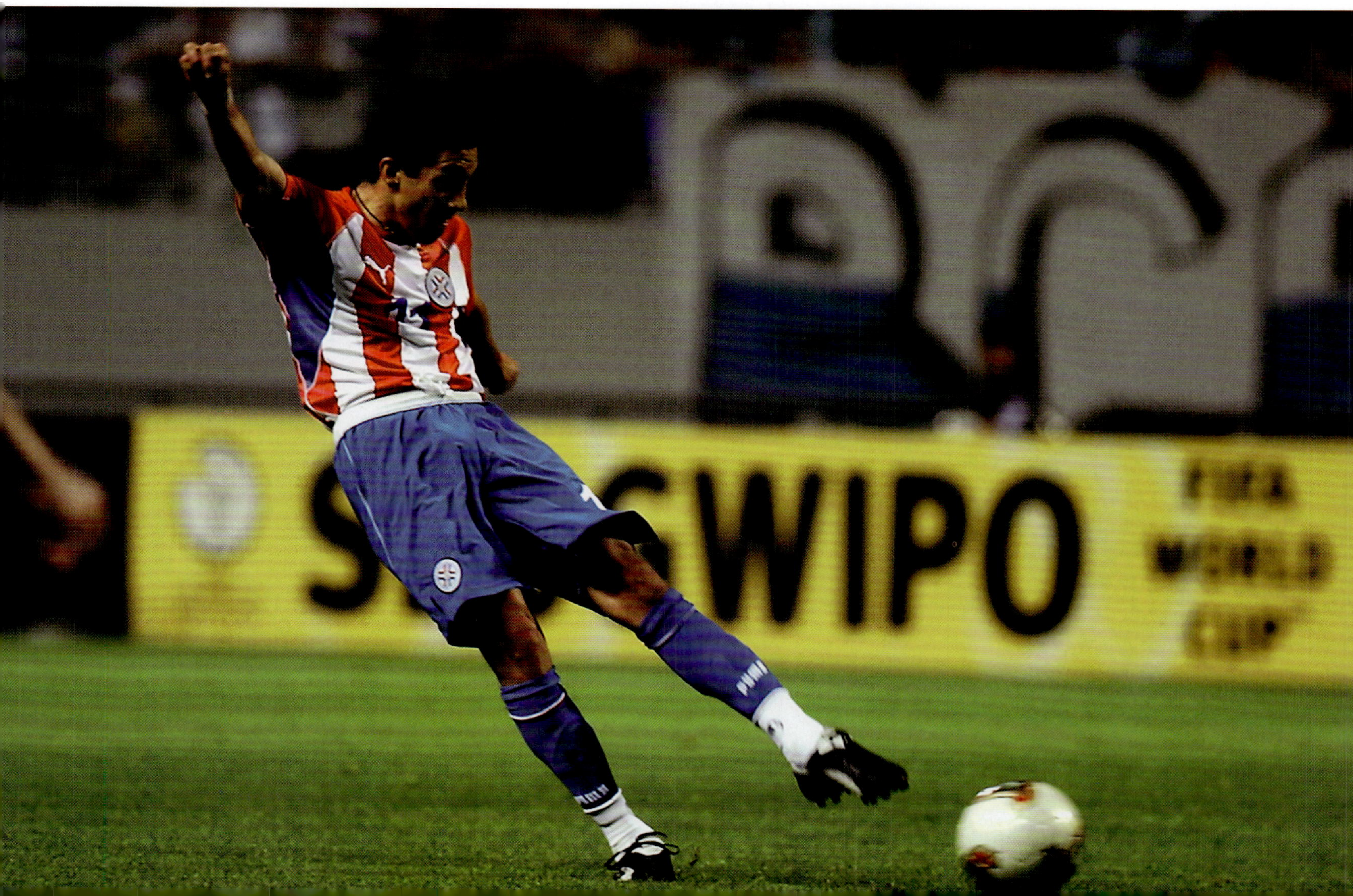

| | | |
|---|---|---|
| Brazil 2 | 1 | Turkey |
| Costa Rica 2 | 0 | China |
| Brazil 4 | 0 | China |
| Costa Rica 1 | 1 | Turkey |
| Brazil 5 | 2 | Costa Rica |
| Turkey 3 | 0 | China |

**Advanced to Knockout Stage: Brazil, Turkey**

Brazil ended up scoring eleven goals in three group-stage games but in their tournament opener they found themselves trailing Turkey 0–1 at halftime. In the second half, veteran stars Ronaldo and Rivaldo came up with big goals to turn it around 2–1. Amazingly, the dynamic duo would score one goal apiece in all three of Brazil's group matches plus the Round of 16 versus Belgium.

**GROUP D: SOUTH KOREA, USA, PORTUGAL, POLAND**

| | | |
|---|---|---|
| South Korea 2 | 0 | Poland |
| USA 3 | 2 | Portugal |
| South Korea 1 | 1 | USA |
| Portugal 4 | 0 | Poland |
| South Korea 1 | 0 | Portugal |
| Poland 3 | 1 | USA |

**Advanced to Knockout Stage: South Korea, USA**

The home team, playing with infectious enthusiasm, began its stunningly deep run into the tournament with victories over longtime European stalwarts Poland and Portugal. The United States also surprised with a win over Portugal and then managed a gritty tie with the inspired South Koreans to advance to the knockouts alongside the hosts.

# THE THREE Rs OF BRAZIL

**Behold, lined up in tandem** on the Brazilian roster, a perfect killers' row at the 9, 10, and 11. Ronaldo 'Fenômeno', the golden boy with the Golden Shoe, flush in his prime at age twenty-five, the best striker in the world. Rivaldo, the brilliant playmaker and wizened elder at age thirty. Ronaldinho, the prodigy just coming into his own at age twenty-two as a world-class magician both in the midfield and on the wing.

The trio scored fourteen of Brazil's eighteen goals in the 2002 World Cup tournament: eight by Ronaldo, five by Rivaldo, and two by the youngster Ronaldinho. One of Rivaldo and Ronaldo would score in every single match and their virtuoso performances in South Korea and Japan contributed to the sentiment that Brazil 2002 had joined their 1970 predecessors in the pantheon of the greatest squads in World Cup history.

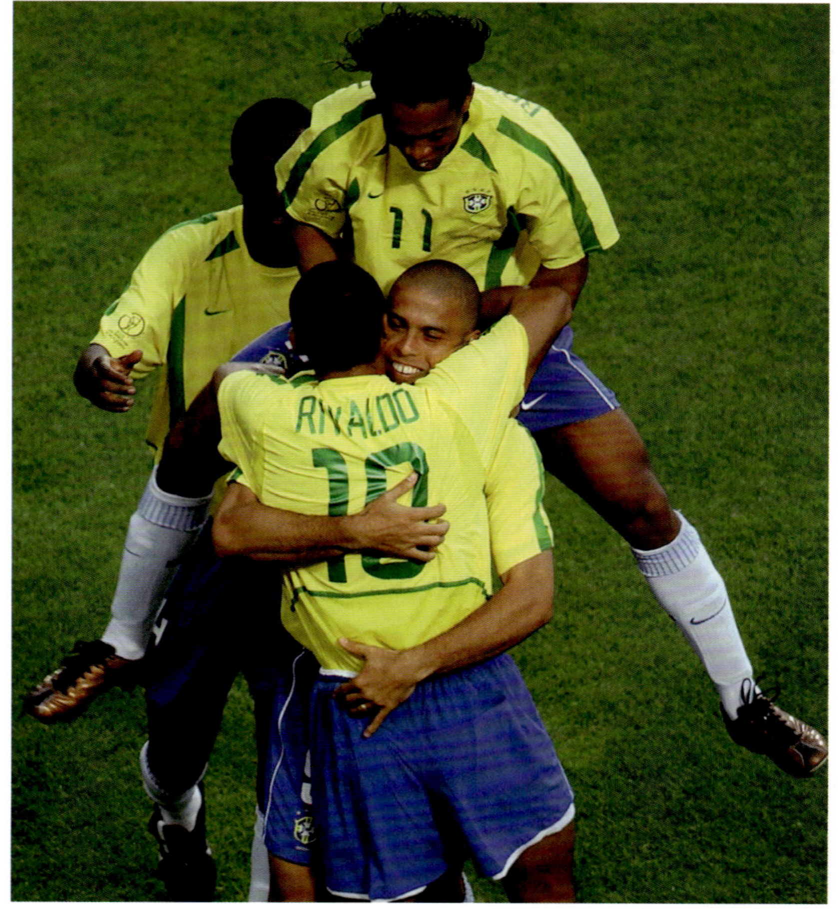

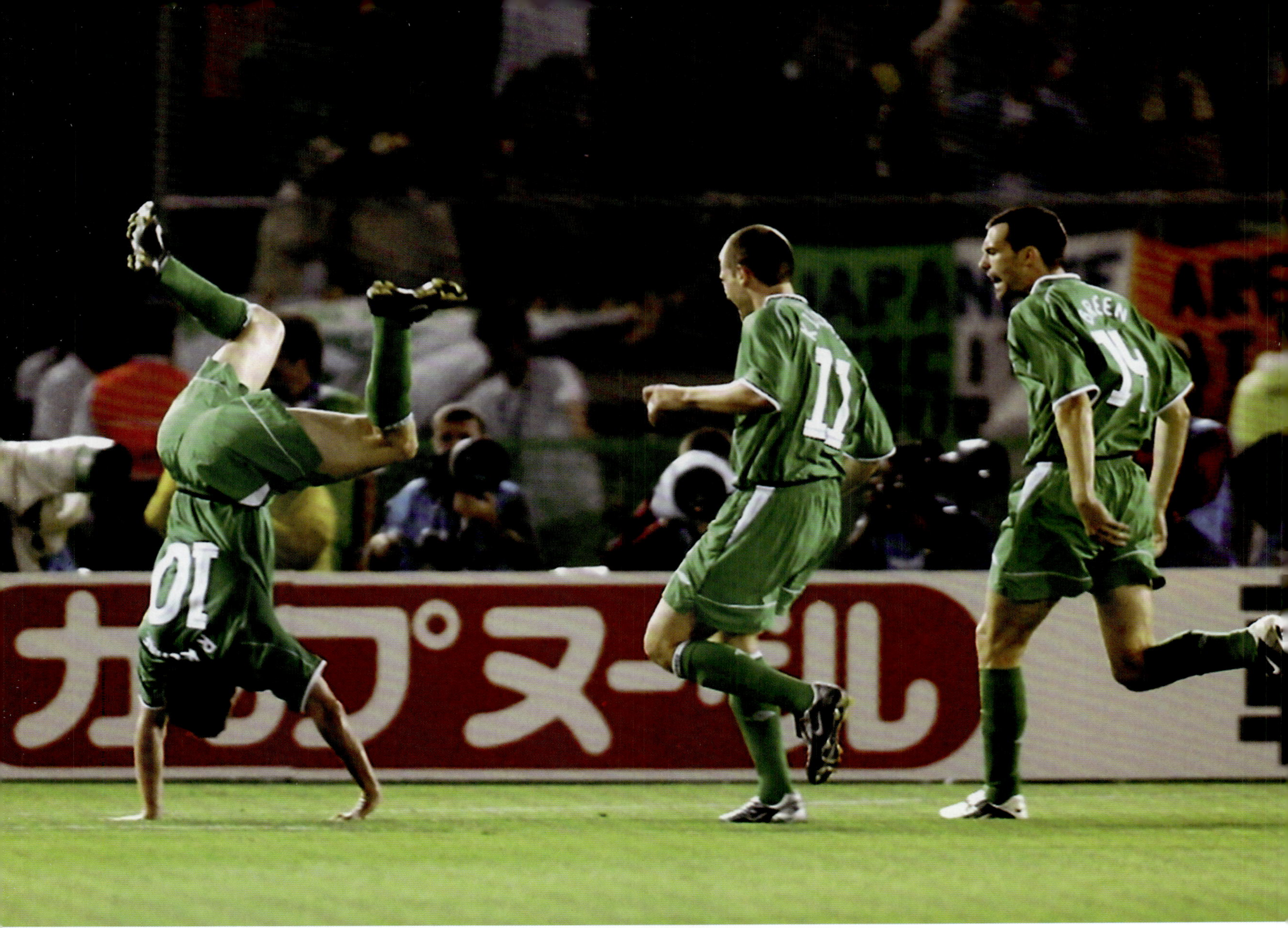

## GROUP E: GERMANY, REPUBLIC OF IRELAND, CAMEROON, SAUDI ARABIA

| | | |
|---|---|---|
| Republic of Ireland 1 | 1 | Cameroon |
| Germany 8 | 0 | Saudi Arabia |
| Germany 1 | 1 | Republic of Ireland |
| Cameroon 1 | 0 | Saudi Arabia |
| Germany 2 | 0 | Cameroon |
| Republic of Ireland 3 | 0 | Saudi Arabia |

**Advanced to Knockout Stage: Germany, Republic of Ireland**

## GROUP F: SWEDEN, ENGLAND, ARGENTINA, NIGERIA

| | | |
|---|---|---|
| Argentina 1 | 0 | Nigeria |
| England 1 | 1 | Sweden |
| Sweden 2 | 1 | Nigeria |
| England 1 | 0 | Argentina |
| Sweden 1 | 1 | Argentina |
| England 0 | 0 | Nigeria |

**Advanced to Knockout Stage: Sweden, England**

One of the tournament's most memorable moments was Irishman Robbie Keane's joyous cartwheel and somersault celebration. A second-half dart past goalkeeper Oliver Kahn in stoppage time equalised against the mighty Germany and helped Ireland join them in the knockout round.

Argentina entered the tournament as co-favourites but David Beckham's penalty just before halftime gave the stout English defence the cushion it needed to overcome the Argentines, 1–0. In the end, Sweden matched England's solid, if unspectacular, level of play to win the group and reach the knockout stage.

**ABOVE** *Ireland's Robbie Keane (far left) with a gymnastic celebration after scoring the opening goal in a 3–0 victory over Saudi Arabia.*

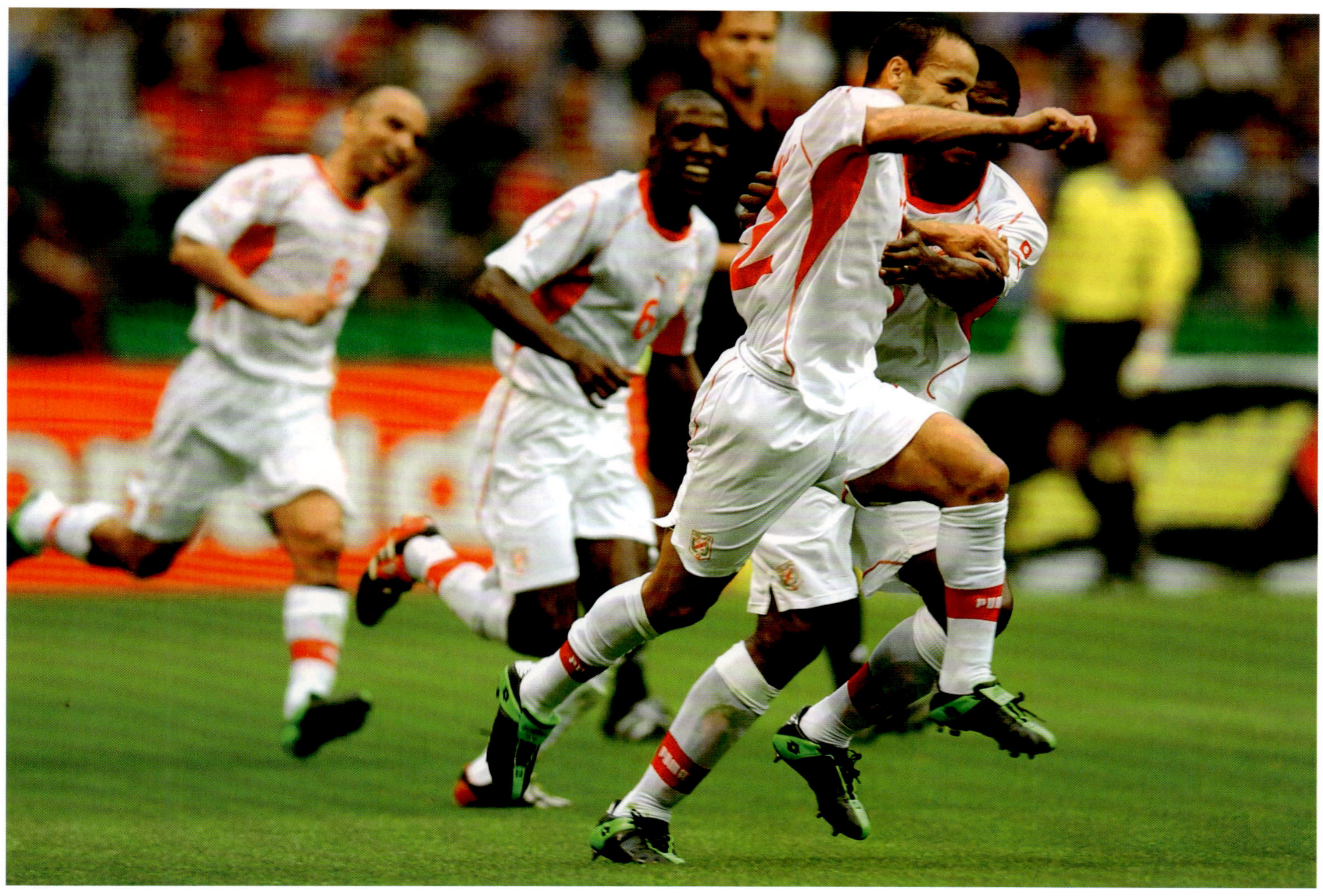

## GROUP G: MEXICO, ITALY, CROATIA, ECUADOR

| | | |
|---|---|---|
| Mexico 1 | 0 | Croatia |
| Italy 2 | 0 | Ecuador |
| Croatia 2 | 1 | Italy |
| Mexico 2 | 1 | Ecuador |
| Mexico 1 | 1 | Italy |
| Ecuador 1 | 0 | Croatia |

**Advanced to Knockout Stage: Mexico, Italy**

## GROUP H: JAPAN, BELGIUM, RUSSIA, TUNISIA

| | | |
|---|---|---|
| Japan 2 | 2 | Belgium |
| Russia 2 | 0 | Tunisia |
| Japan 1 | 0 | Russia |
| Tunisia 1 | 1 | Belgium |
| Japan 2 | 0 | Tunisia |
| Belgium 3 | 2 | Russia |

**Advanced to Knockout Stage: Japan, Belgium**

Mexico's surprising wins over both Croatia and Ecuador and a spirited draw with Italy put them in first place of Group G. Three goals by Christian Vieri helped Italy snag the second spot in the group. Croatia had been in the best position to move on but stumbled badly against an inspired Ecuador side who exited the tournament with a 1–0 win thanks to a stalwart back line and a thundering header by captain Hernán Gómez in the second half.

Japan, playing what one observer called 'fast, exuberant football', became the third Asian team (with Turkey and South Korea) to advance into the knockout round with solid wins over Russia and Tunisia. Belgium needed a victory over Russia in the final game to advance and they got it in an exciting match that came down to a tension-filled final two minutes.

*ABOVE Raouf Bouzaiene of Tunisia is chased down by teammates after his free kick equalises against Belgium.*

# KNOCKOUT STAGE
## ROUND OF 16

| | | |
|---|---|---|
| Germany 1 | 0 | Paraguay |
| USA 2 | 0 | Mexico |
| Spain 1 | 1 | Republic of Ireland |
| | | (3–2 on penalty kicks) |
| South Korea 2 | 1 | Italy |
| England 3 | 0 | Denmark |
| Brazil 2 | 0 | Belgium |
| Turkey 1 | 0 | Japan |
| Senegal 2 | 1 | Sweden |
| | | (after sudden-death extra time) |

Ahn Jung-hwan's golden-goal header sent his fellow South Koreans into flights of euphoria as the home team moved past Italy into the quarter-finals. Senegal became just the second African nation to reach the final eight, and the United States decisively eliminated its CONCACAF rival Mexico, its first-ever win in the knockout stage. With South Korea, USA, Turkey, and Senegal reaching the final eight, it marked the first time that teams from five different continents reached the same World Cup quarter-finals round.

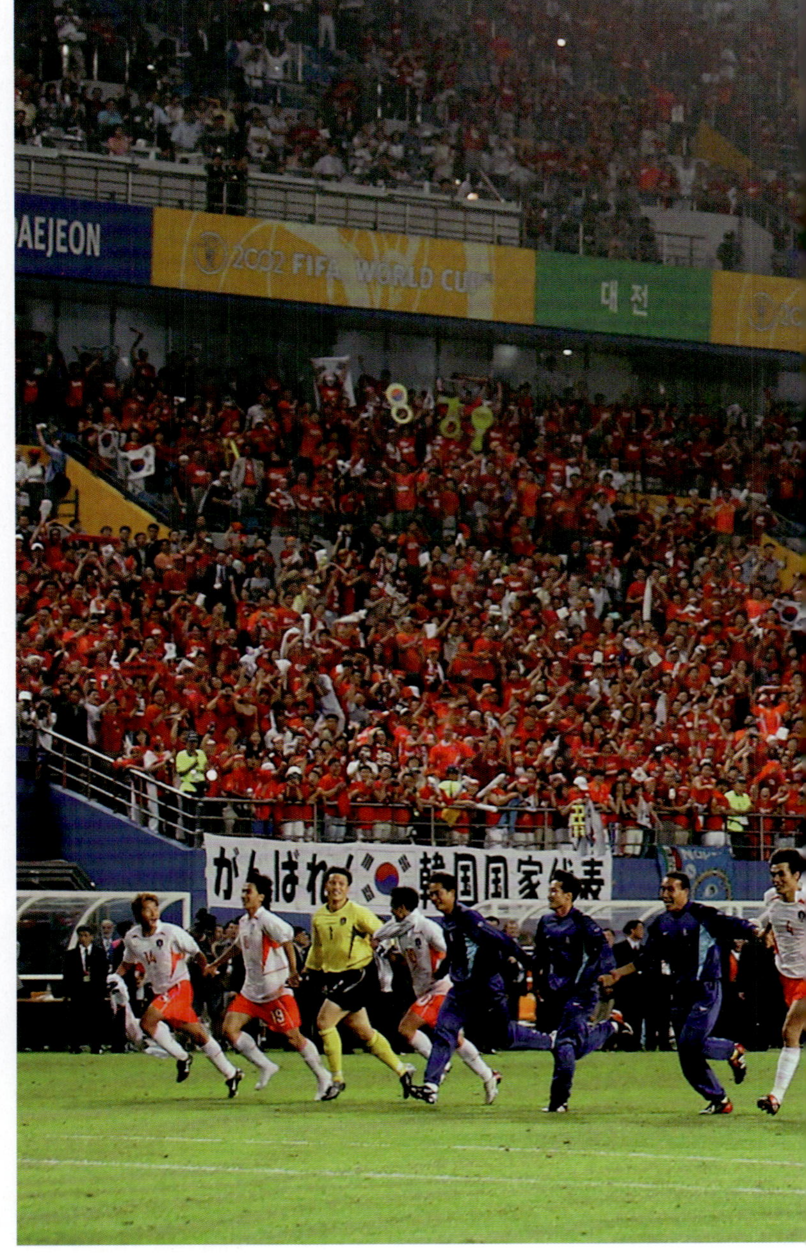

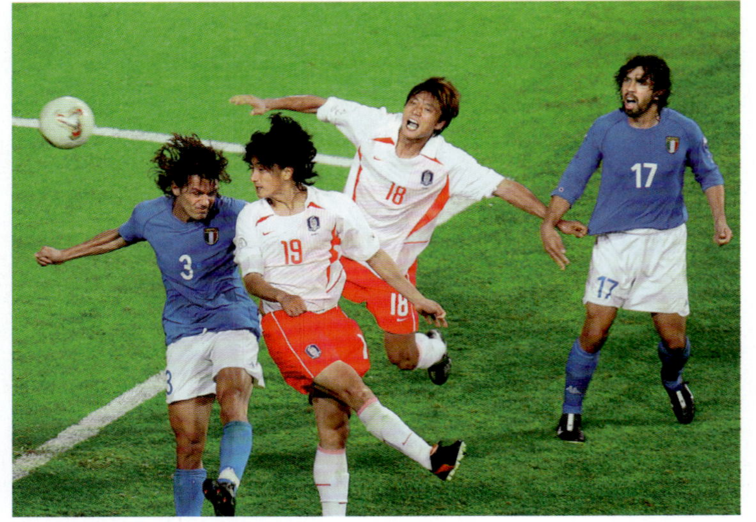

**ABOVE** *The South Korean squad joins hands and runs the length of the pitch to thank their local supporters after a shocking golden-goal upset of Italy.*

**RIGHT** *Ahn Jung-hwan (number 19) beats Paolo Maldini (number 3) in the air for the golden goal.*

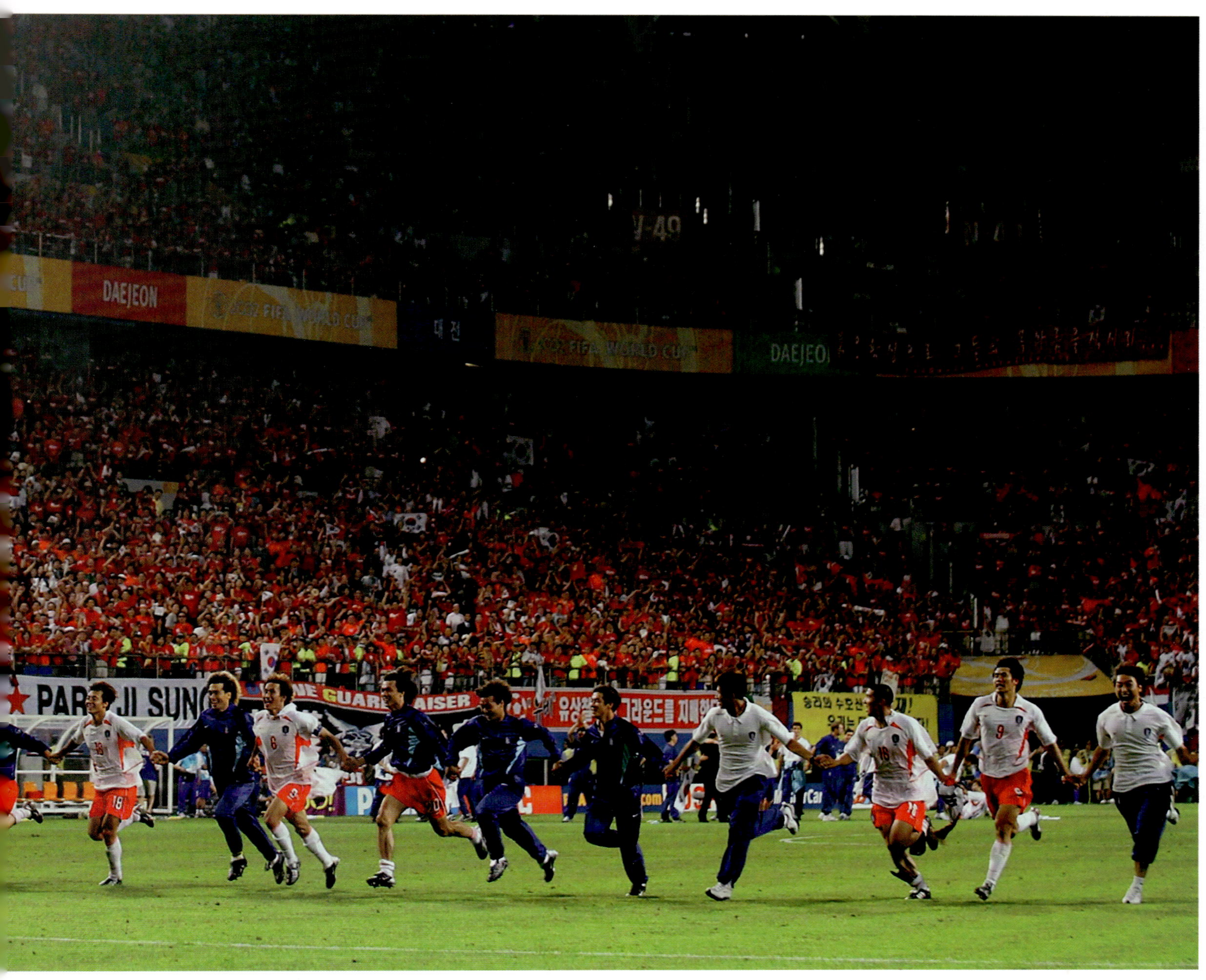

## THE GOLDEN GOAL THAT GOT HIM SACKED

**When Ahn Jung-hwan outjumped** the legendary Italian defender Paolo Maldini and banged home a dramatic header in the 117th minute of a nail-biter in Daejeon, his golden goal put South Korea past Italy into the quarter-finals. Unfortunately, it also angered his Italian boss Luciano Gaucci, chairman of Perugia, the Italian Serie A club that owned the option on Jung-hwan's contract. Afterwards, Gaucci famously said, 'I have no intention of paying a salary to someone who has ruined Italian football.'

As it turned out, getting sacked was very much worth it. Ahn Jung-hwan became a national hero in South Korea. He played professionally for ten more years in Japan and Europe then launched a celebrated career as a TV personality and broadcaster in his home country. Jung-hwan ended up as one of his country's Olympic torchbearers when South Korea hosted the Winter Olympics in 2018.

'The legendary German goalkeeper
known as Der Titan.'


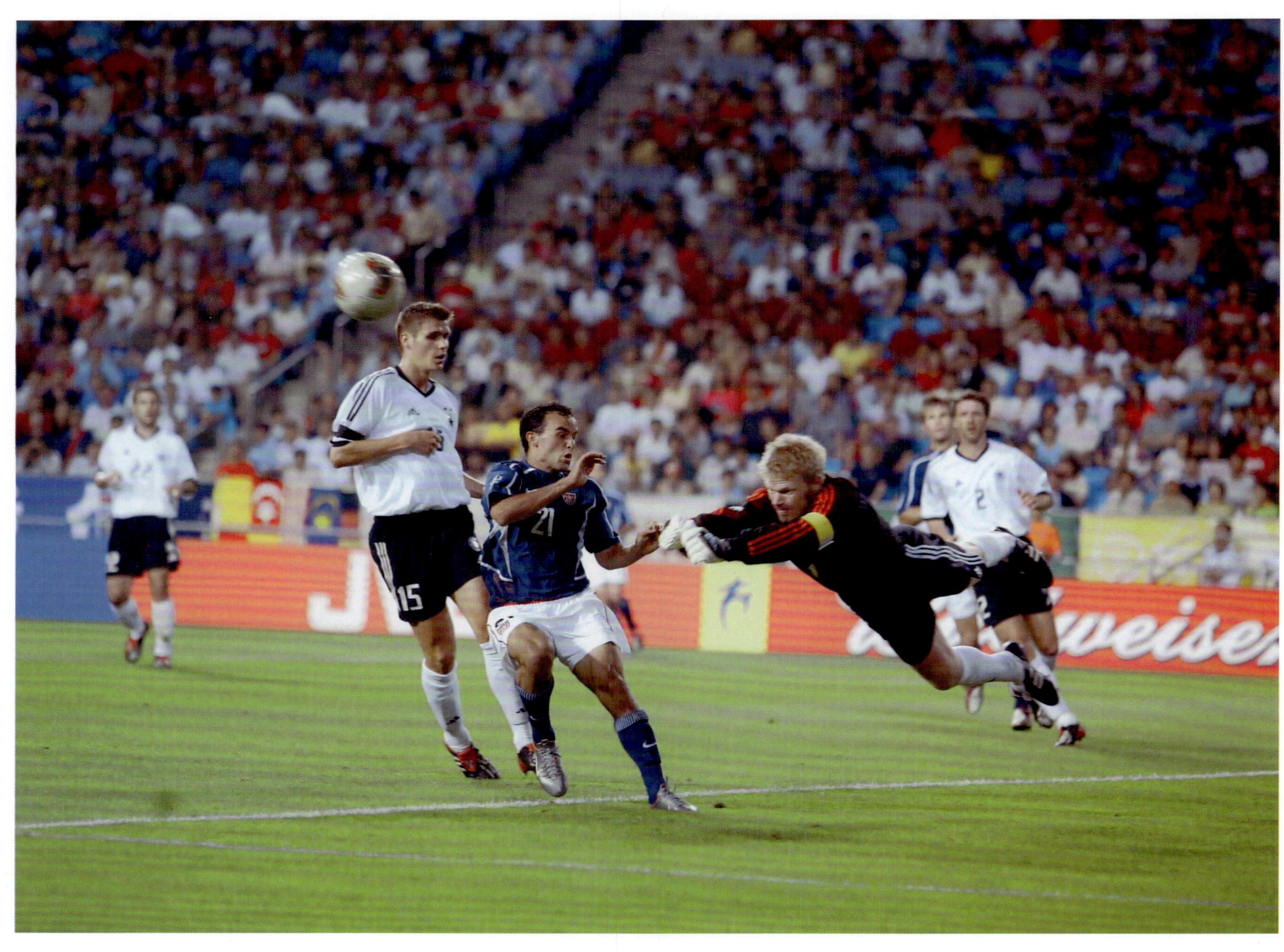

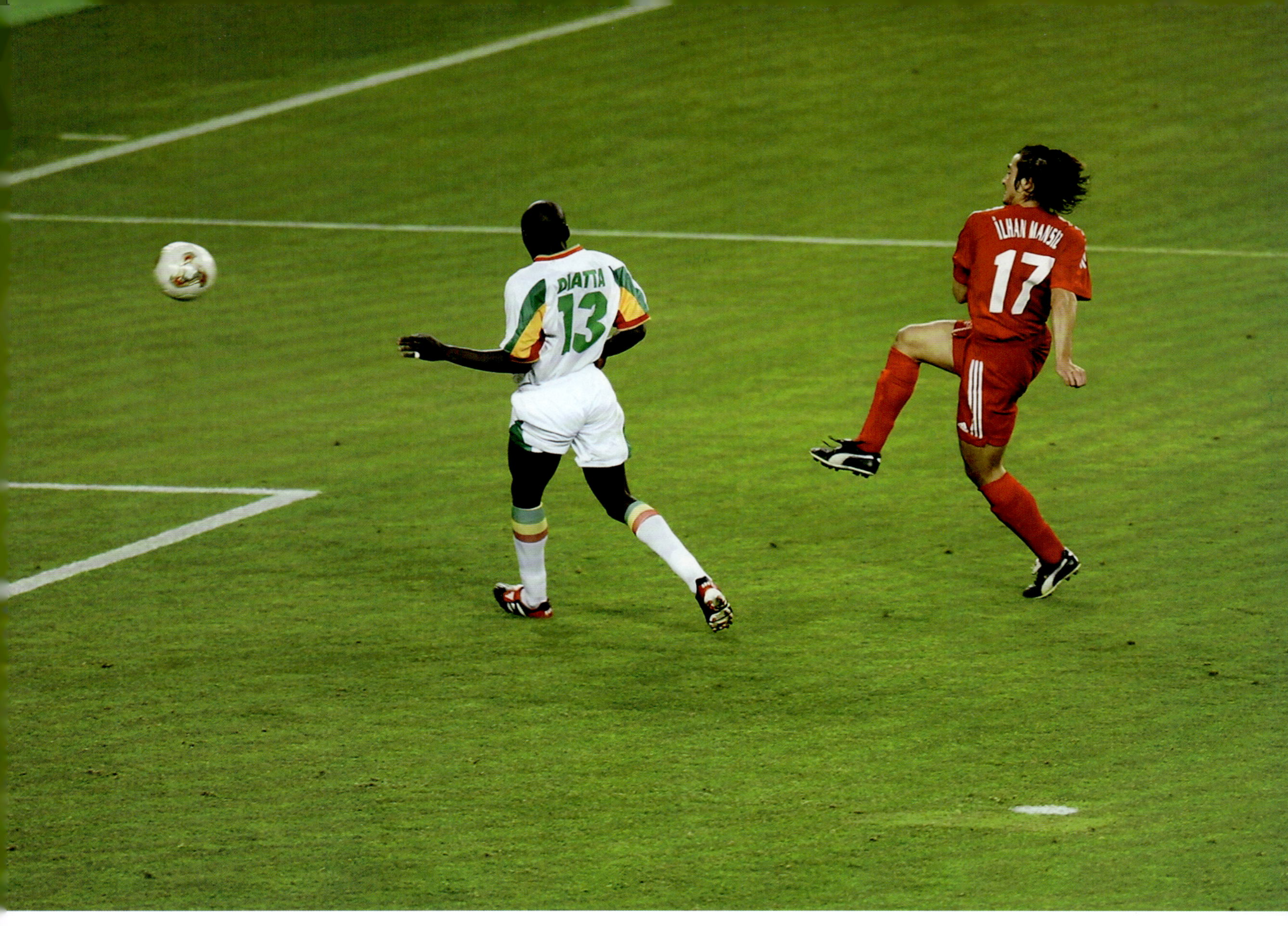

## QUARTER-FINALS

| | | |
|---|---|---|
| Germany 1 | 0 | USA |
| South Korea 0 | 0 | Spain |
| | | (5–3 on penalty kicks) |
| Brazil 2 | 1 | England |
| Turkey 1 | 0 | Senegal |

Brazil earned a solid 2–1 win over England thanks to Ronaldinho's spectacular, bending free kick from well outside the box. Oliver Kahn's series of astonishing saves against the Americans—including several preternatural parries of wicked shots from a twenty-year-old Landon Donovan—kept the relentless Germans on track to the next round. Later, the USA got a consolation nod when Donovan was named Best Young Player of the tournament.

South Korea kept the magic flowing with a perfect five-for-five performance in the penalty-kick shootout to slip past Spain, while İlhan Mansız's golden goal for Turkey beat Senegal and put a second Asian country in the semi-finals.

**OPPOSITE** *German goalkeeper Oliver 'Der Titan' Kahn with a leaping punch, Superman-like, to clear the ball away from USA's Landon Donovan. Khan was instrumental in preserving Germany's 1–0 lead throughout the match.*

**ABOVE** *İlhan Mansız with a thrilling golden goal for Turkey, much to the heartbreak of a tough Senegal side. This would be the final golden goal at the World Cup, as it was retired for 2006.*

## SEMI-FINALS

Germany 1 | 0 South Korea
Brazil 1 | 0 Turkey

South Korea's electrifying march to the semi-finals—beating Poland, Portugal, Italy, and Spain—transfixed the host country and triggered a joyous swell of national pride. An estimated 15 percent (about seven million) of the country's entire population watched the Koreans go toe-to-toe with the Germans for seventy-five minutes. Finally, a late Michael Ballack goal gave Germany the breakthrough.

The other semi-final featured a rare rematch of an earlier Group C game, won by Brazil on a last-minute penalty. Here, Brazil controlled the pace once again with their sparkling brand of attacking football…but once again found it hard to break down the resolute Turkish back line until Ronaldo's superb toe-poke strike a few minutes into the second half.

## KAHN THE IMPENETRABLE

**Outside an early 8–0 outburst** against woefully over-matched Saudi Arabia, Germany's typically lethal attack sputtered badly throughout the 2002 tournament. The Germans scored twice against a weak Cameroon side but managed only single goals against Ireland, Paraguay, United States, and South Korea—and they were shut out by Brazil in the final. How do you make it to a World Cup Final with such an anaemic attack?

The answer, in a word: *Kahn.* In 2002, the legendary German goalkeeper known as *Der Titan* patrolled his box like a great territorial beast. Other than the Irish-man Robbie Keane's brilliant counterpunch at 90+2' of stoppage time in their group-stage match, only the immortal Ronaldo could penetrate the plane of the great Oliver Kahn's goal. Overall, Kahn posted five clean sheets: two in group, then all three knockout matches leading to the Final. All were marked by a string of miraculous saves, including multiple highlight-reel parries against the United States in the quarter-finals. As a result, Kahn became the first and only goalkeeper to win the Golden Ball, the award given to the tournament's most outstanding player.

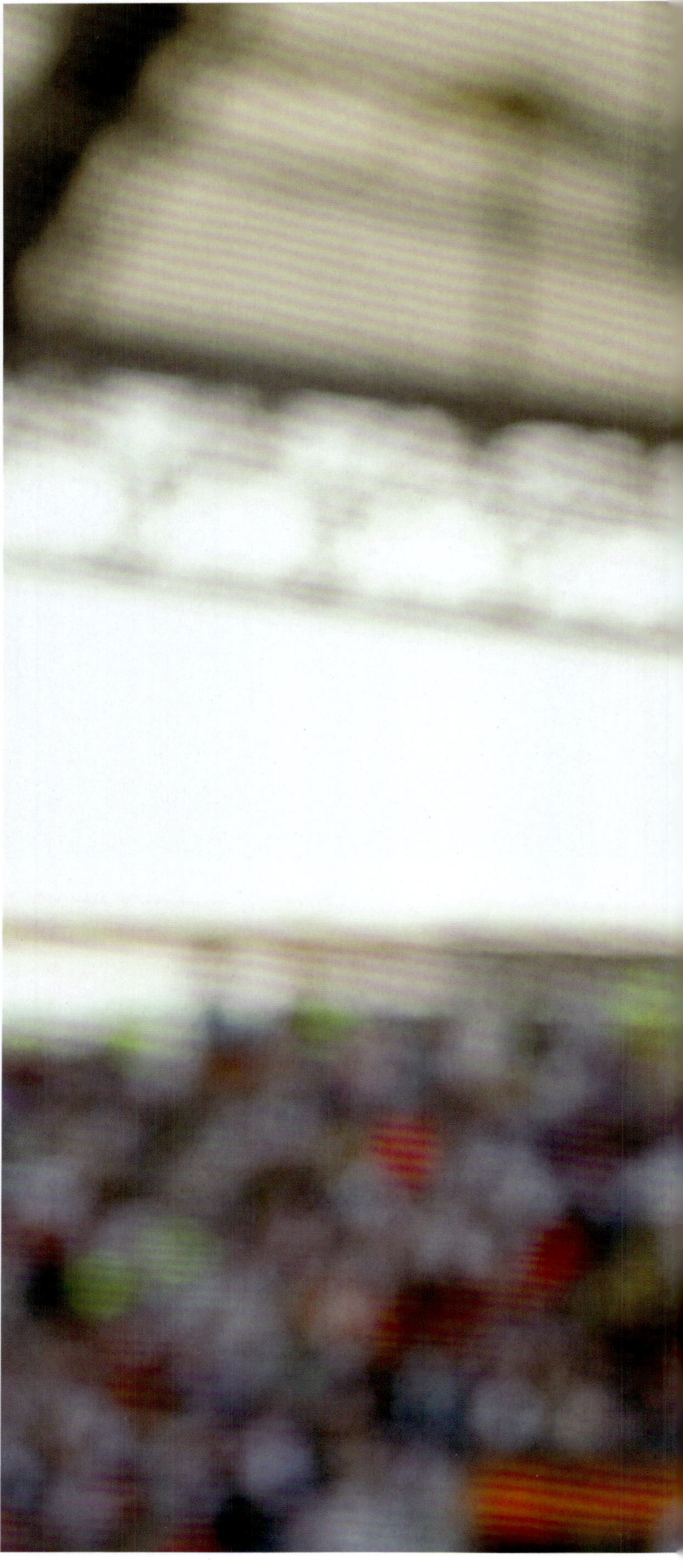

**RIGHT** *Oliver Kahn, winner of the 2002 World Cup Golden Ball.*

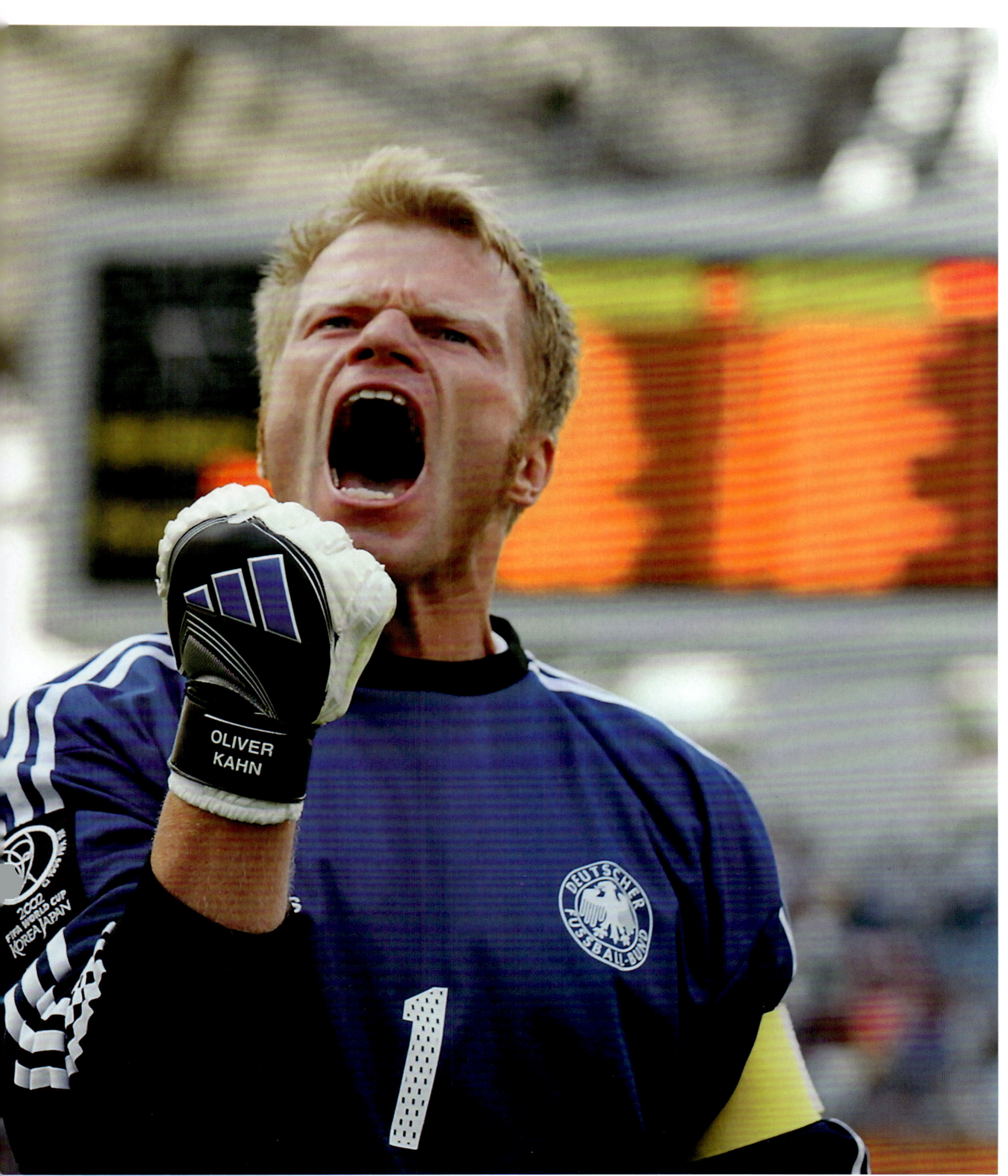

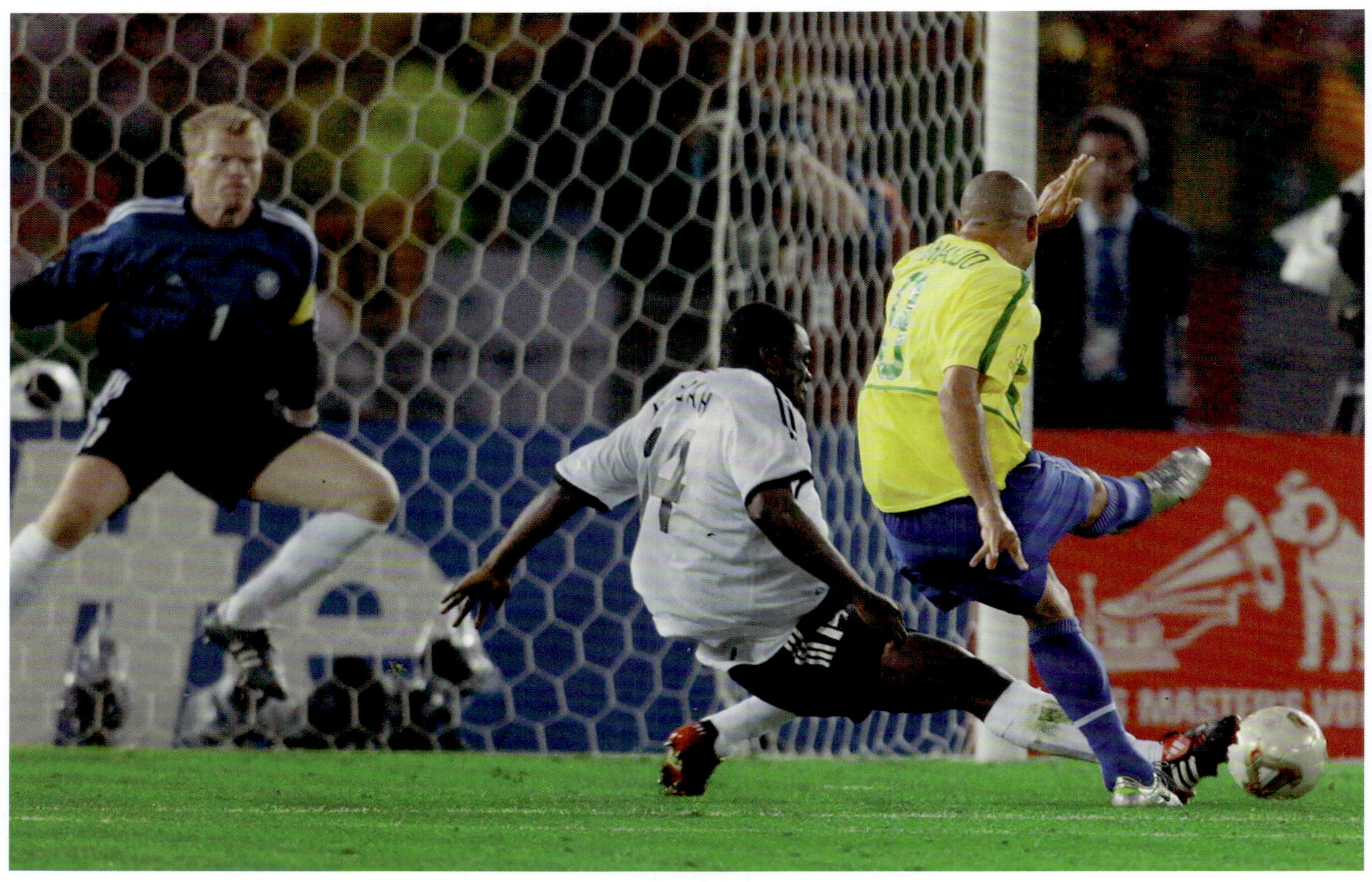

# FINAL

Brazil 2 | 0 Germany
       | (First Place)
Turkey 3 | 2 South Korea
       | (Third Place)

The third-place battle of the Asian powers opened with a Turkish goal by Hakan Şükür a mere 10.8 seconds after the opening kickoff, the fastest in World Cup history. The Turks built up a 3–1 lead in the second half and held on after South Korea notched one last score in stoppage time.

The Cup Final in Yokohama's International Stadium was a fascinating contrast of styles. For well over an hour, goalkeeper Oliver Kahn and his densely organised German defence stymied the supremely talented Brazilian trio of Ronaldo, Rivaldo, and Ronaldinho. But in the sixty-seventh minute, Kahn's failed scoop of Rivaldo's hypersonic missile spilled directly to the predatory Ronaldo, who clattered the ball home. Twelve minutes later, the usually ironclad German defence left Ronaldo completely unmarked at the top of the box, and the Brazilian made them pay with a calm reception, touch, and strike inside the far post.

'The great ones make it look easy,' remarked the BBC, an apt description of Ronaldo with the ball at his feet in a foe's penalty box. Thus, Brazil won a record fifth Cup title and Ronaldo, who won the Golden Shoe after scoring eight goals, officially joined the Brazilian pantheon of football deities.

**ABOVE** *Rivaldo's dummy fake (pretending to go for the ball but allowing it to pass by at the last moment) gave Ronaldo the space he needed to collect the ball and slot it into the net's lower-right corner.*

**OPPOSITE** *Ronaldo celebrates after pouncing on the ball for Brazil's first goal in the final.*

'Ronaldo officially joined
the Brazilian pantheon of
football deities.'

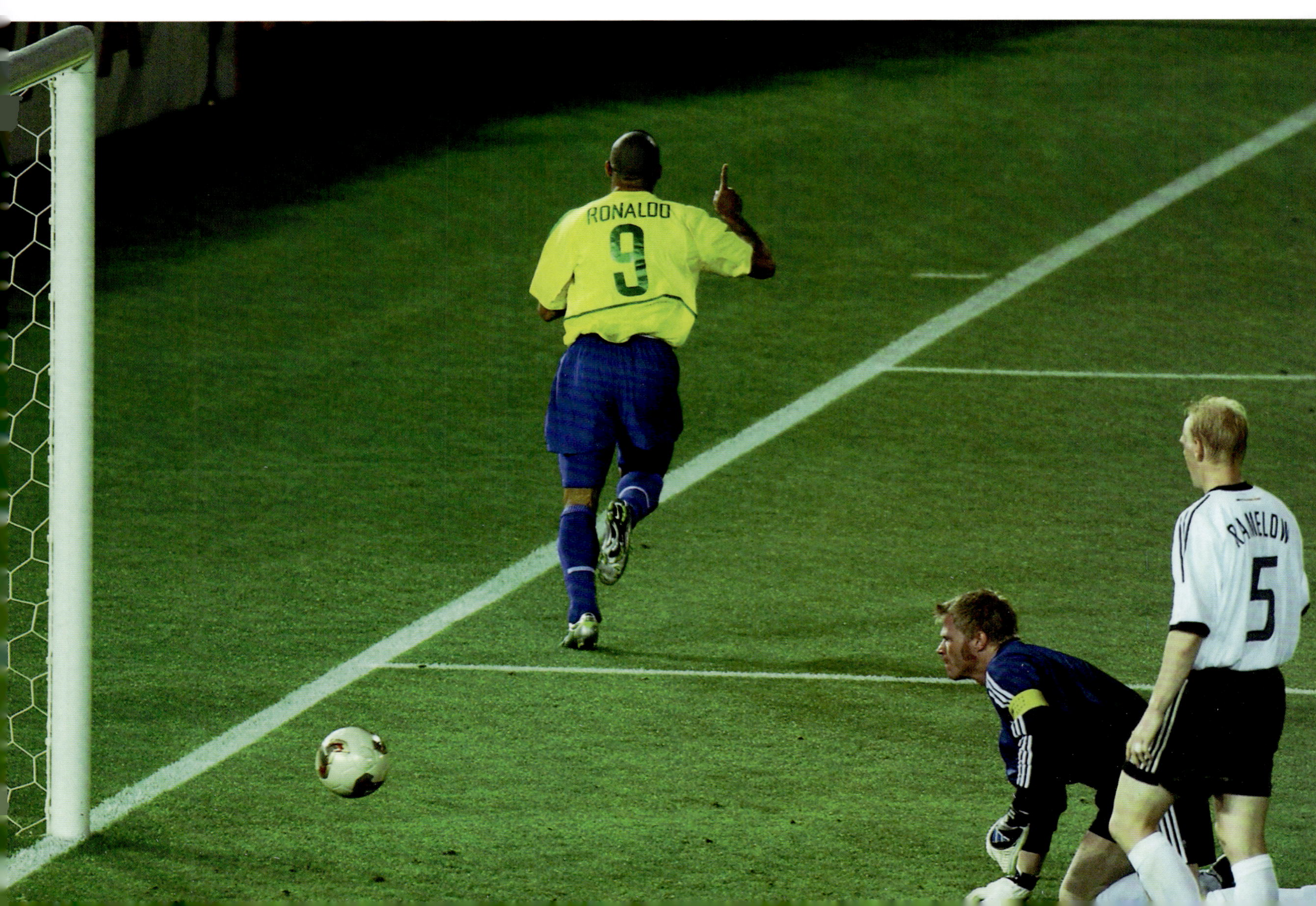

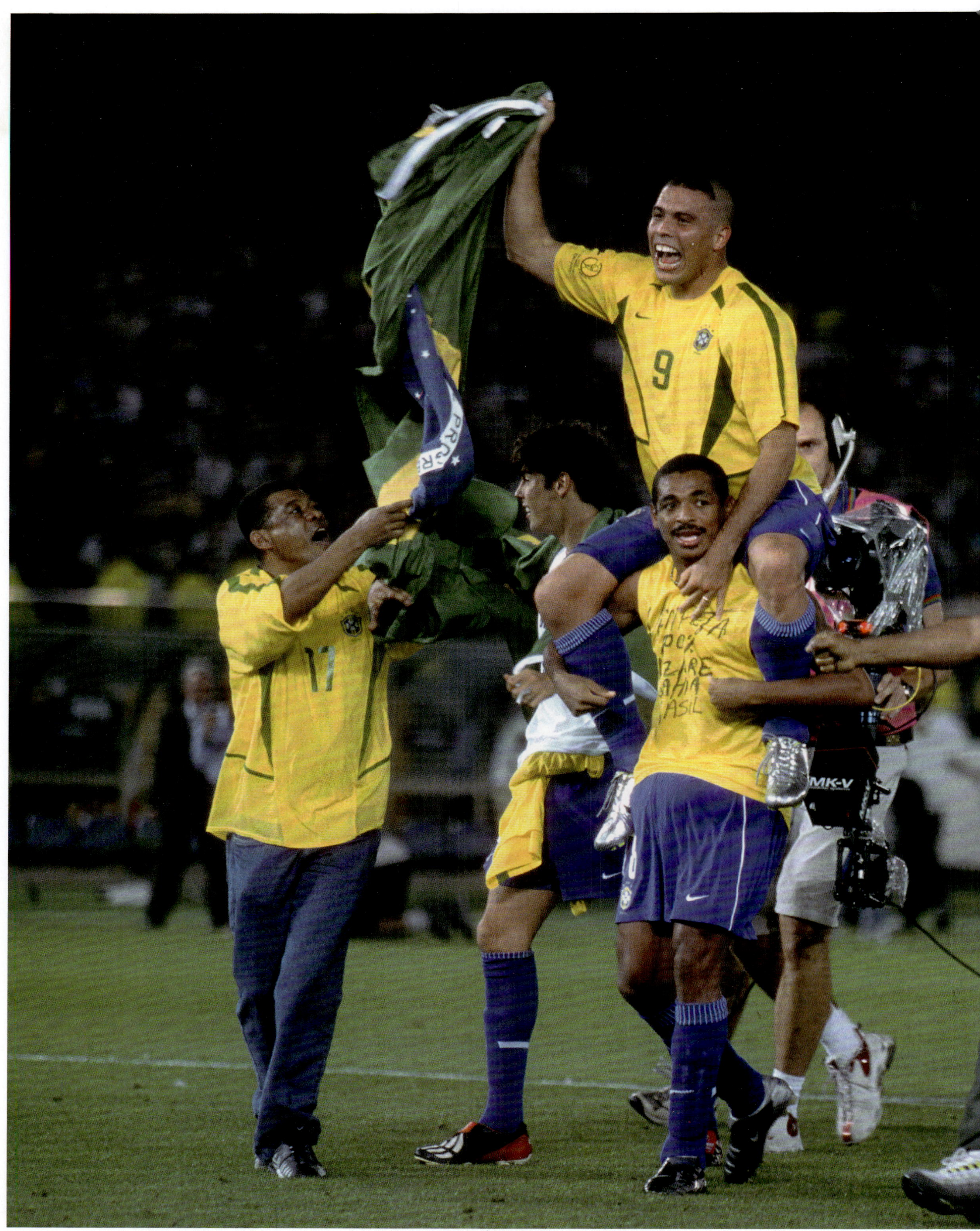

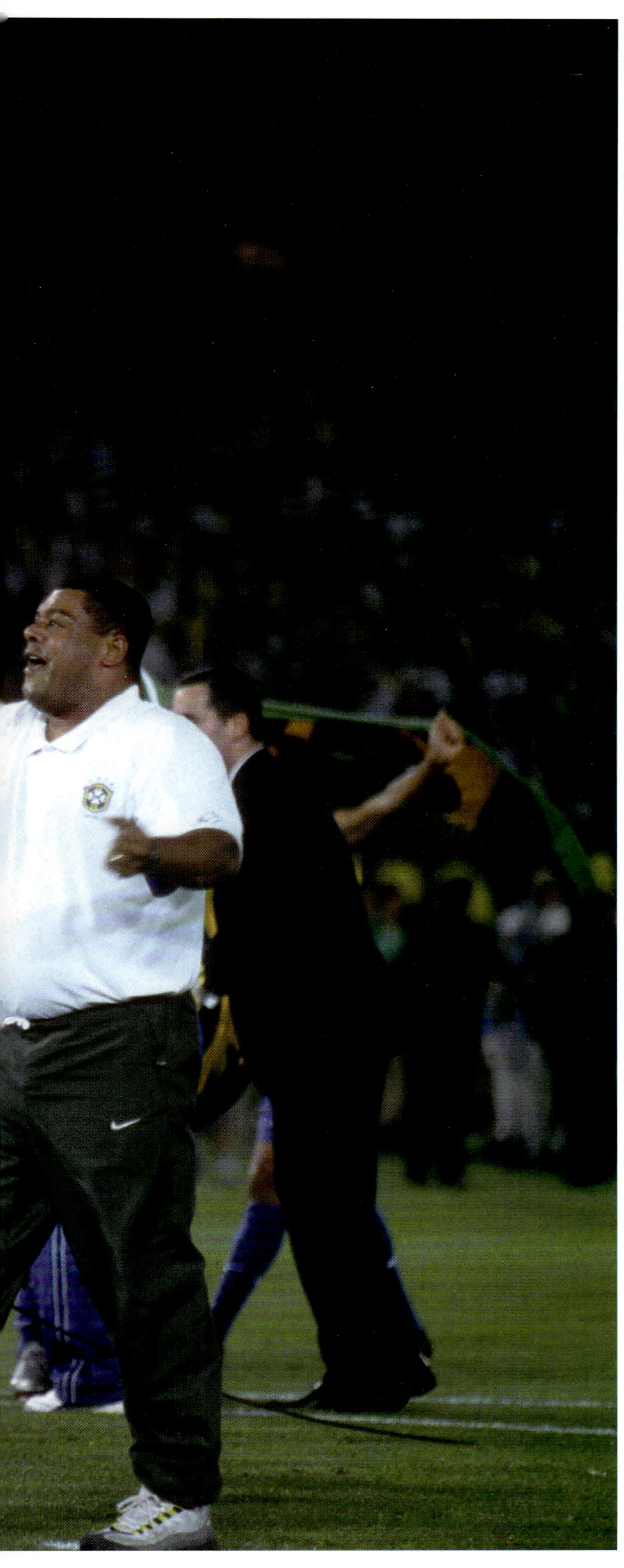

LEFT *Ronaldo triumphantly waves the Brazilian flag atop the shoulders of teammate Vampeta.*

# 2006

HOST COUNTRY: **GERMANY**
CHAMPION: **ITALY**
RUNNER-UP: **FRANCE**
THIRD PLACE: **GERMANY OVER PORTUGAL**

**FIFA chose Germany to stage** the 2006 World Cup. It was the country's second tournament as host, although technically their first was as 'West Germany' in 1974. In those days, East Germany existed as a separate country, part of an Eastern Bloc coalition of communist states aligned with the old USSR. But in 1990, East and West reunited to become simply 'Germany' again. By 2006, their political, economic, and cultural reintegration was complete, inspiring a new bloom of German pride, with the national team's great history of success as a focal point.

That summer's World Cup celebration was rousing and, at times, quite moving. Germans referred to it as the 'Sommermärchen' (summer fairy tale). The official slogan of the tournament was *Die Welt zu Gast bei Freunden*: 'A time to make friends'. The Cup's theme song, 'Celebrate the Day', turned into a popular anthem. A joyous closing ceremony in Berlin's Olympiastadion featured singing by Shakira, Wyclef Jean, Toni Braxton, and Plácido Domingo, as well as a grand work by German composer Matthias Keller, performed by the Munich Philharmonic conducted by Zubin Mehta. 'This really was the most positive and prosperous of modern-day World Cups . . . drenched in Euro boom good times', wrote Barney Ronay of *The Guardian*.

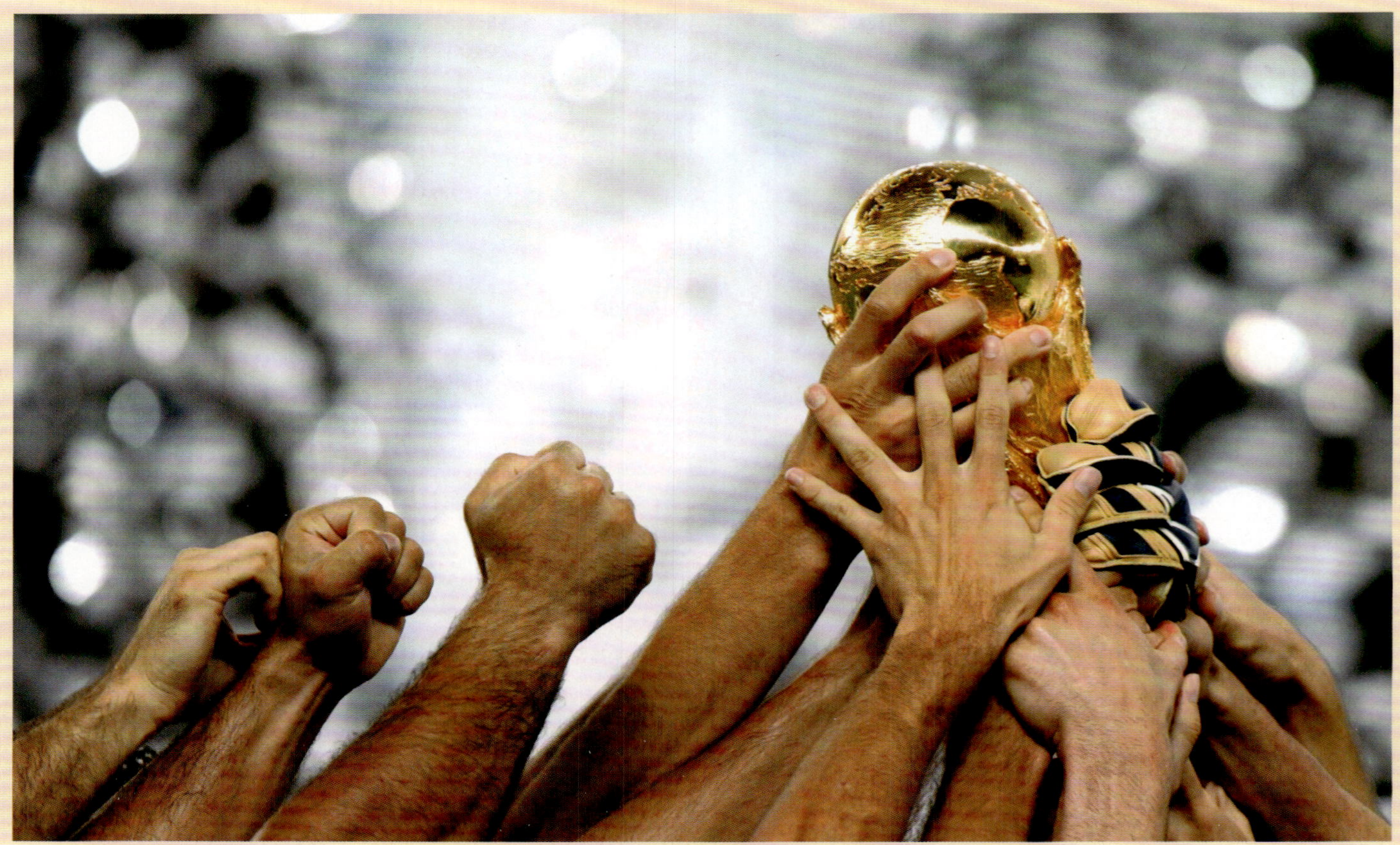

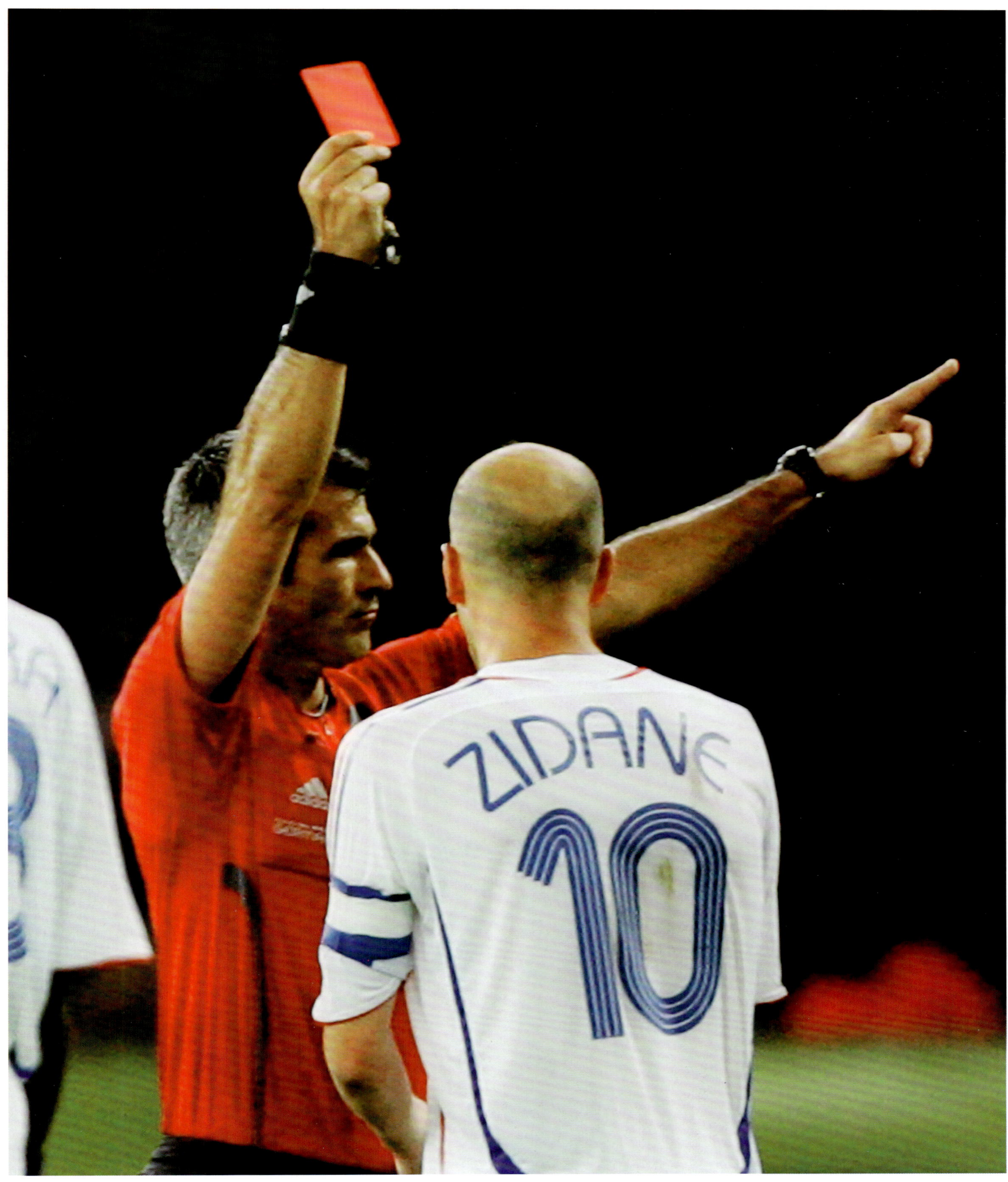



**OPPOSITE** *Italy players reaching for the trophy.*

**ABOVE** *Zinedine Zidane receives a red card for the most notorious foul in World Cup history.*

# Tournament: GROUP STAGE

### GROUP A: GERMANY, ECUADOR, POLAND, COSTA RICA

| | | |
|---:|---|---|
| Germany 4 | 2 | Costa Rica |
| Ecuador 2 | 0 | Poland |
| Germany 1 | 0 | Poland |
| Ecuador 3 | 0 | Costa Rica |
| Germany 3 | 0 | Ecuador |
| Poland 2 | 1 | Costa Rica |

**Advanced to Knockout Stage: Germany, Ecuador**

### GROUP B: ENGLAND, SWEDEN, PARAGUAY, TRINIDAD & TOBAGO

| | | |
|---:|---|---|
| England 1 | 0 | Paraguay |
| Trinidad & Tobago 0 | 0 | Sweden |
| England 2 | 0 | Trinidad & Tobago |
| Sweden 1 | 0 | Paraguay |
| Sweden 2 | 2 | England |
| Paraguay 2 | 0 | Trinidad & Tobago |

**Advanced to Knockout Stage: England, Sweden**

Germany, now coached by Jürgen Klinsmann, got off to a strong start on home soil with three convincing wins and a pair of braces from Miroslav Klose. Ecuador took second place while playing an attacking style, scoring five goals and racking up a pair of convincing shutout wins over Poland and Costa Rica. FIFA and fans were certainly delighted to see eighteen goals scored in Group A. In fact, Germany's 4–2 win over Costa Rica was the highest-scoring Cup opener in history.

Any group with both England and Sweden is likely to feature some stout defence. Sure enough, although they both scored twice against each other, the Swedes and English recorded shutouts in their other two group matches.

**BELOW** Vaunted striker Miroslav Klose with Germany's opening goal in the 2006 World Cup against Ecuador.

**OPPOSITE** Angola's Zé Kalanga and Iran's Mehrzad Madanchi battle for the ball.

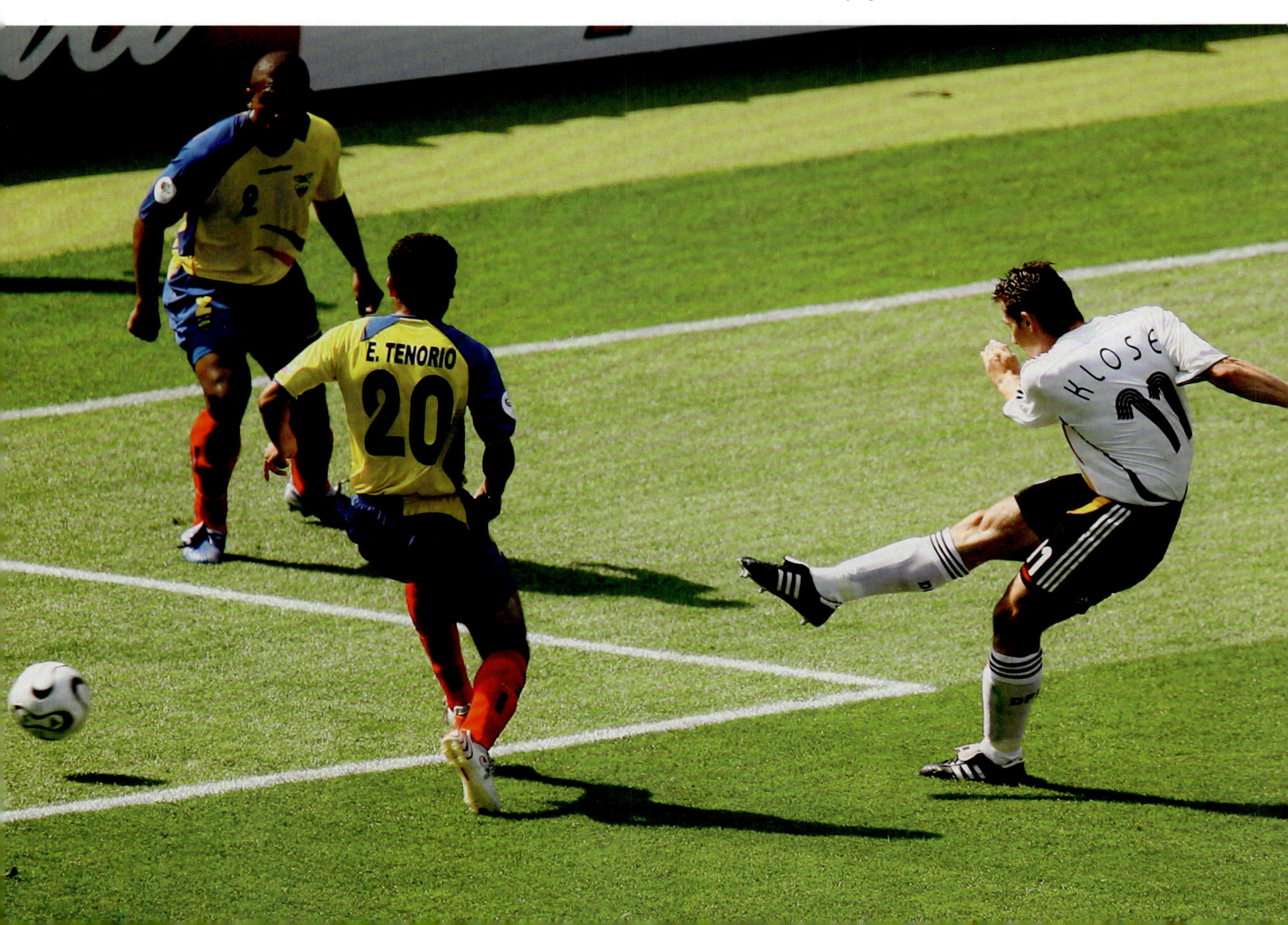

| | | |
|---:|:---:|:---|
| Argentina 2 | 1 | Ivory Coast |
| Netherlands 1 | 0 | Serbia & Montenegro |
| Argentina 6 | 0 | Serbia & Montenegro |
| Netherlands 2 | 1 | Ivory Coast |
| Netherlands 0 | 0 | Argentina |
| Ivory Coast 3 | 2 | Serbia & Montenegro |

**Advanced to Knockout Stage: Argentina, Netherlands**

Group C matched Group A's scoring total with eighteen goals. Argentina's Esteban Cambiasso finished one of the truly great 'team' goals in Cup history by scoring after his side had strung together twenty-one passes in a row. Newcomer Ivory Coast put in an impressive performance but just couldn't slip past the two heavyweights of Argentina and the Netherlands.



| | | |
|---:|:---:|:---|
| Mexico 3 | 1 | Iran |
| Portugal 1 | 0 | Angola |
| Mexico 0 | 0 | Angola |
| Portugal 2 | 0 | Iran |
| Portugal 2 | 1 | Mexico |
| Iran 1 | 1 | Angola |

**Advanced to Knockout Stage: Portugal, Mexico**

Coached by Luiz Felipe Scolari, who guided Brazil to the previous World Cup title, Portugal swept through with maximum points, including a narrow 2–1 victory over the group runner-up, Mexico. The experienced Mexican side was fourth in the FIFA world rankings coming into the tournament but struggled to a 0–0 draw with Angola, who made a respectable showing in their first-ever World Cup appearance.

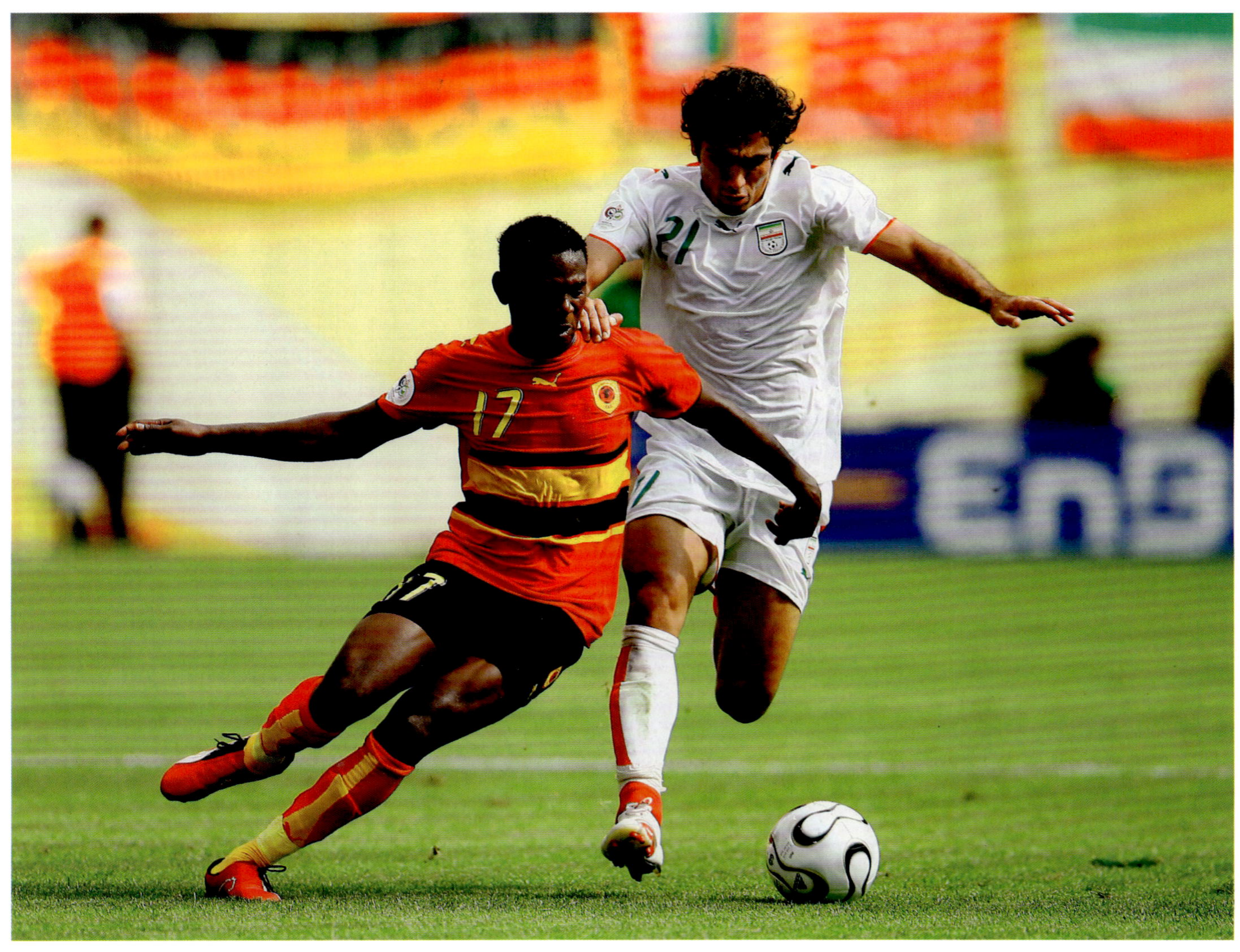

Ghana followed its decisive upset over Czech Republic by knocking a hopeful USA squad out of the tournament. The Americans were fuelled from a bravely fought 1–1 tie with Italy, one of the Cup favourites, that saw three players be red-carded. Italy, ever the defensive stalwarts, conceded just one goal in group play, an own goal versus the United States—a preview of what was to come in the knockout stages.

After a first-half test from Croatia, defending-champion Brazil took charge with a long-range, curling effort from Kaká before sweeping through the group easily. Australia provided the unexpected spark and got through to the next stage. An amusing, well-publicised blunder: Croatia's Josip Šimunić received a second yellow card in the match against Australia but wasn't sent off as required. Three minutes later, he argued heatedly with the ref over a call and was shown a *third* yellow card, after which he was finally tossed from the game. To this day, the only three-card performance in World Cup history… or any history, for that matter.

**BELOW** *Kaká with a curling left-footed shot from range to put Brazil up 1–0 over Croatia.*

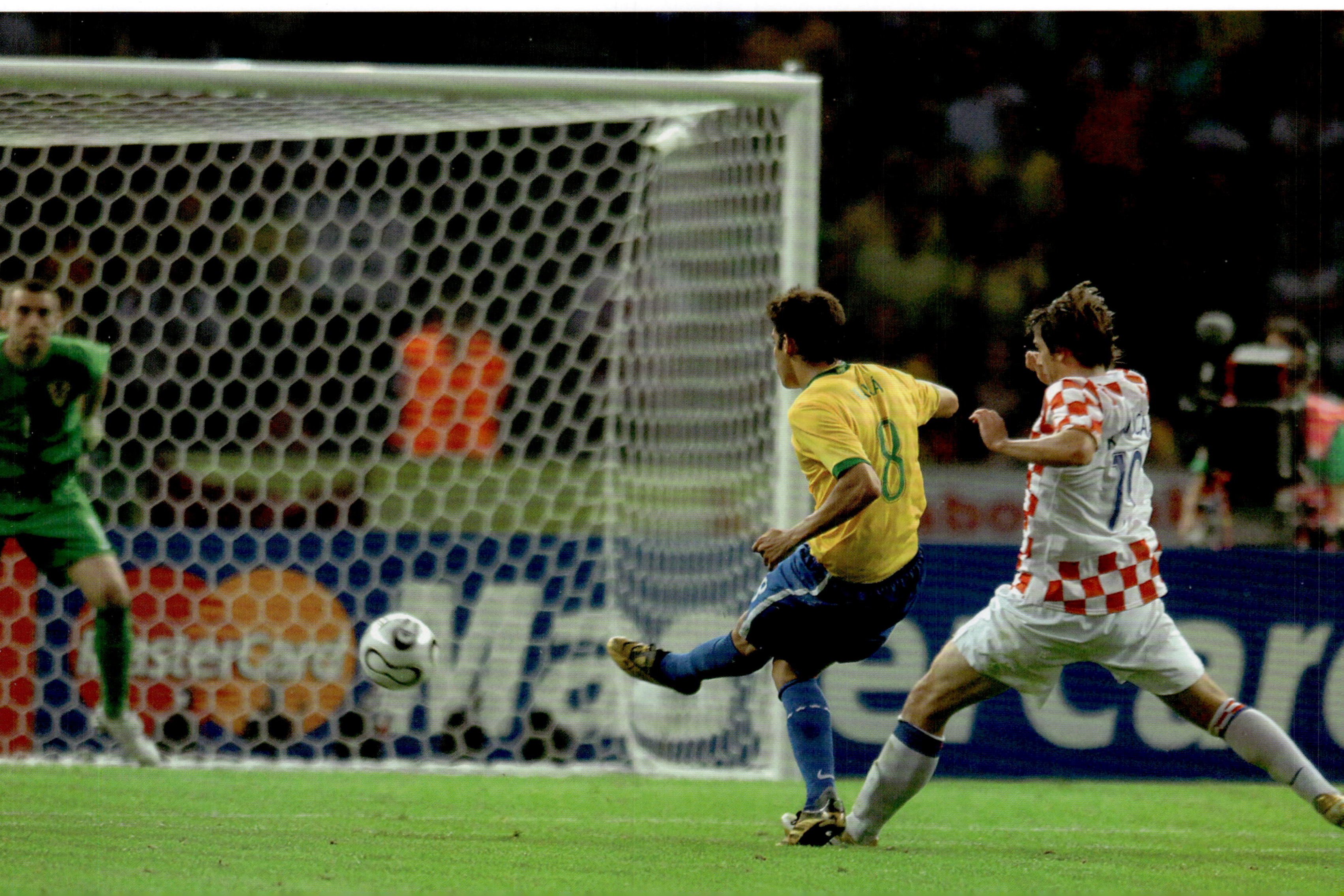

**GROUP G: SWITZERLAND, FRANCE, SOUTH KOREA, TOGO**

| | | |
|---:|:---:|:---|
| South Korea 2 | | 1 Togo |
| France 0 | | 0 Switzerland |
| France 1 | | 1 South Korea |
| Switzerland 2 | | 0 Togo |
| France 2 | | 0 Togo |
| Switzerland 2 | | 0 South Korea |

**Advanced to Knockout Stage: Switzerland, France**

Switzerland posted three shutouts, including a scoreless tie with France in stifling heat, to win the group. France's match with South Korea, another draw, dropped them to second place, but they were determined to redeem themselves after the disastrous 2002 effort and return to the winning ways that saw them crowned in 1998. The French took a step forward with a 2–0 win over unheralded Togo in their third match, despite captain Zinedine Zidane serving a one-game suspension for earning a yellow card in each of France's previous group matches.

**GROUP H: SPAIN, UKRAINE, TUNISIA, SAUDI ARABIA**

| | | |
|---:|:---:|:---|
| Spain 4 | | 0 Ukraine |
| Tunisia 2 | | 2 Saudi Arabia |
| Ukraine 4 | | 0 Saudi Arabia |
| Spain 3 | | 1 Tunisia |
| Spain 1 | | 0 Saudi Arabia |
| Ukraine 1 | | 0 Tunisia |

**Advanced to Knockout Stage: Spain, Ukraine**

Spain won all three matches and looked good doing it, even while playing a full reserve side in their group final versus Saudi Arabia. Despite getting throttled 4–0 by Spain, conceding two goals in the first seventeen minutes, Ukraine bounced back with a pair of wins to take second and advance. In a tense 1–0 win over Tunisia, the Ukrainians were aided by a first-half red card that left the African side playing with ten men.

**BELOW** *Ukraine and AC Milan legend Andriy Shevchenko watches his dynamic header get past Saudi Arabia's Mabrouk Zaid.*

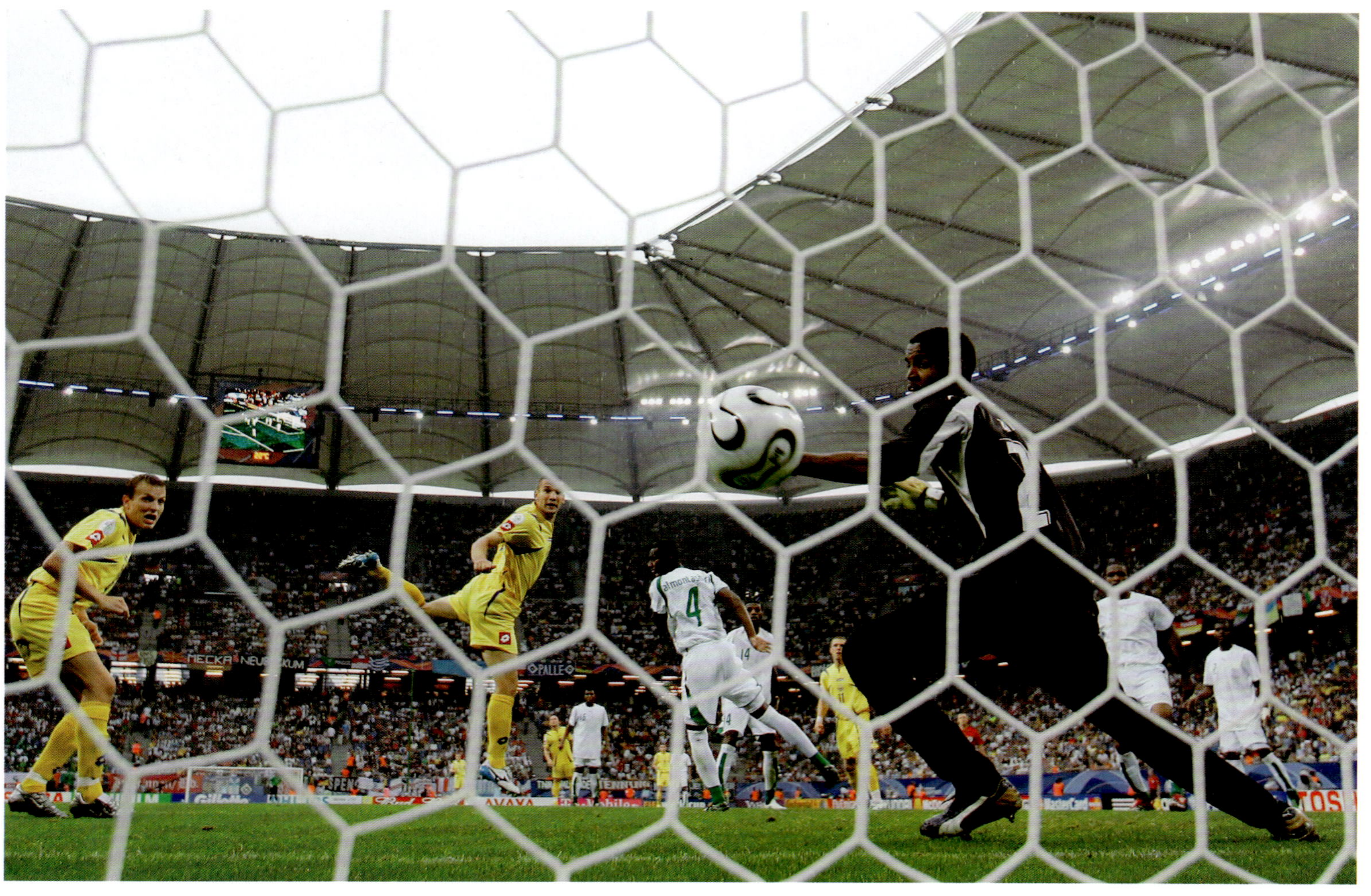

# KNOCKOUT STAGE
## ROUND OF 16

| | |
|---:|:---|
| Germany 2 | 0 Sweden |
| Argentina 2 | 1 Mexico |
| | (after extra time) |
| Italy 1 | 0 Australia |
| Ukraine 0 | 0 Switzerland |
| | (3–0 on penalty kicks) |
| England 1 | 0 Ecuador |
| Portugal 1 | 0 Netherlands |
| Brazil 3 | 0 Ghana |
| France 3 | 1 Spain |

Unlucky Switzerland suffered two unhappy firsts in FIFA World Cup play. First, they became the only team in Cup history that failed to convert *any* of their penalty kicks in a shootout; Ukraine capitalised on the misses to move into the quarter-finals in its first-ever Cup tournament. Second, the Swiss were also the first-ever Cup qualifier eliminated without conceding a single goal. Meanwhile, Ronaldo's goal against Ghana was his fifteenth overall in World Cup competition, moving the Brazilian past Gerd Müller and into first place for all-time scoring. France came from behind to clock Spain, 3–1.

Harkening back to the World Cups of old, the Netherlands–Portugal referee showed an outrageous twenty cards, sixteen yellow and four red, in a rough match that became known as 'The Massacre of Nuremberg'. Argentina struggled into extra time to beat Mexico, Germany dispatched Sweden with ease, and David Beckham's brilliant, bending thirty-yard free kick salvaged a win for England over Ecuador in brutally hot temperatures. Finally, Italy was forced to play a man short for nearly half the match but still managed to eke out a 1–0 win over stubborn Australia, thanks to a penalty shot in the fifth minute of second-half stoppage time.

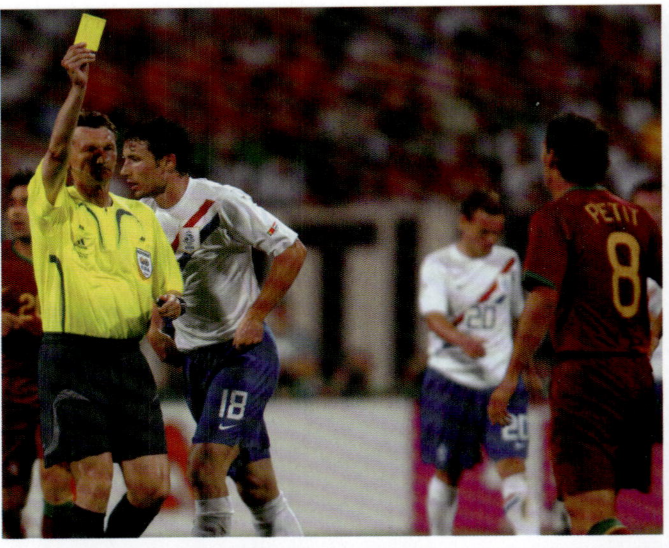

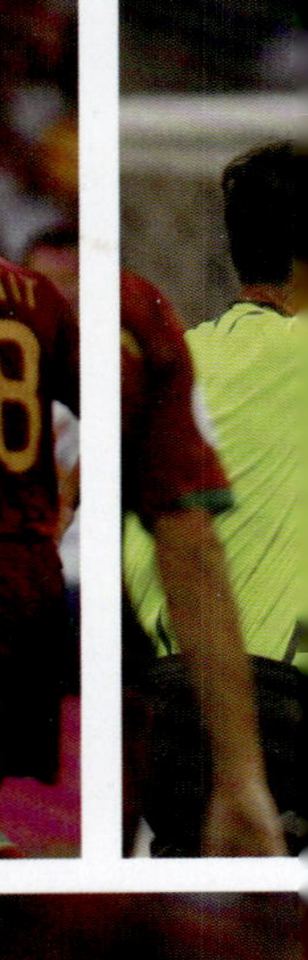

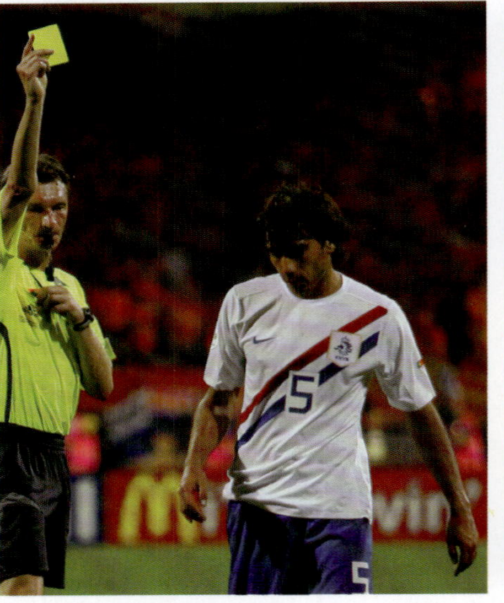

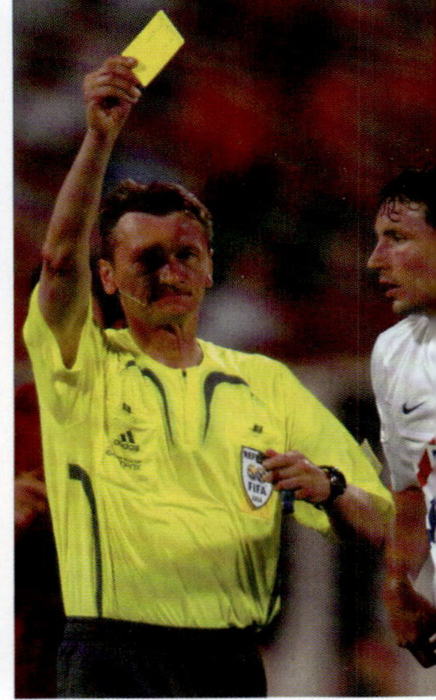

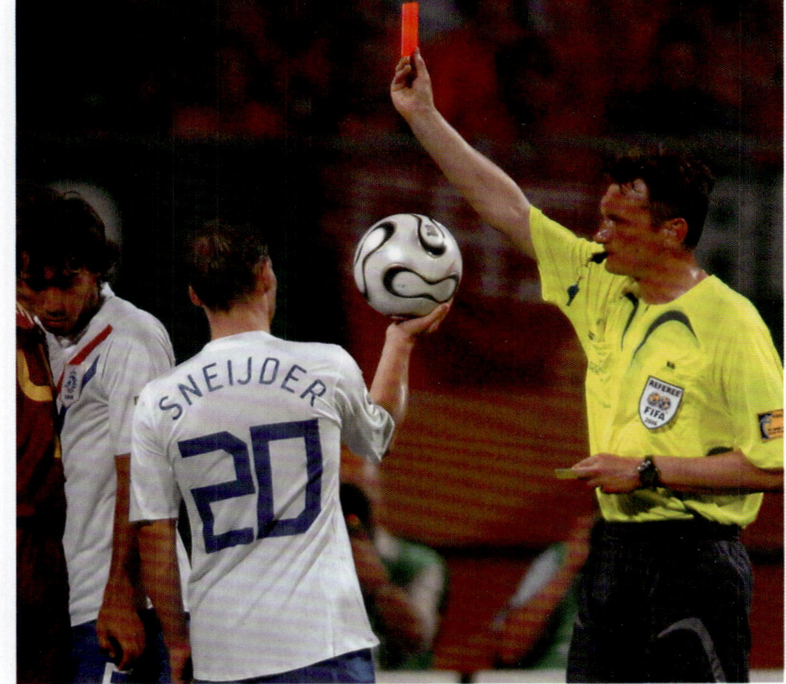

**RIGHT** *A match descends into madness and chaos. Russian referee Valentin Ivano awards nine yellow cards and four red cards in the infamous Round of 16 match between Portugal and the Netherlands.*

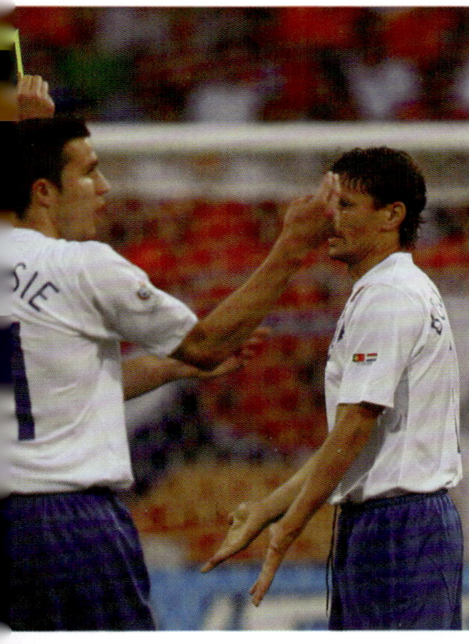
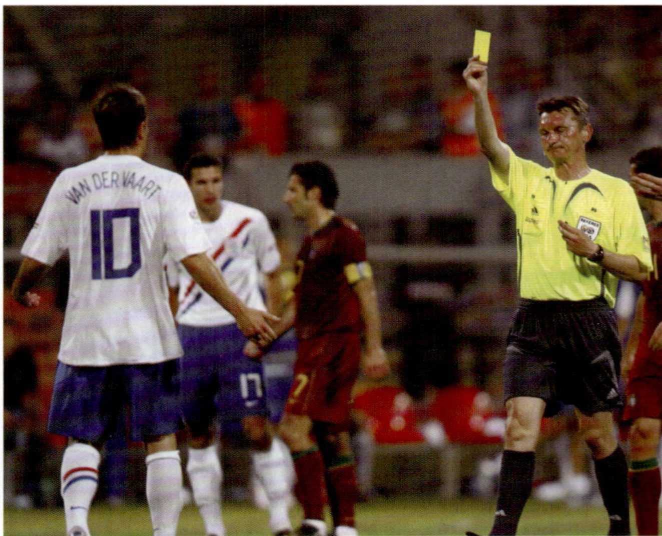
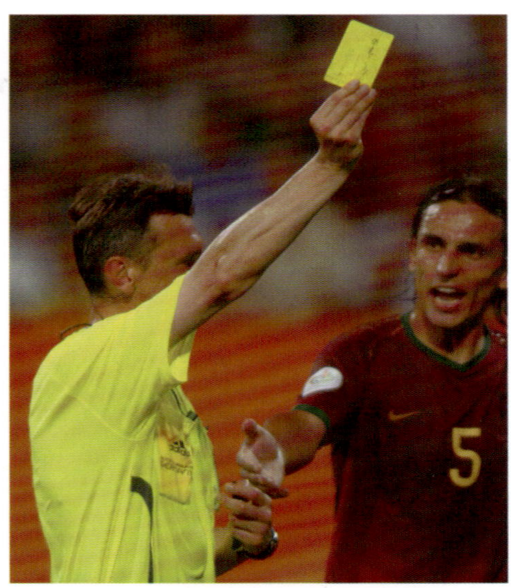
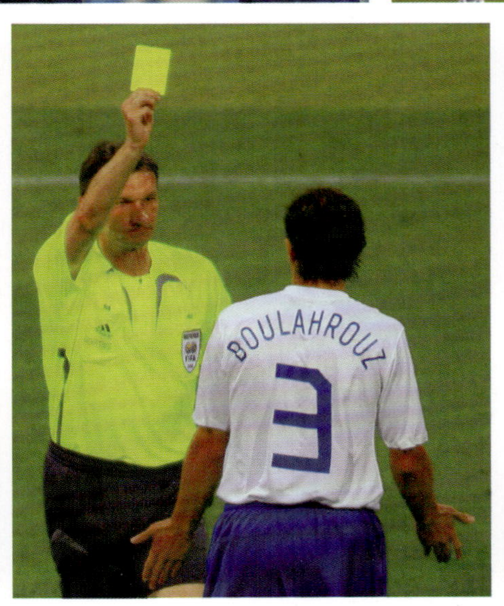
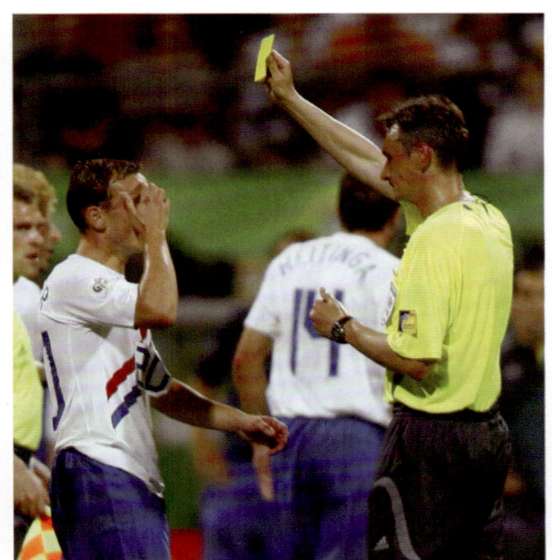
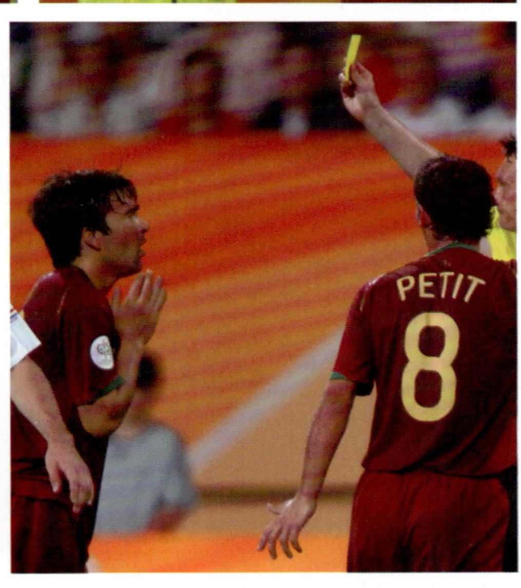
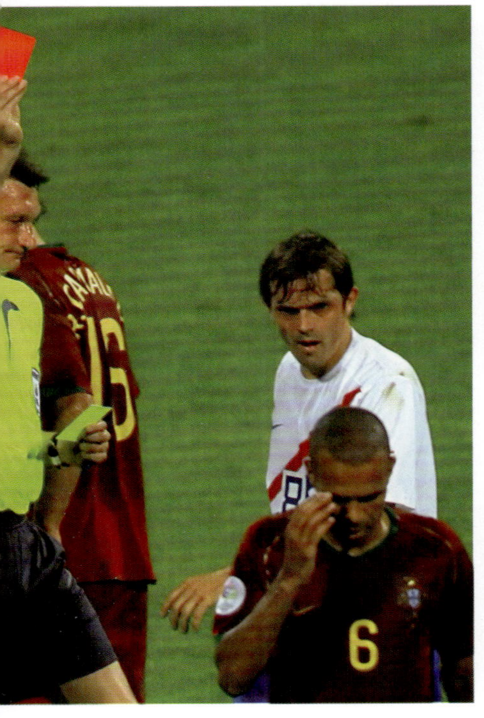
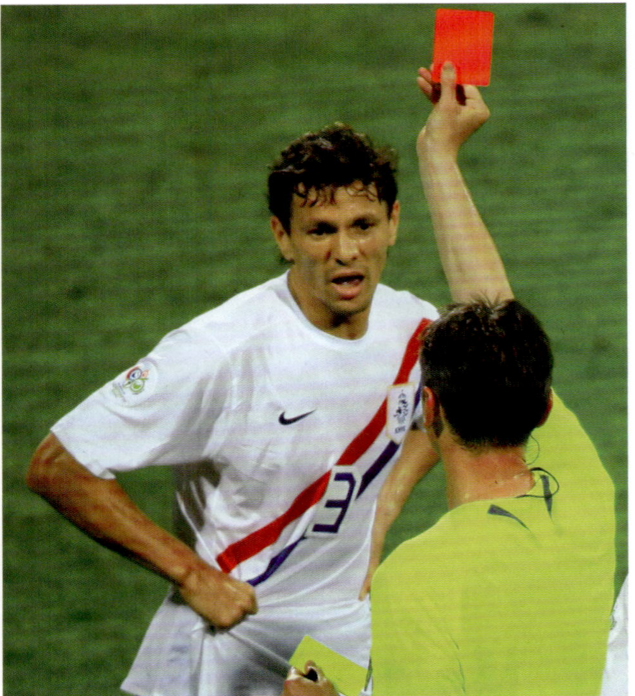
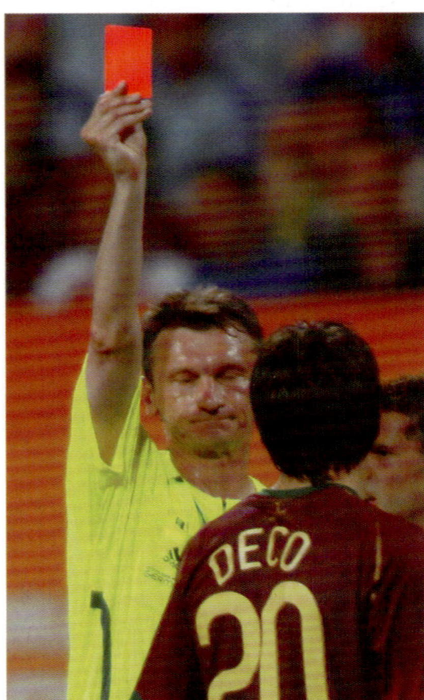

# QUARTER-FINALS

| | |
|---|---|
| Germany 1 | 1 Argentina |
| | (4–2 on penalty kicks) |
| Italy 3 | 0 Ukraine |
| Portugal 0 | 0 England |
| | (3–1 on penalty kicks) |
| France 1 | 0 Brazil |

Zinedine Zidane was absolutely brilliant in France's match with Brazil, asserting full control of the midfield and serving up a perfect free kick to Thierry Henry for the lone goal. Portugal beat England in a shootout to reach its first semi-final round since the great Eusébio-led team of 1966. When Argentina and Germany played to penalty kicks, too, something had to give, as both nations were 3–0 in World Cup shootouts. In the end, Germany won this one on home soil. Finally, Italy crushed Ukraine 3–0 and ended their exciting debut run.

**BELOW** *Zinedine Zidane orchestrating the midfield despite a star-studded Brazilian opposition.*

**OPPOSITE** *Italy set up a wall to defend against a German free kick in the semi-final. (Left to right) Mauro Camoranesi, Alberto Gilardino, Simone Perrotta, Fabio Grosso, Francesco Totti.*

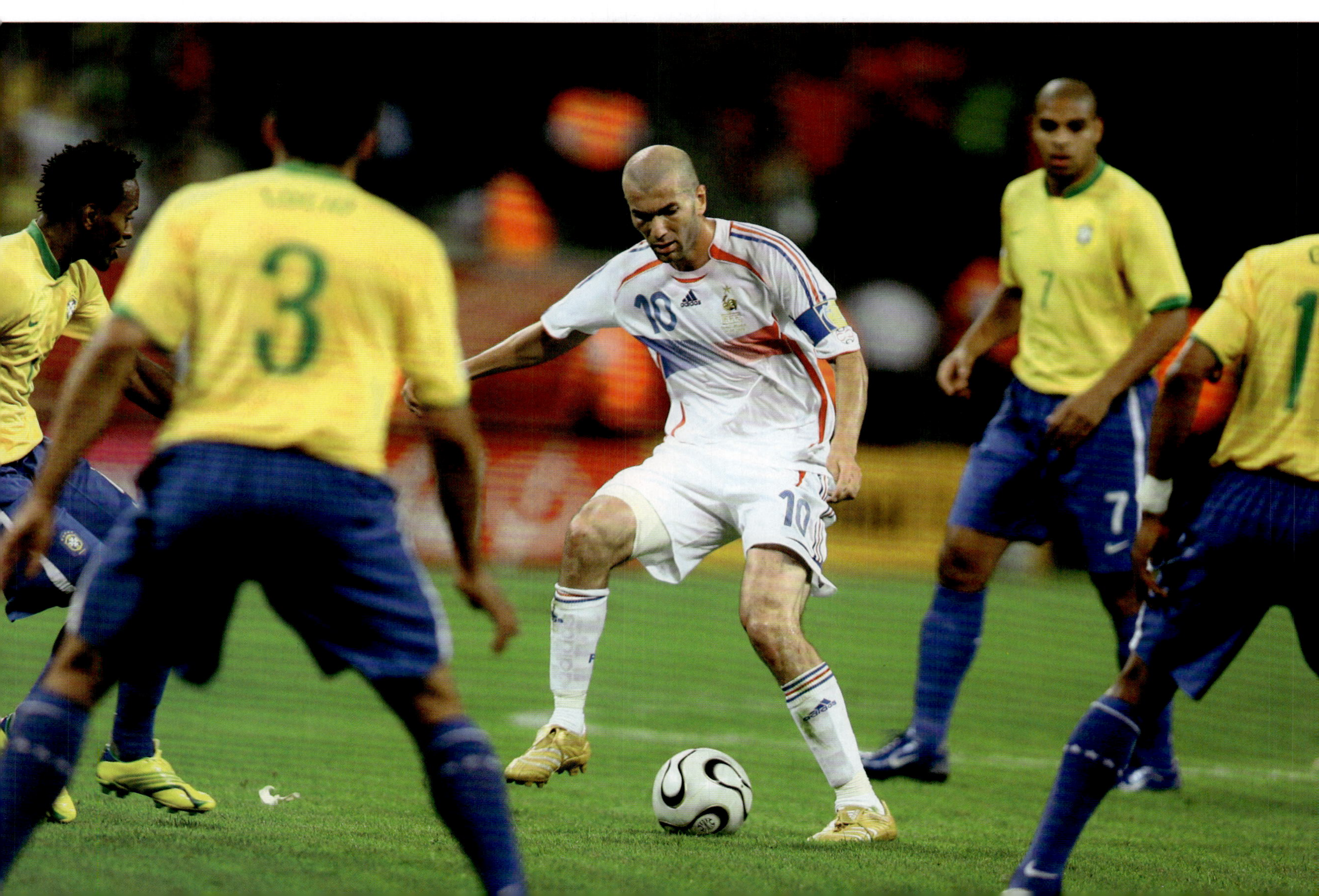

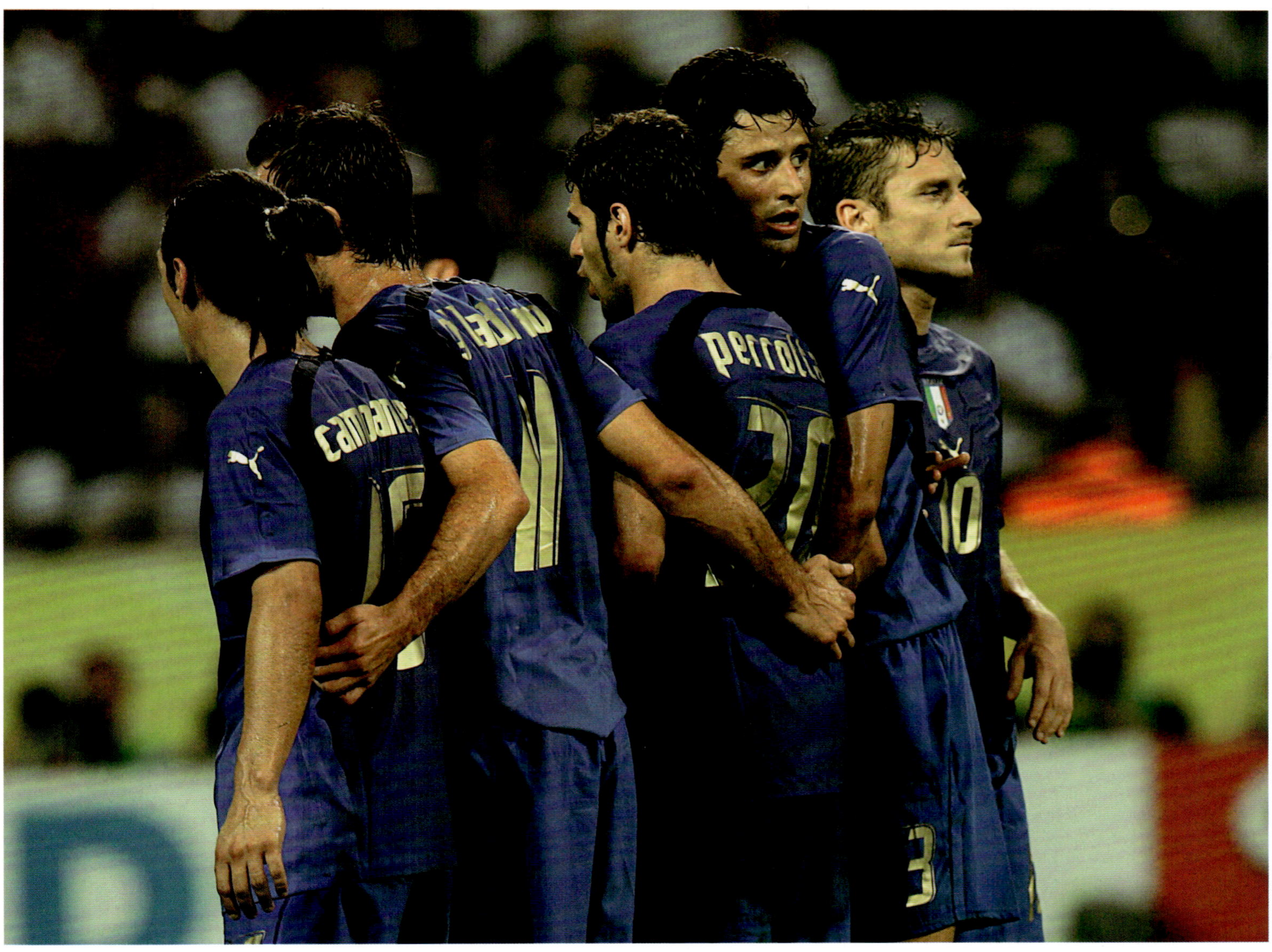

## SEMI-FINALS

Italy 2 | 0 Germany
| (after extra time)
France 1 | 0 Portugal

In the first semi-final, Italy notched its third-straight shut-out in the knockout stage with a 2–0 win over Germany. The match was lively and well-played on both sides. Just two minutes away from a shootout, Italy's late switch to risky attack-heavy tactics paid off with a Fabio Grosso goal. Germany was notoriously clinical from the penalty spot, so Italian coach Marcello Lippi gambled by playing four forwards in the second extra period, hoping to avoid a shootout. With Germany selling out for an equaliser, Italy got a counter and knocked in an insurance goal with time running out.

## THE ITALIAN WALL

**Italy put on perhaps** the greatest defensive performance in World Cup history in 2006. The Blues allowed only two goals in their seven games: one an own goal versus the USA, and the other a penalty kick by Zinedine Zidane in the final. Thus, the 'Italian Wall' didn't allow a single goal (from an opponent) during open play.

The second semi-final had a less stimulating flow, as Zidane converted an early penalty kick and then France settled back and played conservatively for the remainder of the ninety minutes. Portugal produced a few second-half threats but couldn't finish them, in part due to France's back end masterfully dismantling the attacks.

# FINAL

|          |                           |
|----------|---------------------------|
| Italy 1  | 1 France                  |
|          | (5–3 on penalty kicks)    |
|          | (First Place)             |
| Germany 3 | 1 Portugal               |
|          | (Third Place)             |

To the delight of the Stuttgart home crowd, Germany scored three times in twenty minutes in the second half, roaring to a 3–0 lead in the third-place match. All three scores were created by Germany's twenty-one-year-old midfielder Bastian Schweinsteiger: two shots directly into the net, and one from his free kick that ricochetted off Portugal's Petit for an own goal.

## . . . FOR THE AGES

**After all the glorious pregame** pomp and ceremony in Berlin's Olympiastadion, the Cup Final opened on a sour note just seven minutes in when French midfielder Florent Malouda went down in the box and drew a questionable call — replays showed he clipped his own calf and fell. Zinedine Zidane, of course, took the penalty shot. With cheeky arrogance, the French captain lofted a risky 'Panenka penalty', a light chip straight down the middle, pioneered by its Czech namesake Antonín Panenka. Zidane's struck the underside of the crossbar as Italian goalkeeper Gianluigi Buffon dove to his right.

In a dramatic sequence, the ball struck the ground just inside the goal line but bounced straight up, hit the crossbar again, and then rebounded out onto the pitch. The referee called it good. Fortunately, replays showed it was the correct ruling.

Twelve minutes later, Marco Materazzi, who'd been called for the spot foul, got redemption by heading home an Andrea Pirlo corner kick. The rest of the match produced back-and-forth chances but no further results. After ninety minutes, the score remained level. Late in the second period of extra time, Buffon tipped a dangerous header from Zidane over the bar. Just minutes later, with time running down, Zidane and Materazzi had a brief exchange of words . . . and suddenly, the Frenchman slammed his forehead viciously into the Italian's chest, knocking him to the ground. The referee didn't see the strike, but after much consultation with his assistants, he issued Zidane a red card in the 110th minute.

The match went to a shootout. France had only a single miss but Italy, exorcising all demons from 1994, converted all five of its kicks and thus brought home the World Cup for the fourth time. Only Brazil, with five, had more.

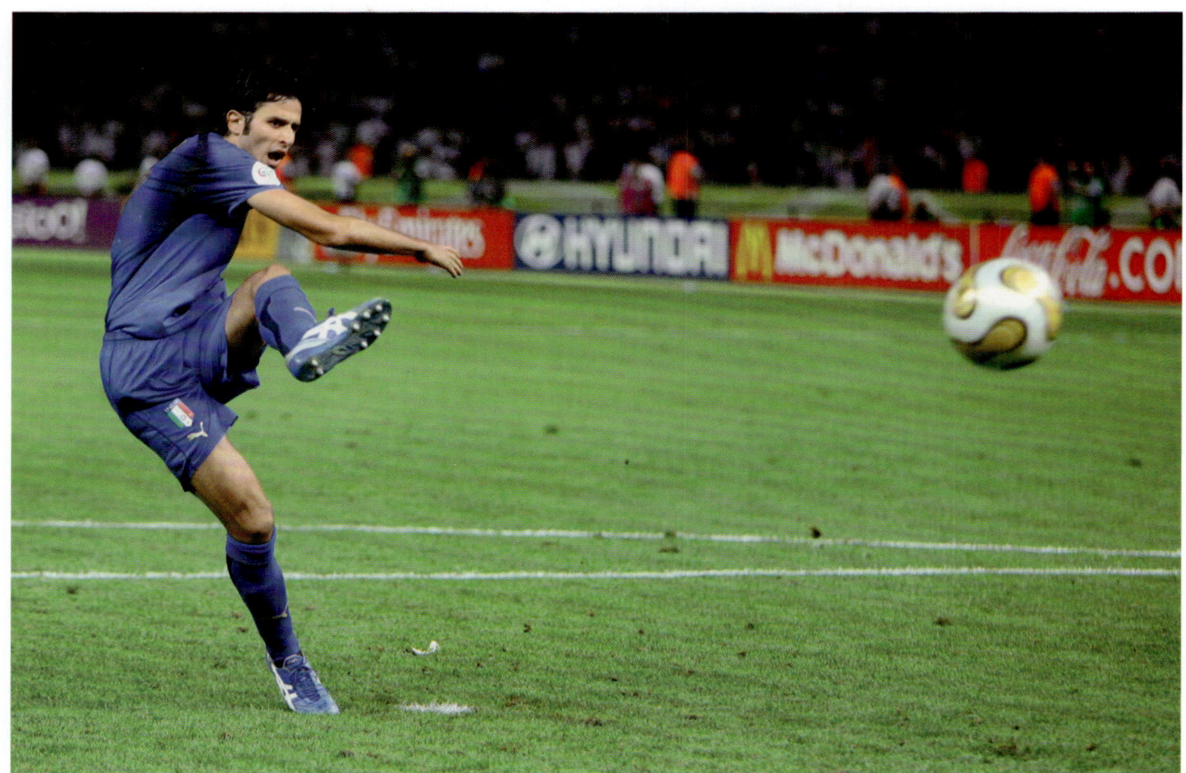

**LEFT** *Fabio Grosso with the winning penalty in the final shootout.*

**OPPOSITE** *The infamous head-butt. Zidane's brilliance made him France's hero in the 1998 final . . . in 2006, his temper made him the villain.*

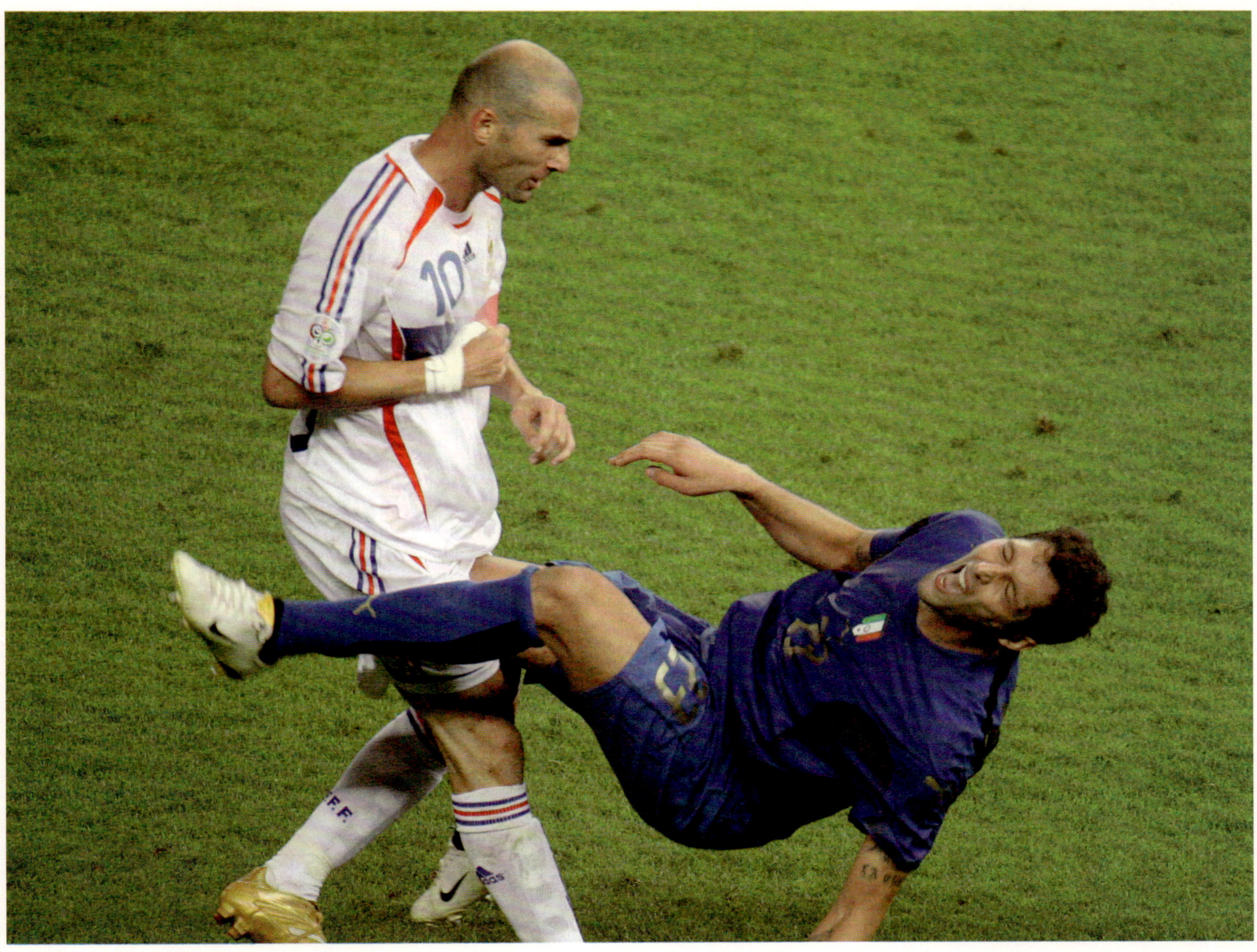

# ANOTHER ZIDANE HEADER

**Zinedine Zidane made history** in 1998 with a pair of powerful headers in the Final that lifted France over Brazil. Eight years later, that explosive forehead would also produce one of the most infamous incidents in modern football: Zidane's dramatic head-butt of Italy's Marco Materazzi. Allegedly, the Italian slyly insulted the Frenchman's sister. The almost inexplicable loss of self-control — with just ten minutes to play in extra time during a Cup Final tied at 1–1 — sent the French captain off with a red card. Although Italy couldn't exploit the man advantage in the waning time, Zidane's absence in the subsequent penalty shootout likely hurt his team, given that he'd missed only four penalty kicks in his long career.

It's certainly unfortunate that such an incident would mar the last minutes of a nonpareil playing career: Zidane had already announced he would retire after the Cup, citing his declining skills. Ironic, too, because Zidane was a master of control on the pitch. His peers worshipped him. David Beckham called him 'the greatest of all time'. Pelé said, 'He made the game beautiful.' And Zlatan Ibrahimović added perhaps the greatest compliment: 'When Zidane stepped on the pitch, the ten other guys just got suddenly better.' He was named FIFA World Player of the Year three times.

The infamous head-butt will live on in football lore, without a doubt, but so will Zidane's eminence as one of the greatest midfielders to ever grace the World Cup. 'People always remember the head-butt,' notes The Guardian. 'They forget that Zidane, in his last appearance as a player at age thirty-four, was also awarded the Golden Ball as best player of the 2006 tournament.' It was no legacy award. Zidane was indeed still the best on the pitch in Germany 2006.

# 2010–PRESENT

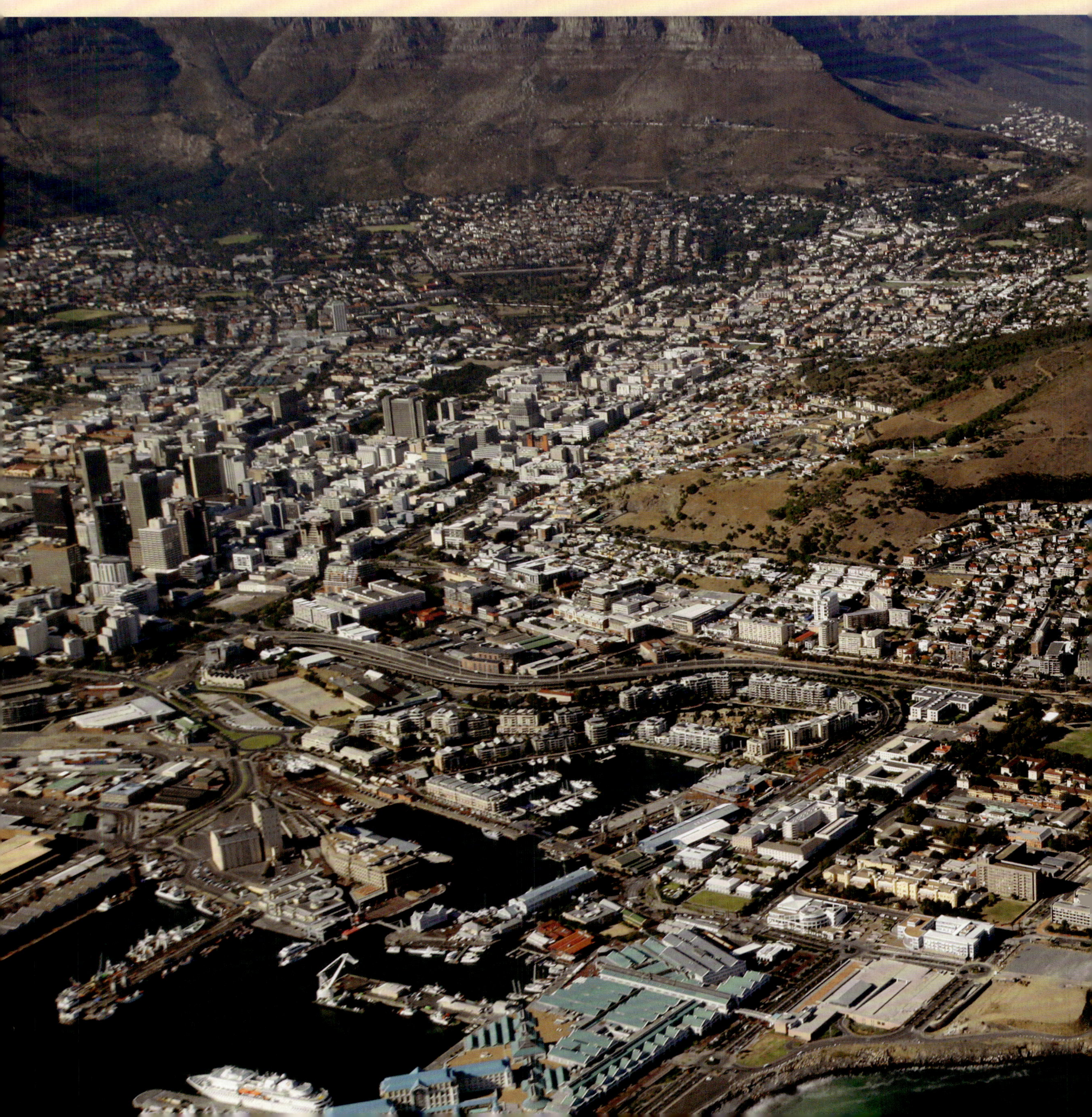

# CHAPTER 9

# *Historic Hosts, Tiki-Taka, the New King?*

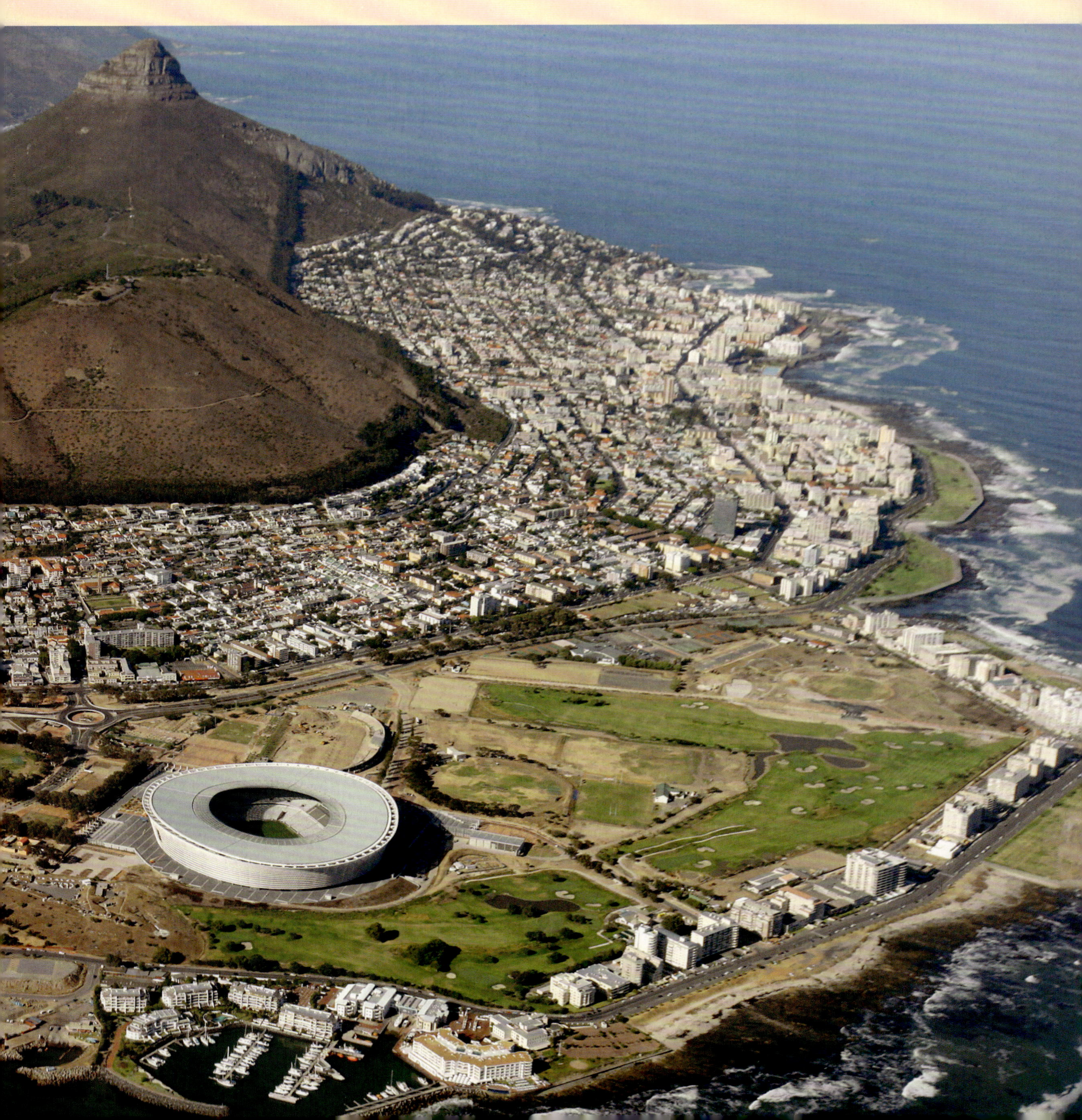

# 2010



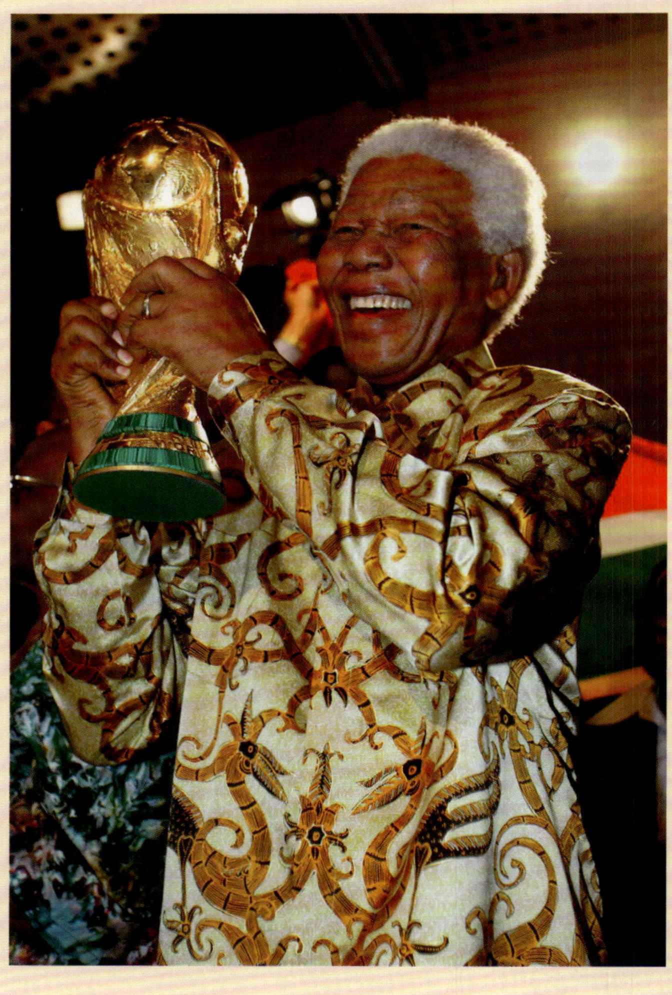

**FIFA had its eyes on** staging an African-hosted World Cup since the mid-1990s, so when South Africa's bid to host the 2010 tournament received a boost from an eminent historical figure, FIFA was ready to listen. Nelson Mandela, a lifelong sports enthusiast, called football 'the people's sport' and spoke of how 'the game made us feel alive and triumphant despite our situation' during his twenty-seven-year imprisonment for opposing the old apartheid system. Mandela's gentle lobbying made the difference, and after the South African proposal was confirmed, FIFA President Sepp Blatter presented the beloved Nobel Peace Prize winner and former South African president with a carefully crafted replica of the World Cup Trophy.

**PREVIOUS SPREAD** *A stunning aerial view of Cape Town, South Africa. At the bottom, just right of centre, is the Cape Town Stadium. Its contemporary design and waterfront location promise a new era for the World Cup.*

**LEFT** *Former South African president, and revolutionary icon, Nelson Mandela lifts the World Cup Trophy as South Africa is announced as the hosts of the 2010*
*World Cup. Zurich, Switzerland. 15 May, 2004.*

**OPPOSITE TOP** *Diego Forlán with a twenty-five-yard goal against South Africa. The Uruguayan veteran was the tournament's Golden Ball recipient, in part due to notching multiple stunners from long distance.*

**OPPOSITE BOTTOM** *South African fans and the polarising vuvuzela horns.*

## DON'T WORRY, 'BE HAPPY!'

**One of the more interesting** and controversial decisions made by the FIFA tournament committee for the 2010 World Cup was to commission a new official match football. Created and manufactured by Adidas, the Jabulani (which translates to 'Be happy!' in Zulu) featured eight spherically moulded panels with uniquely textured surfaces designed to 'improve aerodynamics'.

The result was a ball that served as every goalkeeper's nightmare. When struck with force, the Jabulani exhibited enough movement in flight to rival particles in the quantum realm. Hugo Lloris of France called the ball 'a disaster'. Gianluigi Buffon of Italy called it 'shameful'. Júlio César of Brazil compared it to a cheap supermarket ball; Iker Casillas of Spain called it 'a beach ball'. And David James of England famously said it 'left goalkeepers looking daft'.

But the ball's unpredictable flight path led to some of the most thrilling long-distance strikes in World Cup history. Every well-struck ball became a swerving, dipping, hypersonic missile. Strikers, of course, liked this characteristic. Uruguay's Diego Forlán loved the ball, launching several highly kinetic goals, including a stunning thirty-yard blast so directionally unstable that the South African goalkeeper just stood rooted to the spot. In the end, the Jabulani was deemed too capricious a traveler, and Adidas ended production of the ball two years later.

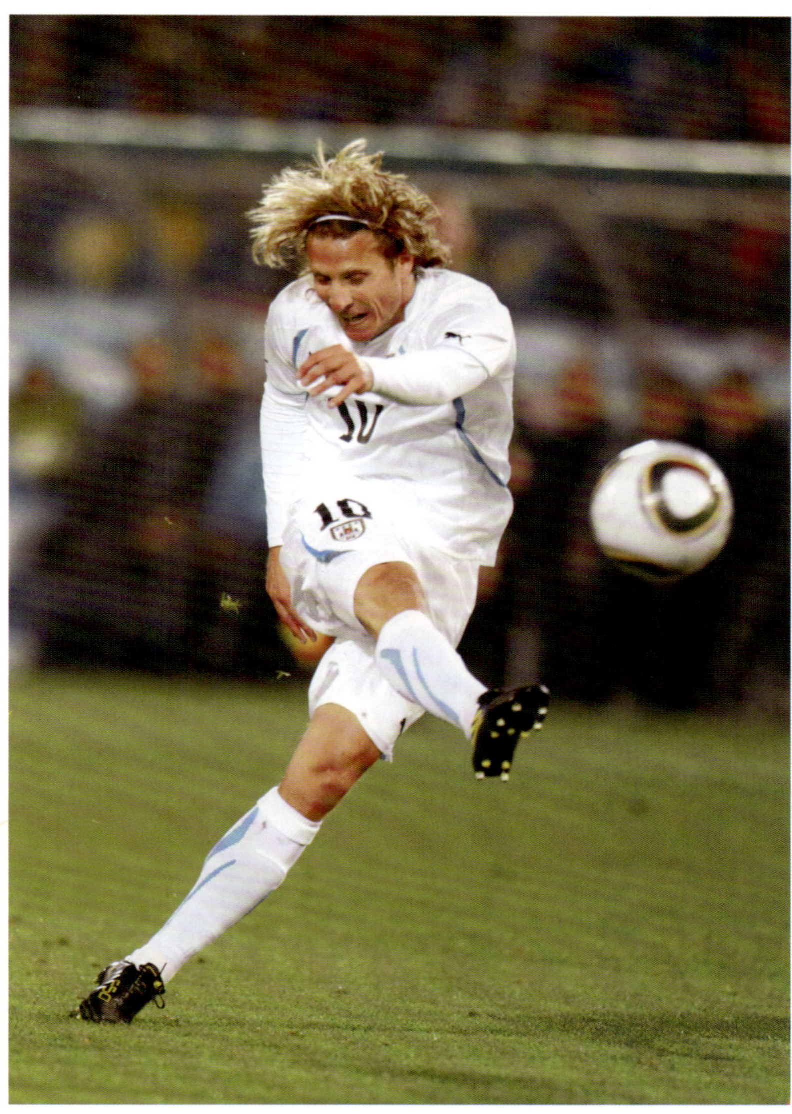

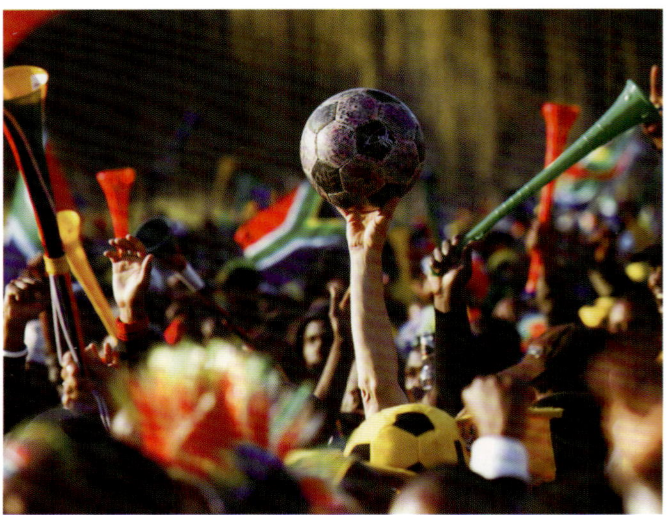

## WHAT'S THAT BUZZING?

The 2010 World Cup introduced the wider sporting world to that now-familiar 'angry hornet swarm' harmonics of the vuvuzela. Tens of thousands of South African fans brought their deafening plastic horns to the stadiums and changed the soundscape of World Cup fanaticism forever. Some people loved the cultural phenomenon . . . some did not. Regardless, you couldn't deny the aural assault in every South African stadium during the summer of 2010. One medical journal estimated that fans in a vuvuzela throng were exposed to an average of 140 decibels — the equivalent of standing next to a jet engine.

# Tournament: GROUP STAGE

### GROUP A: URUGUAY, MEXICO, SOUTH AFRICA, FRANCE

| | | |
|---|---|---|
| South Africa 1 | 1 | Mexico |
| Uruguay 0 | 0 | France |
| Uruguay 3 | 0 | South Africa |
| Mexico 2 | 0 | France |
| Uruguay 1 | 0 | Mexico |
| South Africa 2 | 1 | France |

***Advanced to Knockout Stage: Uruguay, Mexico***

### GROUP B: ARGENTINA, SOUTH KOREA, GREECE, NIGERIA

| | | |
|---|---|---|
| South Korea 2 | 0 | Greece |
| Argentina 1 | 0 | Nigeria |
| Argentina 4 | 1 | South Korea |
| Greece 2 | 1 | Nigeria |
| Nigeria 2 | 2 | South Korea |
| Argentina 2 | 0 | Greece |

***Advanced to Knockout Stage: Argentina, South Korea***

Once again, a finalist from the previous World Cup would fail to emerge from group play. A dissension-racked France scored only one goal and lost twice to end up last in Group A, evoking the debacle from the 2002 tournament. The host South African team, on the other hand, got off to a strong start. In the second half of the opening match against Mexico, Siphiwe Tshabalala fired off an absolute missile of a strike for one of the most explosive, and textbook, first goals in World Cup history. Ultimately, though, South Africa wound up tied with Mexico for second place on points but lost out due to goal differential. Uruguay, led by a veteran Diego Forlán at the peak of his powers and energised by a rising young star named Luis Suárez, finished comfortably at the top.

Against Nigeria, Argentina's dangerous corps of young forwards showed plenty of attacking flair but struggled to finish their chances and ended up with a slim 1–0 win. Perhaps they were distracted by the now-infamous fan in the Ellis Park Stadium stands who kept shining a green-laser pointer pen at Argentine players and coaches during the game.

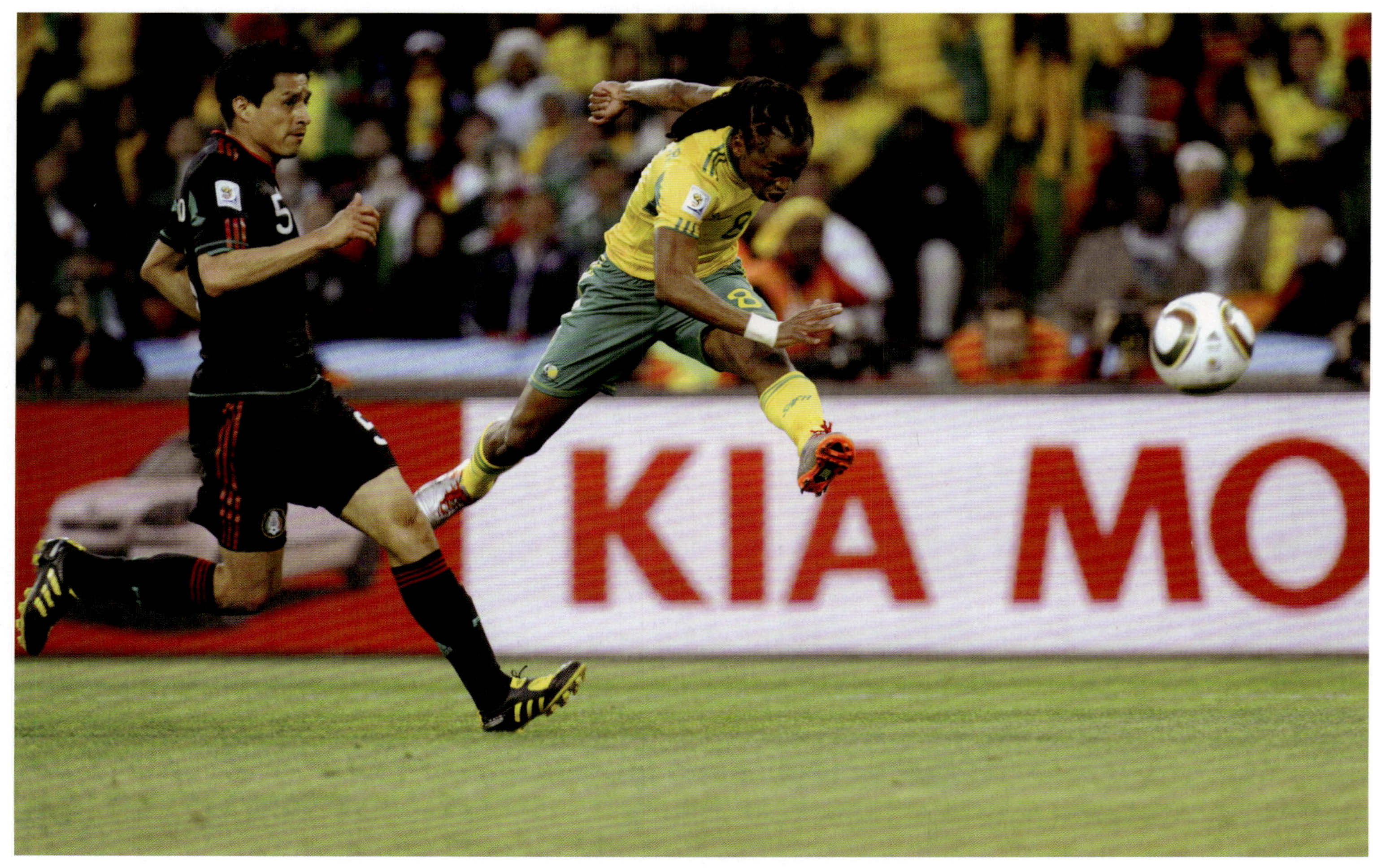

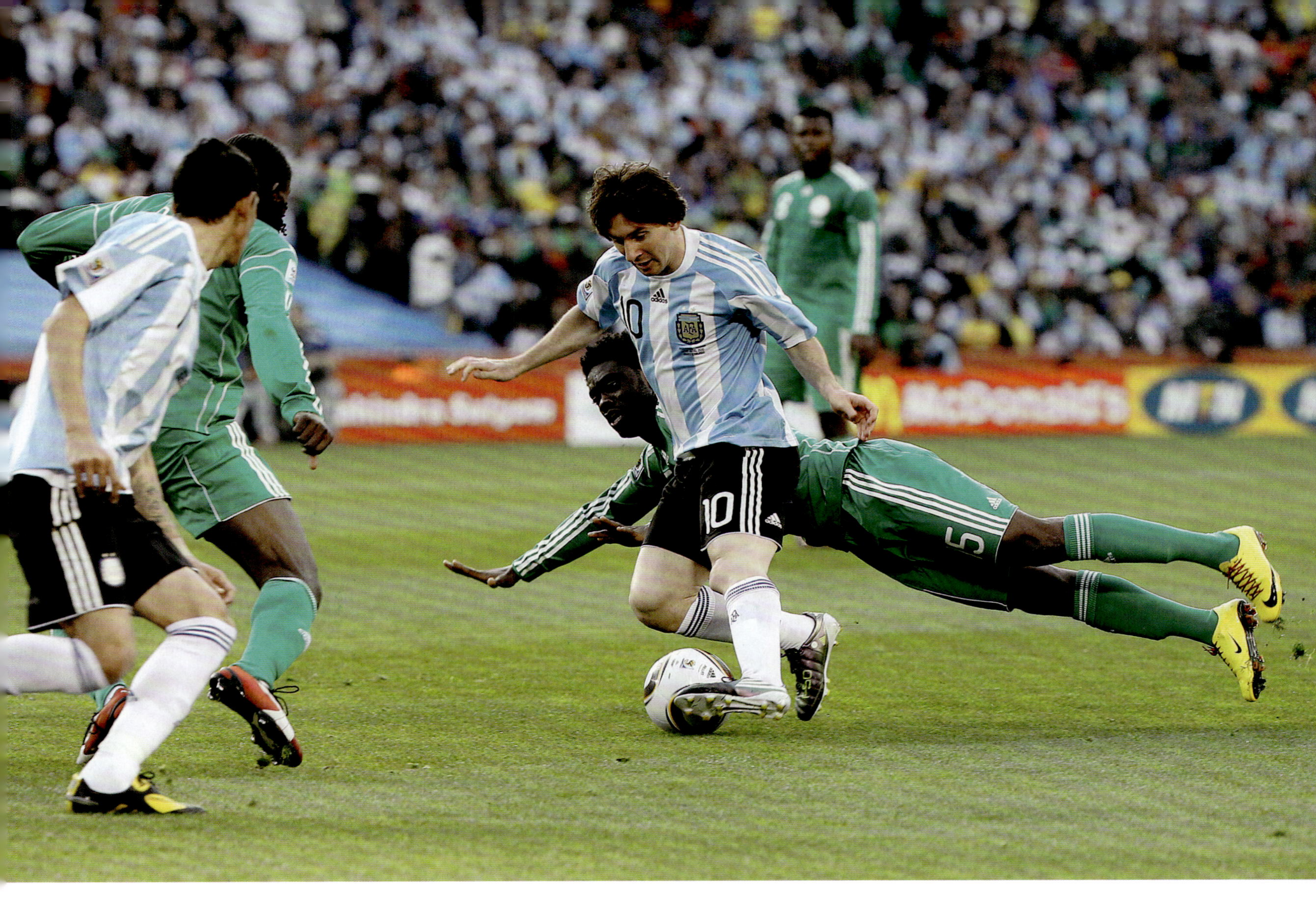

## THE KIDS ARE ALL RIGHT

Argentina featured Diego Maradona as its manager, veteran stars on the roster, and a trio of hungry twenty-two-year-olds in Gonzalo Higuaín, Sergio Agüero, and Ángel Di María. Of course, there was another twenty-two-year-old lad on the roster who was already a superstar. By 2010, Lionel Messi was an established force of nature at his club FC Barcelona. Under manager Pep Guardiola, Messi had won the 2009 Ballon d'Or by tallying forty-one goals and fifteen assists in the calendar year while leading Barcelona to the mythical 'sextuple' of trophies. In Argentina's opening Cup match in South Africa, he gave Nigeria nightmares in what *The Guardian* described as 'a performance of bewitching guile'. Few teams in football history could boast such a deep, dynamic, and youthful core.

**OPPOSITE** *South Africa's Siphiwe Tshabalala (right) launches an astonishing long-range strike for the opening goal of the 2010 World Cup.*

**ABOVE** *Argentina's Lionel Messi displaying his prodigious close-dribbling skills to get around Nigeria's Lukman Haruna.*

**GROUP C: USA, ENGLAND, SLOVENIA, ALGERIA**

| England 1 | 1 USA |
|---|---|
| Slovenia 1 | 0 Algeria |
| Slovenia 2 | 2 USA |
| England 0 | 0 Algeria |
| England 1 | 0 Slovenia |
| USA 1 | 0 Algeria |

***Advanced to Knockout Stage: USA, England***

After draws with England and Slovenia, the latter featuring a stunning Landon Donovan strike from a near-impossible angle, the USA got a dramatic stoppage-time goal against Algeria (again from talisman Landon Donovan) to lock up a surprising group win over the English based on goals scored. Donovan's rousing finish remains a highlight moment of his country's history in World Cup competition—especially because another tie would have dropped them to third place and out of the tournament.

**GROUP D: GERMANY, GHANA, AUSTRALIA, SERBIA**

| Ghana 1 | 0 Serbia |
|---|---|
| Germany 4 | 0 Australia |
| Serbia 1 | 0 Germany |
| Ghana 1 | 1 Australia |
| Germany 1 | 0 Ghana |
| Australia 2 | 1 Serbia |

***Advanced to Knockout Stage: Germany, Ghana***

Germany's stumble against Serbia was facilitated by the sendoff of Miroslav Klose in the thirty-sixth minute, leaving just ten Germans on the field for the rest of the match. Ghana's only two goals in group play came from penalty kicks, one that beat Serbia and another that tied Australia, enough to squeak into second place as the only African team to reach the knockout stage.

**GROUP E: NETHERLANDS, JAPAN, DENMARK, CAMEROON**

| Netherlands 2 | 0 Denmark |
|---|---|
| Japan 1 | 0 Cameroon |
| Netherlands 1 | 0 Japan |
| Denmark 2 | 1 Cameroon |
| Japan 3 | 1 Denmark |
| Netherlands 2 | 1 Cameroon |

***Advanced to Knockout Stage: Netherlands, Japan***

Led by talented forwards Robin van Persie and Arjen Robben, a rejuvenated Netherlands side won all three matches, while Japan was the surprise package, upending both Denmark and Cameroon and advancing to the next round.

**GROUP F: PARAGUAY, SLOVAKIA, NEW ZEALAND, ITALY**

| Italy 1 | 1 Paraguay |
|---|---|
| New Zealand 1 | 1 Slovakia |
| Paraguay 2 | 0 Slovakia |
| Italy 1 | 1 New Zealand |
| Slovakia 3 | 2 Italy |
| Paraguay 0 | 0 New Zealand |

***Advanced to Knockout Stage: Paraguay, Slovakia***

Defending-champion Italy joined fellow 2006 finalist France at the bottom of their respective groups. After Italy's aging squad struggled to a shocking tie with New Zealand, the Azzurri entered their final match needing at least a tie to move on. Instead, they got upended by an inspired Slovakian side that had looked quite pedestrian in its first two matches.

**OPPOSITE** *USA talisman Landon Donovan blasts the ball to score from an exceptionally difficult near-post angle in the Group C match with Slovenia.*

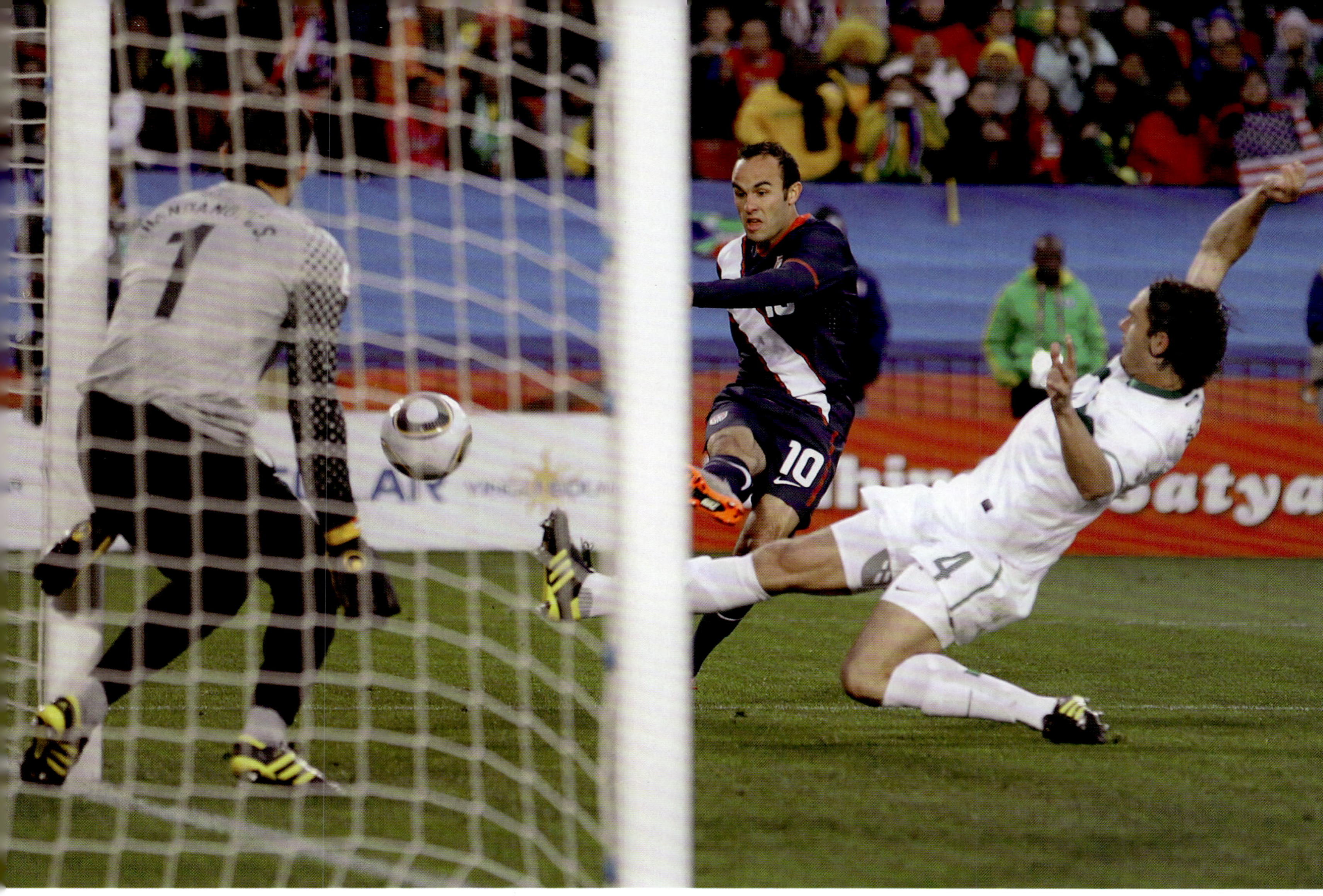

## GROUP G: BRAZIL, PORTUGAL, IVORY COAST, NORTH KOREA

| | |
|---|---|
| Ivory Coast 0 | 0 Portugal |
| Brazil 2 | 1 North Korea |
| Brazil 3 | 1 Ivory Coast |
| Portugal 7 | 0 North Korea |
| Brazil 0 | 0 Portugal |
| Ivory Coast 3 | 0 North Korea |

**Advanced to Knockout Stage: Brazil, Portugal**

Portugal decided to remember the lesson from 1966 in its 2010 rematch against North Korea—this time, six second-half goals buried the North Koreans. Unfortunately, Portugal's much-anticipated final group match versus Brazil did not meet expectations (one writer called it 'a crashing bore'), as both sides played conservatively to preserve qualification for the knockout stage. All the players on the pitch were booed off at the final whistle.

## GROUP H: SPAIN, CHILE, SWITZERLAND, HONDURAS

| | |
|---|---|
| Chile 1 | 0 Honduras |
| Switzerland 1 | 0 Spain |
| Chile 1 | 0 Switzerland |
| Spain 2 | 0 Honduras |
| Spain 2 | 1 Chile |
| Switzerland 0 | 0 Honduras |

**Advanced to Knockout Stage: Spain, Chile**

After a disappointing 0–1 loss to Switzerland, Spain rallied to win its next two. Conversely, Switzerland couldn't match that first effort and lost the next two, allowing Chile to lock down second place. Chile's refreshing style of attack-oriented football, often pushing seven men forward, earned two solid victories and drew a lot of attention. Overall, Group H exhibited some of the tournament's most competitive play—all six matches were tense and closely contested.

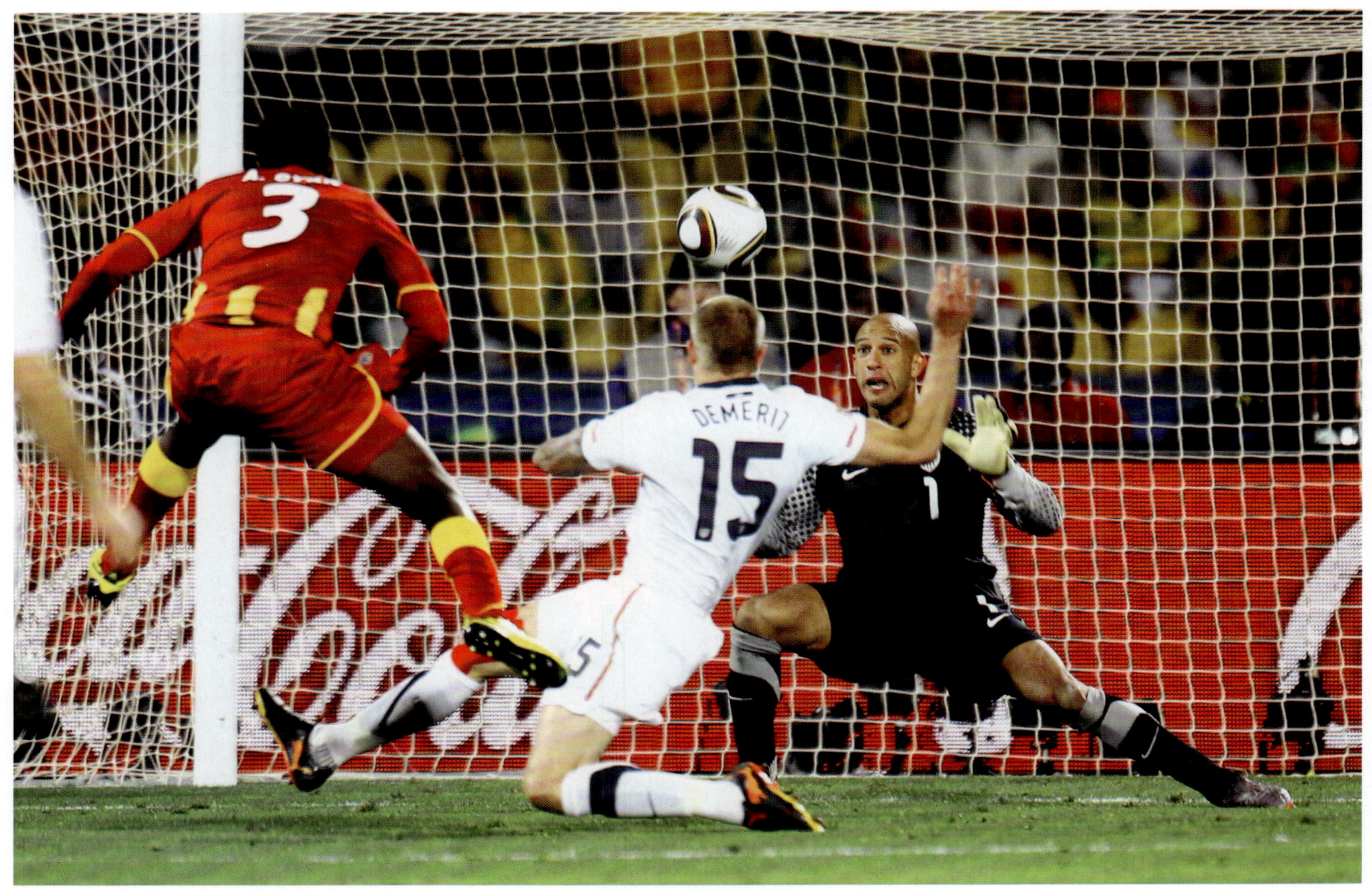

## KNOCKOUT STAGE
## ROUND OF 16

| | | |
|---:|:---:|:---|
| Uruguay 2 | 1 | South Korea |
| Ghana 2 | 1 | USA |
| Netherlands 2 | 1 | Slovakia |
| Brazil 3 | 0 | Chile |
| Argentina 3 | 1 | Mexico |
| Germany 4 | 1 | England |
| Paraguay 0 | 0 | Japan |
| | | (5–3 on penalty kicks) |
| Spain 1 | 0 | Portugal |

Despite the close scoreline, Spain was rarely pressed in beating its Iberian neighbour Portugal. A brace from Luis Suárez advanced Uruguay, the second goal a particularly magnificent looping shot. After a determined American side clawed back from an early one-goal deficit, Ghana's Asamoah Gyan collected a long pass and muscled past a defensive challenge to score in extra time for the win. Carlos Tevez scored two to pace Argentina's easy win over Mexico.

Brazil whisked Chile aside easily, 3–0, but Paraguay needed a shootout to beat scrappy Japan. England's bruising 4–1 loss to Germany was their worst ever in a World Cup tournament. Painfully, an obvious English goal (as seen in replays) was disallowed. That controversy would hasten the advent of goal-line technology, which would be seen at the next Cup in 2014. Finally, creative winger Arjen Robben's return from injury propelled the Netherlands to a win over Slovakia.

**ABOVE** *Xavi Hernández's precise passing and tempo control were instrumental to the implementation of Spain's tiki-taka system.*

**OPPOSITE** *Ghana's Asamoah Gyan shoots the ball past USA's Tim Howard for the 2–1 victory in the Round of 16.*

## TIKI-TAKA

**Spain's successful run** through the 2010 Cup was built on an almost religious adherence to a style of play called 'tiki-taka' football — a label that sounds frivolous but, in execution, can be lethal and deadly serious. A possession-based style characterised by short, quick passes and a high pressing defence, Spain's tiki-taka relied on great technical skill, particularly in tight spaces, and relentless pressure from front to back. Success was built on collective effort and inter-changeable roles, with a tactical flexibility not unlike the 'total football' concept popularised by the Dutch in the 1970s.

True, Spain's style was flowing and often beautiful. Spain's possession rate hovered around a stunning 65 to 70 percent, even against top-rung opponents. But it served very basic, aggressive, sometimes even inelegant purposes — the more possession you have, the more you limit your opponent's options. Defensively, tiki-taka's wilful control of pace and space, and its relentless high-press, was downright brutal.

'Put simply: Spain "defends" by possessing the ball,' wrote analyst Sid Lowe in *Sports Illustrated*. 'If you don't have possession, you cannot attack Spain.' And as the great German striker Miroslav Klose explained: 'When we did eventually win the ball, we were so exhausted from chasing it that we couldn't do anything with it.'

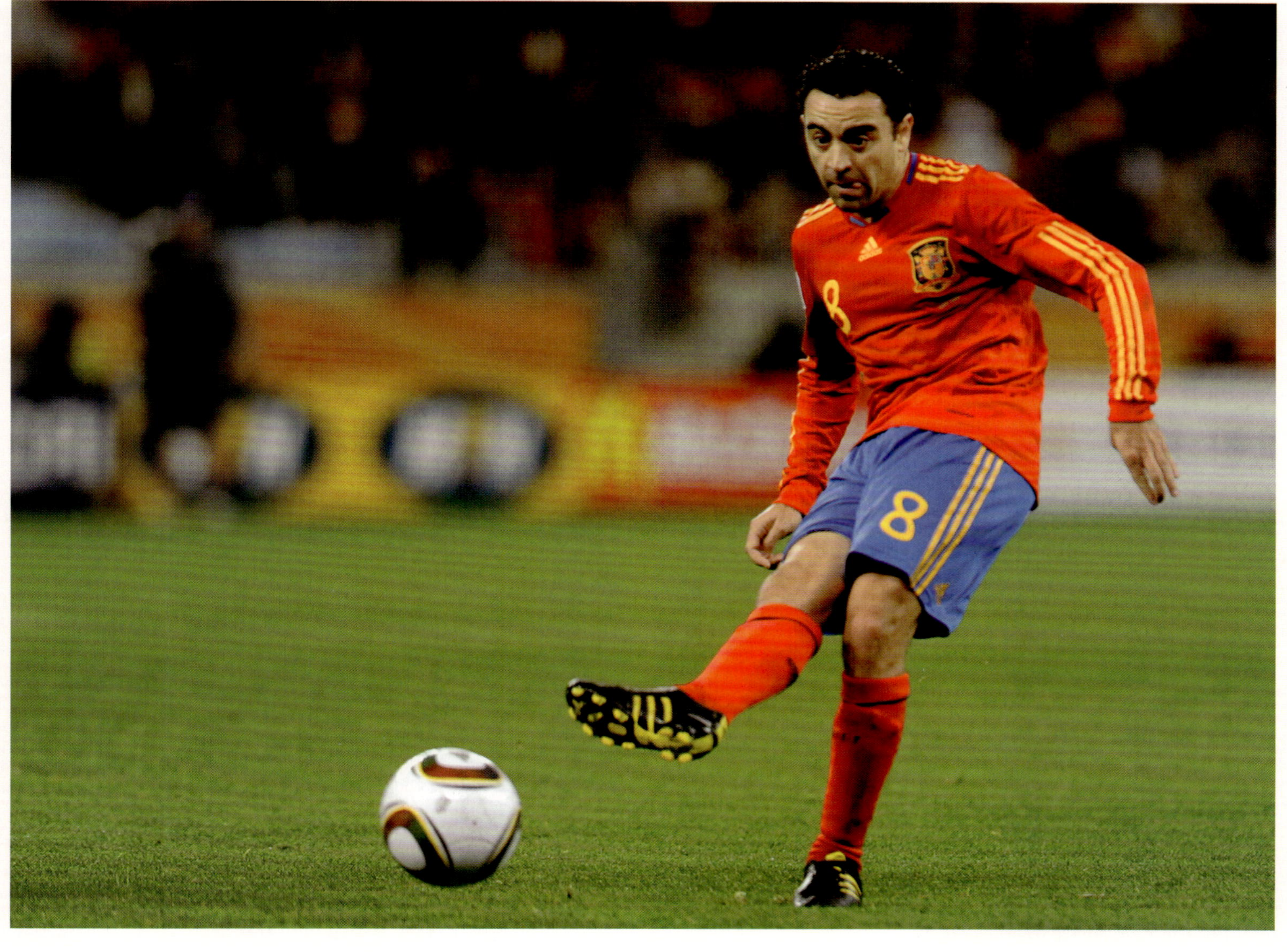

# QUARTER-FINALS

| | | |
|---|---|---|
| Uruguay 1 | 1 Ghana | |
| | (4–2 on penalty kicks) | |
| Netherlands 2 | 1 Brazil | |
| Germany 4 | 0 Argentina | |
| Spain 1 | 0 Paraguay | |

What a finish! At the very end of a 1–1 thriller, Uruguay's Luis Suárez deliberately swatted away a Ghana shot on goal with his hand and was issued a red card…but his desperate ploy paid off when Asamoah Gyan lifted his penalty shot over the crossbar. Uruguay then won the subsequent shootout, 4–2. In Port Elizabeth, the Netherlands came from behind thanks to a Brazilian own goal and brilliant Dutch goalkeeping from Maarten Stekelenburg.

Meanwhile, Germany scored four goals for the third time in the tournament as its fast, powerful front runners laid waste to the Argentine defence. Spain nearly fell behind after an hour in a wild sequence in which Paraguay was awarded a spot kick. But luck was on their side: the Spanish keeper saved the shot and then Spain immediately carried the ball straight to Paraguay's goalmouth, where a lunging foul from the defence gave the Spaniards a penalty kick of their own—which would also be saved. It was David Villa's goal in the eighty-third minute that finally broke the scoreless tie and put Spain into the semi-finals.

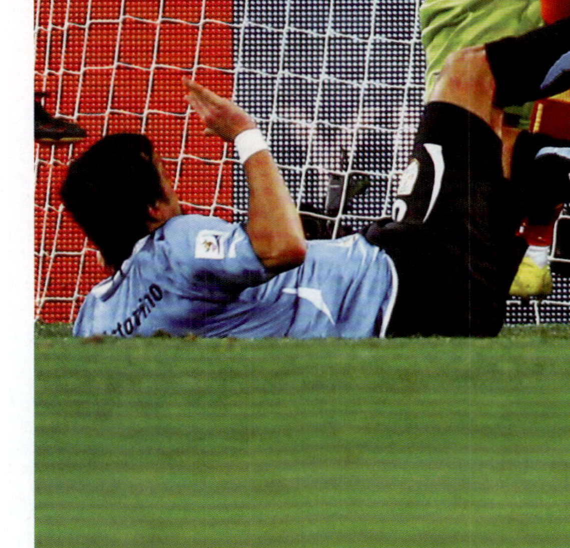

**RIGHT** *Luis Suárez's intentional (and infamous) handball against Ghana keeps the ball out of the Uruguayan net.*

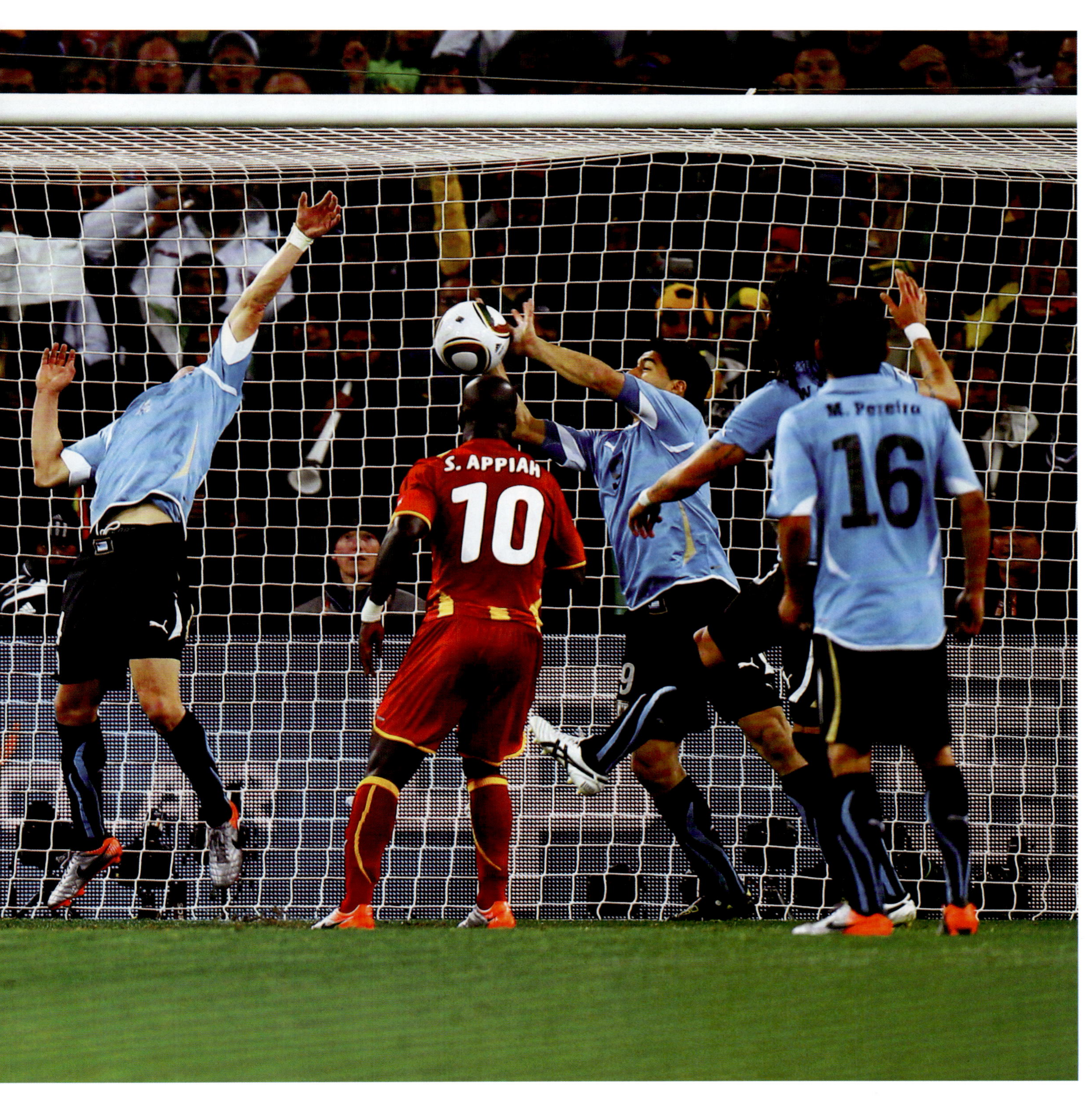


S. APPIAH
10
M. Pereira
16

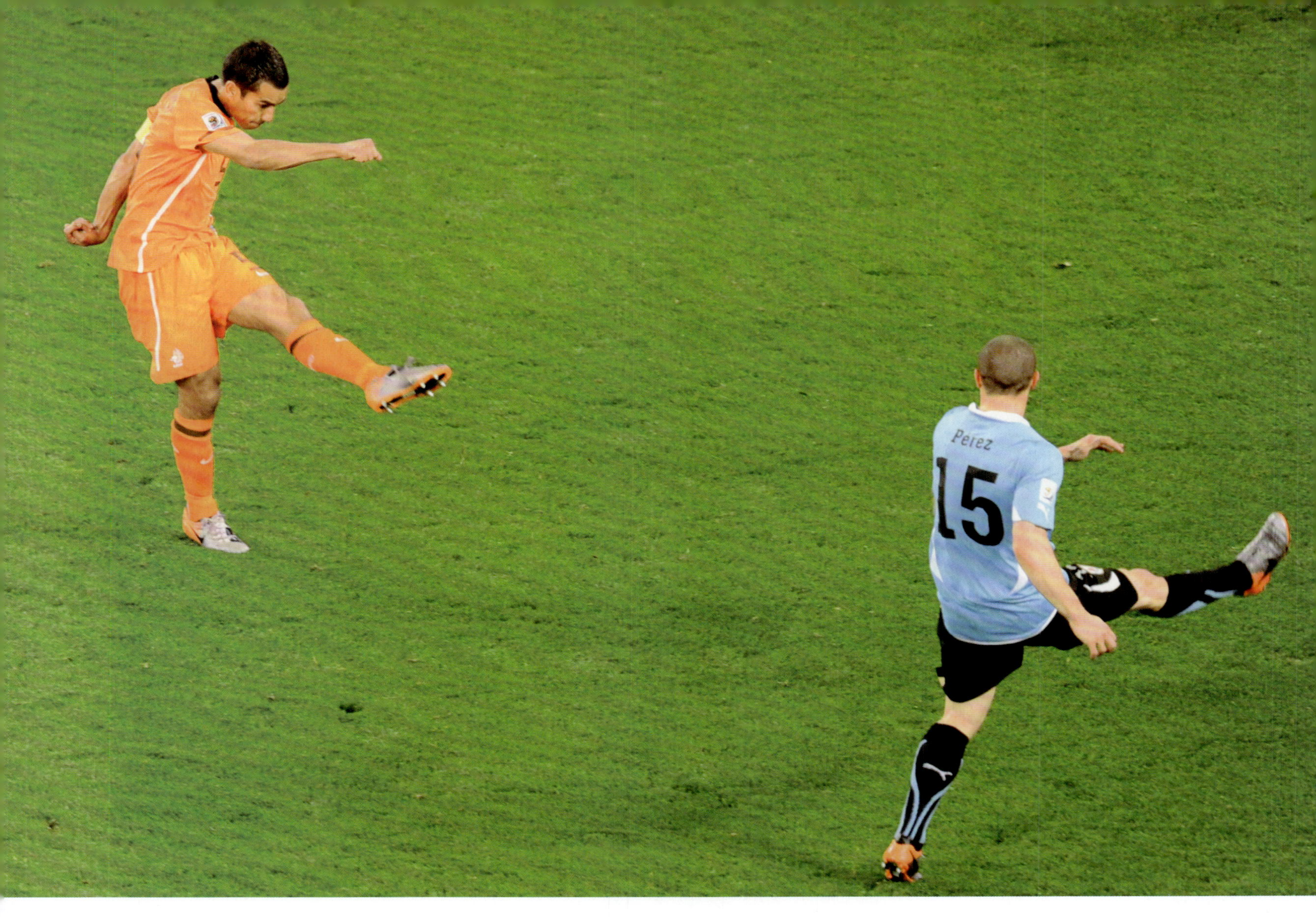

## SEMI-FINALS

Netherlands 3 | 2 Uruguay
Spain 1 | 0 Germany

Spain completed another 1–0 clinical dissection of an opponent, this time by stifling the high-scoring Germans, whose front line had been running rampant through its first five matches. A second-half header by Carles Puyol put the *La Furia Roja* into their first-ever Cup Final. In the other semi-final, the scoreboard had been opened by a pair of outrageous long-distance strikes from the Dutch Giovanni van Bronckhorst and the Uruguayan Diego Forlán. The Netherlands finally broke open the tight 1–1 match in the second half by driving in two shots just three minutes apart. Uruguay's score in stoppage time made things interesting for a few minutes, but the Dutch closed out the win.

The results set up the first Cup Final in history that didn't include at least one of Brazil, Italy, Germany, or Argentina.

**ABOVE** *Dutch defender Giovanni van Bronckhorst with an outrageous strike from distance to open the scoring in the semi-final against Uruguay.*

**OPPOSITE** *Spain's Andrés Iniesta glides past Germany's Per Mertesacker in the semi-final. Iniesta and Xavi are widely considered one of the greatest centre midfield duos in football history.*

# THE YEAR OF LA FURIA ROJA

**Spain's brilliant side in 2010,** known as *La Furia Roja* ('The Red Fury'), came into the World Cup tournament as one of the favourites. They'd won Euro 2008 in convincing fashion and brought most of that victorious squad to South Africa, but a shocking 0–1 opening loss to Switzerland had everyone wondering if Spain would underperform yet again, a common theme in previous Cups. The Spanish rebounded to win their next two behind three goals from star forward David Villa, but questions remained.

What followed was a remarkable string of four 1–0 victories, including Andrés Iniesta's thrilling extra-time goal in the 116th minute of the Cup Final to bring Spain its first-ever World Cup championship. The key to *La Furia Roja*'s success: a disciplined back end that allowed only two goals the entire tournament, both in group play, and a breathtaking style of play that controlled possession like few teams before or since.

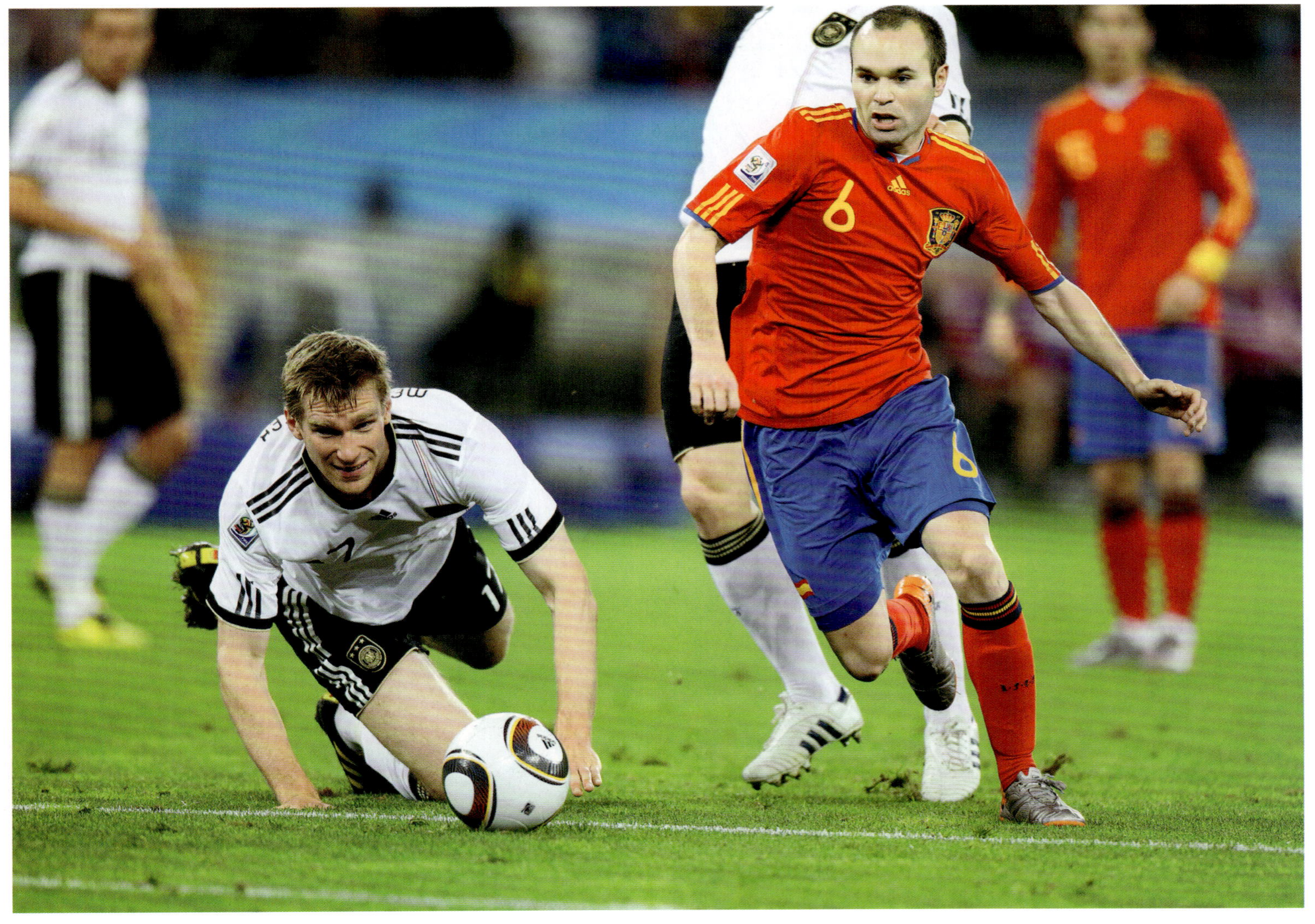

# FINAL

| Spain 1 | 0 Netherlands |
|---|---|
| | (First Place) |
| Germany 3 | 2 Uruguay |
| | (Third Place) |

As is often the case with World Cup third-place matches, where the pressure to win is far less stifling, this one was an entertaining, wide-open, seesawing spectacle. Germany scored first, Uruguay scored twice to take the lead, and then Germany did the same, with midfielder Sami Khedira heading home the game winner with eight minutes left. This was Germany's third win in a World Cup third-place match, more than any other nation.

On the other hand, the Cup Final in Johannesburg was a remarkably tense affair, with fouls galore and fourteen yellow cards handed out. Several golden scoring opportunities for both sides missed or were parried by sharp goalkeeping. The Netherlands deployed aggressive, sometimes-nasty tactics to disrupt the flow of Spanish tiki-taka. This worked to a certain extent…until it backfired late in extra time when Dutchman John Heitinga booked a second yellow card and was sent off at the 109' mark. Not long after, in the 116th minute, Andrés Iniesta took advantage of the extra space to move into an advanced position and receive a ball in the Dutch eighteen-yard box. A slightly awkward first touch had the ball bouncing up on him, but the masterful midfielder reacted quickly to launch a volley that would give Spain the dramatic 1–0 victory.

After the final whistle, the ecstatic Spanish donned their traditional red jerseys (*La Furia Roja!*) to receive their medals and lift the trophy.

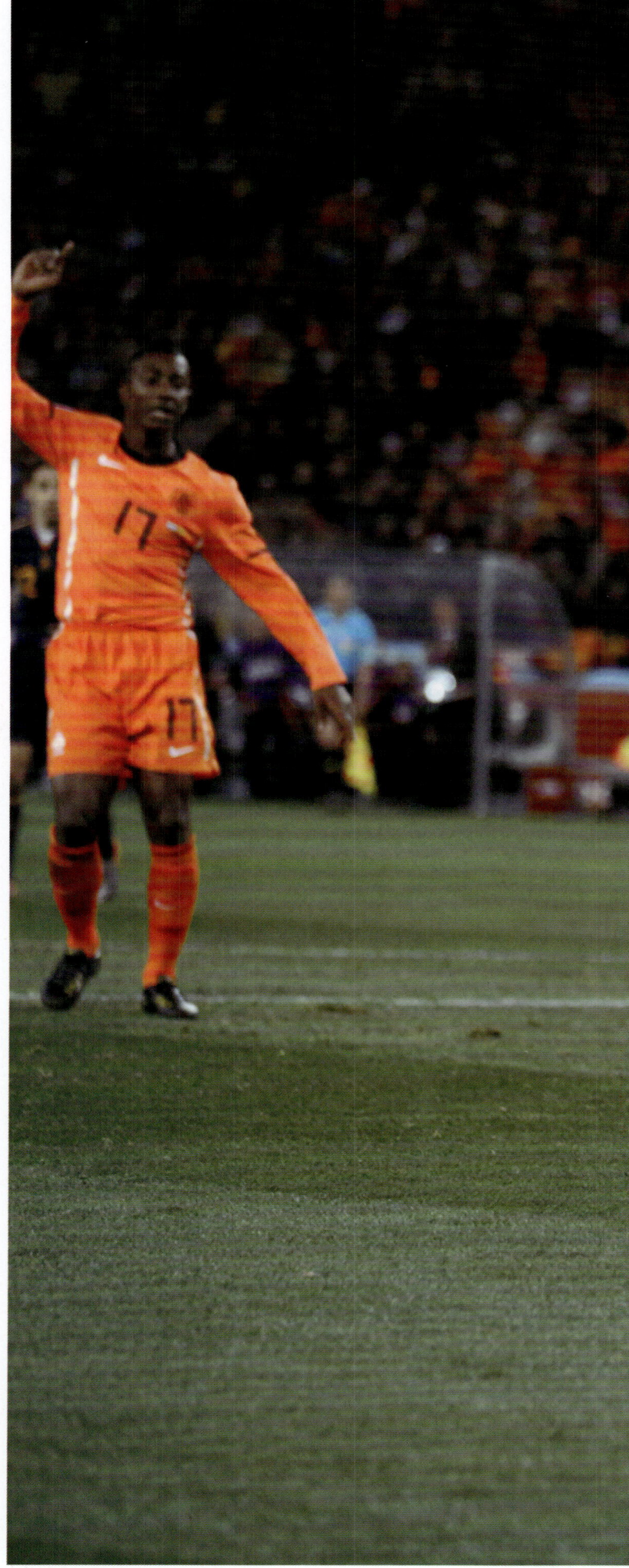

**RIGHT** *Andrés Iniesta's volley in extra time leads Spain to victory over the Netherlands in the final.*

**FOLLOWING SPREAD** *Spain triumphant.*

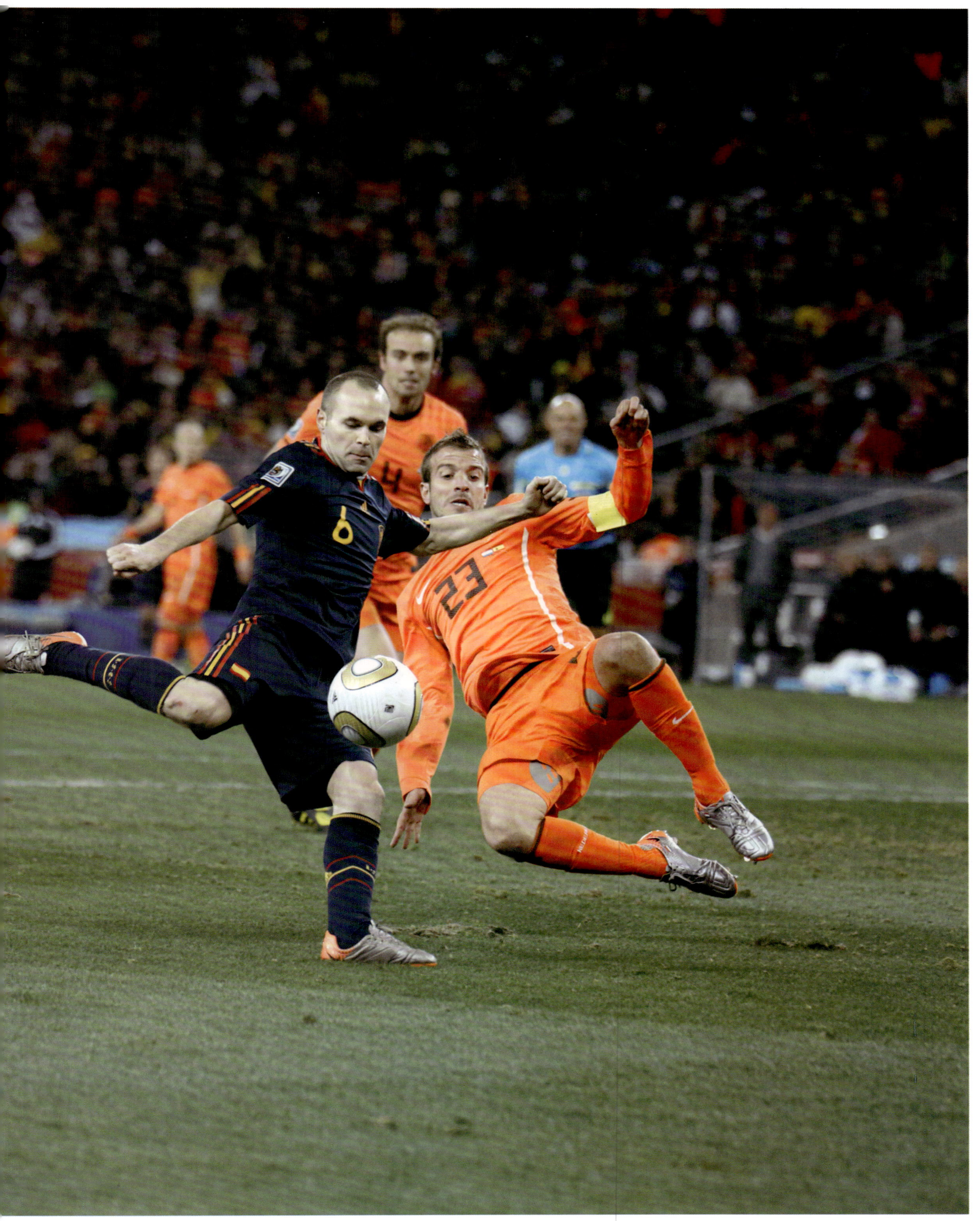

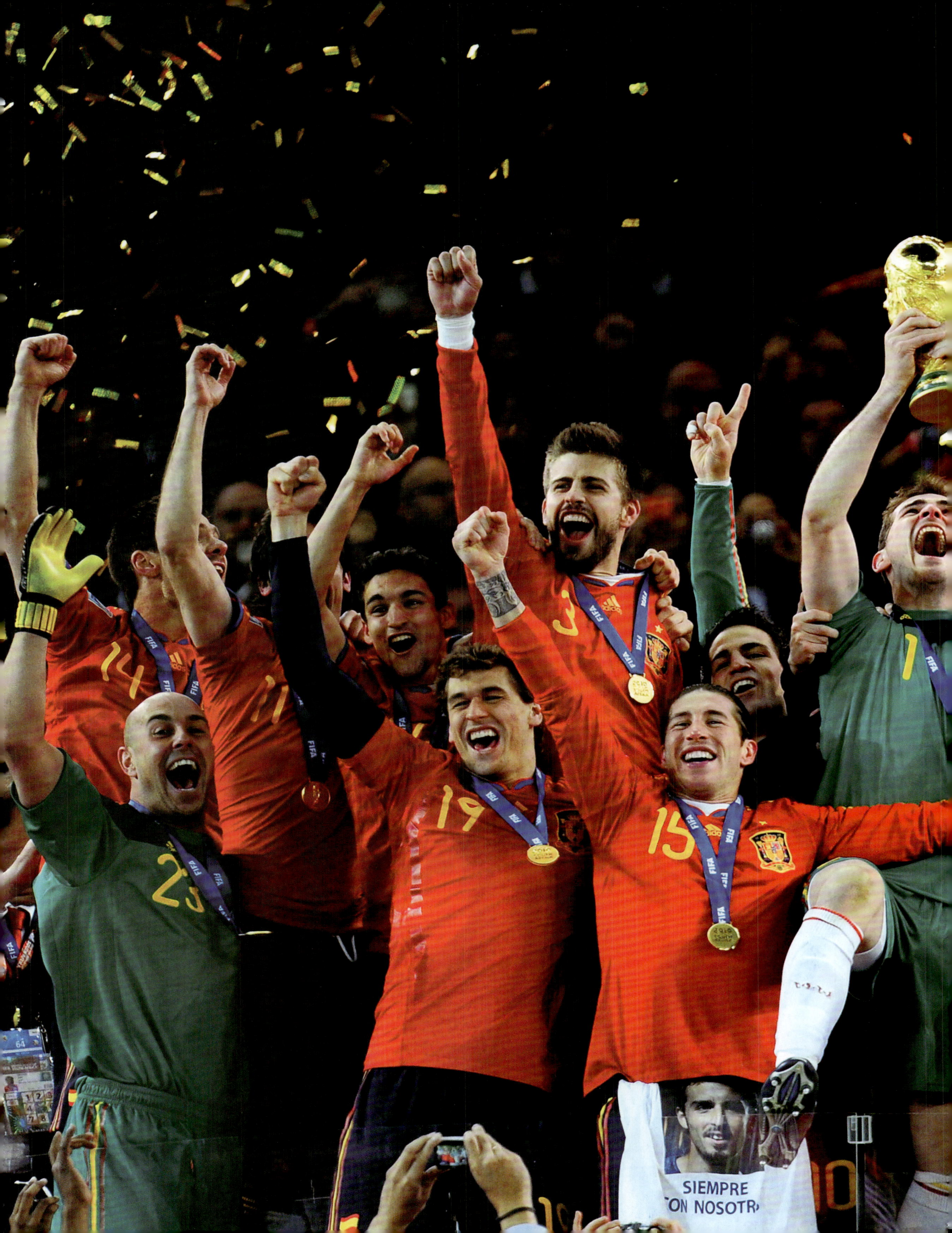
SIEMPRE
CON NOSOTR

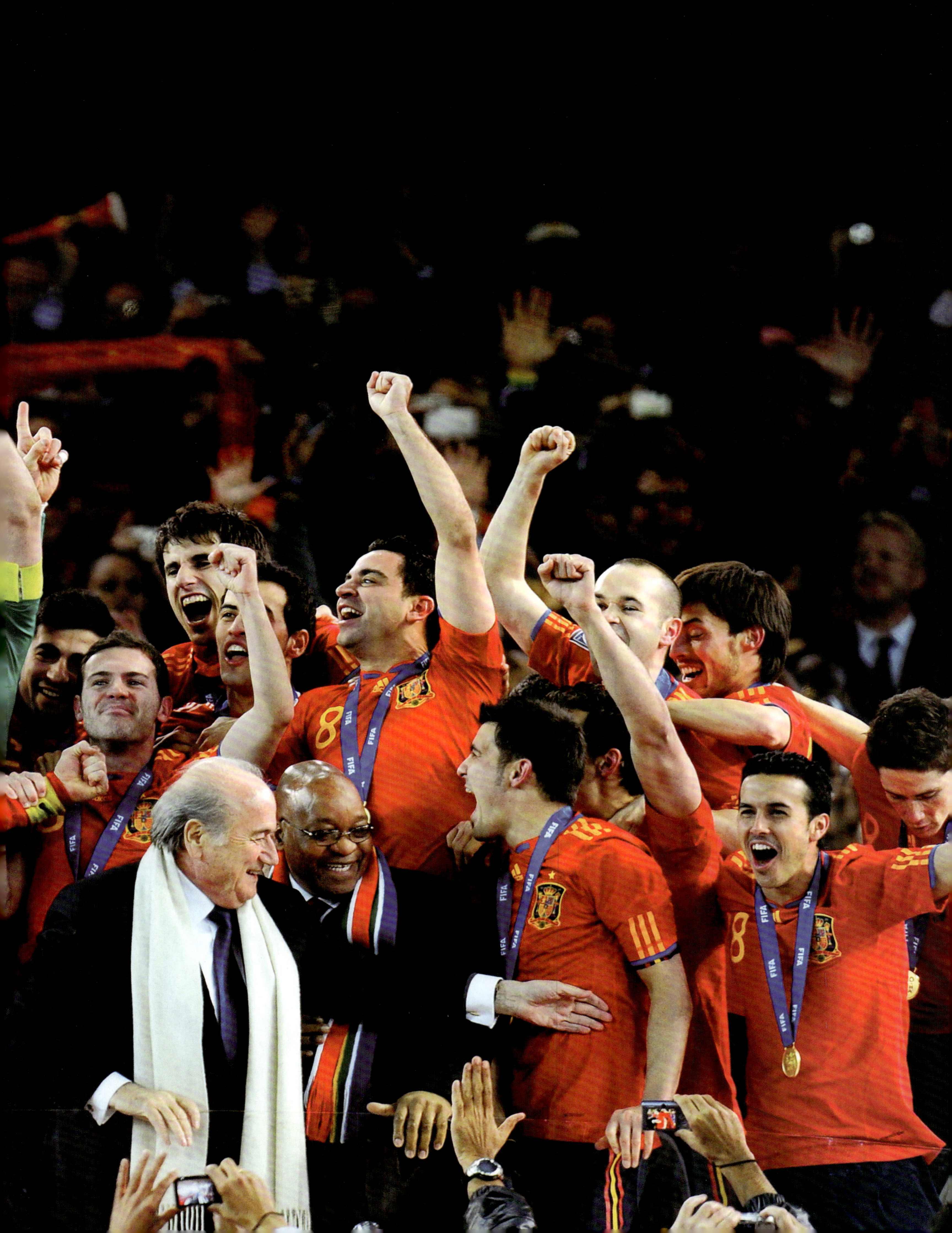

# 2014

HOST COUNTRY: **BRAZIL**
CHAMPION: **GERMANY**
RUNNER-UP: **ARGENTINA**
THIRD PLACE: **NETHERLANDS OVER BRAZIL**

**Back in 2007, FIFA** unanimously chose its only five-time champion to host the 2014 World Cup. Initial response in Brazil was beyond jubilant, as the country had hosted its first Cup in 1950 and spent six decades longing for another chance. But as the true costs piled up over the next five years, the attitude of the Brazilian public began to sour. Projections for combined infrastructure costs, including new stadiums, had grown to more than $16 billion, an alarming number for the many Brazilians who were experiencing financial struggles. In 2013, unrest marred Brazil's staging of the Confederations Cup as large street protests mobilised in response to the Brazilian government's attempt to clear out entire *favela* (slum) neighbourhoods in host cities.

But as the construction, which included seven brand-new venues, and other preparations wrapped up in (the nick of) time for the opening ceremonies of 12 July, 2014, the national mood seemed to shift back to feverish anticipation — after all, football in Brazil is nothing short of a religion. In the end, the World Cup brought an estimated one million visitors from more than 200 countries to the beautiful country with the beautiful game. *Joga bonito!* At the spectacular opening ceremonies in Arena de São Paulo, 660 dancers whirled behind Brazilian singer Claudia Leitte and Jennifer Lopez to celebrate Brazil's dynamic culture and history — a perfect display of the tournament's official slogan: *Juntos num só ritmo* ('Together in a single rhythm').

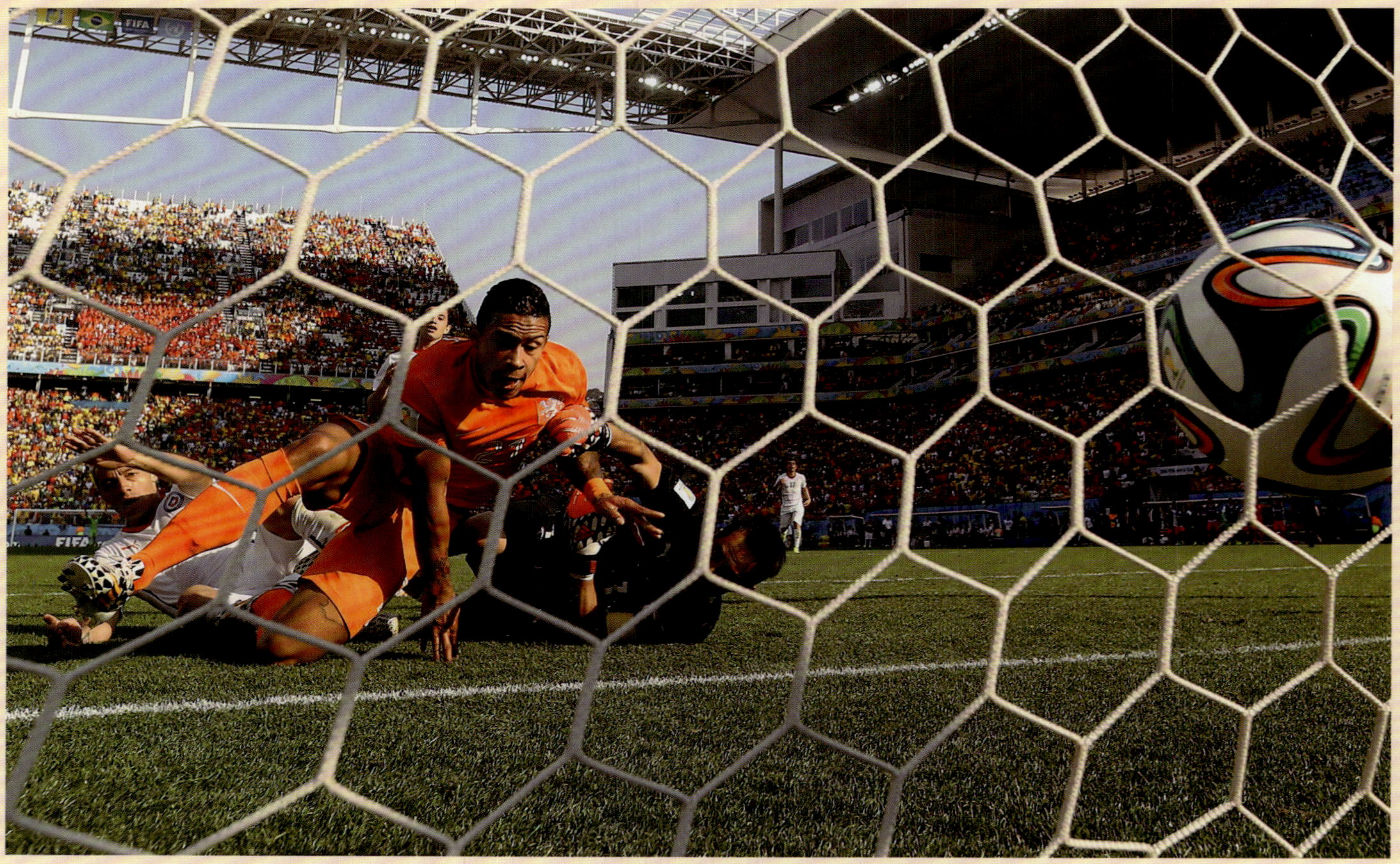

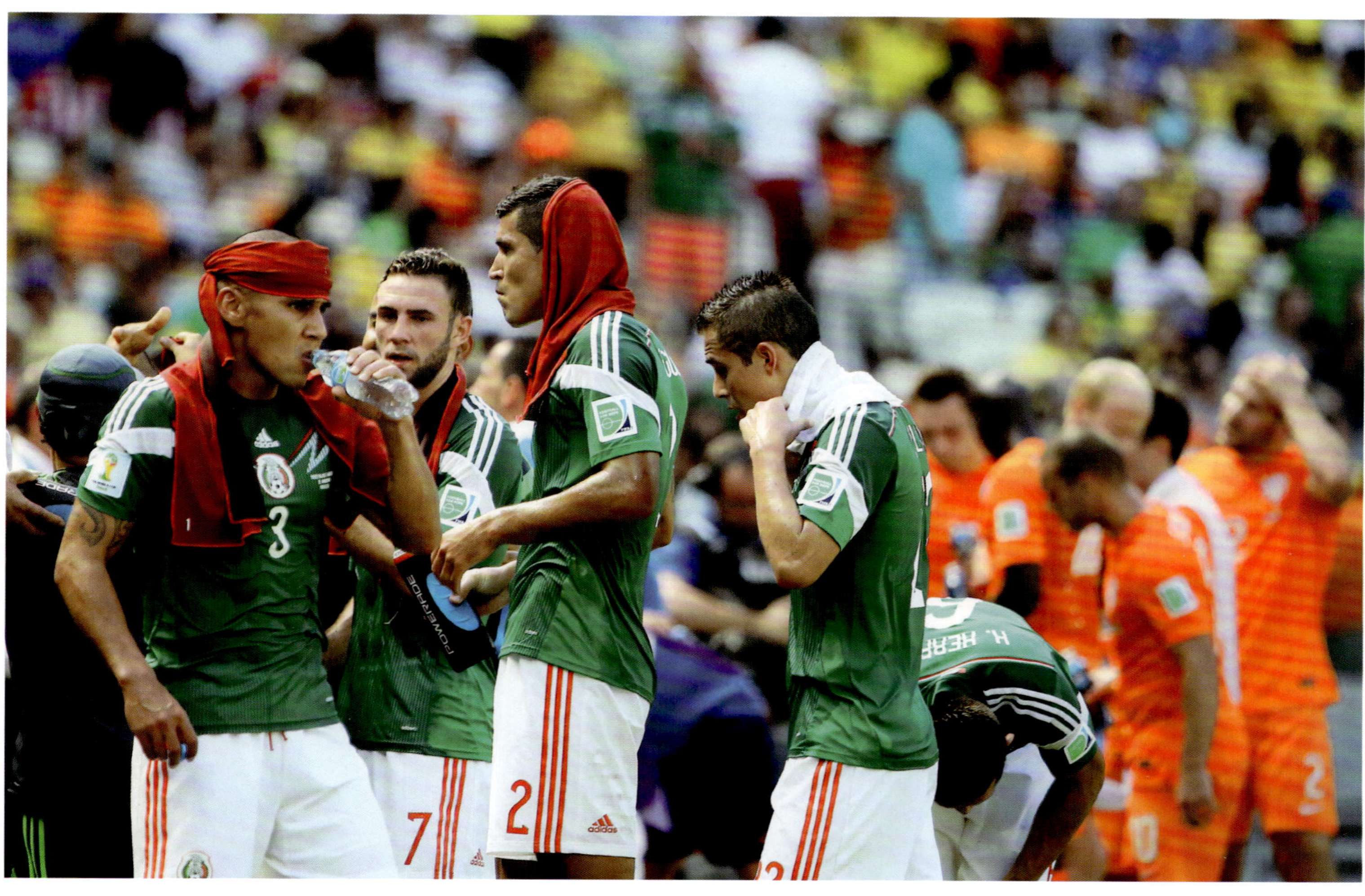

## INNOVATIONS

**Several controversial 'ghost goal'** miscalls over the years had motivated FIFA to develop and introduce fool-proof goal-line technology for the 2014 tournament. The new 'Goal Control' system relied on two sets of seven cameras, one set aimed at each goal. If the cameras determined that a ball had fully crossed the goal line, a watch worn by the referee would vibrate.

FIFA also equipped referees with a special spray paint for free kicks, used to mark the ball spot and the ten-yard line for defenders. This paint was designed to completely disappear after a few minutes. One other smart addition: FIFA introduced three-minute cooling breaks during play to help counter Brazil's high temperatures and humidity in some venues.

**OPPOSITE** *Memphis Depay slides in to get on the end of a cross from Arjen Robben and beat Chile keeper Claudio Bravo for a 2–0 Netherlands lead.*

**ABOVE** *Mexican players during a cooling break.*

# Tournament: GROUP STAGE

### GROUP A: BRAZIL, MEXICO, CROATIA, CAMEROON

| | | |
|---|---|---|
| Brazil 3 | 1 | Croatia |
| Mexico 1 | 0 | Cameroon |
| Brazil 0 | 0 | Mexico |
| Croatia 4 | 0 | Cameroon |
| Brazil 4 | 1 | Cameroon |
| Mexico 3 | 1 | Croatia |

**Advanced to Knockout Stage: Brazil, Mexico**

Brazil's new young superstar, Neymar, made an auspicious debut, scoring twice after his team fell behind Croatia on an early own goal. He added another brace against Cameroon. Meanwhile, Mexico looked dangerous all over the pitch, especially with a world-class goalkeeper in Guillermo Ochoa locking down the back end. Ochoa starred in the 0–0 draw with Brazil and both teams moved to the knockout stage.

### GROUP B: NETHERLANDS, CHILE, SPAIN, AUSTRALIA

| | | |
|---|---|---|
| Netherlands 5 | 1 | Spain |
| Chile 3 | 1 | Australia |
| Netherlands 3 | 2 | Australia |
| Chile 2 | 0 | Spain |
| Spain 3 | 0 | Australia |
| Netherlands 2 | 0 | Chile |

**Advanced to Knockout Stage: Netherlands, Chile**

The rematch of the previous World Cup Final turned into a laugher. Spain took a 1–0 lead on a penalty kick, but the Netherlands equalised with Robin van Persie's highlight-reel diving header from just inside the penalty area. The second half turned into a merciless Dutch barrage of four straight goals. In the end, the usual culprits van Persie and Robben had a brace apiece... and Spain looked broken. When Chile beat Spain in the next round, the Spanish were out and Chile advanced, continuing the unfortunate streak for reigning champions.

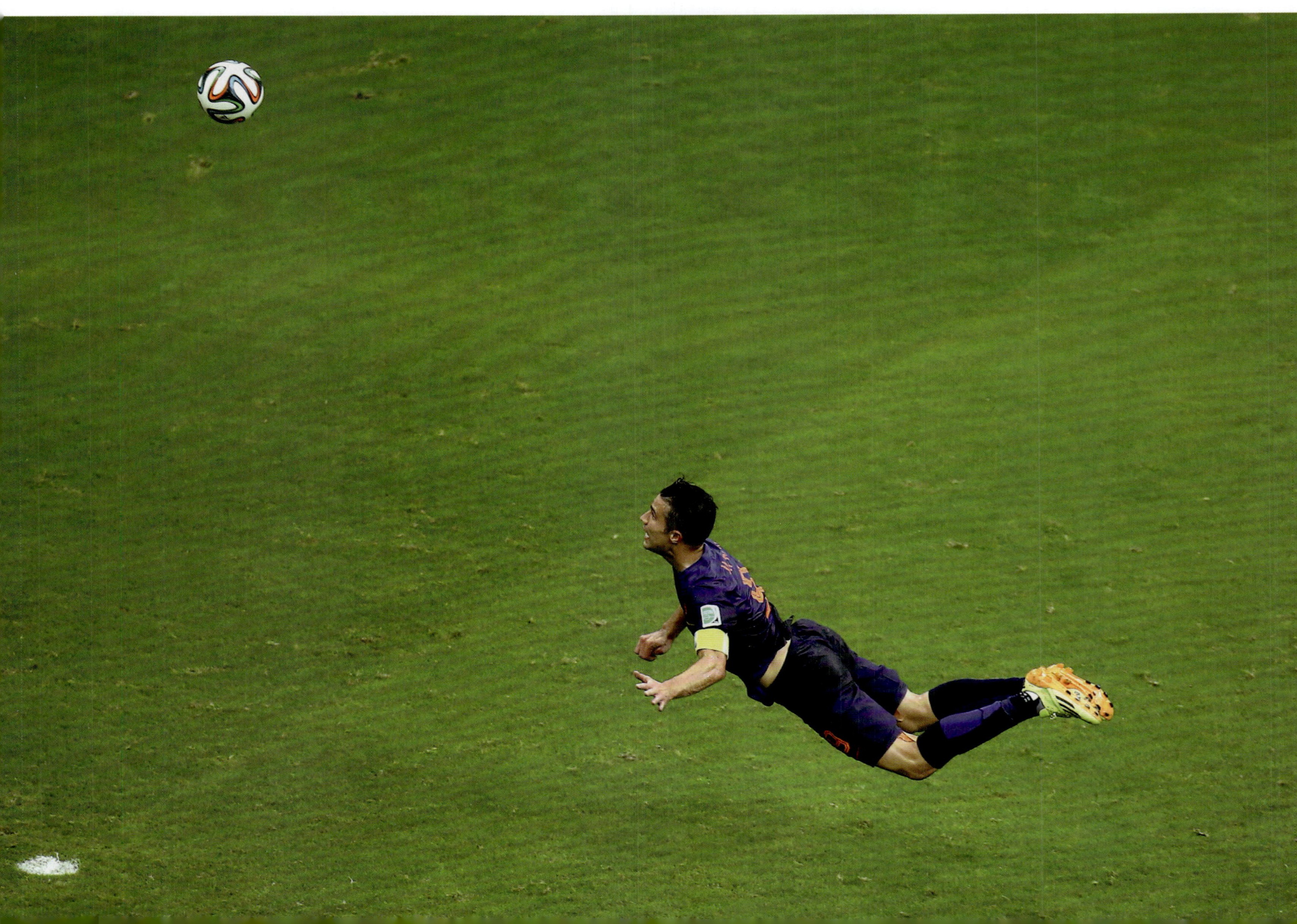

**GROUP C: COLOMBIA, GREECE,
IVORY COAST, JAPAN**

| | |
|---|---|
| Colombia 3 | 0 Greece |
| Ivory Coast 1 | 1 Japan |
| Colombia 2 | 1 Ivory Coast |
| Japan 0 | 0 Greece |
| Colombia 4 | 1 Japan |
| Greece 2 | 1 Ivory Coast |

**Advanced to Knockout Stage: Colombia, Greece**

This group featured four footballing nations ready to play lively and interesting matches. Colombia looked particularly solid and potentially dangerous with its bright young star, James Rodríguez, scoring three dashing goals in group play. Most surprising of all was the quality of Greece, who edged out both the Ivory Coast and Japan to advance past the group stage for the first time in its history.

**OPPOSITE** *One of the definitive goals of the tournament and a re-match of the 2010 World Cup Final between Spain and the Netherlands. Dutch striker Robin van Persie calculates the angle of an incoming cross and perfectly times his jump for a gorgeous diving header of considerable range.*

**BELOW** *Mexican keeper Guillermo 'Memo' Ochoa in rare form against Brazil, holding the hosts to a 0–0 draw.*

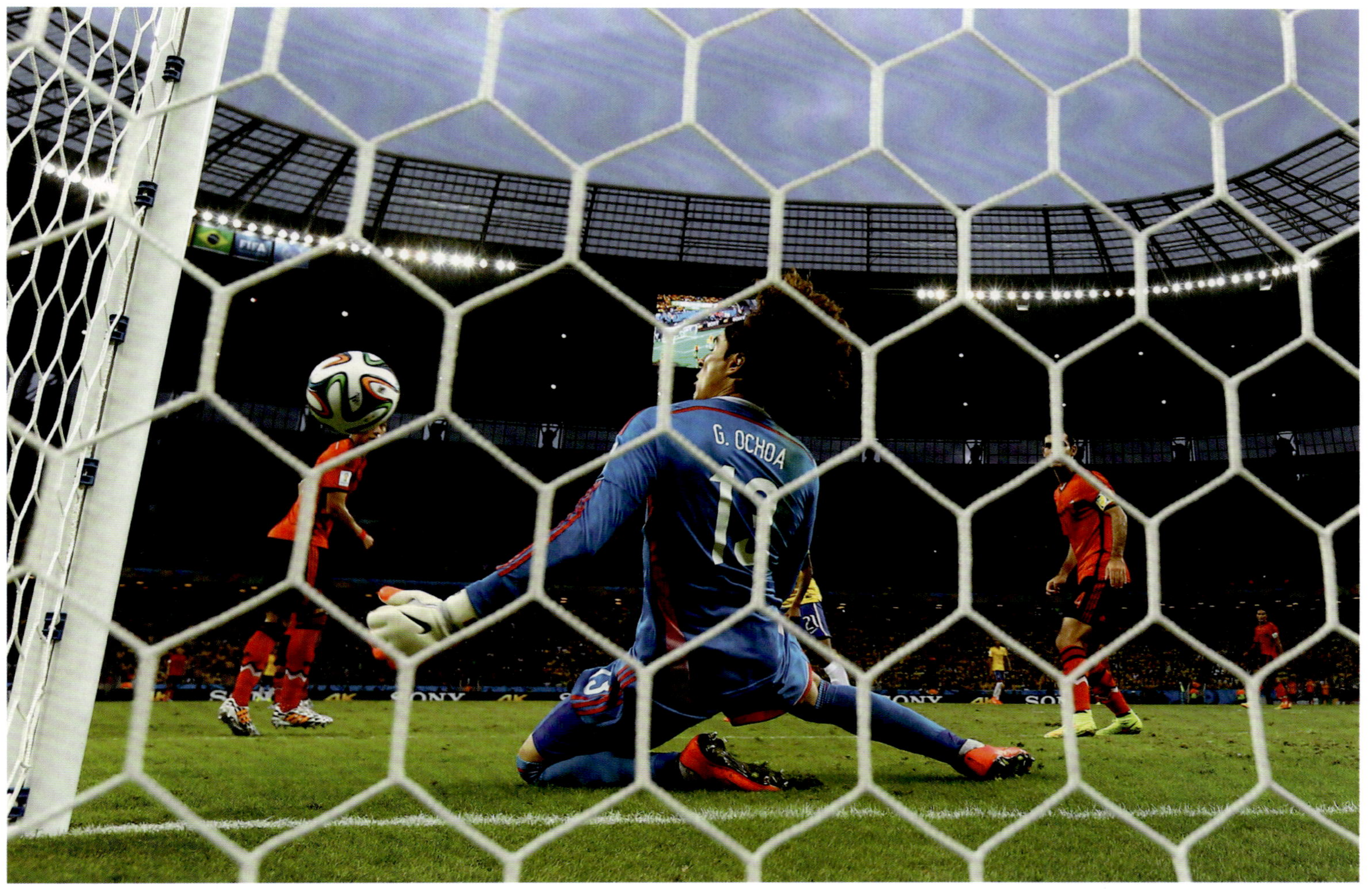

**GROUP D: COSTA RICA, URUGUAY, ITALY, ENGLAND**

| | | |
|---|---|---|
| Costa Rica 3 | 1 | Uruguay |
| Italy 2 | 1 | England |
| Uruguay 2 | 1 | England |
| Costa Rica 1 | 0 | Italy |
| Uruguay 1 | 0 | Italy |
| Costa Rica 0 | 0 | England |

***Advanced to Knockout Stage: Costa Rica, Uruguay***

**GROUP E: FRANCE, SWITZERLAND, ECUADOR, HONDURAS**

| | | |
|---|---|---|
| Switzerland 2 | 1 | Ecuador |
| France 3 | 0 | Honduras |
| France 5 | 2 | Switzerland |
| Ecuador 2 | 1 | Honduras |
| Switzerland 3 | 0 | Honduras |
| Ecuador 0 | 0 | France |

***Advanced to Knockout Stage: France, Switzerland***

With Italy, England, and Uruguay, this group was initially considered the tournament's 'Group of Death', minus the seeming outlier Costa Rica. And it lived up to the billing…just not in the way that anyone expected. Who could foresee an undefeated Costa Rica finishing in first ahead of Uruguay (a top-four team in 2010), while Italy and England were both sent packing? Adding to the surrealism of 2014's Group D was one of the most memorable moments in Cup history: Luis Suárez's bizarre bite on the shoulder of Italy's Giorgio Chiellini that prompted FIFA to ban Suárez from the rest of the tournament. The Group of Death, indeed.

With young stars Paul Pogba and Antoine Griezmann joining prolific forwards Karim Benzema and Olivier Giroud, France had rebuilt a solid foundation to succeed the great Zidane–Henry teams of the previous decade. Pogba was particularly impressive, eventually winning the tournament's Young Player Award. The French swept through the group handily except for a frustrating tie with Ecuador. Switzerland's two victories over the teams from the Americas moved them into second place.

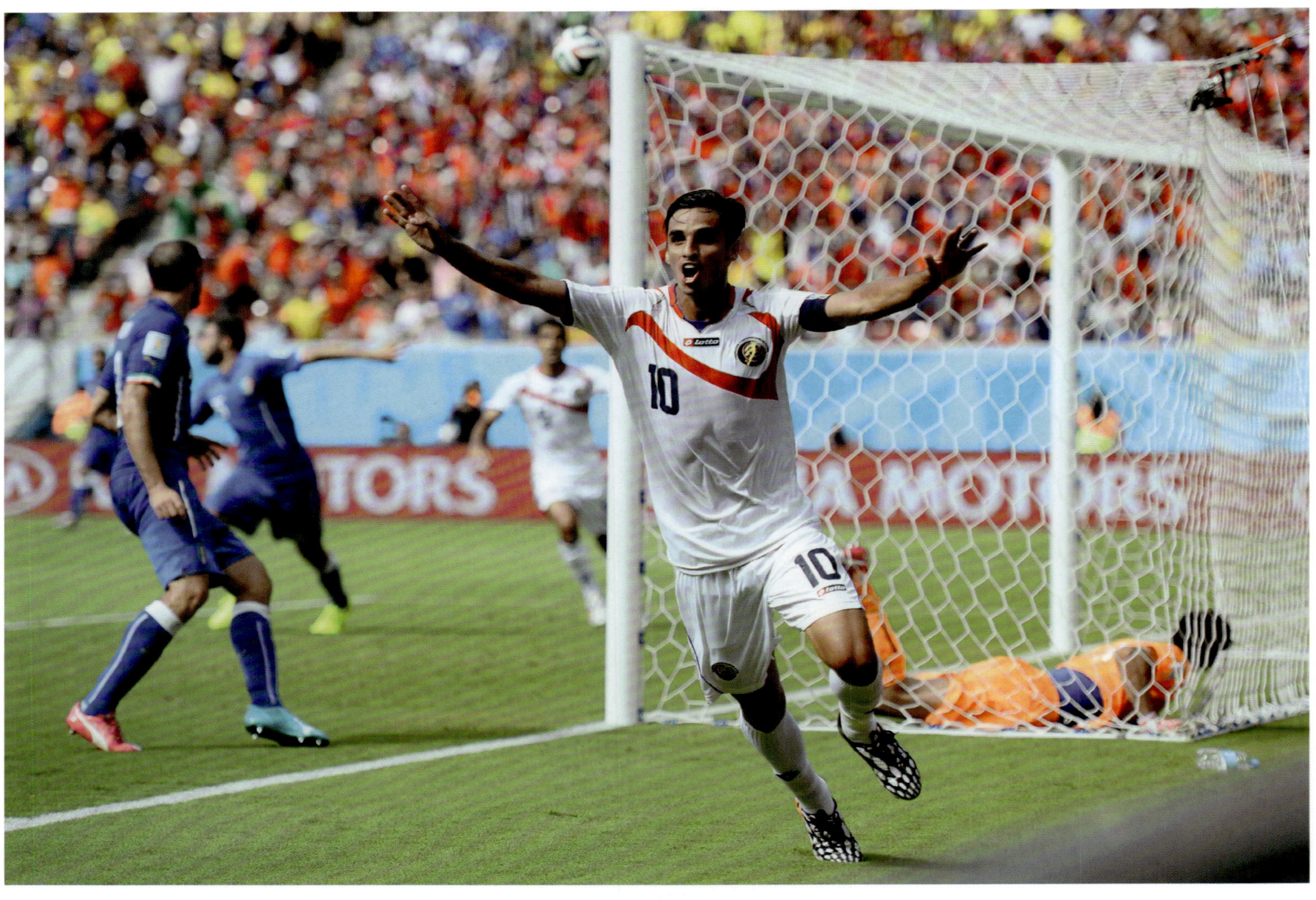

Argentina swept through as expected, but not as easily as anticipated, as each win was by just a one-goal difference. Lionel Messi scored four of his team's six goals in group. Nigeria barely edged into second place.

## ARGENTINA'S 'FAB FOUR'

In the 2010 Cup, a quartet of young Argentine stars finally emerged on the world scene. Four years later, the foursome, now twenty-six and led by Lionel Messi, the four-time FIFA Ballon d'Or winner, formed the heart of their national team. Messi, along with his supporting cast of Gonzalo Higuaín, Sergio Agüero, and Ángel Di María, was widely expected to break through and win this 2014 World Cup, giving him the international championship that would confirm his status as perhaps the greatest footballer of all time. But a resurgent and clinical Germany would obstruct this outcome.

**OPPOSITE** *Many saw Costa Rica as the inevitable prey of Group D, 2014's Group of Death. Bryan Ruiz's game-winning goal against Italy, itself arriving on the heels of a 4–2 upset over Uruguay, confirmed that Los Ticos were, in fact, the predators.*

**BELOW** *Enner Valencia of Ecuador is challenged by Mamadou Sakho en route to a 1–1 draw.*

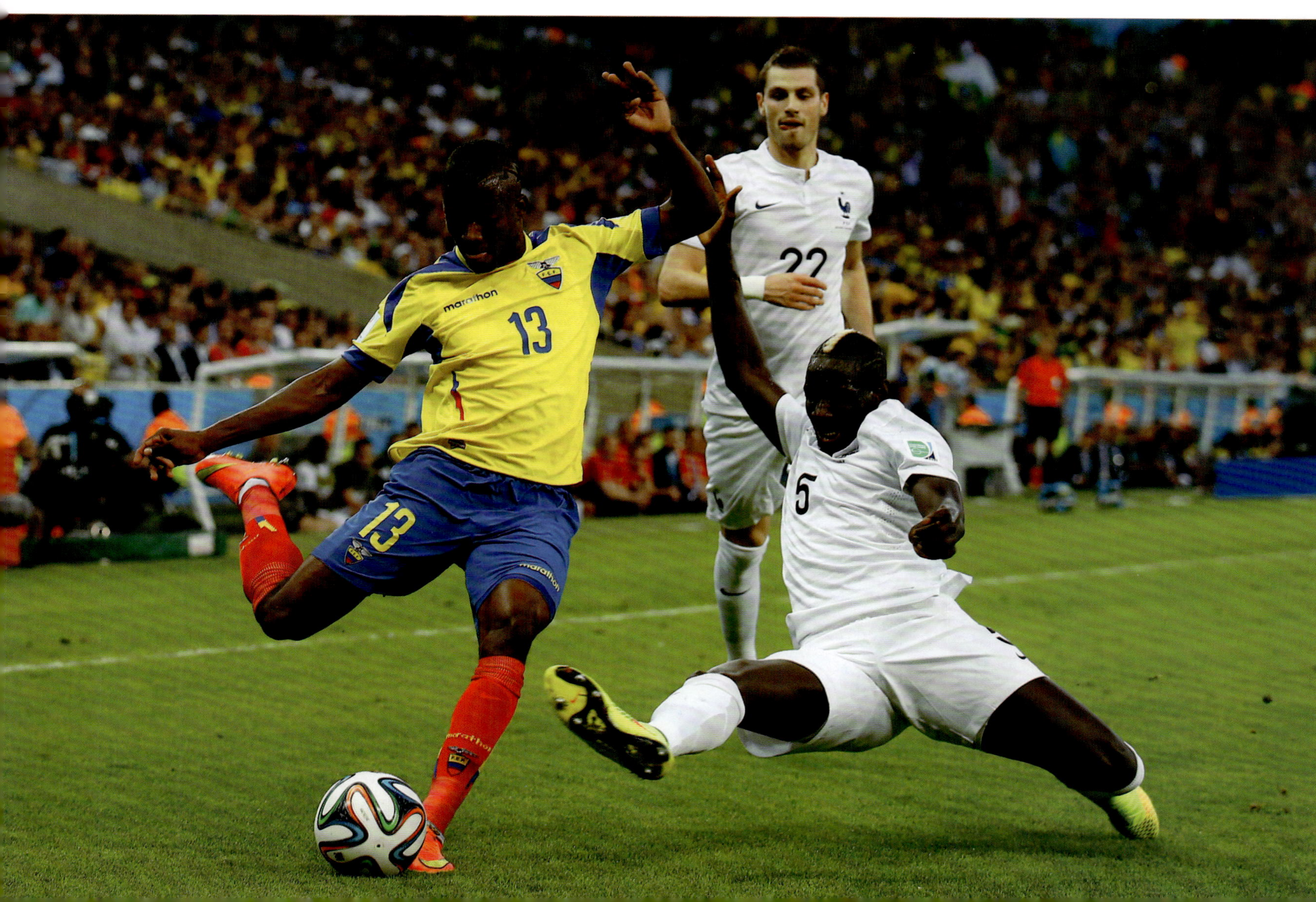

## GROUP G: GERMANY, USA, PORTUGAL, GHANA

| | | |
|---:|:---:|:---|
| Germany 4 | 0 | Portugal |
| USA 2 | 1 | Ghana |
| Germany 2 | 2 | Ghana |
| USA 2 | 2 | Portugal |
| Germany 1 | 0 | USA |
| Portugal 2 | 1 | Ghana |

**Advanced to Knockout Stage: Germany, USA**

## GROUP H: BELGIUM, ALGERIA, RUSSIA, SOUTH KOREA

| | | |
|---:|:---:|:---|
| Belgium 2 | 1 | Algeria |
| Russia 1 | 1 | South Korea |
| Belgium 1 | 0 | Russia |
| Algeria 4 | 2 | South Korea |
| Belgium 1 | 0 | South Korea |
| Algeria 1 | 1 | Russia |

**Advanced to Knockout Stage: Belgium, Algeria**

The USA beat Ghana and had Portugal on the ropes until Silvestre Varela's goal five minutes into stoppage time tied the match. Luckily for the Americans, Germany's earlier 4–0 thrashing of Portugal (fuelled by Thomas Müller's fearsome hat-trick) gave the USA an edge in goal differential. They advanced to the knockout stage in second place behind the indomitable Germans.

Belgium took three one-goal victories to top the group. A surprising Algeria emerged in second place, but only after a controversial goal gave them the tie they needed against Russia in the group's final match.

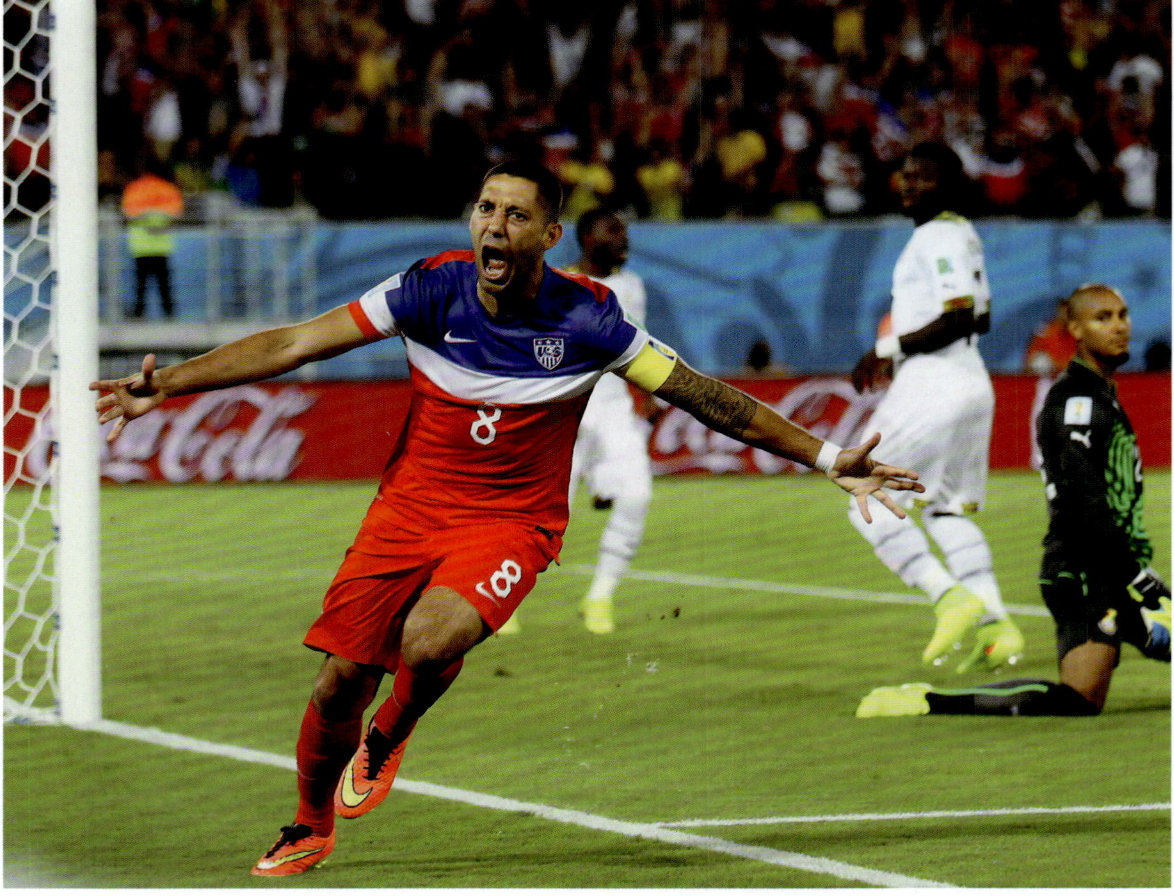

**LEFT** *Clint Dempsey scores just thirty seconds into the USA's tournament opener against Ghana.*

**OPPOSITE** *Bastian Schweinsteiger (left) and Toni Kroos (right), two key cogs in Germany's well-oiled midfield machine.*

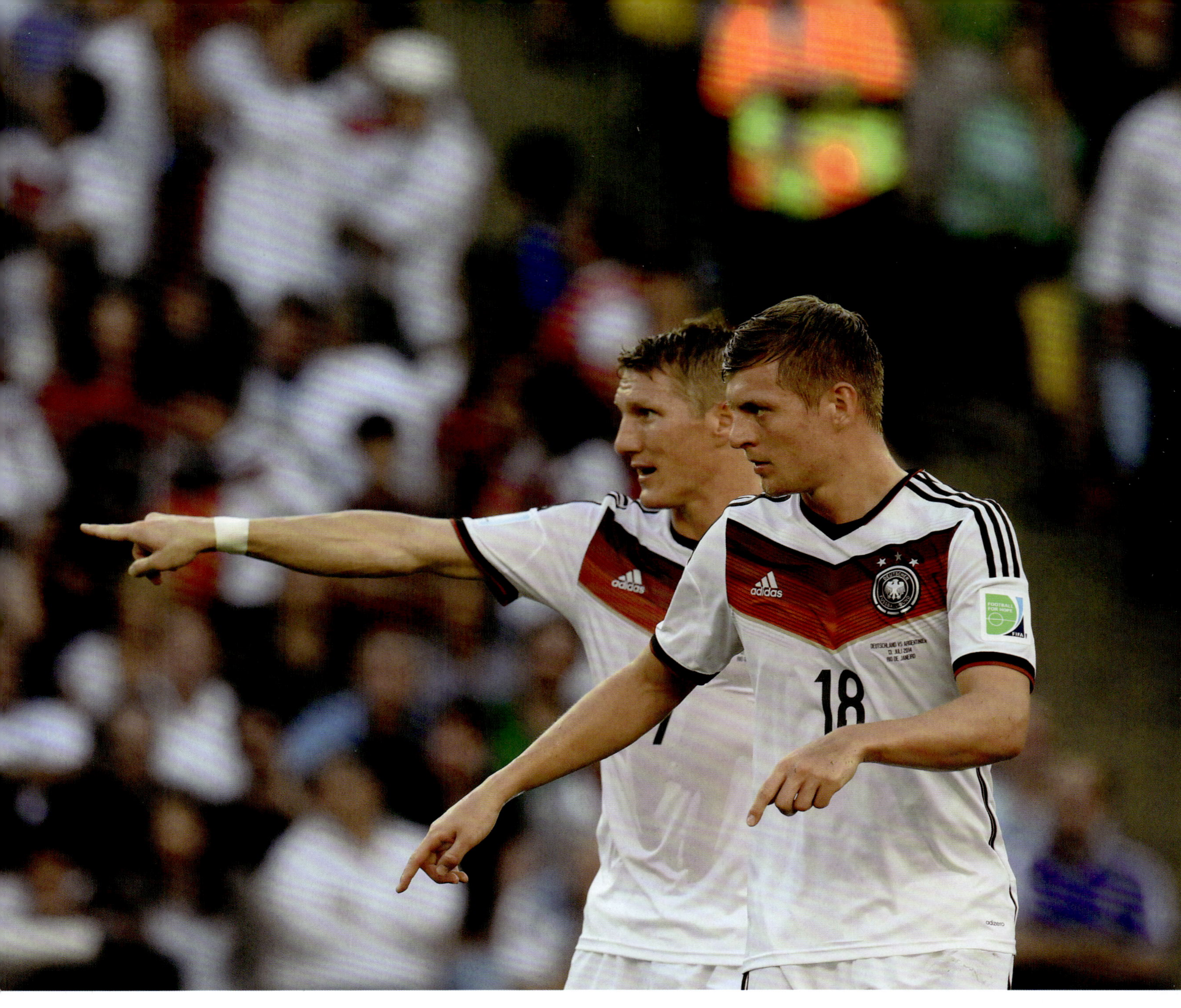

## ALGERIAN LIGHT SHOW

**Group H play included** one particularly dramatic, and somewhat problematic, moment. Algeria, trailing Russia 1–0 in their battle for the group's second spot, was awarded a free kick late in the match. As Algerian midfielder Abdelmoumene Djabou prepared to strike the ball, a green laser light from somewhere in the Algerian section of the crowd shone right into Russian goalkeeper Igor Akinfeev's face, seen clearly in TV replays.

Djabou delivered a quality ball into forward Islam Slimani, who converted with a header, but Akinfeev was clearly distracted by the light and complained vigorously to the referee, to no avail. The 1–1 draw denied Russia the win it needed to advance and sent Algeria on. Later, after reviewing footage of the incident, FIFA fined the Algerian Football Association $60,000 for its fan base's use of lasers to disrupt play.

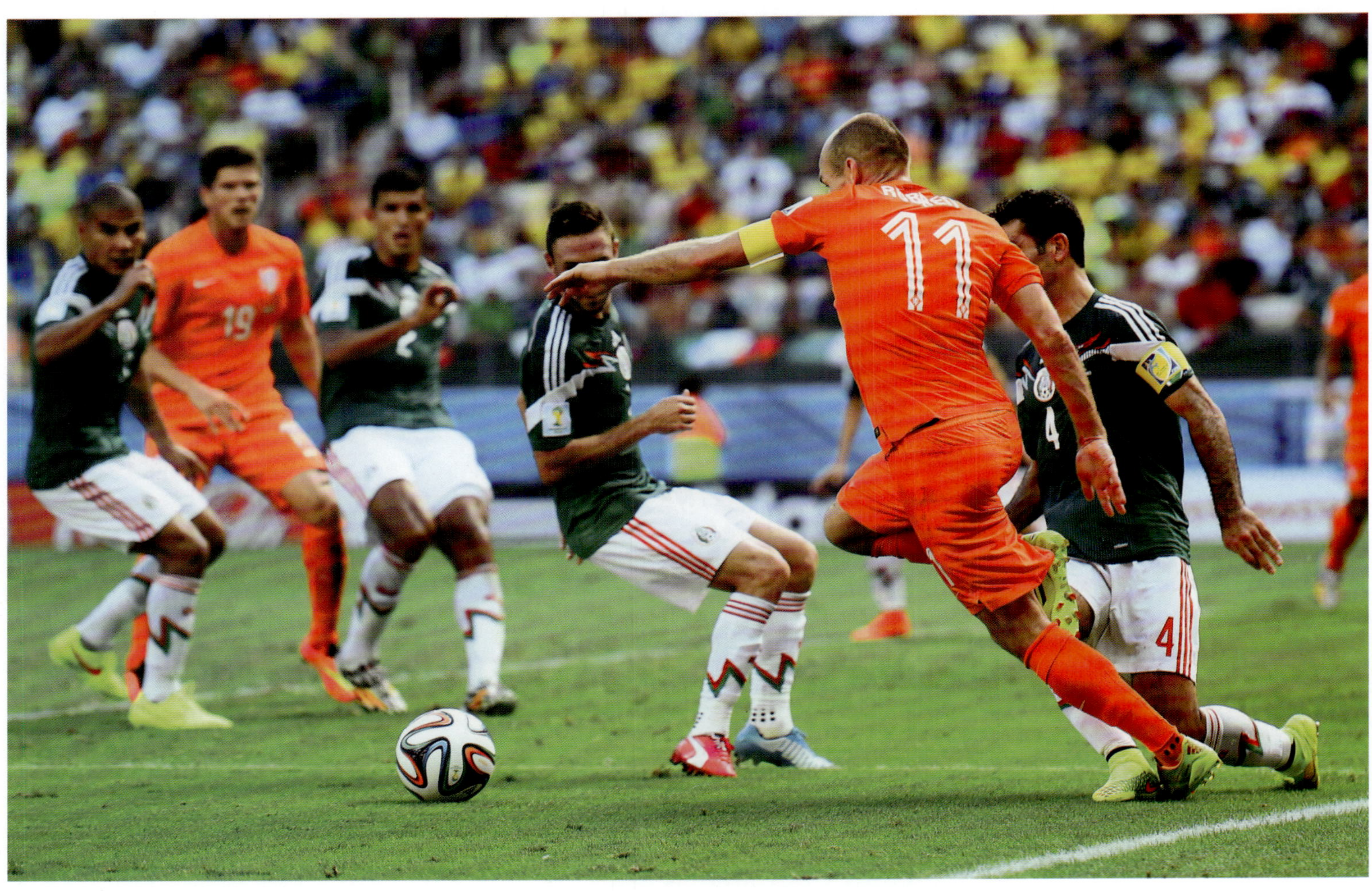

## KNOCKOUT STAGE
## ROUND OF 16

| | | |
|---|---|---|
| Brazil 1 | 1 Chile | (3–2 on penalty kicks) |
| Colombia 2 | 0 Uruguay | |
| France 2 | 0 Nigeria | |
| Germany 2 | 1 Algeria | (after extra time) |
| Netherlands 2 | 1 Mexico | |
| Costa Rica 1 | 1 Greece | (5–3 on penalty kicks) |
| Argentina 1 | 0 Switzerland | (after extra time) |
| Belgium 2 | 1 USA | (after extra time) |

The home team Brazil barely slipped past Chile in a close shootout. Perhaps the most spectacular goal of the entire tournament was the first of two by Colombia's James Rodríguez against Uruguay: he received a ball onto his chest outside the penalty box and then swivelled into a full volley shot, knuckling the ball just under the bar. Meanwhile, Nigeria pushed France hard in the first half but grew fatigued and disorganised as the French patiently notched a late goal. Costa Rica took an early lead against Greece but a 66' red card reduced their side to ten. A dramatic Greek stoppage-time equaliser led to a shootout, but all five Costa Rican shooters connected, and surging goalkeeper Keylor Navas came up with a huge save, to seal the win.

Eventual finalists Germany and Argentina were both pushed into extra time by determined opponents, but both prevailed—Argentina thanks to Lionel Messi's wild run that ended in a clinical assist to Ángel Di María with just two minutes left in extra time. The tournament's most controversial call was an eighty-eighth minute foul that gave the Netherlands a penalty kick against Mexico, which they converted for the 2–1 win. Dutchman Arjen Robben certainly dramatised his fall, and replays suggested it may have been an outright dive. *El Tricolor* had outplayed the Dutch orange for long stretches of the match and *No Era Penal!* ('It wasn't a penalty!') became a rallying cry for the heartbroken Mexican fans.

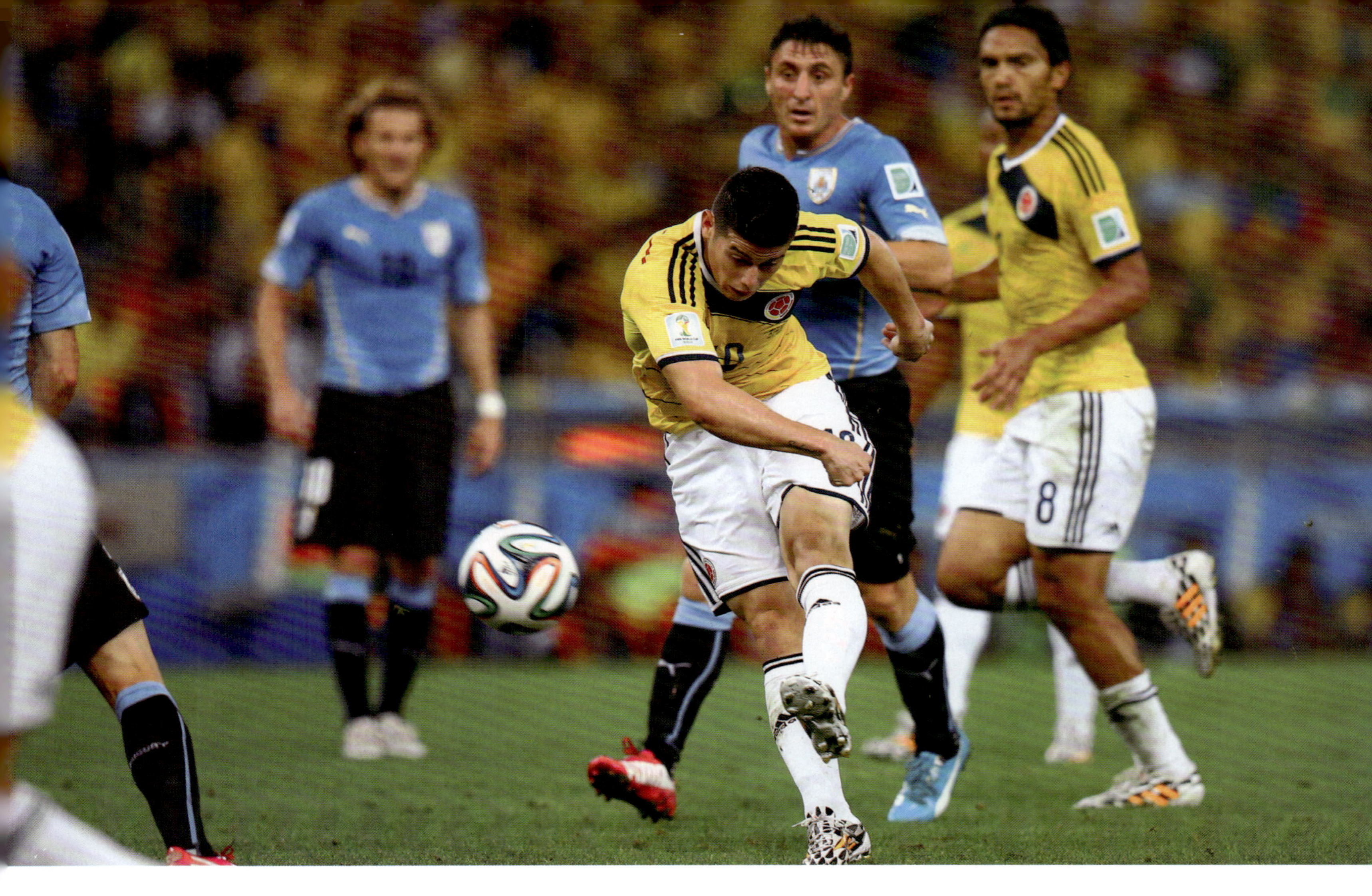



**OPPOSITE** *Dutchman Arjen Robben is seemingly tripped inside the box for a penalty kick in the Round of 16, drawing protest from many Mexico supporters.*

**ABOVE** *Colombia's James Rodríguez, the break-out star of the tournament. Here photographed launching a stunning volley (after a chest trap and 180-degree rotation) against Uruguay en route to a semi-final berth.*

# THE KEEPERS OF NORTH AMERICA

**In the Round of 16,** North American neighbours the United States and Mexico both lost 2–1 heartbreakers to European neighbours Belgium and the Netherlands, respectively. But both games produced Man of the Match goalkeeping from the losing side. Mexico's Guillermo Ochoa burnished his legend with a brilliant athletic display against the Netherlands … just twelve days after his equally impressive shutout of host Brazil in group play.

Meanwhile, the thirty-five-year-old American goalkeeper Tim Howard registered an astounding sixteen saves against an unrelenting Belgian onslaught, setting a FIFA World Cup record for saves in a single game. An amusing sidenote: For a short time, Wikipedia users managed to change the entry for the US Secretary of Defence Chuck Hagel, placing Howard in the White House Cabinet position instead.

And yet, as impressive as those two played, the best North American goalkeeper at the Cup would turn out to be Costa Rica's Keylor Navas. Named Man of the Match an amazing three times in the tournament, and with three clean sheets in his five games, Navas's astounding penalty-kick save in Costa Rica's Round of 16 shootout with Greece led *Los Ticos* to their first-ever quarter-final. His Cup showing was such a revelation that Real Madrid, arguably the biggest club in football history, signed Navas immediately after the tournament. After 162 appearances in all competitions for Real, he moved on to Paris Saint-Germain, where he would add another 114 appearances to his resume. Widely considered the greatest goalkeeper in CONCACAF history, indeed one of the greatest of all time, Keylor Navas's mythos began at this World Cup.

**BELOW** *Costa Rica's legendary goalkeeper Keylor Navas with a penalty-kick save on Greece's Theofanis Gekas in the Round of 16.*

**OPPOSITE** *Tim Howard of USA extends to tip the ball over the bar in the Round of 16. Despite Howard's record-breaking sixteen saves, Belgium would triumph.*

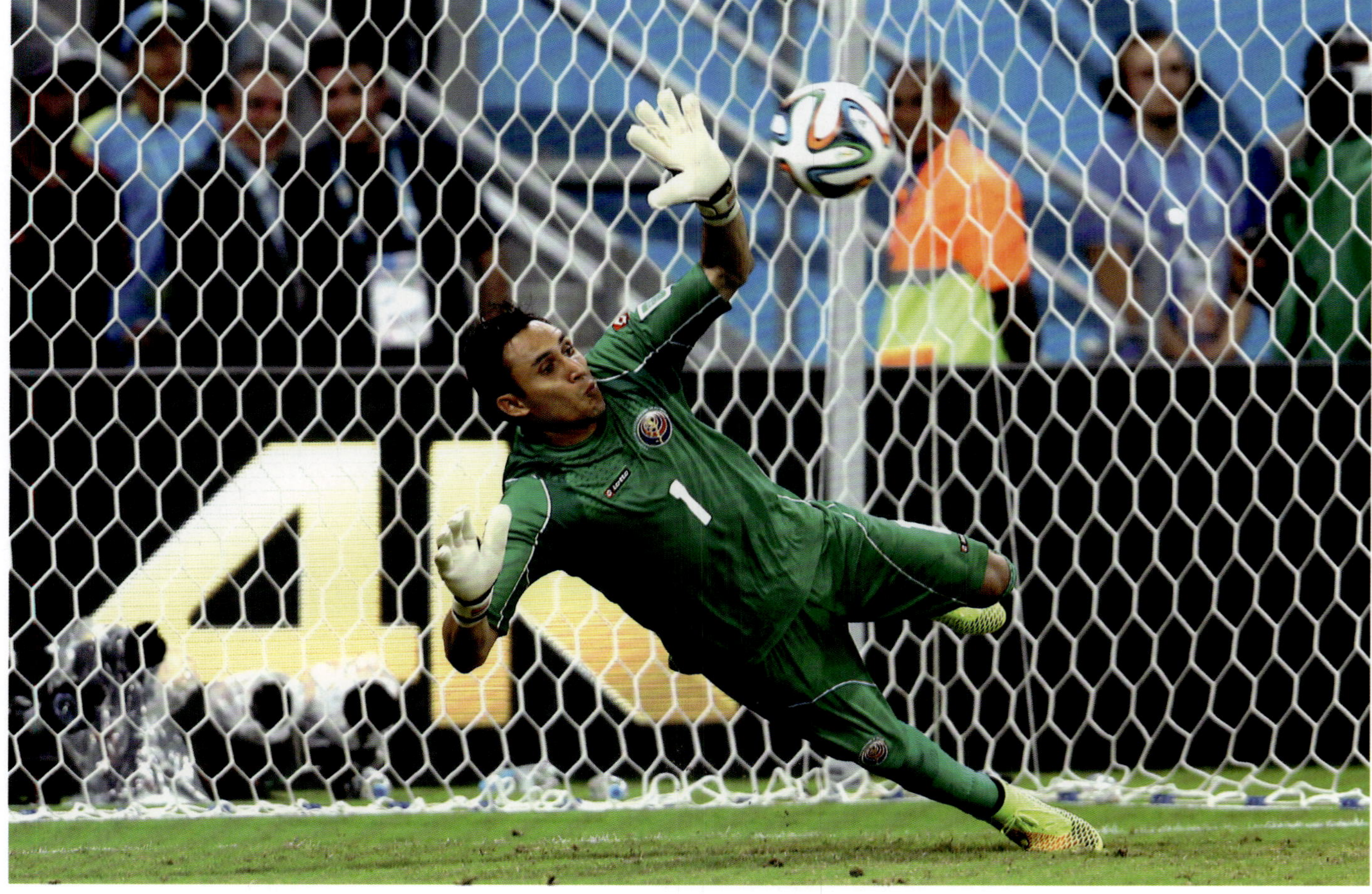

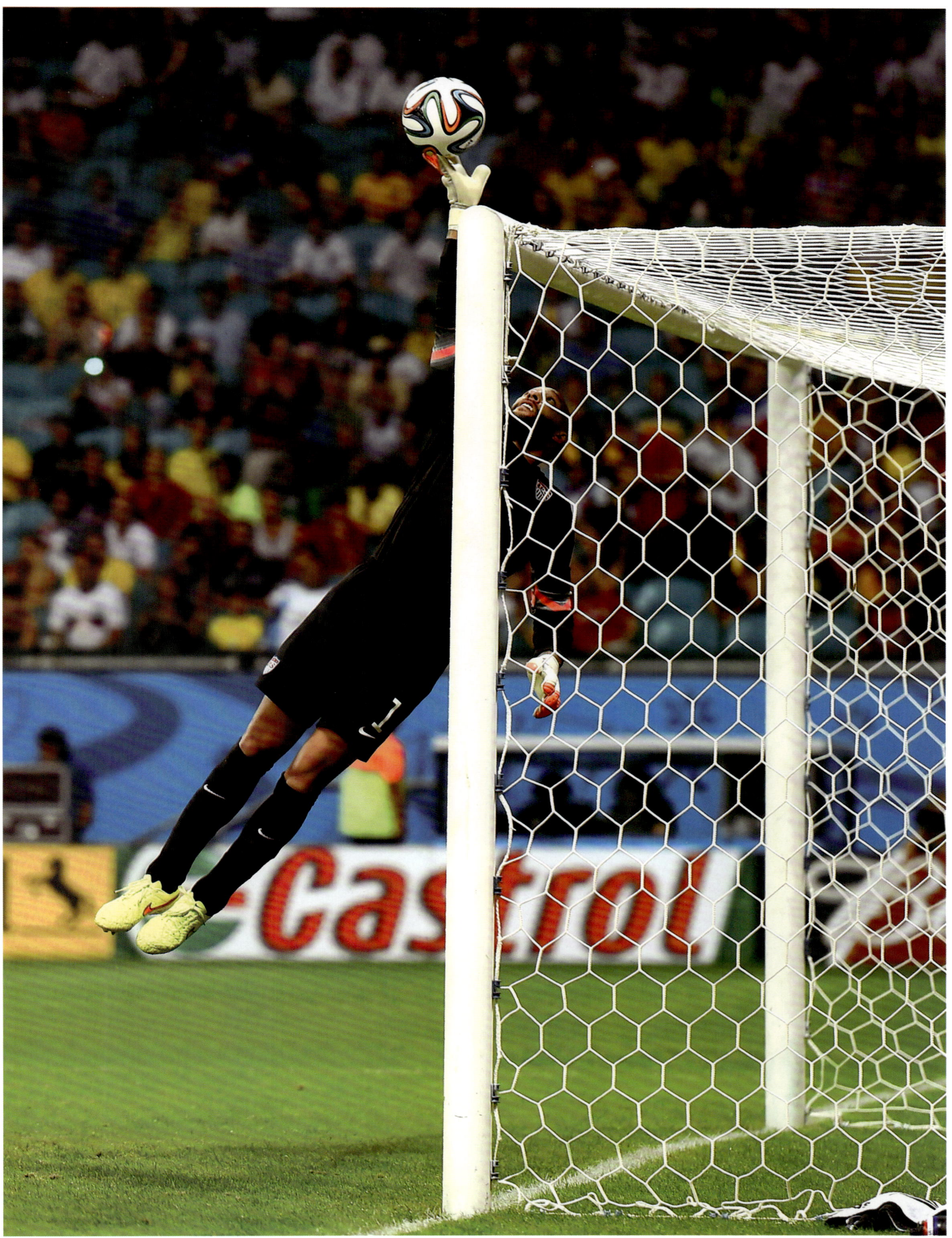

Castrol

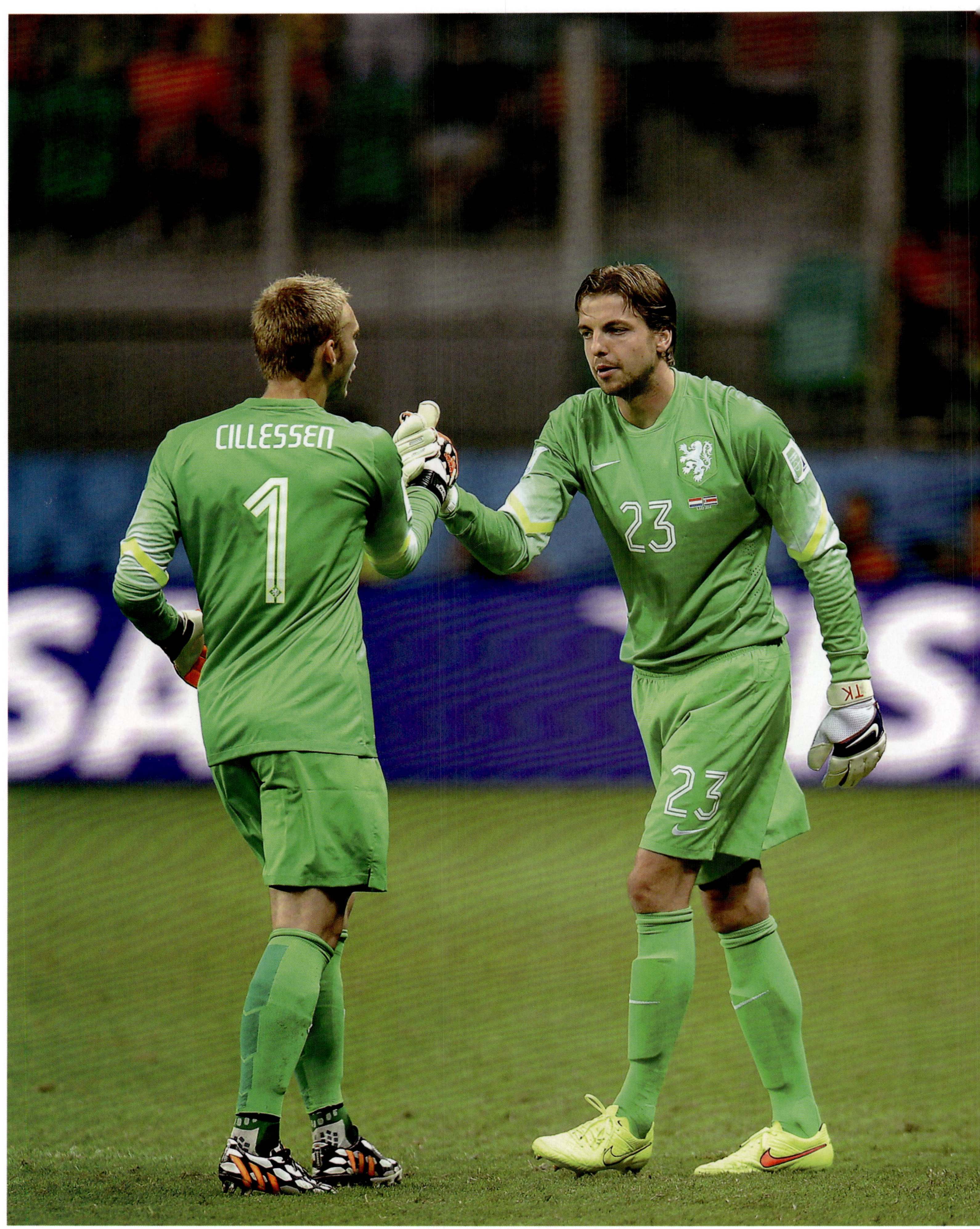

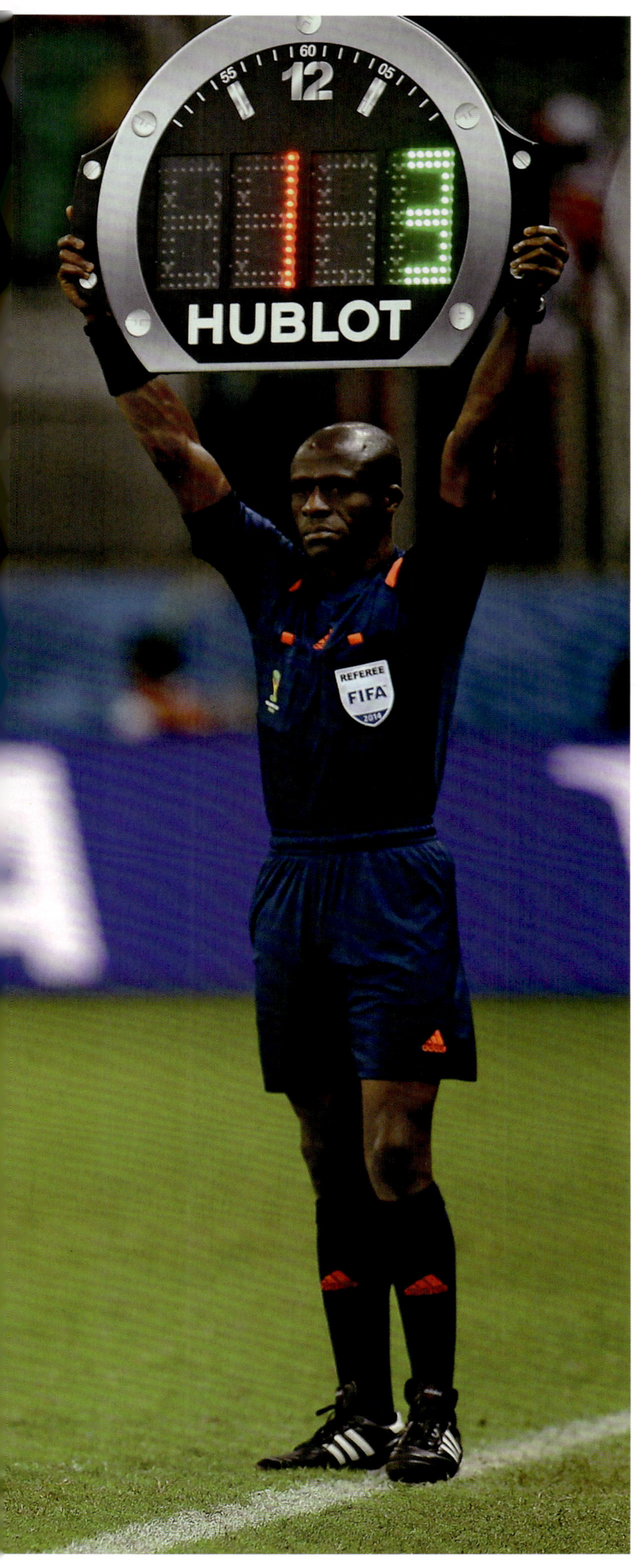

LEFT *Dutch coach Louis van Gaal with a stroke of genius. Penalty-stopping specialist Tim Krul (right) comes on during the closing moments of extra time to replace starting keeper Jasper Cillessen (left). Krul saved two penalties during the shootout to push the Netherlands past an exceptional Costa Rica.*

## QUARTER-FINALS

| | |
|---|---|
| Brazil 2 | 1 Colombia |
| Germany 1 | 0 France |
| Netherlands 0 | 0 Costa Rica |
| | (4–3 on penalty kicks) |
| Argentina 1 | 0 Belgium |

Brazil's 2–1 victory over Colombia proved costly, as Neymar's painful vertebrae injury knocked him out of the tournament. The Germans continued to elevate their level of play, taking an early lead over France and maintaining firm control until the end. This meant that Germany had qualified for their fourth straight semi-final appearance, a World Cup record.

As the Netherlands and Costa Rica struggled through the final minutes of extra time tied at 0–0, Dutch coach Louis van Gaal substituted in his backup goalkeeper Tim Krul, a penalty-kick specialist, for the impending shootout. The gambit paid off nicely as Krul parried away two penalty kicks to send the Dutch into the semi-finals over a superb Costa Rica. In the last quarter-final, Belgium's defence organised early to nullify Messi, although this allowed Gonzalo Higuaín to shake free for a quick goal in the eighth minute. That turned out to be all Argentina needed.

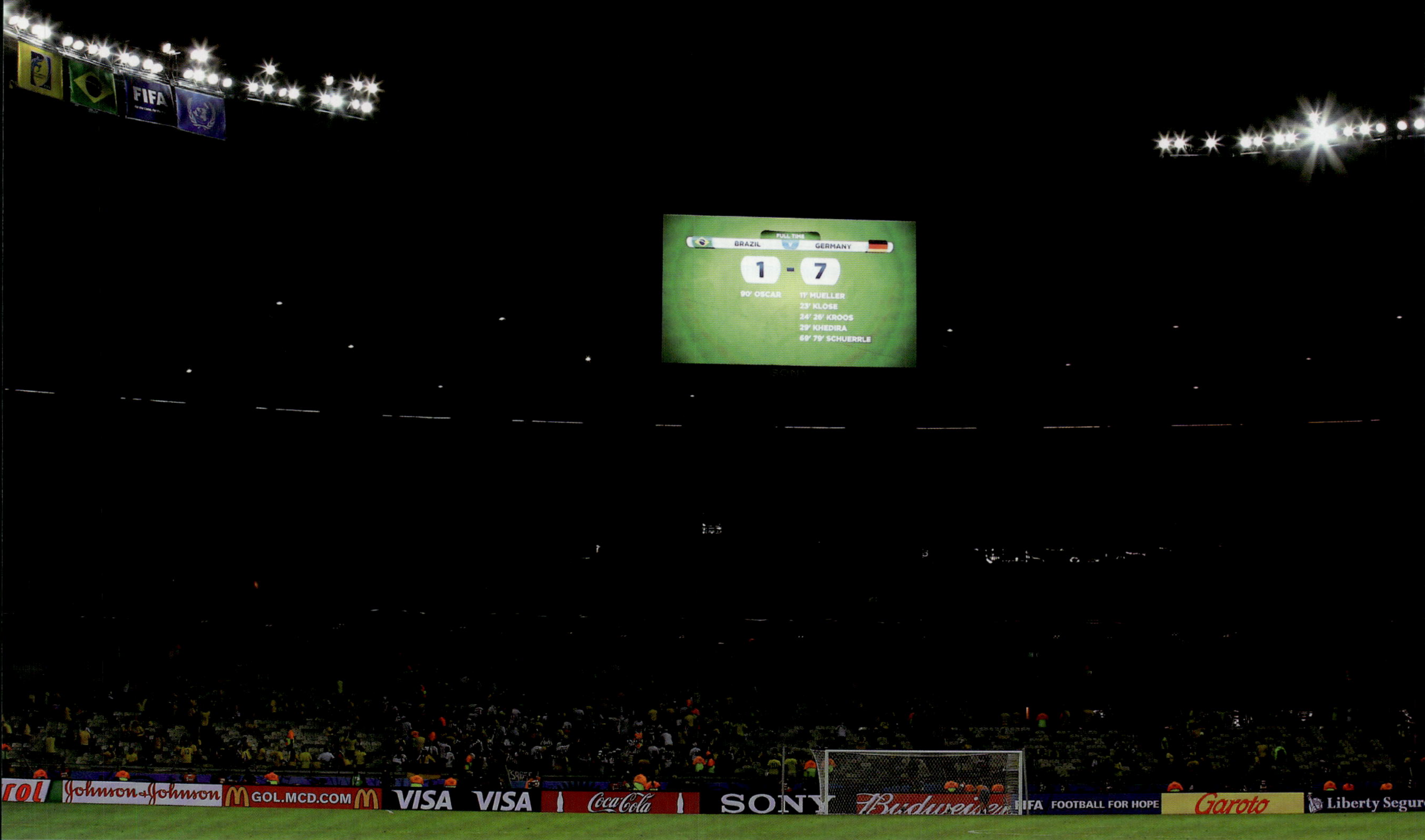


## SEMI-FINALS

| Germany 7 | 1 Brazil |
|---|---|
| Argentina 0 | 0 Netherlands |
| | (4–2 on penalty kicks) |

Germany's 7–1 rout of the home team was astonishing, humiliating, and surreal. It would go down as perhaps the most devastating late-tournament loss in World Cup history and surely brought tears to many more Brazilians than just the fans in the Estádio Mineirão home crowd. Between the twenty-third and twenty-ninth minutes, the Germans scored an unbelievable four times. For Brazilian football, it was arguably more painful than the infamous Maracanazo of 1950. And to add just an extra dash of insult to injury, Miroslav Klose's goal during the romp was his sixteenth in World Cup play...moving him ahead of Brazil's Ronaldo for most-ever World Cup goals.

In the other semi-final, a tactical slugfest on a rainy day in São Paulo made for a somewhat dull match that played out predominantly in the middle third and ended 0–0 after extra time. Dutch coach Louis van Gaal had used up his three substitutions so he couldn't repeat his quarter-final tactic of putting penalty-master Tim Krul in goal for the shootout. Thus, Messi and his cool crew converted all four of their shots while the Dutch missed two of theirs.

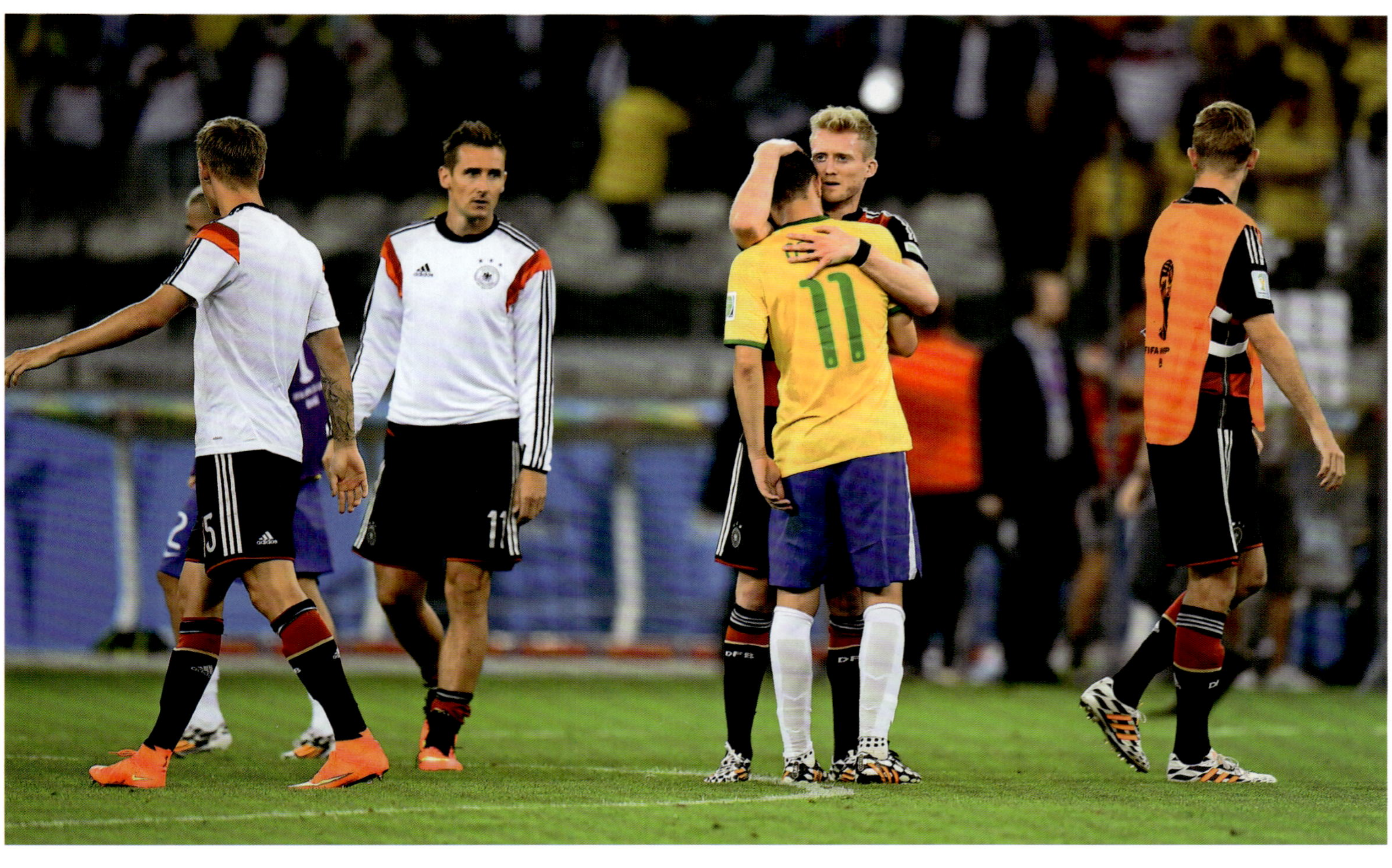


OPPOSITE *Photos of the digital scoreboard would go viral online.*

ABOVE *Germany's André Schürrle comforts Brazil's Oscar (number 11) following the host nation's humiliating 7–1 defeat on home soil.*

FOLLOWING SPREAD *A backdrop of purple hues and bright lights set the stage for Germany's semi-final demolition of host nation Brazil at the Mineirão in Belo Horizonte.*

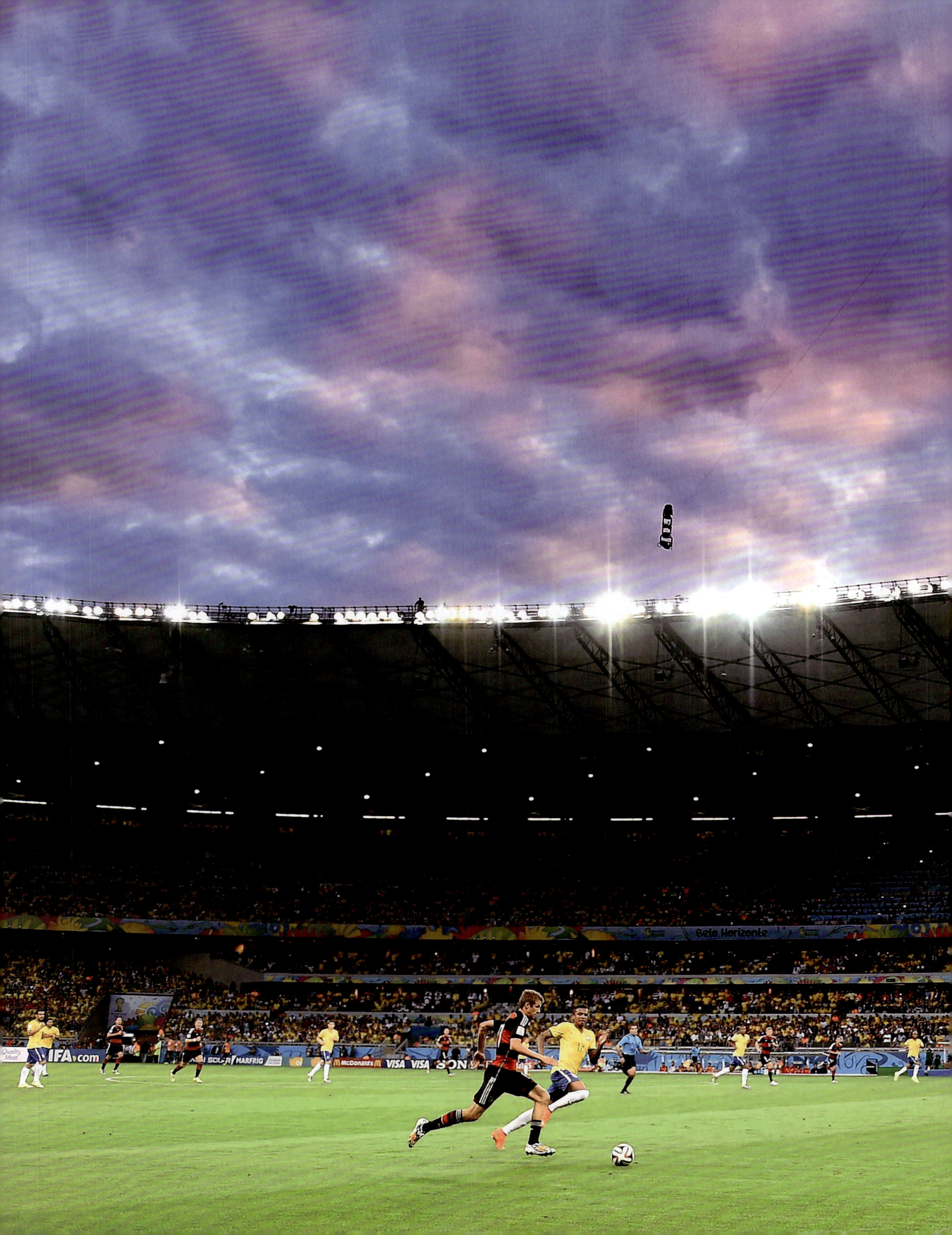

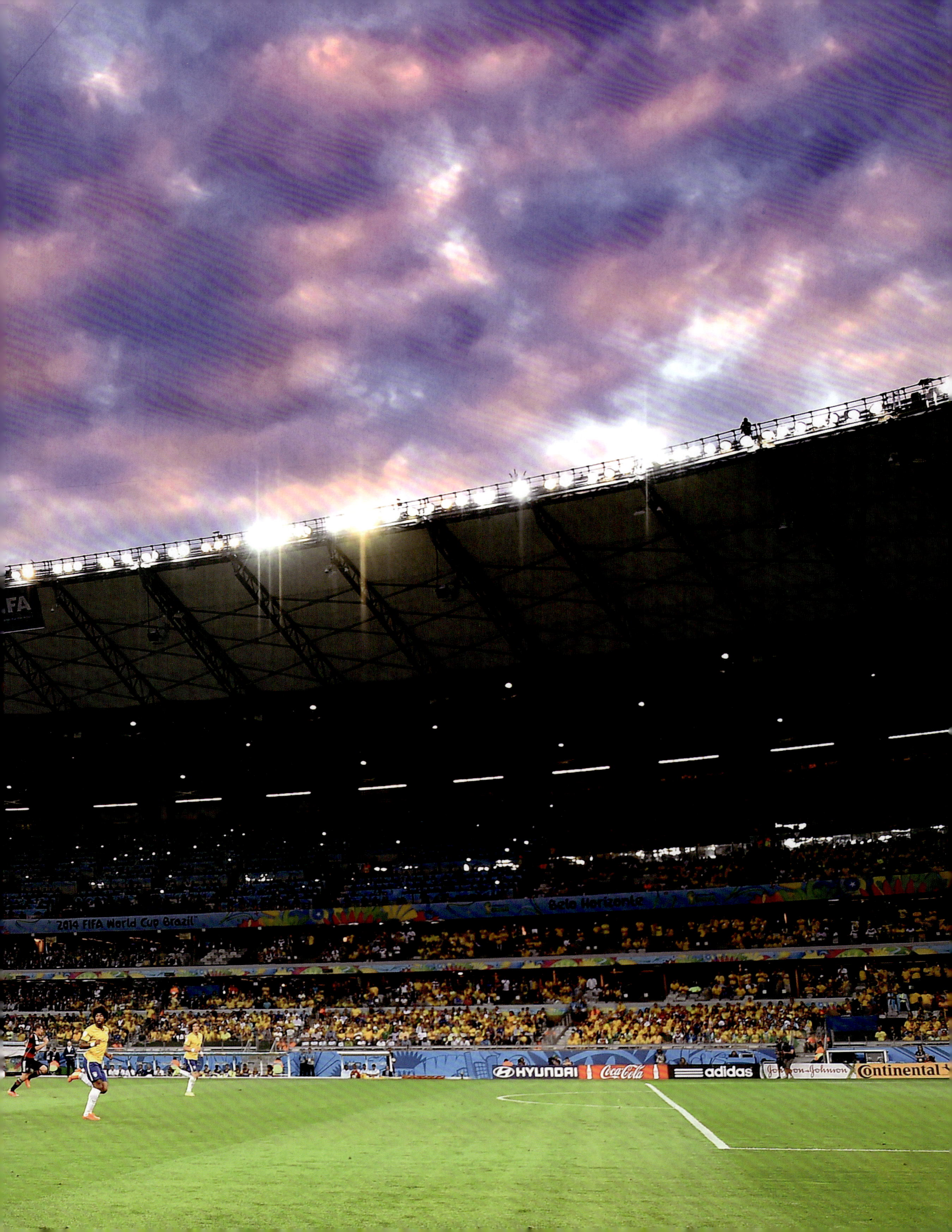
FA
2014 FIFA World Cup Brazil
Belo Horizonte
HYUNDAI
Coca-Cola
adidas
Johnson-Johnson
Continental

# FINAL

Germany 1 | 0 Argentina (First Place)
Netherlands 3 | 0 Brazil (Third Place)

The Netherlands extended Brazilian pain with another beat-down, 3–0, marking a second-straight top-three Cup finish for the Dutch. For Brazil, the semi-final demolition by the Germans had taken a bitter toll. Missing both Neymar and captain Thiago Silva, the South American side appeared rudderless . . . and was roundly booed off the pitch at game's end. For the tournament, the Brazilians had conceded a dispiriting fourteen goals—half of them in their most crucial match. Finishing in the top four was little consolation for a five-time champion hosting the Cup for the first time in sixty-four years.

The finale in Rio de Janeiro's mythic Maracanã Stadium was a fascinating matchup and the third Cup Final to pit the two historic nations against each other. Argentina, led by a Messi at the peak of his powers, was supremely skilled. However, Germany seemed not only more physically imposing but also more tactically cohesive. Most observers predicted a convincing German victory, but Argentina came out on fire. With multiple golden chances at the outset, the Germans were kept on their back foot early on. Dangerous open shots by Higuaín, Messi, and Rodrigo Palacio slid just wide of the German post. Then, as the intense, absorbing match wore on, Germany began to regain and hold possession more, putting the Argentines off-balance and out of rhythm.

Just before regular time expired, Germany substituted their dynamic twenty-two-year-old forward Mario Götze for the aging lion Miroslav Klose. The fresh legs and energy paid off in the second period of extra time when young Götze chested a crossing ball and then slashed a volley past Argentina's goalkeeper Sergio Romero at the 113' mark. Germany held on to win their fourth World Cup championship.

Winning the Golden Ball as the most outstanding player of the tournament did little to assuage Messi's disappointment, as this chance to finally hoist the Cup with his Argentine mates seemed an opportunity tragically lost. 'I would give all my personal records to be world champion,' he said. 'Nothing can console me.' Of no mean importance was the mounting pressure on Messi's shoulders to lead his country to World Cup glory—as his immortal predecessor Diego Maradona had done decades prior.

On the other side, Germany's relatively young squad was flush with confidence. Coach Joachim Löw said, 'We aim to dominate the game for a decade.'

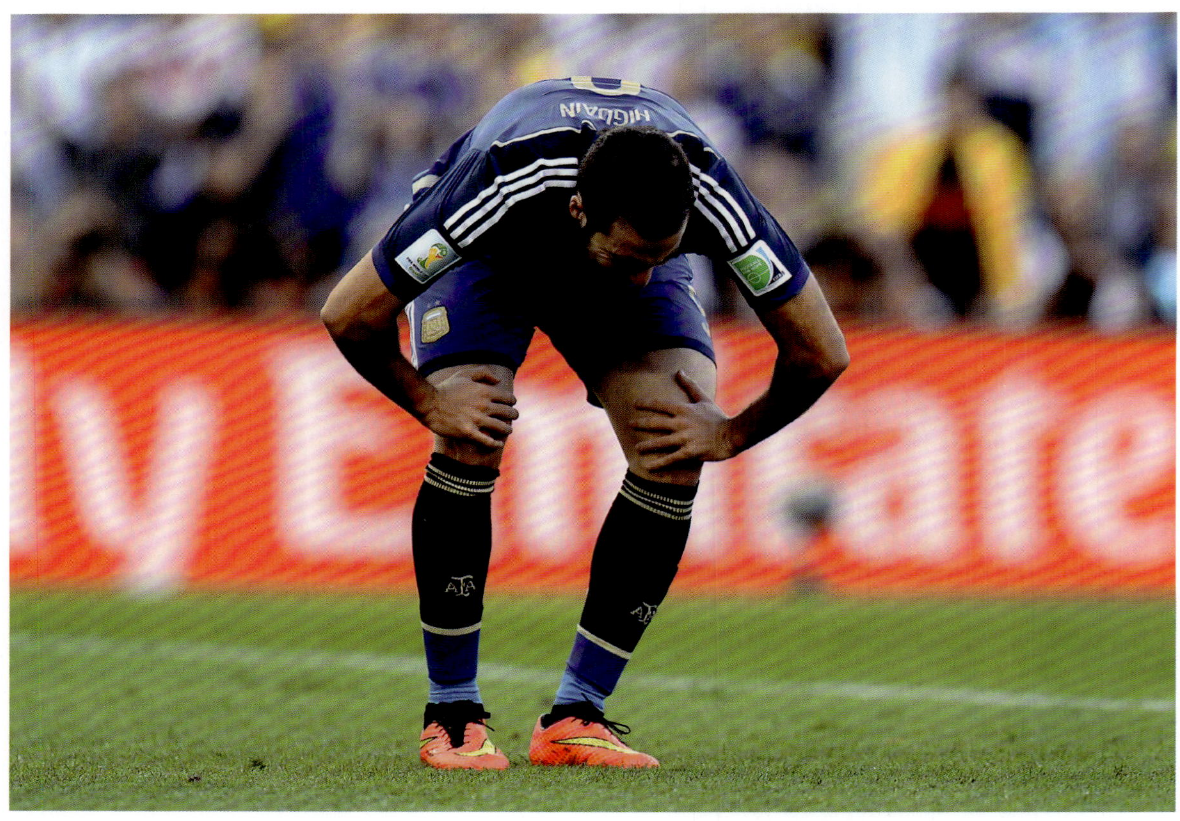

**LEFT** *Argentine striker Gonzalo Higuaín doubled over after a frustrating miss in the final.*

**OPPOSITE** *Germany's Mario Götze with an acrobatic finish in extra time to deny Lionel Messi and Argentina in the 2014 final.*

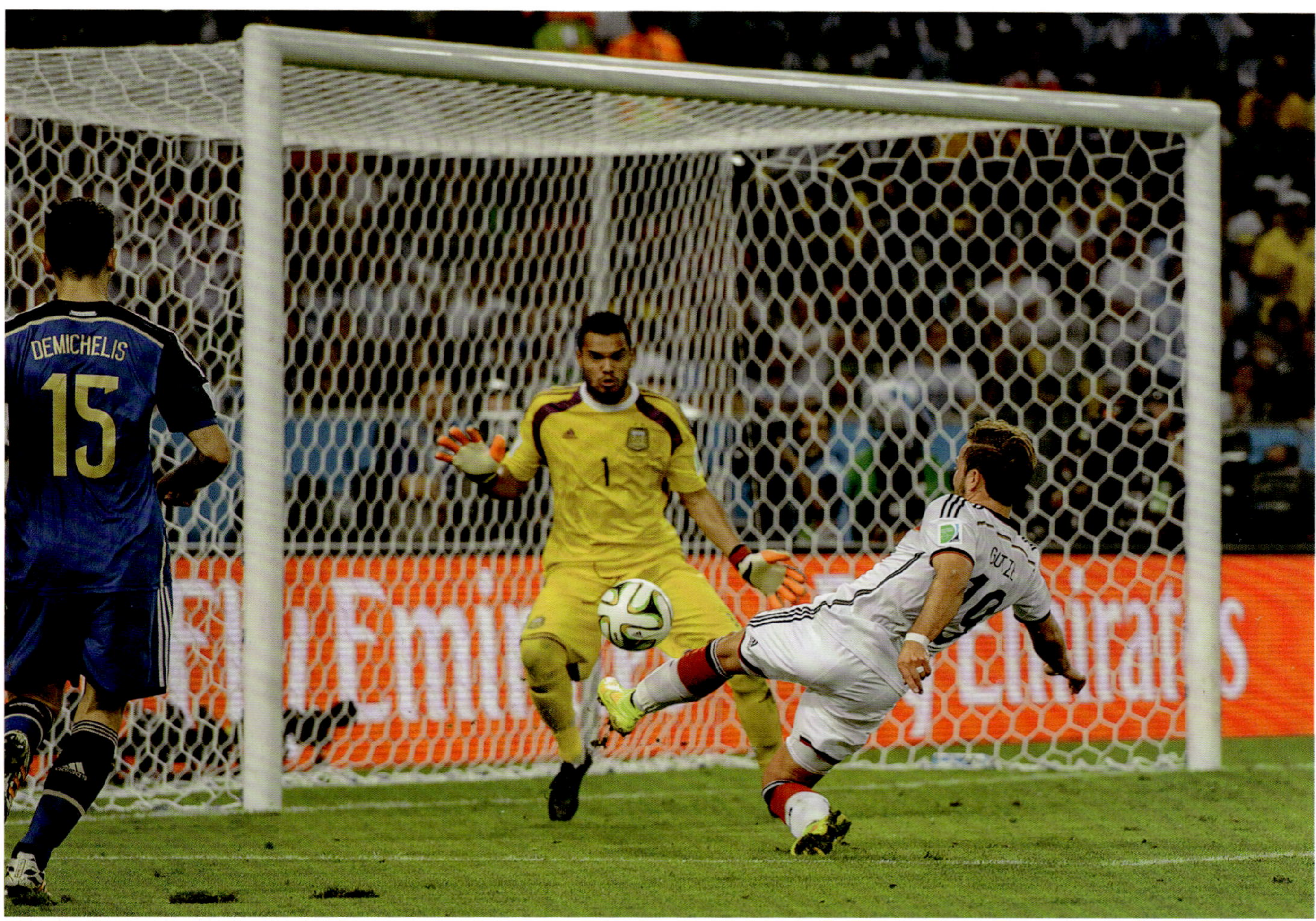

## GERMANY 2014: ANALYTICS, VIRTUOSITY, AND BIG FAST GUYS

**Going back to the 1930s,** German football, at its best, has always been characterised by certain perennial characteristics: rangy athleticism with length and great speed, deadly counterattacks, and overall dominance in the air. Over time, its national teams added geometric precision in the midfield (perhaps first introduced and pesonified by the great Franz Beckenbauer) and disciplined defensive cohesion. In 2014, these traits all coalesced into one of the truly great teams in the sport's history, a juggernaut of efficiency that played its best down the stretch in decisive knockout wins over three highly talented opponents: France, Brazil, and Argentina.

Germany's midfield pairing of Toni Kroos and Bastian Schweinsteiger controlled match tempo with remarkable technical ability and composure, and twenty-four-year-old phenom Thomas Müller joined the national team's all-time leading scorer Miroslav Klose in a lethal front line. The German attack netted a staggering eighteen goals during the tournament — admittedly padded a bit by a Brazilian collapse in the semi-final, but impressive nonetheless. The defence, meanwhile, was disciplined, solid, and backed by a world-class goalkeeper in Manuel Neuer. The German back line gave up just two goals in group play and only two more in its four knockout-stage matches.

Also of note was the German staff's famous employment of real-time data and advanced predictive analytics to break down elements of play, identify opponent weaknesses, and design data-driven game plans and optimised training sessions. Its customised match-analysis tools could track players, generate individual profiles, and design performance goals tailored for each player. The analytics revolution that Germany embraced, and certainly helped promote, has had an undeniable impact on global football . . . but what effect has it had on the state of the 'beautiful game'? A matter of profound debate.

# 2018

HOST COUNTRY: **RUSSIA**
CHAMPION: **FRANCE**
RUNNER-UP: **CROATIA**
THIRD PLACE: **BELGIUM OVER ENGLAND**

When FIFA selected Russia to host the 2018 World Cup, Eastern Europe finally got its long-awaited chance to stage football's biggest event. Like their predecessors, the Russians poured considerable resources (an estimated $14.2 billion) into travel-infrastructure upgrades and venue-development projects to welcome the influx of foreign football fans and press. Of the twelve stadiums used for the tournament, nine were brand-new and the other three were extensively renovated. Overall, more than three million fans attended matches across Russia.

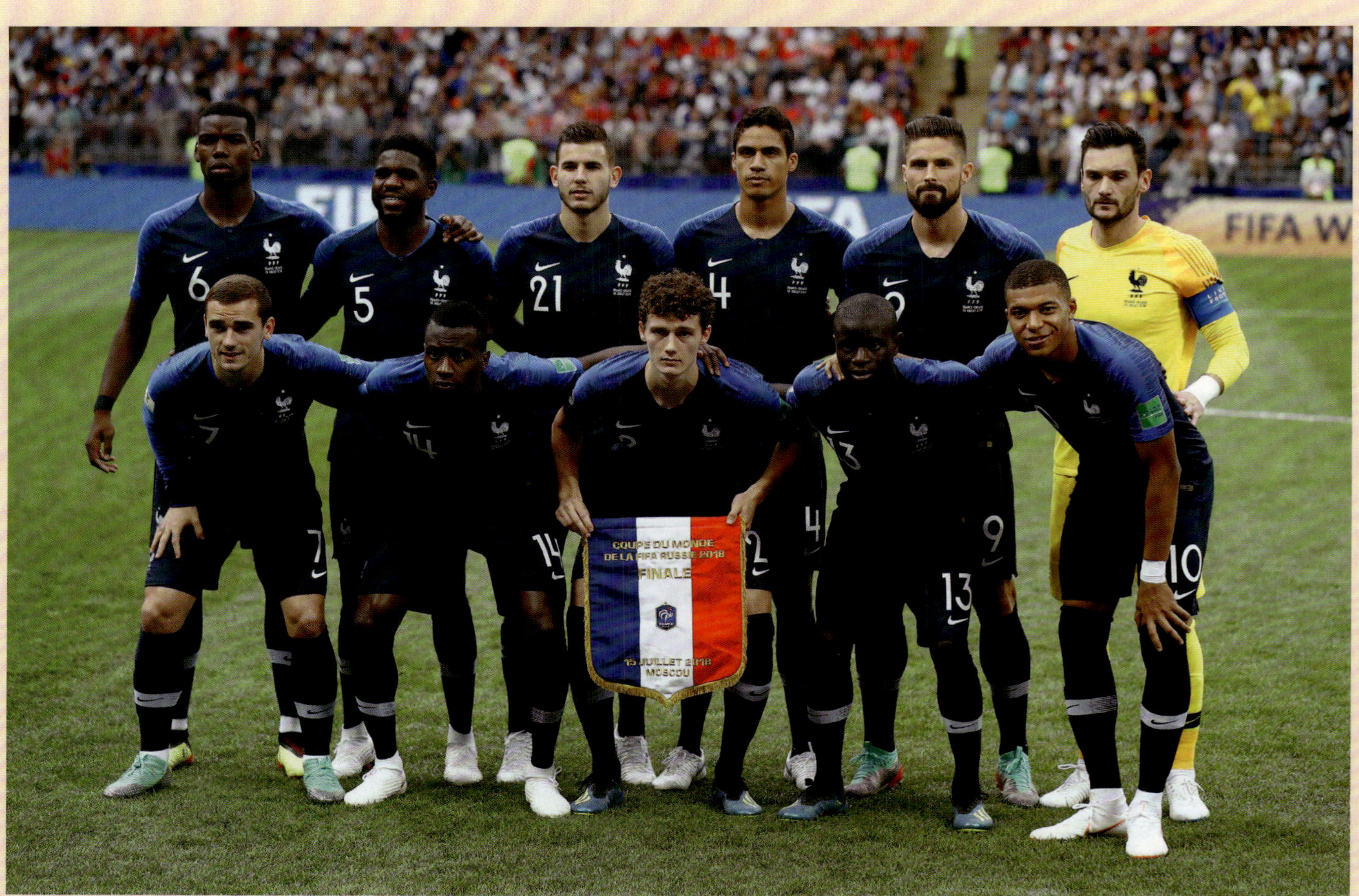

**ABOVE** *France's 2018 line-up promises an exciting new generation of French football.*

# RUSSIA'S MONEY MAN

**To commemorate the 2018 World Cup,** Russia printed a special 100-ruble banknote featuring Russia's most famous footballer: the legendary goalkeeper Lev Yashin. Illustrated on the banknote is a boy watching Yashin dive for a save while wearing a black jersey, emblazoned with Yashin's number 1, in homage to his iconic 'Black Panther' outfit. For almost two decades, Yashin was the surest bet on the Russian national team. The motherland's 'money man' in goal, one might say. Thus, it seemed entirely fitting to highlight him on the national currency.

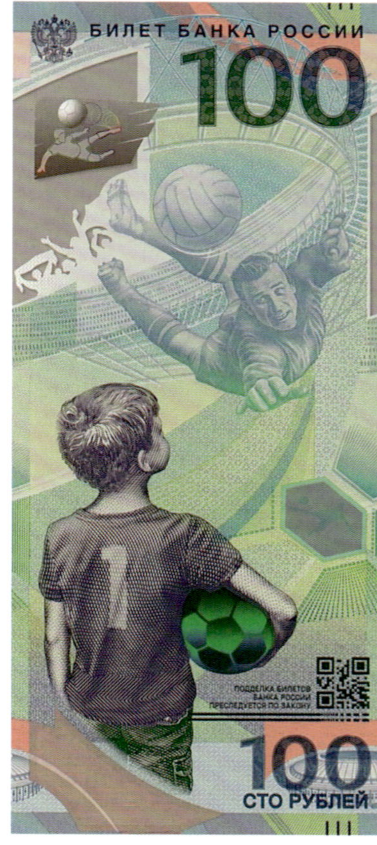
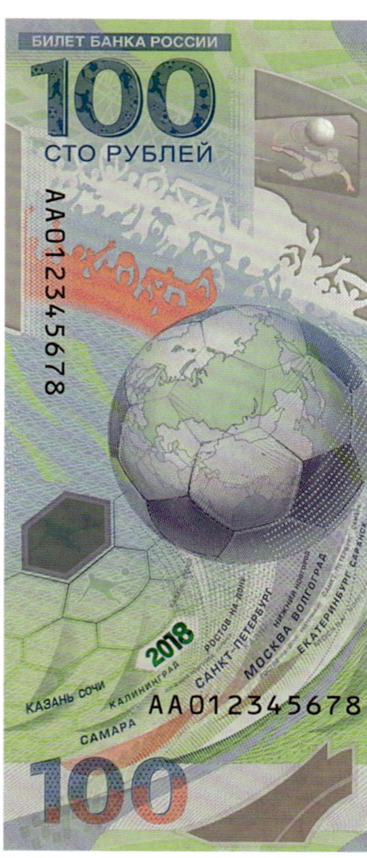

*RIGHT Russian hosts celebrate Lev 'The Black Spider' Yashin, legendary goalkeeper of the Soviet Era, with a 100-ruble banknote.*

*BELOW A large screen in the stadium indicates that VAR is checking for a possible penalty during the 2018 World Cup Final between France and Croatia.*

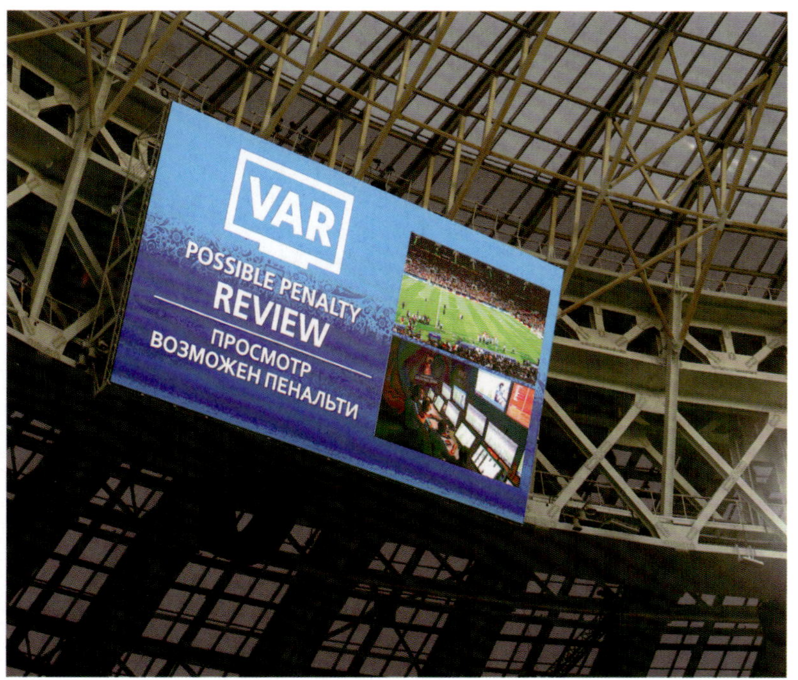


# THE ADVENT OF VAR

**The 2018 tournament would be** the first to employ video assistant referees (VAR), providing video replays from various angles to review and, if necessary, correct difficult calls made or missed by the on-field referee crew. VAR could be used in checking goals and offsides, penalty decisions, mistaken identity, and the proper issuance of red cards.

As it turned out, VAR calls would make a big difference in several 2018 Cup matches and FIFA considered the roll-out an unqualified success, as the tournament featured markedly fewer officiating controversies than in previous Cups. After the tournament, Pierluigi Collina, chairman of the FIFA Referees Committee, praised the new feature and said, 'Believe me, VAR is like a parachute . . . it's better to have it when [you] need it.'

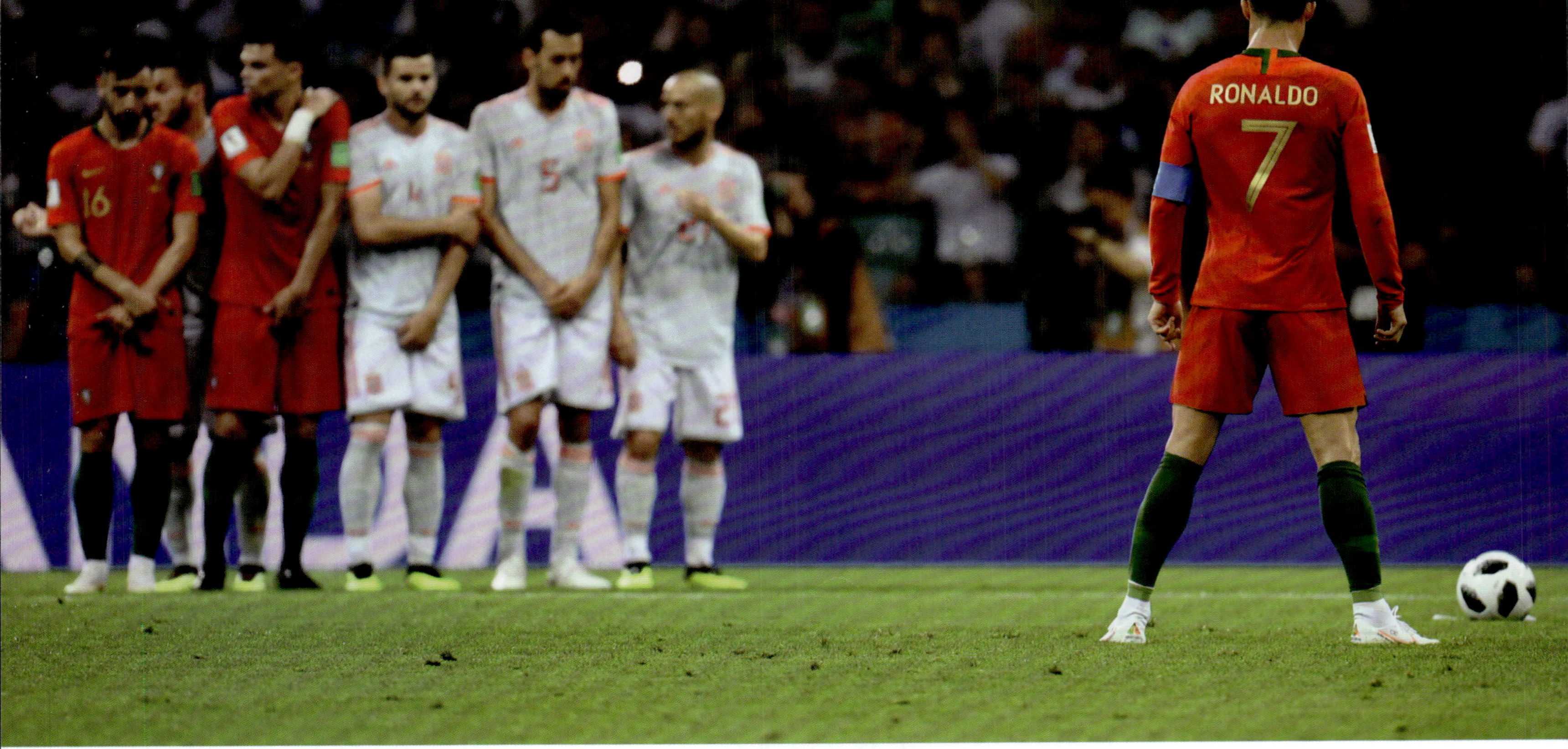

# Tournament: GROUP STAGE

### GROUP A: URUGUAY, RUSSIA, SAUDI ARABIA, EGYPT

| | | |
|---:|---|---|
| Russia 5 | 0 | Saudi Arabia |
| Uruguay 1 | 0 | Egypt |
| Russia 3 | 1 | Egypt |
| Uruguay 1 | 0 | Saudi Arabia |
| Uruguay 3 | 0 | Russia |
| Saudi Arabia 2 | 1 | Egypt |

**Advanced to Knockout Stage: Uruguay, Russia**

### GROUP B: SPAIN, PORTUGAL, IRAN, MOROCCO

| | | |
|---:|---|---|
| Iran 1 | 0 | Morocco |
| Portugal 3 | 3 | Spain |
| Portugal 1 | 0 | Morocco |
| Spain 1 | 0 | Iran |
| Portugal 1 | 1 | Iran |
| Spain 2 | 2 | Morocco |

**Advanced to Knockout Stage: Spain, Portugal**

The host team (ranked seventieth in the world, the lowest of all participants in the tournament) came out sizzling in a 5–0 thrashing of Saudi Arabia and a 3–1 defeat of Egypt. The Russians lost soundly to Uruguay in their last group match but pleased the home crowds by collecting six points and finishing second in group. The stout Uruguayan squad concluded their decade of group-stage dominance with three victories and zero goals conceded.

Spain–Portugal in Sochi was a spirited, back-and-forth affair between the Iberian archrivals that more than lived up to expectations. Cristiano Ronaldo carried his team, the reigning European champions, to a 3–3 draw with a splendid hat-trick (his fifty-first at the time) that included a final equaliser in the eighty-eighth minute—a spectacular free kick. And though eliminated, Morocco's surprising performance would be a harbinger of things to come in four years' time.

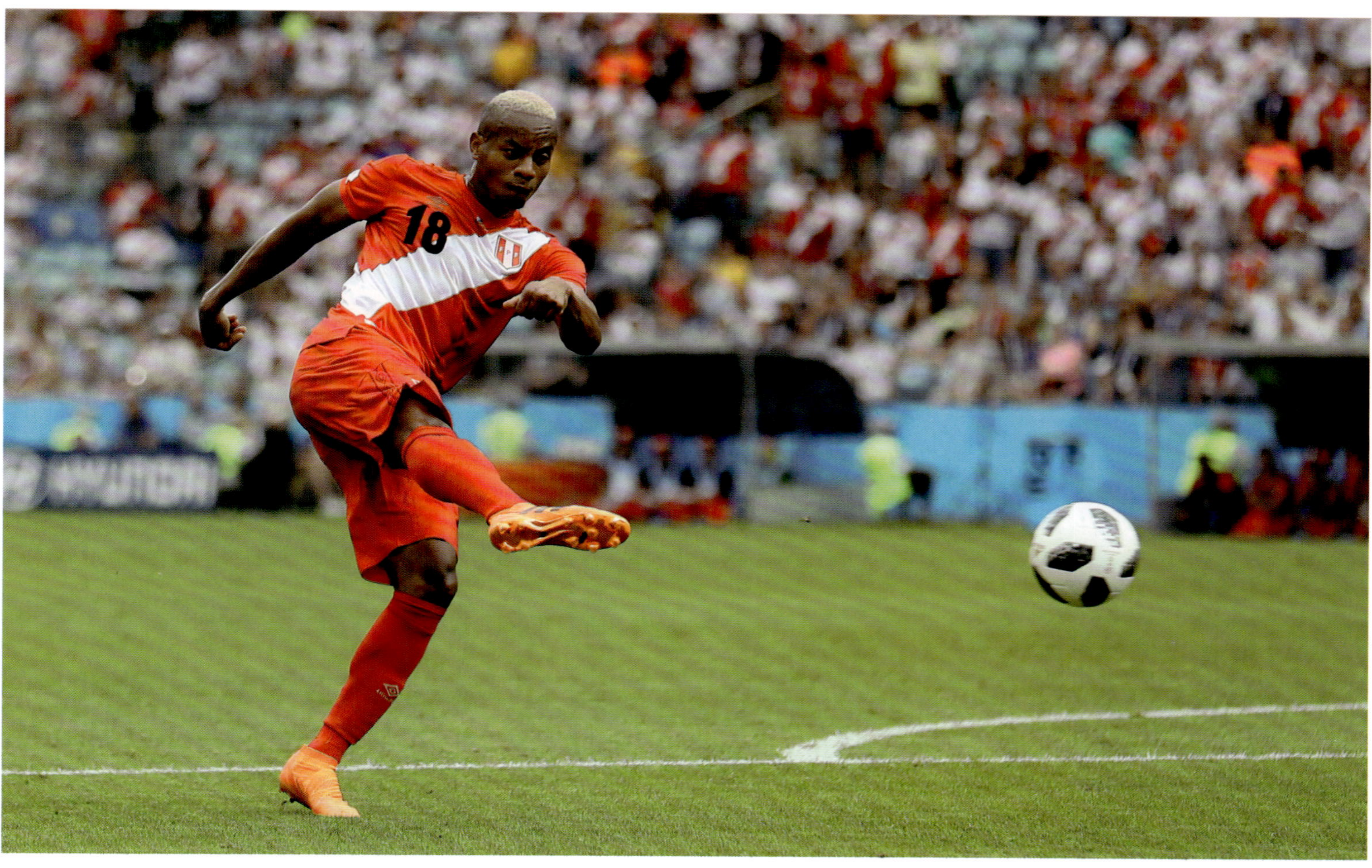

## GROUP C: FRANCE, DENMARK, PERU, AUSTRALIA

| | | |
|---:|:---|:---|
| France 2 | 1 | Australia |
| Denmark 1 | 0 | Peru |
| Denmark 1 | 1 | Australia |
| France 1 | 0 | Peru |
| Denmark 0 | 0 | France |
| Peru 2 | 0 | Australia |

**Advanced to Knockout Stage: France, Denmark**

This low-scoring but gruellingly competitive group produced a historic moment—Kylian Mbappé's first World Cup goal, the game winner for France against Peru. Just 19 years and 183 days old, Mbappé became France's youngest-ever scorer in the World Cup. Peru, finally returning to the tournament after a thirty-six-year absence, surprised the world with its strong and spirited play. A missed penalty against Denmark and the aforementioned Mbappé break-out goal kept them from advancing, but they would get their due against Australia: a sensational volley from André 'La Culebra' Carrillo and a crafty finish from veteran striker Paolo Guerrero ensured that *La Blanquiroja* did not leave Russia empty-handed.

**OPPOSITE** *Portugal's Cristiano Ronaldo before scoring a free kick against Spain to equalise at 3–3 and complete his hat-trick.*

**ABOVE** *Peru's André Carrillo scores an impressive volley against Australia.*

### GROUP D: CROATIA, ARGENTINA, NIGERIA, ICELAND

| | | |
|---:|:---:|:---|
| Argentina 1 | | 1 Iceland |
| Croatia 2 | | 0 Nigeria |
| Croatia 3 | | 0 Argentina |
| Nigeria 2 | | 0 Iceland |
| Argentina 2 | | 1 Nigeria |
| Croatia 2 | | 1 Iceland |

**Advanced to Knockout Stage: Croatia, Argentina**

Cup favourite Argentina barely slipped through to the next stage, suffering a 1–1 tie with upstart Iceland and a ghastly 3–0 loss to Croatia. Critics noted an over-reliance on Lionel Messi that made the South Americans too predictable. The Croatians, led by their brilliant captain Luka Modrić, by 2018 one of the greatest midfielders of all time, swept through the group with full points.

### GROUP E: BRAZIL, SWITZERLAND, SERBIA, COSTA RICA

| | | |
|---:|:---:|:---|
| Serbia 1 | | 0 Costa Rica |
| Brazil 1 | | 1 Switzerland |
| Brazil 2 | | 0 Costa Rica |
| Switzerland 2 | | 1 Serbia |
| Brazil 2 | | 0 Serbia |
| Switzerland 2 | | 2 Cost Rica |

**Advanced to Knockout Stage: Brazil, Switzerland**

Two wins and a tie put them at the top of the table. Switzerland, ranked sixth in the world by FIFA, played well enough to earn second. They suffered an amusing own goal when a late Costa Rican penalty kick struck the bar, ricochetted straight down (and hard) onto the Swiss keeper's head, and then bounced back into the net.

### GROUP F: SWEDEN, MEXICO, SOUTH KOREA, GERMANY

| | | |
|---:|:---:|:---|
| Mexico 1 | | 0 Germany |
| Sweden 1 | | 0 South Korea |
| Mexico 2 | | 1 South Korea |
| Germany 2 | | 1 Sweden |
| South Korea 2 | | 0 Germany |
| Sweden 3 | | 0 Mexico |

**Advanced to Knockout Stage: Sweden, Mexico**

Germany's post-2014 plan to 'dominate for a decade' hit a bit of a snag with a last-place finish in Group F that included shutout losses to Mexico and South Korea. This marked the fourth time in five tournaments that the reigning champion failed to advance out of the group stage. And in shocking fashion, too, as the Koreans scored twice in second-half stoppage time to send them home.

## LES BLEUS 2018

**The stars of France's solid** 2014 Cup squad — including Paul Pogba, Antoine Griezmann, N'Golo Kanté, and Olivier Giroud — had matured into the veteran core of the 2018 side. But the roster also mixed in some truly exciting young talent, including Ousmane Dembélé, twenty-one, and the new boy wonder of the football world, Kylian Mbappé, nineteen. Mbappé and Griezmann would score four goals apiece to power France through the tournament.

**OPPOSITE** *Alfreð Finnbogason of Iceland welcomes doubters and detractors after equalizing against overwhelming favourites Argentina.*

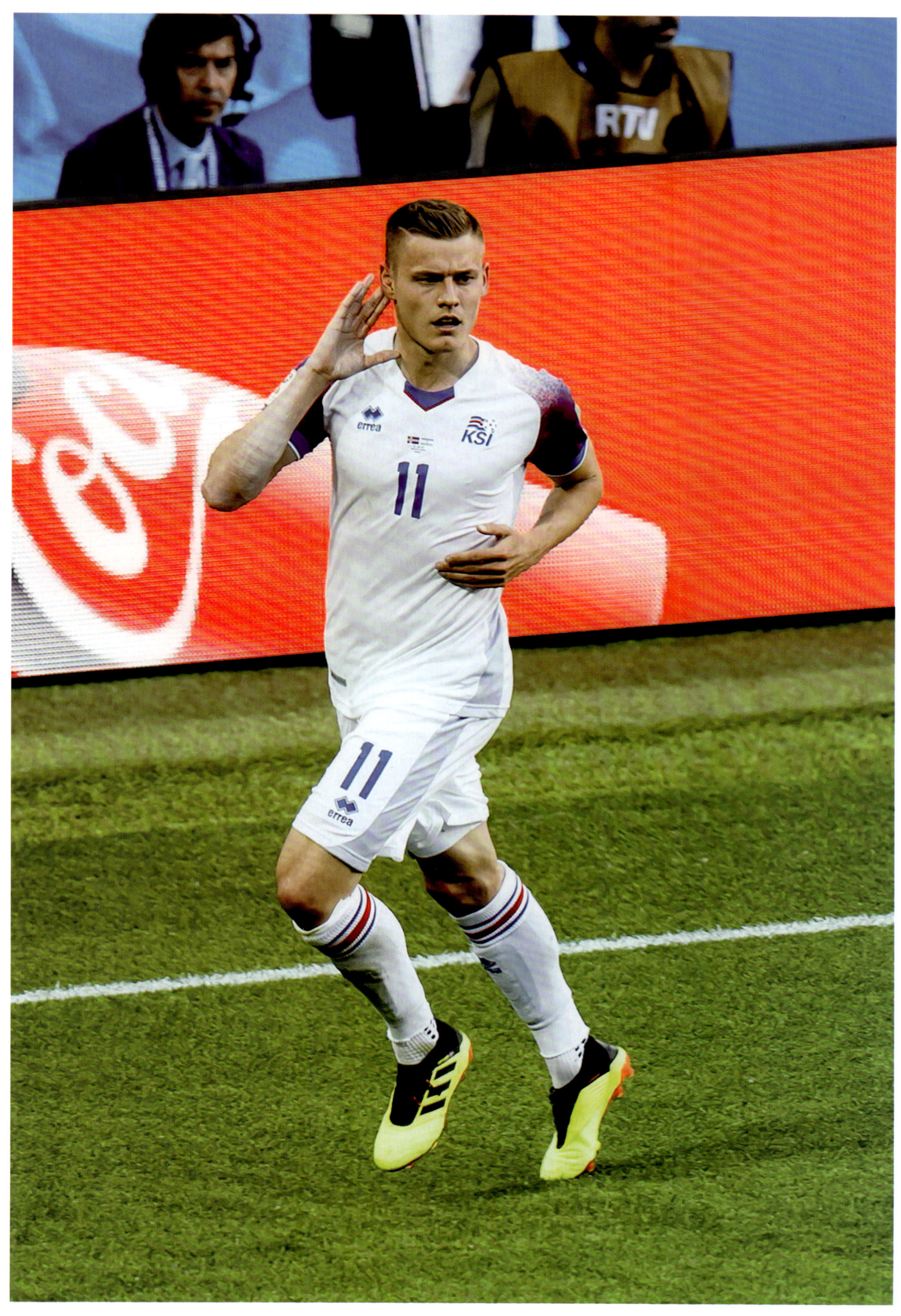

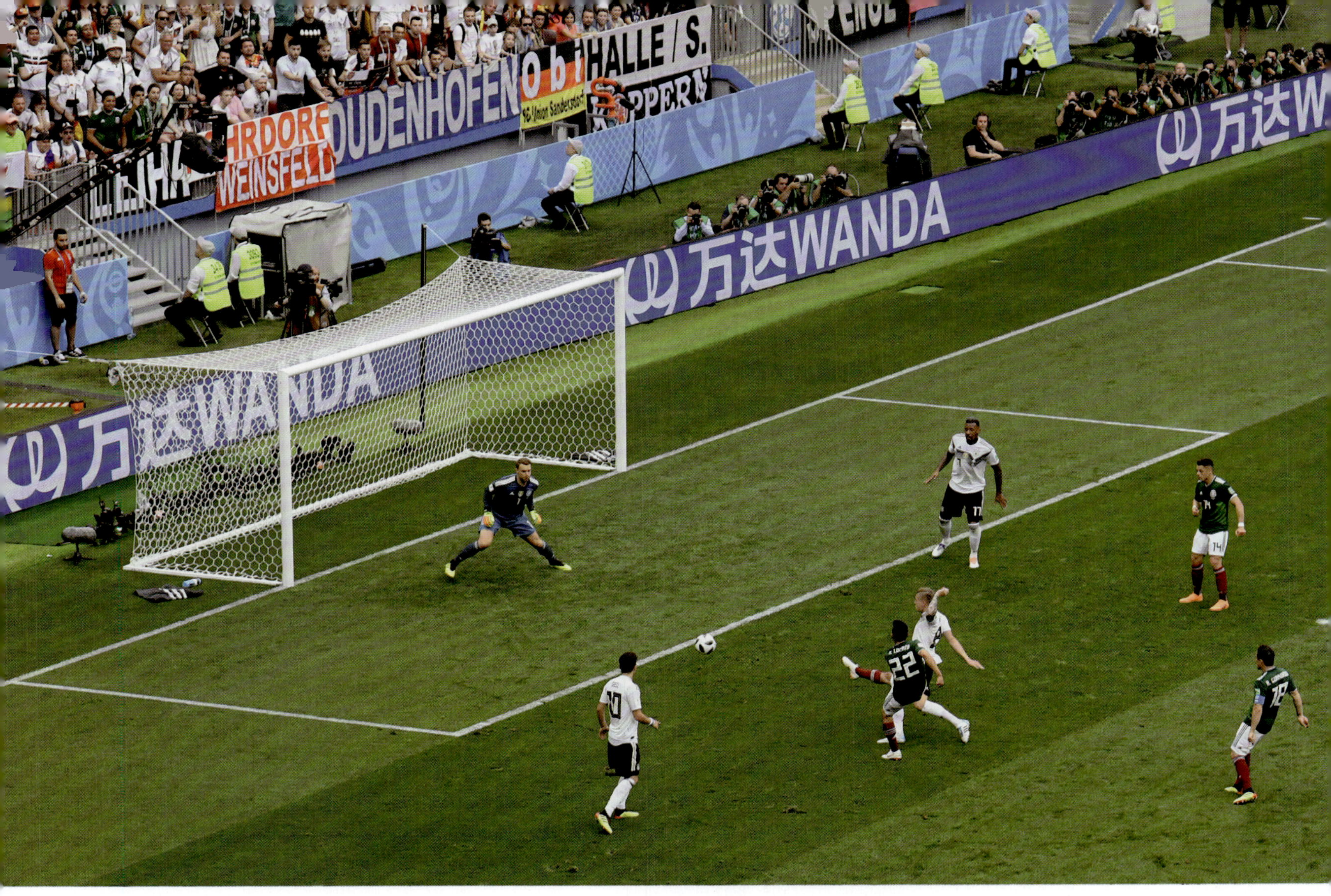

# THE MEXICO CITY 'QUAKE' OF 2018

**On 17 June, 2018,** Hirving 'Chucky' Lozano scored the lone goal in Mexico's stunning 1–0 victory over defending World Cup champion Germany at Luzhniki Stadium in Moscow. The sight of the ball striking the net triggered what was officially noted by one of Mexico's earthquake monitoring agencies as a 'mass jumping event'. Hundreds of thousands, if not millions, of fans at communal watch parties back home in Mexico City went into a joyous leaping frenzy.

Mexican media sometimes refer to Lozano's goal as 'the moment all of Mexico roared'. There was much roaring, no doubt, but the mass jumping at exactly 11:32 a.m., local time, created such a tremor across Mexico City's metropolitan area — population 21.8 million, with most watching the match live, including 75,000 folks hopping in the city's main square — that two regional seismic sensors registered the activity as a minor tectonic event, setting off earthquake alarms.

**ABOVE** *Mexico's Hirving Lozano finds the space to get the shot off, and convert the goal, despite heavy pressure from Germany's defence.*

**OPPOSITE** *Senegal's M'Baye Niang (in green) is shown a yellow card by Serbian referee Milorad Mažić for a foul on Colombia's Yerry Mina (number 13). The hotly contested match would finish 1–0 in favour of Colombia.*

**GROUP G: BELGIUM, ENGLAND, TUNISIA, PANAMA**

| | | |
|---|---|---|
| Belgium 3 | 0 | Panama |
| England 2 | 1 | Tunisia |
| Belgium 5 | 2 | Tunisia |
| England 6 | 1 | Panama |
| Belgium 1 | 0 | England |
| Tunisia 2 | 1 | Panama |

**_Advanced to Knockout Stage: Belgium, England_**

Belgium looked sharp, cruising to easy wins over Panama and Tunisia and then a slightly closer 1–0 win over a young English side. With both sides guaranteed to move on, though, the Belgium–England match featured mostly reserve players. English captain Harry Kane scored an amazing five goals: a hat-trick against Panama and a brace against Tunisia.

**GROUP H: COLOMBIA, JAPAN, SENEGAL, POLAND**

| | | |
|---|---|---|
| Japan 2 | 1 | Colombia |
| Senegal 2 | 1 | Poland |
| Japan 2 | 2 | Senegal |
| Colombia 3 | 0 | Poland |
| Poland 1 | 0 | Japan |
| Colombia 1 | 0 | Senegal |

**_Advanced to Knockout Stage: Colombia, Japan_**

Colombia played well enough to win the group, as expected, but Group H was not without surprises. When Japan and Senegal tied for second place in points _and_ in every scoring-based tie-breaker category, the difference came down to 'fair play points'. In this new FIFA rule, teams with fewer violations (yellow or red cards) in group play accumulate more points. Japan had four yellow cards in group play whereas Senegal had six, so Japan moved on to the knockout stage. To date, this has been the only use of 'fair play' as a tie-breaker in World Cup history.

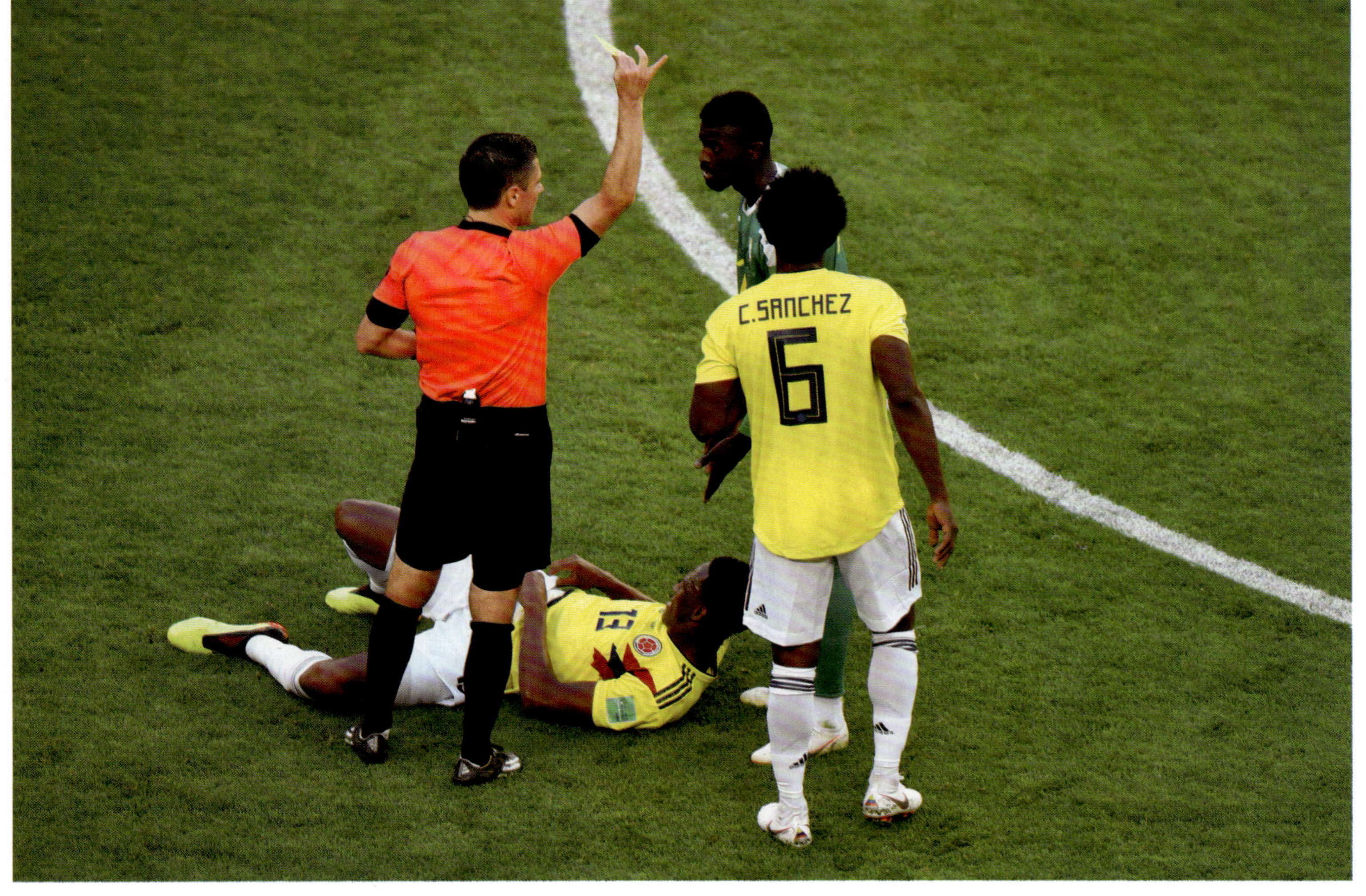

# KNOCKOUT STAGE
# ROUND OF 16

| | | |
|---:|---|---|
| Uruguay 2 | 1 Portugal | |
| France 4 | 3 Argentina | |
| Brazil 2 | 0 Mexico | |
| Belgium 3 | 2 Japan | |
| Russia 1 | 1 Spain | |
| | (4–3 on penalty kicks) | |
| Croatia 1 | 1 Denmark | |
| | (3–2 on penalty kicks) | |
| Sweden 1 | 0 Switzerland | |
| England 1 | 1 Colombia | |
| | (4–3 on penalty kicks) | |

This Round of 16 featured some excellent matches, led by the France–Argentina roller-coaster. On one side of the bracket:

Belgium fell behind 2–0 to Japan but methodically clawed its way back to snag a workman-like 3–2 win, Cristiano Ronaldo followed fellow megastar Lionel Messi out of the tournament after Portugal's 2–1 loss to Uruguay, and Brazil's Neymar ended Mexico's dream by contributing to both goals in an emphatic 2–0 victory.

The other side of the draw featured three pressure-packed shootouts. In the only match decided in regular time, Sweden rode a goal deflected off a defender to a 1–0 victory. In somewhat typical fashion, Spain dominated possession but struggled to finish off their opponent... Russia then won the shootout thanks to two heroic saves by keeper Igor Akinfeev. Croatia and England won their respective shootouts, setting the quarter-final pairings.

## A PEEK AHEAD TO 2022

**France versus Argentina proved** to be one of the best matches in Round of 16 history... and a dramatic preview of the Final four years later. It featured a break-out performance from teenager Kylian Mbappé, whose electrifying seventy-yard run into the Argentine box drew a penalty that put the French up 1–0.

A cracking effort by Ángel Di María was followed up by a diverted Lionel Messi shot that found the back of the net and pushed Argentina up 2–1. But France equalised at 57'... and then young Mbappé took over, slotting home two awe-inspiring goals at 64' and 68'. Messi assisted another goal to Sergio Agüero in stoppage time, but France held on for a thrilling 4–3 win.

**OPPOSITE** *Sweden and Switzer-land in a competitive Round of 16 clash, as evidenced by the challenge between Marcus Berg (left) and Johan Djourou (right).*

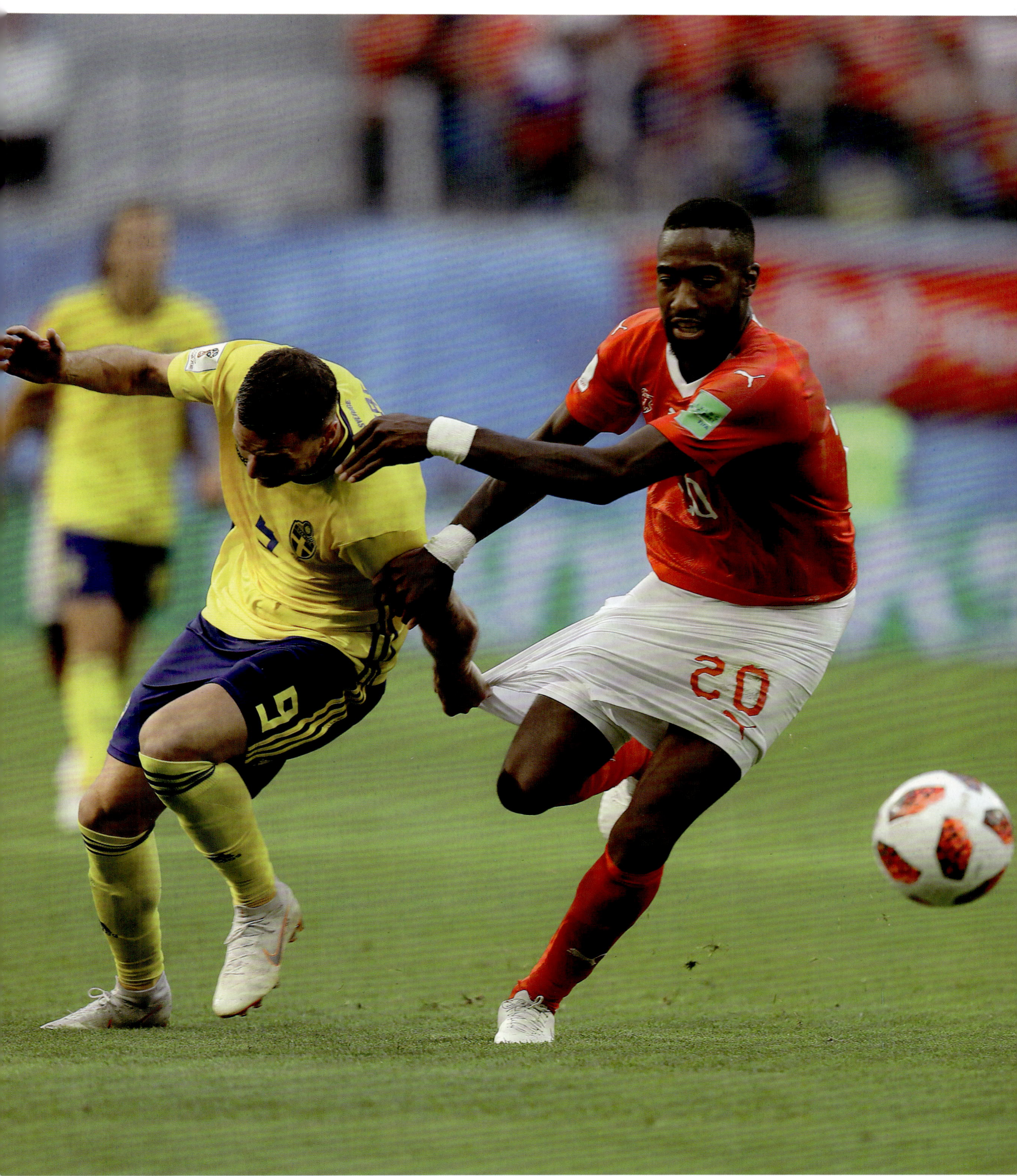

'Croatia went back-and-forth with
the home-fuelled Russians.'

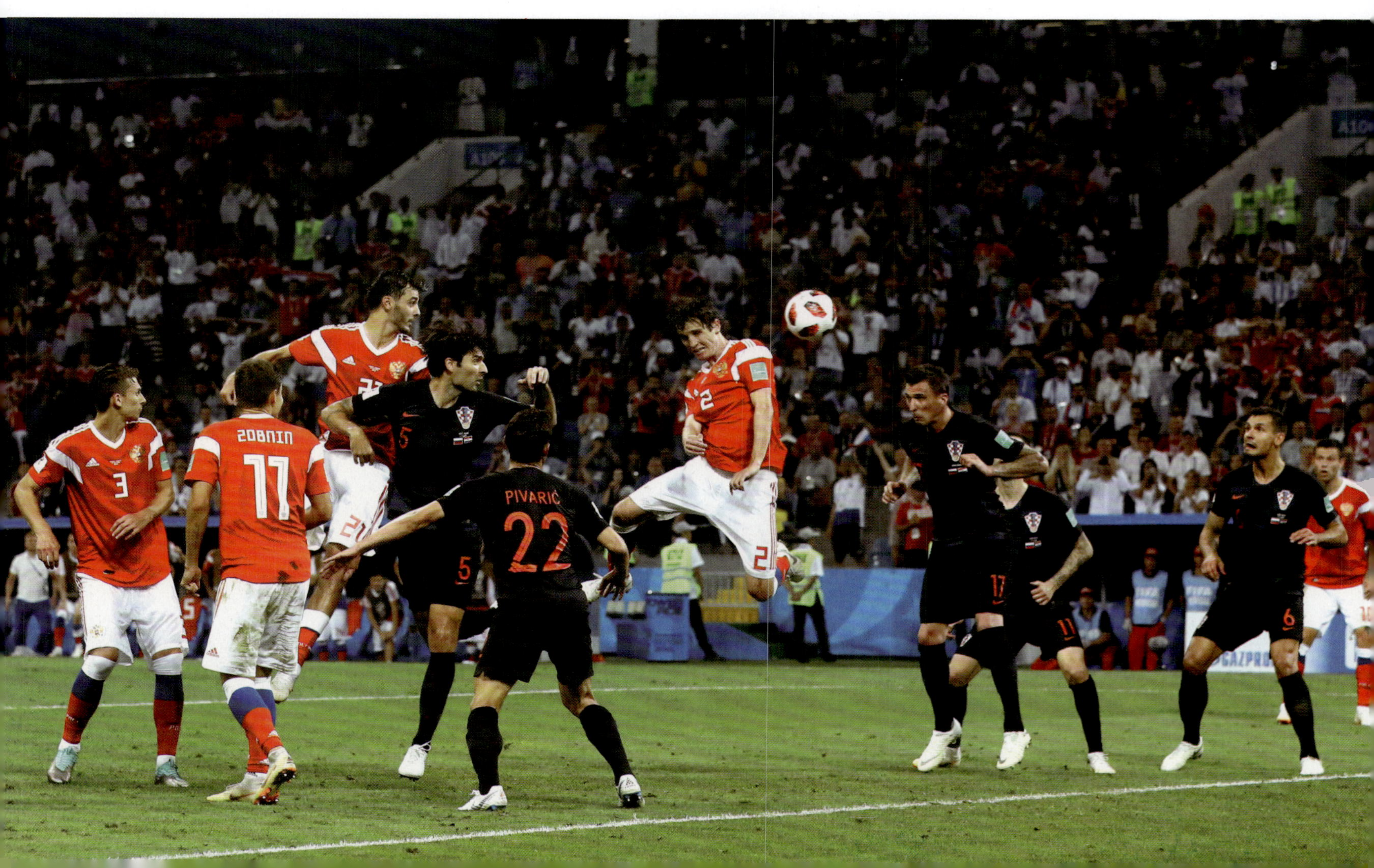

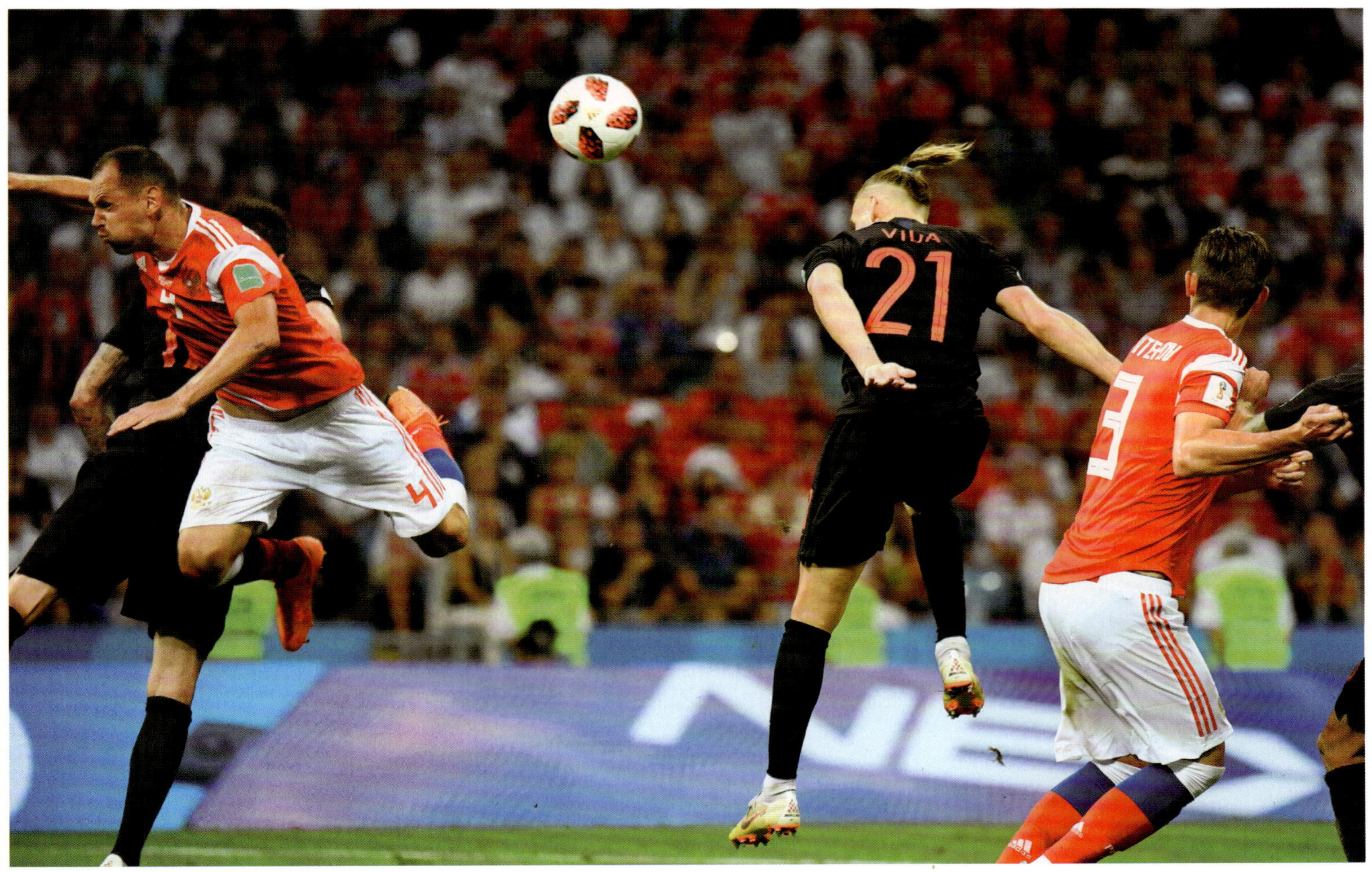

## QUARTER-FINALS

| | |
|---|---|
| France 2 | 0 Uruguay |
| Belgium 2 | 1 Brazil |
| Croatia 2 | 2 Russia |
| | (4–3 penalty kicks) |
| England 2 | 0 Sweden |

France and England both earned comfortable, efficient 2–0 victories. Belgium seemed en route to a similar drama-free result, leading 2–0 after half an hour. But Brazil pressed hard and scored at the seventy-sixth minute. Only brilliant goalkeeping by Thibaut Courtois (including a superhuman fingertip save on a Neymar strike in stoppage time) contained a late Brazilian flurry of attacks. Belgium's advancement meant that the 2018 World Cup semi-final round would be the first since the inaugural Cup in 1930 not to feature Germany or Brazil.

In the last quarter-final, Croatia went back-and-forth with the home-fuelled Russians, as each scored in extra time to force the shootout. A white-knuckle penalty phase ended with a final-shot match-winner from Ivan Rakitić.

**OPPOSITE AND ABOVE** *Back-to-back header goals in extra time. Croatia's Domagoj Vida (top) and Russia's Mário Fernandes (bottom) trade off to send the quarter-final to a penalty shootout.*

# SEMI-FINALS

France 1 | 0 Belgium
Croatia 2 | 1 England
 | (after extra time)

Kieran Trippier's curling free-kick shocker in the fifth minute gave England a lead they carried well into the second half but, as usual, Croatia did not panic. With Luka Modrić directing traffic, Croatia scraped back: Ivan Perišić got the equaliser and then in extra time Mario Mandžukić slotted in the go-ahead at the 109th minute.

In the other semi-final, Belgium started off strong and seemed in good shape. French defender Samuel Umtiti had other ideas, though, hammering home a header off an Antoine Griezmann corner kick just after halftime. From then on, France settled into a disciplined pace and rode out the second half for the 1–0 win.

**BELOW** *Mario Mandžukić fires past England's Jordan Pickford in extra time to take Croatia to the World Cup Final.*

**OPPOSITE** *The ageless midfield titan Luka Modrić (centre left) gets past Argentina's Javier Mascherano (centre right).*

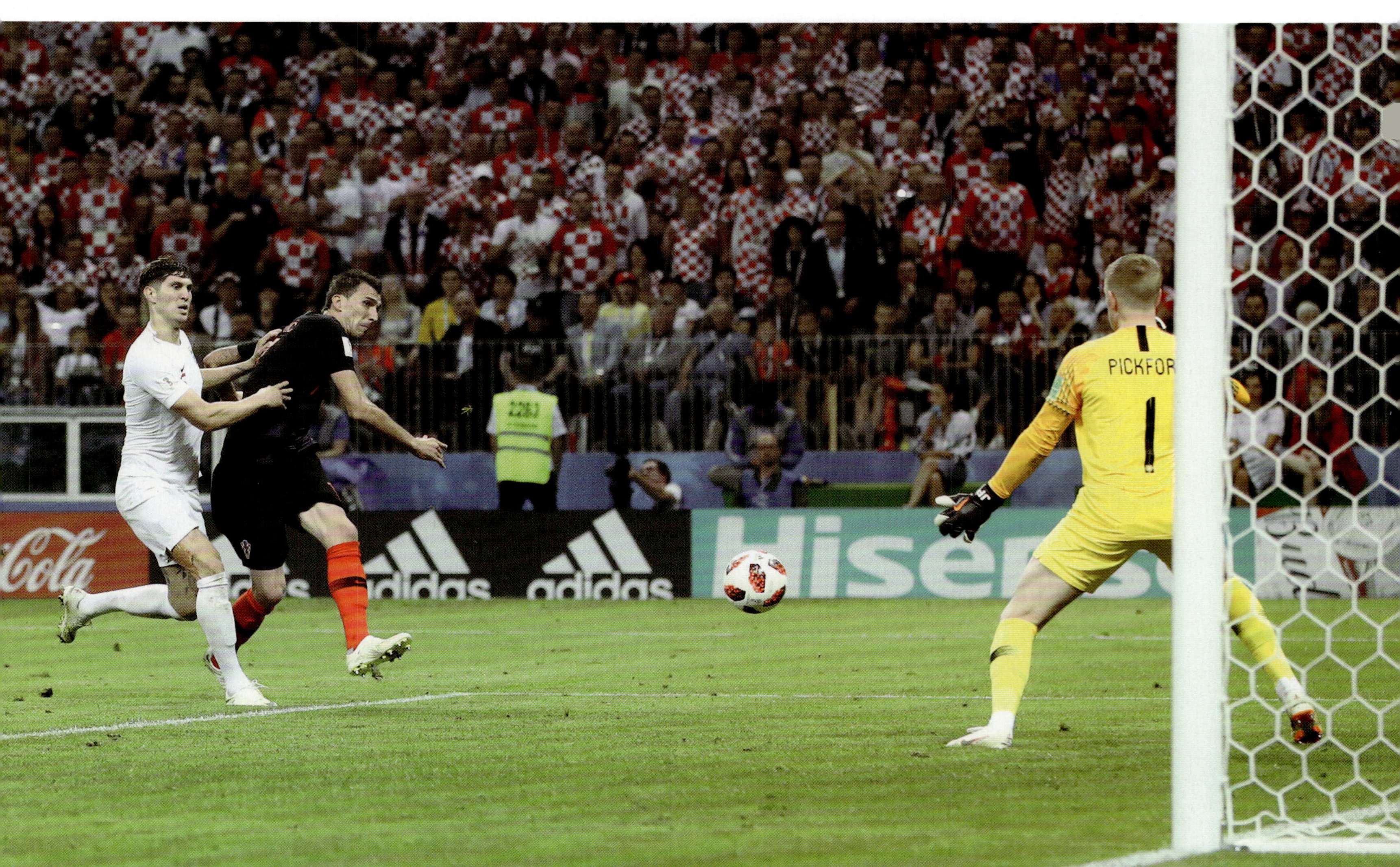

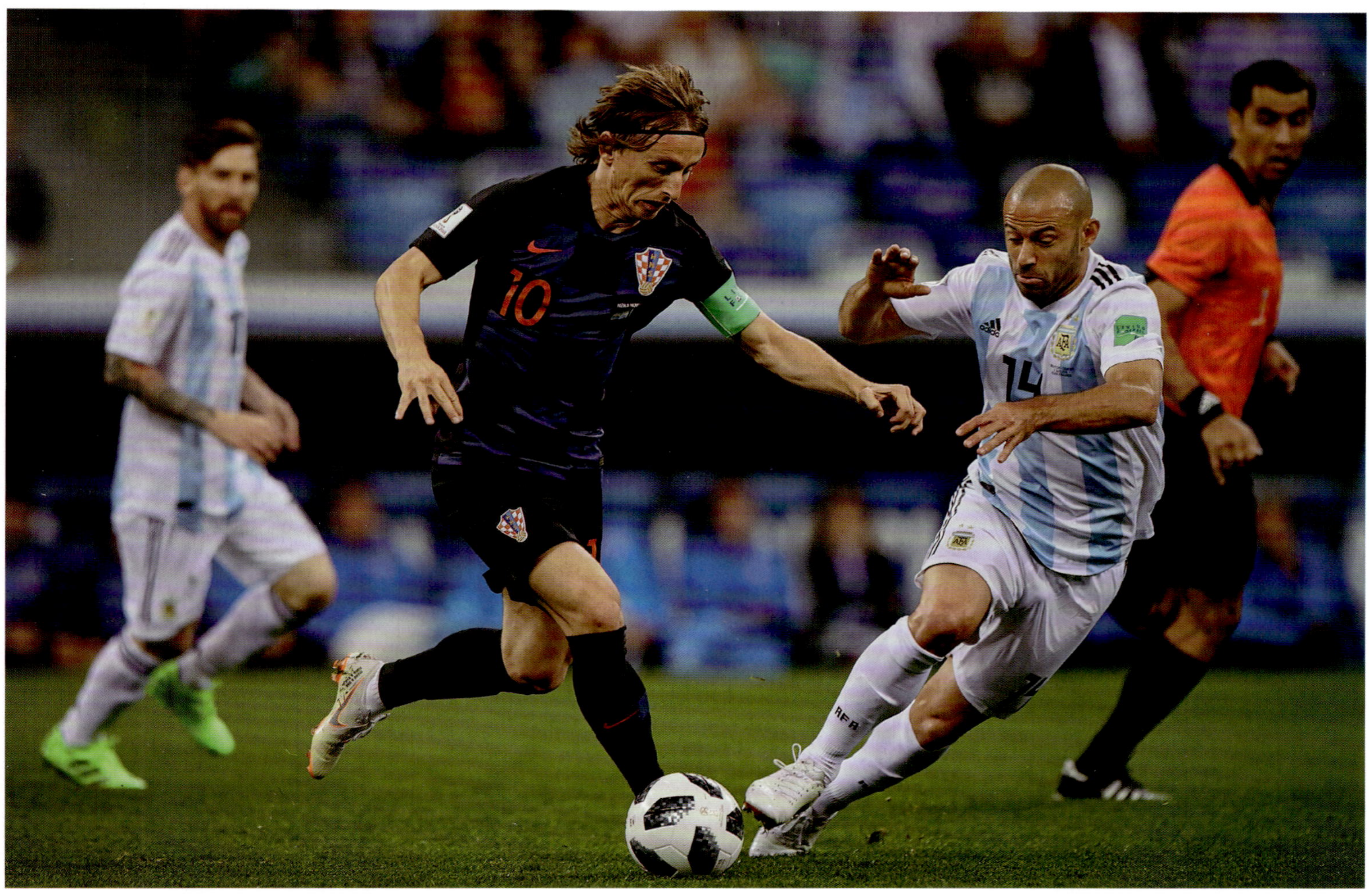

## LUKA'S OLD MEN

**Croatia in 2018 was** one of the scrappiest, most resilient modern-era sides to reach a World Cup Final. They didn't always play the prettiest football, but Croatia consistently found ways to survive and thrive. Though certainly led by captain and midfield conductor Luka Modrić, the team also featured supplementary playmaker Ivan Rakitić and a veteran duo of aggressive goal scorers in Ivan Perišić and Mario Mandžukić. The quartet's respective ages were thirty-two, thirty, thirty-two, and twenty-nine — plenty of seasoning.

The Croatians started off with a shocking 3 – 0 win over Messi's Argentina in group play, but they had to claw through the knockout stage — two gut-wrenching shootout wins over Denmark and Russia, followed by a highwire 2 – 1 extra-time victory over England in the semi-finals. In the end, Modrić would win the Golden Ball as best player in the tournament and Croatia's 'old men' earned the football world's recognition.

# FINAL

|  |  |
|---|---|
| France 4 | 2 Croatia (First Place) |
| Belgium 2 | 0 England (Third Place) |

The third-place contest was a reprise of the Belgium–England group-play matchup, although that one had featured mostly reserve players playing a meaningless game. This time, the regular starters battled hard for national pride. Belgium knocked in a quick goal in the fourth minute and then frustrated the English attack time and again until Belgian captain Eden Hazard broke free late to put the game away, 2–0. England's consolation prize was Harry Kane's Golden Boot award as the tournament's leading scorer, with six goals.

The Cup Final in Moscow turned into a showcase for France's young and dynamic new generation. It started with a French free kick into the box that skimmed off the top of Mario Mandžukić's head into Croatia's net. It was the first-ever own goal in a World Cup Final. Once again, Croatia scrambled back into contention with a Perišić score just ten minutes later. Ten minutes after that, France was awarded a penalty (after VAR review) and Griezmann converted cleanly for the 2–1 lead at halftime.

The second half belonged to France. At the fifty-ninth minute, Paul Pogba unleashed a left-footed blast for 3–1 and then just six minutes later Kylian Mbappé fired in a long-range rocket to end any realistic hopes for another patented Croatian comeback. At nineteen, Mbappé became the second-youngest player to score in a World Cup Final after Pelé, who was seventeen when he scored twice in 1958. Not even a horrible goalkeeper error by French captain Hugo Lloris that gifted a cheap goal to Mandžukić could alter the inevitable outcome.



**OPPOSITE** *In the final, skilful Paul Pogba curls in a left-footed shot from outside the box for France's third goal in an eventual 4–2 win over Croatia.*

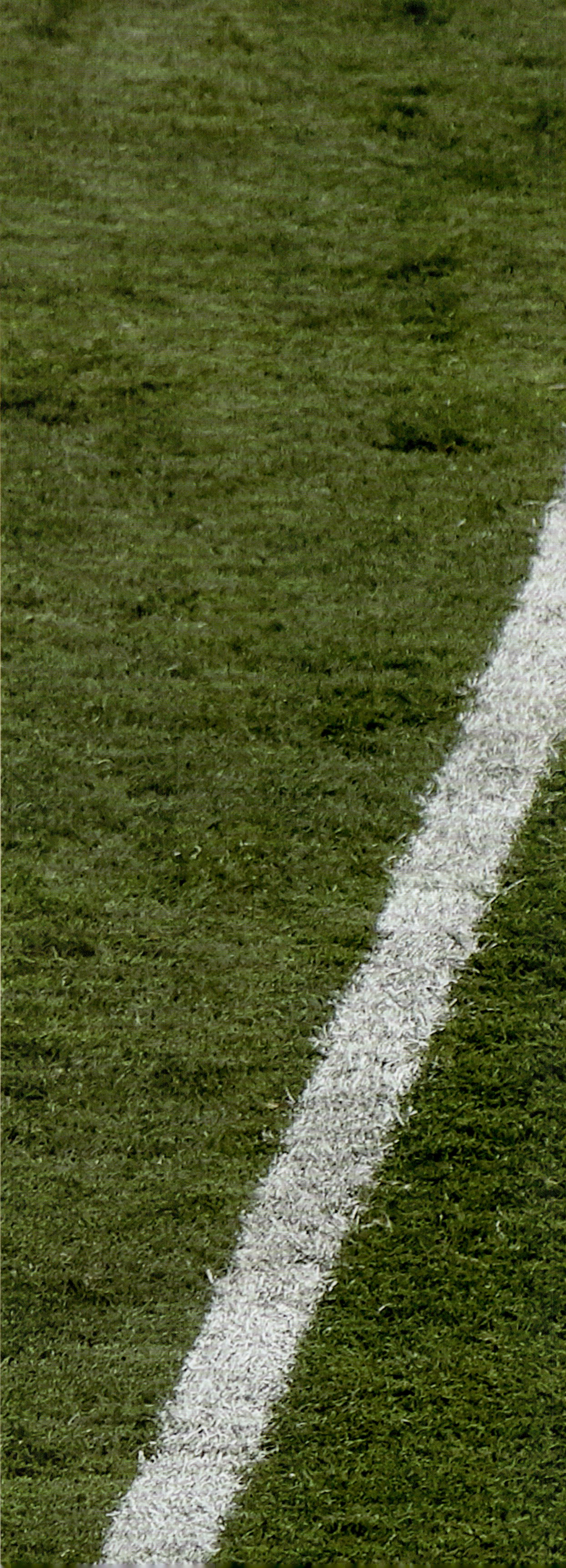

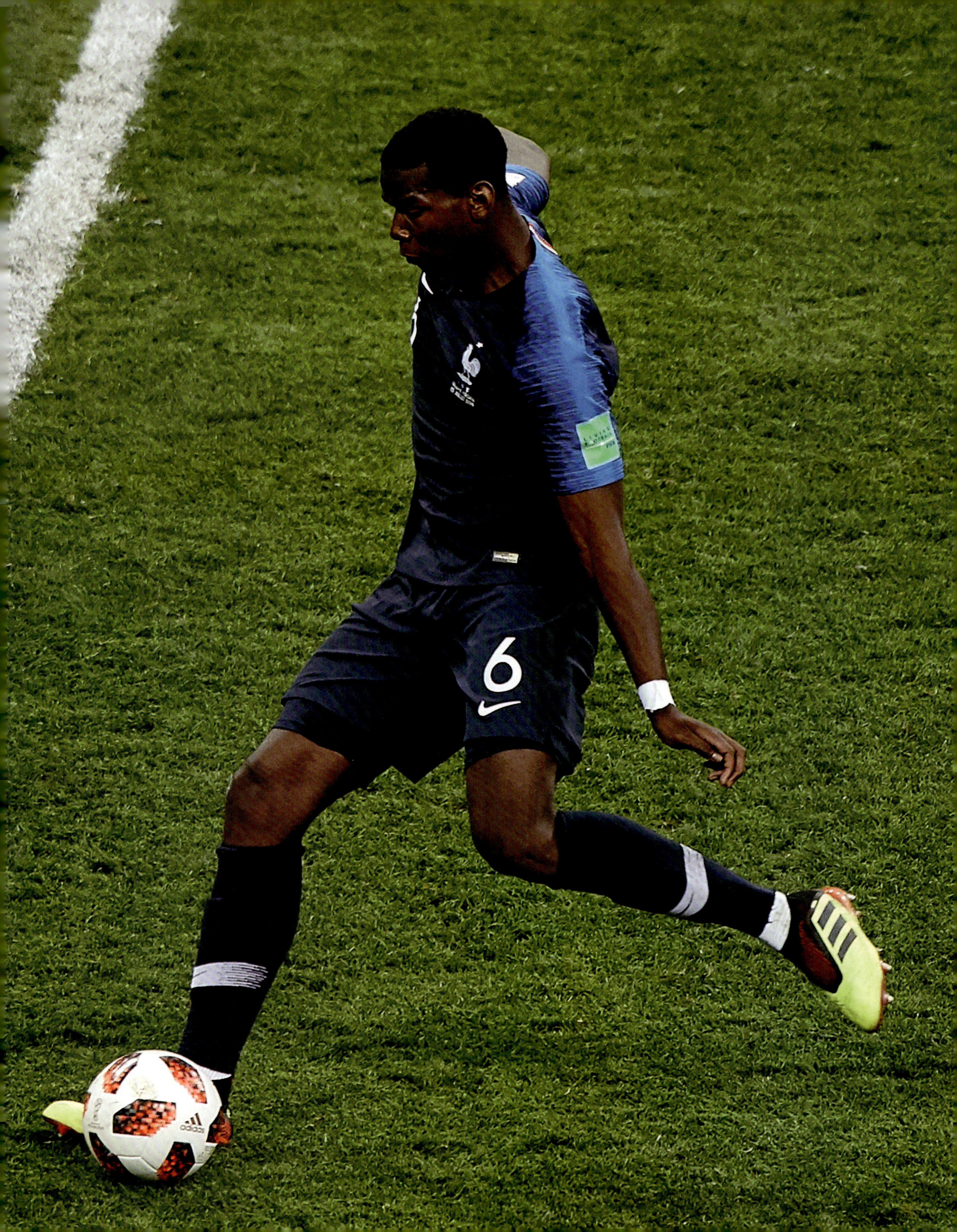

# 2022

HOST COUNTRY: **QATAR**
CHAMPION: **ARGENTINA**
RUNNER-UP: **FRANCE**
THIRD PLACE: **CROATIA OVER MOROCCO**

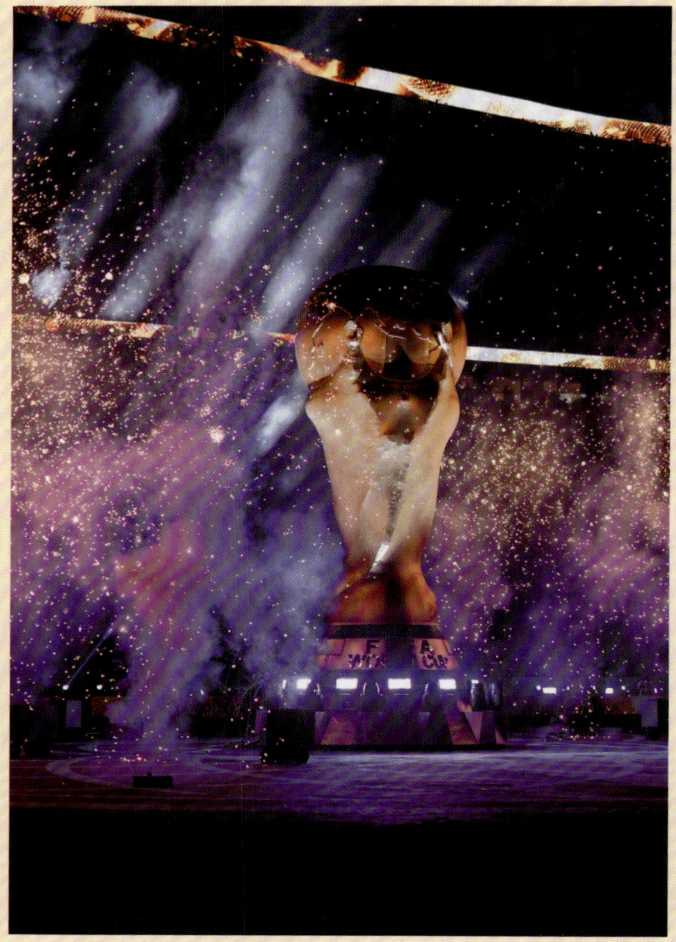

**Qatar was perhaps the most** controversial World Cup host ever chosen by FIFA. First off, its desert climate produced summers so brutally hot that Cup play couldn't start until late November. Second, FIFA member nations had concerns about reported abuse of migrant workers brought in for Qatar's tournament-infrastructure projects. Finally, allegations of bribery and corruption dogged the selection process. None of this lessened FIFA's determination to stage a first-class tournament in Qatar with eight state-of-the-art football venues.

A colourful opening ceremony in Al Bayt Stadium on 20 November, 2022, highlighted Qatari culture and heritage while emphasising themes of hospitality, unity, and, of course, football's unique ability to bring together people from around the world in the spirit of friendly competition. As scathing accusations of 'sportswashing' flooded in, the Emir of Qatar, Tamim bin Hamad Al Thani, was keen to market a warm and welcoming atmosphere. As he put it in his welcoming address: 'People of different races, nationalities, faiths, and orientations will gather here in Qatar . . . How beautiful it is to put aside what divides them in order to celebrate their diversity and what brings them together at the same time.'

**ABOVE** *The opening ceremony at Qatar's Lusail Stadium for the 2022 semi-final between Argentina and Croatia. Despite the lavish adornment, Qatar came under intense scrutiny for allegations of* *human-rights abuses in preparation for the tournament.*

**OPPOSITE** *England talisman Harry Kane takes a decisive penalty in the quarter-final against France.*

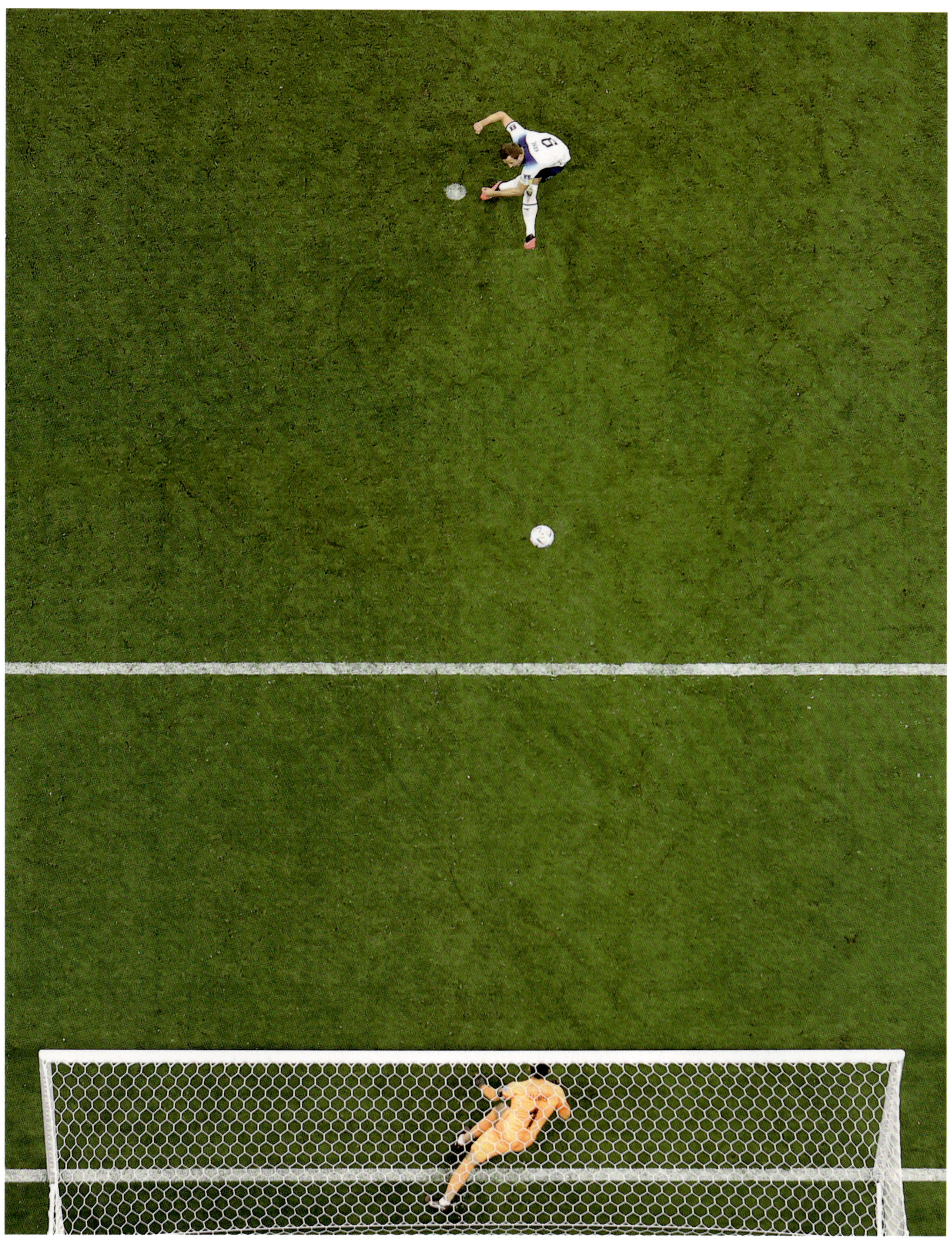

# Tournament: GROUP STAGE

### GROUP A: NETHERLANDS, SENEGAL, ECUADOR, QATAR

| | | |
|---|---|---|
| Ecuador 2 | 0 Qatar |
| Netherlands 2 | 0 Senegal |
| Senegal 3 | 1 Qatar |
| Netherlands 1 | 1 Ecuador |
| Senegal 2 | 1 Ecuador |
| Netherlands 2 | 0 Qatar |

**Advanced to Knockout Stage: Netherlands, Senegal**

### GROUP B: ENGLAND, USA, IRAN, WALES

| | | |
|---|---|---|
| England 6 | 2 Iran |
| USA 1 | 1 Wales |
| Iran 2 | 0 Wales |
| England 0 | 0 USA |
| England 3 | 0 Wales |
| USA 1 | 0 Iran |

**Advanced to Knockout Stage: England, USA**

In the tournament opener, the hosts hoped to pick up a point, or at least score a goal, against Ecuador. They failed to do either. Thus, Qatar became the first Cup host nation to lose its opening match. And then first to lose all three group matches. Against Senegal, they did at least manage to score one goal for the home crowd. Other than a stumbling draw with Ecuador, the Netherlands glided through group play to finish first, with Senegal in second.

The USA posted a disappointing tie with Wales after completely dominating the contest but fought to a well-earned scoreless draw with favoured England. In their final match of the group, young star Christian Pulisic knocked in the winner against Iran to push the Americans through to the knockout stage in second place behind the English. But perhaps the most thrilling match was played by the two squads who didn't make it out of the group. Iran versus Wales was a high-flying, seesaw affair, with Wales controlling the first half and Iran the second. Iran's dramatic goals finally came at 98' and 101' of stoppage time.

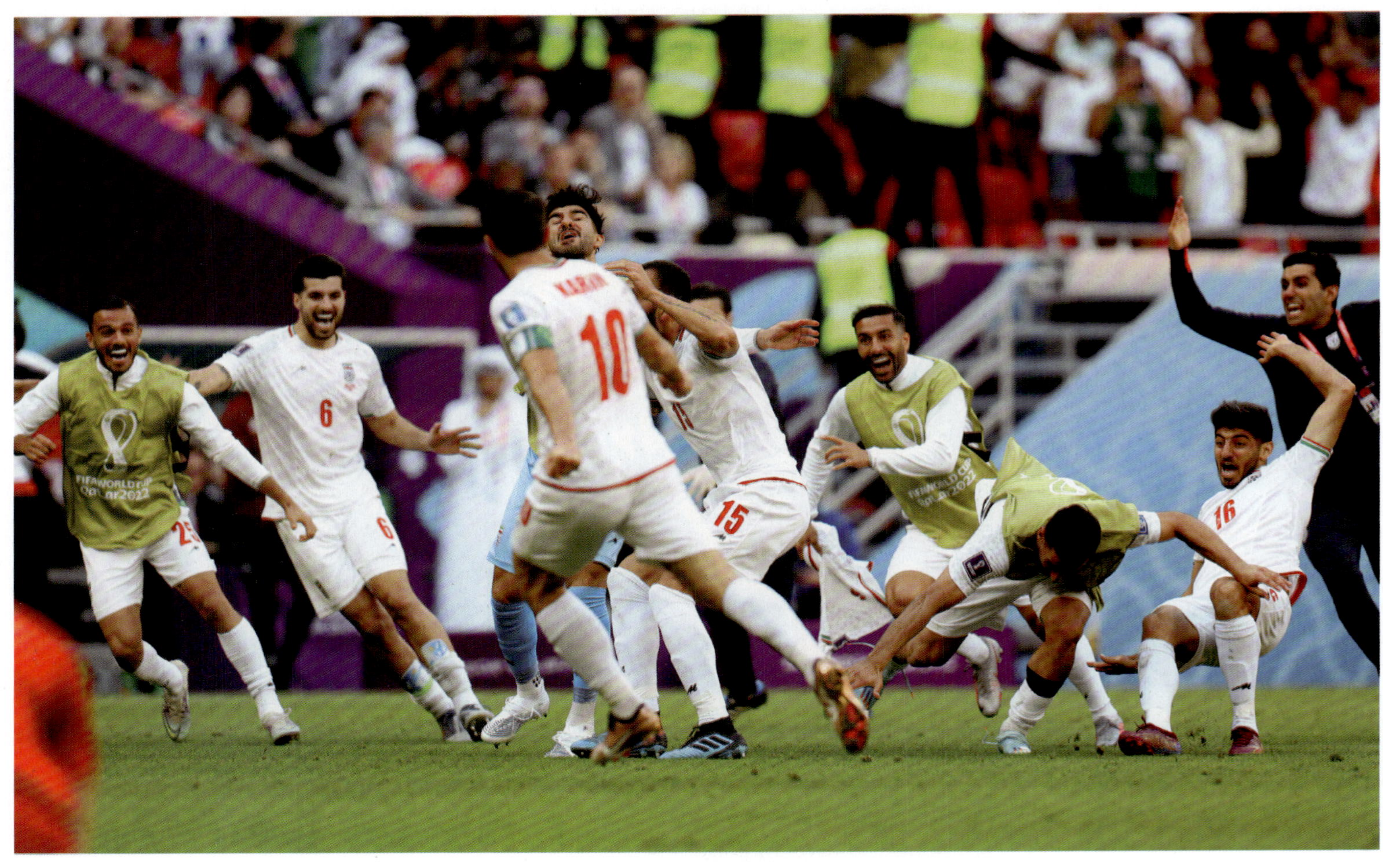

| | | |
|---|---|---|
| Saudi Arabia 2 | 1 | Argentina |
| Mexico 0 | 0 | Poland |
| Poland 2 | 0 | Saudi Arabia |
| Argentina 2 | 0 | Mexico |
| Argentina 2 | 0 | Poland |
| Mexico 2 | 1 | Saudi Arabia |

**Advanced to Knockout Stage: Argentina, Poland**

A truly stunning result! Saudi Arabia over Argentina was one of the biggest upsets imaginable, only magnified in retrospect given how the Argentines would respond in the rest of the tournament. But in their second group match, Lionel Messi quickly righted the ship with a goal and an assist to down Mexico, 2–0. His side then matched that score against Poland to finish top of the group.

**GROUP D: FRANCE, AUSTRALIA, TUNISIA, DENMARK**

| | | |
|---|---|---|
| Denmark 0 | 0 | Tunisia |
| France 4 | 1 | Australia |
| Australia 1 | 0 | Tunisia |
| France 2 | 1 | Denmark |
| Australia 1 | 0 | Denmark |
| Tunisia 1 | 0 | France |

**Advanced to Knockout Stage: France, Australia**

Tunisia's impressive 2–1 victory over defending Cup champion France would have been quite unbelievable, too, if France hadn't already locked up the group and chosen to field mostly reserves. The French controlled the group behind three Kylian Mbappé goals and managed to collect all three points from a tough Denmark, against whom they had only managed a 0–0 draw in 2018.

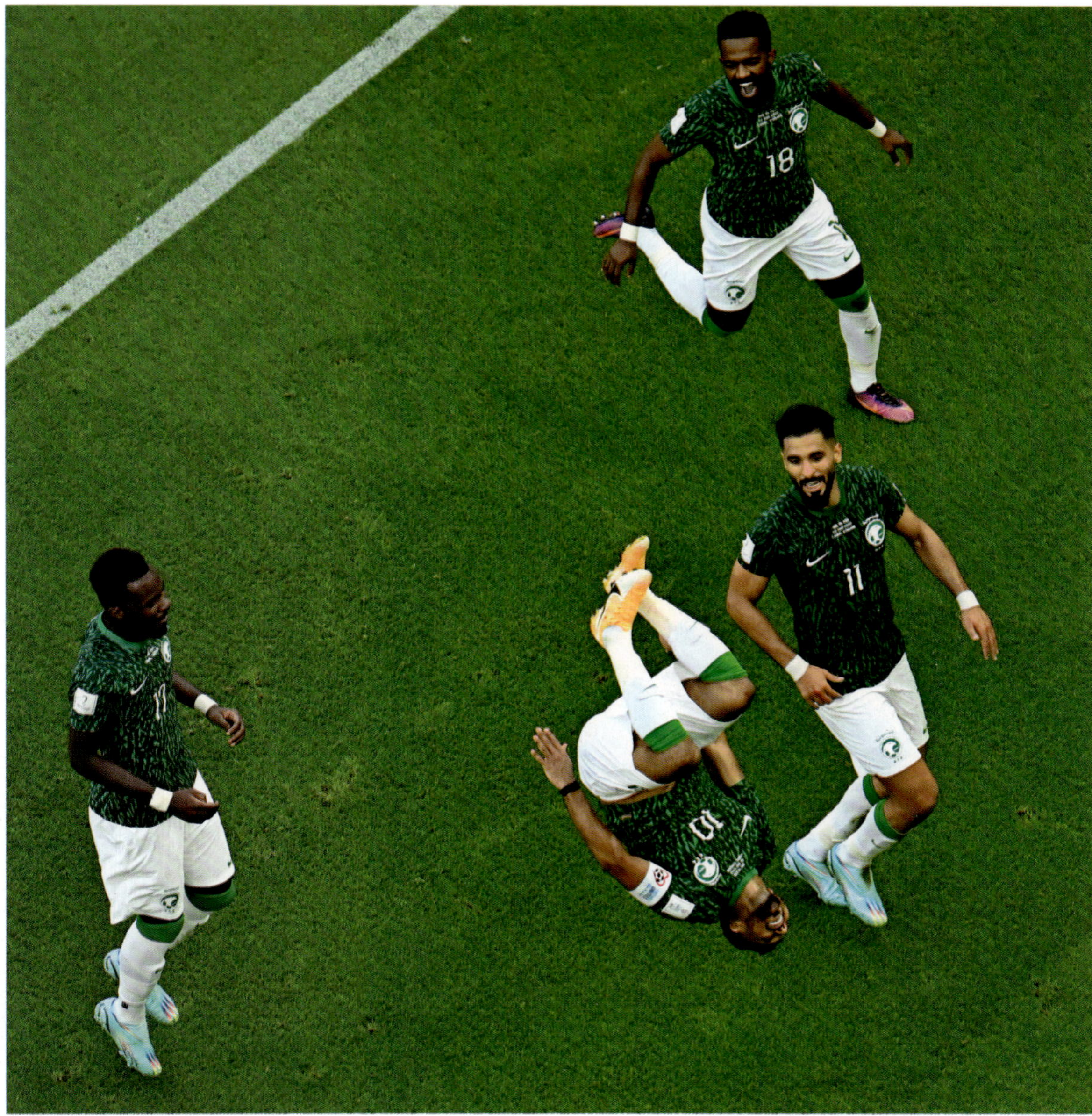

**OPPOSITE** *An exhilarating and dynamic Group B matchup with back-and-forth action. Finally, in the ninety-eighth minute, the Iranian squad celebrate a late opening goal against Wales.*

**RIGHT** *Salem Al-Dawsari with an acrobatic celebration after scoring Saudi Ariabia's winning goal in a shocking upset over Argentina.*

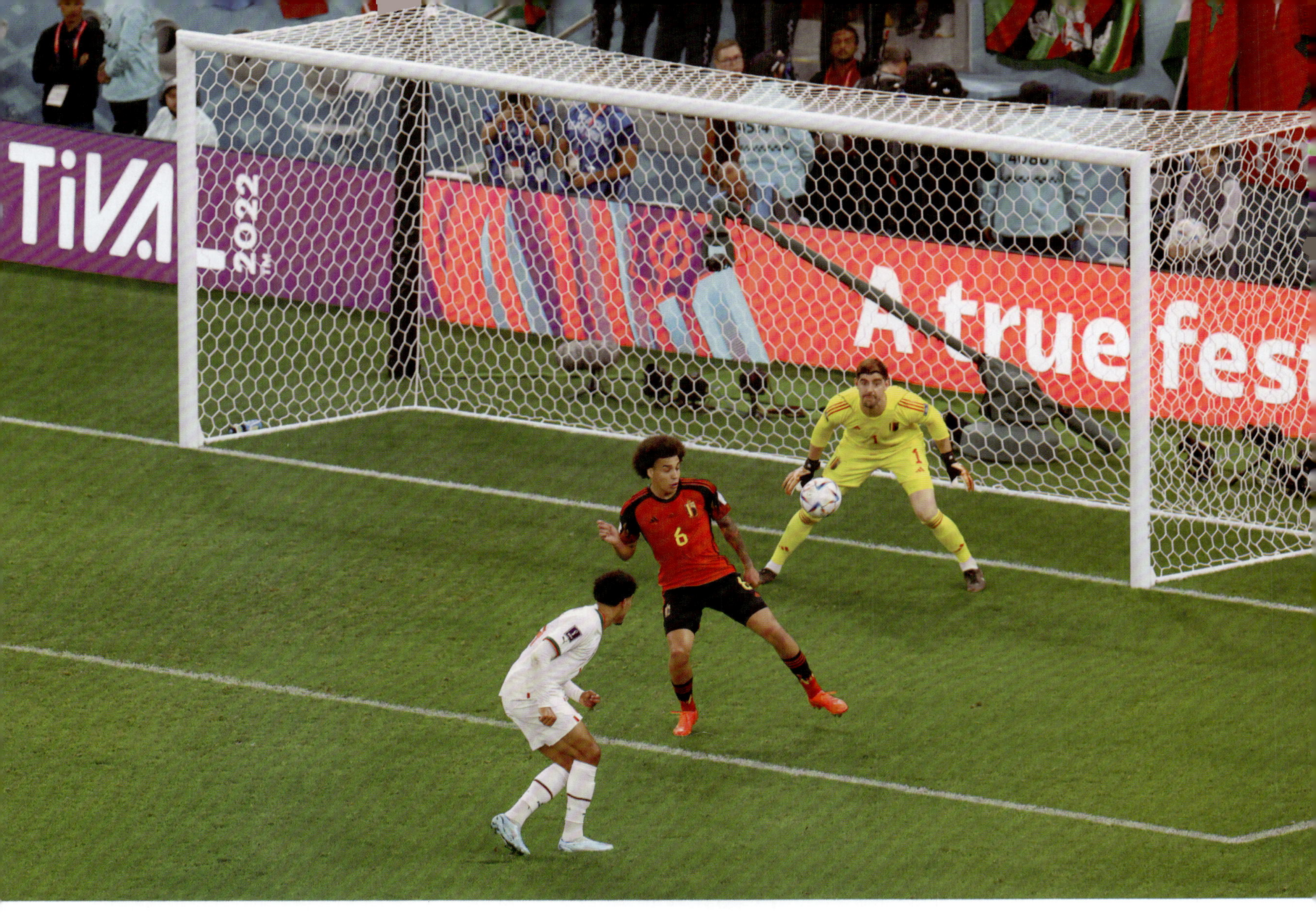



## GROUP E: JAPAN, SPAIN, GERMANY, COSTA RICA

| | | |
|---:|---|---|
| Japan 2 | 1 Germany | |
| Spain 7 | 0 Costa Rica | |
| Costa Rica 1 | 0 Japan | |
| Spain 1 | 1 Germany | |
| Japan 2 | 1 Spain | |
| Germany 4 | 2 Costa Rica | |

***Advanced to Knockout Stage: Japan, Spain***

## GROUP F: MOROCCO, CROATIA, BELGIUM, CANADA

| | | |
|---:|---|---|
| Morocco 0 | 0 Croatia | |
| Belgium 1 | 0 Canada | |
| Morocco 2 | 0 Belgium | |
| Croatia 4 | 1 Canada | |
| Croatia 0 | 0 Belgium | |
| Morocco 2 | 1 Canada | |

***Advanced to Knockout Stage: Morocco, Croatia***

Germany followed its disastrous 2018 Cup performance with one almost as poor, once again flushing out of the tournament after group play. Japan impressed by knocking down both European heavyweights, Germany and Spain, by identical 2–1 margins and finishing first in group. The Samurai Blue broke out of their traditionally patient, methodical approach to unleash a free-flowing, unpredictable style—ESPN writer Gabriel Tan called it 'smash-and-grab football'—to surprise Spain with a pair of rapid-fire goals just six minutes apart.

Belgium came into the tournament ranked second in the world and was considered a favourite to win the Cup. The Atlas Lions of Morocco volunteered to dismiss that notion. After a scoreless draw with previous Cup Finalist Croatia, the energetic Moroccans proceeded to clock the Belgians properly in a decisive 2–0 win. Belgium's subsequent 0–0 draw with Croatia dropped them out of the tourney and left the Croatians in second place behind the exciting African side that had become the talk of the tournament.

# RICHARLISON'S BIKE

**Other goals were more momentous,** but none was as spectacular as Richarlison's acrobatic bicycle against Serbia. Surrounded by three defenders with his back to the Serbian goal at the penalty spot, the Brazilian controlled a centring pass with a single light touch, tapping the ball straight up into the air. Then, with a graceful swivel, he fell backwards and scissored his right foot through the ball, striking a perfect shot into the upper-left corner. As BBC's commentator Peter Drury exclaimed: 'Now, that... that is Brazil!'

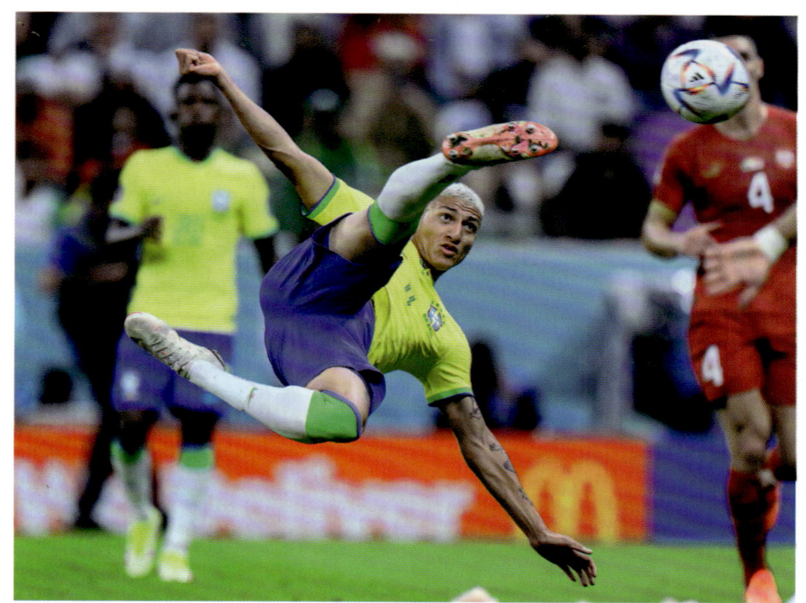

**OPPOSITE** *Morocco's Zakaria Aboukhlal finds the header goal despite a tight angle and stiff opposition from Belgium's renowned goalkeeper Thibaut Courtois.*

**ABOVE** *Richarlison's stunning overhead kick against Serbia.*

## GROUP G: BRAZIL, SWITZERLAND, CAMEROON, SERBIA

| | |
|---|---|
| Switzerland 1 | 0 Cameroon |
| Brazil 2 | 0 Serbia |
| Cameroon 3 | 3 Serbia |
| Brazil 1 | 0 Switzerland |
| Switzerland 3 | 2 Serbia |
| Cameroon 1 | 0 Brazil |

***Advanced to Knockout Stage: Brazil, Switzerland***

Brazil kicked off this tournament as the only nation to have appeared in all twenty-two World Cups. Led by Neymar, Richarlison, and a budding star in twenty-two-year-old Vinicius Júnior, the Brazilians were listed as number one in FIFA's world rankings and Richarlison's astounding bicycle kick against Serbia was a tournament highlight. With first place in group already assured after two wins, Brazil played its reserves against Cameroon and lost 1–0. As a result, Cameroon became the first African side ever to defeat Brazil in World Cup play.

## GROUP H: PORTUGAL, SOUTH KOREA, URUGUAY, GHANA

| | |
|---|---|
| Uruguay 0 | 0 South Korea |
| Portugal 3 | 2 Ghana |
| Ghana 3 | 2 South Korea |
| Portugal 2 | 0 Uruguay |
| Uruguay 2 | 0 Ghana |
| South Korea 2 | 1 Portugal |

***Advanced to Knockout Stage: Portugal, South Korea***

Cristiano Ronaldo's penalty kick against Ghana made him the first man to score in five separate World Cup tournaments—a truly remarkable record. South Korea was a surprise: After knocking off Portugal with a stoppage-time goal, they slid into second place and nailed the coffin of Uruguay's golden generation of the 2010s.

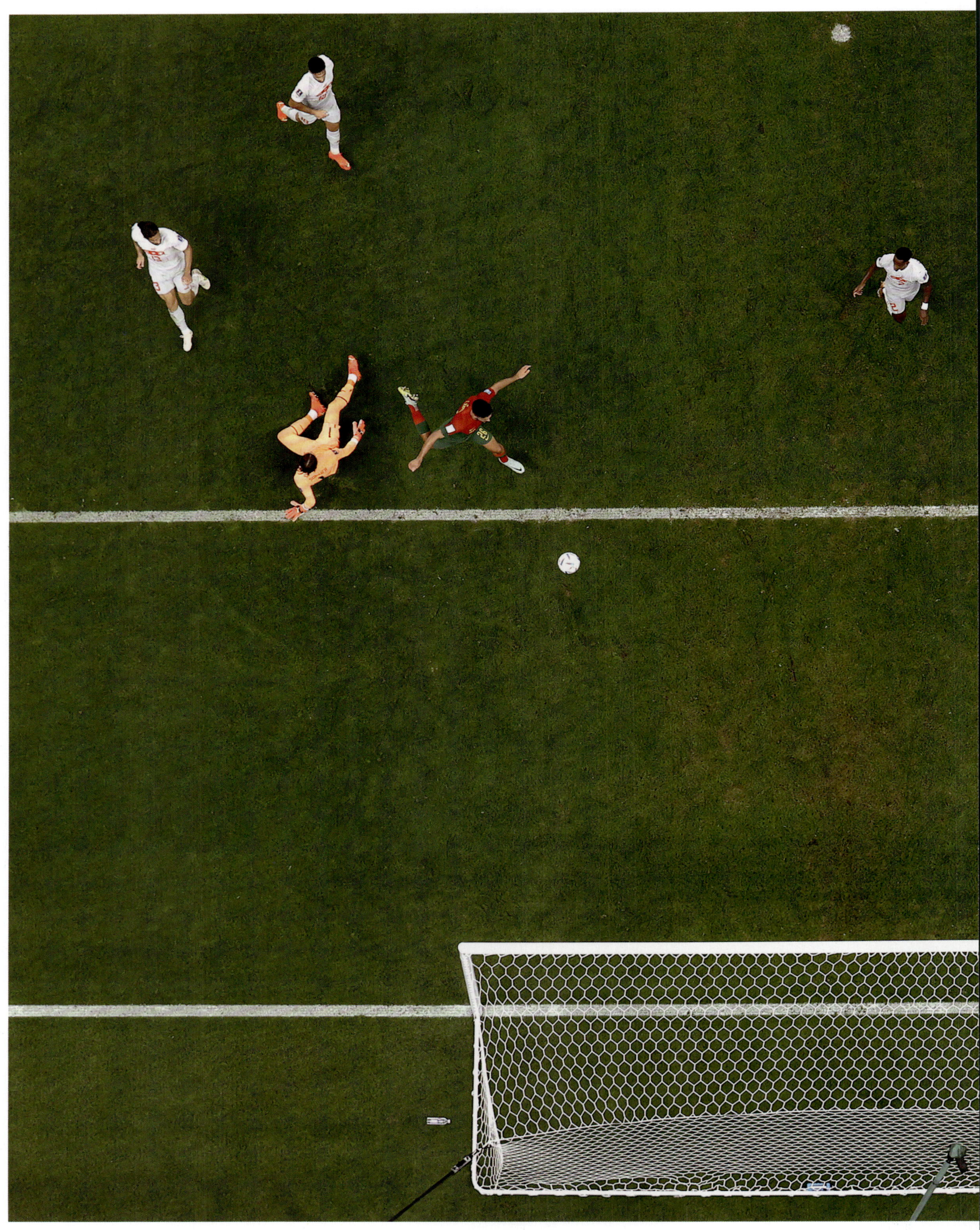

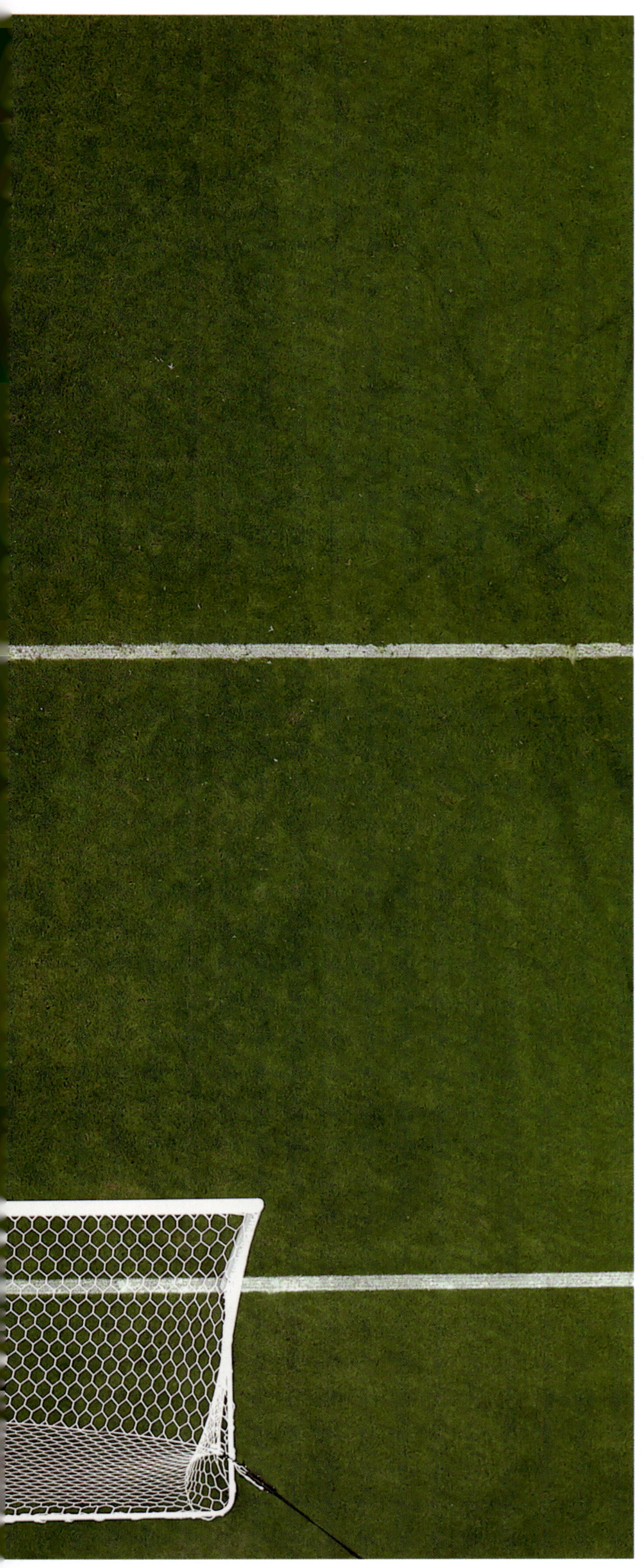

## KNOCKOUT STAGE
## ROUND OF 16

| | |
|---:|:---|
| Netherlands 3 | 1 USA |
| Argentina 2 | 1 Australia |
| Croatia 1 | 1 Japan |
| | (3–1 on penalty kicks) |
| Brazil 4 | 1 South Korea |
| England 3 | 0 Senegal |
| France 3 | 1 Poland |
| Morocco 0 | 0 Spain |
| | (3–0 on penalty kicks) |
| Portugal 6 | 1 Switzerland |

A talented but very young USA squad learned hard lessons from the Dutch, who played with professional calm and then decisively pounced on their opportunities with lethal speed. Argentina dazzled the Australians with goals from Messi and the young Julián Alvarez for a 2–0 lead before conceding an own goal. Japan's Samurai Blue ran rampant in the first half and took a 1–0 lead on Croatia before Luka Modrić led his patient side back to even and then easily won the shootout. Brazil laid elegant waste to South Korea, going up by four goals after just thirty-six minutes.

There was little drama on the other side of the bracket, with England, France, and especially Portugal making easy work of their opponents. Mbappé scored a brace for the French and Gonçalo Ramos netted a hat-trick for Portugal. The nail-biter of the round was Morocco's 0–0 draw with heavily favoured Spain that led to a shocking shootout in which the Spanish converted *none* of their kicks . . . and Morocco moved on to the quarter-finals.

**LEFT** *Overhead view of Gonçalo Ramos's hat-trick (and Portugal's fifth) goal in the Round of 16 against Switzerland.*

# QUARTER-FINALS

| | |
|---|---|
| Argentina 2 | 2 Netherlands |
| | (4–3 on penalty kicks) |
| Croatia 1 | 1 Brazil |
| | (4–2 on penalty kicks) |
| France 2 | 1 England |
| Morocco 1 | 0 Portugal |

Messi guided Argentina to a 2–0 lead but gangly substitute forward Wout Weghorst produced two late goals for the Dutch, including a wildly dramatic equaliser in the final seconds of stoppage time from a clever free kick. After no scoring in extra time, a cool and collected Argentina won the shootout. Meanwhile, France had to rely on Harry Kane's late missed penalty kick to hang on for a 2–1 win in a classic contest of two well-matched teams.

Morocco extended its unprecedented run to become the first African nation to reach a World Cup semi-final. The Atlas Lions beat Portugal with a first-half header and sheer defensive grit despite losing a player to a late red card. The remaining quarter-final pitted Brazil's sizzling attack against Croatia's dominant midfield. Neymar's goal in extra time seemed a game winner, but the always-resilient Croatia equalised when Luka Modrić slid a perfect pass through the defence to Bruno Petković. After that, the Croatians proceeded to convert every one of their kicks in the shoot-out for the win.

**BELOW** *The Netherlands with a deceptive, and brilliant, free kick to equalise against Argentina.*

**OPPOSITE** *Following triumph over Portugal, underdog Morocco stands tall as the first African side to reach a Cup semi-final.*

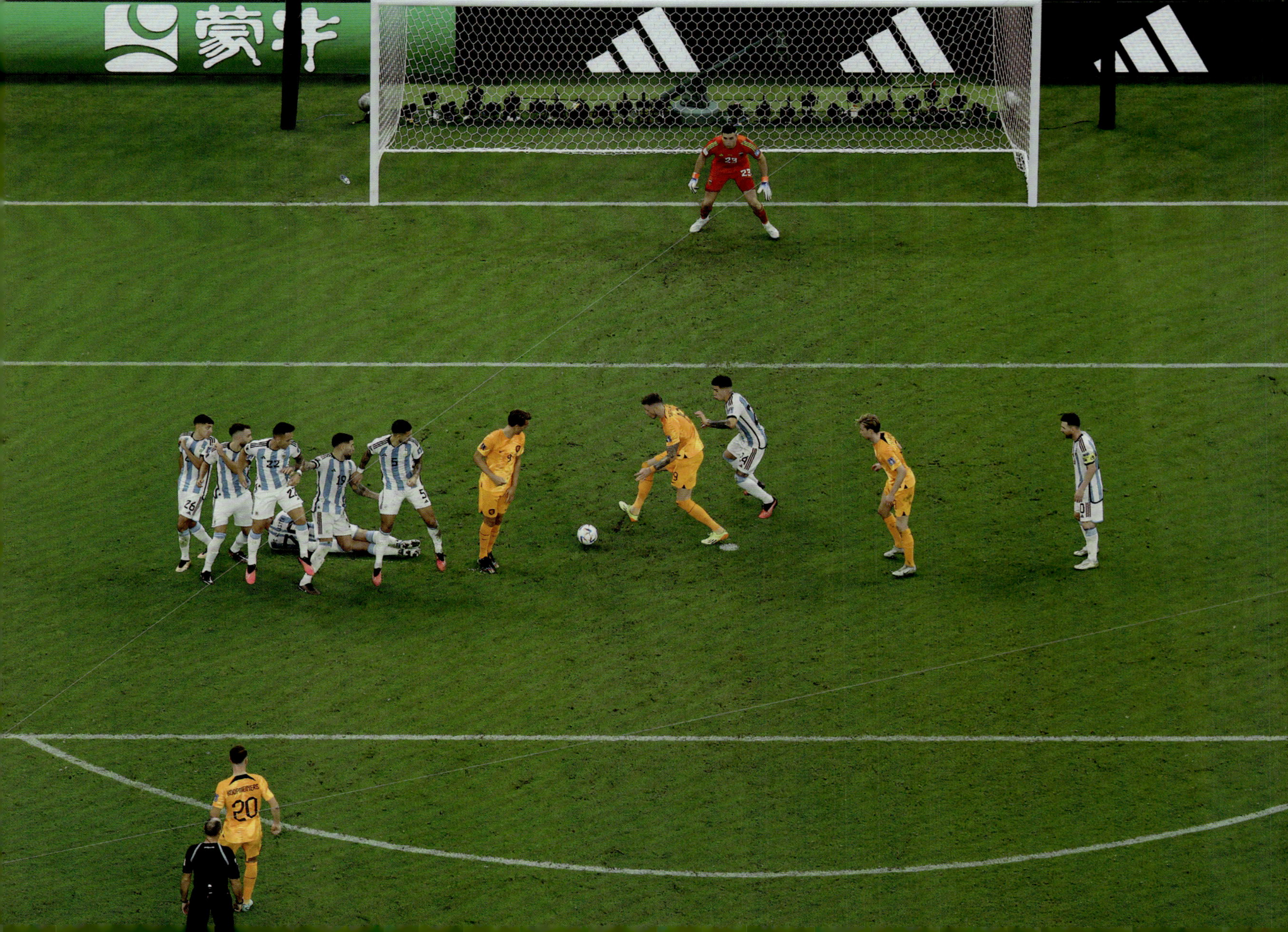

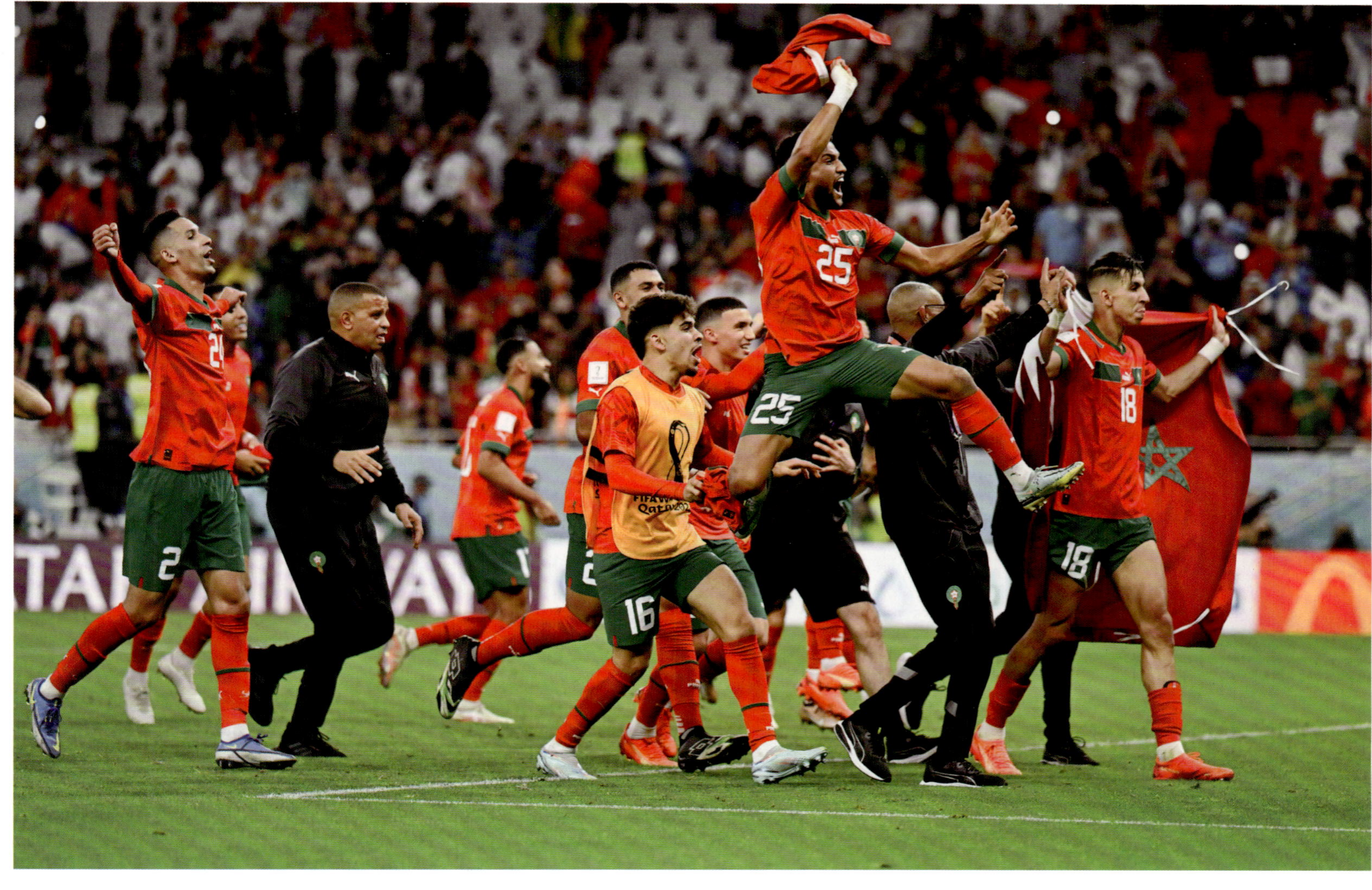

## AND ALSO . . . MOROCCO

**The international media in 2022** tended to focus on the two undeniable stars of the tournament: Messi and Mbappé, now club teammates at Paris Saint-Germain. Given how the tournament played out and culminated in their dramatic duel — the most thrilling and emotional Cup Final in history — that focus was certainly justified. But the other great story of the 2022 Cup was the amazing trajectory and team culture of Morocco.

Known as the Atlas Lions, the Moroccan side played joyful, energetic football all the way to the semi-finals, the deepest run ever by an African team. They tied Croatia, beat Belgium, Spain, and Portugal, and played toe-to-toe with defending-champion France in a stirring semi-final. A well-played rematch with the Croatians in the third-place game ended in a gallant 2–1 loss, but the Lions went home proud.

The best part of the feel-good Moroccan experience for fans around the world was the constant presence of the players' parents and families during postgame celebrations on the field. It was a connection strongly encouraged by Morocco's coach Walid Regragui, who told his team, 'We all have different cultural baggage, but the one thing that unites us is our parents. We won't have any success if our parents aren't happy.'

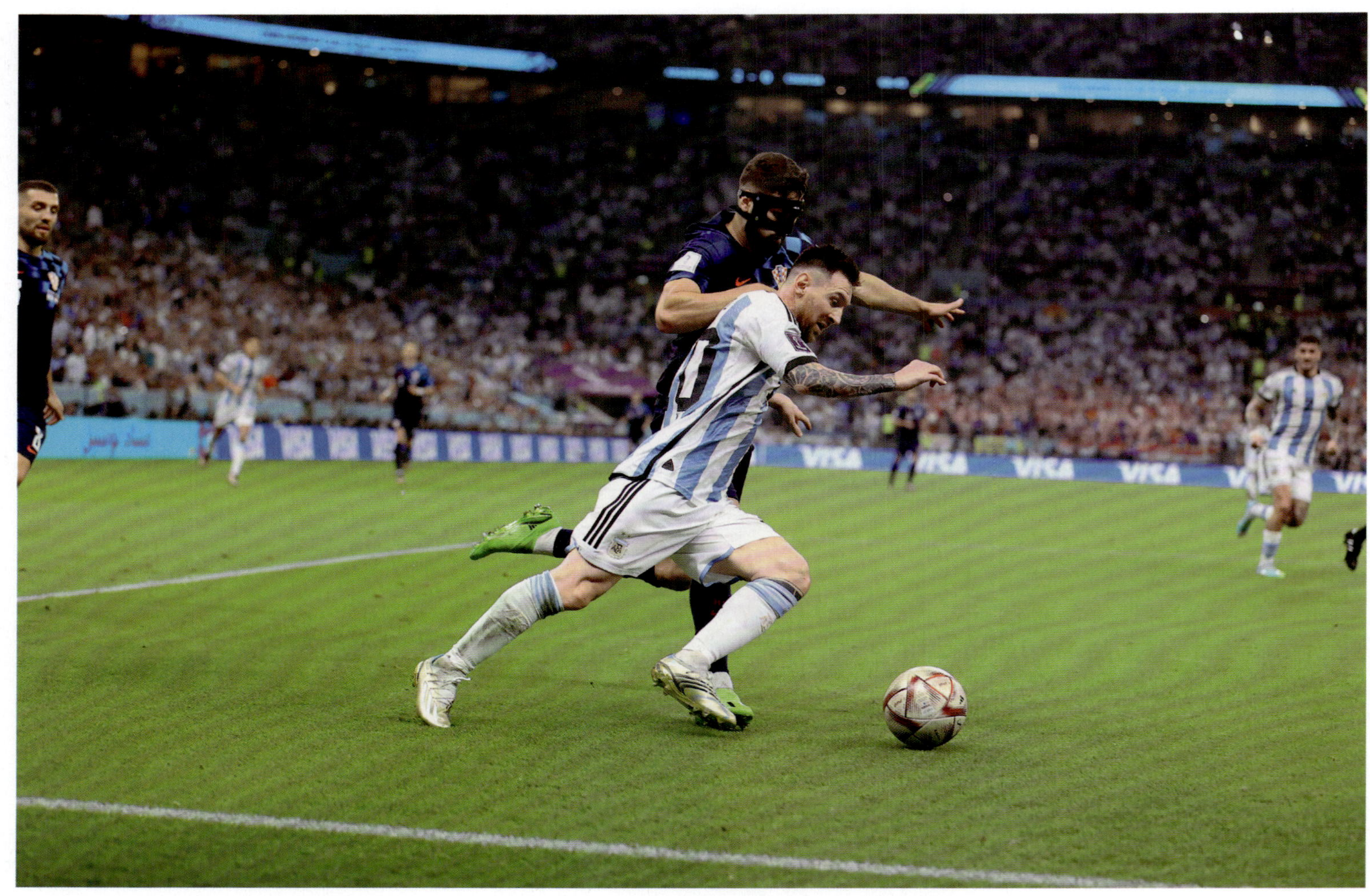

## SEMI-FINALS

Argentina 3 | 0 Croatia
France 2 | 0 Morocco

Lionel Messi led a tactical assault that broke down Croatia's usually ironclad midfield and Argentina led 2–0 at half. A goal by Julián Alvarez in the second half gave him a brace for the game, and the final 3–0 scoreline was perfect payback for the Croatian disassembly of Argentina by the same score at Russia 2018.

In the other semi-final, France jumped out to a 1–0 lead just five minutes in. Kylian Mbappé fired off two quick blocked shots and the second one bounced up high, just beyond the far post where Théo Hernandez somehow extended his left foot over the ball and then slashed it downward into the net. Sturdy Morocco kept their poise and traded even blows, nearly scoring on a dazzling scissors kick by Jawad El Yamiq just before half. They continued pressing hard in the second half, but France got a late counter for the 2–0 win.

*THIS SPREAD Messi displaying his class and determination in a brilliant run (above) to set up Julián Alvarez for Argentina's third goal (opposite) over Croatia.*

‘Messi was resolute to fulfil
the destiny that had long since
been placed on his shoulders.’

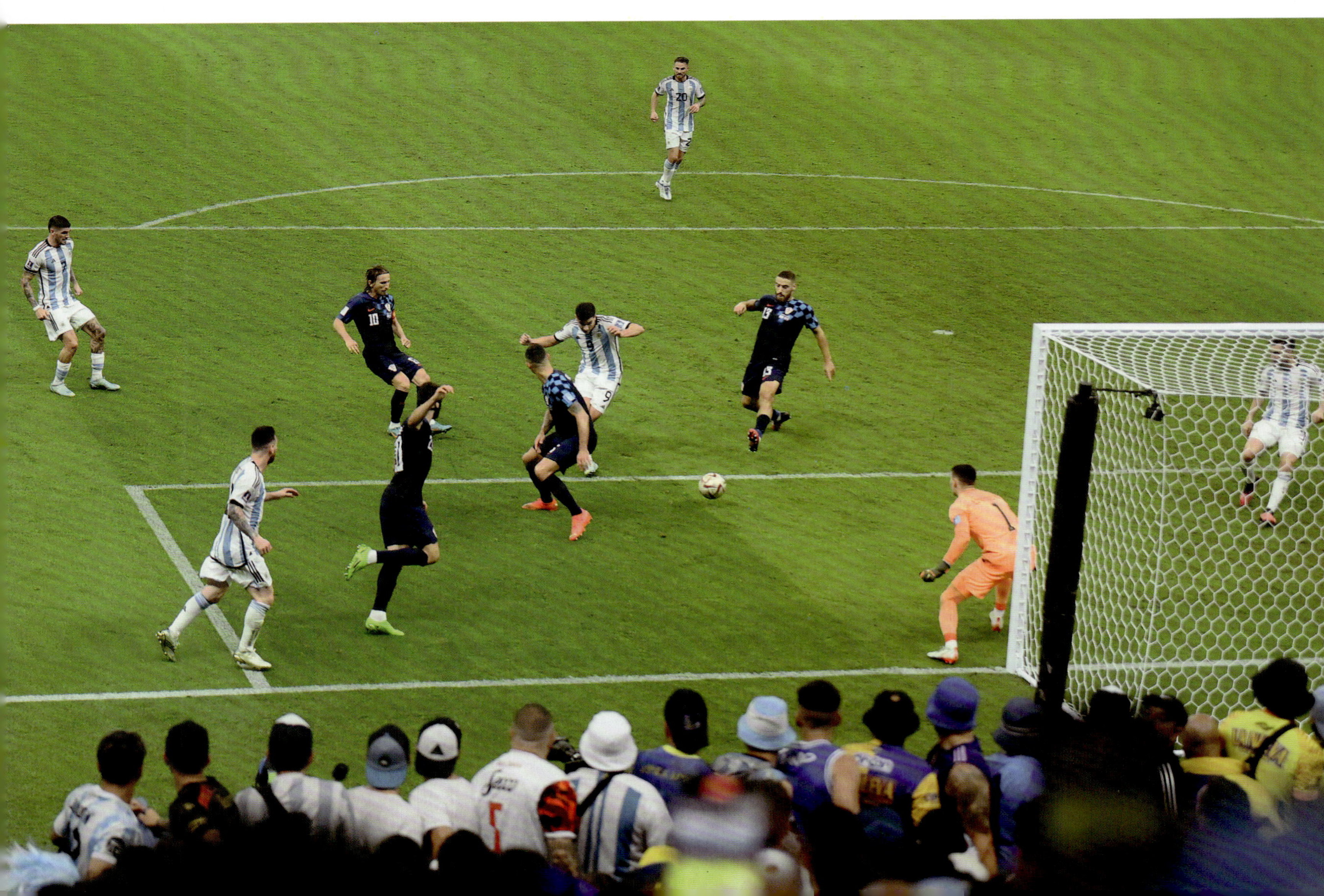

# FINAL

Argentina 3 | 3 France
(4–2 on penalty kicks)
(First Place)

Croatia 2 | 1 Morocco
(Third Place)

In the exciting third-place match, both sides scored in the first ten minutes to start things off with a bang. Croatia got another goal before half and went in with a 2–1 lead. The entertaining second half generated good opportunities for both sides, but neither could score.

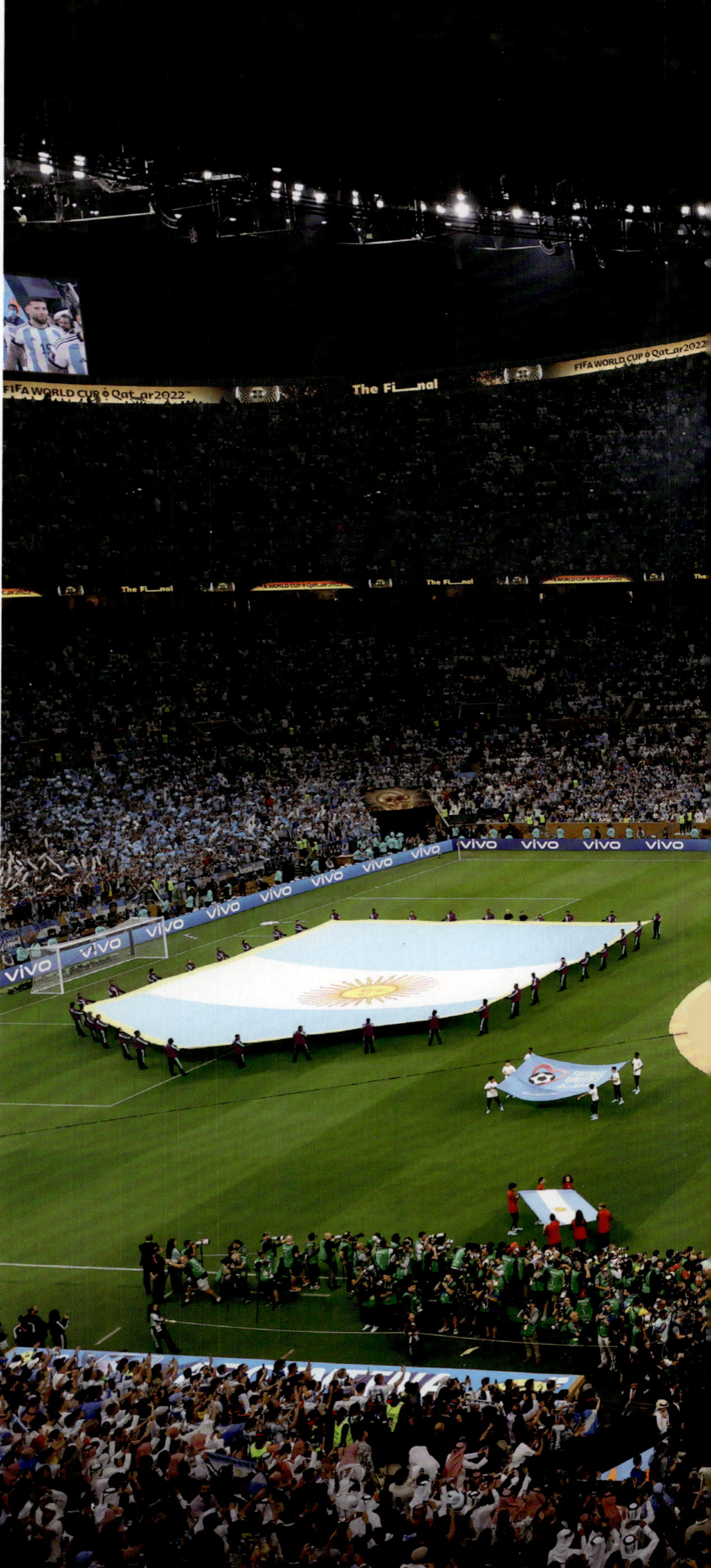

RIGHT *Argentina and France prepare for the 2022 World Cup Final at Lusail Stadium.*

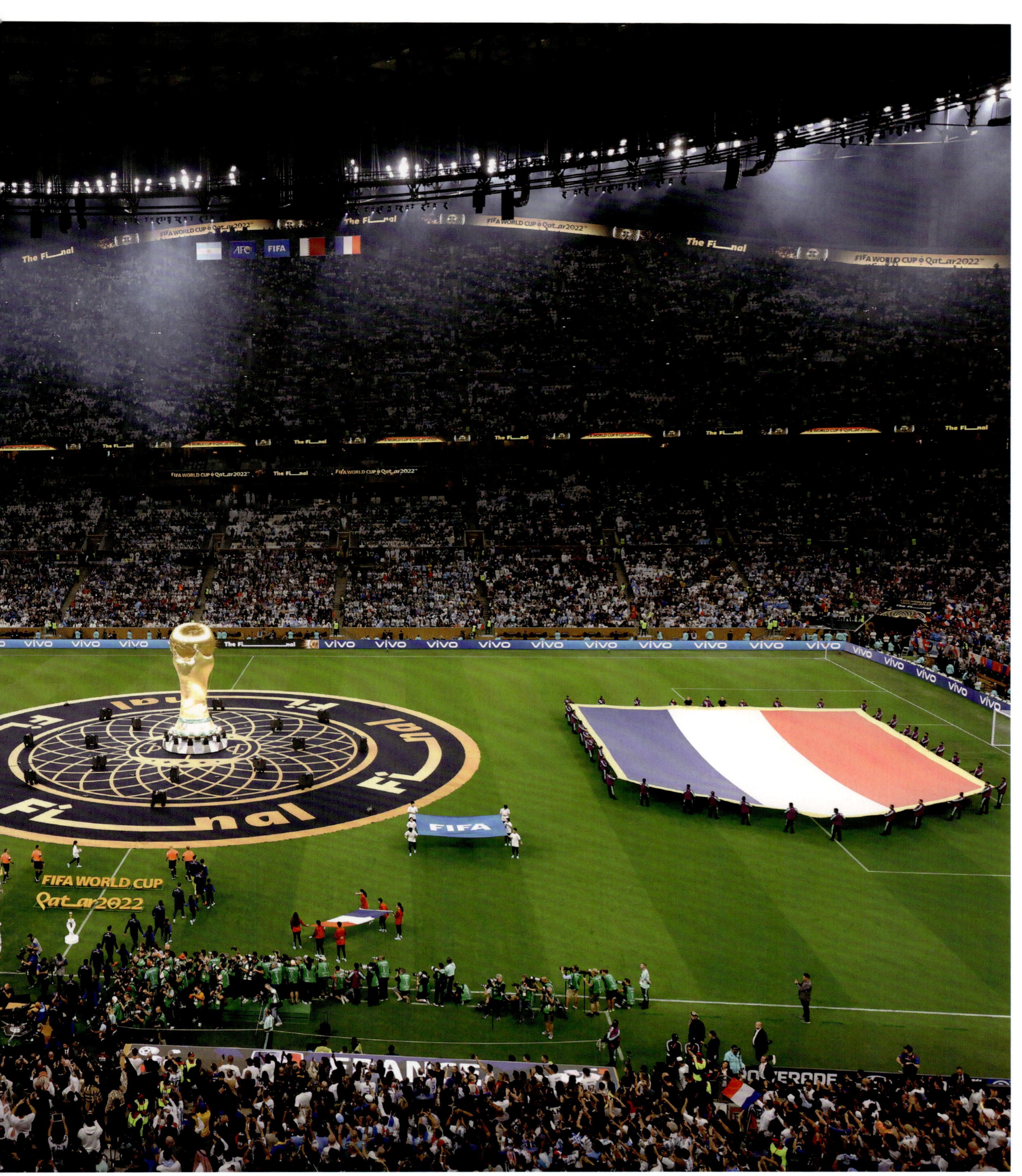

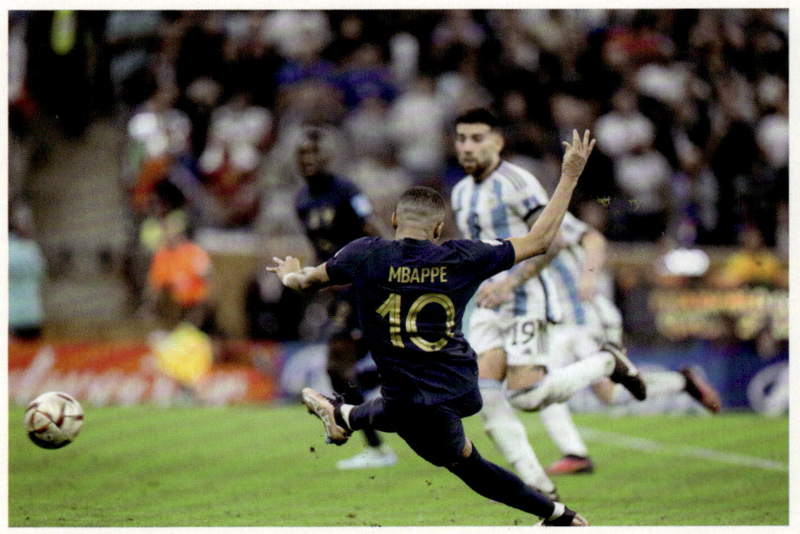

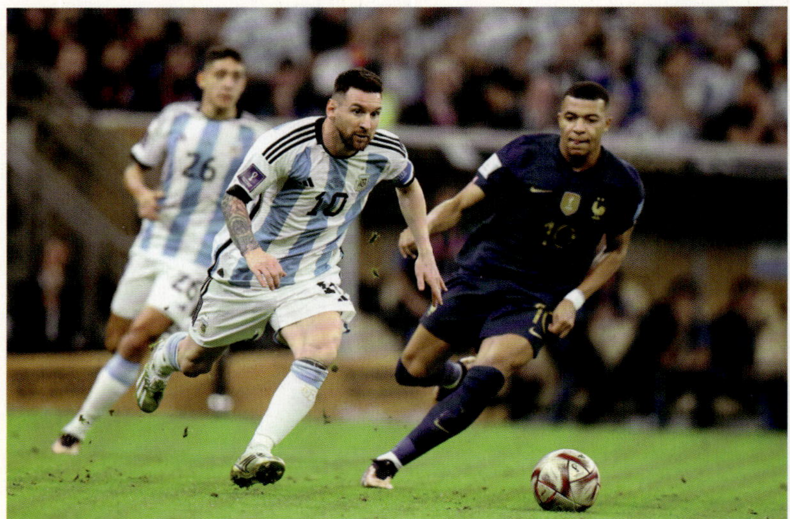

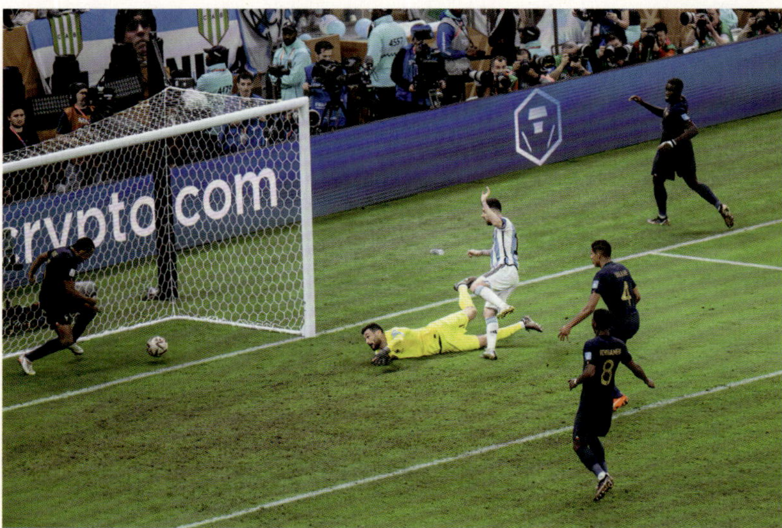

## THE DUEL IN THE DESERT

**Though shamelessly reductive to break** down the complex mechanics of a World Cup Final to a 'duel' between two gunslinging superstars, the narrative was too overwhelmingly perfect to ignore or overcome. Kylian Mbappé, twenty-three, having already scaled the mountaintop in 2018, now sought immortality as a two-time champion at the expense of his storied elder and current Paris Saint-Germain FC teammate — a relationship that some suggested was a bit prickly. Melodrama at its finest.

But beyond melodrama, far beyond that, Lionel Messi, thirty-four, exemplified, more than any other player in history, the incalculable gravity of a World Cup Trophy. Despite having won everything else that could be won in football and despite having broken nearly every individual record conceivable, the elusive crown jewel that is the World Cup was the unbearable cross on his back. For many, he could never, ever be the greatest football player of all time — he could never truly stand side by side with Pelé and Maradona — unless he could lead his country to the ultimate summit. And after being tragically denied in the previous two Cups, Messi was resolute to fulfil the destiny that had long since been placed on his shoulders.

And thus, the stage was set. Messi scored first with a penalty kick and then added an ingenious flick during a mesmerising sequence of five consecutive passes that resulted in Argentina's second goal, a measured strike by Ángel Di María. But at the 80' mark of the second half, Mbappé converted a penalty kick of his own and then, just one minute later, volleyed a lunging, powerful blast past goalkeeper Emiliano Martínez to bring the score level at 2–2. The momentum suddenly flowed in France's direction. Messi and crew looked deflated, anxious.

But extra time produced more scintillating football. After a point-blank shot at the 108' mark by Lautaro Martínez rebounded off French keeper Hugo Lloris, Messi seized his moment, pouncing on the loose ball and putting it in the back of the net. Ten minutes later, with time running out, a hard Mbappé shot caught an Argentine defender's arm to draw yet another penalty. Mbappé converted and the match went to a shootout. Mbappé and Messi each converted the first kick for their respective sides, but a monumental save by Emiliano Martínez, plus zero misses by the four Argentine shooters, saw France fall.

Despite the loss, Kylian Mbappé became only the second footballer in history—along with Geoff Hurst of England in 1966—to score a hat-trick in a World Cup Final. Every one of his goals was a crucial, come-from-behind score, each delivered perfectly under the greatest of pressure. Overall, Mbappé scored eight goals in the tournament and won the Golden Boot. No duel has ever been so entertaining, impressive, and emotionally resonant.

For the tournament, Lionel Messi scored seven goals and added three crucial assists for *La Albiceleste*, a magnificent performance. To quote the postgame poetry of BBC man Peter Drury: 'It is hard to escape the supposition that [Messi] has rendered himself today the greatest of all time. He was the point of difference. He has *always* been the point of difference.' As in 2014, Messi was awarded the Golden Ball as best player in the tournament — the only man ever to win it twice. But this time, it was different. At just eighteen years of age, the deified Diego Maradona had hand-selected his successor: 'I've seen the player who will inherit my place in Argentinian football, and his name is Messi.' Inheriting Maradona's place in the Argentinian pantheon only meant, could only ever mean, one thing. More than fifteen years later, it was achieved.

The immortal moment: hoisting the World Cup Trophy for your country.

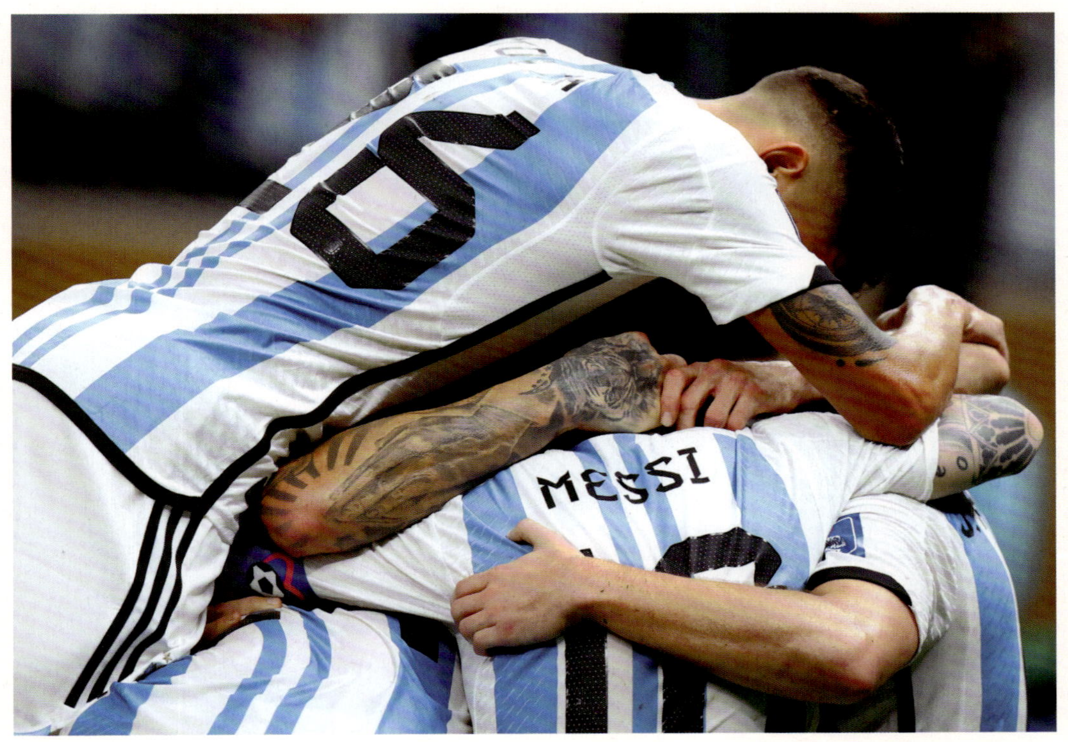

**OPPOSITE TOP** *Kylian Mbappé, one of the heroes of France's 2018 triumph, fires off a rapid volley (while falling) for his second of three goals.*

**OPPOSITE MIDDLE** *Club teammates Lionel Messi (centre) and Kylian Mbappé (right) in a battle for legacy.*

**OPPOSITE BOTTOM** *Lionel Messi gets the ball across the line in extra time for Argentina's third goal.*

**RIGHT** *Lionel Messi is swarmed by his teammates, many of them much younger, who celebrate the culmination of his hard-fought quest to deliver Argentina a World Cup.*

**FOLLOWING SPREAD** *Long ago foretold and long awaited. Lionel Messi, with a truly transcendent display at Qatar 2022, lifts the trophy and rises as the newest king of World Cup football.*

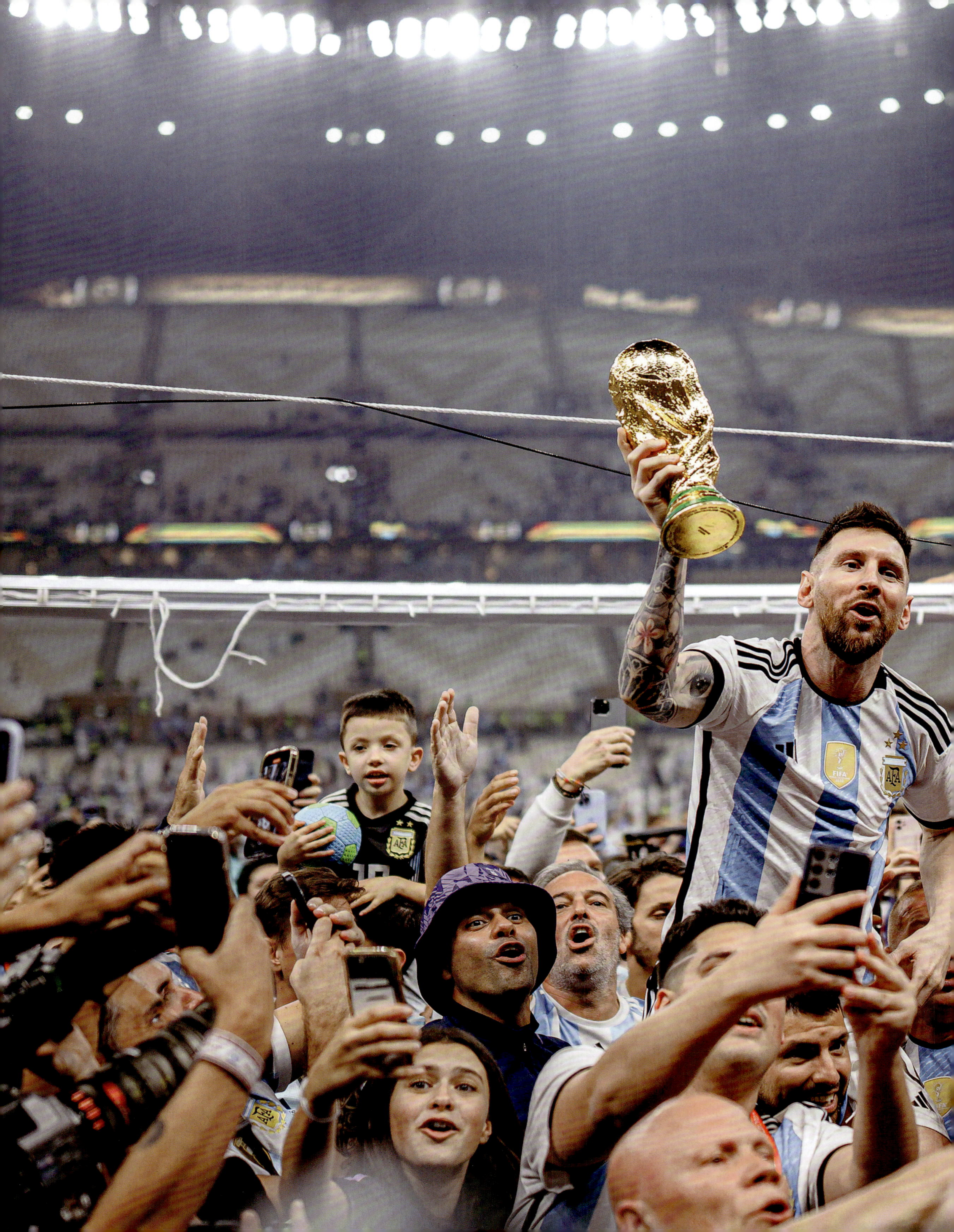

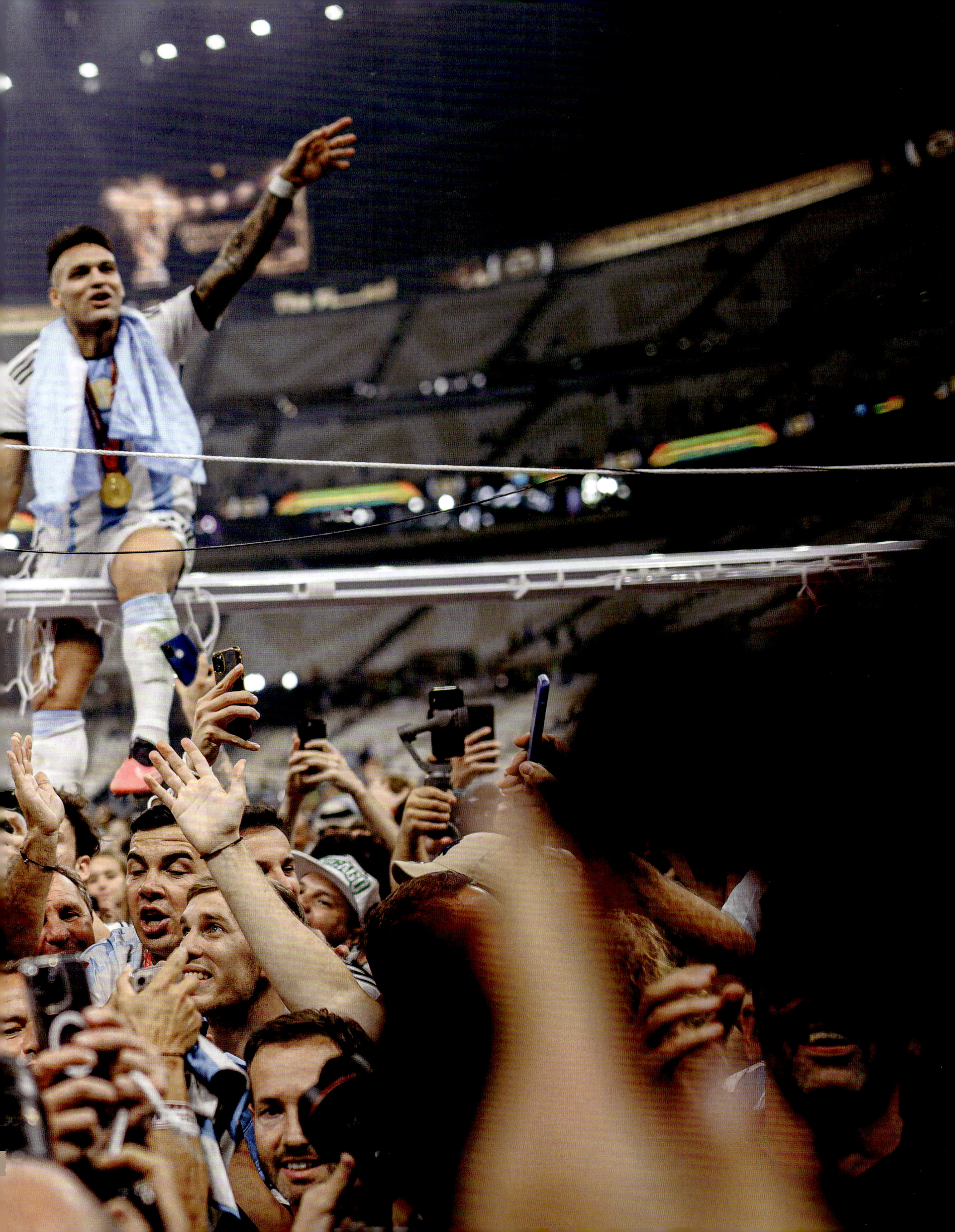

### A GLANCE BACK . . . AND A PEEK AHEAD

**In 1930, Europe floated uneasily** in a trough between two tidal waves of World War. The continent also faced the front edge of the Great Depression, a severe economic downturn that would last a full decade. So, when Jules Rimet and his FIFA colleagues brought together thirteen nations in Uruguay to play football that year, the notion of an international World Cup celebrating the spirit of unity and good sportsmanship seemed quaint, maybe even naive. Indeed, most of Europe's major football powers — Italy, England, Spain, Austria, and Germany among them — turned down invitations to that first tournament.

Over time, of course — as you've witnessed on every page of this book — Rimet's vision proved to be uncannily prescient. Every four years, the World Cup has served as a powerful reminder of our shared humanity. Thanks to the immediacy of modern media, Cup tournaments now transport billions of us across oceans to far-flung venues where people from different lands welcome us with open hearts. Maybe the Cup doesn't solve global problems, but it's certainly become a healing force. It showcases moments of cultural comity and compelling human drama that ripple far beyond the pitch.

'Football is fundamentally an emotional experience, and human emotion is the universal language,' said University of Colorado social psychologist Bernadette Park. Each World Cup is a global communal event that produces powerful spikes of joy and heartbreak that connect us to people who may differ from us culturally, but do not differ essentially. 'These emotions speak to us directly, no translation or filters needed,' said Park. 'Every Cup becomes a repository of all these great human stories that resonate and move us and ultimately unite us.' For a while, we all march together under the human banner.

Of course, the World Cup creates 'superhuman' stories, too, the enduring legends that amaze and inspire us — Pelé, Cruyff, Beckenbauer, Maradona, Zidane, Ronaldo, Messi. Great players making magic. And the Cup also inspires a healthy national pride in its participant countries. Over the years, stunning upsets by resilient underdog nations have literally triggered seismic tremors of joy back home, as in Mexico City in 2018.

Today, as the World Cup matures, it continues to evolve while still tapping into the world's passion for football. This year, we look forward to the debut of an expanded format jointly hosted by Canada, Mexico, and the United States — more teams, more games, more unforgettable stories on the global stage. With forty-eight sides from six confederations playing in sixteen host cities, a knockout bracket starting with a Round of 32, and a total of 104 matches to be played over thirty-nine days, the 2026 FIFA World Cup tournament is on track to be the grandest and most watched ever.

And so, once again, the biggest spotlight in history is set to re-illuminate Jules Rimet's original vision from a century ago: *A worldwide football family, a force for good, fostering healthy competition and friendship between all cultures.*

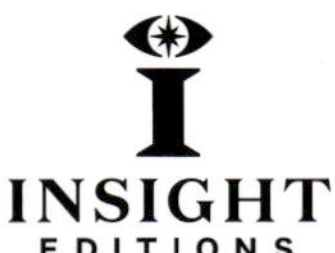

# INSIGHT
## EDITIONS

PO Box 3088
San Rafael, CA 94912
www.insighteditions.com

Find us on Facebook: www.facebook.com/InsightEditions
Follow us on Instagram: @insighteditions



ISBN: 9798337404134

**Publisher:** Raoul Goff
**SVP, Group Publisher:** Vanessa Lopez
**VP, Manufacturing:** Alix Nicholaeff
**Publishing Director:** Mike Degler
**Editorial Director:** Jennifer Sims
**Creative Director:** Josh Baker
**Art Director:** Catherine San Juan
**Designer:** Samuel Louie
**Editor:** Alecsander Zapata
**Editorial Assistant:** Ollie Swasey
**Managing Editor:** Nora Milman
**Production Designer:** Luca Del Carlo
**Senior Production Manager:** Greg Steffen
**Strategic Production Planner:** Lina s Palma-Temena

**Cover Art by:** Charlie Davis

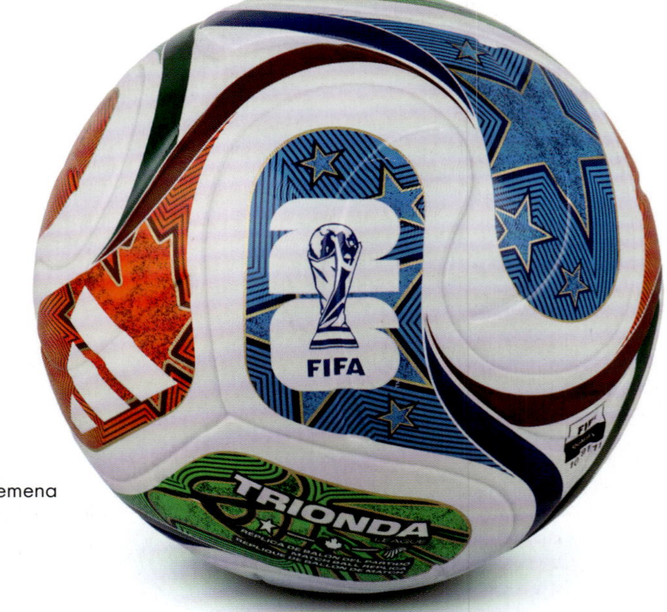

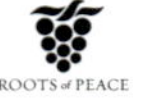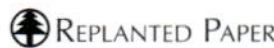

Insight Editions, in association with Roots of Peace, will plant two trees for each tree used in the manufacturing of this book. Roots of Peace is an internationally renowned humanitarian organisation dedicated to eradicating land mines worldwide and converting war-torn lands into productive farms and wildlife habitats. Roots of Peace will plant two million fruit and nut trees in Afghanistan and provide farmers there with the skills and support necessary for sustainable land use.

Manufactured in China by Insight Editions

10 9 8 7 6 5 4 3 2 1